MW00782451

# The Meaning of the Pentateuch

*Revelation, Composition and Interpretation*

John H. Sailhamer

IVP Academic
An imprint of InterVarsity Press
Downers Grove, Illinois

*InterVarsity Press*
*P.O. Box 1400, Downers Grove, IL 60515-1426*
*World Wide Web: www.ivpress.com*
*E-mail: email@ivpress.com*



*InterVarsity Press® is the book-publishing division of InterVarsity Christian Fellowship/USA®, a movement of students and faculty active on campus at hundreds of universities, colleges and schools of nursing in the United States of America, and a member movement of the International Fellowship of Evangelical Students. For information about local and regional activities, write Public Relations Dept., InterVarsity Christian Fellowship/USA, 6400 Schroeder Rd., P.O. Box 7895, Madison, WI 53707-7895, or visit the IVCF website at <www.intervarsity.org>.*

*All Scripture quotations, unless otherwise indicated, are the author's own translation..*

*Design: Cindy Kiple*

*Images:* Two Old Men Disputing *(oil on panel) by Rembrandt Harmensz van Rijn at National Gallery of Victoria, Melbourne, Australia/Bridgeman Art Library*

*ISBN 978-0-8308-3867-7*

*Printed in the United States of America* ∞

*InterVarsity Press is committed to protecting the environment and to the responsible use of natural resources. As a member of Green Press Initiative we use recycled paper whenever possible. To learn more about the Green Press Initiative, visit <www.greenpressinitiative.org>.*

**Library of Congress Cataloging-in-Publication Data**

*Sailhamer, John.*
*The meaning of the Pentateuch: Revelation, composition, and interpretation/John H. Sailhamer.*
*p. cm.*
*Includes bibliographical references and index.*
*ISBN 978-0-8308-3867-7 (pbk.: alk. paper)*
*1. Bible. O.T. Pentateuch—Criticism, interpretation, etc. I. Title.*
*BS1225.52.S25 2009*
*222'.106—dc22*
*2009026590*

**P** *21 20 19 18 17 16 15 14 13 12 11 10 9 8 7 6 5 4 3*
**Y** *26 25 24 23 22 21 20 19 18 17 16 15 14 13 12 11 10*

*To my students*

# Contents

# Preface

The approach taken in this book has a high regard for the questions raised by both the "historical-critical" and classical "biblical-historical" views of the Old Testament Scriptures. I hope this will be evident to the reader, not necessarily by my use of those methods, but by my taking seriously the questions they raise. It is neither "critical" nor "precritical" but noncritical, seeking to understand the meaning of the Pentateuch and the rest of Scripture as we have them in the earliest canonical shapes of our Bible in the late pre-Christian period.

It remains now to acknowledge my debt to some of those who made this book possible. First are the many students to whom I have had the privilege of teaching Old Testament theology and in particular the Pentateuch over the past thirty-five years. It has been a joy. I would also like to acknowledge the editorial staff at InterVarsity Press, and in particular my editor, Dan Reid, without whom this book would never have seen the light of day. Most of all, Patty, my wife, for being a steadfast helper and encourager.

# Abbreviations

**Divisions of the Canon**

| | |
|---|---|
| HB | Hebrew Bible |
| NT | New Testament |
| OT | Old Testament |

**Ancient Texts, Text Types and Versions**

| | |
|---|---|
| LXX | Septuagint |
| MT | Masoretic Text |

**Modern Editions**

| | |
|---|---|
| *BHS* | *Biblia Hebraica Stuttgartensia* |
| $NA^{27}$ | *Novum Testamentum Graece*, Nestle-Aland, 27th ed. |

**Modern Versions**

| | |
|---|---|
| ASV | American Standard Version |
| KJV | King James Version |
| NASB | New American Standard Bible |
| NIV | New International Version |
| NKJV | New King James Version |
| NJPS | *Tanakh: The Holy Scriptures: The New JPS Translation according to the Traditional Hebrew Text* |
| NRSV | New Revised Standard Version |
| RSV | Revised Standard Version |

**Dead Sea Scrolls**

| | |
|---|---|
| 4Q398 | *4QHalakhic Letter*$^{e}$ (4QMMT$^{e}$) |

**Greek and Latin Works**

Augustine

| | |
|---|---|
| *Doctr. chr.* | *On Christian Doctrine* |

Eusebius

| | |
|---|---|
| *Hist. eccl.* | *Ecclesiastical History* |

Irenaeus

| | |
|---|---|
| *Haer.* | *Against Heresies* |

Josephus

| | |
|---|---|
| *Ag. Ap.* | *Against Apion* |

Justin
*Dial.* *Dialogue with Trypho*

**Secondary Sources**

| | |
|---|---|
| AB | Anchor Bible |
| AnOr | Analecta orientalia |
| BAS | Biblisch-theologische und apologetisch-kritische Studien |
| *BBR* | *Bulletin for Biblical Research* |
| BCAT | Biblischer Commentar über das Alte Testament |
| BCOT | Biblical Commentary on the Old Testament |
| BDB | F. Brown, S. R. Driver and C. A. Briggs, *A Hebrew and English Lexicon on the Old Testament* (Oxford, Clarendon Press, 1907) |
| BEvT | Beiträge zur evangelischen Theologie |
| BGLRK | Beiträge zur Geschichte und Lehre der Reformierten Kirche |
| *Bib* | *Biblica* |
| BL | Biblical Languages |
| BZAW | Beihefte zur Zeitschrift für die alttestamentliche Wissenschaft |
| CC | Continental Commentaries |
| FAT | Forschungen zum Alten Testament |
| FSTR | Forschungen zur systematischen Theologie und Religionsphilosophie |
| GKC | *Gesenius' Hebrew Grammar.* Edited by E. Kautzsch. Translated by A. E. Cowley. 2nd ed. (Oxford: Clarendon Press, 1910) |
| GKW | Geschichte der Künste und Wissenschaften |
| *HAL* | L. Koehler, W. Baumgartner and J. J. Stamm. *Hebräisches und aramäisches Lexikon zum Alten Testament.* Fascicles 1-5 (Leiden: Brill, 1967-1995) |
| HAT | Handbuch zum Alten Testament |
| HCOT | Historical Commentary on the Old Testament |
| HKAT | Handkommentar zum Alten Testament |
| HNT | Handbuch zum Neuen Testament |
| HSM | Harvard Semitic Monographs |
| HTS | Harvard Theological Studies |
| ILBS | Indiana Literary Biblical Series |
| JBTh | Jahrbuch für biblische Theologie |
| *JETh* | *Jahrbuch für evangelikale Theologie* |
| JLSP | Janua linguarum: Series practica |
| JSOTSup | Journal for the Study of the Old Testament: Supplement Series |
| KAT | Kommentar zum Alten Testament |

| | |
|---|---|
| KEHAT | Kurzgefasstes exegetisches Handbuch zum Alten Testament |
| KEK | Kritisch-exegetischer Kommentar über das Neue Testament |
| KHC | Kurzer Hand-Commentar zum Alten Testament |
| LBTL | Library of Biblical and Theological Literature |
| LCC | Library of Christian Classics |
| MSt | Monographien und Studienbucher |
| NEchtB | Neue Echter Bibel |
| NThG | Neue theologische Grundrisse |
| OBO | Orbis biblicus et orientalis |
| OBT | Overtures to Biblical Theology |
| OTL | Old Testament Library |
| OTS | Old Testament Studies |
| OtSt | Oudtestamentische Studiën |
| PL | Patrologia latina [= Patrologiae cursus completus: Series latina]. Edited by J. P. Migne. 217 vols. (Paris, 1844-1864) |
| *PTR* | *Princeton Theological Review* |
| *RGG*[3] | *Religion in Geschichte und Gegenwart*. Edited by K. Galling. 3rd ed. 7 vols. (Tübingen: Mohr Siebeck, 1957-1965) |
| *RGG*[4] | *Religion in Geschichte und Gegenwart*. Edited by H. D. Betz et al. 4th ed. 8 vols. (Tübingen: Mohr Siebeck, 1998-2005) |
| SBG | Studies in Biblical Greek |
| SBLDS | Society of Biblical Literature Dissertation Series |
| SBT | Studies in Biblical Theology |
| SDDSRL | Studies in the Dead Sea Scrolls and Related Literature |
| SThH | Sammlung theologischer Handbücher |
| STL | Sammlung theologische Lehrbücher |
| SubBi | Subsidia biblica |
| *TBNT* | *Theologisches Begriffslexikon zum Neuen Testament*. Edited by Lothar Coenen and Klaus Hacker. 4 vols. (Wuppertal: Brockhaus, 1965-1971) |
| *TJ* | *Trinity Journal* |
| *TWNT* | *Theologisches Wörterbuch zum Neuen Testament*. Edited by G. Kittel and G. Friedrich. 11 vols. (Stuttgart: Kohlhammer, 1932-1979) |
| *VT* | *Vetus Testamentum* |
| VTSup | Supplements to Vetus Testamentum |
| *WTJ* | *Westminster Theological Journal* |
| *ZAW* | *Zeitschrift für die alttestamentliche Wissenschaft* |
| *ZDMG* | *Zeitschrift der deutschen morgenländischen Gesellschaft* |

# Introduction

This book is a study of the theology of the Pentateuch. It follows an approach that looks for the biblical author's "intention" in the "verbal meaning" of his book. It seeks the meaning of his words, phrases and sentences. How do the individual pieces fit together within the whole? Central to the aim of this book is the discovery of the compositional strategy of the biblical author of the Pentateuch. This introduction gives an overview of the studies in the book and shows how they affect our understanding of the theology of the Pentateuch.

## Revelation and Religion

The book begins with a discussion of the question of authority. To whom was the Pentateuch written as the norm of biblical faith? For whom was it intended to be normative when first written? Who was its audience? What did it have to say to that audience then, and what, if any, claims does it make on its readers today?

What does it mean to believe that the OT is the Word of God? And what effect does the answer to that question have on an evangelical theology of the Pentateuch?

We begin our study with questions about two central terms that lie behind most of the discussions in this book: *revelation* and *religion*. Revelation, classically understood, is the divine act of self-disclosure put into written form as Scripture by the prophets. God has communicated through his prophets in ways understandable to them and to their readers. In the Pentateuch, as in the rest of the Bible, God used a human language, with its words, phrases and sentences, to make known his will. Revelation was not a mystical divine act of self-disclosure; it was an everyday human act of speaking and writing. God revealed himself in a book, the Pentateuch, made of words, sentences and paragraphs. Through it, one can understand the mind of God, not mystically, but by reading its words. Revelation is not something that occurred only long ago; it continues today in the prophetic words of Scripture. One can know the mind of God *(mens dei)* by reading the words of the human author.

In this book I trace the rise and fall of the modern evangelical view of revelation and show, historically, how the classical evangelical view was replaced by one that builds on the notion of the Bible and religion. That replacement came to mean that for evangelicals, a theology of the Pentateuch was little more than a historical reconstruction of what the Israelites once believed rather than what its readers should believe—not a prescription of what its early readers were to understand as their faith, but a description of what ancient Israel once believed. The only real difference between the evangelical view and the critical view was that for evangelicals, what was thought of as history was limited to what could be read in the Bible. The critical view was grounded in a "real" history that had to be reconstructed from nonbiblical sources. It is not difficult to see that the evangelical view of the Pentateuch was, and still is, in need of hermeneutical adjustment to the message of the NT. If the Bible is the sacred text of ancient Israel, how could its message be applied to the church? What has the church to do with Israel and the OT? The evangelical answer to those questions consisted of a return to the application of NT typology to the OT. Israel in the OT was identified with the church in the NT. That which applied to the people of Israel in the OT was replaced by its application now to the church. Seen in that light, the Pentateuch cannot serve a normative role in the church; it can only point its readers to the religion of ancient Israel as the "faith once given."

One question addressed throughout this book is the locus of meaning in the Pentateuch. Where and in what way do we find authoritative words in the Pentateuch? What, for example, does the Pentateuch tell us about the Mosaic law(s)? Is the Pentateuch written only for the ancient people of Israel? Is its intention primarily the descriptive task of understanding Israel's religion under the Sinai covenant? Or was the Pentateuch written to confront its readers now, as then, with the imperative to live a life of faith exemplified by Abraham's walk with God in the Pentateuch? Is it a "shout out" for Abraham, the believing prophet (Gen 15:6; 20:7), or for Moses, the priest who in the wilderness failed to exhibit his faith (Num 20:12)? How can anyone today read and understand its meaning for his or her life? How can a Christian take its laws and religious rites as something that must be obeyed?

In the first section of this book I argue that the message of the Pentateuch, like the rest of the OT, is not that its readers should become ancient Israelites and worship God in a temple. That surely was the intent of these laws and judgments when first given to Israel at Sinai. Moses, however, did not give them the Pentateuch on Sinai; he gave them the law. Sinai came long before the writing of the Pentateuch. An additional part of the aim of this book is to demonstrate that in the writing of the Pentateuch, various selections of Sinai laws were included to show the great difficulty of living a life of faith under the Mosaic covenant and its law (Num 20:12; Deut 31:29). Israel's religion, established at Sinai with Moses as mediator, was not the ultimate concern of the message of the Pentateuch. The laws are put in the Pentateuch to give the reader a sense of the kind of religion that once characterized the covenant at Sinai. The law given at Sinai neither had the same purpose nor carried the same message as the faith taught by the Pentateuch.

What we have noted here can lead to an important distinction in reading strategies when looking for the message of the Pentateuch. My focus throughout this book is not what the laws meant to ancient Israel at Sinai. Instead, I am asking what the inspired written message of the Pentateuch means to us today, and what the law in the Pentateuch has to do with that. Surely, the author of the Pentateuch wants readers to see that Moses and the Israelites at Sinai were obliged to obey the Sinai laws; just as Noah was called on to obey the divine instructions for building the ark, so also Moses obeyed the Sinai covenant by doing what its laws required (Num 12:7). The author of the Pentateuch shows readers that Abraham lived centuries before the giving of the Sinai law and its authority over him. In making that point, the author was not suggesting that readers submit themselves to a new code of "Abrahamic" laws, but is making the same point that Paul later makes in Romans 4: readers should have Abraham's faith if they want to be counted as fulfilling the law. Abraham fulfilled the Sinai law by living a life of faith (Gen 26:5; Rom 8:4).[1]

[1]See John H. Sailhamer, "The Mosaic Law and the Theology of the Pentateuch," *WTJ* 53 (1991): 24-61; Hans-Christoph Schmitt, "Redaktion des Pentateuch im Geiste der Prophetie," *VT* 32 (1982): 170-89.

This is an amazing "Pauline" statement from within the Pentateuch itself. Long before the coming of Christ, the theology of Jesus and of the apostle Paul is reflected in the author's intent *(mens auctoris)*.

The purpose of the Pentateuch is not to teach a life of obedience to the law given to Moses at Sinai, but to be a narrative admonition to be like Abraham, who did not live under the law and yet fulfilled the law through a life of faith. The Pentateuch is a lesson drawn from the lives of its two leading men, Abraham and Moses.[2] The Pentateuch lays out two fundamentally dissimilar ways of "walking with God" (Deut 29:1): one is to be like Moses under the Sinai law, and is called the "Sinai covenant"; the other, like that of Abraham (Gen 15:6), is by faith and apart from the law, and is called the "new covenant." These two central themes (law and faith) are played out in the Pentateuch and into the prophetic literature as a contrast of two covenants, Mosaic and Abrahamic, or law and gospel. We will see that the prophets were aware of the meaning of the Pentateuch through their own reading and study of it. As a result of that, they helped to preserve it by producing a new "prophetic edition" of the Pentateuch based on their understanding of Mosaic law. This is the "canonical Pentateuch" in our Bible today. Further evidence of the "prophetic update of the Pentateuch" is found in some early texts and versions.[3]

## The Prophetic Echo

Ernst Hengstenberg, a well-known nineteenth-century evangelical OT scholar,[4] sees in the composition of the books of the OT a great deal of interdependence among the biblical writers. The prophets relied heavily on the Pentateuch and on each other's "comments" (e.g, 1 Sam 2:10)[5] and "glosses" on the Pentateuch. Such commentary could be found in the form of the remnants of ancient discussions about the meaning of texts, their translation, and the comments given to the text within the text itself. Just the location and arrangement of a text within or alongside other texts can affect how a reader understands the text. Hengstenberg calls this interdependence of the OT

---

[2]See John H. Sailhamer, *The Pentateuch as Narrative: A Biblical-Theological Commentary* (Grand Rapids: Zondervan, 1992), pp. 1-79.

[3]See John H. Sailhamer, "Biblical Theology and the Composition of the Hebrew Bible," in *Biblical Theology: Retrospect and Prospect*, ed. Scott Hafemann (Downers Grove, Ill.: InterVarsity Press, 2002), pp. 25-37.

[4]Also picked up by C. F. Keil in his commentary on the Minor Prophets. See C. F. Keil, *The Twelve Minor Prophets*, trans. James Martin (BCOT; Grand Rapids: Eerdmans, 1954), 2:96.

[5]Compare in the NT, for example, Matthew 2:15.

authors an "echo." He understands virtually the whole of the messianic message of the OT to be a function of this echo. In the words of the prophets Hengstenberg hears an echo of the words of Moses as well as an echo of the words of other prophets.[6] He says of the prophecies of Joel, "The prophet adheres closely to the outline already given by Moses, with the filling up and finishing of which, all other prophets also are employed."[7] Using the same terminology of an "echo," C. F. Keil says of Habakkuk's vision, "The description of this theophany [Hab 3] rests throughout upon ancient poetic descriptions of divine revelation from Israel's earliest days (i.e., the Pentateuch). Even the introduction (ver. 3) has its roots in the song of Moses in Deuteronomy 33:2, and in the further course of the poem we meet with various echoes of the psalms."[8]

For Hengstenberg (and Keil), the prophets did not merely bounce the words of Moses back and forth to the other prophets; they sent those words back freighted with their own prophetic commentary.[9]

Prophecy thus had an echo effect as it made its way through the books of the OT. One prophet's words were heard by another, exegeted, and sent back as an echo of those earlier prophetic words. Each time the prophet's words were heard and echoed, new clarity and relevance were revealed. It also rep-

---

[6]Walter Kaiser points to a similar feature of OT interpretation and calls it "the analogy of antecedent Scripture." Each biblical writer works within the context of the developing canon of Scripture that has preceded him. The difference between the views of Hengstenberg and Kaiser is that for Kaiser, the prophets played a passive role in recording their own echo of Moses and the other prophets. They did not attempt to read back into the earlier OT Scriptures. They simply recorded their own words in a kind of chronologically correct sequence.

[7]Ernst W. Hengstenberg, *Christology of the Old Testament*, trans. Reuel Keith (1854; reprint, McLean, Va.: MacDonald Publishing, 1972), 1:234.

[8]C. F. Keil, *Biblischer Commentar über die zwölf kleinen Propheten* (BCAT 4/3; Leipzig: Dörffling & Franke: 1866), p. 434.

[9]Kaiser argues for a more passive view of the prophets' work, presumably because he does not want any later viewpoints superimposed back on earlier biblical texts. But that is exactly what Hengstenberg finds of importance in the prophetic word, which is an inspired (but not yet NT) interpretation. The difference between the two can be resolved, I believe, by noting that Kaiser's primary difficulty with such an approach involves principally the NT authors' interpreting the words of the OT in light of their NT fulfillment. But, even though Hengstenberg is also guilty of that charge, he, at least in principle, also wants to allow the OT to interpret itself. This is something that Kaiser is not so much opposed to as something that he does not seem to have considered, at least in an evangelical garb such as Hengstenberg. For Kaiser, this is something too similar to the modern critical concept of "reinterpretation" and thus (rightfully) outlawed at the start. Hengstenberg, however, raises the question within the context of not only a thoroughly orthodox view of biblical authorship, but also in terms of a consideration of the nature of the OT canon. For Hengstenberg, in the early days of the nineteenth century, the OT canon was still a safe haven from the storms of biblical criticism.

resented a distinct historical moment in the progress and unfolding of the whole vision. Within the hallowed halls of the OT Scriptures, Hengstenberg, Keil and others profess to hear the words and commentary of all the prophets, beginning with Moses and ending with Malachi. Some were known by name in Scripture, others were left unidentified. There are many examples of prophetic echoes in Scripture.[10] A notable one is Hannah's poem in 1 Samuel 2:1-10. As she dedicates her son, Hannah offers a song of praise and thanksgiving. At the close of her hymn, Hannah moves to another theme: the prophetic hope of the coming of God's messianic king (1 Sam 2:10). She does this by means of an echo of the poems in the Pentateuch. She says, "May those who contend with the LORD be shattered; against them may he thunder in the heavens, and judge the ends of the earth; may he give strength to his king, and exalt the horn of his anointed." Hannah's "anointed one" and "king" allude to the "messianic king" in the poetry of the Pentateuch (Num 24:7).

Biblical critics have been at a loss to explain how Hannah could have expressed such words. Where could Hannah have gotten a hope in a coming king? Their only explanation is to suppose that a later scribe has rewritten Hannah's praise hymn to make it conform to the messianic beliefs of the later prophets. They have failed to see, however, that Hannah or one of the later "prophetic authors" could have read the Pentateuch or been aware of the prophetic hope in the poems of the Pentateuch. If understood as an echo of the poetry in the Pentateuch, Hannah's words make sense. She, like the prophet Habakkuk, pleads with God to fulfill the messianic hopes that she has learned from the poems in the Pentateuch. Hannah's poem echoes the prophetic hopes of the Pentateuch, and Habakkuk's poem echoes Hannah's. The two poems guide readers in understanding the Pentateuch as messianic.[11] The notion of a prophetic edition of the OT does not, by itself, prove the Pentateuch to be messianic. It does, however, demonstrate that the canonical Pentateuch, as it is in our Bible, makes good sense as a messianic whole.

## THE TANAK

The foregoing observations on the "making" of the Pentateuch and the pro-

---

[10]For example, Zechariah 6:12-13 shows the postexilic interpretation of 2 Samuel 7; Psalm 110; Genesis 14.

[11]See, for example, Genesis 12:2; 18:18; 26:4; Psalm 72:17; Jeremiah 4:2; and Psalm 72:8; Zechariah 9:10.

phetic echo suggest that there is "intelligent life" behind the composition of the biblical books. This raises the question of whether the same sort of intelligent design can be found in the selection and assembly of these books into the whole OT canon (Tanak). I have much to say in this book about the final canonical shape of the OT, arguing throughout that its purpose was to provide the books of the OT with the best possible context for viewing them messianically.

Sometimes, the messianic influence on the final shape is conspicuous. In other cases, it may be merely a matter of what books are placed together and what order they follow (contextuality). The book of Ruth does not stand between the historical books of Judges and Samuel in the Hebrew canon. There, Ruth, whom Boaz called "a virtuous woman," is placed after the poem in Proverbs 31 that begins with the question "Who can find a virtuous woman?"

Those who assembled the OT into its present shape were devout students of Scripture. Many of the individual books of Scripture had been studied and meditated upon for centuries.[12] They had come to be understood not merely as individual books, but as parts of a collected whole. When they were arranged into the OT canon, their framers no doubt were guided by such a holistic understanding of the HB.

Leaders such as Ezra, entrusted with the task of collecting and arranging the OT Scriptures, understood their task as, in part, providing these OT texts with an appropriate commentary. According to Nehemiah 8:8, they read the Scriptures and provided them with commentary and insight as they went. In many cases, their commentary aimed at highlighting the messianic features of these biblical texts. A celebrated example of messianically tinted canonical shape is the notice of the death of Moses at the end of the Pentateuch (Deut 34).[13] That this is not a part of the original Mosaic Pentateuch is clear because it includes an account of the death and burial of Moses.[14] As

---

[12]See I. L. Seeligmann, *Voraussetzungen der Midraschexegese* (VTSup 1; Leiden: Brill, 1953), pp. 150-81.

[13]Franz Delitzsch, failing to see the late canonical significance of Deuteronomy 34:10 (and, in Delitzsch's specific case, any link to Deut 18), remarks, "It is a weighty reason against the single personal and eschatological interpretation of *nabi'* that we never find in the canonical Scriptures of the Old Testament an echo of this promise" (*Messianische Weissagungen in geschlichtlicher Folge* [Leipzig: Akademische Buchhandlung, 1890], p. 45).

[14]There are, of course, literary reasons for distinguishing Deuteronomy 34 from the rest of the Pentateuch—for example, the compositional structure of the whole (narrative/poetry) suggests

messianically shaped, this piece of text is a commentary on the promise of a "prophet like Moses" in Deuteronomy 18:15.[15]

First, Deuteronomy 34 identifies the "prophet" in Deuteronomy 18 as an individual and not as the office of prophet. It does that when it says, "Now a prophet like Moses never arose in Israel" (Deut 34:10). It does not say, "The office of prophecy never arose"; it says, "A prophet [singular] like Moses never arose."

Second, Deuteronomy 34 measures the fulfillment of the promise in Deuteronomy 18 far beyond Moses' own day. Crucial to the time of the composition of Deuteronomy 34 is the statement that "a prophet like Moses never came" (Deut 34:10).[16] This statement not only reflects an awareness of the existence of an office of prophecy,[17] but also is able, within that chronological frame, to draw the conclusion that such an individual prophet (as envisioned in Deut 18!) had not arisen. Neither Joshua, nor Samuel, nor any of the preexilic prophets were in a position to make such a statement. In Joshua's day, the prophetic office had not been established, and in Samuel's day it had only just begun to function. Even during the exile, the office of prophet was still being actively exercised. Deuteronomy 34 says that the prophet promised in Deuteronomy 18 "never came."

The relative time of the comment in Deuteronomy 34 is much later than the time of Moses (and Deut 18) and most of the prophets. The intent of the comment is to call on the reader to trust in God's provision, especially in the absence of the fulfillment of Deuteronomy 18. The fact that the prophet "never came" is intended to spur the reader on to further trust in the hope of his coming. In other words, this last bit of commentary on Deuteronomy 18 in Deuteronomy 34 guides us in understanding Moses' words not as a reference to the coming office of the prophet, but as a historically unfulfilled prophecy of the coming of an individual future prophet.[18]

---

that the Pentateuch concludes with Deuteronomy 32/33.

[15]That it is a part of the canonical linkage between the Pentateuch and the Prophets is also evident because the reference to the death of Moses in Joshua 1:1 presupposes the account of his death in Deuteronomy 34:5. There is no other account of the death of Moses in the Pentateuch. Joshua 1:1 thus must be looking at the account of the death of Moses in Deuteronomy 34:5.

[16]Joseph Blenkinsopp, *Prophecy and Canon* (Notre Dame: University of Notre Dame Press, 1977), p. 86.

[17]Since it suggests a distinct group from which the prophet could be identified as a prophet.

[18]I have in mind the way Deuteronomy 33:4-5 links Moses to the promise of a coming king in the poems of the Pentateuch.

The commentary, or explanation, provided by Deuteronomy 34 reflects the same understanding of Deuteronomy 18 found in the NT. Peter, in Acts 3:22-23, applies the word about the prophet in Deuteronomy 18 (not Deut 34) to Jesus. The promised prophet "never came" until Jesus. Thus Peter, through the eyes of Deuteronomy 34, understood Deuteronomy 18 prophetically, individually and messianically.[19]

## Hermeneutics

The goal of a theological study of the Pentateuch is the biblical author's intent as realized in the work itself. The (human and divine) authors' intent is the "verbal meaning" of the book. The author's intent is what his words say as part of the book.

When talking about the meaning of the words of the Pentateuch, one should be careful to distinguish this from the "things" that the words point to in the real world. The Pentateuch is about real historical events, that is, "things that have happened" *(res gesta)* in the real world. Words are not the things themselves. Words only point to things and tell us about things.

In speaking about historical events (things), one may easily confuse what an author says about these events with the events themselves. As important as history and archaeology are for understanding the "things" that the Bible points to and talks about, they sometimes get in the way of understanding the "words" of Scripture. The Pentateuch may be compared to a Rembrandt painting of real persons or events. We do not understand a Rembrandt painting by taking a photograph of the "thing" that Rembrandt painted and comparing it with the painting itself. That may help us understand the "thing" that Rembrandt painted, his subject matter, but it will not help us understand the painting itself. To understand Rembrandt's painting, we must look at it and see its colors, shapes and textures. In the same way, to understand the Pentateuch, one must look at its colors, contours and textures. To understand

---

[19]If Deuteronomy 34 also tells us that the prophet promised in Deuteronomy 18 "never came" (rather than "has not yet come"), then the former chapter likely was written at a time when there were no more prophets. Prophecy had ceased. Compare 1 Peter 1:10-12: "Of which salvation the prophets have enquired and searched diligently, who prophesied of the grace that should come unto you: Searching what, or what manner of time the Spirit of Christ which was in them did signify, when it testified beforehand the sufferings of Christ, and the glory that should follow. Unto whom it was revealed, that not unto themselves, but unto us they did minister the things, which are now reported unto you by them that have preached the gospel unto you with the Holy Ghost sent down from heaven; which things the angels desire to look into" (KJV).

Rembrandt's painting, one must study the painting itself. To understand the Pentateuch, one must study the Pentateuch itself.

## FINDING THE AUTHOR'S INTENT

How does one go about finding the meaning of a text such as the Pentateuch? The answer I offer is that one should approach the meaning of such a text in terms of its "big idea." There are questions we must ask. What is this book all about? Where is the author going? What is he trying to say? Every part of the Pentateuch has its place within the context of its big idea. The meaning of the whole helps us see the importance and the meaning of each of the parts. This is how texts such as the Pentateuch work. They are not randomly gathered bits of written facts. They give us whole pictures, and the meaning of the whole affects our understanding of the meaning of the parts.

This does not mean, of course, that the individual parts of the Pentateuch have no meaning apart from the whole. They clearly do. It only means that whatever we say about the meaning of the details and parts of the Pentateuch should be brought into line with the author's intent for the whole.

How do we find the big idea of the Pentateuch? The answer to that question is simple: we read it. As we read the Pentateuch, we begin to formulate in our minds a sense of what it is about. Once we begin to get a sense of what the Pentateuch is about, we can test our ideas against what we actually find in the Pentateuch. Does our understanding of the Pentateuch's big idea fit with what we find in the text itself? As one reads the Pentateuch, these are the kinds of questions one should ask: Am I forcing my ideas on the Pentateuch? Does my understanding of the big idea need some adjustment? Is my understanding totally wrong and in of need being replaced?

Obviously, such a process requires a great deal of reading. It also requires humility. If my understanding of the text does not seem to fit the text itself, I have to admit it and start with another big idea. Here, also, is where the help of others comes into play. We often can learn from others' understanding of the Scriptures. A major work such as the Pentateuch has been read for centuries. There are some well-grounded ideas about the Pentateuch, and we should take such ideas into consideration when we read.

How do we know if our big idea fits the text? Here is a basic principle: the best big idea is that which explains the most and the most important features of the text. As we read through the Pentateuch with our big idea in mind, we will soon learn whether that idea helps us understand what is going on. For example, suppose that we had the notion that the big idea of the Pentateuch is "how to ride a donkey." We would not have to read very far before seeing that our big idea is no help. Nothing in the Pentateuch comes anywhere near such an idea. But now suppose that our big idea is "the importance of obeying the Mosaic law." It would soon be evident that such an idea is helpful in reading and making sense of the Pentateuch. Most of the Pentateuch is about the Mosaic law. The Pentateuch is even called "the law" by many today. Undoubtedly, this big idea would help us understand most of what is in the Pentateuch.

But what about the question of what is most important? Does the big idea of "obeying the Mosaic law" help us here? The answer, of course, lies in what we mean by "most important." Most important to whom? To me as a person? To members of my church? To Jesus and the NT writers? To Judaism? Such a question could be answered in many ways.

If we are seeking the author's intent, it seems reasonable to conclude that what is most important in the Pentateuch should be related to the author's intent. What is most important to the author? Our big idea should help us understand not only most of what is in the Pentateuch, but also what is most important to the author. We are beginning to get ahead of ourselves, but it is important at least to introduce the notion of how we determine what is important to the author. The answer is that we should look to those parts of the Pentateuch that most clearly reveal the work of the author. How has the author put the book together? What terms does he repeat? What is the overall outline or structure of the book? These are the kinds of questions that help us see the most clearly defined activities of the author in a book such as the Pentateuch. It is only natural to suppose that such elements will help us determine what is most important to the author of the book.

Let us take an example. It is well known that the author of the Pentateuch writes for more than sixty chapters with hardly a word said about the Mosaic law. If we think that the big idea of the Pentateuch is "the importance of obeying the Mosaic law," why does this idea help us so little to understand the whole first sixty chapters of the book? The Mosaic law does not seem to be most important to the author in the first part of the Pentateuch. Some have suggested the Pentateuch should have begun with Exodus 12:1, which begins the account of the giving of Passover, the first real part of the Mosaic law in the Pentateuch. A better way is to adjust our understanding of the big idea. Perhaps another way of stating our big idea will help explain one of the most important facts about the Pentateuch, which is that it does not immediately deal with the Mosaic law.

In this introduction, for illustration purposes, I will pursue a different big idea for the Pentateuch. I propose that the big idea of the Pentateuch is "the importance of living by faith." Admittedly, when we read through the Pentateuch with this big idea in mind, it does not immediately help us understand most of what is there. Most of what is there is still "law." It does, however, as we will see, help us understand what seems to be most important to the author. It may be that we will have to feel our way along a bit further in formulating our understanding of the big idea of the Pentateuch. If our big idea is to be a good one, it must include both the Mosaic law and the concept of living by faith. At this point, my concern is to introduce the concept of a "big idea" and the way it can help us shape our understanding of the author's central focus in the Pentateuch.

To summarize: We are seeking the author's intent in the Pentateuch. This means that we must seek to understand the meaning of his words and sentences. We do that by understanding his words within the context of the whole of the written Pentateuch. Our clues to the author's big idea are to be sought primarily in those things that he most often writes about and that seem most important to him.

## The Composition of the Pentateuch

What can one say about the way the biblical authors wrote their books? We often assume that biblical books such as the Pentateuch were written as books are today. That is unlikely. From what we can gather from a close study of the Pentateuch itself, the actual work of composition was complex. Many smaller written texts were woven into a single text, much like one would make a quilt or even a scrapbook. The end product demonstrates its unity and singleness of purpose. A close look at the way the Pentateuch was written can give us a clearer picture of the author's meaning.

The author of the Pentateuch apparently started out with two kinds of written sources. It seems that he had several smaller written works that formed the basis of the Pentateuch as a whole. The story of primeval history

(Gen 1–11) or the story of the patriarchs (Gen 12–50) probably already existed in written form when they were used to "make" the Pentateuch. The author also seems to have had a collection of several smaller written records. Some of these were in narrative form, others in poetic. He also had several collections of written laws.

The work of the author, however, was more than merely the compiling of written sources, more than just the making of a scrapbook. The Pentateuch as we now have it is the product of much reflection and organization of its material. There is a strategy in its final shape. Thus, it is important to call its author an "author." His work surely merits that description. The author took written records and wove them together into a coherent whole so that the whole of his narrative has a center, a focus, and tells a complete story of real events. The most direct indication of the author's meaning in the Pentateuch is the overall literary strategy of the book and the verbal seams that unite the final form of the text. The authorship of the Pentateuch is much like that of the Gospels, Samuel and Kings, all of which appear to have used written sources to tell their story.

A question that has interested evangelical biblical scholars is whether the author of the Pentateuch was Moses. I believe that the "biblical" answer to that question comes from Joshua 1:8 and John 5:46. After the death of Moses, Joshua had in his hands a book called "the law" (Josh 1:8). In John 5:46 Jesus said that Moses wrote concerning him. It is reasonable to conclude from these two texts that, as the biblical writers understood their own books, it was Moses who gave Joshua the book called "the law," in which he wrote about the Christ. It is also reasonable to conclude that Moses' "book of the law" in Joshua 1:8 was understood to be the same book as the present (canonical) Pentateuch. This does not mean that Moses wrote about his own death (Deut 33 and Deut 34). So there was material added to the Pentateuch, at least in the last part of the book.

Technically, there are minimally two editions of the Pentateuch: the Mosaic "first edition" of the Pentateuch, and a prophetic "second edition," which included the last two chapters of Deuteronomy (Deut 33–34). Additions appear to have been few, but there were likely some important ones. Deuteronomy 33 probably is the work of Moses, but it appears to have been added by a later "author" (Deut 33:1) because its introduction is clearly aware of the death of Moses" ("before he died").

I do not intend to pursue this question further in this book, but one of the implications of the "two editions" notion of the Pentateuch is that our present Pentateuch is quite close in appearance and shape to the original Mosaic one. The "secondary" nature of the last two chapters of the Pentateuch helps us understand the "original" nature of the rest of the Pentateuch.

***What Pentateuch?*** Evangelical biblical scholars have devoted a fair amount of time discussing who wrote the first Pentateuch. Where we have fallen short is in our lack of attention to the question of who wrote the *last* Pentateuch, that is, the one we now have in our Bible, the one with the notice of the death and burial of Moses in the last two chapters. When and why was that edition published, and why and how was it attached to the earlier edition?

The answer to that question is not hard to find. Judging from what is said in the additional parts of the Pentateuch (e.g., Deut 33–34), I conclude that those last two chapters were meant to provide an explanation of some of the major events in the Pentateuch at a late period in Israel's history. One of the last statements in the Pentateuch tells us that after Moses died, "There never again arose a prophet quite like him" (Deut 34:10). To make that statement, one would have to have lived after the last prophet in Israel. The text does not say, "A prophet like Moses has not yet arisen." That could be said at any point in Israel's history. What the text says is, "A prophet like Moses never arose." That statement could be made only if all the possible "prophets like Moses" had come and failed to measured up to the prophet Moses. It would also indicate that the last edition of the Pentateuch was written late, after the last prophet, Malachi.

Such observations suggest that the present canonical Pentateuch was a second, or final, edition of the "law of Moses." Judging from what we can gather from biblical statements, I conclude that the first edition of the Pentateuch was an early "book of the law" written by Moses (see Deut 33:4). The present edition was written much later than that Mosaic Pentateuch. It is impossible to determine how different the two editions were. We have no "first edition" of the Mosaic Pentateuch.[20] Our primary concern in the task of discovering the theology of the Pentateuch is the need to focus on the

[20]All we have is a second "prophetic edition" written late in Israel's history, much like the books of Kings and Chronicles and the *Vorlage* of the LXX. In many passages Chronicles comes to us as a late "second edition" of Samuel and Kings. With the Greek translations of Kings and Chronicles we also have two editions of the Hebrew of Kings and the Greek (LXX) of an earlier translation of a more recent version of the Pentateuch.

Pentateuch now in our Bible, that is, the "canonical Pentateuch." The Pentateuch was not only historically passed along to and used by the later OT prophets, Jesus and the authors of the NT, but also it was the one around which the theology of the rest of the OT was formed. In effect, it was with the "second edition" of the Pentateuch that the book of the "law of Moses" became an essential part of the OT canon: the Law, the Prophets and the Writings. It is also that edition which Paul identified as the inspired Scriptures in 2 Timothy 3:16. It is the only edition of the Pentateuch we have.

***The audience of the Pentateuch.*** When reading the Pentateuch with its theology in mind, one must identify the particular historical audience it addresses. To do that, several points should be made clear about its audience. First, one must distinguish between the audience *in* the Pentateuch and the audience *of* the Pentateuch. In Genesis 6, when God tells Noah to build an ark, he is not telling the reader of the Pentateuch to build an ark; he is telling Noah in the flood narrative to build one. The reader has no need to escape a universal flood, but in this narrative, Noah does. When God speaks to Moses and Israel at the foot of Mount Sinai, he is not speaking to the readers of the Pentateuch, but to the Israelites in the wilderness narrative (Ex 19–24). Just as with the instructions for Noah's ark, what God tells Moses at Mount Sinai is not what the author wants to tell his readers. Readers should keep their attention on the correct audience of the Pentateuch and interpret it in that context.

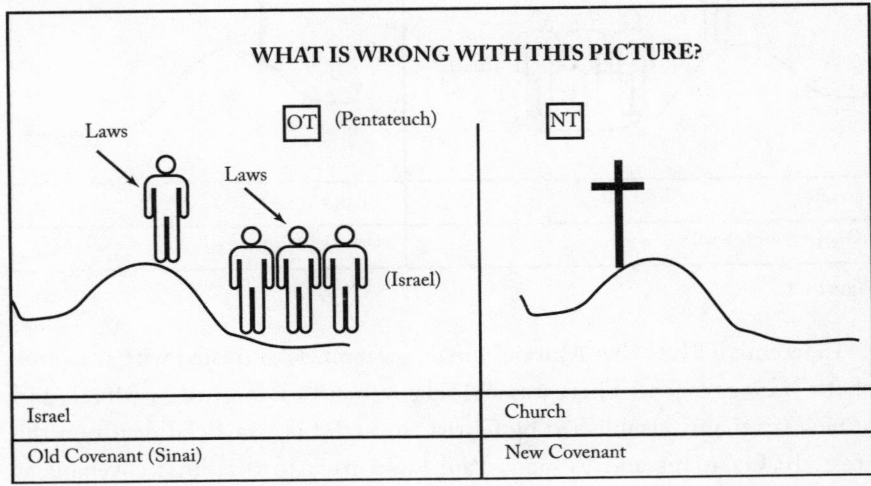


**Figure i.1**

In figure i.1 the Pentateuch is shown as a part of the covenant that God established with Israel at Mount Sinai. In that covenant God gave his laws to Moses, who passed them on to the Israelites standing at the foot of the mountain. Thus, in that view of the Pentateuch, God made a covenant with Israel at Mount Sinai, and it was to teach the Sinai covenant and the law that Moses wrote the Pentateuch. This picture represents a common misunderstanding of the purpose of the Pentateuch. What's wrong with this picture? It identifies the giving of the law with the writing of the Pentateuch. It overlooks that the Pentateuch itself was not written to teach Israel the law. The Pentateuch was addressed to a people living under the law (Deut 30:1-2; Ezra 7:6-10) and failing at every oppportunity (Neh 9:33). The Pentateuch looks beyond the law of God to his grace. The purpose of the Pentateuch is to teach its readers about faith and hope in the new covenant (Deut 30:6). Hence, figure i.2 should be redrawn to show the distinction between the law and the Pentateuch as well as the role of the new covenant in the message of the Pentateuch.

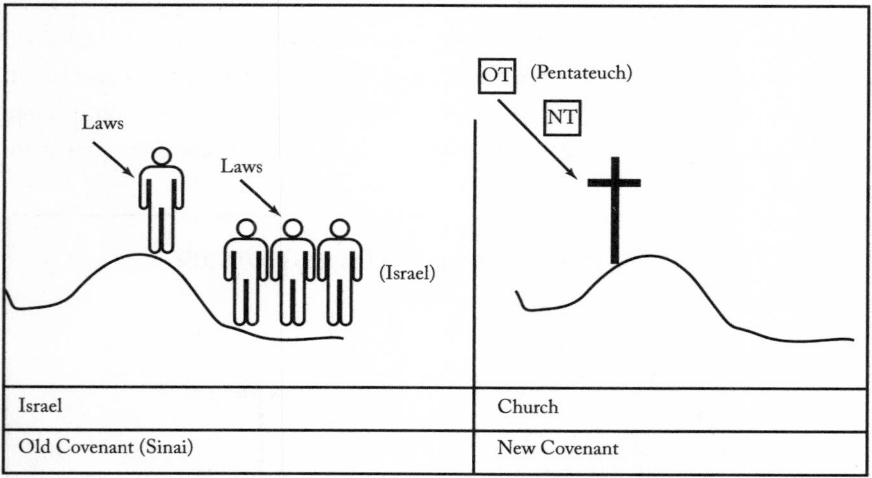


**Figure i.2**

In Jeremiah 31:31 the "Mosaic" Sinai covenant is contrasted with the "prophetic" new covenant. There was an "old covenant" established by Moses, and a "new covenant" established by Christ through his sacrificial death on the cross. In Galatians and Romans Paul looks back to the Sinai covenant as something that failed to bring about faith and divine blessing. Nothing was inherently wrong with the Sinai covenant, but something was fundamentally wrong with Israel's heart: it needed cleansing and filling with God's love (Deut 30:6). But as the prophets saw it, Israel had continued to disobey God's law, and they were in danger of divine correction. Ultimately, the need was to have the law written on their hearts instead of on tablets of stone (cf. Ezek 36:26-27). Israel's prophets and the NT authors frequently looked back at the law as a colossal failure. The Sinai covenant was a broken covenant. The NT contrasted the failure of the Sinai covenant with the new covenant, which succeeded in Christ.

The Pentateuch as we have it in our Bible today is not directly associated with Sinai. To be sure, it tells us about Sinai, but it is not to be identified with the events at Sinai. Keep in mind that it was not at Mount Sinai that Moses gave Israel the present canonical Pentateuch. The Pentateuch was written to Israel at a later time, certainly only after Israel's failures that it records. It was given to tell Israel that the Sinai covenant had failed. As the prophet Hosea saw, the Pentateuch is primarily not about a wedding, but a divorce. In the canonical Pentateuch the prophets also see beyond that divorce to a new covenant "in the last days" (Hos 3:5). In the Pentateuch we are confronted with a call to a new covenant, not to the old. In that respect, the Pentateuch is quite close in meaning to NT book of Galatians. The book of Galatians is also about the Sinai covenant. Paul, in Galatians, raises the question of the continuing validity of the Sinai covenant. According to Galatians, the Sinai covenant failed. In the same way, the Pentateuch confronts its readers with the failure of the Sinai law and the hope of a new covenant. If the Mosaic laws are not written to the readers of the Pentateuch, why are they there?

If the purpose of the Pentateuch is to show that the Sinai covenant and its laws failed, why are there so many laws still in the Pentateuch? We will return to that question in the discussion of the relevance of the Mosaic law in the life of the Christian. For the moment, I want to emphasize that the mere presence of these laws in the Pentateuch is no warrant for taking the Pentateuch as a "book of law." A "book with laws" is not necessarily a "book of law." There may be other reasons why the author included the laws in the Pentateuch. Among them is that perhaps the laws were put in the Pentateuch to show the reader why the Sinai covenant failed. We will return to this question later, when we look closer at the Pentateuch's laws and how they have been positioned within a framework of narratives and poems, suggesting a compositional strategy behind their present location.

***Summary.*** The Pentateuch was not written as modern books are. It is a collection and arrangement of ancient written sources, many of which appear to have been fragmentary and already old by the time of Moses. Indeed, Moses may have had to translate some of them into Hebrew. The Pentateuch represents a literary strategy in which the author strives to teach a theological message. The Pentateuch that we now have is likely a late version of the "book of the law" written by Moses (Josh 1:8). Moses wrote it as a source of divine wisdom and meditation, not as a book of law. It was the later prophets who, after much meditation ("day and night") on the words of Moses, produced the Pentateuch that we have today, the canonical Pentateuch. Through those words, God called them to proclaim his "law" and Israel's failure to obey it. Its purpose was to remind God's people of their commitment to the Sinai covenant and the law given to Israel at Sinai. As I will argue in the rest of this book, the Pentateuch's view of the law is similar to that of Paul in the book of Galatians. The law failed, but the prophets saw in the Pentateuch the revelation of a new and better covenant. The Pentateuch was written not so much to teach Israel about the Sinai covenant as to teach them about the new covenant. Under the new covenant, the law of Moses was to be inscribed by God's Spirit on the heart of every believer. Each one would obey God "from the new heart" that God was yet to give them. As the prophets had come to learn from their own study of the Pentateuch, the temple and priesthood had been replaced by the reading of Scripture. This meant that Israel had become a "kingdom of priests" and a holy nation rather than a "kingdom with a priesthood" (as had happened in Ex 19:24). The prophetic ideal of an individual, personal relationship with God through the reading of his Word had become the rallying cry of the "Israelite church." A future union of believers consisting of Israel and the nations had already been laid out by the prophetic authors of the Pentateuch (Gen 35:11; 48:4; Is 66:18-24). All of these features of the prophetic new covenant were foretold in the canonical Pentateuch.

We are already well on our way to describing the message of the Pentateuch. Provisionally, we might say that the purpose of the Pentateuch appears to be much like the works of Israel's later prophets (Isaiah, Jeremiah, Ezekiel). In their view, the people of Israel had fallen short of what God demanded in the Sinai covenant (see Is 1). What was needed was a new covenant (Jer 31:31-34), one in which Israel was given a new heart and God's Spirit (Ezek 34:24-31; 36:26-27). The human heart had not withstood the test of the tablets of stone given to Israel at Sinai. A new heart was needed. The message of the Pentateuch is like that of the biblical prophets and the NT: God would send his Spirit to renew the human heart and lead people to trust God and obey (Deut 30:6).

All of what I am saying, of course, has to be exegetically tested by evidence from the Pentateuch itself. Like any attempt to determine the big idea in the biblical text, it has to be shown to provide the best explanation of what is actually there in the text of the Pentateuch. Why, for example, does the author of the Pentateuch place the story of the golden calf in such a prominent place in his narrative (Ex 32)? Just at the moment when God was giving Moses the law on Mount Sinai, Israel was breaking it at the foot of the mountain. Israel had just heard the Ten Commandments. God had commanded that they not bow down to idols or have "other gods." Yet, just then, Israel had fashioned a golden idol and was bowing down to it.

To be sure, the author of the Pentateuch is going somewhere with his story. He has a point to make. Our task is to uncover that point anew for ourselves today.

## The Pentateuch as a Whole

Before we examine individual parts of the Pentateuch—for example, the account of the creation (Gen 1) or the exodus (Ex 1–15), it is helpful to look at it from a wider perspective. What is the message of the Pentateuch as a whole? What is its overall purpose? When we have determined something about the Pentateuch from that perspective, we can turn to the smaller parts and ask how they contribute to its overall message.

***The structure of the Pentateuch.*** The most influential, yet subtlest, feature of an author's rendering of historical narrative is the overall framework within which he or she arranges it.[21] Some call this the "context." I call it the "structure" in order to emphasize two important things: (1) a narrative has external boundaries; eventually it stops being something textual, like words and sentences, and becomes part of the real world; (2) a narrative has an internal re-

[21]John Sailhamer, "Exegetical Notes: Genesis 1:1-2:4a," *Trinity Journal* 5, no. 1 (1984): 73-82.

lationship among its own parts.[22] To a large degree, the structure of biblical narratives determines their meaning.

*Definition:* Structure is the total set of relationships within a narrative. It is an expression of the relationship of the parts to the whole and the parts to each other.

In this book I take up two issues about the structure of the Pentateuch. First, how do we go about assessing the meaning of the structure of a work as large as the Pentateuch? Second, what is the meaning, or the message, that comes out of the structure of the Pentateuch? The meaning of a narrative such as the Pentateuch is tied to its shape and progression. What is the author saying in his narrative, and where is he going "in the text"?

***The beginning and the end of the Pentateuch.*** Although it might seem simplistic, one of the most important questions we can ask about the Pentateuch is "Where does it begin, and where does it end?" Only then can we ask, "How does its narrative begin? How does it end? Where is it going?"

*Where does the Pentateuch begin?* It may seem obvious where the Pentateuch begins, but this is a serious matter for many who have studied the Pentateuch. A great Jewish scholar of the medieval period, Rabbi Solomon Ben Isaac (Rashi), taught that the Torah (Pentateuch) did not begin until Exodus 12:1, which starts the account of the establishment of the Passover, the first law in the Pentateuch. For Rashi, all that precedes Exodus 12:1 is but a prologue to the Torah. The Torah (Pentateuch), being a book of laws, begins with its first law.

Modern biblical scholars believe that Genesis 1–11 also is not a part of the Pentateuch. A recent work on the theme of the Pentateuch begins with Genesis 12. Another major study suggests that the Pentateuch originally began not with Genesis 1:1, but with Genesis 2:4a, "This is the history of the heavens and the earth." Genesis 1:1 was added to the Pentateuch by a later scribe, and 2:4a was placed at the end of Genesis 1. I think we can safely say, however, that the Pentateuch in our Bible begins with Genesis 1:1, "In the beginning God created the heavens and the earth."

*Where does the Pentateuch end?* It is harder to determine where the Pentateuch ends than where it begins. There is more than one place that appears to be an end to the Pentateuch.

---

[22]See the notions of "intextuality" and "innertextuality" in John H. Sailhamer, *Introduction to Old Testament Theology: A Canonical Approach* (Grand Rapids: Zondervan, 1995), pp. 207-12.

Those who hold that Moses is the author of the Pentateuch usually argue that the end of the Pentateuch is Deuteronomy 34:4, because Moses' death is reported in the next verse (Deut 34:5). The last eight verses of the Pentateuch, they maintain, were added by Joshua after the death of Moses. But, holding to the same logic, we would have to say that the end of the Pentateuch is more likely to be Deuteronomy 32:52, because the next verse also understands Moses to be dead (Deut 33:1).

Others argue that there never was a "Pentateuch," that is, a five-part book. The original book ended at Numbers 36:13 and was a "Tetrateuch," a four-part book. Deuteronomy was the first part of a larger historical book that consisted of the books of Deuteronomy through Kings.

Still others point to the end of the book of Joshua (Josh 24:26), where it states that Joshua wrote a final copy of the "law of God" (Pentateuch?) that included the whole of the book of Joshua. In that case, they often speak of a "Hexateuch," that is, a six-part book.

If we take the Pentateuch as it comes to us in the OT Scriptures, no doubt it ends with the last verses of Deuteronomy 34 (Deut 34:10-12). Not only is Moses dead and buried by this time (Deut 34:5-9), but also, the writer tells us, "A prophet like Moses never did arise in Israel, one who knew God face to face" (Deut 34:10). That is quite a revealing statement. Clearly, the author who made this statement knows about the entire line of prophets who followed Moses. He also knows that none of them, not even one, was "like Moses." All of them have come and gone, and Moses had no equal. A huge jump is made here at the end of the Pentateuch, taking us from the last days of Moses to the last days of the prophets.

Now that we have noted where the Pentateuch begins and ends, we can raise the question of how it begins and ends. What subject, or ideas and themes, does the author begin with in this work? What subject, or ideas and themes, does the author end with in this work?

*How does the Pentateuch begin?* If Rashi were correct that the Pentateuch began at Exodus 12:1, we would have to say that the Pentateuch begins with the law. Thus, the whole of God's dealings with Israel would be grounded in his giving them the law. This is the view of classical Judaism (covenantal nomism). The Pentateuch is law and must be obeyed as law.

If others were correct who say that the Pentateuch begins with Genesis 12:1, we would have to say that the Pentateuch begins with God's promise to

Abraham (the Abrahamic covenant). This would mean that the Pentateuch grounds God's giving Israel the law in his gracious call and promises to Abraham. Thus, the central issue in the Pentateuch would seem to be the relationship of the gospel and the law (gospel/law).

If the Pentateuch originally began with Genesis 2:4a, "This is the history of the heavens and the earth" (and Gen 1:1 was added later), then Genesis 1 would make no actual statement about creation. It would only be a statement about "nature." The view of Genesis 1 would be that the world of nature was already in existence when God began his work in Genesis 1. "This is the history of the heavens and earth: the earth was formless and void. . . ." Nature, the physical world, is already there as God begins his work of "creation." It is a given that even God must face. If that were the beginning of the Pentateuch, then both the giving of the law and the promises to Abraham would be grounded in nature. The relationship of gospel and law would be subordinated to that of nature and grace (nature/grace).

But we have already seen that the Pentateuch begins at Genesis 1:1, and hence it begins not with law or promise or even with nature as a given; it begins with creation *(ex nihilo)* and thereby establishes a great theological moment at its beginning. All God's acts recorded in the Pentateuch are grounded in the "real world" (biblical realism). Also, the Pentateuch begins with the free act of God in creation. The Pentateuch also moves quickly to tell us that this free act was also for our "good" (e.g., Gen 1:4). Creation thus is cast as an act of grace, unmerited favor. From the point of view of the structure of the Pentateuch, the giving of the law, the promises to Abraham, and nature itself are grounded in God's gracious gift of creaturehood. The Pentateuch ultimately is about creation and grace (creation/grace).

The simple structural observation that Genesis 12:1-3 is grounded in Genesis 1 has many implications. A direct link is established at the beginning of the Pentateuch between God's work of creation and his work of redemption. The call of Abraham and the blessing of the nations (Gen 12:1-3) have as their basis God's original "blessing" in creation (Gen 1:28). The future of humanity is tied to God's gracious election to create humankind. Also, the theme of creation and restoration exhibited in the flood and Noah's sacrifice (Gen 8:20-21) provides the basis for the redemption and blessing promised to Abraham and his seed. It is not by accident that in the rest of Scripture, both the OT and the NT, God's work of redemption is grounded in his act of creation.

The God who is the redeemer in Isaiah is the Lord "who stretched out the heavens and laid the foundations of the earth" (Is 51:13). He hides Jerusalem in the shadow of his hand, "stretching out the heavens and laying the foundations of the earth, and saying to Zion, 'You are my people'" (Is 51:16). Biblical redemption is incomplete until God creates "a new heavens and a new earth" (Is 65:17), and then his people will rejoice in all he has created (Is 65:18).[23]

*How does the Pentateuch end?* Biblical scholars have always thought it unusual that the Pentateuch comes to an end before its narratives are over *(in medias res).* The divine commitments to the patriarchs Abraham, Isaac and Jacob are the centerpiece of the message of hope in the Pentateuch, but they are unfulfilled at the end of the Pentateuch (Deut 34). A central theme in the Pentateuch is God's gift of the land, but at the end of the Pentateuch Israel is not yet in the land. God's last words in the Pentateuch are a reiteration of the promise rather than an anticipation of its fulfillment: "And the LORD said to Moses, 'This is the land which I swore to Abraham, Isaac, and Jacob, saying, "To your seed I will give it." And I will cause you to see it with your own eyes, but you shall not go there'" (Deut 34:4). Moses is barred from enjoyment of God's blessing.

This poses no problem for those who see the book of Joshua as the end of the Pentateuch (Hexateuch). Joshua 21:43 says, "And the LORD gave to Israel all the land he had promised to give their fathers, and they possessed it and dwelt in it." Joshua 21:45 says, "Not one thing from every good thing the LORD had sworn to give to the house of Israel failed to come to pass. Everything came to pass." That is how we might expect the Pentateuch to come to an end: Israel, dwelling safely in the land, enjoys God's good promises.

The fact that the Pentateuch ends with Israel still in the wilderness leads one to draw a remarkable conclusion: the author of the Pentateuch leaves open the question of the time of the fulfillment of the patriarchal blessings. He does not allow the reader to understand the conquest as fulfilled within the Pentateuch. He surely knows about the conquest and its initial successes (Deut 30:1). He even adds a few successes of his own (e.g., Deut 4:38, 46-49). He also knows about Israel's subsequent failures (Deut 30:1-3). It is those failures that occupy his attention. The ending he gives to the Pentateuch as a

---

[23]I cannot emphasize enough that the Pentateuch grounds redemption in creation, not nature. Biblically, creation is the result of a free act of God (grace, election); nature is not free (Eccles 1:4-7), and one day it will make way for the "new heavens and new earth."

whole shows his desire to leave open a possibility that a future remains for God's commitment to Israel. Looking beyond the initial optimism of Joshua 21:45, the author reflects the same sober realization of Israel's later prophets who looked back on a long, dismal history of Israel's failure to keep God's covenant (Is 6; Hos 1). Even the author of the book of Joshua ultimately falls under the influence of the ending of the Pentateuch in its own long-term assessment of the optimism of Joshua 21:45. Ultimately, Joshua must face the reality of the exile as forecast in Joshua 23:15, "But just as all the good things that the LORD your God swore concerning you have been fulfilled for you, so the LORD will bring upon you all the bad things, until he has destroyed you from this good land that the LORD your God has given you."

## POEMS IN THE PENTATEUCH

Genesis 1–11 is a collection of small, self-contained narratives. At the conclusion of each narrative is a poem. The poem is followed by an epilogue. Each poem represents the final word of the central character of that narrative. By means of each poem, the central character makes a programmatic statement about the events of the narrative. The poems are something like the songs in a Hollywood musical. They thematize what the author intends the reader to draw from the narratives. The epilogues return the narrative to its status quo.

In the present shape of the Pentateuch the creation account in Genesis 1–2 concludes with the short poem by Adam regarding his newly fashioned wife (Gen 2:23). Then comes an epilogue (Gen 2:24). The account of the fall in Genesis 3 concludes with a poem (Gen 3:14-19) and an epilogue (Gen 3:20-24). The account of Cain in Genesis 4 concludes with Lamech's poem (Gen 4:23) and an epilogue (Gen 4:24-26). The genealogy in Genesis 5 concludes with the poem of (another) Lamech (Gen 5:29) and an epilogue (Gen 5:30-32). The story of the flood in Genesis 6:1–9:24 concludes with Noah's poem (Gen 9:25-27) and an epilogue (Gen 9:28-29).

After the conclusion of Genesis 9, the pattern (within Genesis 1–11) ceases. The Table of Nations, which follows in Genesis 10, is not a narrative, and there are no further poetic texts in Genesis 1–11. An important feature of the Table of Nations is the additional "narrative insertions" positioned throughout the chapter. Their purpose is to provide the reader with a running commentary of the important events in the lives of these seventy nations. There is an important purpose for attaching Genesis 10 to the account of Noah's poetic discourse in Genesis 9:25-27. Among other things, Genesis 10 gives a preview of the historical identity and implications of Noah's programmatic statement in Genesis 9:27: the sons of Japheth will dwell in the tents of Shem, and the Canaanites will serve them.

The Table of Nations also answers additional questions raised by Noah's poem. It identifies the "descendants of Japheth" who will dwell in the tents of Shem, and it further identifies the "descendants of Shem and Ham." It serves as a summary of what will become of these various people when Noah's "prophetic poem" comes to fulfillment.

According to Genesis 10:2, the sons of Japheth are "Gomer, Magog, Madai, Javan, Tubal, Meshech, and Tiras," and ultimately the "Kittim." Among the sons of Ham who will be subject to Japheth and Shem are Babylon, Assyria, the Canaanites and the Philistines. Among the sons of Shem, in whose tents the sons of Japheth will dwell, are Assyria (or Assur) and Eber. Viewed as a historical and genealogical map of Noah's poem in Genesis 9:27, the Table of Nations shows the reader that the Medes, the Greeks, and the Kittim ultimately will "dwell in the tents of" Babylon and Assyria (=Syria?), along with the Canaanites and the Philistines and, ultimately, Assyria (Syria?) and Eber. All of those events eventually played out in the subsequent historical events of Israel's past.

A further observation is to be made about the compositional shape of Genesis 1–11. Spliced into the final lists of the descendants of Shem in Genesis 11 is a brief narrative account of the building of the city of Babylon (Gen 11:1-9) reminiscent of the story of Cain and the city named after his son Enoch (Gen 4:17). This is the same Babylon that figures prominently in the narrative additions to the Table of Nations (Gen 10:8-12). The people of the city of Babylon want to make a name (Shem) for themselves, but in Genesis 12:1-3, God promises Abram that he will give him a great name (Shem).

To summarize: Viewed as a whole, Genesis 1–11 follows a recognizable compositional strategy that links together an otherwise loose collection of independent narratives. The strategy consists of attaching poems to the end of each narrative. Noah's pronouncement in Genesis 9:25-27 is an example of how programmatic such poems prove to be in the overall context. Noah's poem provides the interpretive context for the Table of Nations and the account of the building of the city of Babylon.

Is there a similar compositional pattern of narrative and poetry elsewhere in the Pentateuch? The answer is that there are four major collections of poems in the Pentateuch: Genesis 49, Exodus 15, Numbers 23–24, and Deuteronomy 32–33. Several features of these poems suggest that they are part of a compositional strategy similar to that in Genesis 1–11.

Genesis 49 comes at the conclusion of the large block of narrative representing the "patriarchal history" (Gen 12–48). Genesis 49:29-33 is an epilogue. The poem in Exodus 15:1-18 concludes the large block of narrative representing the "exodus from Egypt" (Ex 1–14). Exodus 15:19-21 is an epilogue. The poem in Numbers 23–24 concludes the narratives dealing with the wilderness wanderings, which in the present shape of the Pentateuch is Numbers 10–21. Numbers 24:25 is an epilogue. The poem in Deuteronomy 32–33 concludes the narratives of the conquest of the Transjordan of which the book of Deuteronomy is now a part. Deuteronomy 34 is an epilogue.

The arrangment of the larger poems in the Pentateuch reflects a conscious strategy that spans the whole of the Pentateuch from Genesis 1 to Deuteronomy 34. This strategy also appears to be an extension of the compositional strategy of Genesis 1–11.

The focal point of each of these major poems is the promise of a coming messianic king. The three poems in Genesis 49:1, Numbers 24:14, and Deuteronomy 31:29 have an almost identical introduction. In each introduction the central narrative figure (Jacob, Balaam, Moses) calls an audience together (using imperatives) and advises them (using cohortatives) of what will happen "in the last days." The phrase "in the last days" is found only one other place in the Pentateuch: Deuteronomy 4:40.

The phrase "in the last days" occurs fourteen times in the HB—thirteen times in Hebrew, once in the Aramaic of Daniel. It is generally recognized that the phrase has an "eschatological" meaning. It is about the days of the coming messianic king. The same three poems (Gen 48–49; Num 23–24; Deut 32–33) also have considerable cross-referencing between them.

What is said about the king in Numbers 24:9a is a verbatim statement of Genesis 49:9b: "He crouches down, he lays down like a lion, and like a lioness; who will arouse him?" Numbers 24:9b is a direct quotation of Genesis 27:29. Such cross-referencing and quotation shows an author's conscious awareness of the strategic importance of these three poems. The three major poems in the Pentateuch frequently refer to and allude to the smaller poems in Genesis

1–11. In doing so, they link the themes of the poems in Genesis 1–11 to the messianic and eschatological hope expressed in the larger poems.

Central to this connection is the identification of the future warrior of Genesis 3:15 with the messianic king of the larger poems. Along with that is the identification of the nature of the warfare in the remainder of the Pentateuch with the battle between the "seed of the woman" and the "seed of the serpent" in Genesis 3:15. Each of the three large poems is attached to an earlier poem to which it provides additional commentary: Genesis 49 overlays and interprets the poem in Genesis 48 along the lines of the coming king from the house of Judah; the poem in Numbers 24 overlays and interprets the poem in Numbers 23; the poem in Deuteronomy 33 overlays and interprets the poem in Deuteronomy 32. A close study of the additional material in the poems suggests that the overall compositional strategy was made from a messianic perspective. The large poem in Exodus 15 is different from the other poems in the Pentateuch in that it overlays the narrative passage in Exodus 14 and extends the Pentateuch's view of "kingdom" beyond the house of Judah to the eternal reign of God (Ex 15:18).

This consistent pattern of usage of the poems as interpretation is intentional and extends to the scope of the whole of the Pentateuch. The fact that the poems have been extended and linked to the king from the house of Judah (David) suggests that their intent is to identify the king in the poems as a messianic figure. The messianic hope begins to emerge from these poems along with the eternal reign of God as king.

The foregoing observations suggest that the author of the Pentateuch intentionally used the (large and smaller) poetic texts in the Pentateuch to establish a context for reading the narratives. The author wants us to view the stories in the Pentateuch within the context of the prophetic hope in a coming messianic king. Thus, the poems focus attention on the central theme of the need for God's grace and redemption (the small poems of Genesis 1–11) and at the same time link those themes to the coming messianic king and his kingdom (the large poems forming the central structure of the Pentateuch). This suggests that one of the central issues in the message of the Pentateuch is the coming king and his eternal kingdom.

## The Theme of Faith

In the preceding section we looked at the influence of the messianic hope and eschatology in the composition of the final shape of the Pentateuch. We have noted that, viewed as a whole, the compositional strategy of the Pentateuch represents the same hope found in the compositional strategy of the literature of the later prophets: the new covenant. By means of a textual strategy that uses poetic texts to thematize central ideas in the narrative, the events of the Pentateuch are linked to pointers to events that lie in the future. Past events foreshadow the prophetic future. Like the Pentateuch, the prophetic literature also uses the interchange of narratives and poems to express its central themes. In the prophetic literature it is the narrative that interprets the poems. Without the prophetic narratives we would be hard-pressed to understand the poetry of the prophets.

One could point to other compositional strategies in the Pentateuch. One is a strategy that stresses additional prophetic themes that show up in the OT prophetic literature and ultimately in the NT. One prominent theme is faith and trust in God.[24]

I suggested above that the Pentateuch is composed of major units of narrative, such as Genesis 1–11; 12–50; Exodus 1–15; 19–24. These narratives are linked through the author's use of poetry and commentary as well as a common terminology and "lament form." Each of these narrative pieces is marked by the author's use of similar kinds of editorial comments. These comments are remarkable because of their similarity to the themes we find throughout the OT prophetic literature. The comments I have in mind are marked by the recurrence of the Hebrew verb "to believe" *(ʾāman)* and the use of this form: (1) emergency situation, (2) promise given, (3) response of faith or no faith.

According to Hans-Christoph Schmitt, at crucial points in the Pentateuch the author alerts readers to the central importance of the concept of "faith" *(ʾāman).* When Abraham entered a covenant with God, it was based on his faith (*ʾāman* [Gen 15:6]). When Moses heard the call of God and followed his command, it was because "he believed" (*ʾāman* [Ex 4:5]). When Israel heard the words of God and followed Moses and Aaron, it was because "they believed" (*ʾāman* [Ex 4:31]). The whole purpose of God's meeting with the people at Mount Sinai was that they might "believe" (*ʾāman* [Ex 19:9]). Also, when the Israelites refused to take the land God had promised them, it

[24]See Hans-Christoph Schmitt, "Redaktion des Pentateuch im Geiste der Prophetie," *VT* 32 (1982): 170-89.

was because they "did not believe" (*lō-ya'ămînû* [Num 14:11]). Moses and Aaron could not enter the land because they "did not believe" (*lō-he'ĕmantem* [Num 20:12]). At each crucial step along the way of Israel's history in the Pentateuch, we are reminded that the deciding issue in their relationship with God was their faith, or lack of it.

According to some biblical scholars, these "compositional seams" are designed to set up a contrast between the neccessity of "keeping the law" over against that of "having faith." Such a compositional strategy, which I will attempt to retrace through the Pentateuch, helps us see the importance of faith to the author of the Pentateuch and shows us its closeness to the theology of the prophets. Put simply, it suggests that one of the overriding purposes of the Pentateuch is to teach the message of faith and trust in God.

***The literary structure of Exodus 1–14.*** Following the starting point of an analysis of the theme of faith in the Pentateuch is the internal structure of Exodus 1–14, which is an internally self-contained literary unit. The introductory segment, Exodus 1–4, reaches its literary climax in Exodus 2:23-25, God's remembrance of his covenant with the patriarchs. At the conclusion of this introductory segment comes a profound emphasis on faith (Ex 4:31). This emphasis is an echo of the earlier emphasis on the faith that the signs given to Moses were to produce (Ex 4:5). Both of these texts use the same terminology of faith *('āman).* At the conclusion of this literary unit, Exodus 14:31, we find the same terminology of faith *('āman).* In Exodus 4:1 the focus on faith shows it to be a divinely given sign. Faith in the divine promise of salvation is strengthened by the witness of the sign.

***The literary links to the other units.*** An emphasis on faith is also found at crucial points in other larger literary units in the Pentateuch—for example, Genesis 15:6; Exodus 19:9; Numbers 14:11; 20:12. Exodus 19:9 is placed within a text that links the exodus narrative to the Sinai narrative. Exodus 19:4 looks back to the exodus from Egypt, and Exodus 19:5 looks forward to the covenant at Sinai. Within this pericope we also find an emphasis on faith. The nature of Israel's faith in this segment is directed not toward obedience to the Mosaic law, but toward the assurance of becoming "a kingdom of priests and a holy nation" (Ex 19:6). This theme appears repeatedly in the prophetic literature (e.g., Is 61:6) and the NT (e.g., 1 Pet 2:9; Eph 2:8-9).

Genesis 15 is also tied to the notion of faith. The function of Genesis 15:6 is to link the promise of many descendants in Genesis 15:1-5 to the covenant-guaranteed possession of the land in Genesis 15:7-21. In Genesis 15:6 Abraham's faith is presented as a response to God's gracious assurance. In Genesis 15:7-21 his faith is a sign of God's covenant trustworthiness. This linkage of a sign with faith is identical to the theme of faith in Exodus 19. In both texts faith is directed toward a divinely given sign.

Numbers 14:11 and Numbers 20:12 also occur at crucial points in the structure of the Pentateuch. They answer the question of why the whole generation along with Moses and Aaron were not allowed to enter the land. The answer in both passages is the same: lack of faith. In Numbers 14 the Israelites followed the advice of the ten spies and refuse to take the land. Once again their lack of faith is characterized as a refusal to "believe" in the divine "signs" (Num 14:11) performed in their midst.

The final shape of the Pentateuch is characterized not by a haphazard collection of sacred traditions, but by a dynamic compositional schema that is open to a new work of God in the "last days." Like the prophetic literature in general, the Pentateuch stands open and ready before a new work of God and calls for the response of faith.

## THE "BAG OF LAWS" IN THE PENTATEUCH

When God entered into a covenant with Israel at Sinai and gave them his laws, were those laws an essential part of the covenant, or were they merely an addition? Covenant theologians and dispensationalists, though arriving at different conclusions on this question, generally agree on a central matter: they understand the Mosaic law as an essential part of the Sinai covenant. For covenant theologians, the Mosaic law is the basis for their emphasis on the role of the law in the life of the Christian. For dispensationalists, the Mosaic law is the basis for their separation of the Sinai covenant, with its laws, from the life of the Christian.

Historically, there has been little agreement among Christians on the place of the Mosaic law in the Sinai covenant, particularly among covenant theologians. The problem is not new to post-Reformation theology. Beginning with Justin Martyr (A.D. 100–165), a recurring theme occurs in the theology of the church and in Judaism suggesting that the bulk of the Mosaic law given to Israel at Sinai was not originally intended for the Sinai covenant. That covenant, it has been argued, originally was intended as a covenant of grace, and the laws were added secondarily. Justin Martyr says, "Thus also God by the mouth of Moses commanded you to abstain from unclean and improper and violent animals: when, moreover, though you were eating manna in the desert, and were seeing all those wondrous acts wrought for you by God, you made and worshipped the golden calf" (*Dial.* 20). Irenaeus says, "And He did Himself furnish guidance to those who beheld Him not in Egypt, while to those who became unruly in the desert He promulgated a law very suitable [to their condition]. . . . But when they turned themselves to make a calf and had gone back in their minds to Egypt, desiring to be slaves instead of free-men, they were placed for the future in a state of servitude suited to their wish—[a slavery] which did not indeed cut them off from God, but subjected them to the yoke of bondage" (*Haer.* 4.14.2; 4.15.1). These are strong words about the Mosaic law.

Since the time of the Reformation, the chief representative of this view has been Johann Coccejus (1603–1669), the father of covenant theology. Louis Berkhof summarizes Coccejus's view: "Coccejus saw in the Decalogue a summary expression of the covenant of grace, particularly applicable to Israel. When the people, after the establishment of this national covenant of grace, became unfaithful and made a golden calf, the legal covenant of the ceremonial service was instituted as a stricter and harsher dispensation of the covenant of grace. Thus the revelation of grace is found particularly in the Decalogue, and that of servitude in the ceremonial law."[25]

Although Berkhof makes no mention of it, we should note that Coccejus found his primary exegetical support in Galatians 3:19, where Paul says, the law "was added because of the transgressions, till the offspring should come to whom the promise had been made." Berkhof's primary critique of Coccejus lies in his judgment that Coccejus's view could find no support from Scripture. Berkhof says, "These views are all objectionable for more than one reason: (1) They are contrary to Scripture in their multiplication of the covenants. It is un-Scriptural to assume that more than one covenant was established at Sinai, though it was a covenant with various aspects. (2) They are mistaken in that they seek to impose undue limitations on the decalogue and on the ceremonial law."[26] Berkhof's critique is curious not only because Coc-

---

[25]Louis Berkhof, *Systematic Theology* (Grand Rapids: Eerdmans, 1941), p. 299.

[26]Ibid. Berkhof's most regrettable omission is the lack of attention he devoted to Deuteronomy 29:1, which specifically mentions and discusses a covenant with Israel and others that was different and distinct from the Sinai covenant.

cejus did make extensive use of Scripture in his argument,[27] but also because Berkhof offers no evidence from Scripture to refute him.

Coccejus's view of the law seems to find support in the compositonal strategy of the Pentateuch outlined above. When viewed in light of its final composition, the overall literary strategy of the Pentateuch suggests that God's original plan for Israel at Sinai did not include the vast collections of law found in the Pentateuch. Rather, the Pentateuch suggests that the Mosaic law was added to the Sinai covenant because of Israel's many transgressions in the wilderness (cf. Mt 19:8).

## Textual Strata in the Pentateuch

In the Pentateuch there are three major types of literary sources: collections of laws (legal corpora), narratives and poetry. I will briefly discuss two of these (laws and narratives) and then present ideas on their arrangement (compositional strategy) in the final shape of the Pentateuch.

***Collections of laws (legal corpora).*** The legal codes comprise the largest portion of the center section of the Pentateuch.[28] Clearly recognizable collections of laws in the Pentateuch are the Decalogue (Ex 20:1-17), the Covenant Code (Ex 20:22–23:33), the Holiness Code (Lev 17–26), and the Priestly Code (Ex 25–Lev 16). Belonging to this last corpus are the instructions concerning the pattern of the tabernacle (Ex 25–31) and its construction (Ex 35–40). The important task is to discover the purpose of these various collections in the final arrangement and shaping of the Pentateuch. What does each collection contribute to the message of the Pentateuch? Why has the author of the Pentateuch put them where they are in the text? Why so many different collections?

It has long been recognized that basic differences exist between these collections of laws. The requirements for the building of an altar (Ex 20:24-25) in the Covenant Code, for example, are different from those in the Priestly Code. According to the Covenant Code, the altar was to be made of earth or stones and could be set up "in every place" where God caused his name to be remembered (Ex 20:24). This was a simple form of altar reminiscent of the

---

[27]Johann Coccejus, *Summa theologiae ex scripturis repetita*, in *Opera omnia* (Amsterdam, 1701), 7:281-90.

[28]Some of the following discussion of law collections in the Pentateuch is drawn from John H. Sailhamer, *Introduction to Old Testament Theology: A Canonical Approach* (Grand Rapids: Zondervan, 1995), pp. 275-81, 288-89, and is used by permission.

altars in the patriarchal period. According to the Priestly Code, the altar was to be made of acacia wood overlaid with bronze (Ex 27:1-3) and was to be placed in the tabernacle, where only the priests would have access to it. This is a different sort of altar.

There have been numerous attempts to harmonize these two altar laws. According to one traditional harmonization, Israel was to have two altars, an earthen one for the burnt offering and a wooden one for burning incense.[29] The problem with this explanation is that in Exodus 38:1 the altar used for the burnt offering was to be made of wood. Another common harmonization is that the bronze altar of Exodus 27 was to be hollow (Ex 27:8) and therefore to be filled with dirt or stones to make the earthen altar of Exodus 20.[30] Thus, what appears to be a description of two distinct altars is in fact two aspects of one altar. Such attempts underscore the problem rather than provide a solution. Among modern conservative scholars, the tendency is to allow the two passages to stand without a harmonization; the earthen altar is taken merely as a temporary measure.[31] Although this explanation may provide a solution to the historical problem of the purpose of the two altars, it completely misses the literary question of why the two types of altars are prescribed in the Pentateuch without an attempt to harmonize or explain their differences. Our task is to identify the strategy behind the placement of these collections of laws rather than explain them away.

***Narratives in the Pentateuch.*** Numerous narrative texts of varying lengths are also found in the central portion of the Pentateuch. Not only do these texts provide the general framework for the legal collections, but also they are embedded within the various collections of laws. The general framework of this center section comprises three complex narratives: the exodus narrative (Ex 1–18), the Sinai narrative (Ex 19–34) and the wilderness narrative (Num 10:11–21:35). There are several smaller but strategically important narratives within this section that are also related to the larger framework—for example,

---

[29]Michael Walther, *Harmonia totius S. Scripturae* (Strasbourg, 1627), p. 176.

[30]H. S. Horovitz, ed., *Mechilta D'Rabbi Ismael* (Jerusalem: Wahrmann, 1970), p. 242. "Alij melius sic conciliant, internam altaris partem fuisse de terra solida et compacta, externam autem de lignis dictis" (Walther, *Harmonia totius S. Scripturae*, p. 176). "The enclosing copper case served merely to keep the earth together" (Robert Jamieson, A. R. Fausset and David Brown, *A Commentary, Critical, Experimental and Practical, on the Old and New Testaments* [Grand Rapids: Eerdmans, 1945], 1:391).

[31]Walter Kaiser Jr., "Exodus," in *The Expositor's Bible Commentary,* ed. Frank E. Gaebelein (Grand Rapids: Zondervan, 1992), 2:428.

the oppression narrative (Ex 1); the calls of Moses (Ex 3; 6) and of Joshua (Num 27:12-23); the accounts of the faith of Moses, Aaron and the people (Ex 4; 19) and of their lack of faith (Num 13–14; 20); the narratives of Aaron's calf idol (Ex 32) and of Israel's goat idols (Lev 17:1-9); the narratives of Moses and Pharaoh (Ex 7–12) and of Balaam and Balak (Num 22–24). Although each of these narrative units has a discernible internal structure, our interest in them at the present time is their relationship with each other and with the collections of laws discussed above. It is our task to explain the interrelationship of these narrative texts and the collections of laws.

## TEXTUAL STRATEGY IN THE PENTATEUCH

***The collections of laws (legal corpora) and the Sinai narratives.*** A curious feature of the Sinai narratives is the way in which they envelop and thus serve to link the collects of laws in the Decalogue, the Covenant Code and the Priestly Code.

1. The Decalogue follows the account of the covenant ceremony in Exodus 19:1-25. This narrative is complex and includes two major segments. The first is an account of the establishment of an initial covenant on Mount Sinai Ex (19:1-16a), and the second is an account of Israel's fearful retreat from God (Ex 19:16b-25).
2. The Decalogue (Ex 20:1-17), in turn, is followed by a short narrative, again recounting the fear of the people at Sinai (Ex 20:18-21).
3. The Covenant Code is then embedded in the Sinai narrative between Exodus 20:21 and Exodus 24:1-18.
4. That narrative is followed by the Priestly Code (Ex 25–Lev 16).
5. Furthermore, the account of the making of the golden calf (Ex 32) and the reestablishment of the Sinai covenant (Ex 33–34), both parts of the Sinai narrative, break into the Priestly Code just after the instructions for making the tabernacle (Ex 25–31) and before the account of its completion (Ex 35–40).
6. Consequently, the instructions for building the tabernacle are separated from the remainder of the Priestly Code by the account of the failure of the house of Aaron in the incident of the golden calf (Ex 32) and by the account of the renewal of the Sinai covenant (Ex 33–34).

These observations raise important literary questions. What is the effect of the arrangement of the laws and narrative in the present shape of the text? Is there a sense to be gained from the pattern of narratives and laws in the Pentateuch? Is the shape of the text a part of its meaning? I will address this matter by attempting to unravel and reflecting on the literary strategy behind the shape of the Sinai narrative.

By means of the arrangement of the narrative, the Sinai covenant before the incident of the golden calf is characterized by the laws of the Decalogue, the Covenant Code and the instructions for building the tabernacle. However, the Sinai covenant after the incident of golden calf is characterized by the fundamentally different and more extensive Priestly Code (Ex 35–Lev 16). In other words, after the incident of the golden calf, the bulk of the priestly laws (Ex 35–Lev 16) takes the place of the Decalogue, the Covenant Code and the tabernacle (Ex 19–24). The incident of the golden calf has caused a fundamental change in the nature of Israel's covenant relationship.

With the texts positioned in this way, the changes perceived between the laws in the two codes (e.g., two kinds of altars) are presented as part of a larger change in the nature of the Sinai covenant itself, a change resulting from the incident of the golden calf. Rather than attempting to harmonize the differences between the two law codes, the author uses these differences as part of his message. It is these differences that show that a change had come over Israel's covenant with God because of the sin of the golden calf. Israel's initial relationship with God at Sinai, characterized by the patriarchal simplicity of the Covenant Code (Ex 20–23), was now represented by the complex and restrictive laws of the Priestly Code (Ex 35–Lev 16).

What emerges in this way of understanding the narrative strategy is the notion that the biblical portrayal of Israel's relationship with God in the covenant at Sinai was not meant to be read in a static way. The author wanted to show that Israel's relationship with God, established at Sinai, underwent important changes due to Israel's repeated failure to obey God. What began as a covenant between God and Israel, fashioned after that of the patriarchs (the Covenant Code), had become a law code increasingly more complex (the Priestly Code) as Israel failed to obey God. Israel's propensity to follow "other gods," demonstrated in these narratives by the transgression of the golden calf, necessitated God's giving them the additional laws found in the Priestly Code.

The placement of the other law codes throughout this narrative shows further signs of the same strategy on the part of the author of the Pentateuch. The Priestly Code (Ex 25–Lev 16) is followed by the Holiness Code (Lev 17–26). The specifically unique feature of the Holiness Code is that in its introduction, and throughout its laws, the audience that it addresses is not the priests as such, but the whole of the congregation (the priests and the people). It calls them to holiness. As has long been observed, the Holiness Code is not attached directly to the Priestly Code. Between these two legal codes lies an obscure but striking account of Israel's offering sacrifices to "goat idols" (Lev 17:1-9). This short fragment of narrative is the work of the author who portrays the Israelite people as forsaking the tabernacle and sacrificing "outside the camp."

Though brief, the content of this "goat idol" narrative is remarkably similar to the incident of the golden calf. There are also literary parallels between this text and the opening sections of the other law codes—for example, the establishment of the proper place of worship (Ex 20:24-26; 25:1–26:37; Deut 12; cf. Ezek 40–48).[32] The people have ignored the Lord and his provisions in order to worship and follow other gods, in this case, the goat idols. Unlike the narrative of the golden calf, which places the blame on the priests, in this narrative the people are responsible for the idolatry. Thus, within the logic of the narrative, the incident of the people's sacrificing to the goat idols plays a similar role to that of the priests' involvement with the golden calf. Just as the narrative of the golden calf marked a transition in the nature of the covenant and additions to its laws, so here the incident of the goat idols marks the transition from the Priestly Code to that of the additional laws in the Holiness Code. There is an ever-increasing cycle of disobedience and the addition of more laws.

This structure divulges a strategy at a high level in the writing of the Pentateuch. The laws of the Covenant Code are part of the original covenant at Sinai (Ex 19–24). The laws of the Priestly Code, on the other hand, are associated with the "covenant renewal" after the sin of the golden calf (Ex 32–34). The laws of the Holiness Code are placed in the context of the incident of the people's offering sacrifices to the goat idols outside the camp (Lev 17) and the "covenant renewal" in Leviticus 26.[33]

***Summary and conclusion.*** When viewed from the perspective of the Penta-

[32]Alfred Bertholet, *Leviticus* (KHC 3; Tübingen: Mohr Siebeck, 1901), p. 58.

[33]For a fuller development of this literary strategy, see Sailhamer, *The Pentateuch as Narrative*.

teuch's strategy of composition and treatment of the various collections of laws, the narratives present themselves as an extended treatise on the nature of the Sinai covenant. The author of the Pentateuch seems intent on showing that Israel's immediate fall into idolatry with the golden calf brought with it a fundamental shift in the nature of the Sinai covenant. At the outset of the covenant, the text portrays the nature of the covenant in much the same light as that of the religion of the patriarchs. Like Abraham, Israel was to obey God (Ex 19:5; cf. Gen 26:5), keep his covenant (Ex 19:5; cf. Gen 17:1-14), and exercise faith (Ex 19:9; cf. Gen 15:6). Although immediately agreeing to the terms of this covenant (Ex 19:8), Israel quickly proved incapable of keeping it (Ex 19:16-17). In fear, they chose Moses to stand before God while they stood "afar off" (Ex 19:18-20; 20:18-21). In response to the people's fear, God gave Israel the Decalogue, the Covenant Code and the tabernacle. As depicted in the Covenant Code, Israel's relationship with God was based on the absolute prohibition of idolatry and the simple offering of praise and sacrifice. The covenant was still much like that of the patriarchal period.

The people of Israel, however, led by the priests of the house of Aaron, fell quickly into idolatry in the incident of the golden calf. Even while the laws were still being given to Moses on Mount Sinai, Aaron the priest was making the golden calf. Hence, the covenant was broken almost before it was begun (Ex 32). The incident of the golden calf marks a decisive moment in the course of the narrative. In his grace and compassion (Ex 33), God did not cast Israel off. The covenant was renewed (Ex 34). But, in the renewal of the covenant, additional laws were given. These are represented in the remainder of the code of priestly laws (Ex 35–Lev 16). Although these laws appeared to keep the priests in check, it became apparent in the people's later sacrifices to goat idols that more laws were needed. God therefore gave them the Holiness Code (Lev 17–25) and again renewed the covenant (Lev 26).

It should be clear from the foregoing discussion that the narrative strategy outlined above is similar to that which has been read from these texts since the time of Justin Martyr and particularly that developed by Johann Coccejus in his treatment of the place of law in the "covenant of grace." It also reflects the argument of the apostle Paul that the law was added to the covenant because of the transgressions of the people (Gal 3:19).

Above all, the message of the Pentateuch is centered on God's grace. Israel continually fell short of obedience to his will. God did not cast them off. God gave them more laws to guard them and to keep their lives pure and undefiled. The giving of the law to Israel is thus shown to be an act of God's grace. In the end, the Pentateuch makes it clear that something must be done about the human heart. The Sinai covenant was passing away. God's will had to be written on the human heart, not merely on tablets of stone. At the conclusion of the Pentateuch, therefore, Moses calls for a new heart and a new covenant. When that time came, God would "circumcise" Israel's heart so that they would "love the LORD with all [their] heart and soul" and thus would "live" (Deut 30:6). This is the same message as Jeremiah 31:31-32 and Ezekiel 36:24-28. It is also the same message as Romans 8:4, where Paul says that God acts "so that the just requirement of the law might be fulfilled in us, who walk not according to the flesh but according to the Spirit."

## A Compositional Approach to the Old Testament Canon

As noted above, an evangelical compositional approach to biblical authorship identifies Moses as the author of the Pentateuch and seeks to uncover his strategy in putting the book together. The author's intent is reflected in that strategy. In this view, the Mosaic Pentateuch is understood as the original version of the canonical Pentateuch. As far as we know, the Mosaic Pentateuch is identical with the canonical Pentateuch with only few exceptions. Those exceptions consist of parts of the Pentateuch that likely were not the work of Moses. Two notable examples are the account of the death of Moses in Deuteronomy 34 and Moses' final words in Deuteronomy 33. Such comments, though possibly spoken by Moses, were added late in Israel's history, likely as part of a "new edition" of the Pentateuch ("Pentateuch 2.0," in the lingo of today's computer world). Contrary to the prevailing view of biblical authorship, both critical and evangelical, the compositional approach suggests that the Pentateuch was not the product of a long and complicated process of literary growth, but comes to us more or less as an updated edition of a single earlier Mosaic composition. The present canonical Pentateuch is thus an updated version of the Mosaic Pentateuch produced, perhaps, by the "author" of the OT as a whole (Tanak).

The grounds for dating the composition of the canonical Pentateuch so late in Israel's history lie partly in the fact that the numerous glosses and comments that have found their way into the canonical Pentateuch appear not only to be aware of an earlier, or original, Pentateuch in some need of explanation (see Gen 13:10), but also share a common purpose or strategy. A notable example is the Pentateuch's interpretation of Balaam's oracles in light of events forecast in Daniel 11:30. The explanatory nature of the additional material in Balaam's early poems (Num 24:24) suggests that his words were being explained and commented on in order to bring the "Mosaic Pentateuch" up to date compositionally and theologically. These kinds of comments assume that the shape of the first Pentateuch was essentially the same as the present canonical one, although, as already mentioned, still in need of some exposition and commentary along the lines of that described in Ezra and Nehemiah 8:8 (those who understood the OT helped those who did not). The present textual locations of large, theologically dense poetic commentary in the Pentateuch (Gen 49; Num 24; Deut 33) appear to have the same shape and follow the same pattern laid down by the poems that they are intended to explain (Gen 48; Num 23; Deut 32). One set of poems, in Genesis 48, Numbers 23 and Deuteronomy 32, is explained by another set in Genesis 49, Numbers 24 and Deuteronomy 33. In a similar example from the pentateuchal narratives, the last chapter of the Pentateuch (Deut 34) is a theological commentary on the identity of the "prophet like Moses" in Deuteronomy 18 that reflects the anticipation of a temporary end to prophecy and hence a closing of the OT canon. This important commentary at the close of the canonical Pentateuch assumes that Deuteronomy 18 was part of the original Pentateuch, and that its wording was in need of some commentary on the identity of the "prophet like Moses." The comment in Deuteronomy 34 makes it clear that this prophet was to be understood as a particular individual and not merely signifying the office of prophecy in a general sense, as might be argued from Deuteronomy 18 alone. The statement that "the prophet like Moses never came" (Deut 34:10) clarifies the understanding that Deuteronomy 18 speaks of an individual prophet yet to come. Such explanatory comments within the seams that shape the Tanak reflect the same understanding of Deuteronomy 18 as in some NT texts (e.g., Acts 3:22; 7:37). Not only does the last chapter in the Pentateuch record the death of Moses and his burial, but also it makes the sweeping statement that "no prophet like Moses ever arose again" in Israel. The scope of such a comment divulges the viewpoint of one who knows Israel's history from its beginning to its end. It is the view of one for whom the whole array of Israel's prophets have come and gone, each having been disqualified as being a "prophet like Moses." It is, then, the viewpoint of one who knows Scripture from beginning to end and is intent on interpreting Scripture from that perspective. It is the viewpoint of one who sees a genuine continuity between the ancient (Mosaic) Pentateuch and its canonical final form *(Endgestalt).* The shape and the compositional strategy of the Mosaic Pentateuch are preserved by its canonical commentary.[34] Who better to interpret Scripture by Scripture than an "author" of Scripture in its entirety (the OT canon)?

Essential to the compositional approach is its view of the relationship of the individual comments within the Pentateuch to the Pentateuch as a whole. Those comments are not random bits of data intended to clarify isolated features of the text. On the contrary, such comments can be correlated with other similar comments and linked to the central themes and compositional strategies of the Pentateuch. As such, these comments appear to be the work of a single author.[35] He is one who knows thoroughly the shape and strategy of the Mosaic Pentateuch as well as the theology that emerges from that strategy. These numerous comments suggest that the canonical Pentateuch did not originate in a gradual process of redaction or literary expansion. They are, instead, evidence of intelligent design behind the whole of its present shape, and they appear to have originated during a single period as an intentional and sympathetic "retrofit" of the original Mosaic Pentateuch. It was a remake in the sense that it preserved the original Pentateuch by retrofitting it within the broader context of the rest of Scripture as the Tanak.

The account of the death of Moses in Deuteronomy 34:5 can be understood in light of this stage of composition. At the time of the composition of the Mosaic Pentateuch, there were no other biblical texts. In a canonical sense, the Mosaic Pentateuch was all there was of Scripture. It was meant to be read alone, within its own context. By the time of "Pentateuch 2.0," most, if not all, of the canonical Scriptures were complete. They would have included the literary productions of the prophetic scribes and the sages. Also by that time, the gathering and shaping of the various books of Scripture into a canonical whole was clearly well underway. We know from reading the prophetic (and wisdom) books not only that their authors were well versed in the Mosaic Pentateuch as a literary text, but also that the compositional seams of

[34]See Sailhamer, *Introduction to Old Testament Theology*, pp. 239-52.

[35]I do not have in mind here the obvious comments about something that still exists "until this day," which led some to conclude that the Pentateuch left few signs of its compositional origins.

books such as Proverbs often were modeled after and built on the compositional seams of the Pentateuch. The introductory words about Agur in Proverbs 30:1-2 clearly are linked to Balaam's introduction in Numbers 24:3. Prophecy becomes wisdom (Hos 14:9) until the return of a future prophet—a common theme along the seams of the OT canon (cf. Num 27:18 with Deut 34:9; Is 2:1-4). Most of these early canonical books themselves had grown out of the close study of the Mosaic Pentateuch and represented an ongoing attempt of these prophetic authors to apply its lessons to the changing situations in their day. The purpose of this prophetic and wisdom retrofit of the Mosaic Pentateuch was to preserve the original Mosaic Pentateuch by recasting and positioning it within the growing body of scriptural literature (books) that was to become the canonical OT. The final canonical Pentateuch thus was a major step toward the formation of the whole OT canon (Tanak).

The canonical Pentateuch concludes with Deuteronomy 34:5-12, the notice of the death and burial of Moses. In the Hebrew canon Deuteronomy 34 serves as a canonical link to the book of Joshua and the Former Prophets. It is likely that the new canonical edition of the Pentateuch was the work of one or more of the prophetic authors of the rest of Scripture. Hendrik Koorevaar, among others, argues that the author of Chronicles, the final book in many versions of the OT canon (Tanak), was also the "author" of the OT canon.[36] In Deuteronomy 33:4 Moses the prophet (Deut 34:10) is credited with giving God's commandments to Israel, just as Ezra 9:10-11 credits the prophets with carrying out the same task. The work of this anonymous prophetic author might well be similar to that of the Chronicler, who also recasts and retrofits Samuel and Kings within a more recent biblical theological context.

In its view of the shaping of the Mosaic Pentateuch, the compositional approach does not differ significantly from the classical evangelical view. It sees an original Mosaic Pentateuch with several important post-Mosaic additions. Where the compositional view does differ from the classical view is in its attempt to point to meaningful interrelationships between the Mosaic (1.0 version) and the canonical Pentateuch (2.0 version). The present canonical Pentateuch is the same Pentateuch as the Mosaic one, though it is a more recent edition of that Pentateuch and has been refitted (retrofitted) with new "prophetic extras" designed with its new canonical environment in mind. The

---

[36]Hendrik J. Koorevaar, "Die Chronik als intendierter Abschluss des alttestamentlichen Kanons," *JETh* 11 (1997): 42-76.

new Pentateuch interfaces with the rest of the OT canon. It is intertextual and now has connectivity with the whole of Scripture. Much had happened since the first edition of the Pentateuch was written, and this new edition intends to bring its readers into the conversation and in touch with the future of God's work with Israel and the nations. For the most part, the new edition replicates the original Mosaic Pentateuch, but it has a wider screen. Rather than reading the Pentateuch from the viewpoint of the beginning of Israel's history, as no doubt was intended in the original Mosaic Pentateuch, the new edition looks at the Pentateuch from the perspective of the end of Israel's history and God's further work with Israel and the nations. The "beginning times" have become a prophetic symbol of the "end times." This new context is a reflection of the viewpoint of both the biblical prophets and the sages who came at the close of Israel's history. In that sense, the canonical Pentateuch is a prophetic rewrite of the Mosaic Pentateuch.

The value of a compositional approach to the OT canon is that it takes seriously the statements within the Bible regarding Moses as the author of a book (e.g., Josh 1:8) and at the same time acknowledges that the canonical Pentateuch contains material and insights from a time much later than Moses.

The well-known examples of post-Mosaica in the Pentateuch are evidence of the new viewpoint of the canonical Pentateuch. The death of Moses and the list of "kings who reigned in Edom" (Gen 36:31) are recounted in the canonical Pentateuch without a hint of a sense of anachronism. That is because the late viewpoint of the present Pentateuch is itself part of its compositional strategy. As I have suggested, the canonical Pentateuch sees itself within the context of the end of Israel's history and the beginning of God's work with the nations. It intends to be a comprehensive overview of the whole of history, not just its beginnings under Moses at Sinai. Thanks to the author of the book of Daniel and the prologue provided by Genesis 1–11, the Sinai covenant and its laws are now viewed within the scope of the history of the world and all of creation. The "rest of the story" is more than a rerun of the Mosaic Pentateuch; it is a reflective memoir of the life of Moses and an honest critique of Israel's common humanity with Adam. To be sure, this "new" evaluation of Moses and Sinai was itself drawn from the prophetic Scriptures that had taken their place alongside the Mosaic Pentateuch as its interpreters. Those prophetic Scriptures themselves were a product of the Mosaic Pentateuch. They were the work of nameless prophets who had read and studied the Mosaic Scriptures (e.g., Josh 1:8) and were very much aware of their continuing relevance.

To have ignored this "effective history" of the Pentateuch and have kept only the immediate perspective of the Mosaic Pentateuch, which focused on the Sinai covenant and not also the new covenant, would have meant a continual rereading of the canonical Pentateuch solely within the context of the original covenant at Sinai. It would have been a "planned obsolescence" for the Pentateuch as Scripture and would thereby have been destined for the hermeneutical chop shop.

In light of the increasingly pessimistic viewpoint of the prophets regarding the Sinai covenant, merely restating the originally positive aspects of that covenant would have unnecessarily isolated it from the rest of Israel's history and from the prophetic Scriptures' own inspired evaluation of that history. It would have been unnecessary because the Mosaic Pentateuch already contained the seeds of the prophet's pessimism regarding Sinai.[37] In addition, such a restatement would have permanently linked the Pentateuch to the Sinai covenant and suggested its eventual obsolescence with the passing of that covenant. As it now stands, the present canonical Pentateuch is not, and should not, without further reflection, be identified with the Sinai covenant (cf. Deut 29:1). On the contrary, the present Pentateuch cast itself as a revisiting of that covenant and a consequent reevaluation of it in light of the prophetic hope of a new covenant (Jer 31:31). Although the hope for a new covenant was already an essential part of the Mosaic Pentateuch (Deut 30:6), without a reading of the Pentateuch within the context of the message of the prophets and the new covenant, there remained a clear and present danger of that message not being heard. As Ezra 7 and Nehemiah 8 make clear, the Pentateuch continues to stand in need of interpretation by "those who understand it." Even the prophetic literature recognized a need for the clarification and explanation of their message (see Dan 9). It is here we should place the author of the book of Hebrews, who in the same way uses the OT Scriptures (Jer 31) as a critique of the "old covenant" and as the basis of his hope for a future grounded in the "new covenant" (e.g., Heb 8:13).[38]

***Moses and the prophets.*** The compositional approach explains the appearance of the prophets and their message not by assuming that they were reli-

[37]Compare the response to the Pentateuch in 2 Kings 22.

[38]Paul also does this in Romans 10.

gious geniuses,[39] but simply by noting that they had been, as Joshua 1:8 urges, reading the Mosaic Pentateuch "day and night" and were feeling God's call on their lives from within its perspective of hope and divine grace.

An important additional feature of a compositional approach to the Pentateuch and the OT canon is its attempt to describe the theological payoff of the Pentateuch's composition within Israel's subsequent history and to attempt to locate it within the larger parameters of the book as such. It also differs, as I have suggested, in its view of the nature of the canonical Pentateuch. The present canonical Pentateuch is the same book as the Mosaic Pentateuch in the sense that it is a preservation of that original Pentateuch within the context of Scripture and canon. This means that in the canonical Pentateuch we are invited to read the Mosaic Pentateuch within its own effective history, or as Geiger would put it, within its own internal development *(Entwicklung)* within Ur-Judaism and/or Ur-Christianity.[40] There are not two Pentateuchs in the HB, the one Mosaic, the other canonical.[41] There is only one, the canonical Pentateuch. In the OT canon the Mosaic Pentateuch has become the canonical Pentateuch. The OT canon does not aim merely to provide us with a Mosaic Pentateuch to satisfy our historical curiosity. The canonical Pentateuch is the Mosaic Pentateuch to the extent that it is by means of the canonical Pentateuch that the original Mosaic Pentateuch has been preserved and interpreted for us.

***How did Moses "make" the Pentateuch?*** As I described it earlier, the nature of the composition of the Pentateuch is similar to that of the books of Samuel and Kings, as well as the Gospels. Moses used written texts that he gathered from various sources and provided them with commentary, much like a modern producer of a film documentary.

Some aspects of the compositional approach's view of the making of the Pentateuch are similar to the views of earlier evangelical scholars Robert Jamieson, A. R. Fausset and David Brown in their commentary on the OT (ca. 1863). They say in their discussion of the Pentateuch, "It may be conceded that . . . Moses would and did avail himself of existing records which were of reliable authority; . . . he interwove them into his narrative conform-

---

[39]The view of Wellhausen and Kuenen.

[40]Abraham Geiger, *Urschrift und Übersetzungen der Bibel in ihrer Abhängigkeit von der innern Entwickelung des Judentums* (Breslau: Julius Hainauer, 1857).

[41]As there are two histories of Samuel–Kings and Chronicles.

ably with the unity of design which so manifestly pervades the entire Pentateuch."[42] The compositional view is specifically stated in Louis Gaussen's remarkably lucid comment on biblical authorship: "Whether [the biblical authors] describe their own emotions, or relate what they remember, or repeat contemporary narratives, or copy over genealogies, or make extracts from uninspired documents—their writing is inspired, their narratives are directed from above."[43]

This way of framing the question of authorship represents the widely held evangelical view from as early as the late seventeenth and early eighteenth centuries. Campegius Vitringa describes, almost in modern terms, Moses' procedure in making the Pentateuch. According to Vitringa, Moses collected various written documents, sorted them, and prepared them for use by filling in missing details and sections from other documents. These he then "made" (*confecisse* [*conficio*]) into the Pentateuch. It was, he suggests, a process of "collecting, sorting, preparing, and, where they are lacking, filling out and making from them the first of his books."[44]

In a compositional view, passages such as Deuteronomy 34 are considered important additions to the Mosaic Pentateuch. They provide vital clues to how authors at the end of the biblical period (ca. 300 B.C.) understood the Pentateuch. The addition of such formative parts of the Pentateuch was not an afterthought. On the contrary, it was part of the larger compositional strategy that embraced the whole of the OT canon (Tanak). To understand the theology of the Pentateuch, one does well to pay close attention to that strategy. The canonical composition of the Pentateuch *(Endgestalt)* was

---

[42]Jamieson, Fausset and Brown, *Old and New Testaments*, 1:xxxii.

[43]Louis Gaussen, *The Divine Inspiration of the Bible*, trans. David D. Scott (Grand Rapids: Kregel, 1971), p. 25.

[44]"Has vero schedas & scrinia patrum, apud Israelitas conservata, Mosen opinamur collegisse, digessisse, ornasse, &, ubi deficiebant, complesse, atque ex iis primum libroruni suorum confecisse" (Campegius Vitringa, *Sacrarum observationum libri quatuor* [Franeker, 1700], p. 35). Note Fausset's veiled citation of Vitringa's view of Mosaic authorship: "arranging, abridging, selecting, and adapting them to his purpose" (Jamieson, Fausset and Brown, *Old and New Testaments*, 1:xxxi). Since the rise of biblical and historical criticism in the nineteenth and twentieth centuries, the conservative position has, understandably, shied away from talking about "sources" or "written records." But, if pressed, this remains the view of most American evangelical OT scholars today. The only variation on this is that many hold that the "sources" available to Moses were not yet written. Moses relied on oral tradition. This not only fails to deal adequately with the realities of the text itself, but also introduces an unnecessary level of uncertainty into the process. Where would we be today in NT studies if we believed that the Gospels were written from "oral sources"? See Sailhamer, *Introduction to Old Testament Theology*, p. 274.

shaped by, and grounded in, a developed messianic hope already embodied in the Mosaic Pentateuch at a "grassroots" level. Not only do the comments about a future prophet in Deuteronomy 34 reflect on and interpret Deuteronomy 18, but also they are echoed by the same kind of comments lying along the seams of the Tanak as a whole. Those seams are found in Joshua 1; Malachi 4 (3 in HB); Psalms 1–2; 2 Chronicles 36.[45]

Such textual features suggest that during the pre-Christian period there was already considerable discussion about the meaning of the whole of the HB (Tanak). Judging from the kind of theologically motivated themes we find expressed in these canonical seams, we may conclude that those discussions often turned on the question of the messianic and biblical theological import of crucial parts of the HB.[46]

In this introduction I have sought to show the new directions open to an evangelical approach to the OT as Scripture and to sketch out what such an approach might look like. The rest of the book follows this same line of argument with considerably more discussion. This introduction is intended to help readers find their way through the book.[47]

---

[45]An additional element of this (compositional) approach is its sensitivity to the layers of "postbiblical" (and therefore secondary and uninspired) interpretation that accompanied and many times found its way into the Tanak itself. Here I have in mind the version of the HB that lies behind the earliest editions of the OT, such as the Hebrew *Vorlage* of the LXX, the Hebrew texts among the Dead Sea Scrolls, and some parts of the MT (e.g., Jeremiah).

[46]For example, is Numbers 24:7 about Agag or Gog (see *BHS* apparatus ad loc.; cf. Ezek 38:17-18; see also, in chap. 2 below, "The Coming Eschatological King"), and is the "anointed one" of 2 Samuel 23:1-7 David or the Messiah (see Sailhamer, *Introduction to Old Testament Theology*, p. 221)?

[47]Regarding the use of foreign languages and quotations in this book: (1) all quotations in the body of the book are given in English; (2) quotations in the footnotes are given in English if the point being made is essential to the argument; (3) quotations from rare and hard-to-find books are in their original language.

# Part One

# APPROACHING THE TEXT AS REVELATION

*Chapter 1*

# Understanding the Nature and Goal of Old Testament Theology

OT THEOLOGY IS THE STUDY OF THE THEOLOGY and message of the OT.[1] A wide diversity of opinion exists concerning the nature of theology. This diversity arises in large part from how one's understanding of the term *theology* is affected by the word *old* in "Old Testament." Is it correct to say that OT theology is merely that branch of theology that has the OT as its subject matter? Does not the term *old* have a significant qualifying effect on the sense of the term *theology*? Does not the idea of an Old Testament theology suggest a distinction between an Old and a New Testament theology? If so, the sense of the term *theology* may well shift semantically in either case.

## The Nature and Goal of Theology

The term *theology* is sometimes linked to the highly charged notions of "revelation" and "religion." With such a move one often finds subtle shifts in the meaning of the word "theology." Among evangelical biblical theologians and scholars the word *revelation*[2] describes an act of God in which he makes his will known. In this book we take the similar position that God has revealed himself in the OT and in the whole Bible. A theology of the OT in such a setting is understood as a study of divine revelation presented in the OT.

[1]Most of this chapter recasts material found in the introduction of John H. Sailhamer, *Introduction to Old Testament Theology: A Canonical Approach* (Grand Rapids: Zondervan, 1995), pp. 11-25, and is used by permission.

[2]I am using the term *revelation* in the limited sense of the Scriptures as God's special revelation.

In contrast to the term *revelation*, the term *religion* describes the human response to an act of divine revelation. An OT theology that has religion as its object is a study of the human responses to God's revelation and not a study of the divine revelation itself.[3]

When our understanding of the nature and purpose of theology is related to either of these terms, the particular nature and task of theology takes on its own distinct meaning. Such a shift of meaning can have a fundamental effect on our understanding of the terms *religion* and *revelation* and ultimately on the task of an OT theology.

*Theology and revelation.* Theology can be understood as the revelation of divine truth or as the recording of historical divine acts. Evangelical theologians traditionally have understood the task of theology as the study of divine revelation, a "God-given" way of thinking *(habitus Theosdotos divinitus datus).* "With respect to its principle, revealed theology is called a God-given way of thinking *[habitus];* not as though it is immediately infused into one's mind, but because its fundamental basis *[principium]* is not human reason but rather divine revelation. Therefore revealed theology is called wisdom coming from on high."[4]

Theology has its ground in a work of God—a spoken word or a divine act.[5] God has spoken to his human creatures and has acted among them in various ways and times (Heb 1:1-2). He has revealed himself in observable and communicable ways. Theology's task is to pick up the conversation and pursue the line of discourse and disclosure initiated by God.

As a human work, theology cannot claim to speak *with* divine authority, nor can it be handled *as* divine authority, but it can and must attempt to speak *on behalf of* God's revelation, and hence it should be handled with the same care as that authority itself. To the extent that theology can rightly grasp God's revelation and accurately translate it into a particular setting, theology can lay claim to some amount of normativity. "But we have this

---

[3]C. H. Ratschow, "Religion IV B. Theologisch," *RGG*[3], vol. 5, pp. 976-84.

[4]"Respectu cujus principii Theologia revelata dicitur habitus qeovsdoto divinitus datus, non quasi sit immediate infusus, sed quia principium ejus non est humana ratio, verum divina revelatio. Idcirco Theologia revelata vocatur sapientia superne veniens" (David Hollaz, *Examen theologicum acroamaticum universam theologiam thetico-polemicam complectens* [Stargard, 1707], p. 11).

[5]"Requirimus ut Deus ejus specialis sit autor, quia ad scripturam talem non sufficit concursus communis. . . . Necessarius ergo est impulsus peculiaris, qui autoribus omnibus sacris praesto fuit, quotiescumque Deus eorum calamo usus est" (André Rivet, *Isagoge, seu introductio generalis, ad Scripturam sacram Veteris et Novi Testamenti* [Leiden, 1627], p. 8).

treasure in earthen vessels, that the excellency of the power may be of God and not of us" (2 Cor 4:7).

However much theology may claim to speak for God or on God's behalf, as an act of revelation it is a human word. Theology stands on the human side of the divine act of revelation. It is always subject to self-examination and criticism. It is a "mirror viewed darkly" (1 Cor 13:12) through which we must look for a word from God.[6]

In this book the sense of the term *theology* raises several questions. How can an *OT* theology make normative claims to NT Christians? Does not the term *Old* suggest obsolescence? Does it not suggest a replacement by something *New*? Is it not a serious problem to label one part of the Bible "Old" and the other "New" and then hold them both as normative? How can both continue as a single word from God? How can a single word come to us labeled both as "Old" and "New"?[7] The problem itself is not new. It lies in the way of every Christian attempt to understand the meaning of the two Testaments, the OT and the NT.

An understanding of the term *theology* that sees its task as the restatement of God's revelation and hence as normative has far-reaching implications for an evangelical understanding of and approach to OT theology. It will influence much of what is proposed for OT theology in this book.

*Theology and religion.* The term *theology* can also ground its meaning in the notion of religion, a human act of discovering past beliefs about God. In such cases the task of OT theology runs the risk of being understood merely as a human act of discovering and recording religious beliefs of the people in the OT. Emanuel Hirsch argued that this view of theology owes its origin to the eighteenth-century theologian Sigmund Jacob Baumgarten. Baumgarten distinguished divine *revelation* in the Bible from the ancient religion of Israel witnessed to in Scripture. The Bible was no longer approached as revelation, that is, the "manifestation of things previously unknown" *(rerum ignotarum manifestatio)*,[8] but as the written record of revelation played out in historical acts recorded and witnessed *in* the Bible.

---

[6]Karl Barth, *Church Dogmatics*, vol. 1 (Edinburgh: T & T Clark), p. 495

[7]Sailhamer, *Introduction to Old Testament Theology*, pp. 13-14.

[8]Sigmund Jacob Baumgarten, *Dissertatio theologica de discrimine revelationis et inspirationis* (Halle, 1745), p. 6 (Emanuel Hirsch, *Geschichte der neuern evangelischen Theologie: Im Zusammenhang mit den allgemeinen Bewegungen des europäischen Denkens* [Gütersloh: Bertelsmann, 1949–1954], 2:378).

Baumgarten thus tilted the classical view of the Bible as revelation toward the notion of the Bible as the written record of divine acts. The term *inspiration* came to be "the means by which direct revelation was communicated and recorded in books."[9] Thus for Baumgarten, divine revelation was not identified with Scripture, but rather Scripture was identified as a record of that which had been revealed and communicated directly to the mind of the biblical writers. According to Hirsch, "German Protestant theology reached a decisive stage with Baumgarten. It went from being a faith based on the Bible to being one based on revelation—a revelation for which the Bible was in reality nothing more than a record once given."[10]

For Baumgarten the Bible itself was not divine revelation but merely one of many possible responses to divine revelation. It was little more than a religious artifact, not a book where one might hope to find divine wisdom. Such a distinction in understanding the OT meant a removal of the normative status from the concept of theology. Theology was reduced to being merely a restatement of ancient beliefs about God. OT theology was given the task of recounting what the biblical writers believed to be true about God. Theology must only say, "This is what they believed about God." It does not ask, "What does the OT demand of me?" It sought only to discover what its readers in ancient Israel understood about God's demands of them.

*Should theology claim to be normative?* This book is about the classical evangelical view of revelation and the Bible, particularly the Pentateuch, and its meaning for the church today. In dealing with questions such as the above, we cannot avoid difficult questions about the normative status of the theology of the OT.[11] A crucial question it raises for OT theology is whether the OT's theology can be understood as normative for the Christian's life of faith. Is the OT also our NT as it was to Jesus and the early church?[12] Those questions are not the basis for

---

[9]"Medium, quo revelatio immediata mediata facta inque libros relata est" (ibid., p. 16 [quoted in Hirsch, *Geschichte der neuern evangelischen Theologie*, 2:378]).

[10]For Baumgarten, revelation was separated from Scripture, and Scripture was turned into a human expression *(religio)* of divine revelation. "Alles in allem darf man wohl sagen: die deutsche evangelische Theologie ist mit Baumgarten in das entscheidende Stadium des Übergangs vom Bibelglauben zu einem Offerbarungsglauben getreten, dem die Bibel im Wesentlichen nichts ist als die nun einmal gegeben Urkunde der Offenbarung" (Hirsch, *Geschichte der neuern evangelischen Theologie*, 2:378).

[11]See Sailhamer, *Introduction to Old Testament Theology*, p. 16.

[12]For a full discussion of these issues, see Sailhamer, *Introduction to Old Testament Theology.*

proceeding with the description of OT theology, but they help us clarify our understanding of the theological meaning of the OT and its teaching. They affect one's approach to doing OT theology.

The task of biblical theology is to state God's Word (the Bible) to the church clearly and precisely. What could be expected of biblical theology other than an understandable statement of the meaning of God's words that come to us as the Word, "Holy Scripture"? Such a theology does not claim to be normative in the same way the Bible itself makes that claim. An OT theology can only attempt to present the claims of biblical narrative in human terms. Biblical theology of the OT is only a clay vessel for holding the message of the Bible's own written texts.[13]

Such is the understanding of the term *theology* that undergirds this book. Theology is the restatement and explication of God's written revelation, the Bible.[14] It intends to state what should be heard as normative for the faith and practice of the biblical reader.

Theology, like all other fields of study, is a human endeavor. As such, it is subject to all the limitations of human fallibility. No statement of the Bible's theological message can claim to speak with the same authority as the Bible itself. Only the Bible is infallible and authoritative, not our interpretations or theological opinions.

## Old Testament Theology

***Definition of Old Testament theology.*** There is no unanimous opinion about the nature and goal of biblical theology.[15] That is because there is no unanimous opinion about the nature of biblical studies themselves. Many scholars search for the earliest traces of belief in the ancient records lying behind present canonical Scripture. Others look for the meaning that lies in the final shape of the biblical texts *(Endgestalt)*. In the definition of OT Theology followed in this book, the focus falls on the final texts, the OT as we have it today in our Bibles. *OT theology is the study and presentation of what is revealed in the OT.*

***The study of the Old Testament.*** OT theology is grounded in a comprehen-

---

[13]Along with other forms of literary and historical texts such as genealogies, laws and itineraries.

[14]God's Word is not merely *in* the Bible, it *is* the Bible.

[15]See Bernd Janowski, "'Biblische Theologie' (BTh) ist kein eindeutiger Begriff," *RGG*[4], vol. 1, col. 1543.

sive study of the biblical texts of the OT.[16] It includes all the elements of the text of Scripture commonly studied in OT introduction:

OT Hermenuetics (interpretation of texts)[17]

1. Semantics (biblical translation)
2. Exegesis (study of the meaning of texts)

The initial feature of this definition of OT theology is that it assumes the necessity of the serious *study* of the OT. It might rightly be disputed whether the study of the OT deserves a place in the description of OT theology. Is not OT theology the end result of the study of the OT? Does it not come as the capstone of much study and labor in the biblical text? The answer is a qualified yes, but with it a realistic hope that will always stop short of a final result.

### The Presentation

Early biblical theologians often spoke of the skill of understanding the Bible and the skill of explaining the Bible.[18] It is one thing to have a good understanding of what the biblical writers were saying and of their theology, but another to communicate meaningfully one's understanding of that theology. There are a number of ways in which the material can be presented. The focus of much current debate lies in determining the most appropriate shape and arrangement of the material in its final presentation. This step may also be called homiletics.

The biblical writers themselves were theologians, and their writings were their "biblical theologies." The author of the Pentateuch is a theologian working out themes through his arrangement and shaping of the material. If that be the case, the OT should be approached in terms of the shape and mode of presentation reflecting its theology. That shape can be different from modern

[16]See Sailhamer, *Introduction to Old Testament Theology,* pp. 16-21.

[17]"Für eine spezielle biblische Hermeneutik spricht zunächst die Beobachtung, dass die Bibel—wenn sie auch nur ein wenig recht hat—der seltsamste und einzigartigste, ja ein unvergleichlicher Gegenstand ist. Nirgendwo in der Weltliteratur gibt es ein Buch wie dieses" (Gerhard Maier, *Biblische Hermeneutik* [MSt; Wuppertal: Brockhaus, 1990], p. 12).

[18]"Exposuimus libris superioribus subsidia et adminicula hermeneutica. . . . Superest denique, ut ostendamus, qua ratione sensus, istis subsidiis inuentus ac detectus, cum aliis etiam communicari, solide, et salutariter adplicari debeat" (Johan Jacob Rambach, *Institutiones hermeneuticae sacrae, variis observationibus copiosissimisque exemplis biblicis illustratae* [Jena, 1725], p. 272).

conceptions of what a biblical theology should look like.[19] But even if that is the case, there may still be sufficient reason for seeking an alternative arrangement of the OT material or plan or strategy of presentation. As a theological task, OT theology must seek to make the message of the OT as clear and precise as possible to whatever audience it might have. For many audiences, this means that it must present itself as an integrated whole. It must show how the parts fit into the whole. It must present the inherent structure of the biblical message in its entirety and thus squarely face the problem of how to arrange its parts in a meaningful way.

The most common structures of presentation traditionally chosen by OT theologians can be grouped into four types.

1. *Systematic.* Arranging theological systems under major headings, such as God, humanity and salvation.[20] This approach to the presentation of OT theology has been criticized as artificial, one that forces the OT to fit into modern categories of thinking and distorts the biblical meaning. The biblical texts, critics argue, do not fit neatly into such predetermined rubrics. By superimposing alien categories on the biblical text, one may fail to appreciate the perspective of the biblical writers.

2. *Historical.* Ordering the OT's theology after the historical narratives and thus recounting a history of extending from creation to the last centuries before Christ. In many OT theologies the course taken by Israel's history is conveniently understood to be the central organizing principle of the OT.[21] In the last two centuries (particularly the nineteenth century) and continuing to the present, the historical approach has dominated the study of OT theology.[22]

---

[19]A recent example is the canonical approach of Rolf Rendtorff, *Theologie des Alten Testaments: Ein kanonischer Entwurf* (Neukirchen-Vluyn: Neukirchener Verlag, 1999). Rendtorff, however, includes a second volume to his theology that arranges the material more topically and exegetically.

[20]For example, Ludwig Köhler, *Theologie des Alten Testaments* (NThG; Tübingen: Mohr Siebeck, 1966): Erster Teil: von Gott; Zweiter Teil: vom Menschen; Dritter Teil: von Gericht und Heil.

[21]For example, Walter C. Kaiser, *The Promise-Plan of God, A Biblical Theology of the Old and New Testaments* (Grand Rapids: Zondervan, 2008), and Wilhelm Möller, *Biblische Theologie des Alten Testaments in heilsgeschichtlicher Entwicklung* (Zwickau: Herrmann, 1938), p. 527.

[22]Walther Eichrodt speaks of "the tyranny of historicism in OT studies" broken only partially in 1922 by Eduard König's *Theologie des Alten Testaments: Kritisch und vergleichend dargestellt* (Stuttgart: Belser, 1922) and again by his own theology a little more than a decade later in 1933 (*Theology of the Old Testament*, trans. J. A. Baker [OTL; Philadelphia: Westminster Press, 1961], p. 31); see also Gustav Hölscher, *Geschichte der israelitischen und jüdischen Religion* (Giessen: Töpelmann, 1922), p. 267; Rudolf Kittel, *Die Religion des Volkes Israel* (Leipzig: Quelle & Meyer, 1921), p. 210; Eduard König, *Geschichte der alttestamentlichen Religion* (Gütersloh: Bertelsmann, 1912), p. 606;

3. *Central theme.* Arranging an OT theology around a single integrating theme such as covenant, law, promise or blessing. Much debate has centered on the identification of such themes. If a single theme exists, how should it be expressed in the presentation of an OT theology? Should it be stated in categories derived from the OT? Or should one express it in categories that anticipate those of the NT or systematic theology?

4. *No central theme or idea.* Abandoning the attempt to rearrange the existing order and arrangement of the OT's message. In this view, any attempt to superimpose a structure on the OT's own way of presentation runs the risk of distorting the theological picture of the OT, if not even its theology.[23]

***Divine revelation.*** The definition of OT theology offered above assumes that the term *theology* finds its meaning in relation to the concept of revelation. OT theology is concerned with that revelation of God's will contained in the written pages of the OT. It expects to find in its study of the OT knowledge that comes from God, "wisdom from above."

To speak of the OT as revelation is not merely to speak in the past tense. If God has spoken and his voice is heard in the text of Scripture, there is no reason why that Word should be limited to the past. We will argue in this book that his voice can still be heard as it is echoed off the pages of the written Word of the Scriptures. It is in this sense that the OT continues to be a revelation of God's will. This kind of theology of the OT thus seeks to present and proclaim God's Word "as it is written." The task of OT theology implied in such a definition is inherently normative because it takes up the idea of revelation as an act initiated by God though it continues to seek to be a theology like any other.

Because it focuses on the text of Scripture, the aim of this kind of OT theology is not Israel's ancient religion as grounded in the Sinai covenant. Its aim is Israel's "new covenant" with God as grounded in the message of the OT prophetic writings. Simply put, we will argue that the authors of the OT Scriptures were prophets, not priests. Their heroes were not like Moses, who focused on keeping the law, but like Abraham, who focused on a life of faith and was reckoned as one who kept the law (Gen 15:6). Viewed in that light, the Pentateuch appears to have a very Pauline ring to it (e.g., Gal 3:19). We will see that most, if not all, of these Pauline themes are found along the com-

---

Ernst Sellin, *Israelitisch-jüdische Religionsgeschichte* (Leipzig: Quelle & Meyer, 1933), p. 152.

[23]Gerhard von Rad, *Old Testament Theology*, trans. D. M. G. Stalker, 2 vols. (New York: Harper & Row, 1962–1965).

positional seams of the present Pentateuch, which suggests that they are part of the final composition of its author and reflect his overall strategy in the book. This means that although the subject matter of the OT is Israel's failed covenant at Mount Sinai, much hope and blessing awaits them under a "new covenant" with God (Deut 29:1). That view, which echoes through the pages of the prophetic Scriptures and the Pentateuch, shows that for the author of the Pentateuch, God still had plans to make a new covenant with Israel and the nations (Gen 48:4), but it was to be made apart from the one at Sinai (Deut 29:1).

*Chapter 2*

# Finding the Author's Verbal Meaning

In order to understand the Bible, one must read it. One must read it like any other book. That is not to say that the Bible is only another book, but that the Bible *is a book* and should be read the way all books are read. The biblical authors expected their books to be read and understood in that way. They used the language and literary forms common in their day. Their books make sense and reward the patient reader with genuine understanding and insight. The meaning of the Bible is straightforward and unmysterious. Many miracles are recorded in the Bible, but what is most remarkable about the Bible is the Bible itself. In it God speaks through the miracle of a human language.[1] Through language, modern readers can understand the thoughts of biblical authors who lived thousands of years ago in a culture very different from our own.

The study of biblical hermeneutics, or biblical interpretation, is complex, and we should avoid simplistic solutions to the questions it raises. Nevertheless, the complexity of biblical interpretation does not rule out the basic simplicity of the task of discovering the meaning of the OT. The goal of the interpretation of the OT is its author's intent. What is the biblical author saying? What is his point? What do his words say and mean? The goal is always to understand what the author has written.

[1]"Imagine, Mr. Chomsky says, that some divine superengineer, in a single efficient stroke, endowed humans with the power of language where formerly they had none" (Margalit Fox, "A Changed Noam Chomsky Simplifies," *New York Times*, December 5, 1998).

In the case of the Bible, the specific author I have in mind is the human author. To be sure, in the OT there is a divine intent along with the humanity of the author. That intent, as I understand it, is the same as the human author. In my approach to the OT, I always assume that what its human author intended to say is the same as what God intended. If we understand the human author's intent, we will know what God intended.

According to E. D. Hirsch, the quest for an author's intention lies in understanding the author's "verbal meaning."[2] The author's intent is expressed by the words he or she uses in writing the book. That may sound simple enough, and it is, though there are important details in need of some clarification.

The key phrase, "verbal meaning," Hirsch understands as the meaning of the words used by the biblical author. If we want to understand the author, we must assume that the author meant to say what his words say and mean. The meaning of his words represents what he intended to say. If one wants to read and understand what I am now writing in this paragraph, he or she would have to understand the words I am using and the sense they give when they are put together grammatically as I am now doing. One would have to read my words and make sense of them, just as the reader is now doing. Utlimately, the locus of an author's intent lies in the words he or she has chosen. What these words mean, as a part of the language of the Bible, is what one should understand as the author's "verbal meaning."

The expression "verbal meaning" does not mean "literal meaning." If a biblical author writes poetry, the intention of his words would not be found in their literal meaning. The meaning of his words (verbal meaning) would be the sense that his words have within a line of poetry. His words employ images and poetic figures of speech rather than real descriptions of the things to which they refer.

There is no complete agreement among biblical scholars about the nature and importance of the verbal meaning of a text and the intention of its author. Some understand the intention of an author to lie in what the author "intended" to say or "thought" he was saying by the words he used rather than in what the words actually say. It can be argued that an author, being human, has many things in mind when writing a book. A biblical author, in writing a biblical book, may be intending to address a number of issues in his book.

---

[2]E. D. Hirsch, *Validity in Interpretation* (New Haven, Conn.: Yale University Press, 1967).

Before one can understand his words, one must know what kinds of issues the author faced and what questions he might have been addressing. One has to know the kind of thoughts the author was capable of thinking within his ancient cultural setting. One cannot assume that the ancient biblical authors thought the same thoughts as one might in the modern world. The author was addressing a different social setting. His words must be understood not merely as parts of sentences and paragraphs, but within the social and historical context of the issues he faced in his day. Thus, understanding a biblical author's intent requires a great deal more effort than merely reading his words and taking them in their usual grammatical sense. We must locate the author in his historical and social setting and piece together the issues and questions he was facing in his day. Our knowledge of the author's world therefore plays an important role in understanding what his words meant.

This point is well taken by those who stress the importance of reading the OT in light of its historical background. The issue, however, often is complex and can divide over the question of the exact social location of the ancient author. If one is speaking of the context of the author who wrote a particular biblical book, then all is well. If one knows, or has a general idea about, the identity of the author of a biblical book and in what historical period he wrote, then all the information one can gather about that context is important. However, two further issues often go unnoticed that greatly affect the outcome of this question.

First, most OT books are anonymous, and thus one has no way of knowing who wrote them. This usually is considered not to be a major problem in biblical interpretation because it is often possible, or believed to be possible, to surmise the historical location of the composition of a book by attempting to place it within the history unfolded in the biblical narratives. Although there may be serious historical problems related to such an approach, it is a mainstay of evangelical biblical exposition and has some merit when approaching the OT intertextually.

The second issue is related to the first, but is much more serious. Much of the OT consists of historical narratives. The purpose of such literature is to tell a story. As part of a narrative, the events and characters of the stories have their own historical setting. Such information must be kept distinct from the background of the author and the characters of his narrative. We cannot assume that the central character of the biblical narrative was also its author.

That would be similar to assuming that if Jesus is the central character of the Gospels, he must also be the author of the Gospels.

As recorded in the book of Genesis, the narrative events of the life of Abraham occurred in the early second millennium B.C. Fortunately, that is a time about which we know considerable historical detail. The question, however, is the role of such historical information in our understanding of the Abrahamic narratives, since Abraham could not have been the author those narratives. Those narratives were not written at the time they occurred. They may have been written down earlier than the Pentateuch, but as part of a Mosaic composition of the Pentateuch, they likely were used by the author of the Pentateuch at a considerably later period. This means that the historical context of Moses, as the author of the Genesis narratives, is located considerably later than the historical setting of the Abraham narratives.

If we grant the importance or necessity of historical background information in understanding the author's setting, should we also grant it for understanding the life setting of the central characters and events of the narratives? Many biblical theologians see no difference between the historical setting of the author of a biblical book, such as Moses would have written, and the historical setting of the lives of the biblical characters recorded in those books. Important questions of authorship, interpretation and history turn on such seemingly insignificant matters.

There are several reasons why this difference has not received the attention that it merits. Given the eyewitness nature of the Abrahamic narratives, it has become commonplace for evangelicals to read them as if Abraham were the author. At the same time, evangelicals hold to the Mosaic authorship of Genesis and the whole of the Pentateuch. Evangelicals thus are prone to confusion when seeking the historical background of Abraham, as if he were the author of the book of Genesis, and the historical background of Moses, who they believe was the author of the Pentateuch as a whole. Such confusion is evident in the treatment evangelicals give to the historical background of the "author" of the Tower of Babel narrative (Gen 11:1-9). Evangelicals approach the Tower of Babel narrative as if it were about a Sumerian ziggurat and accordingly explain the narrative in light of that context. In doing so, they seem unaware of the fact that such background material comes from a historical context of events that stem from hundreds, or even thousands, of years earlier than Moses. When one reads the Genesis narrative, one seeks to illuminate its events with historical details from the time of Abraham rather than the time of Moses, the author of the Pentateuch. D. J. Wiseman's comments on the story of the Tower of Babel are typical:

> The "Tower of Babel," an expression not found in the OT, is commonly used to describe the tower intended to be a very high landmark associated with the city and its worshippers. It is generally assumed that, like the city, the tower was incomplete (verse 8), and that it was a staged temple tower or multistoried ziggurat first developed in Babylonia in the early third millennium BC.[3]

In such a reading of the biblical narratives, the meaning of the story is not drawn from the words and phrases of the narrative itself, but from information gathered about ziggurats in ancient history. John Davies, having identified the "tower" with a Sumerian ziggurat, concurs with Wiseman that it is usually understood to be a very high landmark associated with the city and its worshipers.[4] From that identification, Davies draws the conclusion that "if the Tower of Babel was indeed the prototype of the later ziggurats, then it may well have represented high-handed rebellion against the true God."[5] In this statement, Davies has imported an external historical meaning into this narrative text. By his own admission, it is a meaning or sense that he has derived not from the biblical narratives and not from the time of Moses, the author of those narratives within the Pentateuch, but from an assessment of historical information drawn from the context of the ancient world at the time the events of the biblical narratives happened. Further examples of such historical readings of biblical narrative are not difficult to find in works by evangelicals.

To be sure, some of this discussion has become highly sophisticated and consequently gives the impression of genuinely illuminating the biblical text. Much of the material is also highly questionable and subject to various interpretations. That notwithstanding, these examples and others show that evangelicals have much to ponder about their approaches to biblical narrative. They should not allow two hundred years of uncritical reflection on their methods to pass as a validation of those methods. These examples point to a basic lack of clarity among evangelicals, particularly in understanding the

---

[3]D. J. Wiseman, "Babel," in *The New Bible Dictionary*, ed. J. D. Douglas (Grand Rapids: Eerdmans, 1962), p. 116.

[4]John J. Davies, *Paradise to Prison: Studies in Genesis* (Grand Rapids: Baker, 1975), p. 146.

[5]Ibid., p. 148.

role of biblical authors when assigning meaning to their texts, and in the judicious use of historical background in biblical interpretation and theology.

As we understand the task of biblical interpretation (hermeneutics), historical questions are of primary importance for apologetics and for introductory issues such as the attempt to identify a book's author or the date of its composition. These are not the kind of questions that should inform us of the biblical author's intent. The historical background of the author of a biblical narrative is a part of the meaning of the narrative insofar as it helps us understand the meaning of his words (philology). One must remember that historical knowledge even about specific details in an author's life and world is not the kind of information that tells us the meaning of his words. What we find in words are specific lexical meanings and usages by which an author gives expression to his intention. That meaning is tied directly to the language used by an author. Words have meaning within the language of which they are a part. A word is meaningless unless it is read as part of a language. Hence, an author has no control or influence over the meaning of the words he uses. That is determined by the uses of those words by all the speakers of a language. All the author can do is use the words of his language according to the rules of grammar of that language and according to the sense of his words. Thus, an author's intent lies in the given meaning of the words he uses and in the way he uses them in a specific work. The meaning is not merely *in* the biblical book; the meaning *is* the book. It is what the author has said by means of his book that constitutes his intended meaning. To understand the biblical author, one must know the meaning of the words he uses within the context of the language in which they are used (or one must at least have a good translation). One must also know the compositional, or literary, strategy within which the author uses his words. This is what is meant by the grammatical-historical approach.

Such a view of the meaning of a book is particularly suited to an evangelical understanding of the doctrine of verbal inspiration (2 Tim 3:16). Simply put, if the words of the Bible are inspired, their meaning is of central importance. This puts the emphasis in the right place: on the meaning of the words as a part of the language of the Bible. To ask why the author wrote the Pentateuch is a valid historical question, but that question should not be construed as an answer to the question of the meaning of the Pentateuch. One finds the meaning and message of the Pentateuch not in asking why it was written or how, but in asking what was written as the book itself. The author of the Pentateuch surely had specific reasons or motives for writing the Pentateuch, but those reasons should not be identified with the meaning of the Pentateuch. The meaning of the Pentateuch as intended by its author lies in its "verbal meaning," be that the literal, figurative, realistic or spiritual sense.

## The Classical and Medieval View of Scriptural Meaning

The meaning of the OT is a function of a context made up of varying assumptions about its words and the nature of the things to which they refer. Those assumptions were laid down over time in the long history of biblical interpretation. Uncovering such well-worn assumptions about the meaning of biblical narratives requires a patient journey back in time. A great reward awaits us at the end of the journey. This reward consists not merely of a better understanding of where biblical interpretations may have erred, but also of a clearer focus on where the meaning of a biblical passage may lie for us today, and a better sense of how we might find a proper warrant for our contemporary understanding. This means not only a focus on how biblical narratives produce meaning and the kinds of meaning they produce, but also a clearer understanding of how larger units of biblical text were linked and shaped into whole books and ultimately into the Bible as such. In short, the formation of the Bible entailed a good deal of interpretation.

Lying behind most Christian discussions of biblical interpretation are the formative ideas of Augustine's *On Christian Doctrine (De doctrina christiana)*. In that work Augustine focuses on the principles and procedures Christians should use to ground their beliefs in Scripture. According to Augustine, the meaning of the Bible is found in the interrelationship of two features of texts: its "words" *(verba)* and the "things" *(res)*[6] to which its words pointed, or the "things" signified by its words.[7]

Augustine believes that the purpose of a "word" *(verbum)* is to point to a "thing" *(res)* in the outside world. A word is a "sign" *(signum)* of a "thing" *(res)*. Augustine further argues that things also pointed to other things. Words point to things, and things point to other things. According to Augustine, the

---

[6]The Latin word *res* means "thing" in the sense of something that is a part of the real *(res)* world referred to in the Bible but lying outside the Bible itself. It is a piece of the outside world identified specifically by a specific "word" *(verbum)*.

[7]Note that the nominative singular and plural of *res* is the same.

meaning of the Bible (OT) lies in the sense of the things to which its words point. Meaning is found not in the biblical words, but in the things to which those words point. Meaning is connected to the role of things *(res)* in the "*re*al" world (*re*ality). Reality, or "thingness," is where the meaning of Scripture ultimately is to be found. To understand the Bible and its words, one has to know the meaning of the "real-world" *(res)* pointed to in the Bible.

Augustine's ideas continue to influence current discussions of the meaning of the Bible. In modern historical approaches to biblical theology, Augustine's view of things *(res)* pointed to by words *(verba)* is a major component of the belief that "historical *re*alities" *(res)*; that is, the "*re*al" *(res)* world of things is the true locus of meaning in the Bible (OT). Biblical theology must be based on a quest for the meaning of things *(res),* that is, "historical reality."

The Latin word for "thing," *res*, is the root from which our words *real* and *reality* are derived. Not a few theologians see the meaning of the Bible in terms of the "historical realities" *(res)* to which its "words" *(verba)* point. By the nineteenth and twentieth centuries, knowledge of historical realities *(res)* had become essential for understanding the Bible (OT). Knowledge of the historical things of Israel's history was identified with the meaning of the Bible (OT). Hence, Augustine's ideas continue to shape contemporary discussion of the meaning of the OT and biblical theology, even if not in the way he originally intended. Augustine's concern was how to relate OT words to the spiritual realities (things) found in the NT. Augustine's focus on the things behind the Bible in his day is today the same as the identification of biblical words with physical and historical realities of the ancient world. The meaning of the Bible is linked to what we know about Israel's history within the context of the ancient world.

Whether or not one agrees with Augustine's ideas about meaning, words, and things, it is clear that nearly two thousand years of discussions on biblical interpretation have followed the lines of thought that he originally laid down.

> All doctrine concerns either things *[res]* or signs *[signa],* but things *[res]* are learned by signs. Strictly speaking, I have here called a "thing" *[res]* that which is not used to signify something else, like wood *[lignum],* stone *[lapis],* cattle *[pecus],* and so on; but not that wood *[lignum]* concerning which we read that Moses cast it into bitter waters that their bitterness might be dispelled, nor that stone *[lapis]* which Jacob placed at his head, nor that beast *[pecus]* which Abraham sacrificed in place of his son. For these are things *[res]* in such a way

> that they are also signs *[signa]* of other things *[res]*. There are other signs whose whole use is in signifying, just as are words *[verba]*. For no one uses words *[verba]* except for the purpose of signifying something *[res]*. From this may be understood what we call "signs" in that they are things *[res]* which are used to signify something. Thus every sign is also a thing *[res]*, for that which is not a thing *[res]* does not exist at all; but not every thing *[res]* is also a sign. (Augustine *Doctr. chr.* 1.2)

Augustine's view was widely represented in the early church. Scriptural meaning was drawn from the relationship of signs *(signa)* to things *(res)* and of things *(res)* to other things *(res)*. Words *(verba)* as signs *(signa)* are a divinely ordained "bridge" to the world of things *(res)*. Through the "words" *(verba)* of Scripture we enter the "world" *(res)* of Scripture. Things *(res)* are what make the world real *(re*al = *res)*. The words *(verba)* of Scripture are what take us into the world of things *(res)*, the *re*al world. That world alone is where we comprehend (and contemplate) eternal and spiritual *re*alities.[8] In that world, says Augustine, there is a sweetness that makes us "blessed" *(beatos)*.[9] That is because, ultimately, it is the world that God himself inhabits. It is the place in which one may find ultimate reality. The Scriptures are what is instrumental in our entering that world and thus obtaining the state of blessedness that is the goal of all Christian living. The Scriptures are not the source of our blessedness *(beatos)*.[10] The words of Scripture are the means by which one enters into the spiritual realities of the world of things *(res)* where one finds blessedness *(beatos)*.

Here, Augustine's thinking takes a surprising turn. Once the words *(verba)* of Scripture have done their part by leading us into the *re*al world of things *(res)* and the blessedness *(beatos)* found there, one has no further need of Scripture and its words. Consequently, Augustine believed, many Christians live happy and blessed *(beatos)* lives without the Scriptures *(sine codicibus)*. The devout but illiterate person who contemplates the spiritual world of things *(res)* is at no disadvantage from the scholar who reads the Bible and meditates on its words *(verba)*. Scripture has accomplished its purpose by bringing one to the point of the contemplation of things *(res)* themselves. The world of things is a further portal to higher worlds of things *(res)*. In such a

---

[8]*Aeterna et spiritalia.*

[9]*Cuius suauitas faceret beatos.*

[10]Note the contrast with Psalm 1:1-3, where the "blessed" person meditates on Scripture.

hierarchy of things *(res)* one is ultimately led closer to God,[11] the ultimate reality, and the blessedness *(beatos)* of his presence.

Augustine's view, to be sure, is not that of the Protestant Reformers *(sola Scriptura).* Nor was it, as we will see, the view of the biblical authors. Augustine's view, however, played itself out fully in medieval biblical interpretation and provided the foundation of most modern "historical" approaches to the Bible.

***The mind of God* (mens dei).** In his discussion of "things" *(res)* and their meaning Augustine raised crucial questions: Without words, what makes "things" meaningful? What gives the world of reality its own distinct meaning? What makes reality real? Augustine answered those questions by appealing to the ultimate knowledge of the world of things, the "mind of God" *(mens dei).* He assumed that the relationship of words to things and things to other things as signs *(signa)* was real (meaningful) because such relationships had been eternally preestablished as such in the mind of God. As the creator of all "things" *(res),* God knew the reality of "things" to be such as they are. To know truth and the meaning of the real world was to see the world as God saw it. It was to know the mind of God. All "things" were certain and meaningful in God's mind *(mens dei),* as were the specific "words" that pointed to them. Also in God's mind were the relationships of "things" to each other. In the mind of God one could know not only the "things" pointed to by the "words" of Scripture, but also the "things" that pointed to other "things." Augustine's notion of history as "things" *(realia)* provided the basic vocabulary in most subsequent discussions of the role of external reality, that is, "history," in biblical interpretation. Talk of "realia" and the "real world," so important after the eighteenth century, was little more than a continuation of Augustine's discussion of "words" *(verba)* and "things" *(res).* Reformed orthodox biblical scholars continued the discussion in the sixteenth and seventeenth centuries, and it continues even today in defining the essential components of evangelical biblical theology.

The classic statement of the evangelical position on meaning and truth is found in Edward Carnell's *Introduction to Christian Apologetics:*

> Truth, then, in its simplest dimension, is a judgment which corresponds to things as they actually are. . . . This definition of truth, however, is deficient

---

[11]Homo itaque fide et spe et caritate subnixus eaque inconcusse retinens non indiget scripturis nisi ad alios instruendos. Itaque multi per haec tria etiam in solitudine sine codicibus vivunt (Augustine *Doctr. chr.* 1.39.43).

> from the Christian point of view, for it does not link truth with the mind of God sharply enough. For the Christian, God is truth because He is the Author of all facts and all meaning. There is no reality apart from the eternal nature of God Himself and the universe which He has created to display His glory. . . . Since the mind of God perfectly knows reality, truth is a property of that judgment which coincides with the mind of God. . . . Truth for the Christian, then, is defined as correspondence with the mind of God. On any level of judgment, therefore, man has truth only as long as he says about facts what God says about these facts.[12]

***The literal sense* (sensus literalis).** The outcome of Augustine's argument was to define the sense of a word in terms of its pointing to something. Hence, the "literal meaning" *(sensus literalis)* of a word is simply the thing it pointed to. The identification of a thing *(res)* to which a word *(verbum)* points is the literal sense of that word (*verbum*). The ordinary task of language is to use its words *(verba)* to name, or refer to, the things *(res)* in the real world *(res)*. Central to this view of Augustine is the belief that the relationship between a word *(verbum)* and the thing *(res)* to which it points is preestablished in language and grounded in a God-given ability to use language properly. The correlations between words *(verba)* and things *(res)* are thus fixed by God's own use of language in Scripture. We know that our view of the real world is the same as God's because in Scripture God uses ordinary language *(verba)* to describe the world of things *(res)*. In his use of a biblical language, God had the same correspondences between words and things as other speakers of that language. God's use of language thus confirms our understanding of language and provides a degree of certainty to our knowledge of the "mind of God" *(mens dei)*.

***The spiritual sense* (sensus spiritualis).** A further role of things *(res)* in Augustine's system of biblical interpretation is to point to other things *(res)*. Spiritual meaning *(sensus spiritualis)*, according to Augustine, is a function of the role of things *(res)* pointing to other things *(res)*. The word *(verbum) tree* (*lignum* in the Vulgate) points to real trees in the outside world. However, any one of those real trees *(lignum)*, if God has so determined in his mind, may be a sign *(signum)* that points to another thing *(res)*, such as the tree *(lignum)* upon which Christ was crucified. In the Vulgate Moses says, "Cursed by God

[12] Edward J. Carnell, *An Introduction to Christian Apologetics: A Philosophic Defense of the Trinitarian-Theistic Faith* (Grand Rapids: Eerdmans, 1948), p. 46.

is the one hanged on a tree *[in ligno]*" (Deut 21:23).[13] Hence, Paul cites this text in reference to Christ in Galatians 3:13.

In God's mind *(mens dei)* there is an eternally preestablished relationship between the word *(verbum)* "tree" *(lignum)* in Exodus 15:25 and a real "tree" *(res)* that is understood to be a sign *(signum)* pointing to the cross (Vulgate: *in ligno*) in Acts 5:30. When, in Exodus 15:25, the Lord pointed *(wayyôrēhû)* Moses to the tree *(lignum)* that would make the water sweet, he was pointing to a real thing *(res)* that itself, as a thing *(res)*, pointed to the cross *(res)*. That cross *(res)*, according to Augustine, points to the "sweetness" of salvation and eternal life.

In God's mind *(mens dei)* there is an established relationship not only between the word *(verbum) tree* and the things *(res)* we know as trees in the real world, but also between the specific tree *(res)* in Exodus 15:25 and the cross *(res)* on which Christ died. In God's mind the word *tree (lignum)*, the thing *(lignum)* to which it points, and the relationship between the two are already established, along with the spiritual thing *(res)* to which it points. For Augustine, a real and necessary relationship existed between the words *(verba)* of Scripture and the things *(res)* to which they point because they had existed eternally in that relationship in the mind of God. God sees the "real world" *(res)* as it is—the things as they are in and of themselves, just as he created them.[14] What is true in God's mind is eternally true and fixed. In the reading of the Bible (OT), the meaning invested in a particular word *(verbum)* is tied to that which it has in God's mind. Its importance rests in the value of the thing *(res)* it points to as a sign *(signum)* of a greater spiritual reality *(res)*.

A major weakness of the Augustinian view is the notion of knowing the mind of God apart from Scripture. Though it may be possible through language to determine what words *(verba)* point to, it is not immediately clear how we can know what things *(res)* point to on their own. Yet this is an essential part of Augustine's system, as well as of those who have followed him to the present day. Without the mind of God to tell us, how do we know the meaning of the "historical things" that other "things" point to? We must know not only what things words point to, but also what things *(res)* signify as signs *(signa)* of other things *(res)*. How does a biblical interpreter know the inherent

---

[13] KJV: "for he that is hanged is accursed of God"; Vulgate: "quia maledictus a Deo est qui pendet in ligno." In the MT "in ligno" is not present.

[14] This is what Kant would later call "das Ding an sich" ("the thing itself").

relationship of things *(res)* to each other? Words are no help in this case because the signification of things lies not in words, but in other things.

To resolve this question, Augustine, and those who followed in his steps, turned increasingly to the authority of the church. The meaning of things *(res)* was located in the meaning that tradition assigned to them. The meaning of the words *(verba)* of Scripture and the things *(res)* to which they pointed, as well as the things *(res)* that pointed to other things *(res)*, was decided by the church and its tradition of biblical interpretation. It was on the authority of the church's tradition that the word "tree" in Exodus 15:25 pointed to the "cross." By means of church tradition, the spiritual meaning of the words of Scripture was located not in the meaning of the words themselves *(sensus literalis)*, but in the interrelationship of the things *(res)* to which they pointed. What this complex relationship of words and things signified came to be known as the "spiritual meaning" *(sensus spiritualis)* of Scripture. To streamline the process of assigning spiritual meaning to specific biblical terms, the church limited its consideration to the "words" of Scripture in Jerome's Latin translation of the Bible, the Vulgate.

The implications of Augustine's approach are not difficult to imagine. The meaning of Scripture and the doctrines of the church came to be formulated in terms of the meanings assigned to biblical words and things *(res)* by the church. The church decided what was in the mind of God. More importantly for the history of biblical theology was the fact that a proper understanding of things *(res)*, not merely words *(verba)*, became an essential part of biblical interpretation. Reading the Bible (OT) came to be a process of watching for the things that words pointed to. This meant, if need be, that the meaning of Scripture could, as easily as not, be investigated apart from the meaning of the words of Scripture.

As long as the church was allowed to identify the things *(res)* that biblical words signified, the system seemed to work. But a new kind of authority was brewing in the eighteenth and nineteenth centuries, one that did not acknowledge the traditions of the church. That new authority was historicism. It acknowledged not the church, but only the mind of the modern historian as the basis for determining the meaning of the "things" to which words pointed. It allowed not church tradition, but only rational and historical proof as the warrant for the relationship of words to things and things to other things. Conditions thus were ripe for a new consideration of the meaning of the things *(res)* referred to in Scriptures. Alongside the church's spiritual interpretation of things *(res)* referred to in Scripture arose a developing historical consciousness that was more than willing to try its hand at determining the meaning of biblical things *(res)*. Under the influence of Augustine's legacy, which valued the things *(res)* of Scripture over the meaning of its words *(verba)*, the meaning of historical things *(res)* took the upper hand in determining the meaning of the words *(verba)*. From there it was only a matter of time before the spiritual things *(res)* that the church had assigned to the "words" of Scripture became the domain of an entirely new kind of search for the meaning of "things," or as "things" came to be known, "historical realities" *(res gesta)*.[15] Whereas meaning, including the spiritual sense, once had been located in the sense assigned to Scripture by the church, it now found its reference point in the "historical realities" *(res gesta)* pointed to by the biblical words. Even now, three centuries later, evangelicals continue to focus on a kind of meaning that lies in the things *(res)* or the historical realities *(res gesta)* to which the Bible refers.

The net loss of the shift in focus in biblical meaning was, at least for evangelical biblical theology, a considerable depletion of the *sensus spiritualis* of the biblical words. Biblical words pointed to real events in history (biblical realism), not to spiritual truth as such. If there were to be a spiritual sense to Scripture, it would have to come from somewhere other than the meaning of the biblical words. Since biblical words pointed to "historical realities" *(res gesta)* that lay beyond the biblical text, for most evangelicals the spiritual sense would have to come from within the context of those historical realities. That was possible only by further assigning a NT spiritual sense to the events *(res)* depicted by the biblical words *(verba)*. That signaled the beginning of the typological approach. Biblical words pointed to real events that pictured, or prefigured, a spiritual sense found in the NT.

The ground thus had shifted under the feet of evangelical biblical theologians. The spiritual sense, which in classical orthodoxy was once the sole domain of the words of Scripture, was now also to be found in the historical realities *(res gesta)* that prefigured and led to the events of the NT. This meant that a NT meaning could be assigned to OT biblical words without depriving them of their basic historical value. It was a historical meaning that found its

---

[15]Latin for "things that have happened."

ultimate reference point in the NT. In the hands of evangelical historicists, such historical moments of spiritual significance quickly began to form a new kind of historical reality, a type of "holy" history that played itself out within an increasingly secularized flow of real events.

One troubling aspect of this shift in meaning was that it occurred largely unnoticed by evangelicals. The reason may have been the safe haven evangelicals had found in Reformed orthodoxy in the late sixteenth century and the seventeenth century. Before the rise of the historical method, orthodox biblical hermeneutics had devoted considerable effort to nailing down the link between words and things. Their concern was not merely with words and historical events *(sensus literalis)*, but with the links between biblical words *(sola Scriptura)* and the spiritual sense of Scripture *(sensus spiritualis)*. In Reformed orthodoxy, biblical words could refer to either historical or spiritual realities *(res)*, but not both at the same time. Having thus grounded the "real" and the "spiritual" meaning in biblical words alone, evangelicals were at a loss on how to deal with the historicist's reattachment of those same biblical words to newly discovered secular historical realities *(res)*. Evangelicalism thus was locked into its seventeenth-century (precritical) retreat from historicism. The spiritual *(sensus spiritualis)* and real *(sensus literalis)* meaning of the words of Scripture were again being detached from their lexical meaning and reattached to a meaning derived from a newly reconstructed, less friendly series of historical events.

The influence of Augustine's focus on things *(res)* was again making itself felt in both secular and evangelical versions of historicism. This meant not only that the spiritual meaning *(sensus spiritualis)* of the Bible (OT) had been reassigned a "real" *(res)* meaning along with its spiritual one, but also that its value as a "word" (*verbum*) was to be renegotiated outside, rather than within, the canonical Scriptures. Words that had once had a spiritual sense were being assigned a historical meaning depleted of any spiritual sense. To be sure, this new evangelical historical meaning of biblical words was still very different from the historical realities reconstructed by critical biblical historians. The new evangelical historical realities that were engendered by a residual respect for biblical words offered a history that looked much the same as the history they had previously drawn from the biblical narratives. The major difference was that this new "biblical" reality was located outside the text of Scripture and thus far out of reach of any control by the biblical words. It was a kind of "history within a history," a holy history within the ordinary history of the ancient world. It was a real *(res)* history, but it still depended primarily on the NT for its spiritual sense. It also was a history whose meaning was a function not of the words depicting it, but of the events themselves understood as real events. The primary means of knowing this history was the biblical text, though it was a text not to be read as a text per se, but one to be understood as if it were the historical event itself. Reading biblical history had come to mean not reading words on the pages of Scripture, but viewing, or picturing, events as historical events seen through the words of the text.

The result for evangelical biblical theology was a demand not merely for a new kind of interpretation, that is, typology; the demand was also for an interpetation that focused not in the grammatical meaning of words alone, but within the understanding of the flow of historical events issuing out of the biblical text but extending beyond the range of the biblical words themselves. That course of biblical history, arising as it did out of the text and flowing alongside it, became the basis for the development of a new typological method that treated biblical narratives as real history within which events were still tied closely to the meaning of biblical words and whose spiritual meaning lay in its close proximity to NT persons and events. It was a way of finding NT spiritual meaning in events that remained outside the range of the increasingly threatening historical-critical realities. When the dust had settled at the end of the eighteenth century, what remained of the orthodox view of the spiritual meaning of Scripture was a reading of the Bible that left a considerably important part of its meaning—its spiritual content—largely unattached to the words of the OT Scriptures and highly vulnerable to both private experience (pietism) and public knowledge (historical method).

The resistance to Augustine's notion of the meaning of things *(res)* over the words *(verba)* of Scripture was already remarkably strong among the Reformers. John Calvin's distaste for the meaning of "things" apart from the "words" of Scripture is forcefully stated in his commentary on 2 Corinthians 5:7 ("for we walk by faith, not by sight"): "For 'we look into a glass darkly' (1 Cor 13:12); that is, in place of things *[res]* we rest content in words *[in verbo]*."[16]

---

[16]"(1 Cor 13:12, videmus enim, sed in speculo et aenigmate) hoc est loco rei in verbo acquiescimus."

The Reformation's Scripture principle *(sola Scriptura)* was an intentional move away from church tradition and back to the written words *(verba)* of Scripture. It was also a move away from the world of "things" in which the church had so heavily invested as the warrant for its doctrine. In the Disputation of Leipzig (1519) Luther forthrightly expressed his commitment to the words of Scripture alone:

> Not the tradition that comes from the church fathers, not the councils, not the Pope—Holy Scripture alone [*allein*] is the fountain and judge in all questions of faith and teaching. From here on it is a matter of Scripture alone [*sola scriptura*]. This is because the Bible regards itself as the most clear, most simple, most appropriate interpreter of itself, examining, judging and illuminating all of everything.[17]

Hans-Joachim Kraus sees the Reformers' call for *sola scriptura* as the beginnings (*die Anfänge*) of a serious interest in biblical theology. But it was only the beginning, since the Scripture principle raised as many questions as it answered.[18] Although it was true that the study of biblical theology could have arisen only out of a commitment to *sola scriptura*, such a commitment by itself proved unable to address the questions it had raised. What, for example, is the relationship of the OT Scriptures to the systems of doctrine developed from the NT by the Protestant churches?[19] If not the authority of the church, then by whose authority must one judge the meaning of the words of Scripture? Do we rest only on the words *(verba)* of Scripture, or do the things *(res)* to which those words point have a role to play in the process of divine revelation and hence biblical theology?

The full implications of these questions have been the object of much discussion,[20] but rarely has that discussion been played out within the context

[17]Luther: "Nicht die von den Kirchenvätern ausgehende Tradition, nicht die Konzilien, nicht der Papst—allein die Heilige Schrift ist *fons et judex* in allen Fragen des Glaubens und der Lehre. Fortan gilt es: *sola scriptura*. Denn die Bibel stellt sich selbst dar als 'ipse per sese certissima, facillima, apertissima, sui ipsius interpres, omnium omnia probans, judicans et illuminans'" (quoted in Kraus, *Die biblische Theologie*, p. 17).

[18]"Doch alle unter dem Prinzip 'sola scriptura' vorgelegten theologischen Entwürfe der Reformatoren geben keine klare Antwort auf die methodologische Frage, welche Konsequenzen sich aus dem Primat der Schrift und mithin aus dem Primat der Exegese für die Ausbildung und Gestaltung christlicher Lehre ergeben" (Kraus, *Die biblische Theologie*, p. 17).

[19]"Doch zugleich bricht das angezeigte methodologische Problem auf: Wie verhalten sich Bibel-Theologie und Lehrsystem zueinander? Wie und wo kann der Primat der Exegese zur Geltung kommen, ohne dass die Schriftaussagen den Gestaltungskategorien der doctrina verfallen?" (ibid., p. 18).

[20]See Kraus, *Die biblische Theologie;* D. L. Baker, *Two Testaments, One Bible: A Study of Some Modern*

of evangelical theology. My purpose is to return briefly to these questions within the specific context of an evangelical understanding of Scripture and biblical theology. That story has not yet been told. It therefore is necessary at the start to set the stage for a biblical theological understanding of evangelicalism. A full treatment of such a topic would require a book in itself. My aim is merely to set out the broad lines along which recent evangelical biblical theology has pursued its task. The overriding question is how the meaning of the OT came to be largely identified with the historical reference of its words. The question I am raising is not whether the historical link between the words of Scripture and the "things" to which it refers can be dispensed with. Such a state of affairs cannot be identified as evangelical. Evangelical biblical theology insists on the historical veracity of such a link. The question is this: Where we are to locate the locus of meaning, in the words or in the "things" to which they refer?

## Scripture *Is* the Word of God

Two broad themes emerge from a survey of the literature. First, in its formulation of biblical theology, evangelical theology contains a strong commitment to the centrality of Scripture. However much the centrality of Scripture may or may not play into one's definition of evangelicalism, it is clear that mainstream evangelical theology has remained committed, at least in theory, to the Reformers' belief in Scripture as the central locus of divine revelation.

A second broad theme within evangelical biblical theology is its equally strong conviction regarding the role of history in understanding and defending Scripture. Whatever else may characterize evangelical theology, there is no denying that the concern for historical validation of the biblical message is central to evangelical biblical theology.[21] This means that evangelicalism has deep roots in the nineteenth century's quest for historical truth and is in no mood to question those roots or seek to replace them with another foundation. In an earlier book I attempted to show how evangelicals' concern for historical truth (biblical accuracy) has shaped their understanding of the nature of biblical interpretation and hermeneutics. While seeking to demon-

---

*Solutions to the Theological Problem of the Relationship between the Old and New Testaments* (Downers Grove, Ill.: InterVarsity Press, 1976); John H. Sailhamer, *An Introduction to Old Testament Theology: A Canonical Approach* (Grand Rapids: Zondervan, 1995).

[21]See, in reponse to Hans Frei, Carl F. H. Henry, "Narrative Theology: An Evangelical Appraisal," *TJ* 8 (1987): 3-19.

strate the historical accuracy of the Bible, evangelicals too often have identified the Bible's accuracy with its meaning and its theology. Though both concerns are an important part of evangelicalism, a demonstration of the accuracy of the Bible does not have the same goal as the search for its meaning. The first is the aim of biblical apologetics. The second is the aim of biblical hermeneutics. Both are essential to an evangelical biblical theology based on the Scriptures alone.

Though not speaking specifically of evangelical biblical theology, Hans Frei argues that Christian theology in general has increasingly blurred the lines between using historical events (ostensive reference) as a means of defending Scripture (the task of apologetics) and the use of those same events for determining the meaning of Scripture (the task of hermeneutics). If that is true for theology in general, it is all the more true of evangelical biblical theology, which largely identifies itself in terms of the truthfulness of Scripture. On the question of the meaning of Scripture as "ostensive reference," evangelical biblical theologians differ little from their critical counterparts described by Frei. For both, the meaning of the OT Scriptures is understood primarily in terms of the historical facts *(res)* that lie behind the biblical words. Critical scholars are considerably more skeptical of the biblical narratives than are evangelicals. Evangelicals believe the Bible has proven itself to be historically reliable and in difficult passages should be given the benefit of the doubt. Thus, the difference between historical-critical approaches and evangelicalism lies principally in the degree to which evangelical biblical theologians may or may not distance themselves from the Scripture's own version of the historical events. Both evangelical and critical biblical theologians accept the historical events referred to in the Scriptures as the locus of Scripture's meaning. The difference comes in the degree of accuracy accorded the scriptural account of those events by evangelicals.

As important as that difference may be, one should not overlook the equally important similarities between the two approaches. Ironically, in its quest for the "historical" meaning of the OT, evangelicalism has returned to Augustine's focus on "realia" *(res)*. On the question of the meaning of history in biblical theology, evangelicalism has tended to follow the theological trends of biblical criticism rather than the Reformers.

Evangelicalism's return to the "realia" of Scripture as the locus of its meaning has led to a fundamental readjustment of its view of biblical history. On this subject I have written at considerable length and so will devote little attention to it here.[22] I must, however, touch on some of the important moments of that discussion in what follows. My purpose is to argue that if evangelicalism is to remain true to its rich biblical heritage, the goal of an evangelical biblical theology must be refocused on the meaning of the Scriptures themselves *(sola Scriptura)*. What do the words of Scriptures tell us about the "things" *(res)* to which they point? I am not suggesting that the Scriptures are not about real things *(realia)*. I believe that they are. What I am suggesting is that the theological meaning of the Scriptures lies in the meaning of its words as parts of sentences, paragraphs, and whole texts. The words of Scripture are part of the language of Scripture, and they have meaning within the context of that language. The meaning of the words of Scripture lies in their expression of the intention of the writers and authors of Scripture. Those authors used words with a distinct understanding of their meaning, and they expect us to know those words and what they mean. Thus the meaning of the "things" to which the Scriptures point must be gathered from the meaning of the words found in Scriptures and what they tell us about the things to which they point.

## The Classical Evangelical View of Verbal Meaning

I have argued above that the formulation of the Reformation Scripture principle *(sola Scriptura)* represented a major step toward framing the task of biblical theology. That task, which began as early as Augustine's treatise on Christian doctrine, is still largely incomplete, at least as far as evangelicalism is concerned. The issue raised by the Reformers was how a normative Christian theology could be grounded solely in the meaning of an ancient text, that is, apart from the authority of the church tradition. In attempting to address that question, many biblical theologians have returned to Augustine's identification of the meaning of words with the things *(res)* pointed to by those words. "Things" have been identified both in terms of the relationship of language to the "mind of God" *(mens dei)*, particularly as represented in Christian doctrine, and the relationship of language to the historical "realia" drawn from the study of the "things" *(res)* lying behind and pointed to by the biblical texts.

---

[22]See Sailhamer, *Introduction to Old Testament Theology*, pp. 36-85.

My focus is on those evangelicals who, at least in theory, have continued to embrace the Scripture principle. That is not to say that evangelicalism has retained, in practice, the same "precritical" position held by their Reformed forebears. I have argued elsewhere that a central characteristic of contemporary evangelicalism is its move away from an authentic precritical view of Scripture.[23] This means that the evangelical view of Scripture is precritical only in theory; that is, it confesses to believe in a correspondence between the words of Scripture and the events recorded by those words. It thus believes that "the OT narratives record real historical events that provide the framework for the early history of the world and humanity, and it is precisely that history that envelops the history of the New Testament, the church."[24] Although that might be true in theory, in practice evangelicals have long since abandoned the precritical view, choosing instead to identify the meaning of Scripture with the sense found in the meaning of the "things" *(realia)* pointed to by biblical words. Thus, in theory evangelical biblical theologians see themselves as faithful to the Reformers' call for a theology based on Scripture alone, but in practice they have moved a considerable distance from that view.[25]

In the classical evangelical view of the "verbal meaning" of Scripture, the meaning assigned to the things *(res)* referred to by the words of Scripture is found in the meaning of those words *(verba)* as parts of the ancient biblical language. The biblical words point to and assign meaning to the extrabiblical things *(res)* in the *re*al *(res)* world. Whether or not the things *(realia)* in the real world have their own meaning as parts of that world, the meaning as-

---

[23]Ibid., p. 37.

[24]Ibid.

[25]Brevard Childs takes issue with my statement "The pre-critical view is, in fact, virtually the same as that of modern evangelicalism" (Sailhamer, *Introduction to Old Testament Theology*, p. 37). Childs rightly contends, "The Reformers in the 'pre-critical' era were still able to *assume* the coherence of text and historical reference. Following the challenge of the Enlightenment, this *assumption* was no longer possible" ("Hermeneutical Reflections on C. Vitringa, Eighteenth-Century Interpreter of Isaiah," in *In Search of True Wisdom: Essays in Old Testament Interpretation in Honour of Ronald E. Clements*, ed. Edward Ball [JSOTSup 300; Sheffield: Sheffield Academic Press, 1999], p. 98). However, my remark cited by Childs is qualified, in the sentence preceding it, by the assumption that "Frei's categories are helpful *if we allow for* the continuing validity of the pre-critical understanding of narrative" (italics mine). Although Frei sees no possibility of holding the precritical view after "the challenge of the Enlightenment," he makes it clear that he does not intend this statement to apply to evangelicals, even though in the monograph to which Childs refers and in the present book the intent is to demonstrate that Frei's statement does apply to evangelicalism. The fundamental flaw in evangelical biblical theology is that Frei's understanding of the "eclipse" of the "precritical" view fits evangelicalism's hermeneutic all too closely.

signed to them by the Bible is the only meaning that is theologically relevant to an evangelical biblical theology. A reader of Scripture who understands the language of Scripture (or who has a good Hebrew grammar and lexicon) can understand the meaning of the things *(res)* that Scripture is about. Their meaning lies in the meaning of the words within the language of the Bible.

Historically and hermeneutically, the Reformers' call for *sola scriptura* was a response to the instability of the meaning of things *(res)* in the medieval system of interpretation. As suggested above, within that system (based not on the Hebrew text, but on a common Latin translation), things *(res)*, not words *(verba)*, were the yardstick by which the meaning of the text was measured. Hence, for the Reformers, *sola scriptura* meant a return to the sense of Scripture as it could be gathered from the sense of the scriptural words *(sensus literalis)*. This also meant a return to the study of biblical languages, such as Hebrew, and a focus on translations in the everyday languages (vernacular) of the people. The beginning of the Reformation thus was marked by a strong desire to read and understand the Bible in one's own vernacular. That was because the meaning of Scripture was tied directly to the meaning of its words *(verba)*.[26]

The resultant focus on the meaning of words *(verba)* as the locus of the meaning of texts is similar to Hans Frei's description of the "precritical" mind:

> Western Christian reading of the Bible in the days before the rise of historical criticism in the eighteenth century was usually strongly realistic, i.e., at once literal and historical, and not only doctrinal or edifying. The words and sentences meant what they said, and because they did so they accurately described real events and real truths that were rightly put only in those terms and no others. . . .
>
> The preeminence of a literal and historical reading of the most important biblical stories was never wholly lost in western Christendom. . . . Most important were three elements in the traditional realistic interpretation of biblical stories. . . .

[26]The foregoing discussion assumes the proper role of philology and the difference between it and the historical method. Philology produces lexicons and grammars of ancient languages such as biblical Hebrew. It compares stages of a language with earlier and later stages and compares the meaning of words in texts from various time periods of the language. History attempts to reconstruct and date past events and institutions. Philology is the study of ancient written texts. History is the study of past events and their meaning. These two sciences are not the same. Although there are historical components of philology, and philology contributes greatly to the study of history, the two sciences have distinct purposes and objects.

> First, if it seemed clear that a biblical story was to be read literally, it followed automatically that it referred to and described actual historical occurrences. The true historical reference of a story was a direct and natural concomitant of its making literal sense. . . .
>
> The second element in precritical realistic reading was that if the real historical world described by the several biblical stories is a single world of one temporal sequence, there must in principle be one cumulative story to depict it. Consequently, the several biblical stories narrating sequential segments in time must fit together into one narrative. The interpretive means for joining them was to make earlier biblical stories figures or types of later stories and of their events and patterns of meaning. Without loss to its own literal meaning or specific temporal reference, an earlier story (or occurrence) was a figure of a later one. The customary use of figuration was to show that Old Testament persons, events, and prophecies were fulfilled in the New Testament. . . .
>
> In the third place, since the world truly rendered by combining biblical narratives into one was indeed the one and only real world, it must in principle embrace the experience of any present age and reader. Not only was it possible for him, it was also his duty to fit himself into that world in which he was in any case a member. . . . He was to see his disposition, his actions and passions, the shape of his own life as well as that of his era's events as figures of that storied world.
>
> A story such as that of man's creation and "fall" (Genesis 1–3) made sense in its own right and as part of the larger story into which it was incorporated by Christian interpreters, beginning with St. Paul. But in addition, figuration made sense of the general extra-biblical structure of human experience, and of one's own experience, as well as of general concepts of good and evil drawn from experience.[27]

Frei's description of a precritical reading and understanding of Scripture can be summarized in the following points.

**1. *Biblical realism.*** In a precritical reading of the Bible (OT), it was taken for granted that if a biblical narrative was realistic (which they almost always are!) it must also be real, that is, historically true. A realistic narrative must also be a "historical" narrative. If a narrative was about real events *(res),* that is, "historical," then those events must be true. It was taken as a fundamental premise about the nature of the Bible and its authorship that the biblical authors would

[27]Hans Frei, *The Eclipse of Biblical Narrative: A Study in Eighteenth and Nineteenth Century Hermeneutics* (New Haven, Conn.: Yale University Press, 1980), pp. 1-3.

never narrate something in a realistic manner unless it had actually happened. The Bible would not narrate something that did not happen; and if something did happen, the Bible would narrate it just as it happened, that is, realistically.

**2. *A single story.*** If the many individual real (true) stories in the Bible (OT) are part of one real world, they must all also be a part of the same real story, one that includes the NT stories and the storied world of the reader in all ages. Each real story was meaningful as part of the whole story. The meaning of each story would arise out of its being connected to the one whole story.[28] This is the basis for the way scriptural narratives have meaning in the lives of individual readers of the Bible.

**3. *Figuration.*** The many and various connections between the stories in the Bible (OT) are a function of a process called "figuration." Figuration is a way of recounting events so that their basic similarities and interconnectedness become apparent. The events are real and to a large extent connected historically, but through figuration a deeper link is established. The "similarities" drawn between otherwise dissimilar stories in the Bible are meant to signal a connectedness of the stories and the events they recount. They belong together and are part of a single whole. In figuration, each individual story is cast as a figure, or similarity, of other stories. OT stories thus can be figures of NT stories, and biblical stories in general can be figures of events in the life of individual readers. Discovering connections through meditation on Scripture thus becomes the central means of spiritual enlightenment and understanding (cf. Josh 1:8; Ps 1:2). This does not mean that OT stories can be read as "types" or "symbols" of NT stories. It means that "in reality," real events recounted in the OT have a basic similarity to real events recounted in the NT and events in the "real life" of individual readers of both. For there to be figuration, the events of both Testaments must be real. Only in that way can a real (historical) connection exist between the two events.

**4. *The Bible is my story.*** Since the world rendered by the cumulative biblical narratives is conceived of as the only real world *(res)*, it follows that it includes the world of the reader. It is thus the duty of the reader to fit his or her life into the events of the biblical story. In that way, as suggested above, the reader's everyday world is made a meaningful part of the whole world in which God is actively at work.

---

[28]See the book of Esther.

## The Loss of Biblical Narrative

An important theme for Hans Frei is that the "precritical" view of the Bible as described above was unable to withstand the challenges of a growing modernity at the beginning of the eighteenth century. In hindsight, it is clear that it had already begun to unravel by the end of the seventeenth century.[29] In some respects, its demise followed closely on the heels of the increasingly popular historical-critical method,[30] but the two are not the same and therefore must be understood separately.

According to Frei, fault for the final collapse of the precritical view can be laid at the feet of English Deism and its challenge to the long-cherished precritical (and biblical) notion of divine providence. To be sure, there had been early warning signs. Johann Coccejus, for example, in his commentary on the book of Isaiah, believed that he had found in Isaiah 33:7 a reference to the tragic death of Gustavus Adolphus at the Battle of Lutsen (1812).[31] As far as Coccejus was concerned, the meaning of the biblical text could be located in, and identified with, important though ordinary historical events *(res)*, sometimes even those in his own day. Such examples show that Coccejus and others like him had already begun to loosen the ties between textual meaning (located in the words *[verba]* of Scripture) and ostensive reference (which pointed to events in the "real *[res]* world"). The biblical world, by taking on the attributes of ordinary history, was unwittingly being sheared not only of its prophetic grandeur, but also, even more importantly, of its precritical status as the primary arena of divine activity. History was being divested of its claim to be a place where God acts and was increasingly identified merely as a place where ordinary things *(res)* happen *(res gesta)*.

In the long run, such blurring of the lines would considerably undermine precritical efforts to confront the contemporary world with biblical reality. With an increased dependence of biblical studies on the historical method,

---

[29]See Klaus Scholder, *Ursprünge und Probleme der Bibelkritik im 17. Jahrhundert: Ein Beitrag zur Entstehung der historisch-kritischen Theologie* (Munich: Kaiser, 1966).

[30]See Hans-Joachim Kraus, *Geschichte der historisch-kritischen Erforschung des Alten Testaments*, 2nd ed. (Neukirchen-Vluyn: Neukirchener Verlag, 1969).

[31]Coccejus's comment on Isaiah 33:7: "Haec optime conveniunt in Gustavum Adolphum" (*Synopsis Prophetiae Jesaiae*, in *Opera omnia*, 3:21). Also, "Tale quid vidimus, cum in ultimo conflictu Rex Sueciae occubuisset & Caesarani caesi essent" (*Curae majores in prophetiam Esaiae*, in *Opera omnia*, 3:280).

the "biblical world" came to look increasingly less like the world one actually sees in the Bible and increasingly more like the world of the modern historian. As long as the picture of reality generated by the historian bore a reasonable likeness to the biblical narratives, no loss was felt in viewing it through the lens of the modern historian. Indeed, to the seventeenth-century exegete and biblical theologian, the historical details of the death of Gustavus Adolphus appeared to cast considerable light on Isaiah's prophecy. Frei's point, however, is that the historical method eventually came to be identified with the task of biblical interpretation. The meaning of words was understood in terms of the world of external events *(res)*. Once established, the making of connections between the words of Scripture and their ostensive reference in the "real" *(res)* world became a habit that was hard to shake. By the end of the seventeenth century, the hermeneutical weight had so shifted to the side of "real" *(res)* things, that biblical theology appeared to have reached a kind of irrecoverable tilt. There could be no turning back to a precritical frame of mind. The biblical world, as such, had given way to a modernized reconstruction of the distant past, a kind of theme park "Frontier Land" complete with modern conveniences such as drinking fountains, restrooms and souvenirs. Even if one were so inclined, there was little the biblical theologian could do to halt the erosion of the biblical world in the hands of the "modern" historian.

To understand the precritical world, it is important to recall its dependence on the belief in divine providence. In the precritical world, it went without saying that God was active in human history *(res gesta)*. The world of things *(res)* does not play itself out alone. All things *(res)* are providentially ordered and governed by a sovereign God. In the Bible, God is at work in many, if not all, ordinary events. What gave a meaningful cohesion to God's many acts in the Bible and in history was the basic similarity of the two activities. God's acts, as recorded in the Bible, were like his actions in historical events. The Bible and the events of the real world were the same. By learning to see God at work in biblical events, one came to see God's work also in the world outside the Bible. Together, these two acts of God stood in a closed relationship that Erich Auerbach called "figuration."[32] In figuration, patterns of divine

[32]"Figural interpretation 'establishes a connection between two events or persons in such a way that the first signifies not only itself but also the second, while the second involves or fulfills the first. The two poles of a figure are separated in time, but both, being real events or persons, are within

activity written in the Bible were seen, writ large, in the world of ordinary human affairs. The notion of figuration itself could be seen as an historical reality (*re*al) because it was understood that the Bible and the whole of human history were guided by one God's providential hand.

Divine providence is a notion that Deism could not abide. In order to make rational sense of the world, the deist was obliged to rule out divine providence. Though divine providence was essential for making sense of the biblical world, in Deism (and the modern mind in general) it was virtually the only biblical notion that could not be accommodated to the modern world. Deism, in order to ground itself securely in human reason, could not allow for divine acts in the real world. Divine acts, if granted as possible, could jeopardize the rational laws of nature. A suspended law was no law at all.

As understood by orthodox theologians, the biblical God was above and beyond the laws of nature. In classical orthodoxy, the biblical God was not bound by his own natural laws, and if necessary, they could be suspended and miracles could be allowed to happen. But to the deist, laws of nature, if they were truly laws, could not be suspended, not even to make room for genuinely biblical divine acts (miracles). To the modern historian, the meaning of history could be explained only by the application of the rules of reason (eighteenth century) or by accepted historical procedures (nineteenth and twentieth centuries). If the biblical worldview was to retain its credibility in the modern world of the eighteenth and nineteenth centuries, its view of biblical history was obliged to lay aside the notion of divine providence and miracles.

Few orthodox biblical theologians were willing to follow through with such a program. Many were forced to retreat to mediating positions. The story of biblical theology in early evangelicalism, by whatever name it should be called during the eighteenth through twentieth centuries, is one of cautious accommodation of revelation to reason, and the Bible to history.

Along with the notion of divine providence, which evangelicals were unwilling to lay aside, many mediating positions were forged. What often did not make the final cut for evangelicals was the retention, unaltered, of the

temporality. They are both contained in the flowing stream which is historical life, and only the comprehension, the *intellectus spiritualis*, of their interdependence is a spiritual act'" (Erich Auerbach, *Mimesis: The Representation of Reality in Western Literature*, trans. Willard R. Trask [Princeton, N.J.: Princeton University Press, 1953], p. 73).

classical (precritical) notion that God works directly and miraculously in his governance of the world. Miracles increasingly gave way to historical explanations. The result of the various mediating positions during this period (seventeenth through nineteenth centuries) was an increasingly natural view of the real *(res)* world. Miracles could and did happen, though there were limits to when and how they occurred. In addition to those limitations there was a growing loss of a sense of figuration in the actual events *(realia, res)* of the historical world. Any recognition of similarities between the real world and biblical events, apart from the already shrinking arena of "salvation history," was either downplayed as largely coincidental or validated somehow by historical means. If the book of Exodus described Moses' turning the Nile River into blood as a figuration of the death of the firstborn Egyptians and the slaying of the Israelite sons, its theological import rested no longer on an appeal to God's direct activity in history, as was the likely meaning of the text, but rather rested on a rationally verifiable appeal to historical realities such as the excessive rainfall at the sources of the Nile and the consequent coloration of the river by a massive drain-off of red clay.[33]

The story of what eventually happened to the precritical view at the beginning of the nineteenth has not been fully written. Most would agree that by the eighteenth century, the precritical view of the Bible had given way, even among some of the most conservative biblical theologians, to at least four diverse and often competing hermeneutical options: biblical criticism, typology, biblical realism and salvation history. Each of these options sought a way to replace divine providence with a more or less plausible notion of history while at the same time not entirely excluding God's actions from some *real (res)* events. Within each of these approaches, the task of holding the *real (res)* world together and giving it meaning through figuration was increasingly left in the hands of the historian. Given the shift from understanding verbal meaning in terms of the grammaticality of Scriptural words *(verba)* to that of the "meaning" of the things *(res)* pointed to by the words, it seemed most natural to look to the historian rather than the exegete (philologist) for Scripture's meaning. The historian's newly found task became that of connecting verbal meaning to the everyday (ancient) world of "things" *(res)*. Consequently, figuration, if there was to be any, was in-

[33]See Sailhamer, *Introduction to Old Testament Theology*, pp. 80-81.

creasingly relegated to a small and special realm of history *(res)* in which it could still be maintained that God had truly (historically) acted. His actions there were, of course, construed to be in conjunction with the things referred to by the words *(verba)* of Scripture, apart from and largely in opposition to the rest of history *(realia)*.

That part of history to which God had voluntarily limited his divine activity was increasingly understood to be a special realm, or place, where history is holy and leads toward a grand act of human redemption. It thus came to be called a "salvation history" *(Heilsgeschichte)*. It was a real history, if not an ordinary one, where God acted and in which God was increasingly becoming more active on humankind's behalf. Though a special kind of history, its domain was still "historical," and the task of finding its meaning as such was increasingly allotted to the historian. God could be known by the historian through his special acts in history because God's acts, being real history, conformed for the most part to the laws of real historical events. This meant that throughout the nineteenth and twentieth centuries, biblical theology, even among evangelicals, could be understood principally as a historical discipline. Hence, throughout this period, evangelical biblical theologians viewed their task as forging real, historical links between the words *(verba)* of Scripture and the things *(res)* to which they pointed in the real world.[34] Such links between "words" and "things" were no longer to be found in the mind of God *(mens dei)*, as Augustine had argued, nor were they found in the divinely ordained interconnectedness of events *(providentia Dei)*, as the Reformers believed; they were to be found in a historical (and scientific) method that was willing, if not eager, to accept an occasional miraculous, or "supernatural," intervention. All other events, even when the Bible appeared to suggest otherwise, would have to fall in line with those "ordinary events" that were the domain of the modern historian.

To the evangelical mind, God was not being squeezed out of history. God was, rather, being ushered into his own special history in which his divine acts could be accommodated to the laws of ordinary historical events.

One could make sense of the *real (res)* world, and hence a significant portion of biblical theology, only by means of the cause-and-effect relationships established by the modern historian and archaeologist. If God was to play a

[34]The primary mechanism for evanglicals from the mid-nineteenth century through the twentieth century was the amazingly productive and still successful model of biblical archaeology.

part in historical events, it would have to be according to the rules of the rest of history, or else he would be required to limit his activity to the special part of human history allowed to him, which dealt only with events identified and assigned meaning by the Bible (salvation history). Although that history, in theory at least, could still be understood by means of the words *(verba)* of Scripture, it could no longer be identified with the whole of history as a single story. History had grown larger than the Bible, and biblical history could locate its meaning only from within the coordinates of that larger history.

If God's acts within historical events conformed to the progress of ordinary historical events, then the record of those events in Scripture could also be taken as conforming to ordinary history. This meant that the words of Scripture and the recording of its events could also be taken as a part of ordinary history and could thus be understood, as history, by the informed historian. The Bible thus was taken as a collection of historical "facts" that needed only to be interpreted as such by qualified historians. Theologians therefore were required to be historians and to interpret the text not in terms of an authorial will lying behind a compositional, or literary, strategy of verbal meaning, but as a sequence of ordinary historical events (e.g., Charles Hodge) whose meaning could be unlocked only by a commitment to the historical method. One thus confronted history in the words of the biblical text in a way comparable to watching a live event on television. What one saw was only words on a page, or pixels on a screen, but one reacted to them as if they were the real thing. A biblical theologian thus would also have to be a biblical historian, whose task was to approach the Bible (OT) as one would approach historical events in need of interpretation.

Although Charles Hodge of Princeton was not, strictly speaking, a biblical theologian, he established the proper method of biblical theology for most evangelicals of the nineteenth century and even the twentieth. For Hodge, the starting point of a biblical theology is the collection and observation of all the "facts" of Scripture, followed by a complete description and explanation of every part. The Bible (OT) and all of its historical bits and pieces are to be approached as a huge unknown in need of a scientific explanation. Only one who could grasp the whole and thereby assign meaning to each of the parts need apply for the job of a biblical theologian. According to Hodge,

> The Bible is to the theologian what nature is to the man of science. It is his

> store-house of facts; and his method of ascertaining what the Bible teaches, is the same as that which the natural philosopher adopts to ascertain what nature teaches. . . . The duty of the Christian theologian is to ascertain, collect, and combine all the facts which God has revealed concerning himself and our relation to Him. These facts are all in the Bible.[35]

This quotation makes clear that the theologian was not being assigned the task of discovering the biblical authors' meaning or the literary arguments of the various authors of the Bible. There is no notion of a textual or compositional strategy to be uncovered by the reader. The Bible is approached as a brute fact containing many smaller facts, all in need of a brilliant explanation. The ultimate meaning behind the "facts" in the Bible is to be found in the evidence they provide for discovering God's purpose. That divine purpose must be discovered inductively from the "historical" facts supplied by the Bible (OT). The validity of one's explanation rests not on how well it explains the text, but on how well it explains the facts that come incrementally out of the text as bits and pieces of unassembled history. In that sense, the task is much like that of piecing together a jigsaw puzzle.

> The true method of theology is, therefore, the inductive, which assumes that the Bible contains all the facts or truths which form the contents of theology, just as the facts of nature are the contents of the natural sciences. It is also assumed that the relation of these Biblical facts to each other, the principles involved in them, the laws which determine them, are in the facts themselves, and are to be deduced from them, just as the laws of nature are deduced from the facts of nature.[36]

How similar Hodge's theological method is to the first major biblical theology to come out of the old Princeton school, Geerhardus Vos's *Biblical Theology*. Vos calls attention to the similarity by pointing to the only difference between his biblical theology and the systematic theology of Hodge and others.

> Biblical Theology . . . differs from Systematic Theology not in being more Biblical, or adhering more closely to the truths of the Scriptures, but in that its principle of organizing the Biblical material is historical rather than logical. Whereas Systematic Theology takes the Bible as a completed whole and endeavors to exhibit its total teaching in an orderly, systematic form, Biblical

---

[35]Charles Hodge, *Systematic Theology* (New York: Scribner, Armstrong, 1873), 1:10-11.
[36]Ibid., p. 17.

Theology deals with the material from the historical standpoint.[37]

In the end, the task of biblical theology, which Vos preferred to call "history of special revelation,"[38] was "the study of the actual self-disclosures of God in time and space which lie back of even the first committal to writing of any Biblical document, and which for a long time continued to run alongside of the inscripturation of revealed material."[39]

[37]Geerhardus Vos, *Biblical Theology: Old and New Testaments* (Eerdmans: Grand Rapids, 1948), p. i.
[38]Ibid.
[39]Ibid., p. 13.

*Chapter 3*

# What Is the "Historical Meaning" of Biblical Texts?

THE APPROACH ADVOCATED IN THIS BOOK is the "historical-grammatical" method as originally practiced by evangelical biblical scholars. In this section I trace the development of this approach by beginning with the formative work on biblical hermeneutics by Johann August Ernesti. I contend that from its inception in the eighteenth century to the present it has undergone considerable development and change in some of its key tenets. As originally conceived, the approach was an attempt to read the Bible (OT) as an ancient book, viewing the "history it records" in terms of the "grammatical sense of its language," that is, ancient Hebrew. The "historical" part of the approach was the recognition that the Bible's content and subject matter is a narration of past events. The biblical narratives give us "history." For that matter, the biblical narratives *are* "history." The "grammatical" part of the approach was its attempt to understand the Bible (OT) in terms of the grammatical rules of its three languages: Hebrew, Aramaic and Greek.

Many contemporary evangelicals see the aims of the historical-grammatical method differently. For them, the "historical" part of the approach is not defined in terms of the kinds of narrative one finds in the Bible, that is, "historical" narratives. The "historical" part of the method is, rather, that it attempts to understand the biblical narratives by viewing them as if they were the "historical" events themselves. It shifts the focus from the biblical narratives, as historical accounts of real events, to the events themselves *(res)* lying outside the narratives. Thus, the task of the study of biblical "history" in this new orientation of method consists of clarifying, explaining and adding to the biblical narrative depictions of biblical events. We do so by filling in the details of the events from our growing knowledge of ancient history. Our knowledge of ancient history supplements what we know of the events from the biblical narratives. By placing the biblical narratives in the context of what we know of ancient history, we give them new meaning, and we gain a bigger picture of the actual events. We see the biblical events beyond and apart from how they are depicted in the biblical narratives. Our broader knowledge of ancient history and archaeology gives us a larger context for viewing the biblical history. Biblical interpretation comes to mean viewing the events of the biblical narratives through the eyes of historians rather than of the authors of the biblical narratives themselves. We look at the words on the page as if they were the events themselves and attempt to explain them as we would any other ancient historical evens. Hence, we come to see the events apart from their biblical setting and within the new context of the ancient world.

The differences between these two views of the historical-grammatical approach are considerable. Given the way the approach is understood today, the kind of skills one would need to carry out its tasks would consist principally of those historical tools that enable us to reconstruct past events and life situations. Contemporary evangelical OT scholars, for example, have focused much of their attention on the *realia* behind the biblical narratives, relying heavily on studies in archaeology and ancient history. Their aim is to view biblical events not merely through the eyes of the biblical authors (as written accounts of those events), but also through the eyes of historians as if we were gazing upon the actual events through the words of the text.

As the historical-grammatical approach was originally conceived, the skills it required were of a different sort. They were of the sort that enabled one to read texts and understand literature. The historical skills it required were, among other things, a facility in ancient languages and an understanding of the nature of biblical composition. How were the books of the OT written? What strategies were used, and how are the texts to be read today? As the historical-grammatical method was understood, knowledge of biblical history came not from a historical analysis of the events recorded in Scripture, but from a literary and linguistic understanding of the biblical text and its composition. Consequently, a biblical theology of the OT (Pentateuch) based on such a historical-grammatical method would focus primarily on reading the biblical text rather than on extensive studies in archaeology and ancient history. It would, of course, use tools such as archaeology and ancient history to show, apologetically, the historical trustworthiness of the biblical narratives, since they are about real events *(realia)*, but at the same time it would insist that those narratives are, above all else, written texts that recount for their readers a narrative version of the events they contain. They are, of course, not the events themselves; they are verbal versions of those events. In this sense, history, as a study of real events, is an essential part of an evangelical approach to the Bible (OT), but it is not the central focus of a biblical theology.

## The Bible Is God's Revelation

The changing evangelical view of the role of "history" in biblical interpretation is a story that requires more attention than can be given here.[1] Given its commitment to the Bible as the necessary starting point of a biblical theology, evangelicalism must continue to rethink itself in light of its starting point, if only to avoid reinventing itself in a way that distances it from the OT as inspired Scripture.

An evangelical view of Scripture starts with an understanding of the Bible as the inspired locus of divine revelation. There are other approaches to Scripture that are not characteristic of evangelicalism, and there are approaches to hermeneutics other than that of evangelicalism. There are possibly other definitions of the evangelical view of Scripture, but the view described here is the view rooted in classical Reformed orthodoxy and reflected in the creeds that came out of the Reformation.

## Historical Reconstructions

As understood by many evangelicals, the aim of a historical approach to biblical theology is to reconstruct as nearly as possible the actual events that lie behind the historical narratives of the OT. It is taken for granted that these events contained divine revelation, and that the more we understand the meaning of these events, the more we can know of God's revelation in them. It is not that these evangelicals do not consider the scriptural narratives to be revelatory. They do. But many evangelicals also believe that over

[1]See John H. Sailhamer, *An Introduction to Old Testament Theology: A Canonical Approach* (Grand Rapids: Zondervan, 1995), pp. 36-85.

and above the divine revelation found in Scripture there is additional revelation to be found in the historical events themselves.[2] A trained historian, studying past events, is able to piece together a larger picture of the events recorded in Scripture. By discovering or reconstructing the missing pieces of events that expand the biblical picture of what happened, historians sometimes are able to understand better the events depicted in the biblical narratives.

A more consistently evangelical approach looks primarily to the biblical text itself for an understanding of divine revelation and God's acts in history.

Before the rise of the historical method, sometime during the sixteenth or seventeenth century, the biblical narratives generally were taken at face value as more or less exhaustive accounts of what could be known about the events recounted in the OT. Explaining the meaning of those events was a function of explaining the verbal sense of the historical narratives depicting them. With the increasing attention given to the ability of the historical method to penetrate into the meaning of past events came a new confidence in the historian's ability to get back to the biblical events themselves and to explore them as parts of a larger historical picture. The new confidence in the historical method threatened to minimize the importance of paying close attention to reading the text. In this section I attempt to trace the increasing attention given to the historical reconstruction of biblical (OT) events at the expense of the meaning embodied in biblical narratives.

I will approach the question from the point of view of the history of interpretation. Elsewhere I have given a lengthy discussion of the central issues relating to the evangelical view of Scripture.[3] I argue that in the evangelical view, history and especially the discipline of philology (the study of ancient texts) are rightly assigned a central role in gaining an understanding about the biblical texts. Who was the author? When was it written? Why was it written? What was the lexical meaning of its individual words? History also plays a central role in the apologetic task of defending the veracity of the biblical record. Are the patriarchal narratives historically reliable? Were the biblical authors influenced by ancient myths? Did Jesus rise from the dead? Such questions and many others are linked to the larger question of the nature of history and historical method.

---

[2]See ibid., p. 40.

[3]See Sailhamer, *Introduction to Old Testament Theology*.

When, however, it comes to the meaning of the biblical texts as historical narrative, the evangelical view of history is such that historical reconstructions of the biblical events and narratives cannot and should not be allowed to take the place of the close study of the written texts and the meaning they give to the events they recount.

It is not a question of whether one can accurately fill in the historical details that have been left out of the biblical picture. Evangelicals have always believed that they could do so successfully. The ability to fill out the biblical picture is at the heart of the problem. Using modern historical tools, we have the same ability to fill in the historical details of scriptural narratives as we have of painting intricate details of seventeenth-century life over the shadows of a Rembrandt painting. By painting shadows, Rembrandt deliberately left out many historical details that would have given us much information about the events he recorded on canvas. Historians who understand the culture and life setting of seventeenth-century Europe could easily replace Rembrandt's dark shadows with historically accurate details of the world around him. In the same way, historians of the ancient world could fill in many historically accurate details about the events recorded in the biblical narratives. They could, for example, help us to better understand the nature of biblical covenants by comparing them with ancient treaty documents. There is no end to the amount of material now available to "fill in" the biblical picture. The problem is that this would have the same effect on the biblical (OT) narratives as on Rembrandt's paintings. Filling in the biblical narratives with additional historical material may teach us things about the events of which the biblical writers were speaking, but the evangelical's goal in interpretation and biblical theology is not an understanding of those events as such. The goal, as evangelicals must see it, is the biblical author's understanding of those events in the inspired text of the Bible (OT). We should not seek to know what lies behind or beneath Rembrandt's shadows. It is the shadows that are a central part of the paintings, not the historical details that lie behind the shadows and are thus not in the painting. Rembrandt's meaning lies as much in what is not seen in his painting as in what is seen. The shadows, by blocking out the irrelevant details, help us focus on what is seen. The effect of our adding more details to the painting would be to lose Rembrandt's focus. The task for evangelicals is to recover the sense of what the biblical texts intend to tell us about the events they are recounting. We can arrive at that goal only by an exegesis of the text.

The task of understanding the events themselves is the task of biblical historiography. That is an important part of an evangelical approach to the Bible (OT). It is not, however, the task of biblical hermeneutics and theology. Hermeneutics, as evangelicals have understood it, is devoted to discovering the meaning of the biblical text. To quote Meir Sternberg, "The text itself has a pattern of meaning."[4] The task of biblical theology is to represent the meaning of the biblical text and to represent it as a word from God.

## History of Interpretation

An understanding of the history of biblical interpretation is a prerequisite for addressing the changing role of "history" in evangelical biblical hermeneutics.[5] Over a relatively short period of time, the phrase "grammatical-historical method" went from being a description of the primarily textual procedure of studying written narratives to an almost exclusive search for the meaning of the historical events *(realia)* lying behind those narratives. The evangelical understanding of the terms *grammatical* and *historical* was ably defended in the late eighteenth century by Johann August Ernesti.[6] In Ernesti's view, "historical" meant simply the "grammatical" meaning of the words of Scripture. The "historical" meaning was the "grammatical" sense. Ernesti's view was immediately heralded as the classical expression of both the historical nature of the biblical texts and the nature of the history that the biblical texts depict. Ernesti's view remains today the definitive statement of the grammatical-historical approach, though this was not accomplished without it undergoing major changes in the hands of later generations.

Since Ernesti, many shifts have occurred in the meaning of the expression "grammatical-historical method," all of them laying claim to represent the views of Ernesti. The most notable shift in the meaning of Ernesti's views was the transition from the phrase "grammatical-historical method" to the phrase "historical-critical method." The story of the rise of the critical approach to the Bible has been told many times, and I need not repeat it here.[7]

---

[4]Meir Sternberg, *Poetics of Biblical Narrative: Ideological Literature and the Drama of Reading* (ILBS; Bloomington: Indiana University Press, 1985), p. 15.

[5]The following discussion includes and builds on material found in John H. Sailhamer, "Johann August Ernesti: the role of history in biblical interpretation," *JETS* 43, no. 2 (June 2001): 193-220, and is used by permission.

[6]Johann August Ernesti, *Institutio interpretis Novi Testamenti* (Leipzig, 1761).

[7]See especially Hans-Joachim Kraus, *Geschichte der historisch-kritischen Erforschung des Alten Testaments,* 2nd ed. (Neukirchen-Vluyn: Neukirchener Verlag, 1969).

Our focus is on how the meaning of the phrase has shifted within the context of evangelical biblical scholarship. Within that context there have been many subtle changes in Ernesti's method. These have come to have a fundamental effect on evangelical hermeneutics and biblical theology.

The grammatical-historical approach of Ernesti came to the nineteenth-century American evangelical public in the form of Moses Stuart's highly successful English translation of Ernesti. Stuart, himself a highly acclaimed evangelical biblical theologian, had his own ideas about hermeneutical method and the importance of historical studies in biblical interpretation. He also had made a lifelong commitment to introducing the American public to the results of continental biblical criticism. In light of such matters, it is of interest that Stuart's translation of Ernesti presented to the English-speaking world a considerably nuanced picture of Ernesti and his approach to historical events. Stuart accomplished this, as we will see, in both his translation of Ernesti's work and the copious notes that accompanied his translation.

Broadly speaking, it was through Stuart's translation that the grammatical-historical method became a safe haven from the destructive influences of the newly developing historical-critical method. Stuart presented Ernesti as a kind of halfway position on the question of the use of history in biblical interpretation. It was presented as a way of using the results of some aspects of the historical method without committing oneself to the full war chest of critical tools. In his translation of Ernesti, Stuart advocated the use of history to uncover the meaning of biblical events but was careful to warn his readers against a negative critical understanding of history. In Stuart's translation of Ernesti, evangelicals were offered a sense of safety in the dark waters of the historical-critical method, as long as they could still see the lighthouse of Stuart's Ernesti on the horizon. Stuart's translation of Ernesti was both a guide through the waters of the historical method and an opening of the floodgates. But that was not the intent of Ernesti's work. Ernesti had intended to move in the opposite direction toward a closer focus on the scriptural text. In his day, the historical method was tilting heavily away from a focus on the biblical text. It was Ernesti's aim to reverse that trend and move readers and biblical theologians safely back to the text.

To gain a sense of Ernesti's approach to biblical interpretation, it is helpful to use one of Ernesti's own principles: pay careful attention to the way words are used. In Ernesti's case, the two words he used to describe his approach are "grammatical" and "historical." Ernesti advocated the use of a "historical-grammatical" method, and he had a specific meaning for each of those two terms.

He used "grammatical" and "historical" because those terms were part of the standard vocabulary of hermeneutical works on the Bible. For Ernesti, there was little difference in the meaning of the two. Sometimes they were hyphenated, as in "historical-grammatical method." At other times the two terms were connected by the Latin conjunction *sive*, meaning "namely" or "that is to say." The approach thus was identified as the "grammatical, namely *[sive]* historical" method or the "historical, that is to say, grammatical" method. The "historical" was the "grammatical" method. Ernesti was particularly careful to use these terms in this way and thus to identify the "historical" part of his method with the "grammatical." What this specifically implied was that the biblical text itself is the object of a "historical" study of the Bible. The "grammatical" part focused on the elements of the language of the Bible in which these narrative texts were written. Discovering the meaning of "history," in Ernesti's way of thinking, meant "reading" the biblical historical narratives. It did not mean what many now think the word *history* should mean. Today the word *history* brings to mind the actual occurrence of past events, not necessarily the written accounts of those events. For Ernesti, however, history was something that could and should be approached grammatically through the process of reading a biblical text.

After Ernesti, biblical scholars such as Karl August Keil[8] launched a concerted and successful effort to move these two terms in a different direction than Ernesti had intended. The new direction can be seen in the way biblical scholars had begun connecting them with the conjunction *et* ("and"). This was an important shift in meaning from the conjunction *sive* ("namely"). It reflected a genuine change in the understanding of the task of biblical interpretation. In effect, the use of the conjunction *et* pointed to the fact that the terms *historical* and *grammatical* were no longer considered synonyms. The meaning of the two terms had begun to fall apart. Ernesti's single-step "historical, *namely*, grammatical" method was becoming a two-step method in Keil's "grammatical and *[et]* historical" method. Step one, the "historical" part of the method, sought to examine the *realia* that lay behind the biblical narratives.

---

[8]Karl August Keil, *Keilii opuscula academica ad N.T. interpretationem grammatico-historicam et theologiæ christianæ origines pertinentia*, ed. J. D. Goldhorn (Leipzig: Barth, 1821).

Step two, the "grammatical" part, focused on the textual meaning of the biblical narratives themselves. The first task was a historical investigation of *realia*, and the second was a literary and linguistic search for meaning.

To understand the shift that these two words experienced in the hands of a growing number of biblical scholars, one must give attention to the course taken by Ernesti's Latin text before its translation into English by Moses Stuart.[9]

It is generally believed that the hyphenated form "grammatical-historical" originated in the Latin translation of Karl August Keil's German work on NT hermeneutics. In Goldhorn's Latin translation, Keil's work was described as an *interpretatio grammatico-historicus*,[10] that is, "a historical, along with a grammatical, interpretation." Whether or not this was the first instance of a hyphenation of the two terms, it is widely accepted that Keil's work was the first major study to give the hyphenated form its new meaning. Keil's goal in doing so was to update the central thesis of Ernesti that the Bible should be studied like any other book from the past. For Keil, this meant that the Bible should not merely be read as history, but also that it should be studied as history according to the newly developed historical consciousness introduced into biblical studies by Johann Salomo Semler (1753–1791).

Semler was a transitional figure in the history of theology. A student of the celebrated Sigmund Jakob Baumgarten at the University of Halle in the early eighteenth century, Semler read biblical texts not as histories themselves, but as written sources from which one might draw historical conclusions. Both Semler and Baumgarten saw the biblical narratives, and particularly the OT narratives, as human records of past revelatory events rather than direct sources of revelation itself. Hence, according to historian Emanuel Hirsch, it was with Baumgarten that "German Protestant theology reached a decisive stage. . . . It went from being a faith based on the Bible to being one based on revelation—a revelation for which the Bible was in reality nothing more than a record once given."[11] The Bible and revelation were not

[9]Moses Stuart, *Elements of Interpretation: Translated from the Latin of J. A. Ernesti and Accompanied by Notes, with an Appendix Containing Extracts from Morus, Beck and Keil* (Andover, Mass.: Flagg & Gould, 1822).

[10]For contrast the earlier edition was Karl August Keil, *Elementa hermeneutices Novi Testamenti*, trans. Christoph August Emmerling (Leipzig: Vogel, 1811).

[11]"Alles in allen darf man wohl sagen: die deutsche evangelische Theologie ist mit Baumgarten in das entscheidende Stadium des Übergangs vom Bibelglauben zu einem Offenbarungsglauben getreten, dem die Bibel im Wesentlichen nichts ist als die nun einmal gegeben Urkunde der Of-

synonymous, as they had been to the Reformers. Revelation was increasingly understood as a past act of God to which the Bible was a witness or written record. The Bible was thus a record of a past revelatory event. The Bible was the means of making known a divine revelation that had occurred as a historical event. The locus of divine revelation was a historical event, and the Bible had assumed the role of being merely a record of that past event. The Bible was not the actual event, and thus it could not itself be revelatory. In this way, with Semler and Baumgarten, and eventually with Keil, the Bible came to forfeit its status as divine revelation and became merely a historical source of a past divine revelation.

Throughout the seventeenth century, evangelical biblical scholars treated the notion of history as an attribute of the biblical text. What was recorded in the Bible was identified as what had happened, that is, history. It was not a question of whether the Bible had recorded the events accurately. That was taken for granted. It was, rather, a matter of how a biblical event was understood to have happened. From a historical viewpoint, the events recounted in the Bible happened as they were recorded in the biblical narratives. The event recorded in the Bible was treated as if it were the event that happened rather than being an account of the event that happened. Narrated events in the Bible were treated as if they were the actual events (realism). There was little thought of these biblical events as written records of real happenings *(res gesta)*. Biblical narratives were simply taken as if they were the real event itself. The biblical event as narrated was then approached "historically," not in terms of its narrative depiction, but from the viewpoint of a historian looking at actual past events and making sense of them as history. As such, biblical narratives were treated as revelatory events in themselves. It helped that the biblical events were so much like real events (biblical realism) that they could easily be treated as if they were the actual events.

For a theologian such as Johann Coccejus (1603–1669), the preeminent evangelical biblical scholar of his day, the series of events recorded in the Scriptures was identical to the series of events in real-time history. To understand history, one need only read the biblical text. To experience biblical revelation, one need merely experience the narrated events as written in the biblical text. To be sure, divine revelation was to be found in historical events,

---

fenbarung" (Hirsch, *Geschichte der neuern evangelischen Theologie*, 2:378).

but in order to gain access and understand those events, one must know them only as they happened in Scripture. Scripture depicted historical events along with the meaning of those events. Hence, in Scripture one was put into immediate contact with the real events of the biblical past. The phrase "biblical history," then, denoted only a series of real events as they were referenced and depicted in the Bible.

Recent studies in the history of biblical interpretation, such as those by Hans Frei[12] and Hans-Joachim Kraus,[13] argue that a fundamental shift in the meaning of the notion of biblical history swept over Europe during the eighteenth century. It was a shift in which the "historical" meaning of the Bible ceased being located in the words and sentences of the biblical narratives and came instead to be located in the actual (real) events referred to by those narratives. Hence, divine revelation was not to be found in Scripture as such, but in the real events referred to in Scripture. Though subtle, the shift was real, and it is not hard to imagine how it led to a fundamentally different view of biblical history. In a word, the meaning of "history" was no longer to be gathered from the statements and events depicted in the biblical narratives. The meaning of history was to be found from a historical analysis of the events themselves with little or no connection to the depiction of them in the text of Scripture. The meaning of history was no longer the same thing as the meaning of the Bible.

This story of the "eclipse" of biblical narrative has been told numerous times. In order to understand evangelical biblical theology, this story is not enough. One must look further at these same events from another perspective. Most, if not all, accounts of the development of the "grammatical-historical" method have been aimed at explaining the rise of the "historical-critical" method. As important as that historical development was, it is equally important for evangelicals to look at these same events from the perspective of important evangelicals of that period. What did the shift in biblical interpretation mean to evangelical biblical theologians? How did they respond to the new focus on history and the eclipse of the biblical narratives? How did this shift affect their view of the Bible as an inspired text?

For the most part, those responsible for the shift in focus from text to events were, at this early point, essentially evangelical in their theology.

[12]Hans Frei, *The Eclipse of Biblical Narrative* (New Haven, Conn.: Yale University Press, 1980).
[13]Kraus, *Die biblische Theologie.*

Among other things, this meant that they believed in the divine inspiration of the biblical texts. They thought of the Scriptures as the Word of God. They adhered to the major creeds. The story of the rise of the historical-critical method is thus the story of the loss of the sense of Scripture as the Word of God and the shift to a new focus on historical events as a means of divine revelation. This raises the question of the viewpoint of those who remained evangelical in their theology during this time. How did they respond to the shift of focus from revelatory text to revelatory events? How did they reconcile their belief in an inspired text with a growing focus on real events as the locus of revelation?

Some evangelicals during this period openly traded in their notion of scriptural inspiration and eventually found their way into various forms of the historical-critical method. What course did others take? What approaches to scriptural interpretation were open to those evangelicals who stayed the course and retained the notion of an inspired biblical text?

In the end, evangelicals during the late eighteenth and early nineteenth centuries opted to hold fast to the phrase "grammatical-historical method" and looked upon it as their most distinguishing trademark. It is possible that such a decision was apologetically motivated. Whatever lay behind their choices, our task is to raise the question of the effect of their decisions on the meaning of the phrase "grammatical-historical."

## Words and Things

In order to understand the sense of the phrase "grammatical-historical method," we must return to two terms discussed above, "words" *(verba)* and "things" *(res)*.[14] Ernesti begins with a paraphrase of Augustine: "Corre-

[14]As I have suggested, these terms have been essential to the discussion of biblical texts almost from the start. It was not without purpose that up to and including the work of Ernesti, treatises on biblical hermeneutics almost always were written in Latin. This was even long after vernacular languages had begun to be used in biblical studies and theology. For the same reason, even in the nineteenth century, Keil's work on biblical hermeneutics, originally written in German, was translated into Latin. A long-standing use of Latin terms had been maintained in hermeneutical works at least since the publication of Augustine's *On Christian Doctrine*. Some of these terms have come over into English, such as the "literal sense" *(sensus literalis)* and the "historical sense" (*sensus historicus*). Augustine's two most essential terms, "things" *(res)* and "words" *(verba)*, were not properly adjusted to English usage. As I have shown above, Augustine's simple formula was "words signify things." Words are parts of language; things are what words point to. Throughout the history of biblical interpretation, the major treatises begin by laying this basic groundwork. Ernesti was no exception.

sponding to every word *[verbum]* in Scripture there is an idea or notion of a thing *[res]* which we call the sense *[sensus]*."[15] For Ernesti, "meaning" *(sensus)* is achieved when words are matched up to "things" *(res)*. The history of Christian biblical interpretation is a history of the attempt to narrow or to expand the range of the term "things" *(res)*. Medieval interpretation, both Christian[16] and Jewish, was characterized by the links they drew between words and things, and between things and other things. What often appears as an arbitrary labeling of words and meanings is the result of a carefully drawn matrix of "words" and "things" along with "things" and what other "things" they signify. The control factor is often little more than the acceptance of the links drawn between "things" and other "things." In the medieval church those links were established by the force of tradition. It is therefore no surprise that the early Protestant treatises on hermeneutics were preoccupied with nailing down links between words and things. Since there could be only a single meaning to the text, any particular "word" in Scripture could only signify a single "thing." At the same time, Protestants were concerned to maintain the "spiritual sense" of Scripture, particularly the OT, as it was understood by Jesus and the NT. If the words did not seem to point to that "spiritual sense," then it may, or must, be found in the thing to which the words refer.

The resolution of this problem played itself out in at least two ways: the Lutheran and the Reformed approaches. Lutherans such as Salomon Glassius saw every "word" in Scripture as referring either to a thing *(res)* or a "mystery" derived from a thing *(res)*.[17] The single meaning *(sensus)* of Scripture Glassius identified as that which the Holy Spirit intended, either the thing itself or the "mystery" that lies in the "word." Glassius identified the thing referred to by the words as "the literal, or, the historical sense."[18] The

---

[15]"Omni verbo respondere debet, in sacris quidem libris semper et haud dubie respondet, idea, seu notio rei, quem sensum dicimus" (Ernesti, *Institutio interpretis Novi Testamenti*, p. 15).

[16]Augustine, and the medieval intellectual tradition that followed him, saw in the relationship of words to things the possibility for accounting for both a literal and a figurative interpretation of biblical texts. Words point to (signify) things, but also things can point to (signify) other things. All things get pointed to by words (literal sense), but some things also point to other things (figurative sense). For Augustine, the "wood" that Moses cast into the bitter waters (Ex 15:25) was both a "thing" to which the word "wood" pointed and a "thing" that points to another thing, the cross ("wood") of Christ.

[17]"Ergo praeter sensum literalem, qui ex verbis colligitur, mysticum etiam dari, qui ex rebus ipsis hauritur, negari nulla ratione potest" (Salomon Glassius, *Philologia sacra* [Leipzig, 1705], p. 350).

[18]"Literam seu historiam" (ibid.).

literal sense of a biblical "word" was the historical sense of the "thing" pointed to by the word.

In Reformed hermeneutics, the literal meaning *(sensus literalis)* of Scripture lay not in "things" themselves, but in the linguistic sense (Hebrew meaning) of the biblical "words" *(verba)*. The words of Scripture were either intended in their proper sense, in which case they pointed to things *(res)*, or they could be taken in a typological sense, in which case they pointed to future spiritual realities *(mysterium)*.[19] When words pointed to things, this was simply called "history," or *res gesta* ("things that happen"). In Reformed hermeneutics, contrary to Augustine and the medieval church, "things" *(res)* had no inherent possibilities for meaning. Meaning *(sensus)* resided only in words. It was the words that rendered things (history) meaningful. What this meant was that meaning, whether literal or spiritual, could only be read as "words" off the surface of the biblical page. There could, then, be only one meaning, and that was the literal sense, but that literal sense could, and often was, understood "spiritually."[20]

In Reformed hermeneutics, the meaning of "history" was, and still is in many cases, tied securely to the meaning of the biblical "words" (texts). For Lutherans, however, the meaning of Scripture was detachable from words and could become resident in "things."

Since Ernesti was a devout Lutheran, we must take a closer look at the Lutheran notion of things and words. In Lutheran hermeneutics, the *sensus* of Scripture was located either in the words or in the *mysterium* pointed to by the things. Thus, meaning *(sensus)* often was only indirectly connected to the words of Scripture. Though not intended to be so, in this system of interpre-

[19]"Ubi unicum tantum esse scripturae sensum, eumque literalem, asserit; Et locos illos in quibus praeter historiam, eamque veram & gestam, significatur aliquid futurum typicè, non duos habere sensus, sed unicum, cumque literalem, verum tamen integrum sensum & totum non esse in verbis proprie sumptis, sed partim in typo, partim in re ipsa quae gesta fuit" (William Whitaker, *Disputatio de sacra Scriptura*, quest. 5, chap. 2); "Sensum verbi divini per se tantum umicum esse, eum nimirum, quem intentioni dicentis, & rei significatae natura importat, qui quidem literalis sive grammaticus dici solet" (Bartholomaus Keckermann) (both quoted in Rivet, *Isagoge*, p. 214).

[20]One can see in this not only how such a hermeneutic (Reformed) provided a firm basis for the typological interpretation that developed in Reformed orthodoxy in the seventeenth century (Coccejus), but also why questions about the role of history in biblical interpretation have not dogged Reformed hermeneutics quite so much as Lutheran. Another, less charitable, way to put it is that one can see why classic Reformed theologians often see themselves as taking a historical approach to exegesis, when in reality they are doing little more than retracing the history recorded in the biblical narratives themselves. In my opinion, there is inherently nothing wrong with such an approach as long as one recognizes it for what it is—a textual approach.

tation the things of Scripture enjoyed a significant degree of independence from the words. Only the literal sense *(sensus literalis)* was securely tied to the words. Consequently, in Lutheran approaches to the Bible, the things of Scripture often could become the means whereby, apart from the words, outside meaning was imported into the text. This worked well in allowing freedom for christological interpretations of the OT, but there was a price to be paid. Allowing christological meaning to reside in the things pointed to by words opened a door into Scripture so wide that both orthodox scholars and pietists could import their own doctrines and personal beliefs by truckloads into the text.

By the eighteenth century, it was nearly impossible for the meaning of the words to have any effect on the meaning of the things behind the words. It was one of Ernesti's primary goals to secure the legitimate control of the words of Scripture over the meaning of the things. This was necessary and important for Ernesti because he believed that it was the words of Scripture, not the things, that were divinely inspired. His basis for that view was the same as all orthodox (evangelical) theology in his day, Paul's sweeping statement in 2 Timothy 3:16: "All Scripture [words] is inspired."

Behind the writing of his work on biblical hermeneutics was Ernesti's concern that the meaning *(sensus)* of Scripture had become vulnerable in the hands of the historian, just as the meaning of Scripture had once been vulnerable in the hands of the theologians and pietists. Historians too had gained remarkable access to the things *(realia)* of Scripture. Given Lutheranism's stress on the importance of things in deciding the meaning of Scripture, the historian's newly gained knowledge of things was quickly put into service in discovering the sense of Scripture.

For several reasons—the most important being his concern for verbal inspiration—Ernesti established his first basic rule of Scriptural interpretation: the meaning *(sensus)* of Scripture could come only through the words of Scripture. Regarding that rule, Ernesti says, "Entirely deceitful and fallacious is the approach of gathering the sense of words from things. Things, rather, ought to be known from words."[21] Ernesti looks on this issue as a major obstacle for understanding the meaning of Scripture. The point, however, was largely lost on his successors.

[21]Ernesti, *Institutio interpretis Novi Testamenti*, p. 13.

In the sixteenth and seventeenth centuries, Protestant biblical scholars had used the term "history" to refer to the "things" pointed to by the "words" of Scripture. This did not mean that they understood the term "history" as we do today. Lutheran and Reformed biblical scholars understood the concept of "history" *(res)* not so much as a flow of past events guided and governed by the will of God, but as a final shape given to past events for the spiritual purpose of instruction in the will of God. History, viewed in its totality, had a divine lesson to teach, and its shape was an important part of that lesson. Biblical history was presented as a timeless, comprehensive figuration of divine and human activities—events linking God and Israel as well as Israel and the church.

John Calvin understood biblical history not, as most would today, as a series of causes and effects, but in terms of a theological lesson on the nature of divine covenants: "The covenant made with all the patriarchs is so much like ours in substance *[substantia]* and reality *[re ipsa]* that the two are actually one *[unum]* and the same *[idem]*. Yet they differ *[variat]* in the mode of dispensation *[administratio]*."[22] All covenants are "one and the same" in substance. There are not "new" covenants and "old" covenants per se. The "new" of the "new covenant" is new because its administration is new, just as the "old" is "old" only in its administration under law. Biblical history thus was a web of theological and doctrinal symbols, not merely something that had happened in the past. In biblical history the church found its identity as the church alongside Israel in a common covenant with variant administrations. By the same token, Israel's identity was shaped by its administration under law. Kraus's term for that early understanding of biblical history is "dogmatic biblicism."[23] It is the belief that all the doctrines (dogmatic) of the church have found their expression in the comprehensive totality of biblical history (biblicism).

This early view of biblical history, so different from a modern view of history, did not outlast the seventeenth century by more than a couple decades. By the early nineteenth century, the modern view of history as "past events" was beginning to take root. The shift in the meaning of the term *history* happened in two further stages.

---

[22]John Calvin *Institutes* 2.10.2 (*Institutes of the Christian Religion,* ed. John T. McNeill, trans. Ford Lewis Battles [LCC 20; Phildelphia: Westminster, 1960], 1:429). "Patrum omnium foedus adeo substantia et re ipsa nihil a nostro differt, ut unum prorsus atque idem sit. Administratio tamen variat."

[23]See Sailhamer, *Introduction to Old Testament Theology*, p. 120.

The first stage was the introduction into biblical study of the notion of time periods, a system of biblical interpretation associated with Johann Coccejus. Coccejus understood the history portrayed in the Bible as, itself, an actual flow of events, changing with time, and leading to a definite conclusion.[24] Biblical history was no longer understood as a static picture that could be contemplated in its totality. History was increasingly coming to be known more like a motion picture that could be approached only in terms of its temporal sequence. With Coccejus, the "things" to which the biblical words referred were forever changed into dynamic, unrepeatable events. They continued to be recorded in Scripture as "events," but they were no longer viewed as "verbal events" portrayed only in words. They were understood as real events that had happened *(res gesta)*. One could understand biblical events only by becoming part of them, as events, and experiencing them in terms of their momentary and sequential movement. Reading about history was no longer adequate; history now had to be experienced for it to be understood.

For Coccejus, and those after him, biblical history remained biblical. It consisted only of those things *(res)* to which the words of the Bible had referred. The whole of "history," as such, was contained within the cumulative range of all the words *(verba)* of Scripture. Biblical history was not yet submerged into the ocean of world history, but world history was still viewed within the panorama of the events in the Bible. In Coccejus's system, "history" was controlled by divine providence. It was a history read off the pages of the Bible. There was no thought of a history whose central events and meaning could be known apart from the biblical text.

In the early eighteenth century there was a subtle but significant reversal of this view of biblical "history." It came under the influence of the Lutheran theologian Franz Buddeus.[25] Buddeus was thoroughly orthodox, but he became the first biblical scholar to approach the events and meaning of biblical "history" independently of the words of Scripture.[26] Buddeus took it for

---

[24]Kraus, *Die biblische Theologie*, p. 21.

[25]Franz Buddeus, *Historia ecclesiastica Veteris Testamenti*, 2 vols. (Halle, 1715–1719).

[26]"Der Begriff 'oeconomia' wird durch 'historia' ersetzt. Heir dämmert die historische Idee" (Kraus, *Die biblische Theologie*, p. 24). Buddeus's new understanding of history is developed in detail in Ludwig Diestel's description of his major work on biblical history. Buddeus, in very learned comments, enumerated and critically evaluated a large number of viewpoints about the meaning of various events recorded in the Bible. His primary purpose was to explain with the strictest objectivity the biblical events and those of the ancient world. He did so in terms of the general condi-

granted that what could be said about "things" could also be said of the "words" that referred to those "things." The meaning of the words of Scripture thus was identified with what could historically be known about "things." Buddeus had reversed the order of meaning in history. Instead of the words giving meaning to the things, the things were now giving meaning to the words. It was at that point, Kraus argues, that a genuine "historical" consciousness made its way into orthodox (evangelical) biblical interpretation.

## Johann August Ernesti

Ernesti's primary goal was to provide an exegetical approach to the Bible identical to the newly developed philological approach taken in the study of other ancient literature. Only in that way, Ernesti argues, could biblical exegesis free itself from arbitrary interpretation. By "arbitrary interpretation" Ernesti means a meaning derived from "things."[27] His basic thesis is that a text can have no other meaning than its grammatical, or historical, sense. That meaning, which Ernesti calls the "literal sense," is located in individual words. It is the lexical meaning of a word. As Ernesti understands it, the sense, or meaning, of a word is assigned to the word by "human arrangement and custom."[28] Today we would call this a "linguistic convention." That sense consisted of a specific idea, or mental notion, of a thing.[29] Words assign meaning to things. The fact that the sense of words is dependent on human custom means that its relationship to things is arbitrary.[30] Ernesti does not mean to say by the term *arbitrary* that there are no real reasons for the meaning of words. He means simply that the reason for a word's meaning is not arrived at logically. It is a function of whatever particular language the word is a part of and how it functions in that language. When, in a certain language and at a certain time and place, a sense is assigned to a thing by a word,

---

tions and wide range of historical activity during the biblical time period. In doing so, Diestel argues, Buddeus still understood himself to be explaining the meaning of the text (*Geschichte des Alten Testamentes in der christlichen kirche* [Jena: Mauke, 1869], p. 463).

[27]Gottlob Wilhelm Meyer, *Geschichte der Schrifterklärung seit der Wiederherstellung der Wissenschaften* (GKW 11/4; Göttingen: Römer 1802–1809), 5:494-95.

[28]"Eum sensum verba non habent per se; sunt enim non naturalia aut necessaria rerum signa: sed ab institutione humana et consuetudine, per quam inter verba et ideas rerum copulatio quaedam inducta est" (Ernesti, *Institutio interpretis Novi Testamenti*, p. 9).

[29]"Omini verbo respondere debet, in sacris quidem libris semper et haud dubie respondet, idea seu notio rei, quem *sensum* dicimus, quod eius rei, quae verbo exprimitur, sensus audiendo verbo instaurari in animo utcumque debet" (ibid., p. 3).

[30]"Sed ea [sensus] cum esset ab initio, et institutione, arbitraria" (ibid., p. 8).

that sense becomes the necessary meaning of the word.[31] It is for this reason that hermeneutics is grounded in historically conditioned situations, and hence the sense of words must be investigated by means of a proper philological method.[32] This means that the sense of the words should be discovered from the usage *(usus loquendi)* of the words at the time of the writing of the biblical books.

For Ernesti, the notion of the "use of words" *(usus loquendi)* is what distinguished him from the historical method in his day. What Ernesti sees as the "historical" dimension of the meaning of a word is the "fact" that at a certain place and time in the past a living human being recorded a word in a text in such a way that its meaning (usage) could be derived by reading that text. A historical moment was preserved in an ancient text, lexically, grammatically and physically, as a mark on a page or clay tablet. The historical moment preserved was not the event recorded, but the recording of the event. An event *(res)* had become a word *(verbum)*. To discover the meaning *(sensus)* of that word, one must look at the word in context of other words at the time of the recording of the event.

Ernesti is emphatic that to understand the meaning of words, one should not look at the things to which the words pointed. Since the relationship of words to things is arbitrary (unpredictable), it can be discovered only by noting the usage of a word at a particular moment in time and place. Ernesti believed that the relationship between words and things[33] could be radically altered at different times, places, and within different settings. It is the task of the philologist to discover the "usage of words" in specific written texts within various historical contexts. That goal remains today the goal of the science of philology.

The hermeneutical aim of the historical method applied to "words" was, and continues to be, to discover the "sense" of ancient words by reconstructing the world of thought of the ancient writer who used the words. For the historian, the sense of words is gained from knowledge of what the words are

---

[31]"Semel constituta per consuetudinem facta est necessaria" (ibid.).

[32]Meyer, *Geschichte der Schrifterklärung*, 5:494-95.

[33]"Usus autem loquendi multis rebus definitur, tempore, religione, secta et disciplina, vita communi, reipublicae denique constitutione: quae fere efficiunt characterem orationis, qua quisque scriptor tempore quoque usus est. Nam ab iis rebus omnibus vel oritur vel variatur modus verborum usurpandorum: aliterque saepe idem verbum in vita communi, aliter in religione, aliter in scholis Philosphorum dicitur, quae et ipsae non consentiunt satis" (Ernesti, *Institutio interpretis Novi Testamenti*, p. 11).

about; that is, it is gained from knowledge of "things." Such a historical approach is recognizable from Keil's description of the sense of Scripture. According to Keil, to know the sense of the words of Scripture, one must think the same thoughts as the biblical writer when he was writing the book.[34] The meaning, for Keil, is not in the words of the author, but in his mind *(mens scriptoris).* To know the mind of a biblical author is to know the sense of Scripture.[35] It was for this reason that Keil understands the investigation of the sense of words to be a historical task.[36]

For Keil, the investigation of the historical sense of a word is a task different from that of finding its grammatical sense. The sense of a biblical book must be drawn first from the words.[37] The words are a necessary help[38] that the writers use for getting their thoughts across to the readers.[39] But knowing the meaning of the words is not enough. The sense of a book cannot always be known solely from the words of the book.[40] For Keil, there are also other matters to consider. One must have, for example, a ready command of those things that enable us to better grasp the mind of the author.[41]

Ernesti and Keil are in fundamental disagreement on this point. Ernesti, in fact, argues just the opposite. Instead of the meaning *(sensus)* of the words being derived from things, as Keil maintains, Ernesti stresses that the meaning of things ought to be derived solely from the words. It is important to stress that Ernesti could not have been clearer on this point. Hear him again:

> Altogether deceitful and fallacious is the approach of drawing the sense of words from things, since things, rather, ought to be known from words and their sense investigated through legitimate means [philology]. For something may be true which is not in the words, but that which is to be maintained about the things themselves, ought to be understood and judged from the words of the Holy Spirit.[42]

---

[34]"Sensum orationis aut libri cognoscere nihil aliud est, quam iis occupatum eadem cogitare, quae, dum composuit, auctor ipse cogitauit" (Keil, *Keilii opuscula academica*, p. 11.).

[35]"Quod ubi in quopiam locum habet, is recte scriptoris mentem cepit" (ibid.).

[36]"Unde patet, indagationem, quae circa sensum orationis aut libri versatur, esse historiam" (ibid.).

[37]"Hic vero unus librorum N.T. sensus necessario primum e verbis, quae auctores in singulis locis adhibuerunt, cognosci debebit" (ibid., p. 13).

[38]"Velut adminiculo" (ibid.).

[39]"His enim, velut adminiculo, illi ad designandas, quas cum lectoribus communicare volebant, notiones et cogitationes usi sunt, neque uti non potuerunt" (ibid.).

[40]"Sensus libri non semper unice e verbis in illo obuiis cognosci potest" (ibid., p. 14).

[41]"Ut res quoque eae in promtu sint, quarum est vis aliqua in definienda accuratiusque cognoscenda scriptoris mente" (ibid.).

[42]Ernesti, *Institutio interpretis Novi Testamenti*, p. 13.

It is instructive to compare Moses Stuart's note on this last point by Ernesti:

> By things, [Ernesti] means the application of our previous views of things to the words of an author, in order to elicit his meaning, instead of proceeding to our inquiries, in the way of grammatico-historical exegesis. Not that our previous knowledge of things can never aid us, for it often does so; but that this can serve for nothing more than an assistant to our philological efforts.[43]

Stuart completely reverses Ernesti's point. Ironically, he does so by suggesting that Ernesti really does not mean what he says. Stuart suggests that what Ernesti really means to say is that we should look at the things of Scripture without prejudice. In other words, we should look at them as objective historians. But it is clear that Ernesti does not say that. He says exactly what his own words say. He means to say that we should not attempt to understand the words of Scripture by investigating the things to which they refer. We can understand the things only by looking at what the words tell us about those things.

Ernesti acknowledges that sometimes words are ambiguous and texts are unclear. In such cases, things can assist an interpreter to "select some one particular meaning." But here, he says, we must use only those things known to us from the words of other texts. "For," he concludes, "when we investigate the sense in any other way than by a grammatical method, we effect nothing more than to make out a meaning, which in itself perhaps is not absurd, but which lies not in the words, and therefore is not the meaning of the writer."[44] For Ernesti, the intention of the author *(mens scriptoris)* is clearly only to be found in the meaning of the words.

The effect on American evangelicalism of later interpretations of Ernesti by Keil and Stuart is clear from Milton Terry's *Biblical Hermeneutics*, which continues to wield considerable influence among evangelicals. According to

---

[43]Stuart, *Elements of Interpretation*, p. 17.

[44]"Itaque res et analogia doctrinae, quam dicunt, hactenus modo prodest in interpretando, ut in verbis vel a multitudine significationis, vel a structura, vel alia qua caussa, ambiguis, ducat nos ad definiendam verborum significationem, sive ad delectum significationis. In quo tamen et ipso cautio est, ut res, quibus ad definiendum utimur, ductae sint ex verbis planis et perspicuis et certo cognitis aliorum locorum, nec adversentur verba, quorum sensum quaerimus. Cum autem aliter, aut per eam solam, sine grammatica ratione, sensus quaeritur, nihil aliud efficitur, nisi, ut sensus repertus in se fortasse non absurdus sit, non ut in verbis lateat, sitque menti scriptoris consentaneus" (Ernesti, *Institutio interpretis Novi Testamenti*, p. 13).

Terry, "The grammatico-historical sense of a writer is such an interpretation of his language as is required by the laws of grammar and the facts of history." For Terry, the historical sense is "that meaning of an author's words which is required by historical considerations. It demands that we consider carefully the time of the author, and the circumstances under which he wrote." Terry then quotes Samuel Davidson to show that the two terms, grammatical and historical "are synonymous."[45]

At first glance, Terry appears to be following Ernesti fairly closely, but then he begins to specify more precisely what he has in mind. Even though the terms *grammatical* and *historical* "are synonymous," there is a difference in meaning between them. They differ, says Terry, because although the laws of grammar are universal, the special uses of grammar *(usus loquendi)* are determined by "the religious, moral, and psychological ideas, under whose influence a language has been formed and molded."[46] Hence, "all the objects with which the writers were conversant, and the relations in which they were placed, are traced out historically."[47] The grammatical and historical sense of Scripture thus differs in its usage because of the role that things ("all the objects with which the writers were conversant") have in determining the meaning of words. It is clear that Terry (and Davidson) have parted company with Ernesti on the crucial issue of the role of history in biblical interpretation.

Only a few pages later, Terry demonstrates how much he has learned from the later versions of the grammatical-historical method in works such as Keil's or Stuart. In discussing the importance of "the historical standpoint," Terry says,

> The interpreter should, therefore, endeavor to take himself from the present, and to transport himself into the historical position of his author, look through his eyes, note his surroundings, feel with his heart, and catch his emotion. Herein we note the import of the term grammatico-historical interpretation. We are not only to grasp the grammatical import of words and sentences, but also to feel the force and bearing of the historical circumstances which may in any way have affected the writer. . . . The individuality of the writer, his local surroundings, his wants and desires, his relation to those for whom he wrote,

---

[45]Milton S. Terry, *Biblical Hermeneutics: A Treatise on the Interpretation of the Old and New Testaments* (1883; reprint, Grand Rapids: Zondervan, 1974), p. 203.

[46]Ibid., p. 204.

[47]Ibid.

> his nationality and theirs, the character of the times when he wrote—all these matters are of the first importance to a thorough interpretation of the several books of Scripture.[48]

How different from Ernesti! Particularly problematic with what Terry says in this quotation is that he presents his remarks as a description of "the principles so ably set forth by Ernesti [that] were further elaborated . . . by Karl August Keil, whose various contributions to biblical hermeneutics [here he refers to the grammatical-historical method] did much to prepare the way for the solid and enduring methods of exegesis which are now generally prevalent in Germany, England, and America."[49] Whether Terry's approach to the use of historical reconstruction is valid in hermeneutics today, I leave to the reader to decide. The point is that Terry's approach clearly does not represent the grammatical-historical method envisioned by Ernesti.

I will conclude these remarks on the grammatical-historical method with a brief look at the assessment of Ernesti by the standard work on the history of biblical interpretation in his own lifetime, that of Gottlob Wilhelm Meyer.[50] What one misses most from Ernesti, Meyer says, is instructions on the use of the historical method. One should, however, not expect to find such instructions in Ernesti because, Meyer asserts, Ernesti relied solely on a grammatical interpretation.[51] Meyer goes on to argue that it was only with Semler (independently of Ernesti) that we find an interest in historical interpretation as part of the sensus *literalis*.[52]

If, today, evangelicals desire to reclaim their focus on an inspired text (words), they would do well to heed the advice of one of their most gifted forebears, Johann August Ernesti. History has an important role to play in telling us about the Bible, its authorship, time and place of writing, but when

---

[48]Ibid., p. 231.

[49]Ibid., p. 708.

[50]Meyer, *Geschichte der Schrifterklärung*.

[51]The full quotation: "Aber noch mehr vermisste man in dieser Ernestischen Anwerfung, da sie zunächst auf die grammarische Interpretation allein berechnet war, eine Anleitung zur historischen Interpretation . . . und besonders eine Anleitung, die Herablassung Jesus und seiner Apostel zu den nationalen und temporellen Begriffen ihrer Zeitgenossen zu beachten, und aus den Apokryphen des A.T., wie aus andern lautern Quellen, diese Zeitvorstellungen möglichst genau zu erforschen" (ibid., 5:499).

[52]"So suchte bald darauf Semler durch ähnliche belehrende Winke neben der grammatischen noch die historische Auslegung des N.T. zu empfehlen, und selbst an seinem Theile zu befördern" (ibid., 5:501).

it comes to the meaning *(sensus)* of the Bible, there is no substitute for focusing on its words and their grammatical-historical sense.

Ernesti's contribution to biblical study centers on two points. First, what we commonly think of as the grammatical-historical method underwent significant changes in the hands of evangelical biblical scholars in the nineteenth century. One should exercise caution in linking Ernesti to those who, like Terry and Stuart, later identified their approach with his.[53] As Ernesti understood it, the grammatical-historical method was not a warrant for the introduction of all kinds of historical material into biblical interpretation. Ernesti was clear in his belief that historical research, that is, historical reconstructions of the events recorded in the Bible, should not take the place of a sound philological understanding of the meaning of words. It is the meaning of the words, gained through the study of ancient texts, that informs us about biblical events.

Second, Ernesti is a helpful example of how one's view of inspiration can, and perhaps should, affect a hermeneutical method. What characterizes Ernesti's approach more than anything is the importance he placed on the meaning of the words of Scripture. It is true that Ernesti was trained in philology and that he had a greater appreciation for it than the historical method as such, but the more important factor in Ernesti's approach is the reason why he preferred philology to history. The reason lay in his understanding of biblical inspiration. Ernesti held to the classical orthodox view of inspiration. The words of Scripture were inspired, not the historical events (things). Consequently, the method that best rendered the meaning of the words of Scripture was to be preferred. Ernesti may have been the last important biblical scholar to hold fast to the doctrine of biblical inspiration in the classical sense of identifying inspiration with the words of Scripture. By the beginning of the nineteenth century, the accepted view of inspiration had so shifted its focus that it was linked no longer to Scripture as such (words), but to the events (things) to which the Scriptures made reference. Instead of a "holy Bible" as the locus of divine revelation, evangelicals in increasing numbers looked to a "holy history" as the locus of divine revelation. It is therefore no

[53]Gerhard Maier links the expression "grammatisch-historisch" collectively to Ernesti "und seine Schule." "Andrerseits wählten Ernesti und seine Schule gerade den Begriff 'grammatisch-historisch,' um ihre Art von Schriftauslegung zu charakterisierun" (*Biblische Hermeneutik*, pp. 296-97).

surprise that evangelical biblical hermeneutics was eager to make the shift away from the meaning of words to the meaning of things.

In Ernesti's own day there were already strong forces at work making the transition of evangelical biblical theology to revelatory events even more pronounced. This time, however, it was coming from outside the evangelical camp in Friedriech Schleiermacher's critique of the orthodox (evangelical) understanding of the OT. Although many evangelicals valiantly resisted the largely negative influence of Schleiermacher, by mid-nineteenth century their efforts had begun to unravel, leaving them with a view of the OT and its relationship to the NT that closely approximated his in some important ways. Even in their public discourse, evangelical biblical theologians felt free to acknowledge what they believed to be the positive influence of Schleiermacher on their understanding of biblical theology.

## Friedriech Schleiermacher and the Old Testament

The importance of Schleiermacher, for evangelical biblical theology, lies in his radical view of the nature of the OT and its relationship to the NT. Evangelical biblical theologians were unfavorable to Schleiermacher's views in general, but certain aspects of his view of the OT and the Christian faith were appealing to those seeking to wed biblical faith to a historical understanding of religion. I will attempt to show that the most wide-ranging influence Schleiermacher had on evangelicalism, and biblical theology in general, was his belief that the OT had only a secondary historical role to play in defining the Christian faith. After Schleiermacher, it was generally believed by evangelicals that if there was to be a viable link between the OT and the NT, it must grow out of some genuinely "historical" connection.[54]

Schleiermacher, in his critique of the OT,[55] dismisses the notion of a "real" *(res)* theological relationship between the OT and the NT on the grounds that the two parts of the Christian Bible stemmed from two distinct religious viewpoints, Mosaic legalism (OT) and faith (NT). The only link between the two parts of the Christian Bible, he argues, lay in the otherwise incidental fact that Jesus was born in a Jewish home. That, however, is hardly enough

[54]Friedrich Schleiermacher, *The Christian Faith*, trans. H. R. Mackintosh and J. S. Stewart (Edinburgh: T & T Clark, 1928), §12, pp. 60-62.

[55]See Emil Brunner, "The Significance of the Old Testament for Our Faith," in *The Old Testament and Christian Faith: A Theological Discussion*, ed. Bernard W. Anderson (New York: Herder & Herder, 1969), pp. 243-64.

to serve as a basis for a Christian theology of the OT. For Schleiermacher, the OT did not naturally or historically lead to the NT and hence was not essential for the Christian.

Schleiermacher's argument rests on his identification of the OT with ancient Judaism, which he understands as Mosaism. Unfortunately, he thought it unnecessary to give an exegetical defense of that premise. For example, he makes no attempt to demonstrate exegetically from the OT Scriptures that they are an expression of the Mosaic religion that he characterizes as legalism. He assumes that if the OT is historically linked to ancient Judaism, it also teaches the religion of Judaism. The OT teaches adherence to the law, and the NT teaches grace. In advancing such an argument, Schleiermacher brought about a subtle yet fundamental shift in the Christian understanding of the OT. It was a move from the textually based understanding of the meaning of the OT in classical orthodoxy to a location of that meaning in its subject matter, that is, the supposed beliefs of ancient Judaism (Mosaism). Rather than drawing his understanding of the OT from the Scriptures themselves, Schleiermacher identifies the meaning of the OT with the religious beliefs of its historical context. The question of whether or not Schleiermacher's assumptions are valid we can leave to the historians of religion. Our question is the influence that Schleiermacher's assumptions had on evangelical Christian understanding of the OT.

After Schleiermacher, biblical critics were willing to concede only the slightest historical connection between the two Testaments, treating the OT as a part of ancient Judaism and the NT alone as belonging to the Christian church. There was no other link between the OT and NT—certainly not one upon which a Christian biblical theology could be erected.

To be sure, evangelical biblical theologians watched Schleiermacher from a relatively safe distance and with considerable caution. Nevertheless, they were by no means immune to his ideas and critiques of the OT. Although, unlike Schleiermacher, they were willing to accept the biblical version of its own history at face value,[56] under his influence an increasing number of evangelicals turned away from a grammatical reading of the text to a focus on historical events as the locus of biblical meaning.

---

[56]Although many looked at this as a fundamental flaw in Ernst Hengstenberg's apologetical approach.

Some evangelicals openly acknowledged agreement with Schleiermacher. A leading evangelical OT scholar and student of Ernst Hengstenberg, Heinrich August Hävernick, actually made a midcourse correction toward Schleiermacher's views between the first and second volumes of his influential three-volume *Introduction to the Old Testament*.[57] Hävernick's introduction began as a summation of Hengstenberg's orthodox views of the OT. Along the way, Hävernick came under the influence of Schleiermacher, toward whom the direction of Hävernick's OT introduction took a decisive turn. To be sure, most evangelicals such as Hävernick did not go all the way over to Schleiermacher, but they remained deeply influenced by his views of the OT and passed many of them on to their colleages and students. J. A. Dorner, in his foreword to Hävernick's posthumously published *Lectures on the Theology of the Old Testament (Vorlesungen über die Theologie des Alten Testaments),* an influential evangelical work in its day, acknowledged and even praised Hävernick's acceptance of Schleiermacher's focus on historical events *(res)* as the proper basis of a biblical theology.

> Many also will, I hope, recognize that it would be an injustice to the blessed Hävernick if one wished to judge him only by the first volume of his introduction to the Old Testament. He himself later did not highly value that work (although with respect to its learned material it still remains of value), at least since he developed a freer standpoint under the influence of his continual learning from Schleiermacher and Neander. Indeed, whoever desires to do so may learn something of his amazing progress by looking at his commentary on Ezekiel. I hope that this book *[Lectures in Old Testament Theology]* will demonstrate to the theological public that Hävernick belonged neither to the unhistorical right or left, but went his own way, or rather, avoiding any kind of forced historical interpretation, he allowed the material, with which he had identified and in which he had immersed himself deeply, to speak for itself. I may in this regard point to the quite remarkable third section of this book *[Lectures in Old Testament Theology],* which deals with the development of the idea of salvation, the real heart of the Old Testament. In this voluminous, exhaustively detailed, study, Hävernick traces the developmental history of prophecy, in part in a truly masterful way.[58]

---

[57]Heinrich A. C. Hävernick, *Handbuch der historisch-kritischen Einleitung in das Alte Testament*, 3 vols. (Erlangen: Heyder, 1836–1849).

[58]"Mancher auch, hoffe ich, wird erkennen, dass man dem sel. Hävernick Unrecht thun würde, wenn man ihn etwa nur nach den ersten Abtheilungen seiner Einleitung ins A.T. beurtheilen

Schleiermacher's understanding of the OT and, in his view, its minimal historical links to the NT fundamentally shaped the direction and aims of evangelical biblical theology in the nineteenth and twentieth centuries. In the face of Schleiermacher's critique of the OT, those evangelicals who attempted to hold fast drifted in two directions. One direction was toward approaches to OT theology that were either narrowly focused on NT aspects of the OT, such as messianism (Hengstenberg), or driven by issues that arose out of orthodox creeds, such as law and covenant (Vos). It was widely believed among evangelical theologians at the time that Hengstenberg's rebuttal of Schleiermacher in his *Christology of the Old Testament* was wide of the mark, largely because Hengstenberg had properly understood neither the force of the historical arguments of his opponent nor the weaknesses of his own arguments. Be that as it may, Hengstenberg's work was the first of many evangelical biblical theologies that focused almost entirely on "messianic prophecies" and "promise and fulfillment" strategies drawn more from the NT than the OT.

Another direction taken by evangelical biblical theologians in response to Schleiermacher's critique of the OT is seen in the numerous attempts to ground evangelical views of the OT in historical "facts" *(realia)*. That move on the part of early evangelicals inevitably led to what came to be a characteristic evangelical response to the challenge of the OT's historicity: the identification of the message of the OT with historical reconstructions of ancient Israelite religion (Vos). Although enjoying widespread acceptance in evangelical circles, such "salvation-historical" theologies demonstrated little effectiveness against Schleiermacher's negative view. Though wanting to meet the challenges to the historicity of the OT directly and with apologetic in-

---

wollte, die, wenn sie auch in Beziehung auf den gelehrten Stoff immer von Werth bleiben werden, doch später auch von ihm selbst nicht überschätzt wurden, seit er besonders durch Schleiermacher und Neander sich fortbildend einen immer freieren Standpunct gewann. Doch, wer da wollte, der konnte von seinem rüstigen Fortschreiten sich schon aus seinem Commentar über Ezechiel überzeugen. Dieses Werkchen aber hoffe ich, wird dem theologischen Publikum beweisen, dass Hävernick weder zu den Unhistorischen auf der Rechten noch auf der Linken gehört, sondern seinen selbständigen Gang geht, oder vielmehr, dass er abhold aller Geschichtsmacherei die Sache walten lässt, in die er sich mit treuer Innigkeit vertieft hat. Namentlich darf ich in dieser Beziehung auszeichnend den dritten Abschnitt hervorheben, der die Entwicklung des Heilsbegriffs, des Kernes im A.T. behandelt. In grossen aber sichern und auf gründlichen Detailstudien ruhenden Zügen ist hier auch die Entwicklungsgeschichte der Profetie, zum Theil wahrhaft meisterhaft, geschildert" (J. A. Dorner, foreword in Heinrich A. Hävernick, *Vorlesungen über die Theologie des Alten Testaments*, ed. H. A. Hahn [Erlangen: Heyder, 1848], pp. vi-vii).

tent, evangelical responses frequently accomplished little more than a concession to Schleiermacher's central point, which is that the meaning of the OT narratives consists of the mere fact of their historicity.

To be sure, an important aspect of Schleiermacher's critique of the OT was the challenge it presented to evangelical theologians to come to terms with their own long-held views of the role of history in theology, particularly their view of revelation in history. Although evangelical theologians devoted considerable thought to the question of history and revelation, they were unable to produce an effective response to Schleiermacher. Coming out of the eighteenth century, with its general loss of biblical history, evangelical biblical theologians were able to marshal a defense for the OT based only on a superficial understanding of biblical narratives *(verba)* vis-à-vis actual historical events *(res)*. Many evangelicals, such as Hengstenberg and C. F. Keil, were unable to understand biblical history outside the narrow range of what Hans Frei called the "history-likeness"[59] of the biblical narratives. This is not to say they were wrong in assigning historical value to the biblical narratives, or that the biblical narratives were less than real history. Frei's point in calling the biblical narratives "history-like" is that although they are only written texts, they are so realistic, or so "like history," that biblical historians have treated them as if they were the actual events ("real events" *[res]*). The "history-

[59]Frei's use of "history-like" is often misunderstood to mean that he believes that the biblical narratives are not about real history, but are only "like history," that is, fiction. Regardless of what Frei believed about the factuality or truthfulness of the biblical narratives, which was very little, he used "history-like" as a way of saying that the biblical narratives are "realistic" and hence very much "like" the actual events they depict. The biblical narratives are realistic. Biblical narratives, in fact, depict events so realistically that readers respond to them as they would to the events themselves. Like actual historical events, the meaning of biblical narratives lies in their shape and the sequence of events they depict. Frei's use of "history-like" does not entail a belief that the events actually happened or that they did not happen. It simply means that the events are depicted and set before the reader so realistically that reading them is tantamount to seeing the actual events. Frei's book *The Eclipse of Biblical Narrative* is about the loss of the notion of being "history-like" and its replacement by the sense of the narratives's factuality. The biblical narratives are so realistic that they tended to be overlooked in favor of the actual events they depicted. Frei states, "A realistic or history-like (though not necessarily historical) element is a feature, as obvious as it is important, of many of the biblical narratives that went into the making of Christian belief. . . . It is fascinating that the realistic character of the crucial biblical stories was actually acknowledged and agreed upon by most of the significant eighteenth-century commentators. But since the precritical analytical or interpretive procedure for isolating it had irretrievably broken down in the opinion of most commentators, this specifically realistic characteristic, though acknowledged by all hand to be there, finally came to be ignored, or—even more fascinating—its presence or distinctiveness came to be denied for lack of a 'method' to isolate it. And this despite the common agreement that the specific feature was there!" (*The Eclipse of Biblical Narrative*, p. 10).

likeness" of biblical narratives often has contributed to misinterpretations of biblical events. As historians, they set out to read the OT as they would "events" in ancient history—raw facts in need of explanation. As literarily competent theologians, they read the biblical text as they would great epic literature—living within the narrative world depicted by the biblical story.

By calling the biblical narratives "history-like," Frei means that their realism often is mistaken for the realness of the events themselves, and as such, they are assigned a meaning not in terms of their actual status as written narratives, but of being isolated historical "facts" needing to be understood against the background of their ancient Near Eastern setting. In that sense, Frei's notion of an eclipse of biblical narrative also amounts to an eclipse of the biblical author. The narratives as such were so "life-like" that one easily overlooked the fact that they were written depictions *(verba)* of realia *(res)* with a meaning that should be identified as part of an author's intent *(mens auctoris)*. That being so, evangelical theologians such as Hengstenberg and Keil treated the biblical narratives not merely as written accounts *(verba)* of actual events *(res)*, but as the events themselves *(res gesta)*. They thus understood the biblical narratives not to be only accounts of ancient history, but the actual real events, which could, and should, best be explained and verified by historical methods. Hengstenberg, who held such a view, seemed to be unaware of why his understanding of biblical history was not taken seriously by biblical historians. He believed, as other biblical theologians believed, that a historically "true" biblical narrative was one that depicted its events "just as they happened."[60] Since the OT did that, it was historical.

Throughout the nineteenth and twentieth centuries, evangelical biblical theologians devoted considerable effort to formulating a proper response to Schleiermacher's view of biblical history and the limited historical connection it allowed between the OT and the NT, not always knowing, or wanting it known, that it was Schleiermacher they were responding to. The effect those efforts had on evangelical biblical theology was what Frei describes as an "eclipse" of biblical narrative. Narratives as such were seen not as written accounts of events, but as the actual events to be treated in terms of the developing historical methodologies. Understood in terms of *real* history, biblical narratives (as opposed to real events) were used by evangelical theologians to

[60]Kraus, *Geschichte der historisch-kritischen Erforschung des Alten Testaments*, p. 372.

expand Schleiermacher's minimalist historical link between the OT and the NT. Whereas Schleiermacher could accept as historical only the minimal fact that Jesus was of Jewish descent, evangelicals believed that it was possible by means of the "realistic" biblical narratives to extend the small bit of history that it represented into a wide range of actual events linking the OT with the NT. This was particularly the case if they were allowed to draw also from the intertestamental literature. If Jesus was of Jewish descent, then anything we might learn about Judaism in the first century or earlier could, and should, be considered appropriate historical background for a biblical theology wishing to connect the OT and the NT "historically." As such, among evangelicals at least, the historical relationship between the OT and the NT, the very question on which Schleiermacher initially had focused his assault on the OT, became the unlikely ground on which they prepared to mount their counteroffensive for biblical theology.

One can see this equation of biblical narratives with actual historical events in the early works of nineteenth-century evangelicals such as von Hofmann, Rothe, and Keil.[61] Keil, seeking to know why the "Ishmaelites" in Genesis 37:25 are later in the same chapter called "Midianites" and "Medanites" (Gen 37:28), an essentially textual question, suggests not that this was a result of the orthography of the various texts used in the composition of Genesis, but reasons as a historian and geographer that because Judah was a stranger in this part of the land, he was unable to distinguish the various people groups of that region. Keil comments,

> The different names given to the traders—viz. *Ishmaelites* (vers. 25, 27, and 28b), *Midianites* (ver. 28a), and *Medanites* (ver. 36)—do not show that the account has been drawn from different legends, but that these tribes were often confounded, from the fact that they resembled one another so closely, not only in their common descent from Abraham (xvi. 15 and xxv. 2), but also in the similarity of their mode of life and their constant change of abode, that strangers could hardly distinguish them.[62]

Keil thus offers a historical-demographic answer to what was likely only a literary question that could be explained by textual variations in the written accounts of the names of the peoples who sold Joseph into Egypt.

---

[61]See Sailhamer, *Introduction to Old Testament Theology*, pp. 36-85.

[62]C. F. Keil and F. Delitzsch, *The Pentateuch*, trans. James Martin (BCOT; Grand Rapids: Eerdmans, 1971), p. 337.

Other equally important evangelical theologians responded to Schleiermacher's critique of the OT by attempting to return to the precritical past of the seventeenth century, treating the biblical text as raw historical data in need of scientific (historical) explanation (Ernst Hengstenberg, Charles Hodge, Benjamin Warfield).[63]

Evangelical biblical theology in the nineteenth and twentieth centuries took (unwittingly?) its defensive starting point in Schleiermacher's critique of the classical (evangelical) view of the OT as God's written Word.[64] It was in defending the OT against Schleiermacher's critique that evangelical biblical theologians forged new and lasting attitudes toward the OT and biblical history. In responding to Schleiermacher, evangelical biblical theologians sometimes drew from and hence tacitly accepted Schleiermacher's assumptions about the OT. Today, important aspects of those assumptions and the approaches they engendered have become essential parts of the evangelical view of the OT.

Schleiermacher's aim, in sympathy with the emerging historical consciousness of the nineteenth century, was to approach the OT in terms of its specific historical context. That context, Schleiermacher believed, was the religion of ancient Judaism. The OT, the HB, was the Bible of Judaism (Mosaism). In taking that starting point, Schleiermacher knowingly reversed the church's central beliefs about the OT, particularly its veneration of the OT as God's written Word.[65] Although Christians were disinclined to dispute the notion of the OT as the Bible of (ancient) Judaism, neither were they ready to concede that it was not a central and essential part of their own Bible. Jesus and the NT apostles understood the OT to be the Word of God, and the church, following them, acknowledged that the OT was its Scriptures. The church thus knew the OT both as the Bible of (ancient) Judaism and as a major part of its own Bible. It was the same HB (OT) in both.

---

[63]Repristination: "Die Verbindung der Spätromantik mit den Rest der konservativen Aufklärung, die Besinnung auf die fortdauernde rechtliche Geltung der Bekenntnisschriften, die positive Wiederaufnahme des biblisch-dogmatischen Erbes durch die massgebenden theologischen Neubildunger hatten den Boden für die Auferstehung der altprotestantischen Theologie bereitet" (Horst Stephan and Martin Schmidt, *Geschichte der evangelischen Theologie in Deutschland seit dem Idealismus*, 3rd ed. [Berlin: de Gruyter, 1973], p. 203).

[64]"Für das Grundverständnis des Alten Testaments im 19. Jahrhundert hatten die systematischen Erklärungen Schleiermachers eine nicht geringe Bedeutung. . . . Seine kritischen Äusserungen . . . wollen den Zeitgenossen helfen, ein neues Verhältnis zum Alten Testament zu gewinnen" (Kraus, *Geschichte der historisch-kritischen Erforschung*, p. 170).

[65]Ibid., p. 171.

It soon became obvious to most evangelical theologians that there were unanticipated implications to Schleiermacher's reassessment of the OT. Schleiermacher himself wasted no time in uncovering those implications. If the OT was the Bible of Judaism, he argued, it was necessary to view it not in terms of Christianity, but within the context of the religion of Judaism. The same books cannot at the same time be both the Bible of Judaism and the Bible of Christianity, at least not without some confusion. For Schleiermacher, this meant that the message of the OT would have to be reevaluated within its newly understood context of ancient Judaism and the Mosaic law.[66] The OT, being the embodiment of the law and the Sinai covenant, is difficult to understand positively as a preparation for the gospel. Thus, Schleiermacher believed, the OT must be understood in terms of a system of law that by the end of the first century had played itself out in opposition to the Christian gospel. The OT, as Schleiermacher had come to view it, must be understood in the context of the Sinai covenant, which he took to be legalism. To be sure, the use of the OT by the early church was aimed at identifying Christ as the Jewish Messiah promised in the OT, but Schleiermacher argued that this was merely a missiological expediency in view of the early church's missionary outreach to Judaism. Many members of the early Christian communities came out of Judaism. They were familiar with the OT, and it was a help to them to understand Jesus within the context of their own religion. Schleiermacher argued that this was the only justification for the NT church's appeal to the OT.

Although many of Schleiermacher's views were the result of his radical application of biblical criticism to the OT, the weight of his arguments about the OT appear to have been keenly felt even among evangelical theologians who did not hold those same critical views. The net effect of Schleiermacher's understanding of the OT was to remove it from use by many in the Christian church, thereby leaving individual Christians and communities little historical or theological foundation for their faith. There was a considerable net loss for Christians and their use of the OT. The notion of fulfilled OT messianic prophecy had been a mainstay of orthodox evangelicalism. From the NT, it

[66]By "Judaism" Schleiermacher meant "the Mosaic institutions," which included the religion of Abraham and the later communities that followed the Babylonian captivity (see Schleiermacher, *The Christian Faith*, §12, pp. 60-62). When I need to distinguish this from modern Judaism, I refer to it as "ancient Judaism."

was clear that the use of biblical prophecy to validate Christianity was already part of Jesus' (and the apostles') understanding of the OT. With Schleiermacher, the notion of fulfilled messianic prophecy was largely overlooked.[67]

Schleiermacher, a pietist by upbringing, compensated for the loss of historical warrant by stressing the importance of individual faith. The grounds for the truth of Christianity did not rest so much on historical arguments, such as the fulfillment of OT messianic prophecy; it rested, rather, on simple faith in Christ.

In spite of these negative features of Schleiermacher's view of the OT, his influence continued to be felt among evangelicals. Evangelical biblical theologians acted as if accepting some of his views here and there would not necessitate abandoning the essentials of their theology. Under the influence of Schleiermacher, evangelicals, in practice if not in theory, edged increasingly closer to the notion that the OT did not belong to the church but was more nearly associated with the religion of ancient Judaism. Such a view was considerably at odds with the classical orthodox view of the OT.

Whatever one's response to the negative aspects of Schleiermacher's views may have been, it was widely acknowledged that his ideas could and did cast a new light on traditional evangelical ways of thinking. For most theologians of his era, Schleiermacher represented a form of Christianity that had to be reckoned with. Many were eager to take advantage of whatever elements of his views they could safely import into their understanding of the Bible, not always aware of what other changes such views might entail down the road.

The positive side of Schleiermacher's view, at least for evangelicals, was the apologetic value he assigned to faith. As a pietist, Schleiermacher taught that personal faith in Jesus Christ was a historical fact of immense certitude. In appealing to personal faith as a historical fact, he believed that he had found a ground of certainty for the truth of the Christian religion. Schleiermacher's appeal struck a positive note with the evangelical revivalism of the early decades of the nineteenth century. On the negative side, Schleiermacher's view failed to provide a historically warranted link between Christianity and the OT. When the dust had settled, it was clear to all that Schleiermacher had dismantled centuries, if not millennia, of his-

[67]"Für ein freudiges Werk kann ich dieses Bestreben, Christum aus den Weissagungen zu beweisen, niemals erklären, und es tut mir leid, dass sich noch immer so viel würdige Männer damit abquälen" (Kraus, *Geschichte der historisch-kritischen Erforschung*, p. 172).

torical and religious ties between the OT and the NT.

Schleiermacher approached the OT solely in terms of what he believed to be its historical religious foundation, ancient Judaism. Since he believed that ancient Judaism was a legalistic religion of law, he also believed that of the OT. Schleiermacher did not appear to have drawn his conclusions about the OT from a study of the OT itself. He had, of course, read the OT and knew its contents, but it was not on that basis that he judged the OT to teach a religion of legalism. He identified the OT as law purely on the basis of its association with ancient Judaism.

From a modern perspective, Schleiermacher's assumptions about ancient Judaism and the OT are far from adequate. In his own day, however, Schleiermacher's view of the OT and ancient Judaism appears to have been widely received. Today, Schleiermacher's description of both ancient Judaism and the OT as legalistic finds little support. This does not mean that no one today holds Schleiermacher's view of the OT, nor does it mean that those who do hold Schleiermacher's views got them directly or indirectly from him. Regardless of where or how one may arrive at the conclusion that the OT teaches legalism, Schleiermacher's views on the matter are crucial for seeing the larger picture of the attitude about the OT both today and during the later stages of classical orthodoxy (early eighteenth century).

Schleiermacher's understanding of the OT as law contrasted sharply with orthodox views of the OT. Throughout the seventeenth and eighteenth centuries, orthodox Christians understood the OT, along with the NT, to be an expression of their Christian beliefs. As the Bible of the ancient church (biblical Israel), they understood the NT to teach that the OT reflected Christian ideas identical to those of the NT. They also understood the NT to teach that Jesus (Jn 8:56), Paul (Rom 4:1-3), and other NT authors (Heb 6:15) believed that Abraham's faith was identical to their gospel (Rom 16:25-27). This view of the OT was bequeathed to evangelical Christian theology by the Reformers and the orthodox theologians of the seventeenth century.

Schleiermacher acknowledged that the Reformers had drawn their understanding of the OT from the NT. He believed that as they approached the question of the meaning of the OT Scriptures, orthodox theologians had simply taken the view of Jesus and the NT authors at face value. Hence, for the orthodox theologians, the OT was an essential part of the NT, the written Word of God. It was, along with the NT, a full and equal part of the

Christian Bible. David Hollaz, a representative evangelical theologian from the later period of Protestant orthodoxy (early eighteenth century),[68] represents one of the last expressions of the orthodox evangelical view of the OT.

> Holy Scripture is the word of God consigned to writing by the immediate inspiration of the Holy Spirit by prophets in the Hebrew language of the Old Testament and by apostles in the Greek language of the New Testament, teaching the sinner that he must have true faith in Christ and having been reconciled to God, that he should live in holiness and obtain eternal life by the beneficence of God.[69]

Orthodox theologians in the eighteenth and nineteenth centuries commonly believed that at the time of Christ, the OT was the Bible of ancient Judaism, which itself was a linear descendant of the religion of the patriarchs such as Abraham, Moses and David. The OT thus teaches the beliefs of biblical Israel (the ancient church), including the views of all believers from the time of the garden of Eden up to the present age. The OT was an authoritative witness to the religion of ancient Judaism, which itself was the Jewish "church" at the time of the composition of the OT. The faith of ancient Judaism (e.g., the faith of Abraham, Moses and David), which found expression in the OT, was identified with the faith of Christ and the NT believers. The OT was just as much the Bible of Jesus, the apostles, and the early church as it was the Bible of the patriarchs,[70] Moses and David. There was no difference between the faith expressed in the OT and the religious beliefs of Jesus and the apostles. It was against such an understanding of the OT that Schleiermacher directed his critique.

Orthodox attitudes toward the OT were decidedly positive. Those attitudes easily found their way into the Christian beliefs of many evangelical

---

[68]"Als Vertreter der orthodoxen Schriftlehre werden hauptsächlich Calov, Quenstedt und Hollaz zitiert, weil Semler seinen Angriff vor allem gegen diese Dogmatiker der Hoch- und Spätorthodoxie gerichtet hat" (Gottfried Hornig, *Die Anfänge der historisch-kritischen Theologie: Johann Salomo Semlers Schriftverständnis und seine Stellung zu Luther* [FSTR 8; Göttingen: Vandenhoeck & Ruprecht, 1961], p. 40).

[69]"Sacra Scriptura est verbum DEI a Prophetis in Veteri Testamento Hebraeo, & in Novo Testamento ab Apostolis Graeco idiomate ex immediata Spiritus Sancti inspiratione literis consignatum, paccatorem instruens, ut veram in CHRISTUM fidem concipiat, DEOqve reconciliatus sancte vivat, ac tandem vitam aeternam beneficio DEI adipiscatur" (David Hollaz, *Examen theologicum*, p. 106).

[70]Orthodox theologians believed that the patriarchs had "the Scriptures" in an unwritten form as "primeval revelation" *(Uroffenbarung)*.

biblical theologians. John Calvin's *Institutes of the Christian Religion* is a classic statement of the orthodox view of the OT. Calvin saw little difference between the religion of the OT and the Christian faith. He believed that, like the NT, the faith of the OT was grounded in the notion of covenant. The single covenant (Lk 1:72) through all ages was ultimately sealed by Christ's blood on the cross. Central to Calvin's view of the OT was his rejection of the notion of multiple covenants. He thus refused to accept the idea that God's covenant with Israel was in any way at variance with his covenant with the church. For Calvin, all the biblical covenants were specific administrations of a single covenant that began with God's pledge to Abraham in Genesis 15. That covenant continued to define the church in both the OT and the NT.[71]

In Calvin's view, the OT was both the Bible of Judaism and an essential part of the Christian Bible. What that meant for Christian theology was that the NT was not "new" in the sense that it was a "new religion." The NT was "new" only in the sense of being a more recent version of the OT covenant. The OT was "old" in the sense that it had been God's Word in Judaism long before the birth of the NT church. Hence, Calvin believed that the NT was a direct descendant of the OT. The OT was the NT before the NT had been written. The OT, combined with the NT, were two parts of one Christian Bible. The OT pointed to the coming of Christ, and the NT proclaimed his arrival.

The orthodox view of Scripture was developed in the sixteenth century within the context of the Reformers' opposition to the medieval church's doctrine of Scripture. The views of the medieval church represented an infallible "tradition" alongside the Bible, just as the NT represented the meaning of the OT. The Reformers rejected that claim.

The Protestant argument stressed the sufficiency of Scripture. They argued that Scripture alone *(sola Scriptura)* was the source of divine revelation. The medieval counterargument pointed to certain aspects of the Protestant view of Scripture that, they claimed, acknowledged the necessity of "tradition." The medieval argument observed that patriarchs such as Noah and Abraham did not have the written Scriptures, yet they appeared to know the faith taught in Scripture. Those who lived before the Scriptures were written,

---

[71]John Calvin *Institutes* 2.10.

they argued, must have had unwritten tradition to guide them. Did not the OT patriarchs worship God and live lives of faith (Gen 15:6) and obedience (Gen 26:5) long before they had written Scriptures? Did this not prove their reliance on tradition? If Abraham's religious faith was dependent on unwritten tradition, how could the Reformers deny its value?

The Protestant reply to the medieval church's appeal to oral tradition had far-reaching consequences for biblical theology. When the medieval theologians accused Protestants of having their own form of tradition, evangelical orthodox theologians insisted that Abraham and the other patriarchs relied not on "unwritten tradition," but on "unwritten Scripture." They contended that before the OT was committed to writing, the "church" at that time, which had existed long before the writing of Scripture, already had "biblical" revelation in its prewritten form. Before and during the days of the patriarchs, the Bible existed in unwritten form and, as such, was a necessary part of the patriarchs' religious faith. The patriarchs were partakers of divine revelation first hand: "[It was a] heavenly doctrine, which had been committed to the patriarchs from the beginning of the world and which had been revealed to Moses."[72]

It was clear to the Reformers from their reading of the biblical narratives that Abraham and his descendants were aware of the biblical revelation. They knew such things, the Reformers argued, because they experienced revelation firsthand. They were part of the biblical events as they happened and thus clearly understood their meaning. They viewed the Bible in this early stage of development as a kind of "living picture" for those who were part of the events recounted in the Bible. They were there as it happened and understood the events as eyewitnesses. The OT church did not preserve a tradition of scriptural interpretation; rather, it possessed an unwritten record of divine revelation. In orthodox evangelical theology this early, unwritten "biblical"

---

[72]Martin Chemnitz, *Examination of the Council of Trent,* trans. Fred Kramer (St. Louis: Concordia, 1971), 1:55. The full quotation: "These testimonies of the Scripture show how, after these sacred books had been written, the church of the children of Israel was a pillar and ground of the truth, because to them had been committed the oracles of God (Rom. 3:2). But this did not give them license either to establish anything arbitrarily or to impose upon the church from unwritten traditions as dogmas for faith things other and different from those which had been written. They were commended to be the guardians of the Scripture, in which God by His divine inspiration had caused to be committed to writing the heavenly doctrine, which had been committed to the patriarchs from the beginning of the world and which had been revealed to Moses."

revelation was considered a kind of "primeval revelation" *(Uroffenbarung)*.[73] It was an essential part of their doctrine of Scripture.

> The word of God is one and the same as that which the prophets and apostles, informed by divine inspiration, preached with living voice *[viva voca]* and which they inscribed with letters and characters on pages and expressed. Diverse ways of propounding and communicating, which is delivered either in writing or orally, does not introduce diversity of the object or the material contained in the written or spoken word. To this extent, the word of God εγγραφον, that is, written, does not differ in reality from the word of God αγραφω, that is, unwritten, whether by instruction or preaching, nor is it that distinction of genus in its species, or a totality in its integral parts, but of a subject with respect to its accidents.[74]

An important outcome of the orthodox view of primeval revelation *(Uroffenbarung)* was the identification of the written words and texts of Scripture with the actual historical events recounted by those words. Using the language of medieval scholasticism, orthodox theologians argued that Scripture as "words" *(verba)* and as "things" *(res)* is identical in terms of its substance but distinct in terms of its specific accidents, that is, as "written" and "unwritten." It was not merely that orthodox evangelical theologians believed the biblical accounts to be historically accurate, as the issue later became. They did, of course, believe in the historical accuracy and reality of the events recorded in Scripture. The issue that concerned them was their belief that the content of Scripture, its ideas and subject matter, was actually known and understood by OT believers within the context of their daily lives. They contended that in these early ages of biblical history God used an unwritten "prophetic history"

---

[73]The term *Uroffenbarung* was not used by the Reformers.

[74]"Unum enim & idem Dei Verbum est, quod Prophetae & Apostoli, per divinam inspirationem edocti, viva voce praedicarunt, & quod per literas & characteres in charta signarunt & expresserunt. Diversitas modi proponendi & communicandi, qui est vel scriptio, vel oralis traditio, non infert diversitatem objecti vel materiae in verbo scripto & tradito contentae. Adeoque Verbum Dei eggrafon seu scriptum, a Verbo Dei agrafw, non scripto seu tradito & praedicato non differt realiter, nec est divisio illa generis in suas species, vel totius in suas partes integrantes, sed subjecti duntaxat in sua accidentia" (Johann Andreas Quenstedt, *Theologia didactico-polemica*, chap. 4, §1 [Wittenberg, 1685], p. 54). Also: "Hinc orta distinctio Verbi in agrafon & eggrafon; quae non est divisio generis in species, ut Pontificii statuunt; quasi aliud esset Verbum non scriptum a scripto: sed est distinctio subjecti in sua accidentia, quia eidem Verbo accidit, ut fuerit non scriptum olim, & nunc sit scriptum: agrafon ergo dicitur, non respectu temporis praesentis, sed praeteriti, quo visum est Deo Ecclesiam sola viva voca & non scripto edocere" (Franciscus Turretin, *Institutio theologiae elencticae* [Geneva, 1688], p. 64).

*(die weissagende Geschichte),*[75] one that was experienced by the biblical characters but not written down *(die weissagende Offenbarung in Wort),* to reveal himself to the earliest patriarchs. That revelation was the same from its beginning in the lives of the biblical characters until its "inscripturalization" on the pages of the OT.[76] This view of revelation, which to some extent Schleiermacher himself shared with orthodoxy, was an early version of what later was known as "revelation in history" or "salvation history."

On the whole, Schleiermacher's understanding of the OT was at odds with the view of classical orthodoxy. In some areas, however, there was unexpected common ground. Although they were not always conscious of it, both Schleiermacher and Hengstenberg held similar views on the notion of primeval revelation *(Uroffenbarung).* They both believed, for example, in a prescriptural revelation in historical acts *(res gesta).*

Schleiermacher's tacit acceptance of the notion of a primeval revelation, along with his insistence on the importance of faith, opened unexpected areas of common ground between him and those who, like Hengstenberg, had experienced the evangelical revivals. Hengstenberg believed that personal conversion in the context of a religious revival was similar to the experience of a biblical prophet. Both involved a genuine and personal divine work. Both also resulted in new ways of viewing the world and knowing God's will. In both conversion and prophecy one was confronted with a "real" (historical) work of God.

Drawing on his own religious experience of conversion as a "real" event, Hengstenberg believed that he had discovered a significant foundation for predictive (messianic) prophecy. He believed that the absolute certainty of

---

[75]Franz Delitzsch, *Die biblisch-prophetische Theologie: Ihre Fortbildung durch Chr. A. Crusius und ihre neueste Entwickelung seit der Christologie Hengstenbergs* (BAS 1; Leipzig: Gebauer, 1845), p. 171.

[76]Vos still represents this early notion of *Uroffenbarung*: "The most important function of Special Revelation . . . consists in the introduction of an altogether new world of truth. . . . As to the form of direct intercourse, this is objectified. Previously there was the most direct spiritual fellowship; the stream of revelation flowed uninterruptedly, and there was no need of storing up the waters in any reservoir wherefrom to draw subsequently. Under the rule of redemption an external embodiment is created to which the divine intercourse with man attaches itself. . . . Where an ever flowing stream of revelation was always accessible, there existed no need of providing for the future remembrance of past intercourse. But a necessity is created for this in the looser, more easily interrupted, only in principle restored, fellowship under the present enjoyment of redemption. Hence the essential content of the new redemptive revelation is given a permanent form, first through tradition, then through its inscripturation in sacred, inspired writings" (*Biblical Theology*, pp. 29-30).

religious conversion could be used as a ground of defense for messianic prophecy. Both conversion and the gift of prophecy were miraculous works of God involving a divine call and a special sort of divine revelation. If conversion was possible and defensible, as Schleiermacher had argued, why not also messianic prophecy?

Armed with the certitude of personal faith and religious conversion (which, ironically, he shared with Schleiermacher), Hengstenberg set out on a lifelong mission of defending the orthodox view of the OT and messianic prophecy against the critiques of Schleiermacher. Schleiermacher and Hengstenberg thus were in substantial agreement on the orthodox notion of *Uroffenbarung*. In the case of Schleiermacher, that agreement was grounded in a special interest in the historical context *(res)* of Scripture *(verba)* and its relationship to the religion of ancient Israel. For Schleiermacher, understanding primeval revelation was the aim of the historical-critical method. Hengstenberg's understanding of primeval revelation was motivated less by historical interests and more by the task of defending the historicity of the biblical narratives.

Given Schleiermacher's notion of primeval revelation—biblical revelation is grounded in concrete historical acts—it is clear why he understood the meaning of the OT *(verba)* to be equivalent to the historical meaning of the religion *(res)* of ancient Judaism. The problem, however, is that in drawing that conclusion, Schleiermacher appears not to have raised or attempted to resolve in his own mind a deeper historical question of the nature of the religion that the OT represented. For whom did the OT speak? Was there only one voice in ancient Judaism? Did the OT speak for all? Schleiermacher's view of the "Mosaic institutions" appears not to have gone beyond what was a common assumption about ancient Judaism in his day: legalism. However, in the minds of two prominent biblical scholars, Julius Wellhausen and Abraham Geiger, Schleiermacher had raised even deeper questions about the OT and the religion it represented.

Was not ancient Judaism a more complex religion than Schleiermacher had supposed? Did not the OT, which claimed to represent ancient Judaism, bear marks of a greater diversity than Schleiermacher was willing to concede? Schleiermacher had opened a door on the question of the nature of the religion of the OT without finding a sufficient answer. He had gone in search not of diversity per se, but of distinctions in religious ideas. His focus was not the distinct nature of the religion, or religions, of the OT, but rather the differences that he believed lay between the OT and the NT.

## Julius Wellhausen and Abraham Geiger

Unlike Schleiermacher, Wellhausen looked for that diversity within the OT itself. That diversity, he believed, lay embedded in layers of early documents and "redactions" that he believed could be separated from the OT and reconstructed back to their original shape. The task he set for himself was to discover the textual remains of that early diversity. There, he believed it possible to uncover and reconstruct the original documents that reflected the ancient faith of the patriarchs and thus come to a better understanding of the nature of their faith and of the faiths that followed them. Wellhausen was on a quest for the Ur-document (original document) that lay behind the Ur-faith (original faith) of both the OT and the NT. For Wellhausen, the link between the OT and NT had been laid down long before the earliest written documents of the Pentateuch were penned. Wellhausen believed that the real story of the Pentateuch, and of the OT as a whole, was the shift in Israel's religion from the earliest days to the era of the postexilic priesthood. To find the original voice of the OT and relate it to the NT, Wellhausen believed, one must move backwards through the OT, past the priestly laws and prophetic preaching, to the earliest stages of the patriarchal narratives and thence to the patriarchal religion itself. Wellhausen's program called for a quest for the original, pristine faith of the earliest documents, which he believed he could recover in the various documents that lay embedded in the present "Pentateuch."

Geiger, on the other hand, believed the historical realities *(res)* of the religion of ancient Judaism were not to be found, as Wellhausen had supposed, deep within the documentary history of the OT and its earliest layers of texts, but rather lying along the literary surface of its final canonical shape. To Geiger, the OT was a monolithic whole that contained only surface traces of its compositional, and canonical, history. One could, like Wellhausen, cut a deep trench into the Pentateuch and attempt to retrace the layers of written texts, peeling them off like wallpaper, or one could, like Geiger, conduct a surface survey of artifacts and written remains of the ancient occupants of the text.

Both Wellhausen and Geiger had set out to pursue their objectives within the context of Schleiermacher's understanding of the OT. The OT was a necessary pathway to understanding the history of Israel's religion, while at the same time the history of Israel's religion was a necessary pathway to understanding the OT.[77] Israel's history could be uncovered both in the layers of early documents that Wellhausen believed he had discovered within the OT and, as Geiger believed, amid the surface debris laying atop the final canonical shape.

Geiger believed that at the time the OT was receiving its final, canonical shape, there were numerous schisms within ancient Judaism. Each of these alternative views likely had its own community and way of handling the OT Scriptures. One would also expect that each point of disagreement left its mark on the OT along with much surface debris reflecting "the internal development of ancient Judaism" *(innern Entwicklung des Judentums)*.[78] Geiger believed that much of the debris could still be found in the textual and post-compositional history of the OT text and its ancient versions. References to the conflicting views of priests and prophets within[79] the OT suggested to him the likelihood that the religious ideas of such groups ultimately found their way into the present biblical text.[80]

One thing Geiger was certain of: there was much diversity within ancient Judaism, and in one form or another the OT had absorbed a good deal of it. After Schleiermacher, the question came to be how one should proceed in locating and describing the various viewpoints in the textual debris. Should one, like Wellhausen, dig a trench through the Pentateuch and prophetic books to chart its documentary stratigraphy, or, like Geiger, should one survey the surface of the final shape *(Endgestalt)* of the Pentateuch? In the first case (Wellhausen), one looked for literary strata; in the second (Geiger), one looked for literary strategy and artifactual debris. Who were the first to occupy the pentateuchal territory? What remains did they leave behind? Where did they go? Who did they become?

Wellhausen and Geiger were prepared to carry out Schleiermacher's vision of the OT, but not in a way anticipated by him. Schleiermacher stopped short of either Wellhausen or Geiger in attempting to follow the implications of his

[77]Geiger gives expression to this proposal: "Die Untersuchung über die innere Entwickelung des Judenthums wird uns der sicherste Wegweiser sein, und sie wird ebensowohl zur Aufhellung der Geschichte des Bibeltextes und der Uebersetzungen beitragen, wie sie selbst von der Betrachtung dieser Geschichte Licht empfangen wird" (*Urschrift und Übersetzungen der Bibel*, p. 19).

[78]Ibid.

[79]For example, Jeremiah 8:8.

[80]For example, Jeremiah 33 (cf. Jer 23), where the Davidic kingship is assumed by the priesthood.

views. He understood the OT as little more than a relic of a religious past. To Geiger, the OT was also a relic, but it was a relic of inestimable value. As a living relic, the OT had preserved the religious heritage of a part of Judaism not widely known or understood. In the care it took to preserve the HB, that community became a spokesperson for its early form of Judaism. We use the term *pre-Judaism*. Judging from the nature and extent of the textual depris on the surface of the HB, it represented those who saw themselves closely linked to Judaism but considerably removed from its ancient form.

For Schleiermacher, the relevance of the OT to the church stopped short of the status it was given as Scripture in evangelical orthodoxy. Regardless of whether and to what extent his views were influential on later scholars such as Wellhausen and Geiger, Schleiermacher had made an indirect but lasting contribution to evangelical biblical theology and its view of the OT. For better or worse, Schleiermacher had done so by tacitly identifying the OT with the religious faith of ancient Israel. Having identified the OT solely in terms of ancient Judaism, Schleiermacher left Christians in his day with very little to interest them in the OT. For everyone except Schleiermacher's radical evangelical opponents (Hengstenberg), the Scriptures *(verba)* had become a convenient means for recovering the religion *(res)* of ancient Judaism. In search of Israel's earliest religious heritage, critical biblical scholarship followed Wellhausen in peeling the onion skins of the OT documents back to their original sources. Their efforts, it is safe to say, produced predictable and largely negative results.

For whatever reasons, Geiger's program in his own day failed to attract the attention or capture the imagination of biblical scholars. His proposal has remained largely unnoticed. There are, however, signs of more recent appreciation of Geiger's view. The discovery of ancient biblical texts in the caves of the Dead Sea and their importance for understanding the early versions of the OT (e.g., the LXX) have drawn recent attention to Geiger, as also has the renewed attention given to the final stages *(Endgestalt)* of biblical texts. Michael Fishbane stresses the importance of Geiger for contemporary biblical studies: "Geiger not only demonstrated that the major textual versions (the LXX, Targumic, and Samaritan recensions) reflect reworkings of the Hebrew Bible in the light of post-biblical social and theological concerns, but that the Hebrew Bible is itself the product (and source) of such reworkings."[81]

---

[81]Michael Fishbane, *Biblical Interpretation in Ancient Israel* (Oxford: Clarendon Press, 1985), p. 5.

Apart from Wellhausen and Geiger, Schleiermacher's viewpoint made major inroads into evangelical biblical theology. Franz Delitzsch saw traces of Schleiermacher in most all of the major evangelical biblical theologians, such as von Hofmann, Rothe, Bengel and even Hengstenberg, especially in their understanding of the orthodox concept of "primeval revelation" *(Uroffenbarung)*.[82]

By following Schleiermacher and his latent acceptance of primeval revelation and by thus identifying OT revelation with OT history, Johann von Hofmann, an evangelical to be sure, was able to move easily between his evangelical assessment of the OT as Scripture *(verba)* and his appreciation of the historical realities of the religion of ancient Judaism *(res)*. With Schleiermacher, the meaning of the OT Scriptures, even among evangelical theologians, became firmly fixed to the historical reconstruction of the religion of Judaism.

In time, the attempt to work out the implications of Schleiermacher's identification of the OT with the religion of ancient Judaism brought to light hidden stress points in his argument. One such tension point was Schleiermacher's insistence on identifying the meaning of the OT with the priestly religion of the Second Temple period. That identification led him and others to equate the OT narrowly with only a limited number of religious parties within ancient Judaism. Schleiermacher, for example, like most in his day, for the most part had overlooked the role of the prophets in the production of the OT and thus failed to pursue further links between a "prophetic OT" and the NT. For Christians, this appeared to give Schleiermacher's viewpoint a decidedly negative slant. Although some identification of the OT with postexilic Judaism is beyond doubt, one is not free merely to choose which religious group of the various parties within ancient Judaism was most compatible with the OT Scriptures. There are ways of understanding texts and their contexts, and these can help, not so much in discovering the identity of a particular biblical author as in providing a social and religious profile of the authors of some biblical books.[83]

Schleiermacher was aware that Jesus, Paul and the writers of the NT held views of the OT very near those of Protestant orthodoxy, but he also believed that the time had come for a major rethinking of the orthodox view and NT view. Such a rethinking, Schleiermacher believed, would lead to a new his-

---

[82]Delitzsch, *Die biblisch-prophetische Theologie*, p. 171.

[83]William M. Schniedewind, *How the Bible Became a Book: The Textualization of Ancient Israel* (Cambridge: Cambridge University Press, 2004).

torical appreciation of the OT within the context of ancient Judaism. But that did not happen. In the end, Schleiermacher was unable to part with the old orthodox identification of the faith of Judaism (for him a historical question) with the religion of the OT (a theological question of revelation). The identification of the OT with a series of events and institutions had resulted for Schleiermacher in considerable confusion about the nature and reference of biblical narrative. It also, ultimately, hid from view the alternative likelihood that the OT was not so much the product of the Mosaic institutions of ancient Judaism as it was a by-product of the religion that arose out of the words and activities of Israel's early prophets. Had Schleiermacher given more attention to other voices in the OT, he might have positioned himself closer to the prophetic writings and with that also the NT Scriptures.

In 1857 Abraham Geiger published a five-hundred-page monograph to which he gave the unassuming title *The Original Text and Translations of the Bible and Their Dependence on the Inner Development of Judaism (Urschrift und Übersetzungen der Bibel in ihrer Abhängigkeit von der innern Entwickelung des Judentums).*[84] In this work, as he acknowledged in his preface, Geiger mapped out a view of the HB that was destined to open new avenues of study of the meaning of both the HB and the history of Judaism.

In developing his argument, Geiger begins with the observation that the Hebrew MT (A.D. 900) is significantly different in many details from the ancient translations of the HB of an earlier period (e.g., the LXX). How is it, he asks, that such a careful scribal tradition could have resulted in so many important differences? This could not have been a random process, because the differences that Geiger notes followed divergent lines of interpretation and reflected not merely variant text types, but variant points of view as well. Geiger argues that between 100 B.C. and A.D. 900 something had happened within Judaism that set off a series of intense discussions about the meaning and final shape of the HB. These discussions ultimately ended in major differences in points of view about the Bible. It is likely, Geiger contends, that such discussions centered on religious issues in Palestine in the first century. By the second century A.D., as is reflected in some early translations and manuscripts at Qumran, the dust had begun to settle and the lines had been drawn. Those lines had

---

[84]Compare Delitzsch: "den Entwickelungsgang der Heilsoffenbarung . . . als ein lebendig organisches, als ein nach göttlichem Plane mit dem Verlauf der Geschichte Israels innigst" (*Die biblisch-prophetische Theologie*, p. 166).

cut a deep path through almost every section of the HB. By the first century B.C., the HB had become the rallying point for the identity of various parties within ancient Judaism. Geiger believed that given the proper methodology, one could examine the textual surface of the HB and discover the traces left behind by centuries of debates and theological skirmishes. Geiger's aim was to develop an approach to the HB sensitive enough to identify and, if possible, retrace the course of those debates and skirmishes. That, in turn, could be used to cast new light on religious developments that centered on the HB.

Geiger's approach had demonstrated that the interpretation of the HB had not reached its full development until the middle of the second century A.D., the time when major talmudic authorities were already exerting their influence on Judaism.[85] It was also the beginnings of the activities of the Masoretes. During that same time, elements of early discussions were making their way into the three major revisions of the Greek Bible (the LXX)—Aquila, Symmachus, Theodotion—along with the Syriac translation. In these early versions one can see, among other things, the remains of the LXX's adjustment to the developing Hebrew (Masoretic) text,[86] showing that the traditional (Masoretic) HB had already begun to part company with the Hebrew *Vorlage*[87] of the LXX.

This concentrated activity surrounding the developing HB was accompanied by similar changes in biblical interpretation. Judging by the compositional nature of the meaning reflected in the early stages of the HB, it appears that biblical interpretation had largely focused on textual meaning at a "holistic" level. There is mounting evidence that the earliest approaches to the individual biblical books and sections of the OT canon were already conscious of the meaning of the whole Bible and how that played into larger OT themes. The aim of biblical interpretation was to arrive at the sense of the whole of Scripture and how its parts were to fit into that whole. This is also noticeable in the interbiblical readings of the Pentateuch by the prophets and the framers of the OT canon.[88]

Unexpectedly, in approaches to biblical interpretation beginning in the first century, one can begin to see signs of a shift of focus on isolated individual words and minor details of words and texts. At a later period, this growing

---

[85]Geiger, *Urschrift und Übersetzungen der Bibel*, p. 2.

[86]Something important that Geiger does not point to is that it is also at this time that the Christian apologists, such as Justin Martyr were engaging leading Jewish scholars (Trypho [ca. 135]) in debates over the messianic meaning of the HB.

[87]The term *Vorlage* refers to the Hebrew text of the translators of the LXX.

[88]Sailhamer, *Introduction to Old Testament Theology*, pp. 239-52.

"atomistic" approach to interpretation came to characterize almost the whole of rabbinical and Christian interpretation of the HB. What this came to mean for biblical interpretation was a lessening of focus on the reading of the whole of Scripture and the author's intention in favor of a corresponding relocation of that meaning to seemingly insignificant details—details largely outside the control of the authors of these texts. A focus on individual textual details meant that biblical meaning could be shifted and adjusted with minimal textual "mutations."[89] The hermeneutical center of gravity was beginning to shift from the "the mind of the author" to that of the biblical interpreter.

By the sixth and seventh centuries, the vowel signs were added to the Hebrew consonantal text. This was a move that reflected and further aided the interpretive shift to the smallest textual minutiae. By the ninth century, the process had come to a rapid conclusion in the large Masoretic manuscripts, codices and treatises, in which every letter, vowel and accent was registered and assigned a permanent meaning, often in conformity not so much to the text as such as to secondary literature such as the Jerusalem[90] and Babylonian Talmuds. The final stage of the HB, represented in the MT, marked the beginning of the peshat[91] commentaries of Saadia and Rashi. These commentaries made no effort to change or alter the text as it had been permanently established. They focused, rather, on explaining the sense of the minutiae of the existing Masoretic manuscripts. After the formation and stabilization of the MT, only occasional questions were raised about the condition and originality of the MT.[92] It was accepted as the *textus receptus* (received text). The MT still holds the

---

[89]The word *mutations* is helpful here because it suggests that these changes were not conscious distortions of the text. They were part of a larger process of consolidation and accommodation of the text to the accepted understanding of the communities that preserved the various versions of biblical texts.

[90]Geiger, *Urschrift und Übersetzungen der Bibel*, p. 4.

[91]See Sailhamer, *Introduction to Old Testament Theology*, pp. 133-42.

[92]Elias Levita (1469–1549), for example, demonstrated that the vowels and accents were added to the HB after the talmudic period (second–fourth centuries A.D.). Although Levita's thesis created a firestorm within Protestant Christian scholarship, it seemed to have little effect on Judaism and Catholicism; both groups had long laid their principal stress on tradition. In this same century, another Jewish scholar, Azariah de Rossi, raised the question of the difference between the MT and the early versions in his publication of a scholarly work, *Imre binah* (Mantua, 1574). De Rossi's views were also ignored within Judaism. Three hundred years later, Zacharias Frankel (1801–1875) reintroduced the question of the differences between the MT, the LXX, the Targum and the Vulgate. S. D. Luzzatto (1847) explained the differences between the MT and LXX as the attempts of the scribes to adjust the Bible to the needs of the average layperson, whom they did not want to be led astray into misunderstanding (Geiger, *Urschrift und Übersetzungen der Bibel*, pp. 18-19). These changes could be at the level of the vowels and accents, as well as consonants,

honor of being the received text among Jews and most Christians.

Geiger's point in rehearsing this brief survey of the development of the HB was to show that too little attention had been given to the sometimes minor differences between the MT and the earlier versions (the LXX). Such variants, when seen within the larger context of early biblical interpretation, often served as biblical support for major theological issues. A rabbinical maxim states, "The whole universe can be suspended on a single letter." Textual minutiae in the HB cannot be dismissed as irrelevant to larger theological issues. Although it probably was not the intention of the historical authors of the HB to hang their thoughts on textual minutiae, such was the eventual outcome that atomistic biblical interpretation had on the HB. Understanding the "original meaning" of the biblical text often means removing the textual debris that has accumulated from centuries of theological debate. The text itself is thus a living witness to the discussions that have centered on the HB over the centuries.

For Geiger, there was an area of unfinished business in the intellectual and religious history of Judaism. It was the study of the causes that lay behind the shifts in biblical interpretation as reflected in the differences between the MT and the earliest versions (the LXX). The task as Geiger saw it was ultimately to recover the HB laying beneath the debris of tradition and textual commentary, much of which had become part of the permanent surface texture of the MT. Geiger says,

> We must search out and find and coherently restore (from its gradual change of shape) the original Hebrew text, which the later tradition has preserved from the earliest period but which partly has been combined with it and has conformed it to the concerns of later times, and so allow the witness to the original sense of the text to live again from the earliest period in order, through listening and testing it. Only then can a firm foundation be established under our feet and dark areas given a new light; we will then for the first time recognize and grasp the great inner-religious struggle that has shaped present-day Judaism.[93]

words and phrases.

93"Wir werden die Trümmer, welche die spätere Tradition aus der altern Zeit aufbewahrt, aber theilweise mit ihren Producten vermischt, theilweise ihnen die Färbung ihrer Zeit gegeben hat, aufsuchen, aussondern und einheitlich wie in ihrer allmäligen Umgestaltung zusammenfügen müssen, so die Zeugnisse aus der Vorzeit wieder beleben, um durch Anhörung und Prüfung derselben uns den Thatbestand vergegenwärtigen zu können. Erst dann wird ein sicherer Boden gewonnen werden, dunkle Gebiete eine neue Beleuchtung erhalten; wir werden dann erst den innern grossartigen Kampf des Judenthums erkennen und begreifen, wie es seine gegenwärtige Gestalt erlangt hat" (Geiger, *Urschrift und Übersetzungen der Bibel*, p. 19).

*Chapter 4*

# Finding the Big Idea in the Final Composition of the Text

I HAVE ARGUED THAT WHEN SPEAKING of the meaning of the "words" *(verba)* of the Pentateuch, we should be careful to distinguish between the author's meaning and the "things" to which his words point, which as such have a meaning of their own. The Pentateuch is about real events, and its words point (literally or figuratively) to things in real life. One must keep in mind that the author's words are not the things themselves. The words only point to those things. You cannot smoke the word *pipe.* The thing to which that word points, however, you can smoke.

To illustrate a similar point, the Belgium artist René Magritte painted a realistic picture of a pipe. A caption on the painting reads, "This is not a pipe." Magritte's point, of course, was that the pipe was a painting of a pipe and not the pipe itself.

When the Bible describes "things" in the outside world, like pipes, it does so with words. The biblical authors did not draw pictures. They "wrote" pictures using words, much like an artist uses paint and brush strokes. Each word is an author's brush stroke. The Pentateuch is thus much like a verbal painting of historical events. Its words point to real events, and they tell us about those events. To experience the events, all we need to do is read the Bible. It is the next thing to being there. It is the closest we have to being there. To experience the biblical events as the author intended, one must keep a close eye on the author's words. We would miss his point if we tried to find out about those events apart from his words.

Since the biblical narratives are like an artist's painting, in order to understand a painting, we must look at what the artist has painted on the canvas. We would not attempt to understand a Rembrandt painting by taking a photograph of his model and using it to fill in places in the painting that are not clear or are cast in the shadows. That may help us see or understand the people and places Rembrandt painted, that is, his subject matter, but it would not help us understand the painting itself. To understand a Rembrandt painting, one must look at it and see its colors, shapes and textures. One must understand what he meant to do with each brushstroke. In the same way, to understand the Pentateuch, one must look at it and the words of its author.

Not all biblical texts are historical narratives. There are many poems in the Pentateuch, as well as large collections of laws and genealogies. In the many poetic texts in the Pentateuch, one must seek to understand the poetic images to which the author's words point. What, for example, is the author's meaning of the poetic line that calls Judah "a young lion" (Gen 49:9)? What does the word "scepter" express as a picture in the same poem (Gen 49:10)? In poetry, the meaning of the words the author uses may have a figurative, or nonliteral, sense. Ultimately, our task in interpreting the various books of the OT is to discover the meaning of the author's words, that is, the "verbal meaning" of the author.

## Finding the Author's Intent (Verbal Meaning)

How does one go about finding the meaning of the words and the text that they embody? One must start, of course, by reading the text. But we must go further than that. We must approach the meaning of a text such as the Pentateuch in terms of its "big idea." The text was written with the author's intention in mind. The author is going somewhere with his text. One must learn to track with the author and watch carefully where he takes us with his words.

Behind texts and their words stand authors. Authors have a purpose in writing books. The Pentateuch is no exception. Its author is getting at something. As he writes his book, he has its purpose in mind. One should expect that his purpose affects our understanding of every detail in the book. Every part of the book has its place within the context of the author's big idea. Every piece of the jigsaw puzzle makes its unique contribution to the sense of the whole puzzle. An individual piece may or may not have a meaning of its own.

Although one may look at each piece under a microscope and see all its details, it is only when the piece finds its place within the puzzle as a whole that its meaning can be appreciated. The meaning of the whole puzzle helps one see the importance of the shape and meaning of the parts.

In the same way, the Pentateuch has a big idea. A big idea is like the picture on the cover of a jigsaw puzzle box. Ultimately, everything in the Pentateuch is meaningful, insofar as it is part of its central meaning. That is how whole texts such as the Pentateuch work. They are not randomly collected bits and pieces of data or information. Nor is the Pentateuch an anthology of individual, self-contained texts. The Pentateuch is a meaningful (whole) text made up of words and bits and pieces of smaller texts. The meaning of the Pentateuch as a whole effects our understanding of the meaning of its parts. The big picture tells us how we should understand the smaller parts. It shows us how the parts fit together. The Pentateuch, like a jigsaw puzzle, has many parts, and each one has its place.

This does not mean that the individual parts of the Pentateuch have no meaning apart from the whole. Clearly, they do. But whatever one says about the meaning of the details and parts of the Pentateuch should be brought into line with the author's intent, or the big picture of the whole. In this way, the meaning of the whole of the Pentateuch is governed by the author's intent. The author's intent acts as a kind of control on the meaning we assign to the pieces.

How, then, do we find the big idea of a large text such as the Pentateuch? How do we formulate a big idea to help us make sense of the Pentateuch? The answer is surprisingly simple. We find the big idea by reading and rereading the text in its parts and as a whole. As we read the text, we begin to formulate a sense of what the text is about (subject matter), and where the author is going with it (compositional strategy). Most of the time, we do this unconsciously, but as we reread the text, we should also do this consciously and intentionally. We should look for where the author is taking us in the Pentateuch. What kinds of topics and events are important to him? What is he writing about? What is he saying? Those questions help us get a sense of what the Pentateuch is about.

Once we get a clearer sense of what the Pentateuch is about, we can test our idea against our rereading of the Pentateuch. Rereading is an important step in the interpretation process. Our rereading of the Pentateuch acts as a check on our understanding of its big idea. We learn more about the Pentateuch as we reread it, and we can check our understanding of it by further rereading. This procedure is already anticipated in two of the major compositional seams of the OT, Joshua 1:8 and Psalm 1:2: the wise and understanding are those who "read" the Scriptures day and night.

Here we ask whether our understanding of the Pentateuch's big idea fits with what is actually in the text. And, does it fit well? Am I forcing my big idea on the Pentateuch? Does my concept of its big idea help me understand more as I read, or does my concept of its big idea sometimes get in the way of understanding what is actually in the text? Does my big idea need additional adjustments? Continual rereading may also suggest that one's idea of the meaning of the Pentateuch is basically wrong and in need of being replaced. We may also find that parts of the big idea do fit, but other parts do not.

Obviously, such a process requires a great deal of time in reading the Pentateuch. Commentaries and books about the Pentateuch may be helpful, but ultimately, it is reading and rereading that tell us what the Pentateuch is about and what it intends to say.

Finding the big idea of the Pentateuch also requires humility. If our understanding of the Pentateuch does not appear to fit our reading of it, we must be willing to admit that and attempt to reformulate our big idea. Here, also, is where the help of commentaries and other studies on the theology of the Pentateuch can be useful. One can learn much from others in understanding the Scriptures. The Pentateuch has been read and interpreted for at least three millennia. It has a rich history of interpretation and commentary. We would be remiss not to tap into this "effective history" *(Wirkungsgeschichte),* if only for a broader view of the Pentateuch outside our limited horizons.

The fact that we must read the Pentateuch within a limited horizon raises important questions. How do we know if our big idea is a good fit for the text? How do we get outside our own reading of the Pentateuch and view ourselves critically? How do we evaluate our understanding of the Pentateuch's big idea?

Here is the principle I will follow: the best (most valid) big idea is the one that explains the most and the most important parts of the Pentateuch.

Obviously, our big idea of what the Pentateuch is about will help us understand the Pentateuch. Our big idea should also help us see the most important elements of the Pentateuch. When we read the Pentateuch with the help of a big idea, we soon learn whether or not our big idea is of any help. Elements of the text that resonate with the big idea begin to stand out. We see things we had not noticed before. Themes and key terms become apparent where previously they had lay undetected. When that happens, it is a sign that our big idea is on track with that of the author.

Suppose that our big idea for the Pentateuch is that it teaches "legalism," that is, the necessary obedience to the Mosaic law. The author wanted to show the blessings that come from a strict obedience the Mosaic law. Such a big idea appears helpful. Even an initial perusal of the Pentateuch reveals its interest and focus on the Mosaic law. With the help of that big idea, one is helped to see that throughout the Pentateuch stress is put on the importance of obedience to the Mosaic law. It goes without question that in sheer number of examples, most of what is in the Pentateuch is hundreds of laws given by Moses at Mount Sinai.

But, as weighty a factor as sheer volume might be in assessing an author's intent, there is the additional need to examine the importance of this material within the Pentateuch as a whole. This raises the question of what is most important in the Pentateuch? Does the big idea "obedience to the Mosaic law" help us see what is most important? The answer, of course, lies in what one means by "most important." To answer that question, we must ask another: "To whom is this big idea important?" Are we seeking to know what is most important to ourselves? To our families? To members of our church? To Jesus and the NT writers? To ancient Israel? There are many ways that the question of what is most important can be framed.

As a guide to answering that question, we must recall the initial discussion of the author's intent. The goal of our interpretation of the Pentateuch, I suggested, is the author's intent. That starting point should prove helpful in identifying what is most important in the Pentateuch. If we are seeking the author's intent, it follows that what is most important in the Pentateuch should be related to the author's intent. We should ask, "What is most important to the author?" Our big idea not only should help us understand (quantitatively) most of what is in the Pentateuch, but also it should help us discover (qualitatively) what is most important to the author.

How do we determine what is most important to the author? Here I can give only a preliminary answer to that question. As it will be worked out in the remainder of this book, I will focus on those parts of the Pentateuch that most clearly reflect the work of the author in making the Pentateuch. It was the author who gave us the Pentateuch, and it was the author who gave the Pentateuch its present shape. He put it together. He "made" it, and he "made" it as it is. So we should ask these questions: How has the author gone about his task? How has he put the Pentateuch together? What shape has he given it? Where does it begin? Where does it end? How do its pieces fit together? What verbal clues does the author use to emphasize or signal to readers the path of meaning to be followed through the Pentateuch? Are there key terms to which he repeatedly returns? Is there an overall outline or structure to the book? Does its plot unfold predictably? What kind of compositional strategy guides the work along? Our understanding of the author's work lies in the answers we give to these questions.

In this book on the theology of the Pentateuch, I spend considerable time investigating these kinds of questions. They are the primary means of discovering the author's intent. It is not enough to have an idea of what we think the Pentateuch is about. We must support that notion with hard exegetical evidence that points to the author's intent. We must keep our eye on the author and follow him throughout his work.

In beginning the Pentateuch, the author writes for more than sixty chapters before making any mention of or reference to the Mosaic law.[1] Interest in the Mosaic law begins in Exodus 12. That should strike us as unusual if Schleiermacher is correct that the intent of the Pentateuch is to stress the necessity of obedience to the law (legalism). If we suppose the big idea of the Pentateuch to be "the importance of obedience to the Mosaic law," why the seeming neglect of the law at the beginning of the book? How can the Mosaic law be most important to the author if he rarely mentions it in these opening sections of the book? We might also note in passing, and return to it later, that in the first sixty chapters the author devotes considerable attention to the notions of "faith" and "righteousness" (e.g., Gen 6:8-9; 15:6).

The law receives so little mention at the beginning of the Pentateuch that some have suggested that the Pentateuch actually begins in Exodus 12:1, the account of the giving of the first law, the Passover.[2] This would, of course, as-

[1]There are occasional exceptions to this observation, such as Genesis 26:5, "Abraham obeyed me and kept my service, my commandments, my statutes, and my laws," but these serve to show how rare such statements are in the first part of the Pentateuch.

[2]Rashi: "Rabbi Isaac said: The Torah, which is the Law book of Israel, should have commenced with the verse (Exod. XII.1) 'This month shall be unto you the first of the months,' which is the

sure that the Pentateuch conforms to the big idea of the Mosaic law, but it would do so at the expense of failing to explain the Pentateuch that we have before us, which begins with creation, not the giving of the law. A better way to approach the Pentateuch's early focus on topics other than law is to adjust our understanding of the Pentateuch's big idea to include something other than the Mosaic law. Perhaps there is a way to adjust our big idea so that it helps us see the Mosaic law as a part, but not the whole, of what is most important in the Pentateuch. Perhaps our big idea will have to be more complex. This reshaping of our big idea helps us to consider the possibility that the author's delay in discussing the law may have a larger strategic purpose in mind. There may be a reason why the author of the Pentateuch does not immediately bring the Mosaic law into view, but does so only gradually.[3] The fact that the law comes later may be a part of the author's strategy. How different the Pentateuch would be if it began with the statement "In the beginning God gave Moses the law" rather than "In the beginning God created the heavens and the earth." As it is, creation precedes law, or the law comes only after creation and not as a part of it. Given that in the Pentateuch creation is presented as an act of divine grace, it is of no little consequence that grace precedes law in the overall structure of the Pentateuch. Each of these broad themes (law and grace) appears to be an important aspect of the big idea of the Pentateuch. It is only by sifting through the various possibilities that we can arrive at an understanding of the book as a whole. Once we come to the point of formulating a big idea, we must be prepared to follow it through the Pentateuch and allow it to interpret the details of the book on its own. Only then can we expect to arrive at a consistent and warranted interpretation of the theology of the Pentateuch.

Our interest to this point has been the notion of reading the text in light of what we propose to be its big idea. I will return to this topic when I am ready to develop my own understanding of the Pentateuch's big idea. Here I will conclude the discussion with a brief summary of where I think the big idea of the Pentateuch will take us.

Although many have insisted that the big idea of the Pentateuch is focused on the centrality of obedience to the Mosaic law, my reading of the Penta-

---

first commandment gien to Israel" (*Pentateuch with Rashi's Commentary: Genesis*, trans. M. Rosenbaum and A. M. Silbermann [London: Shapiro, Vallentine, 1929], p. 2).

[3]Note how elements of the Mosaic law are worked into the early chapters of the Pentateuch (e.g., Gen 1:14-31; 7:8).

teuch will take us along a broader path. We will begin that journey in a preliminary way with the suggestion that the "big idea" of the Pentateuch is about both "obedience to the Mosaic law," and "living by faith." Admittedly, my reading of the Pentateuch within the context of "faith" will not initially point us to most of what is in the book. Most of what is in the Pentateuch consists of law or discussions of law. From Exodus 12 on, it is almost entirely about the laws given Israel at Sinai.

We will find that the big idea of "faith" helps us to see what is most important to the author. As we locate and isolate and ultimately describe the work of the author, it becomes increasingly clear that his interest is to develop an understanding of "faith and trusting God." The law, as such, takes on secondary importance, even though the author devotes considerable time and attention to it.

Throughout this book I attempt to feel a way along a path laid out by the author of the Pentateuch as I attempt to formulate an understanding of its big idea. I will have to formulate for a big idea that includes both the notion of obedience to the Mosaic law and the concept of living by faith. Ultimately, I believe, these two themes of law and faith will find their place alongside each other as a juxtaposition of law and gospel. The gospel, that is, justification by faith, is God's means for our fulfilling the law.[4] This statement immediately strikes us as "Pauline," but not in the sense of reading Paul's theology into the Pentateuch. The theology of the Pentateuch is "Pauline" in the sense that we must read the Pentateuch's theology into Paul. Paul's line of thought about the law and faith is drawn from the theology of the Pentateuch, not the other way around. To be sure, an exegetical validation of the Pauline concept "faith" in the Pentateuch remains to be seen. At this point, my concern is to introduce the concept of a big idea and the way one must shape an understanding of it in the Pentateuch. However one may eventually formulate an understanding of the Pentateuch, its warrant or validity must be sought exegetically in the statement of its big idea.

## WARRANT (VERBAL MEANING LINKED TO THE BIBLICAL TEXT)

The importance of formulating an understanding of the central message of the Pentateuch obliges us to think about the proper warrants for doing so.

---

[4]As in Romans 8:4: "so that the requirement of the Law might be fulfilled in us, who do not walk according to the flesh but according to the Spirit" (NASB).

Although this is not the place to give a detailed explication of the various means for validating our understanding of the Pentateuch's big idea, we must explain some of the general principles followed in this book.

Shimon Bar-Efrat suggests four textually based levels from which our understanding of the meaning of biblical narratives can be assessed and validated: verbal, narrative technique, narrative world, thematic. Each level of structure in biblical narrative provides a perspective for viewing the author's shaping of the biblical material. This will give us what Wolfgang Richter has called a "text immanent"[5] warrant for the meaning we assign to the biblical text. Richter has in mind grounding the textual meaning in the text itself as it has been constructed "from the ground up." It is an attempt to understand the text in terms of its own range of meaning without importing ideas and meanings from outside sources. The various levels of structure in narrative must be anchored to each other and to the text as a whole. Tracing the author's work at each level is essential for finding the proper warrant for an interpretation of narrative.

***Verbal level.*** The starting point in approaching the meaning of biblical narrative is located in the words themselves. This is what Bar-Efrat designates as the verbal level. At this level, meaning is a function of the grammar and syntax of the original language of the text (Hebrew) or a translation (e.g., English). Whatever is said about the narrative and its structure must ultimately find its support in the words of the author and the ways they are grammatically construed. There is no substitute for a thorough reading of the Pentateuch at its verbal level. Its meaning cannot be detached from its words and the syntactical patterns that govern them.

***Narrative technique.*** The study of the narrative technique of a biblical text concentrates on the technical means that the author uses to replicate events in the real world. Narrative technique includes features such as how the author begins and ends a narrative, as well as how the author connects the narratives into a single whole. Here one may think of Otto Eissfeldt's concept of "back-reference" and "fore-reference"[6] as a primary means of linking smaller texts into a literary unity. We will see much of this in the Pentateuch. Also, there

[5]See Wolfgang Richter, *Exegese als Literaturwissenschaft: Entwurf einer alttestamentlichen Literaturtheorie und Methodologie* (Göttingen: Vandenhoeck & Ruprecht, 1971), pp. 179-87.

[6]Otto Eissfeldt, "Die kleinste literarische Einheit in den Erzählungsbüchern des Alten Testaments," in *Kleine Schriften*, ed. Rudolf Sellheim and Fritz Maass (Tübingen: Mohr Siebeck, 1962), 1:144-45.

are important questions to be asked in regard to biblical narratives: Who is allowed to speak for the author within the narrative? Where is the voice of the narrator located? How are elements such as time, directionality and movement handled? Narrative technique must be closely tied to the verbal level of the text.

At the level of the language of biblical Hebrew, these questions translate into the author's use of specific verbal forms such as *wayyiqtol* and *qatal* to mark sequence and background in the text.[7] This will become a central part of the argument for the meaning of the Sinai narrative (Ex 19–24) and its role within the compositional strategy of the Pentateuch. Of curse, the discovery of these narrative features requires a certain level of expertise in biblical Hebrew.

Biblical Hebrew is an ancient language that must be studied without the aid of living informants. Nevertheless, the contribution of narrative technique to the meaning of the biblical narratives has been increasingly acknowledged and should be an essential part of any attempt to find theological meaning in the shape of the Pentateuch.

***Narrative world.*** The nature of the narrative world depicted in the Pentateuch is a function of the author's use of narrative technique. By casting the narratives in the form of a true story, the author assumes the role of what Hans Frei,[8] Erich Auerbach[9] and, in particular, Nelson Goodman[10] understand as "ways of worldmaking." The Pentateuch, and the Bible as a whole, presents its readers not merely with a narrated segment of their own world, but with a world entirely of the biblical author's making, or better, in the case of the Bible, entirely of God's making. As the author of the Pentateuch understands it, God created a world, the only world, "in the beginning," and through the act of reading the Pentateuch he brings its readers into the reality *(res)* of that world. In the Pentateuch both God and the author "make" a world. In creation, God "makes" the real *(res)* world. In writing the Pentateuch, its author explains God's world to the readers. Without the Pentateuch, we would know the world only as we see it. By means of the narrative of the Pentateuch, we see the world as God sees it, and we are invited to live our lives in that world.

---

[7]See Wolfgang Schneider, *Grammatik des biblischen Hebräisch: Ein Lehrbuch* (Munich: Claudius, 2001), pp. 177-97.

[8]Hans Frei, *The Eclipse of Biblical Narrative* (New Haven, Conn.: Yale University Press, 1980).

[9]Erich Auerbach, *Mimesis: The Representation of Reality in Western Literature,* trans. Willard R. Trask (Princeton, N.J.: Princeton University Press, 1953).

[10]Nelson Goodman, *Ways of Worldmaking* (Indianapolis: Hackett, 1992).

In the Pentateuch we see God's world through the eyes of its privileged narrator.[11] The world of the Bible is thus a part of our experience of the real world as well as a map of its ways of being that are otherwise unknown to us (Deut 29:29). What makes the biblical world assessable (as well as accessible) to us as readers is that its portrayal conforms to the accepted standards of narrative technique (storytelling and history writing) and Hebrew grammar. Thus, our perspective on the biblical depiction of the world should be grounded in both the level of narrative technique and the verbal level.

***Thematic level.*** The thematic level of the biblical narratives is the primary focus of a biblical theology. Bar-Efrat warns against detaching biblical themes from their moorings in the other levels of meaning. Too often one's understanding of a theological theme has little or no basis (exegetical warrant) in Scripture itself. Biblical theological themes should be grounded in the narrative world, the narrative technique used in depicting that world, and the words of the Bible that convey that world by means of its narrative technique. This means that our understanding of biblical theological themes must be tied to the author's intention (verbal meaning) and linked even to his choice of words, the development of his story, and the nature of the world that he depicts in his narratives. An idea must not be allowed to drift like a distant cloud over the textual horizon. It must always be tethered to the text in ways directly associated with the intention (vebal meaning) of the author. Only then can such ideas be considered part of the author's intention and find exegetical warrant in the text.

***Summary.*** The goal of biblical interpretation (hermeneutics) is to find the author's intent. One must seek to understand the meaning of the words and sentences that the author uses. We do that by understanding the author's words within the context of the grammar of biblical Hebrew and the literary shape of the whole of the Pentateuch (verbal meaning). Our clues to the author's big idea are to be sought in those things about which the author most often writes and that seem most important to him. Ultimately, we discover the meaning of a book such as the Pentateuch by reading it and asking the right questions. Behind our quest for the (human) author's intent is, of course, the conviction that the divine intention of Scripture is to be found in the human author's intent.

---

[11]Meir Sternberg, *The Poetics of Biblical Narrative* (Bloomington: Indiana University Press, 1987), pp. 59-85.

The exegetical warrant for our understanding the message of the Bible, and the Pentateuch in particular, is to be found in a fourfold linkage of perspectives at the verbal level, the level of the narrative technique, the narrative world, and the thematic structure. An exegetically warranted interpretation of a biblical text such as the Pentateuch must be grounded in each of these levels of narrative.

## Biblical Theology and Composition

In seeking to find and describe the theology of the Pentateuch, we will focus on the final shape of the HB as the Tanak.[12] This raises the question of whether a biblical theology that includes both the Tanak and the NT is possible. Can a theology of the whole OT as the Tanak play a role in a Christian biblical theology? Is there an exegetically warranted unity between the HB as Tanak and the NT?

***The final shape of the Old Testament.*** A working definition of the "final shape" of the OT is "the compositional and canonical state of the HB at the time it became part of an established community." This occurred for the OT sometime before the first century B.C. That date is not absolute, as there were multiple communities at that time, and each community looked on the Hebrew Scriptures as their Bible. Given the community nature of ancient texts such as the Tanak, one would expect to find multiple "final shapes" of the HB coming out of the pre-Christian era.

The two categories "composition" and "canon" are descriptive of how an author might have composed books and arranged them like those in the OT. The notion of the interrelationships between texts and communities is called "consolidation." It is an attempt to respond to recent observations about the nature of ancient written texts and the influence that they have on and receive from the communities that preserve them. Religious communities such as Judaism and Christianity derive their essential identity from texts. Biblical texts receive their final shape from such communities. Communities endorse and impose restrictions on their foundational texts. In this book we explore the idea that the consolidation of OT texts includes elements of composition

---

[12]This discussion of biblical theology and composition is substantially drawn from John H. Sailhamer, "Biblical Theology and the Composition of the Hebrew Bible," in *Biblical Theology: Retrospect and Prospect*, ed. Scott J. Hafemann (Downers Grove, Ill.: InterVarsity Press, 2002), pp. 25-37, and is used by permission.

as well as canonization. Communities not only produce canonical texts, they also create (composition) new texts.

The presence of text-communities is reflected to some degree in the textual history of the OT. Ancient manuscripts, such as those from Qumran, and various versions, such as the LXX, give ample evidence that biblical interpretation in the pre-Christian era was anything but uniform. Pre-Christian communities no doubt varied distinctly in their understanding of the meaning of biblical texts, and such differences surely made their way into the final shape of the Tanak to a greater or lesser degree.

The remainder of this chapter is an attempt to trace the inner workings of biblical interpretation within existing manuscripts and ancient versions belonging to various communities from this period. It is an attempt to chart the theological history of the pre-Christian communities that left their indelible mark on the final shape of the HB. Although largely unnoticed by modern scholarship, the work of Abraham Geiger has paved the way for much of the following reflections on the final shape of the HB.

***Problems of biblical theology.*** The focus in this chapter is on a biblical theology of the final shape of the HB. Two problems that directly relate to it must be addressed.

The first problem is the need for a text-model. A text-model is a description of the formation of the HB that adequately explains its present shape. Wolfgang Richter calls it a "theory of literature."[13] If we are going to talk about the final shape of the HB, we should have an idea of how it arrived at that shape and how that shape has changed over time. All biblical studies work with such theories, consciously or not. My aim is to develop a model consciously and to do so along lines consistent with an evangelical view of Scripture.

The second problem is the need to relate the shape of the HB to its connection to the NT. I am not suggesting that the NT has a final shape as a whole, though that is no doubt a question that ought to be raised. Our concern is to raise the question of how the final shape of the HB relates to the NT's reading of the "Old Testament." Does the NT show any awareness or concern to read the OT in terms of the meaning that may lie in its final shape? We will return to that set of problems later in this chapter and throughout this book. Here, we turn to a description of a text model of the OT.

---

[13]Richter, *Exegese als Literaturwissenschaft.*

*A Text-Model of the Old Testament.* The text-model, or general understanding of the biblical text, proposed here is drawn directly from an informed understanding of the theological and hermeneutical nature of the final shape of the HB. In the definition of "final shape" mentioned above are three central components: (1) the composition of a specific biblical text; (2) the canonical shaping of biblical texts and its influence on biblical communities; (3) the consolidation of a text within a specific "biblical" community. My text model views the biblical text at the point of intersection of those three coordinates.

*Composition.* The model proposed here takes seriously the notion that biblical texts have authors, and that authors' meanings can be discovered by reading their texts. The notion of authorship is a recognition of a decisive moment in the history of a text when it becomes an entity within itself and is thus capable of being read in terms of its wholeness and its parts. Authorship implies intentionality, purpose and meaning. It is a recognition of intelligent design in the shape of a text. In this way of thinking about the "final" shape, composition is viewed neither in terms of a dynamic process, as is common in biblical studies, nor a rigid status quo, which often was the view of earlier evangelical approaches to the OT. My understanding of biblical composition views it as other ancient books, representing a creative and decisive moment in the history of the formation of a text.

The phenomenon of multiple Hebrew texts for the book of Jeremiah offers an interesting insight into the nature of the composition of biblical books. Comparing the MT with the Hebrew *Vorlage* of the LXX of Jeremiah suggests that the book comes to us in two "final" shapes, the MT and the (LXX) *Vorlage.* In the view of contemporary textual critics, both shapes appear destined for two quite different communities.[14]

In the prophetic narrative of Jeremiah 27:16, during the last days of the Judean monarchy, the prophet Jeremiah confronts the false prophets of his day with a message of divine judgment. The country is on the brink of destruction. The devastation of Jerusalem is imminent. Yet the response of the false prophets is that Jeremiah has overstated his case, and that Judah's troubles will soon be over. Relief is in sight. As evidence to back up their claim, the message of the false prophets is that the temple vessels in Babylon will

[14]See Emanuel Tov, *Textual Criticism of the Hebrew Bible* (Minneapolis: Fortress, 1992), pp. 320-21; Eugene Ulrich, *The Dead Sea Scrolls and the Origins of the Bible* (SDSSRL; Grand Rapids: Eerdmans, 1999), p. 69.

soon be returned to Jerusalem. But Jeremiah has a different word for Judah and Jerusalem. Captivity will not be over so soon. Seventy years will pass before the temple vessels are returned. The word of the false prophets is that relief will come shortly, but according to Jeremiah, it will come only after seventy years. The textual issues of this chapter in Jeremiah are complex, but they shed considerable light on the nature of biblical composition.

In the MT Jeremiah proclaims, "Do not listen to the words of your prophets who are prophesying to you, saying, 'Behold, the vessels of the LORD's house will now shortly be brought back from Babylon,' for it is a lie that they are prophesying to you." It is clear that in the MT the optimistic word of the false prophets is wrong. They might prophesy that the temple vessels will soon be returned, but that word will prove false. The vessels will not return soon. It will take seventy years.

The apparatus of *BHS* shows that the word "shortly" is not in the LXX and thus not likely in the Hebrew manuscripts *(Vorlage)* used by the LXX translators.[15] In that version *(Vorlage)* of Jeremiah 27 the false prophets say only that the vessels will be returned. They do not say that they will be returned "soon" or "now shortly." Jeremiah, in the Hebrew *Vorlage* (to the LXX), leaves a door open for the false prophets' reading of Jeremiah that the vessels of the Lord's house will be returned, making no mention of the "now shortly." The vessels eventually were returned to Jerusalem, but not quickly or soon, thus confirming Jeremiah's word against them.

Jeremiah appears to insist in one version of the story *(Vorlage)* that the vessels will not be returned. That posed a problem because the vessels were returned seventy years later. In another version of the story Jeremiah says that the vessels will not return "quickly," as happened with the seventy years delay. Given Jeremiah's simple statement in one version of the story *(Vorlage)* that the vessels will not be returned, it might give the appearance that the false prophets got it right. The vessels eventually were returned.

The problem does not exist in the MT. There, Jeremiah quotes the false prophets as saying that the temple vessels will be returned "shortly." The word "shortly" changes everything. Although the vessels eventually did return to the temple, they were not returned shortly. The word of the false prophets thus was not substantiated, and Jeremiah's words eventually were confirmed.

---

[15]Tov, *Textual Criticism of the Hebrew Bible*, p. 320.

This, of course, is not a serious exegetical problem and represents a common textual difficulty. Within the context, the false prophets clearly meant to say that the temple vessels would be returned "shortly." They were not thinking of Jeremiah's seventy years. Their message was that help was on the way. Jerusalem should resist and stand firm. If this were merely a text-critical problem, one would likely say that the MT offers a longer, more difficult and therefore secondary text. It is a gloss of a scribe who wanted to supply a helpful, valid and needed comment. Thus, the LXX represents a more original and, given its implications, more difficult text.

The larger question involves what we are to make of this gloss in light of the composition of the book of Jeremiah. Is this an isolated textual gloss, or is it the work of an "author"? To address that question, two additional observations are necessary. First, this gloss is part of many similar glosses in Jeremiah that seem to fill in for the reader numerous historical details. They are comments from the hand of a scribe who seems to known "the rest of the story" and is intent on helping the reader understand the book from that perspective. This feature of the MT of Jeremiah has led some to suggest that the two versions of Jeremiah, the MT and the LXX Hebrew *Vorlage*, represent preexilic and postexilic editions of the book. The MT of Jeremiah was produced by a "scribal author" who fills in many of the historical details that he is aware of but that were unknown to Jeremiah in his time. It is likely that such a situation may have been the case, but if so, it is not the whole story. To see the whole story, one must take a closer look at the interpretations of Jeremiah's words reflected in these two texts, the MT and the Hebrew *Vorlage* of the LXX.

This leads to the second observation. It is clear from the textual history of these two versions of the book of Jeremiah that both versions survived the exile and became a part of the canon of two distinct postexilic communities. In one community there was a conscious decision to transmit the book of Jeremiah as it had been received. That version is represented in the Hebrew *Vorlage* of the LXX. Even though that version of Jeremiah cast some doubt on Jeremiah's words, it was taken as sufficiently clear and left as is. In the other version of Jeremiah, represented by the MT, its community felt it necessary to add a comment to Jeremiah's words to insure that they were not misunderstood. Thus, two quite different approaches to the meaning of the book of Jeremiah are represented in its textual history. Textual history becomes a function of theological meaning.

When we take into consideration the other textual variants in the book of Jeremiah, it becomes apparent that the community represented by the MT had focused Jeremiah's prophecies on the historical events of the return from Babylonian captivity. When, to mention another example, in some texts Jeremiah speaks merely of a people "from the north," the MT goes to considerable lengths to identify them as Babylon and King Nebuchadnezzar.[16] Again, the "scribal author" is reading Jeremiah in terms of "the rest of the story," which he knows and is concerned that the readers of this book do not overlook. The MT has a decided historical cast to its reading of the book of Jeremiah. It understands Jeremiah's words in light of the immediate events of "world history."

In the text of the LXX, however, Jeremiah's words are not tied to specific historical events—this in spite of the fact that the edition continued for several hundred years as a part of the canon in its community. The implication appears obvious. Even after the exile, and all those events that informed the reading of the MT of Jeremiah, this community appears to have been little concerned about the relationship of Jeremiah's words to the historical realities of his own day. Their focus remained simply on Jeremiah's original words about an invasion of his country by a people "from the north," a theme in Jeremiah similar to Ezekiel 38–39. There was, at least in their version of Jeremiah, still the possibility of a future referent to Jeremiah's words—a referent that looked beyond the seventy years of the Babylonian captivity to an enemy much like that envisioned by Ezekiel. For this community, Jeremiah's words had not been exhausted in the events of Israel's past.[17] There was still a future in his words.

What is remarkable about the *Vorlage* (LXX) to the book of Jeremiah is how well it fits with Daniel 9. In Daniel 9 we see a godly Israelite, still in exile, pondering the meaning of these same chapters of Jeremiah. His question was not how Jeremiah's words had been fulfilled in the Babylonian captivity,

---

[16]"The intention of the exegetical expansions in MT is to identify Judah's enemy with Babylon and, more particularly, with Nebuchadrezzar, whereas in Sept[uagint] there is no further elucidation of the 'enemy from the north'" (William McKane, *A Critical and Exegetical Commentary on Jeremiah* [ICC; Edinburgh: T & T Clark, 1986], 1:xxi).

[17]"In Sept[uagint] . . . there is no further elucidation of the enemy from the north. According to Sept[uagint], Judah, because of its lack of trust in Yahweh and disobedience (v. 8), is about to be vanquished by an enemy from the north who will devastate both Judah and the countries surrounding her, and leave behind a scene of desolation which will evoke astonishment and terror (v. 9)" (ibid., p. 627).

which had been the focus of the MT of these chapters. His question was why Jeremiah's words still will not be fulfilled "for many days hence" (Dan 8:26). Daniel was dismayed that he must seal up the vision until a later time. In Daniel 9 Daniel tries to understand Jeremiah's prophecy of the seventy years in this new light. The answer he receives is that Jeremiah's vision of the future was to be fulfilled not in seventy years, but in seventy weeks of years. In Daniel, Jeremiah's words point far beyond the events of the return from exile—far beyond Nebuchadnezzar and Babylon. The author of Daniel 9 would have had no use for a book of Jeremiah with glosses about Nebuchadnezzar. He would have had no use for the MT of Jeremiah. For him, there was still a future for Jeremiah's word. His words had not been exhausted by the events of the past.

These texts provide a firsthand look at the nature of biblical composition. The kinds of differences that exist between these two "editions" of Jeremiah are not merely scribal. They are compositional in nature. Daniel 9 shows the kind of situation that might give rise to two compositions, or two books, of Jeremiah. The simultaneous existence of both texts suggests multiple communities and diverse interpretations of the same OT book.

One should also note that the differences in the text of Jeremiah are accompanied by a large rearrangement of the contents of the book. The oracles against foreign nations in the MT, Jeremiah 46–51, are located in the LXX version of Jeremiah after the prophecy of the seventy years (Jer 25:15-26).[18] This, incidentally, is the shape of the book as it is reflected in the version of the book published by Baruch in Jeremiah 36:2 and the Hebrew *Vorlage* of the LXX. Moreover, the Dead Sea Scrolls show us that the LXX translators were following closely their own Hebrew texts of Jeremiah. These differences between the two texts of Jeremiah were likely already in early Hebrew manuscripts.[19]

Another interesting feature of the differences between these two versions of Jeremiah is that the additional material in the MT contains numerous examples of rabbinical techniques such as *atbash*, whereby ciphers are created by reversing the alphabet (Jer 25:25-26; 51:1, 41). In this sense, the

---

[18]It is just at this point in the book (Jer 25:13b-14a) that someone, presumably the narrator or the author, begins to speak directly to the readers about the book we are now reading. In text linguistics this is known as a metacommunicational gloss. This comment is not in the LXX.

[19]Tov, *Textual Criticism of the Hebrew Bible*, p. 320.

additional material in the MT is midrashic in nature—a point that should not go unnoticed.[20]

These two versions, or variant texts, of Jeremiah do not merely represent two distinct editions of the book. Both texts also appear to be unique books in their own right. Furthermore, both books were part of communities that in all likelihood accepted them as canonical in the late postexilic period. As such, these various versions of Jeremiah suggest that the composition of a biblical book such as Jeremiah was the work of a distinct community, at a definite moment in time, and representing a particular theological point of view.

*Canonization*. Canonization, the next coordinate in my text-model, looks at the point where a book becomes part of a larger collection and contributes to its overall shape. In current biblical studies, composition generally has been taken to precede canonization. Books received their final shape before they became part of a canon. Composition is seen as an historical process, whereas canonization is a theological one. I agree to some extent with those who separate canon from composition in this way. The final literary shape of the OT books is not always identical with the canonical shape. It does not follow, however, that the formation of the OT canon was the result of purely theological forces. The two versions of Jeremiah, for example, show that composition can, and even does, occur after canonization. The nature of harmonistic textual variants like the addition of "now shortly" in Jeremiah 27:16 shows that the earlier version was already considered canonical, since they are attempts to harmonize an authoritative text. To the extent that such glosses are compositional in nature—that is, they reflect concern for the shape of the whole book and are interconnected with similar kinds of additions—one can say that there are compositional elements in the final canonical shape of the HB. Hence, some composition continues after canonization. It is also clear that some compositional elements were theologically motivated. This means that in classical terms of authorship, the shape of the OT canon as a whole must be taken seriously and integrated into my text-model. Not only do the books of the HB have authors, but also the HB as a whole, and as a canonical shape, is the product of composition and authorship.

Thus, in my understanding of the "final" text, the concept of "canon" does not follow a single trail to each and every canonical shape. Rather than speak-

[20]See I. L. Seeligmann, *Voraussetzungen der Midraschexegese* (VTSup 1; Leiden: Brill, 1953), pp. 150-81.

ing of a process of canonization, I prefer to borrow a term from the field of biology and speak of the OT canon as a "punctuated equilibrium." It is "punctuated" in that it is the result not of a continuous process of development, but of creative moments of formation that can arise within multiple canonical contexts. It is an "equilibrium" in that once established, the canonical shape continued in a more or less steady state until something catastrophic, such as the destruction of the temple, triggered a major shift in the focus and shape of a book or collection of books.

One further observation about canonization warrants mention. What I have said and will say about the compositional formation of the OT canon suggests that it was the work of an individual, not a community as such. Individuals are part of communities—they are shaped by communities, and they speak for communities—but the work of both composition and canonization is the work of individuals.

*Consolidation*. The third notion in our model of the final shape of the HB is "consolidation." Here the issue is the further adjustment of a canonical text to a specific community environment. An example is the adjustment of the LXX to NT quotations of the OT, or to Origen's fifth column in the Hexapla, as well as the adjustment of the MT along the lines of the emerging rabbinical exegesis.

A good deal of the Masoretic activity in the HB appears to center on texts that form the exegetical basis for established core beliefs. The two *yod*s in the account of the creation of man (Gen 2:7: וייצר) likely were preserved in the MT text because they reflect the rabbinical commentary that man was created with two natures (יצרים [cf. Rashi]). In the same way, the single *yod* in the identical verb used for the creation of the animals (Gen 2:19: ויצר) supports the rabbinical doctrine that the animals have only one nature (יצר). This does not mean that this shape of the text should be traced back to the intent of the author of Genesis. That would make it a matter of composition. The preservation of a form of the MT that supports a specific element of rabbinical exegesis is a function of consolidation. At the most, the notion of consolidation means only that once texts become a part of a community, they take on the essential characteristics of the core beliefs of their community.

To summarize the point of these pages: The final shape of the HB is best described in terms of three intersecting coordinates: composition, canonization, consolidation. Composition preceded canonization, but it did not stop there. Canonical books continued to take on varying compositional shapes that reflected the theological viewpoints of their communities. Once established within a specific community, OT texts began to take on essential characteristics of those communities in a way that stopped short of new composition. The result was the production of various versions and shapes of the Hebrew Tanak: the Law, the Prophets, the Writings.

If my text model is valid, it suggests that lying behind the varying shapes of the Hebrew Tanak are various text-communities, in part drawing their theological identity from those shapes. Elsewhere I have suggested that the Hebrew Tanak is shaped around two sets of compositional seams, Deuteronomy 34 and Joshua 1, as well as Malachi 3 and Psalm 1.[21] Both Deuteronomy 34 and Malachi 3 look forward to the return of an age of prophecy. Moses the prophet is dead, and Joshua has taken his place. Joshua is characterized in these seams not as a prophet, but as a wise man. The wise man who meditates on written Scripture has taken over the role of the prophet who speaks directly with God. Scripture, along with the prophetic word within Scripture, are now the locus of divine revelation. Of course, the hope for a return of prophecy in the future still exists. The Scriptures themselves (e.g., Deut 18) point in that direction. In the meantime, one "prospers" and becomes "wise" by meditating on the written Scripture.

These canonical seams suggest a conscious composition of the whole. Its ranking of a collection of written texts over the gift of prophecy strongly suggests that its threefold shape is the form in which it was first received as canon. The shape of the Tanak implies its status as written Scripture. Finally, we know from the history of the HB within Judaism that it was in the shape of the Tanak that the HB was consolidated within medieval Judaism. Indeed, the whole of the Masorah that accompanied the HB was oriented toward this threefold division.

*The Tanak and biblical theology.* Questions about the meaning and shape of the OT lead to the second problem raised by a biblical theology of the final shape of the text. How does the theology reflected in the shape of the Tanak relate to the NT?

Few would contest the notion that the HB existed in a threefold form at some place and point in time during the pre-Christian period. This was not

---

[21]Sailhamer, *Introduction to Old Testament Theology*, pp. 239-352.

its only form or even its most durable or authoritative form. Along with other possible forms, the Tanak existed in its threefold form for a considerable period of time and for a significantly large portion of Judaism. According to Luke 24:44, the Tanak was the "final shape" of the Bible of Jesus. Judging by the prologue to the book of Sirach, it already had that shape a century earlier, even in its Greek form.[22]

Those evangelical biblical theologies embracing a "salvation-historical"[23] approach to biblical theology no doubt will hesitate to acknowledge the theological significance of the final shape of the Tanak. The arrangement of the books in the Tanak does not always follow the "history of salvation." Ruth, for example, is not listed with the Former Prophets, but follows the book of Proverbs. Chronicles falls at the end of the books or before the book of Psalms. The salvation-historical approach has attempted to answer the question of the unity of the two-part Christian Bible (OT/NT) by locating that unity in the historical events leading from Judaism to Christianity. In that historical development, the OT reached its final goal in the events of the life of Christ and the early church. The unity of the two Testaments lies not in the shape of the HB, but in the revelatory progression of salvation history.

The second attempt to link the Tanak with the NT is represented by Rolf Rendtorff's theology of the OT. Rendtorff presses the point that the OT (as the Tanak) was already a distinct entity in its final shape before the formation of the NT.[24] There is thus an inherent diversity between a theology of the Hebrew OT and a NT theology. Such diversity stems, Rendtorff suggests, from the fact that the Tanak is a product of pre-Christian Judaism. That notwithstanding, Rendtorff believes that Christian theologians are obliged to treat the Tanak as the OT component of a biblical theology linked to the NT.[25]

---

[22]An important implication of the prologue to Sirach is that even the OT in Greek was read in a threefold form. This still tells us nothing about the specific makeup of the Tanak at these various times. There continued to be considerable discussion about the details of which books were in and how they were to be arranged.

[23]Here I have in mind those approaches to biblical theology that focus on the salvific events of Israel's history as revelatory in addition to the biblical text. See Sailhamer, *Introduction to Old Testament Theology*, pp. 54-85.

[24]"Die Hebräische Bibel war aber bereits davor die jüdische Heilige Schrift" (Rolf Rendtorff, *Theologie des Alten Testaments: Ein kanonischer Entwurf* [Neukirchen-Vluyn: Neukirchener Verlag, 1999], 1:4).

[25]Rolf Rendtorff, "Toward a Common Jewish-Christian Reading of the Hebrew Bible," in *Canon and Theology: Overtures to an Old Testament Theology*, trans. Margaret Cole (OBT; Minneapolis:

A third attempt to link the Tanak with the NT is made by Hartmut Gese.[26] Gese sees the Tanak as a past stage in the OT's revelatory tradition history. Gese argues that the OT that one is to connect to the NT in a biblical theology is a distinct entity only in the final shape given it by the early church. The formation of that OT is the result of a complex process of interpretation and reinterpretation that has been shaped and ultimately embraced by the formation of the NT. The OT represents the final form of Israel's long and drawn out tradition history. The inherent diversity of the multiple traditions in the OT is a result of a tradition-historical process that culminated in the rereading of the OT by Jesus, the early church and ultimately those who shaped the NT canon. Unity comes out of a complex but singular line of reinterpretation.

A fourth response views, with Rendtorff, the "final (threefold) shape" of the Tanak as already fixed in the pre-Christian period, it representing the form of the OT that must be united with the NT. However, there was not one, but two (or multiple) versions of the Tanak within ancient Judaism. One therefore must not ask simply how the Tanak relates to the NT, but which form of the Tanak should be read alongside the NT. While it may be correct to say that the NT does not wholly conform to the Tanak of later Judaism, it may be possible that the NT does conform to another version of the Tanak. Since no single community represented the entirety of early Judaism, there likely was no single version of the Tanak. In the form we now have it, the (pre-Christian) Tanak that lies in the Hebrew *Vorlage* of the LXX shows considerable similarity to and unity with the NT. Contrary to Gese's view, the OT that one should attempt to link to the NT is neither the OT of the early church nor the canonical form in which it was received by the first Christian communities, that is, the Alexandrian LXX. The OT of the early church may, rather, be found in one of the pre-Christian Tanaks that belonged to the various communities within pre-Christian Judaism.

*Daniel and the end of the Tanak.* I will illustrate by returning to the example of Daniel's reading of Jeremiah. Canonically and compositionally, the book of Daniel raises a perplexing question: What is the appropriate location of Daniel within the Tanak?

---

Fortress, 1993), pp. 31-45.

[26]Hartmut Gese, *Zur biblischen Theologie: Alttestamentliche Vorträge* (Munich: Kaiser, 1977), pp. 23-30.

David Freedman addresses this question in his study of the shape of the Tanak in the pre-Christian period.[27] Freedman finds a great deal of symmetry and order in the Tanak,[28] but he also shows that the symmetry is largely missing if Daniel is included. In effect, Freedman's observations suggest that within the history of the OT canon we must reckon with the possibility of both a "Tanak with Daniel" and a "Tanak without Daniel."

Now, the book of Daniel is not one of those books whose omission or inclusion would make little difference. This is especially true if the larger question is the relationship of the Tanak to the NT. Freedman shows that the major fluctuations in the order of the Writings largely turn on the position assigned to Daniel.

In the earliest complete medieval manuscript (Codex B19a), Daniel falls nearly at the end of the Tanak. It is followed only by the book Ezra-Nehemiah, a single book in the HB. With that arrangement, the edict of Cyrus (Ezra 1:2-4)—the decree to return and rebuild the temple, which plays a central role in the "messianic" schematic of Daniel 9—immediately follows the book of Daniel and provides the introduction to the last book, Ezra-Nehemiah. In that position, the edict of Cyrus identifies the historical return under Ezra and Nehemiah as the fulfillment of Jeremiah's vision of seventy years. It is as if Daniel 9, and its view of seventy weeks of years, were nowhere in sight.

In another arrangement of the last books of the Tanak (Babylonian Talmud, *Baba Batra* 14b), the book of Chronicles comes last and closes with a repetition of the edict of Cyrus (2 Chron 36:23). As Freedman points out, this arrangement of Chronicles and Ezra-Nehemiah is noticeably out of chronological sequence. After the close of Nehemiah, the Chronicler begins his narrative with Adam![29] This suggests that the book of Chronicles was deliberately placed at the end of the Tanak, after the books of Ezra-Nehemiah and after the book of Daniel. It also suggests a conscious effort to close the Tanak with a restatement of the edict of Cyrus at the end of Chronicles.

[27]David N. Freedman, *The Unity of the Hebrew Bible* (Ann Arbor: University of Michigan Press, 1991).

[28]"The correspondences among the major segments are so close, and the symmetry so exact, that it is difficult to imagine that these are the result of happenstance, or that a single mind or group of individuals was not responsible for assembling and organizing this collection of sacred works" (ibid., pp. 79-80).

[29]The order of the OT books followed by the English translations has corrected this by placing Ezra at the end of Chronicles, but with the consequence of a redundant and immediate repetition of Cyrus's edict (2 Chron 36:23; Ezra 1:2-4).

There appears to have been at least two contending "final shapes" of the Tanak. One of them closes with the book of Ezra-Nehemiah. In that version, the edict of Cyrus finds its fulfillment in the historical return from exile. The other shape of the Tanak closes with Chronicles and a repetition of the edict of Cyrus. In that arrangement, the edict of Cyrus has a shorter form than in Ezra-Nehemiah (Ezra 1:2-4), so that it concludes with the clause "Let him go up" (2 Chron 36:23). In the book of Chronicles, the subject of that clause is identified as he "whose God is with him." For the Chronicler, this had a "messianic" turn to it (cf. 1 Chron 17:12). Cyrus says, in effect, "Let him (whose God is with him) go up to Jerusalem." To arrive at that dramatic conclusion, the Chronicler had to omit nearly two verses from the original edict in Ezra-Nehemiah. Those verses link the edict to the historical events of the return from exile.[30] Without them, the fulfillment of the Tanak's final words is left open to the future.

The central role of the edict of Cyrus at the conclusion of the Tanak appears to be driven by the expectation injected into the end of the Tanak by Daniel 9. In Daniel 9 Jeremiah's expectation of a return to Jerusalem is projected beyond the immediate return from Babylonian captivity. Jeremiah's promise of a return after seventy years is extended to seven times seventy years, or 490 years, way beyond any future event known at the time including the Maccabean period.

Regardless of how one might interpret these events, it is clear that they hinge on the timing of "the publication of the word to restore and build Jerusalem" (Dan 9:25). The fact that one version of the Tanak ends with just such a decree (the edict of Cyrus) can hardly be coincidental. Moreover, in the introduction to the edict (2 Chron 36:21), the Chronicler himself consciously links the edict to Jeremiah's prophecy of the seventy weeks, which is precisely the passage Daniel is pondering in Daniel 9.

At least two "final shapes" of the Tanak appear to emerge from these compositional considerations. One leaves us with a Tanak that concludes with Ezra-Nehemiah and identifies the return from Babylonian exile as the fulfillment of Jeremiah's prophecy of seventy years. This represents a Tanak

[30]In contrast to 2 Chronicles 36:23, the subject of the verb "let him go up" in Ezra/Nehemiah is "the heads of fathers' households of Judah and Benjamin and the priests and the Levites . . . even everyone whose spirit God had stirred to go up and rebuild the house of the LORD which is in Jerusalem" (Ezra 1:5).

with a historical fulfillment that it seeks to identify with the immediate postexilic age. The return from Babylon was a well-known reference point in early biblical interpretation. The other Tanak finds its reference point in the book of Daniel, particularly Daniel 9, and closes with the book of Chronicles (2 Chron 36). In doing so, it extends Jeremiah's seventy years beyond the time of the return from Babylon, closing the whole of the Tanak with a decidedly future reference. That shape fits well with the sense one gains from the study of the Hebrew text *(Vorlage)* of the LXX of Jeremiah and the reading of these texts by the NT. Both this Tanak and the NT are open to events that look beyond the return from Babylonian exile.[31]

The points raised in this chapter show that changing attitudes toward the OT have opened the door to a range of new possibilities for constructing a biblical theology of the Old and New Testaments. There will continue to be those who seek the earliest forms of the OT texts, but a growing number of others have turned their attention to the "final shape." This should not be construed as a turn away from an interest in history; rather, it is a focus on a largely overlooked and textually prolific stage of Israel's history, namely, the history of Israel immediately prior to the coming of Christ and the writing of the NT.

Along with an interest in the final shape of the OT has also come a renewed focus on composition. Rather than seeking to discover the literary "strata" behind the biblical text, researchers have shifted their attention to the literary "strategy" of the biblical text. The quest for strategy has replaced the quest for strata. The convergence of these two interests leads to a necessary recasting of the basic questions of a biblical theology of the Old and New Testaments. This is true in at least three important ways.

First, a focus on the final shape of the HB and its link to the notion of canon leaves little doubt that the OT can and should be approached theologically. In the past, biblical theologies have devoted much attention to the question of the theological purpose of the OT as such, with largely negative results. The results have been negative because biblical composition has been viewed apart from the stage where Scripture was recognized as authoritative, that is, at the level of the canonization of Scripture. By contrast, Rendtorff's recent OT theology, which concentrates on the OT canon, has only one sentence devoted to this question. In that sentence, the first in the book, Rendtorff says simply, "The

[31]Note that the final piece of canonical "Velcro" is centered on the notion of fulfilled prophecy (2 Chron 36:22).

OT is a theological book."[32] Had Rendtorff been seeking any level other than the final canonical shape, he would have been obliged to say much more.

A focus on the final shape of the HB considerably reduces the time gap between the OT and the NT. If the formation of the Tanak took place during the second century B.C. or later, the OT is virtually laid at the doorstep of the NT. In a real sense, the OT, as the Tanak, belongs to the intertestamental period. The Tanak does not conclude in the same way as the history of Israel, that is, with the Babylonian captivity. Nor does the OT first come into being with Judaism, that is, in the priestly circles of the second temple. This discussion has shown that at the end of at least one version of the Tanak we find ourselves already in the world of ideas of the NT.

A focus on the final shape, or final shapes, of the HB raises the possibility of an early (pre-Christian) version of the OT that intentionally links the book of Daniel to the edict of Cyrus in 2 Chronicles 36:22-23. To be sure, there are surface disturbances in that shape, such as the variant Hebrew versions of Jeremiah and the canonical location of the books of Daniel and Chronicles. But these very disturbances reveal the deep-seated disagreements over the meaning of Scripture that existed in the postexilic and pre-Christian period. If we follow closely the nature of those disagreements, a picture begins to emerge. The line that runs through and divides the early versions of the Tanak is the same line that separates John the Baptist from the religious leaders of his day. The Tanak closes with the expectation of a new work of God. This work includes the return of prophecy characterized by both Moses (Deut 34) and Elijah (Mal 3) and extends beyond the events that immediately surround Jerusalem and the early centuries of the second temple. It is along that story line that the NT writers pick up the narrative thread and take us into the world of the NT canon.

***Evangelical approaches to biblical theology.*** It is widely recognized that the question of method in OT studies is in a state of flux. Rendtorff has spoken of a "change of paradigm." By which he means, "The paradigm within which Old Testament scholarship has worked for more than a century, namely the old German Literarkritik, has lost its general acceptance." According to Rendtorff,

> It is no longer possible to maintain that serious Old Testament scholarship has to be indispensably tied to this set of methodological principles. So far there is

[32]"Das Alte Testament ist ein theologisches Buch" (Rendtorff, *Theologie des Alten Testaments*, p. 1).

> no alternative concept that has been generally accepted. . . . Old Testament scholarship now is in a stage of transition, and we cannot know whether there will be a new paradigm or if the near future will be characterized by a plurality of approaches and methods.[33]

The current state of transition in OT studies may be an opportune moment for evangelicals to examine afresh their own approaches to biblical theology and how they are affected by prevailing trends. Such an examination could provide a broader view of the kinds of biblical theologies we might expect under the heading of "evangelical." The following discussion of possible evangelical options is not intended to be such an examination in an exhaustive or comprehensive way. Its aim is to put into context the kind of biblical theology I intend to develop in this book.

*Evangelical options for biblical theology.* In the following discussion of evangelical options in biblical theology I understand "evangelical" to apply to approaches that take their starting point in a commitment to the biblical text as divinely inspired. There are other concerns of evangelical method, some having to do with apologetics and some with hermeneutics and exegesis. A central concern for the historicity of the biblical narratives, for example, is shared by all evangelicals. To be sure, evangelical biblical studies cannot afford to diminish its ongoing interest in historiography and adjacent studies, but neither should it emphasize such interests at the expense of its primary concern for the meaning and final authority of the biblical text.

In the face of the current transitional nature of OT studies in general, one might think of evangelical options under three broad headings: (1) stay the course; (2) eclecticism; (3) final shape *(Endgestalt)*.

*Stay the course.* It is reasonable to suppose that in the near future many evangelicals will opt for approaches to biblical theology that could be characterized as "stay the course." They will continue the process of doing biblical theology begun in the late eighteenth and nineteenth centuries. Their primary focus will be the historical development of biblical ideas, such as "covenant," "promise" and "law," treating the written biblical narratives as if they were actual historical events finding their meaning both within the language of the text and historical and literary analogies in ancient Near East. The similarity between contemporary evangelical biblical theologies, like those of

[33]Rendtorff, *Canon and Theology*, pp. 29-30.

Vos and Kaiser, and earlier nineteenth-century approaches, such as those of Hengstenberg and Oehler, suggests that "stay the course" has been an important evangelical option in the past and will continue to be in the future. Taking this option will mean a continued acceptance of the revelatory nature of historical events (salvation history), both as written narratives and as actual events explained by means of the historical method. In doing so, evangelicals will continue to view both the actual history and the biblical narratives as the locus of divine revelation. One can only guess what the eventual outcome of such a position will be.

Has the current generation of biblical theologies laid an adequate foundation for such discussions? To take one example, in pursuing the question of the nature and role of the authorship of biblical books, evangelicals have hardly begun to address some of the most basic questions, such as how divine revelation can be found in historical events and at the same time be viewed as a function of human authorship. Where do the biblical authors and the meaning they have assigned their texts come into play alongside the role that continues to be given to biblical historians? Although contemporary evangelicals have no qualms about focusing both on biblical texts and historical events, it is inevitable that the question of authorship will overtake them. There has been little evidence in their work to date to suggest what direction that discussion might take. It is not merely a question of the final authority of inspired authors of biblical texts. It is self-evident that for evangelicals, the final authority will go to the inspired biblical author, unless they decide, as their nineteenth-century counterparts did, that the events themselves are also inspired.[34] Evangelicals have, in general, resisted such a position.

Another issue that will continue to demand evangelical attention in a "stay the course" approach is the continuing need for a theoretical, or theological, defense of its understanding and use of history. V. Philips Long has made an impressive start.[35] His purpose is to raise the level of evangelical discussion of the task of both defending and making sense of biblical history. Long addresses the problem of the linkage between biblical narrative and real history by an appeal to Christian theism that assumes the link. Although it is an important evangelical option, Long's appeal to theism raises the question of

---

[34]This was the view held by von Hofmann (see Sailhamer, *Introduction to Old Testament Theology*, pp. 61-62).

[35]V. Philips Long, *The Art of Biblical History* (Grand Rapids: Zondervan), 1994.

whether a biblical theology with such commitments can claim to be "biblical" in the ordinary sense of the term. Theism is, after all, a theological system.

A further issue raised by Long's book is one I discussed earlier about Frei's term "history-like" when applied to biblical narrative. Long, incorrectly in my view, takes Frei's term to be an apologetical claim about the lack of historical accuracy or truthfulness in biblical narrative. The long-standing nature of this problem among evangelicals is illustrated by the fact that Long himself builds his argument on a statement made by Geerhardus Vos in 1906.[36] Like many evangelicals, Long understands the issue of history and the Bible to be a question of the capacity of the biblical narratives to record real events accurately. He suggests that the biblical narratives are like an oil painting, which is capable of representing both the artist's conception and the real nature of the subject matter. Long points out that no two artists paint the same picture the same way. A realistic (history-like) painting is as much a product of the artist's intention as it is the nature of its subject. The biblical authors, Long maintains, are like artists who use their paint both creatively and realistically, presenting their unique view of the events they record. We should not expect biblical accounts of historical events to be exactly alike, though we should expect them to be an accurate depiction of the real events.

Long's use of the artist metaphor is correct as far as it goes, but it leaves several of Frei's questions unresolved. Put simply, in Long's metaphor, an artist's use of paint *(res)* is not analogous to the biblical authors use of words *(verba)*. The artist's paint, unlike the words an author writes down on a page, is part of the real *(res)* world and has its meaning within the *realia* of that world. That is unlike the meaning of words in a language. An artist can paint a red hat on a canvas with virtually the same color as a red hat in the real world. That is not the case with biblical narrative. In a written text, the red color of a hat cannot be shown with the actual color red; it can only be described as being red by the use of words that mean "red" in a given language. A narrative text, which depends only on words *(verba)*, can only narrate with words that the color of someone's hat is red. In a narrative description of "a person in a red hat," the hat is not depicted as red in color, nor, for that matter, is it really a hat. In both cases, it is not red as such, and it is not a hat. All one

[36]Ibid., p. 90. The Vos article is "Christian Faith and the Truthfulness of Bible History," *PTR* 4 (1906): 289-305.

can do in a narrative is to state that a hat is red in color. Words describe or depict things such as a real red hat, but the word *hat* is not a hat itself, and the word for its color, *red*, is not itself red but is only the word used to describe that color. There is no inherent link between the color red and the word *red* either in English or Hebrew.

The word *red* belongs to a different level of *realia* than the color red. If that is true, Long must expand and further develop his metaphorical explanation of the artist's painting to explain the relationship between the depiction of things with words in biblical narrative and the use of the color red in an oil painting. Frei did this by the use of the expression "history-like," but his point has been largely missed. The importance of the issue remains, however, and presents evangelicals with a genuine challenge to clarify the discussion.

Words are not the things that they point to in the same way that the color red is the same as the actual color, say, of the red cord in Rahab's window. In narrative texts, it is enough that the word *(verbum) red* has a verbal meaning that corresponds to the physical color red in the real world. Long's painting metaphor is just that, a metaphor, and thus not an entirely adequate representation of the nature of biblical narrative, which can use only words and not colors or things to depict realia. It would be an appropriate model if the biblical narratives had color pictures to go with them. Even realistic narrative is already a step removed from the "things" *(realia)* that it depicts.

Evangelicals who choose to "stay the course" in biblical theology face difficult tasks. One can only hope that they will be transparent in facing the implications of treating both history and texts as the locus of revelation and inspiration.[37] This would mean continuing a kind of biblical theology centered on both textually based meaning and historically reconstructed events and ideas. It would make historians and archaeologists into biblical expositors. There would thus be a continuation of the kind of OT theologies produced by Vos[38] and Kaiser,[39] as well as the classical works of Hävernick,[40] Oehler[41] and König,[42] but they should not be mere duplications of past

[37]Compare Richard Rothe, K. C. von Hofmann and William Temple in Sailhamer, *Introduction to Old Testament Theology*, pp. 59-67.

[38]Vos, *Biblical Theology*.

[39]Walter C. Kaiser Jr., *Toward an Old Testament Theology* (Grand Rapids: Zondervan, 1978).

[40]Hävernick, *Theologie des Alten Testaments*.

[41]Gustav F. Oehler, *Theologie des Alten Testaments* (Stuttgart: Steinkopf, 1882); English translation: *Theology of the Old Testament*, trans. Ellen D. Smith (New York: Funk & Wagnalls, 1883).

[42]König, *Theologie des Alten Testaments*.

works.[43] The days of nineteenth-century evangelical reprints are over.

If evangelicals stay the course, it will likely be in the form of an occasional expansion or updating of existing works. A biblical theology based on the historical conclusions of William Albright would need to be updated, or re-defended, in light of current reconstructions of ancient Israelite history. Also, the problems inherent in staying the course, such as the quest for a center,[44] and the nature of historical events as a locus of divine revelation,[45] almost surely will weaken the appeal of staying the course, since there is little in the approach itself that is able to correct these methodological pitfalls. Many of them are perennial problems inherent in the method itself.

*Eclecticism.* Eclecticism has been a favorite approach of many evangelicals in search of a method in biblical theology. Evangelicals likely will continue to produce biblical theologies that reflect the current state of change and transition in OT studies, thus drawing from the best of methods such as canonical criticism, historical research and archaeology, and narrative studies. This may be the direction in which most evangelicals will move. The obvious appeal of the approach is the freedom to pick and choose that it allows. The drawbacks will come from its inherent lack of consistency and coherency, as well as its inability to take seriously the genuine and unique contribution that a consistently evangelical biblical theology could make. An eclectic approach can never improve on itself; to improve, it must wait on the approaches from which it borrowed.

*Final shape* (Endgestalt). An important focus in recent OT studies has been the growing interest in the theological relevance of the final shape of the biblical text *(Endgestalt)*. That focus has brought evangelicals a step closer to current discussions in OT studies and hence uniquely positioned to make a serious contribution to biblical theology. Evangelicals have always stressed the importance of the text because they believe that it is the only part of the communication chain that is inspired. An evangelical approach that is grounded in a commitment to biblical inspiration is uniquely disposed to

[43]It is hard to project how a "stay the course" approach will fare with future evangelicals. With the help of recent materials focusing on the meaning of texts and language (see Robert-Alain de Beaugrande and Wolfgang Ulrich Dressler, *Introduction to Text Linguistics* [London: Longman, 1981]), one can hope that evangelical biblical scholars and theologians who stay the course will feel compelled to address these difficult questions.

[44]Rudolf Smend, *Die Mitte des Alten Testaments* (BEvT 99; Munich: Kaiser, 1986).

[45]Kraus, *Die biblische Theologie*, pp. 240-53.

place a high value on language, textuality and composition. An evangelical commitment to an inspired text offers a credible basis for a biblical theology that is text-immanent, nondogmatically grounded and is based on the final form of the biblical text.

An important measure of where evangelical OT studies have moved, or may be moving, is the question of the authorship of the Pentateuch. This is also an issue that lies at the heart of a biblical theology of the Pentateuch that is text-focused. In the past, much of the evangelical discussion of the authorship of the Pentateuch focused on this historical question: Who wrote the Pentateuch? In focusing on that question, evangelicals often said little about the literary question of how the Pentateuch was written. As a measure of where evangelicals are on the question of methodology, and as an attempt to understand the various evangelical biblical theologies, I will assume the historical question of who wrote the Pentateuch and raise only the literary question of how evangelicals presently understand the notion of the (Mosaic) authorship of the Pentateuch to work.

Many evangelicals have dismissed the Mosaic authorship of the Pentateuch in an effort to seek greener theological pastures. Since they rightly consider the Pentateuch to be an anonymous work, they make little or no attempt to identify its author. The reasons for holding such a position are many and varied and lie outside our immediate concern. It is safe to say, however, that among evangelical biblical scholars who do not hold to the Mosaic authorship of the Pentateuch, there is a general belief that at least some or much of the material in the Pentateuch can ultimately be traced back to Moses or to credible traditions (oral or written) about Moses. In the past, such views would not have been considered evangelical, and we need not review that history here. Few, however, would deny that status to such evangelicals today, though one gets the impression that even those who take such a position are not entirely comfortable with the view as evangelical. Old habits wear long. This surely is a sign that the issue, which at one time was an undisputed litmus test of evangelical orthodoxy, has been stretched to the point that it is no longer a reliable yardstick. This is not to say that evangelicalism has lowered its standard of doctrinal integrity. It is only to acknowledge that as times change, so do issues, and the question of Mosaic authorship may be reaching the end of its shelf life. As important as the identification of Moses with the author is, an equally important question today is how evangelicals understand the nature of biblical authorship in general and how and to whom they seek to defend those beliefs. In terms of the inspiration and authority of Scripture, an argument against the Mosaic authorship of the Pentateuch may prove more evangelical than an argument for it. The point is that evangelical positions on biblical authorship nowadays have become so nuanced and qualified that a mere affirmation of belief in the Mosaic authorship of the Pentateuch is meaningless without a description of how such a belief would play out and be defended within evangelicalism.

The question to which we now turn is how contemporary evangelicals have understood and conceptualized their beliefs about Mosaic authorship. My goal is not to determine which views are evangelical and which are not, nor is it my purpose to determine which views are correct and which are not. My aim is to uncover the various evangelical approaches to OT theology as they are reflected in evangelical views of Mosaic authorship.

Although among evangelicals today there is not a great volume of work on the Pentateuch and its theology, I will attempt to group together some distinctly evangelical views of Mosaic authorship and highlight the implications of those views for biblical theology.

*Evangelical views of Mosaic authorship. Protestant orthodoxy and Mosaic authorship: Did Moses write the Pentateuch or did he only write it down?* For nearly two centuries, the view of the Mosaic authorship of the Pentateuch held by Protestant orthodoxy was little changed. It was one with the view of the early Reformers. Calvin understood the role of Mosaic authorship in passive terms. As author of the Pentateuch, Moses wrote down what had long been common knowledge among God's people. Moses did not write of "things before unheard of,"[46] but rather "for the first time [he] consigned to writing facts which the fathers had delivered as from hand to hand, through a long succession of years, to their children."[47] As Moses set out to write the Pentateuch, a great body of "revealed" knowledge was at his disposal. This body of knowledge was identical to that which Moses eventually wrote down in the Pentateuch. It had been passed down orally from Adam, through each of the patriarchs (who added to it their own stories), and eventually made its way to Moses, who assigned it completely to written form. Calvin held that Adam

---

[46]John Calvin, *Commentaries on the First Book of Moses Called Genesis*, trans. John King (Grand Rapids: Baker, 1979), p. 58.

[47]Ibid.

was "well-instructed" in the details of creation. Adam, in turn, passed on his knowledge to Noah, and Noah to his sons, and they to Abraham. Hence, Moses "does not propound it as something new, but only commemorates what all held, what the old men themselves had received from their ancestors, and what, in short, was entirely uncontroverted among them."[48] In the view of the Reformers, the need to commit this knowledge to writing arose only out of a concern to preserve it from error, since oral tradition, they believed, was not as secure as written. Unlike their medieval counterparts, Reformers such as Calvin believed that there was nothing inherently inadequate or lacking with this "tradition" in its unwritten form as Scripture. Scripture was Scripture, written or not.

This orthodox view of Mosaic authorship was grounded in an apologetic concern for the Protestant "scripture principle" *(sola Scriptura)*. The Reformers believed that Scripture, not tradition, was divine revelation.[49] Hence, in identifying written Scripture with the "Word of God" (the same, ironically, whether in oral or written form), the Reformers were taking aim at the heart of a central tenet of the Counter Reformation: the notion of an authoritative oral tradition over against Scripture.

In the mid-sixteenth century medieval biblical scholars mounted a major assault on the Reformers' rejection of church tradition. The official position of the medieval church was formulated at the Council of Trent (1546). The position taken by the council laid equal stress on both Scripture and church tradition: "The sacred and holy, ecumenical, and general Synod of Trent . . . following the example of the orthodox Fathers, receives and venerates with an equal affection of piety and reverence, all the books both of the Old and of the New Testament—seeing that one God is the author of both—*as also the said traditions*" (fourth session, April 8, 1546 [italics mine]). The council thus rejected the Protestant principle of the sole authority of Scripture *(sola Scriptura)*.

Perhaps the most capable defender of the medieval position was Robert Bellarmine, in *Disputationum de controversiis Christianae fidei* (1581–1593). What made Bellarmine's arguments particularly telling was not merely that he was a learned and able opponent, but that he launched his attack on the Protestant position from within a clear understanding of that position. Among other things, he understood that the Protestant position rested not

---

[48]Ibid., p. 59.

[49]The term *revelation* as used here is that of special revelation only.

only on Scripture alone, but also solely on Scripture as the written word. In light of that, Bellarmine maintained that the basic flaw in the Protestant position was its failure, within its own understanding of Scripture, to appreciate the central role it had assigned to oral tradition. In essential agreement with the Reformers on the question of the importance of written Scripture, Bellarmine pointed to the long-established Protestant view, noted above, that in writing the Pentateuch, Moses had relied on oral tradition. Moses did not invent the stories in Genesis, nor did he write his books out of his own imagination. Both Catholic theologians and Protestants agreed that from Adam to Abraham and from Abraham to Moses there were as yet no written Scriptures. There was only an unbroken line of authoritative oral tradition. Bellermine believed that what the Reformers had failed to consider in developing their position on Scripture was that oral tradition played the same role that Scripture would later play in offering providential guidance to the church. If during those earlier times the church thrived on oral tradition alone and without written Scripture, it seemed reasonable to conclude that it could continue to do so from Moses to the present.[50] For that reason, it made sense that oral tradition could still play a role in God's economy.

The Protestant response to Bellarmine was successful, but it required a subtle distinction in the meaning of the term *tradition*. Protestant theologians insisted on making a distinction between oral tradition as such, and oral revelation as "unwritten Scripture." Protestants identified the medieval view of pre-Mosaic (oral) tradition with what they understood to be pre-Mosaic (unwritten) Scripture, or primeval revelation *(Uroffenbarung)*.[51] Abraham did not live out his life

[50]"Primum probo ex variis aetatibus Ecclesiae. Nam ab Adam usque ad Mosen fuit Ecclesia Dei aliqua in Mundo. Et colebant homines Deum Fide, Spe, et Charitate, et externis ritibus, ut patet ex Genesi, ubi introducuntur Adam, Abel, Seth, Enoch, Noe, Abraham, Melchisedech, et alii homines justi, et ex Augustino lib. 11. Civit. Dei, et sequentibus ubi deducit Civitatem Dei ab initio Mundi usque ad finem: at nulla fuit Scriptura divina ante Mosem, ut patet, tum quia omnium consensu Moses est primus scriptor sacer: tum quia in Genesi non sit mentio doctrinae scriptae, sed solum traditae, Gen. 18. Scio, inquit Deus, quod Abraham praecepturus sit filiis suis, et domui suae post se, ut custodiant viam Domini. Igitur annis bis mille conservata est religio sola Traditione; non est igitur Scriptura simpliciter necessaria, Quomodo enim conservari potuit antiqua illa religio sine Scriptura ad duo millia annorum, ita potuit doctrina Christi s(c)onservari sine Scriptura ad mille quingentos" (Robert Bellarmine, *Disputationum Roberti Bellarmini: De controversiis Christianae fidei* [Naples: Giuliano, 1856], p. 119).

[51]Paul Althaus, *Die christliche Wahrheit: Lehrbuch der Dogmatik* (Gütersloh: Bertelsmann, 1947), 1:61-62.

in accordance with "early (oral) tradition," as medieval theologians had argued; rather, Abraham lived according to "early (unwritten) revelation" of divine truth, a "prewritten" revelation. Orthodox evangelical scholars believed that Scripture was a revelation identical in every respect to the later written Scriptures, except that, materially, it was not yet in written form. God had not bequeathed to Adam and the fathers an oral tradition; instead, he had revealed himself to the fathers by means of a "primeval" unwritten revelation. It was a revelation that needed only to be committed to writing at a later date. As the author of the Pentateuch, Moses' task was to translate this "unwritten revelation"[52] to written form. What he wrote was verbatim[53] the Pentateuch as it had existed in unwritten form for thousands of years. Writing it down did not change it or make it any more or less the Pentateuch we have today. It was already the Pentateuch in unwritten form. Moses simply committed it to writing.

Much of the polemical theological debate between the Reformers and Rome was shaped by the role assigned to "oral tradition" by the Council of Trent and the Reformers' response to it. It was also the case that much of the "friendly" discussion among the Reformers themselves continued to be shaped by the early formulations and counterarguments against the views of Trent. The Reformers' notion of an unwritten revelation had a lasting effect on the theological landscape of subsequent centuries. It formed the basis of the Protestant orthodox view of Scripture and its relationship to the history recorded in those Scriptures. Without seeing how the notion of primeval revelation played out in Protestant orthodoxy, it is almost impossible to understand the positions taken by evangelical OT scholars such as Hengstenberg, Vos and Kaiser. All three have grounded their approaches to biblical theology in the Protestant orthodox notion of a primeval revelation.

The biblical theology of Geerhardus Vos and its continued reception by contemporary evangelicals show how deeply rooted in evangelical thought are the notion of an unwritten "primeval revelation" *(Uroffenbarung)* and the Protestant "scripture principle" *(sola Scriptura)*. Vos's concept of an unwritten

---

[52]In later discussions of this *Uroffenbarung* Protestant biblical scholars were forced into holding the position that such a "primeval revelation" was no different in kind from the Scriptures themselves. Adam, they insisted, had "Scripture" in its "prewritten" stage. The "Scripture" that Adam had was the same as we now have, though it was not yet written in a book. See Sailhamer, *Introduction to Old Testament Theology*, p. 68.

[53]The view was similar to the early Jewish notion that God created the world following the plan of Genesis 1.

"scriptural" revelation provided him with a crucial link between the written Scriptures and the "historical" world depicted in them. The concept of a primeval unwritten revelation enabled Vos, and many like him, to accomplish the seemingly impossible task of identifying the written Scriptures *(verba)* with the unwritten revelatory events *(res)* of early biblical history. For Vos, it was natural to identify the Scriptures with the primeval history they recorded, as well as with the further history of Israel, right up to the events of the NT. Says Vos, "Biblical Theology deals with the material from the historical standpoint, seeking to exhibit the organic growth or development of the truths of Special Revelation from the primitive preredemptive Special Revelation given in Eden to the close of the New Testament Canon."[54]

There could be no clearer statement of the concept of an *Uroffenbarung*, or primeval revelation. For Vos, special revelation, which evangelical theology has almost always limited to the written Scriptures, extended from the garden of Eden to the end of the NT. Like Calvin, Vos believed that the task of Moses, as the author of the Pentateuch, was to record in writing this unwritten special revelation. In that context, Mosaic authorship of the Pentateuch was important because of the boundaries it provided for special revelation. Linking Mosaic authorship to "primeval revelation" *(Uroffenbarung)* ensured that it would be identified solely with scriptural revelation *(sola Scriptura)*. That being so, it could not extend beyond the writings of Moses and thus become what medieval scholars saw as oral tradition accompanying written Scripture. It was the importance of oral tradition, as opposed to primeval revelation, that medieval biblical scholars were attempting to affirm. As the Reformers understood it, special revelation *(Uroffenbarung)* was identical to the Mosaic Scriptures and not something added to Scripture or merely accompanying Scripture. It was "prewritten" Scripture in oral form.

An important implication of this view is the picture it gives of the role of Moses and the revelatory value of the history of God's dealings with humanity before (and after) him. The role of Moses as author of the Pentateuch was not so much to "write" the Pentateuch as to "write down" the Pentateuch, which was orally already known to him in the exact form we now have it in the written Scriptures. From that viewpoint, the natural assumption is that Abraham would have already had, in oral form, both the substance and the

---

[54]Vos, *Biblical Theology*, p. i. In this, Vos is following Turrettini (see Sailhamer, *Introduction to Old Testament Theology*, p. 68).

material content of the biblical theology that is now reflected in and available as the written narratives of Genesis 1–11. Abraham would have had a very small, unwritten Bible, but it still would have been the Bible we have in our possession today. This means that the Protestant view of Scripture and, consequently, the notion of the Mosaic authorship of the Pentateuch were on a collision course with later views of biblical authorship. Given the nature of the unwritten Pentateuch that Moses "wrote down," the picture of Moses as an author who might have used "sources" would create problems and undermine the notion that he already had a primeval revelation *(Uroffenbarung)* on a par with Scripture. Evangelicals thus were predisposed to rejecting the notion of written sources, which was to become a central plank in the argument of later critical approaches to the Pentateuch.

Walter Kaiser, like many modern evangelicals, follows a similar line of argument. In doing so, he identifies Scripture with primeval, unwritten revelation. The theological and exegetical substance of what is now contained in the Pentateuch was already known, in a prewritten form, by those whose lives are depicted in the Pentateuch. For Kaiser, the pentateuchal theology of the "seed" promised to Eve (Gen 3:15) is unfolded in the "literary" shaping of the flow of events in Genesis 1–11. To demonstrate this, Kaiser uses all the necessary exegetical procedures to explain the meaning of the text of Genesis 1–11. As Kaiser sees it, the early doctrine of the promised seed was already known to those who lived in the "prepatriarchal era" (his term for Gen 1–11). Thus, when God revealed his promise to Abraham in the "patriarchal era," he did so by building on and adding to what he had already revealed to Eve. This early theology on which revelation to Abraham builds is what Kaiser calls "the theology of antecedent Scripture." All revelation is given in the context of previous revelation, ultimately (as Vos also believed) tracing back to the garden of Eden. Abraham thus understands God's words of promise to him, much as one reading a written Pentateuch, because Abraham knew the promises in the context of the theology of the "unwritten Scriptures," Genesis 1–11. Kaiser does not believe that the written text of Genesis 1–11 existed in Abraham's time or when Moses wrote the whole of Genesis as part of the Pentateuch, but he insists that for Abraham and Moses, the unwritten "antecedent Scripture" was there. Abraham knew it and added significantly to it. Abraham knew the meaning and theology of Genesis 1–11 as it now appears in the written Scriptures, even though those parts of the Pentateuch (e.g.,

Gen 1–11) were not recorded in writing until Moses wrote the Pentateuch, long after the time of Abraham. Kaiser writes,

> When Yahweh appeared to Abraham after the patriarch had arrived at Shechem, that ancient word about a "seed" was again revived and now directed to Abraham (Gen. 12:7). . . . Eve had been promised both a "seed" and a male individual. . . . Now the progress of revelation with greater specification elaborated on both the corporate and representative aspects of this promised "seed."[55]

Kaiser's point is more than the notion of progressive revelation, that is, that further revelation was added to what Abraham already knew from oral tradition. Of course, it includes that idea, but for it to work as Kaiser intends, Abraham would have had to have a "textual" understanding of the "ancient word about a 'seed,'" even if still in unwritten form. It had to be "textual" because Kaiser himself derives it from his own exegesis of what is now Genesis 1–11 in written form. Kaiser treats the "ancient word about a 'seed'" known to Abraham not as an isolated "word," but as part of the literary strategy embodied in Genesis 1–11. Kaiser suggests that Abraham would not merely have known about the "seed" promised to Eve through oral tradition, he also would have understood it in the same way we now do, by exegetically following Kaiser's exposition of Genesis 1–11. Abraham, of course, has this "text" only in a "prewritten" (oral) form. Although it was only orally known to Abraham, Kaiser proceeds as if it was already in the shape it now has as part of the Mosaic Pentateuch, that is, as part of the canonical written Scriptures. Before Moses wrote it down, it had what we might call a compositional strategy already in a prewritten (oral) form. It had the same literary structure and compositional features that it later was to have as part of the book of Genesis and the Mosaic Pentateuch. Its meaning was a function of that "prewritten" shape that it would later bring with it when it became part of the Pentateuch. Kaiser thus gives an exposition, or exegesis, of this "prewritten" revelation by giving us an exposition, or exegesis, of the textual strategy it now has in its written form in Genesis 1–11, a written form recorded, but not initiated, by Moses in writing down the Pentateuch. Kaiser explains the "promised seed" in Genesis 1–11 as it was known to Abraham:

> Consequently, "seed" was always a collective singular noun; never did it appear as a plural noun (e.g., as the "sons"). Thereby the "seed" was marked as a unit,

---

[55]Kaiser, *Toward an Old Testament Theology*, p. 88.

> yet with a flexibility of reference: now to the one person, now to the many descendants of that family. This interchange of reference with its implied corporate solidarity was more than a cultural phenomena or an accident of careless editing; it was part and parcel of its doctrinal intention.[56]

Here Kaiser suggests that Abraham understood the "doctrinal intention," that is, the biblical theology, of Genesis 1–11 in the same terms as Moses recorded it centuries later in the early chapters of the Pentateuch. Kaiser's comment that the sense of Genesis 1–11 as Abraham knew it was more than "an accident of careless editing" further suggests that he believes the authorial process by which the Mosaic Pentateuch came into being was already a feature of the narratives of Genesis 1–11 and hence part of the theology of Abraham's antecedent Scripture. Abraham understood the "promise doctrines" in the same way that Moses later recorded them editorially as the author of the Pentateuch. Such a view was possible because Kaiser and Vos, following Hengstenberg, are working under the assumption of the orthodox Protestant notion of an *Uroffenbarung* that envisioned a prewritten, authoritative and meaningful revelation that was identical to Scripture and already in place long before Moses "wrote," or "wrote down," the Pentateuch. The compositional strategy of the Mosaic Pentateuch was there for Abraham to know, though in an unwritten, or "prewritten," form. It was there for Abraham to know because it had been given him as part of the "primeval revelation" to the various individuals whose lives we see depicted in written form in Genesis 1–11.

*The classical model and Mosaic authorship.* Considerable shifts in the Protestant orthodox view of Mosaic authorship were already underway by the late seventeenth century and continued throughout the eighteenth century. Most of the movement was the result of pressures from historical criticism. By the beginning of the nineteenth century, evangelical views of Mosaic authorship had begun to lean more heavily on historical explanations. On the surface, evangelical views of Mosaic authorship were, for the most part, indistinguishable from contemporary critical approaches. What the evangelical view asserted—Moses wrote the Pentateuch—the critical view denied. Whether they affirmed or denied Mosaic authorship, they were in basic agreement about what it was they were affirming or denying. Amidst the scholarly debate and largely unaffected by it, Hengstenberg and those who followed him

---

[56]Ibid., pp. 88-89.

succeeded in winning popular support in their efforts to revive (repristination) the older orthodox view, including its notion of primeval revelation. What became the classical view was forged in the attempt by Hengstenberg to turn back the clock on the increasingly popular historical and critical approaches to the Bible, Mosaic authorship and biblical theology. The classical view that came out of the nineteenth century was a cross between what had survived of Hengstenberg's orthodoxy and what evangelicals believed could safely be borrowed from the increasingly secular historical criticism.

The impetus of the development of the classical model in the early nineteenth century was Hengstenberg's opposition to the historical criticism of Wilhelm de Wette. De Wette, a student of Johann Philipp Gabler at Jena, and a friend and colleague of Schleiermacher at Berlin, has been widely recognized as the instrumental cause of the introduction of "the methods of exact historical-critical study."[57] De Wette's views were characteristic of critical OT scholarship throughout the remainder of the nineteenth century. The immediate question, raised by de Wette, was the christological nature of the OT and its relationship to the NT. The underlying issue was the role of the historical method in biblical theology. De Wette, like Gabler, understood the historical method to call for minimizing the role of faith *(Glaube)* in understanding the past.

In opposition to de Wette, Hengstenberg, following Calvin, believed that faith enters the picture as an affirmation of the truth of what the Bible reveals.[58] If the Bible claims that Moses wrote the Pentateuch, which Hengstenberg believed to be the case, then the task of a "historical method" is to read the Pentateuch as a book written by Moses. Faith meant the conviction that the Bible means what it says. This was not so much an attempt to prove the Bible to be true as it was a means of showing the proper way to understand the Bible and the necessary convictions one must have about the Bible, given its divine authority.

De Wette's historical criticism cast a different light on the importance of faith. In his view, the task of the historian was not to embrace the past in faith, but to make sense of the past that has been handed down to him. For de Wette, faith had little place in the process of understanding historical events. Understanding the past meant using the tools of the historical method

---

[57]Kraus, *Geschichte der historisch-kritischen Erforschung*, p. 174.

[58]Compare Calvin on the internal witness of the Spirit.

to enable one to relive events of the past. For both de Wette and Hengstenberg, this meant relying on eyewitnesses, something about which both theologians had widely divergent views. Hengstenberg understood the notion of eyewitnesses in terms of the orthodox view of "primeval revelation." For de Wette, the quest for eyewitnesses led to a critical evaluation of the early sources in the Pentateuch and to the conclusion that they were written by multiple authors, each dated subsequent to the time of Moses. From that perspective, it was unlikely that Moses could have been the author of the Pentateuch. He would have been older than his sources.

> The opinion that Moses composed these books, is not only opposed by all the signs of a later date, which occur in the book itself, but also by the entire analogy of the history of Hebrew literature and language. But even admitting it was probable, . . . still, even then, it would be absurd to suppose that one man could have created beforehand the epico-historical, the rhetorical and poetic style, in all their extent and compass, and have perfected these three departments of Hebrew literature, both in form and substance, so far that all subsequent writers found nothing left for them but to follow in his steps.[59]

Both Hengstenberg and de Wette believed that they had grounded their views of Mosaic authorship in real "history." Both also had very different views of what that meant. For Hengstenberg, the historical problem of Mosaic authorship of the Pentateuch amounted to a simple question, "Did Moses write the Pentateuch?" It was a factual question. For Hengstenberg, any amount of "proof" that could be brought to bear on the likelihood or possibility of that question was taken as factual "historical" evidence in its favor. As to the exact nature of how Moses wrote the Pentateuch, Hengstenberg had little to offer. For Hengstenberg, Mosaic biblical authorship of a book such as the Pentateuch amounted to the secretarial task of writing down what the forefathers had passed on as "primeval revelation." Hengstenberg believed that anyone who had lived during the events of the "primeval" period and knew the "primeval revelation" could be considered an "eyewitness" to those events, even without having actually "seen" them happen.

For de Wette, unlike Hengstenberg, the historical question was not who wrote the Pentateuch but how was it written. If Hengstenberg had been

[59]Wilhelm M. L. de Wette, *A Critical and Historical Introduction to the Canonical Scriptures of the Old Testament*, trans. Theodore Parker, 5th ed. (Boston: Rufus Leighton, 1859), 2:160-61.

asked, "How was the Pentateuch written?" he would have answered, "It was written by Moses." If de Wette had been asked the same question, he would have answered, "By the use of ancient sources and documents." Had de Wette been asked if Moses wrote the Pentateuch, he would have replied that Moses could not have written the Pentateuch because the sources used in writing the Pentateuch did not yet exist in his time. Had he been asked whether or not the sources of the Pentateuch were historical, he would have answered in the negative because he believed that their age precluded them from having been eyewitnesses to the events of the Bible.

De Wette refused to concede the "historical" nature of Hengstenberg's approach because he sensed that it was grounded in faith, not in a critical view of eyewitness accounts. Hengstenberg believed that since the whole of the Pentateuch was merely the written version of the eyewitness accounts of "primeval revelation," one could say that it was built on the testimony of eyewitnesses and hence met de Wette's criterion of historical fact. Hengstenberg believed that through a long chain of events the biblical eyewitness accounts of primeval revelation were passed on as "unwritten narrative" that was eventually written down by Moses. Moses was not an eyewitness to the early events of the Pentateuch, but he relied heavily on the unwritten eyewitness account of primeval revelation that had been passed down to him. For that reason, Hengstenberg insisted, the Mosaic Pentateuch was a definitive record of the real, historical events of Israel's past.

Hengstenberg believed that the unwritten version of the original "primeval revelation" was an eyewitness account older than Moses. As author of the Pentateuch, Moses' primary task was to commit the ancient oral "primeval revelation" to writing. Hengstenberg believed that what Moses recorded in Scripture *(sola Scriptura)* was historical and based on the eyewitness (unwritten) accounts of biblical events. The whole of the Pentateuch, from Adam to Moses, was "prewritten" and eventually passed on to Moses by eyewitnesses.[60] That meant that as "primeval revelation," the Pentateuch was the work of eyewitnesses and hence should be treated as genuine history. Hengstenberg believed that even after it was recorded in writing by Moses, it continued to enjoy that status.

---

[60]Compare Vos's view of biblical theology as "the organic growth or development of the truths of Special Revelation from the primitive preredemptive Special Revelation given in Eden to the close of the New Testament canon" (*Biblical Theology*, p. v).

If the Scriptures stated that Moses wrote the Pentateuch, Hengstenberg believed that he could take that as a historical fact because the Scriptures were based on eyewitness accounts. This was not because Hengstenberg assumed that the Bible was true; it was because Hengstenberg, and most evangelicals at the time, believed that the Bible in its "prewritten" form was the work of eyewitnesses.[61] The Scriptures, as recorded by Moses in the Pentateuch, were eyewitness accounts of events as early as the garden of Eden. What the written Scriptures recounted as past events, Hengstenberg understood to be written versions of the unwritten eyewitness accounts of those events (e.g., Ex 17). The biblical narratives, as "inscripturated events," are the primary, if not only, means of recovering the eyewitness accounts of revelatory events.

What this meant for Hengstenberg was that biblical history began in "prewritten" versions of the historical narratives, poems, laws and itineraries. Reading the Bible, or the Pentateuch, correctly was not merely reading under the assumption that it was an accurate account of the events it recorded. Though it included that, reading the Bible was an encounter with the actual events that Moses had brought to the reader for the first time in written form. The Bible (Pentateuch) therefore was more than an accurate history of the past. The Bible was that history itself as lived in and recorded by Moses in written form. It preserved the events, even the details of those events, by the

[61]The nature of Hengstenberg's position largely has remained unexplored by those who view him through the eyes of the historical-critical method. John Rogerson, for example, following Gustav Oehler (*Prolegomena zur Theologie des Alten Testaments* [Stuttgart: Liesching, 1845]), cast the difference between Hengstenberg and de Wette in terms of the difference between Hengstenberg's assumption of the historical trustworthiness of Scripture and de Wette's dependence on the negative results of historical criticism. As I have argued above, the difference between the two and the positions they represented went much deeper. It was a debate not, as John Rogerson suggests, between "two sides: the Confessionalists accepted the witness to faith in the Old Testament (as seen through Protestant eyes), assumed the authenticity of the historical narratives in which the witness was expressed, and used scholarship to defend the authenticity of Old Testament writings and history. Those who embraced the critical method approached the Old Testament with a variety of assumptions . . . but they were agreed that the historical-critical method was the basis upon which the 'true' course of Old Testament religion was to be discovered" (*Old Testament Criticism in the Nineteenth Century: England and Germany* [Fortress, 1985], pp. 82-83). That was, to be sure, the way Oehler and other conservatives in the nineteenth century viewed Hengstenberg's opposition to de Wette, but that is not how Hengstenberg himself viewed it, nor was it the heart of the debate. The heart of the debate was Hengstenberg's acceptance of the Protestant orthodox concept of "primeval revelation" as an eyewitness account of early patriarchal religion. Hengstenberg believed that this view, which had once been successful against the Catholic Counter Reformation, could also in his day be applied to de Wette's historical approach. That belief proved untenable.

process of inscripturation. All that one had to do to live out that history and experience its meaning was read the Bible. The nature of the Mosaic authorship of the Pentateuch thus consisted of little more than his "writing down" the "prewritten" primeval revelation *(Uroffenbarung).* To say that Moses wrote the Pentateuch was not to say that he "composed" the Pentateuch, but rather that he recorded what had already been "composed" in unwritten form by eyewitnesses in the gradual progress of the primeval revelation. Any structure or compositional strategy given to the shape of biblical history was not so much the work of Moses as author of the Pentateuch as it was the work of God in shaping the original revelatory history experienced and preserved in unwritten form by eyewitnesses.

Hengstenberg formed his view of biblical history as an attempt to revive the orthodox view of Scripture as primeval revelation. His intent was to block what he viewed as the rival and destructive historical views of de Wette. Hence, as with the orthodox view earlier, the classical model formed by Hengstenberg originated in the debate over the Protestant scripture principle *(sola Scriptura).*

In this debate, the Protestant orthodox view of Scripture clearly was on the line. Unlike the earlier debates in the days of the Counter Reformation, in which each side understood the position of the other side as well as its own, in this debate neither side seemed to understand the other, nor did either side appear willing to address the issues raised by the other. Both sides tried to take the high ground by claiming to be historical. For de Wette, the historical task was to move beyond the biblical text and its theological assertions to the world of the ancient past. De Wette's goal was to follow Schleiermacher in immersing himself in those past events and thus come to experience them firsthand *(Einigkeit).* Only then, he believed, could he understand the Bible as part of its world. De Wette had no desire to know past events as "prewritten" versions of the Bible. His aim was to understand past events as experienced by those to whom they happened.

For Hengstenberg, the real world behind the biblical text looked the same as the events recounted in the Bible (Pentateuch). The biblical narratives, however, are the inscripturation of real past events, not those events themselves. Hengstenberg never seemed to get that point, nor has evangelicalism today. Although they are written records of past events, Hengstenberg believed that they should be approached as the past events themselves, just as they were seen and experienced by the biblical characters. They are prerecorded versions of the events in which Abraham participated as a real person, and in which the reader of the Pentateuch could also participate by reading them. Because they are eyewitness accounts, Hengstenberg believed that the biblical narratives present the events just as they happened in real life; they are "history-like" even though they are textual *(verba)* in nature and thus in reality worlds apart from real events *(realia)*. Thus, Hengstenberg believed that one should understand them as real events, not as written narratives.

The introduction of the historical method, as de Wette understood it, meant an end to the old Protestant orthodox view that Hengstenberg had tried unsuccessfully to revive. Its loss did not put an end to the orthodox claim that the Bible (Pentateuch) was true, but it was a repudiation of the Bible's historical worth as a written version of the past. As Hengstenberg understood it, the historical argument of de Wette was grounded in a theological rejection of Scripture not as history per se, but as inscripturated revelational events—salvation history.

Such discussions within evangelicalism permanently altered the landscape of the question of the Mosaic authorship of the Pentateuch and, more importantly, the nature of biblical theology in texts such as the Pentateuch. At stake was not merely the historical question of who wrote the Pentateuch, but the literary-critical question of what kind of book it was and how one should make sense of its literary focus on historical events. The issue had become not whether Moses could have written the Pentateuch, but whether the Mosaic authorship envisioned by Protestant orthodoxy was viable. Did Moses merely record in written form what was already Scripture (primeval revelation), or did he compose the Pentateuch out of ancient written sources? If so, how ancient were those sources? Did they predate or, as de Wette believed, postdate Moses? Around these questions the lines were drawn for a vigorous debate over the authorship of the Pentateuch. It was a debate over the changing view of how to interpret biblical narratives that depict past events realistically.

Evangelicals after Hengstenberg and before Wellhausen conceded some historically plausible models of Mosaic authorship. They granted the possibility that Moses had used written sources.[62] Not everything in the Pentateuch was "primeval history" *(Uroffenbarung)*. Such concessions were meant

[62]See Sailhamer, *Introduction to Old Testament Theology*, p. 274.

not so much to buttress the historical probability of Mosaic authorship as to add to the historical picture of Moses as an ancient author. It was a way of adding historical realism to the prophetic notion of primeval revelation. What this ultimately would mean for the notion of Mosaic authorship of the Pentateuch was a new openness to the addition of historical details to the biblical picture of Moses, details that in the orthodox view were outside the realm of "primeval revelation" *(Uroffenbarung)*. It thus meant conceding some of the earlier ground won against the Counter Reformation by accepting the existence of a marginal and nonscriptural "tradition" alongside the primeval revelation.[63]

The monumental evangelical commentary on the whole Bible by Robert Jamieson, A. R. Fausset and David Brown readily concedes that "in the composition of those parts of the Pentateuch relating to matters which were not within the sphere of his personal knowledge, Moses would and did avail himself of existing records which were of reliable authority; . . . he interwove them into his narrative conformably with that unity of design which so manifestly pervades the entire Pentateuch."[64]

Under the influence of Hengstenberg, evangelical OT scholarship was increasingly content to rest its case for Mosaic authorship on the grounds of what was believed to be the OT's claims. The assumption was that the Pentateuch made numerous claims to have been written by Moses. Questions about how the Pentateuch was written, which for evangelical scholars had not yielded positive results, were traded for what was left of questions about the historical plausibility of the biblical picture of Moses as author. While conceding some undisclosed form of Mosaic authorship of the Pentateuch, evangelical scholars gave little attention to details about sources or the nature of making biblical books. In the end, concentrating on historical questions, and avoiding such literary questions as de Wette was intent on raising, left the evangelical position ill-prepared to face the challenges from Wellhausen in the next half century. With Wellhausen in the latter third of the nineteenth century, the central question of who wrote the Pentateuch was recast as a question about how the Pentateuch was

[63]It was at this point that the evangelical interest in history found its place, not only as a means of defending the historicity of the Bible but also in filling out the historical details of the narratives themselves.

[64]Robert Jamieson, A. R. Fausset and David Brown, *A Commentary, Critical, Experimental and Practical, on the Old and New Testaments* (Grand Rapids: Eerdmans, 1945), 1:xxxii.

written and when. Evangelical biblical scholars, however, for the most part did not follow Wellhausen. They chose, instead, to draw in their line of defense as close to Hengstenberg as possible. If, in the mid-nineteenth century, there was a conscious attempt to gain new ground in the resurgence of the classical evangelical position on the Mosaic authorship of the Pentateuch, it lay unheeded in a score of erudite, but untranslated, German evangelical volumes responding to the new questions raised by Wellhausen and others.[65] Even today these lay beyond the reach of modern evangelical scholarship. The numerous translations of the works of Hengstenberg are a notable exception.[66] Wellhausen's questions about the Pentateuch received little attention from orthodox evangelical scholarship in the classical period.

In light of its own history, the evangelical view of biblical authorship and its move toward an appreciation of the textual nature of biblical theology face at least three sets of questions. First, it must investigate the smallest segments of the biblical texts, attempting to discover what they tell us about the work and intentions of the biblical authors. What, for example, is the compositional role of small, self-contained narratives such as the building of the city of Babylon in Genesis 11:1-9? How does it fit into the larger strategy of Genesis 1–11? Second, an evangelical position on authorship must uncover how the author of the Pentateuch groups these literary segments, such as the primeval history in Genesis 1–11, into the larger literary units that form the body of the Pentateuch. Third, it must show how larger literary units are combined to form books and whole texts such as the Pentateuch and the OT canon in its totality. Insofar as evangelicals believe the texts of Scripture have authors, they must seek to describe the concrete nature of the authors' compositions, beginning with the smallest segments of the Pentateuch and moving to the level of the whole book.[67]

---

[65]Works by König, Delitzsch, Hävernick.

[66]Some works by Franz Delitzsch were published in translation, but not always as faithful stalwarts in defense of the faith. More often than not they were given as examples of some who went over to Wellhausen's views and the other side. In the foreword to Delitzsch's new commentary on Genesis, the reprint editor felt it necessary to warn the evangelical reader, "While Franz Delitzsch held to certain theories regarding the authorship and text of Genesis, this was done with reservation, and his views on these issues may largely be attributed to the times in which he lived." Whatever his views on biblical criticism were, it is clear that Delitzsch felt it important to respond to Wellhausen's views from the inside.

[67]See John H. Sailhamer, "Exegesis of the Old Testament as a Text," in *A Tribute to Gleason Archer*, ed. Walter C. Kaiser Jr. and Ronald F. Youngblood (Chicago: Moody Press, 1986), p. 293.

*The British model.* British evangelicals have focused considerable attention to alternative models of Mosaic authorship. These models begin with the expectation that biblical books such as the Pentateuch achieved their final form reasonably early, though not necessarily during the lifetime of Moses. The Pentateuch is anonymous. Its content consists of traditional material that is thoroughly Mosaic at its core. The actual "making" of the Pentateuch consisted principally of the task of preserving the Mosaic tradition.

What characterizes the British evangelical model, in contrast to other evangelical approaches, is its willingness to work within contemporary literary-critical assumptions about the use of sources, or documents, in the composition of the Pentateuch. It is from within those assumptions that the British model attempts to arrive at an essentially biblical picture of Mosaic authorship, that is, a picture of the composition of the Pentateuch that is consistent with the sequence of events that make up the biblical history of post-Mosaic Israel. Whether or not it achieves that goal varies among its practitioners. What is essential to the approach is its commitment to carving out an evangelical position "on the merits" as laid out by modern historical-critical method.

To take one example, for Gordon Wenham,[68] Moses is a shadowy figure that emerges only occasionally in the background of his discussion of the authorship of Genesis and the Pentateuch. Wenham concentrates on the nature of the composition of the Pentateuch in traditional literary-critical terms of J (a Yahwistic source) and P (a Priestly source), passing over any identification of Moses as a real author. Wenham's move toward Mosaic authorship, or something close to it, is best seen in his preference for the antiquity of both the P source and the J source, and his viewing these "sources" as primarily fragmentary. Lying behind both the P and the J source materials is a basic narrative framework drawn from analogies to ancient literature. According to Wenham, J gave the book of Genesis and the Pentateuch its final shape, adding occasional comments to parts of the Pentateuch commonly assigned to P.[69] Since it is widely acknowledged that the P material in the Pentateuch provides the broad outline of the book as a whole, early P and J sources would result in an early author (Moses?). Wenham's view has the advantage of working within the framework of contemporary OT scholarship, but it is not too

[68]Gordon J. Wenham, *Genesis 1–15* (WBC 1; Waco, Tex.: Word, 1987).
[69]For example, Genesis 5:29, a J comment on P.

closely tied to current critical views. In the event of a total meltdown of the documentary hypothesis, Wenham could go it alone with his source analysis of the book of Genesis.

*Post-Mosaica (status a quo).* Another evangelical approach to Mosaic authorship of the Pentateuch builds on the classical model (Hengstenberg), including its lack of a clear picture of the process of authorship or the making of the Pentateuch. This view, which may be called the *status a quo* approach, begins with *(a quo)* a Mosaic Pentateuch, written essentially without secondary sources. From that early work, about which we know little, the Pentateuch developed further through minor additions to its original shape. It is essentially the canonical Pentateuch to which has been added numerous minor glosses and comments of non-Mosaic origin. In this view, each gloss reflects its own time of origin,[70] with none acting particularly in concert with the others to form a coherent pattern or theme. The biblical Pentateuch is the Mosaic Pentateuch with a few "post-Mosaic" additions, such as the account of the death of Moses (Deut 34:5) and the mention of the Israelite kingship (Gen 36:31).

This view does not move us beyond the classical concessions to post-Mosaica in the Pentateuch. In fact, it differs little from the classical view of the Pentateuch. It also offers little help in explaining how Moses wrote (or "made") the Pentateuch. In this view, the post-Mosaic parts of the Pentateuch are little more than random glosses and thus are not indicative of a second edition of the Pentateuch. This is the most common evangelical view of Mosaic authorship of the Pentateuch.

*Status a Mosaica.* Recently, Dan Block has revived an earlier theory of the Mosaic authorship of the pentateuchal sources.[71] Moses is the author of the Pentateuch, or at least Deuteronomy, by virtue of the fact that he wrote the sources that were used to make the Pentateuch. In Block's view, yet to be fully developed, Moses' speeches in Deuteronomy constitute the central message of the book of Deuteronomy and are the core around which the whole of Deuteronomy and the Pentateuch were built. The poem in Deuteronomy 32 originally was transcribed and passed along by Moses. Through a process on

[70]Deuteronomy 34, for example, is understood to be post-Mosaic. See Michael A. Grisanti, "Inspiration, Inerrancy, and the OT Canon: The Place of Textual Updating in an Inerrant View of Scripture," *JETS* 44 (2001): 577-98.

[71]Dan Block, "Recovering the Voice of Moses: The Genesis of Deuteronomy," *JETS* 44 (2001): 385-408. In this regard, this view is the same as Richard Simon's "public scribes" view.

which Block does not elaborate, the written "Mosaic sources" were passed on and preserved by later inspired writers for the purpose of making the Pentateuch. Their use of written Mosaic records was similar to God's inspiring Moses to write of events in the book of Genesis. The records used in the writing of the Pentateuch (except Genesis) originated at the time of Moses, but the actual authorship of the Pentateuch occurred at a later time.[72]

*Compositional approach.* An evangelical compositional approach to biblical authorship identifies Moses as the author of the Pentateuch and seeks to uncover his strategy in "making a book." The author's intent is reflected in that strategy. In this view, the Mosaic Pentateuch is understood as the original version of the canonical Pentateuch. As far as we know, the Mosaic Pentateuch is identical with the canonical Pentateuch with few exceptions. Those exceptions consist of parts of the Pentateuch that likely were not the work of Moses. A notable example is the account of the death of Moses in Deuteronomy 34 and Moses' final words in Deuteronomy 33. Such comments, though originally spoken by Moses, were added late in Israel's history, likely as part of a "new edition" of the Pentateuch ("Pentateuch 2.0," in the lingo of today's computer world). Contrary to the prevailing view of biblical authorship, both critical and evangelical, the compositional approach suggests that the Pentateuch was not the product of a long and complex process of literary growth, but rather is something that comes to us as a more or less updated edition of a single earlier (Mosaic) composition. The present canonical Pentateuch is thus an updated version of the Mosaic Pentateuch produced, perhaps, by the "author" of the OT as a whole (Tanak). The canonical identification of Moses as the author of an early book does not merely assume the historical reality of these texts, but it does take seriously their place and importance within the canonical seams. Very clearly in those seams Moses is credited with the authorship of a "Torah book" immediately after his death (Josh 1:8) and within the last prophetic words given to Israel (Mal 4:4 [3:22 MT]). Subsequent biblical narratives view the "book of Moses" as having dropped from sight early in Israel's history (Josh 2:10) and then later discovered during repairs to the temple (2 Kings 22:8).

The grounds for dating the composition of the "canonical" Pentateuch late in Israel's history lie partly in the numerous glosses and comments that have

---

[72]König held this view, as did Astruc. See Eduard König, *Einleitung in das Alte Testament: mit Einschluss der Apokryphen und der Pseudepigraphen Alten Testaments* (SThH 2/1; Bonn: Weber, 1893).

found their way into the present Pentateuch. Those glosses show an awareness of an earlier version of the Pentateuch in some need of explanation (see Gen 13:10). Their purpose looks to a strategy aimed at providing just that sort of explanation or commentary. A notable example is the Pentateuch's interpretation of Balaam's oracles in light of events forecast in Daniel 11:30. The expositional nature of the expanded material in Balaam's early poems (Num 24:24) suggests that his words were being explained and brought up to date as commentary within the Pentateuch as a whole.[73] These kinds of comments suggest that the shape of the first Pentateuch was essentially the same as the present canonical one, though in some need of further exposition; Scripture requires commentary. The context is reminiscent of passages such as Nehemiah 8:1-8 and 2 Chronicles 17:7-9, where it proved necessary to send out those who understood Scripture (Torah) and could teach it to others. The distribution of theologically dense poetic commentary in the Pentateuch (Gen 49; Num 24; Deut 33) follows a similar distribution and pattern laid down by the ancient poems they are intending to explain (Gen 48; Num 23; Deut 32). One set of poems (Gen 48; Num 23; Deut 32) is explained by another set (Gen 49; Num 24; Deut 33).

In a similar example from the pentateuchal narratives, the last chapter of the Pentateuch (Deut 34) appears to be a theological comment on the identity of the "prophet like Moses" (Deut 18) that anticipates a temporary end to prophecy and a closing of the OT canon. This interesting commentary at the close of the canonical Pentateuch suggests that Deuteronomy 18 was at one time part of an earlier Pentateuch whose wording was in some need of commentary on the identity of the "prophet like Moses." The statement in Deuteronomy that "the prophet like Moses never came" (Deut 34:10) suggests that it reads Deuteronomy 18 as a reference to a future individual prophet. These explanatory comments found within the seams give the Tanak its present shape and reflect the same understanding of Deuteronomy 18 as some NT texts (e.g., Acts 3:22; 7:37). Not only does the last chapter in the Pentateuch record the death of Moses and his burial, but also it makes the sweeping claim that "no prophet like Moses ever arose again" in Israel. The scope of such a comment reflects the viewpoint of one who knows Israel's history from its beginning to its end. It is the view of one for whom the whole of Is-

[73]For a more detailed discussion of these texts see John Sailhamer, "Creation, Genesis 1–11, and the Canon," *BBR* 10, no. 1 (2000): 89-106.

rael's prophets have come and gone, each having been dismissed without a word identifying him as the "prophet like Moses." This is the viewpoint of one who knows Scripture and is intent on interpreting Scripture from that perspective. It is the viewpoint of one who sees a genuine continuity between the ancient (Mosaic) Pentateuch and its canonical *Endgestalt*. The shape and compositional strategy of the Mosaic Pentateuch is preserved by its canonical commentary.[74] Who better to interpret Scripture than the author of Scripture in its totality?

Essential to a compositional approach is its view of the relationship of the individual comments within the Pentateuch to the Pentateuch as a whole. Those comments are not random bits of data intended to clarify isolated features of the text. On the contrary, these comments can be correlated with other similar comments and linked to the central themes and compositional strategies of the Pentateuch. As such, these comments can be taken as the work of a single author,[75] one who understands the shape and strategy of the Mosaic Pentateuch as well as the theology that emerges from that strategy. These numerous comments suggest that the canonical Pentateuch did not originate in a gradual process of redaction or literary expansion. They are, rather, evidence of intelligent design behind the whole of its present shape and appear to have originated during a single period. They reflect strategy rather than strata. They are an intentional and sympathetic "retrofit" of the original Mosaic Pentateuch. It was a remake in the sense that it preserved the original Pentateuch by retrofitting it to the Scriptures as the Tanak.

The account of the death of Moses in Deuteronomy 34:5 can be understood in light of this stage of composition. Given what we know about Israel's history at the time of Moses, one can imagine that at the time of the composition of an original Pentateuch there were no other biblical texts. The Mosaic Pentateuch was all there was of Scripture in a canonical sense. The Pentateuch would have been intended to be read alone, within its own context. By the time of the "Pentateuch 2.0" edition, most, if not all, of the Scriptures were complete. They would have included the literary productions of the prophetic scribes and wisdom literature. Also by that time, the gathering and shaping of the various books of Scripture into a canonical

[74]See Sailhamer, *Introduction to Old Testament Theology*, pp. 239-52.

[75]I do not have in mind here the obvious comments about something that still exists "until this day," which led some to conclude that the Pentateuch had left few signs of its compositional origins.

whole would have been well underway. We know from reading the prophetic (and wisdom) books not only that their authors were well-versed in the Mosaic Pentateuch as a literary text, but also that the compositional seams of books such as Proverbs often were modeled after and built on the compositional seams of the Pentateuch. The introductory words about Agur in Proverbs 30:1-2 are clearly linked to Balaam's introduction in Numbers 24:3. Prophecy becomes wisdom until the return of a future prophet—a common theme found along the seams of the OT canon.[76] Most of these early canonical books themselves had grown out of the close study of the Mosaic Pentateuch and represented an ongoing attempt of these prophetic authors to apply its lessons to the changing situations in their day. The purpose of this prophetic and wisdom retrofit of the Mosaic Pentateuch was to preserve the original Mosaic Pentateuch by recasting and positioning it within the growing body of Scriptural literature (books) that was to become the canonical OT. The final canonical Pentateuch was thus a decisive step toward the formation of the OT canon in its totality (Tanak).

The canonical Pentateuch concludes with Deuteronomy 34:5-12, the notice of the death and burial of Moses. In the Hebrew canon Deuteronomy 34 is linked to the beginning of the book of Joshua and the Former Prophets. Compositionally, the final form *(Endgestalt)* of the Pentateuch is an important part of the final form of the Tanak. This raises the question of the relationship of the new canonical edition of the Pentateuch to the work of one or more of the prophetic authors of the rest of Scripture. Hendrik Koorevaar, among others, argues that the author of Chronicles, the final book in many versions of the OT canon (Tanak), was the "author" of the OT canon in its entirety.[77] In Deuteronomy 33:4 Moses the prophet (Deut 34:10) is credited with giving God's commandments to Israel, just as Ezra 9:10-11 credits the prophets with carrying out the same task. The work of this anonymous prophetic author might well be similar to that of the Chronicler, who also recasts and retrofits Samuel and Kings within a more recent biblical-theological context.

In its view of the shaping of the Mosaic Pentateuch, the compositional approach does not differ significantly from the classical evangelical view. It

---

[76]For example, Joshua's spirit of prophecy in Num 27:18 becomes a spirit of wisdom in Deut 34:9.

[77]Hendrik J. Koorevaar, "Die Chronik als intendierter Abschluss des alttestamentlichen Kanons," *JETh* 11 (1997): 42-76.

sees an original Mosaic Pentateuch with several important post-Mosaic additions. Where the compositional view differs from the classical view is in its attempt to point to meaningful interrelationships between the Mosaic Pentateuch ("1.0" version) and the canonical Pentateuch ("2.0" version). The present canonical Pentateuch is the same Pentateuch as the Mosaic one, though it is a more recent edition of that Pentateuch and has been refitted (retrofitted) with new "prophetic extras" designed with its new canonical environment in mind. The new Pentateuch interfaces with the rest of the OT canon. It is intertextual and front-loaded with connectivity to the rest of Scripture. The meaning of the rest of Scripture (Tanak) is scripted at the beginning in the narrative of Genesis 1–11.[78] Much had happened since Moses wrote the Pentateuch, and the new edition intended to bring its readers into the conversation and in touch with the future of God's work with Israel and the nations. For the most part, the new edition replicates the original Mosaic Pentateuch, but it has a wider screen. Rather than reading the Pentateuch from the viewpoint of the beginning of Israel's history, as no doubt was intended in the original Pentateuch, the new edition looks at the Pentateuch from the perspective of the end of Israel's history and God's continuing work with Israel and the nations. The "beginning times" have become a prophetic picture of the "end times"; the last days are like the first days. This new canonical context is a reflection of the viewpoint of both the biblical prophets and the sages who came at the close of Israel's history. In that sense, the canonical Pentateuch is a prophetic rewrite of the Mosaic Pentateuch.

The value of a compositional approach is that it takes seriously the statements within the Bible regarding Moses as the author of a book (e.g., Josh 1:8), at the same time acknowledging that the canonical Pentateuch contains material and insights that are much later than Moses.

The aforementioned examples of post-Mosaica in the Pentateuch are evidence of the new viewpoint of the canonical Pentateuch. The death of Moses and the list of "kings who reigned in Israel" (Gen 36:31) are recounted in the canonical Pentateuch without a hint of a sense of anachronism. This is because the late viewpoint of the present Pentateuch itself is part of its compositional strategy. As I have suggested, the canonical Pentateuch sees itself within the context of the end of Israel's history and the beginning of God's

[78]Similar to the introduction of Isaiah 1 to the rest of the book of Isaiah.

work with the nations. It intends to be a comprehensive overview of the whole of history, not just its beginnings under Moses at Sinai. Thanks to the author of the book of Daniel and the prologue provided by Genesis 1–11, the Sinai covenant and its laws are now viewed within the scope of the history of the world and all of creation. The "rest of the story" is more than a rerun of the Mosaic Pentateuch; it is a reflective memoir of the life of Moses and an honest critique of Israel's common humanity in Adam. To be sure, this "new" evaluation of Moses and Sinai itself was drawn from the prophetic Scriptures that had taken their place alongside the Mosaic Pentateuch as its interpreters. Those prophetic Scriptures themselves were a product of the Mosaic Pentateuch. They were the work of nameless prophets who had read and studied the Mosaic Scriptures "day and night" (Josh 1:8) and were much aware of its continuing relevance.

To have ignored this "effective history" of the Pentateuch and have kept only the immediate perspective of the Mosaic Pentateuch, which focused on the Sinai covenant and not also the new covenant, would have meant a continual rereading of the canonical Pentateuch solely within the context of the original covenant at Sinai. It would have been meant as a kind of "planned obsolescence" for the Pentateuch as Scripture and thereby would have predestined it to the hermeneutical chop shop of Wellhausen.

In light of the increasingly pessimistic viewpoint of the prophets regarding the Sinai covenant, merely restating the originally positive aspects of that covenant would have unnecessarily isolated it from the rest of Israel's history and from the prophetic Scriptures' own inspired evaluation of that history. It would have been unnecessary because the Mosaic Pentateuch already contained the seeds of the prophet's pessimism regarding Sinai.[79] It also would have permanently linked the Pentateuch to the Sinai covenant (contra 1 Sam 15:22-23) and suggested that the Pentateuch eventually would become obsolete with the passing of that covenant. As it now stands, the present canonical Pentateuch is not, and should not, without further reflection, be identified with the Sinai covenant (cf. Deut 29:1). On the contrary, the present Pentateuch presents itself as a revisiting of that covenant and a consequent reevaluation of it in light of the prophetic hope of a new covenant (Jer 31:31). Although the hope for a new covenant was already an essential

---

[79]Compare the response to the Pentateuch in 2 Kings 22.

part of the Mosaic Pentateuch (Deut 30:6), without a reading of the Pentateuch within the context of the message of the prophets and the new covenant, there remained a clear and present danger of that message not being heard. As Ezra 7 and Nehemiah 8 show, the Pentateuch remained, and still remains, in need of interpretation by "those who understand it." Even the prophets recognized a need for the clarification and explanation of their message (cf. Dan 9). It is here we should put the author of the book of Hebrews, who in the same way uses the OT Scriptures (Jer 31) as a critique of the "old covenant" and the basis of his hope for a future grounded in the "new covenant" (e.g., Heb 8:13).[80]

The compositional approach explains the appearance of the prophets and their message not by assuming that they were religious geniuses,[81] but rather by noting the simple fact that they had been, as Joshua 1:8 admonishes, reading the Mosaic Pentateuch "day and night" and feeling God's call on their lives from within its perspective of hope and divine grace.

An important additional feature of a compositional approach to the Pentateuch is its attempt to describe the theological payoff of the Pentateuch's composition and to locate it within the parameters of the whole book. It also differs, as I have suggested, in its view of the nature of the canonical Pentateuch. The present canonical Pentateuch is the same book as the Mosaic Pentateuch in the sense that it is a preservation of that original Pentateuch within the context of Scripture and canon. This means that in the canonical Pentateuch we are invited to read the Mosaic Pentateuch within its own effective history, or as Geiger would put it, within its own internal development *(Entwickelung)* within Ur-Judaism and Ur-Christianity.[82] There are not two Pentateuchs in the HB, the one Mosaic and the other canonical.[83] There is only one, the canonical Pentateuch. In the OT canon, the Mosaic Pentateuch has become the canonical Pentateuch. The OT canon does not aim merely to provide us with a Mosaic Pentateuch to satisfy our historical curiosity. The canonical Pentateuch is the Mosaic Pentateuch to the extent that it is by means of the canonical Pentateuch that the original Mosaic Pentateuch has been preserved and interpreted.

---

[80]Paul also does this in Romans 10.

[81]The view of Wellhausen and Kuenen.

[82]Geiger, *Urschrift und Übersetzungen der Bibel.*

[83]As there are two histories of Samuel-Kings and Chronicles.

## How Then Did Moses "Make" the Pentateuch?

As I noted earlier, the nature of the composition of the Pentateuch is similar to that of the books of Samuel and Kings, as well as the Gospels. Moses used written texts that he gathered from various sources and provided them with commentary, much like a modern producer of a documentary film.

Some aspects of the compositional approach's view of the making of the Pentateuch are similar to the views of earlier evangelical scholars Robert Jamieson, A. R. Fausset and David Brown in their commentary on the OT (ca. 1863). They say in their discussion of the Pentateuch, "It may be conceded that . . . Moses would and did avail himself of existing records which were of reliable authority; . . . he interwove them into his narrative conformably with the unity of design which so manifestly pervades the entire Pentateuch."[84] The compositional view is specifically stated in Louis Gaussen's remarkably lucid comment on biblical authorship: "Whether [the biblical authors] describe their own emotions, or related what they remember, or repeat contemporary narratives, or copy over genealogies, or make extracts from uninspired documents—their writing is inspired, their narratives are directed from above."[85]

This way of framing the question of authorship represents the widely held evangelical view from as early as the late seventeenth and early eighteenth centuries. Campegius Vitringa describes, almost in modern terms, Moses' procedure in making the Pentateuch. According to Vitringa, Moses collected various written documents, sorted them, and prepared them for use by filling in missing details and sections from other documents. These he then "made" (*confecisse* [*conficio*]) into the Pentateuch. It was, he suggests, a process of "collecting, sorting, preparing, and, where they are lacking, filling out and making from them the first of his books."[86]

---

[84]Jamieson, Fausset and Brown, *Old and New Testaments*, 1:xxxii.

[85]Louis Gaussen, *The Divine Inspiration of the Bible*, trans. David D. Scott (Grand Rapids: Kregel, 1971), p. 25.

[86]"Has vero schedas & scrinia patrum, apud Israelitas conservata, Mosen opinamur collegisse, digessisse, ornasse, &, ubi deficiebant, complesse, atque ex iis primum libroruni suorum confecisse" (Campegius Vitringa, *Sacrarum observationum libri quatuor* [Franeker, 1700], p. 35). Note Fausset's veiled citation of Vitringa's view of Mosaic authorship: "arranging, abridging, selecting, and adapting them to his purpose" (Jamieson, Fausset and Brown, *Old and New Testaments*, 1:xxxi). Since the rise of biblical and historical criticism in the nineteenth and twentieth centuries, the conservative position has, understandably, shied away from talking about "sources" or "written records." But, if pressed, this remains the view of most American evangelical OT scholars today. The only variation on this is that many hold that the "sources" available to Moses were not yet written. Moses relied on oral tradition. This not only fails to deal adequately with the realities

In a compositional view, passages such as Deuteronomy 34 are considered important pieces of compositional strategy that support and light up the meaning of the Mosaic Pentateuch. They provide vital clues to how authors at the end of the biblical period (ca. 300 B.C.) understood the Pentateuch. The addition of such formative parts of the Pentateuch was not an afterthought. On the contrary, it was part of a larger compositional strategy that spanned the whole of the OT canon (Tanak). To understand the theology of the Pentateuch, one does well to pay close attention to that strategy. The canonical composition of the Pentateuch *(Endgestalt)* was shaped by, and grounded in, a developed messianic hope already embodied in a Mosaic Pentateuch at a "grassroots" level. Not only do the comments about a future prophet in Deuteronomy 34 reflect on and interpret Deuteronomy 18, but also they are echoed by the same kind of comments lying along the seams of the Tanak as a whole. Those seams are found in Joshua 1; Malachi 4 (3 in HB); Psalms 1–2; 2 Chronicles 36.[87]

Such textual features suggest that during the pre-Christian period there was already considerable discussion about the meaning of the whole of the HB (Tanak). Judging from the theologically motivated themes we find expressed in these canonical seams, we may conclude that those discussions often turned on the question of the messianic and biblical theological import of crucial parts of the HB.[88]

The common assumption has been that the shape of the OT canon is a function of its historical development or growth. As each inspired book was written, it was added to an established list of canonical books. It was that order which came to be the final accepted shape of the OT canon.[89] In such

---

of the text itself, but also introduces an unnecessary level of uncertainty into the process. Where would we be today in NT studies if we believed that the Gospels were written from "oral sources"? See Sailhamer, *Introduction to Old Testament Theology*, p. 274.

[87]An additional element of this (compositional) approach is its sensitivity to the layers of "postbiblical" (and therefore secondary and uninspired) interpretation that accompanied and many times found its way into the Tanak itself. Here I have in mind the version of the HB that lies behind the earliest editions of the OT, such as the Hebrew *Vorlage* of the LXX, the Hebrew texts among the Dead Sea Scrolls, and some parts of the MT (e.g., Jeremiah).

[88]For example, is Numbers 24:7 about Agag or Gog (see *BHS* apparatus ad loc.; cf. Ezek 38:17-18; see also, in chap. 2 below, "The Coming Eschatological King"), and is the "anointed one" of 2 Samuel 23:1-7 David or the Messiah (see Sailhamer, *Introduction to Old Testament Theology*, p. 221)?

[89]Among evangelicals, this view has been ably argued and defended by Herbert Edward Ryle (1899) and developed further by Gleason Archer. The beginnings of the historical-critical method can be traced first to Counter-Reformation attacks on the autonomy of the Protestant canon and then to

a view, there would have been little expectation, if any, of a conscious reflection on the meaning of the shape of the OT canon.

In recent years, the question has been raised of whether the present (canonical) form is more than the end result of an historical process. Is the present shape of the OT theologically relevant? Is its shape a reflection of its framers' theological convictions and their understanding of the OT as a whole?[90] The OT canon represents a considerable amount of work and attention devoted to viewing the OT as a whole. It is likely that such efforts were motivated by a single theological vision.

Much of the recent interest in the "final shape" of the OT as a whole has been stirred by new evidence of variant canonical shapes in the biblical texts at Qumran (the Dead Sea Scrolls) and by reassessments of existing evidence regarding the formation of the OT canon in general. According to many biblical scholars, interpretation of the "hard evidence" for both the traditional view and various recent views has reached something of an impasse. The external historical witnesses to the process of canonization of the OT are remarkably silent about important factors of their history, apart from the fact that they are often open to conflicting interpretations. Some have suggested that we must go back to the drawing board and view afresh the internal evidence from the OT texts to see whether there is in them any literary and canonical shaping that might suggest a theological motive. It is ultimately from those texts alone that we must begin to discover the meaning of the OT that lies behind the various shapes of the OT canon. As H. G. L. Peels concludes,

> There is reason to say, in our opinion, that the external evidence concerning the closing phase of the history of the Old Testament canon offers us insufficient information for making definitive judgments. This does not mean that in the meantime we must therefore simply give up. Alongside the study of the external witnesses of the history of the canon, to which up until now a great deal of energy has been devoted, interest in the internal evidence pertaining to the history of the canon has grown in recent years. Perhaps up until now there has been far too little of it. Does the canon of the Old Testament itself deliver signals of an intended close? Was there a purposeful final redaction not only of the individual books but also of the books of the Old Testament as a whole?

---

Enlightenment attacks on the tradition behind the same canon. Until recently, conservatives, or orthodox, theologians often sought refuge in the relative stability of the OT canon.

[90]Evangelicals such as Hengstenberg and Delitzsch had raised this question, but it was soon lost behind the historical interest in the growth of the HB.

> Is it possible to trace the "redactional glue" between the different sections of the canon? Hopefully, as we seek to answer this kind of question, fresh light will fall on the final phase of the history of the Old Testament canon.[91]

Peels takes us to the heart of our question. As he suggests, we must raise the question of the specific shape of the OT Scriptures at the time of their formation as such and ask if that shape reflects a consistent line of interpretation. Is there an "intelligent design" or purpose reflected in the final shape of the OT Scriptures as a whole? If so, what is the sense of that design? Does the shape of the OT (Tanak) play into the shape and meaning of the various parts of OT books such as the Pentateuch? Is there a meaningful design and shape to the OT Scriptures?

There are at least three ways one can track "intelligent design" in the present shape of the OT canon. The first way is to look at the shape of the OT canon itself. What was the final shape *(Endgestalt)* given the OT canon (Tanak) at the time of the formation of the canon? The second way is to look at what theological forces and textual strategies lie behind the formation of the Hebrew OT's present shape.[92] A third way is to note the theological nature of the latest sections of the Pentateuch—for example, Deuteronomy 33–34, which presuppose the death of Moses and span the entire scope of the canon.

Much has been said about how Jesus read his OT Bible. Too little has been said, however, about the nature and shape of the Bible he read. It is unlikely that someone in his day would have had a single, complete copy of the entire HB, at least in the sense of our OT today. A single biblical scroll could contain, at most, a book the size of Isaiah. In Jesus' day, one would not likely carry around an entire OT. We can assume that Jesus had access to all the books in the complete Bible, and we can assume he knew the Bible in its entirety and probably also as an entirety. There was likely a complete copy of the Hebrew OT on hand in some synagogues (see Lk 4:17) and in the Jerusalem

[91]H. G. L. Peels, "The Blood 'from Abel to Zechariah' (Matthew 23,35; Luke 11,50f.) and the Canon of the Old Testament," *ZAW* 113 (2001): 600-601.

[92]"Therefore, the discovery and circumscription of this and similar tools of literary craftsmanship, because of their very technical nature, may provide more objective means for tracing the composition and literary history of a given unit or 'book,' and possibily of the canon as a whole, than appears to be the case with other historico-critical methods, such as 'source criticism,' which, to a degree, are based on impressionistic criteria" (Shemaryahu Talmon, "The Presentation of Synchroneity and Simultaneity in Biblical Narrative," *Scripta Hierosolymitana* 27 [1978]: 17).

temple.[93] But for someone in his day, the impossible logistics of handling all the necessary manuscripts would have fundamentally altered what it meant to read the whole Bible.

In terms of everyday realities, the OT at that time did not have a specific physical shape. Multiple copies of the whole or parts of the HB were not widely available, even in fragmentary form, much less single manuscripts or whole books (codices). Such things were a physical reality only much later, from the time of the development of the codex, or single book. Any talk of a specific shape of the OT canon at that time would necessitate approaching it not in terms of its physical reality, but as a mental construct.

Regardless of its lack of physical shape, the OT likely was construed in terms that reflected a "semantic shape" and a theological profile. The OT would have been akin to the unassembled pieces of a jigsaw puzzle still in the box. As with the picture of the puzzle on the box, one could have a mental construct of how the pieces fit together, and that construct would be a way of showing the meaning of the individual pieces within the whole. Given the mental force of such a construct, a physical copy of the OT canon would have been unnecessary.

Such a mental construct played a key role in understanding the individual pieces of the OT puzzle. A mental construct was just as important, or more so, than the actual physical shape of the OT canon. The meaning of each piece was largely determined by this construct. Understanding the OT and its parts was a function of such a construct. An individual reader would have read perhaps only a small fragment of a text, yet he or she could have understood it from within the larger context of this mental construct. Like a piece of a jigsaw puzzle, the section of Scripture made sense as part of, and even physically apart from, a larger whole.

At some point early in its history, theologically important agreements were reached about the proper shape (or shapes)[94] of the OT. At least an informal reading sequence was drawn up. From that sequence and shape, one can now draw certain conclusions about its meaning.

Judging from the present shape of the OT, there probably was little debate about where to locate its beginning. It is likely that all agreed on Genesis 1:1 as the most appropriate starting point. Along with this, I will suggest below

---

[93]Tov, *Textual Criticism of the Hebrew Bible*, pp. 32-33.

[94]When speaking of the OT canon, we must not limit its shape to a single form. There probably were several forms and shapes to the HB during these early stages of its development.

that the first word in the Pentateuch, "the beginning," is closely linked to the three major poems in the Pentateuch whose introductions begin with the word "the end."

A greatly debated question about the shape of the Pentateuch and the OT as a whole has focused on where to locate the ending of both the Pentateuch and the OT. I have suggested already that the book of Daniel played a crucial role in discussions about the end of the OT, and in particular, the passage about the "Messiah" in Daniel 9:25-26.

Also playing an important role is the canonical location of the book of Chronicles within the OT (Tanak). Was Chronicles to be read before the book of Psalms, where it occurs in many OT lists and manuscripts, or was it to be read as the last book in the HB? This question ultimately was reduced to whether the HB should end with Ezra-Nehemiah, considered one book, or with the book of Chronicles. Both locations are represented in the early versions of the OT canonical order.

Ezra-Nehemiah and Chronicles contain duplicate versions of the edict of Cyrus—the command to return and rebuild Jerusalem. In the Bible, this event is understood as a defining moment for the people of God. It was a new beginning, and it signified a return to a position of divine blessing. In Daniel 9:25 the edict is identified as a "word to rebuild Jerusalem."

Thus, the edict of Cyrus falls, compositionally, both at the beginning of the book of Ezra-Nehemiah and at the end of Chronicles. If the "word to rebuild Jerusalem" in Daniel 9 is identified with Ezra-Nehemiah's citation of the edict of Cyrus, then the Messiah of Daniel 9:24 would be reduced to a symbol of those who returned from Babylonian captivity. The fulfillment of Daniel 9 would then be realized in the reforms and rebuilding of Jerusalem in the postexilic period. That would amount to a "historical" fulfillment of Daniel's messianic vision.

If, on the other hand, Daniel 9 is linked to Cyrus's edict at the close of Chronicles, and thus at the end of the Tanak, its fulfillment would not be linked to the return from Babylon, but would lie open to a new and undefined future. Such a view of the end of the OT is consistent with Daniel 9:25-26, which sees the fulfillment of Jeremiah's "seventy years" not in the events of the return from exile, but in the coming of a "messiah" *(māšîaḥ)* after many "weeks of years." Fulfillment is cast in terms of a personal messiah and a distant future.

All of this suggests that at this early stage in the formation of the HB there may have already been contending views about the meaning of the OT as a whole. Different shapes of the OT canon reflect different views on the OT. According to the view that placed Ezra-Nehemiah last in the canon, the events of the return from exile were the resolution and final act in Israel's "biblical past." According to the view that placed Chronicles last, there was still much more waiting to come in Israel's "biblical future." Those who assigned the book of Chronicles to the position preceding the book of Psalms at the beginning of the third part of the OT canon apparently were satisfied with an understanding of Jeremiah's prophecies of seventy years as fulfilled at the time of the return from Babylonian exile. Those who positioned the book of Chronicles (and thus the edict of Cyrus) as the last book of the OT Bible appear to have understood its last words as a pointer to a still relevant future that could rightly (given Dan 9:25-26) be called "messianic."

These two arrangements of the OT canon may also be connected to other features of the HB such as the well-known problem of the two versions of the book of Jeremiah.[95] In one version of the book (MT), Jeremiah's prophecy of seventy years of captivity is related to the destruction of Jerusalem by Nebuchadnezzar. The MT of Jeremiah identifies the completion of the seventy years of captivity with the fall of Babylon and the rise of the Persian Empire: "Behold, I will send for all the tribes of the north, says the LORD, and for Nebuchadrezzar the king of Babylon, my servant, and I will bring them against this land and its inhabitants, and against all these nations round about; I will utterly destroy them, and make them a horror, a hissing, and an everlasting reproach" (Jer 25:9). Another version of the book of Jeremiah (LXX *Vorlage*) connects Jeremiah's seventy years to an invasion of a mighty nation from the north. In that version there is no mention of Israel's historical enemies, Nebuchadrezzar or Babylon: "Behold, I [the Lord] will send for the tribe of the north, and I will bring them against this land and its inhabitants, and against all the nations round about; I will utterly destroy them, and make them a horror, a hissing, and an everlasting reproach" (Jer 25:9). The version

[95]"Most of the omissions in the Greek seem to demand a shorter form of the Hebrew text. The discoveries of the DSS at Qumran have revealed MS fragments of both the longer and the shorter forms of the text. The Hebrew MS (4QJerb) follows the shorter text appearing in the LXX. This has confirmed a tentative judgment, long held by textual critics, that there was more than one recension of the Book of Jeremiah. It best explains the existing difficulties" (Charles L. Feinberg, *Jeremiah* [Grand Rapids: Zondervan, 1982], p. 16).

represented in the Hebrew *Vorlage* of the LXX looks beyond the events of the immediate return from exile. Just as in Daniel 9, the completion of the seventy years lies in the distant future.

Neither version of the canonical OT (Tanak) continues the course of Israel's history beyond the return from Babylonian exile. Both end far short of the conclusion of the history of Israel. At the close of the OT, Israel's history is just getting back on track. Although that history will continue for several hundred years, from a biblical perspective, it is passed over in nearly complete silence.[96] It passes by without notice from the OT canonical Scriptures. There are many histories of Israel that continue their story, but the OT is not one of them.

According to the version of the Tanak that ends with Ezra-Nehemiah, there are no significant events expected in Israel's subsequent history. The future, so far as it can be made out of the biblical texts, will be either a continuation of the present or an extension of the past. In the version of the Tanak that ends with Chronicles, the next biblical events are to be the coming of the Messiah (Dan 9:25), the death of the Messiah (Dan 9:26) and the destruction of the temple (Dan 9:26b). These events, all taken from Daniel 9, are projected on to the screen of the future by 2 Chronicles 36 at the close of the Tanak. Those events take us directly into the first century.

These observations raise the question of why neither version of the OT seems especially interested in continuing Israel's history. Some would say that the OT concludes where it does because prophecy had ceased just at that point.[97] There were no more prophetic voices to carry on either a new course of events or the writing of their history. This explanation may be true, but if so, it is not the whole truth.

Something more near the truth may be connected to the fact that the ending of the OT is fixed by its reference to Daniel 9, the last great prophetic word recorded in the Tanak. This is the prophecy of Daniel's seventy weeks (Dan 9). In that prophecy it is explicitly stated that the Messiah will come after sixty-nine "weeks of years." The countdown begins with "the issuing of a decree to restore and rebuild Jerusalem" (Dan 9:25). It is that decree of Cyrus that brings the OT to its proper conclusion. At the same time, that

---

[96]Compare the references to the time period in Daniel 11.

[97]"From Artaxerxes to our own time the complete history has been written, but has not been deemed worthy of equal credit with the earlier records, because of the failure of the exact succession of the prophets" (Josephus, *Ag. Ap.* 1.41).

conclusion also signals an important new beginning. It is the beginning of the countdown to the coming of the biblical Messiah. Once that is begun, nothing in Israel's subsequent history remained of importance to the framers of the HB. The countdown had begun, and along with it the waiting for the fullness of time (seventy weeks of years [Dan 9]). By marking the effective end of the Tanak with Daniel 9, the framers of the OT canon were making a statement that the next great event in Israel's history was the advent of the Messiah (Dan 9:25). There was little left to do but wait for that event. All else, biblically as well as historically, was put on hold.

The renewed interest in the compositional shape of the OT books and canon has important implications for biblical theology. Among other things, it provides new perspectives on old problems, such as the theological unity of the Old and New Testaments.[98] The ideas and themes inherent in the compositional strategies of the individual OT books, as well as those of the OT canon as a whole, suggest that there are genuinely historical (real) links between the Old and New Testaments. Viewed in such terms, OT textual strategies, both compositional and canonical, appear poised to move directly and intentionally into the theological world of the NT.[99] Such textual strategies suggest that the NT is a true descendant of the OT. It also suggests that some of the framers of the OT Tanak had ties to early "pre-Christian" believers like those in the early parts of the Gospels and included men and women of the likes of John the Baptist, Simeon, Zacharias and Anna (Lk 1–2). The historical faith that lies behind the shape of the OT canon anticipates the faith of the early Christian communities. A focus on the compositional shape of the HB and its links to the NT therefore is essential to understanding either

---

[98]"It has been possible to say without fear of exaggeration that the hermeneutic problem of the OT is *the* problem and not merely *a* problem of Christian theology" (Antonius Gunneweg, "Christian Hermeneutics," in *The Jewish Bible and the Christian Bible: An Introduction to the History of the Bible*, ed. Julio Trebolle Barrera, trans. Wilfred G. E. Watson [Leiden: Brill, 1998], p. 518). "The hermeneutic problem of the Christian Bible, OT versus NT, derives from the fact that despite many points of contact between the old and the new, the old does not necessarily flow into the new and the new does not flow spontaneously from the old. Christian faith does not arise from the scriptures but from faith in the saving act made manifest in Christ, which has to be understood by turning to the old scriptures" (ibid.). See also Emil Brunner, "The Significance of the Old Testament for Our Faith," in *The Old Testament and the Christian Faith: A Theological Discussion*, ed. Bernard W. Anderson (New York: Herder & Herder, 1969), pp. 243-64.

[99]See John H. Sailhamer, "Biblical Theology and the Composition of the Hebrew Bible," in *Biblical Theology: Retrospect and Prospect*, ed. Scott Hafemann (Downers Grove, Ill.: InterVarsity Press, 2002), pp. 25-37.

in its totality. The two steps of composition and canon are both theologically and historically necessary and relevant. Attempts at constructing a biblical theology that includes both the Old and New Testaments surely must pay attention to these links and lines of OT interpretation, especially where they might lead into the composition and shape of the NT.

What can be said about the shape (or mental construct) of the OT at the time of Jesus? Was it similar to the present three-part OT, the Tanak (Torah [Law], Nebiim [Prophets], Kethubim [Writings])? Luke 24:44 suggests that this was one of the shapes of the OT in Jesus' day. A reference in Sirach also suggests that as early as the second century B.C. many understood the OT as a three-part book. Also, a text from the Dead Sea Scrolls refers to the OT as "the book of Moses and the books of the prophets and David" (4Q398 frags. 14-17, col. 1:2-3).

Some diversity in the order of the books was tolerated within the threefold shape. A book's order within a canonical list no doubt played a role in determining its meaning. If nothing more, it was a reflection of the book's relationship to other books in the list. The fact that Ruth occurs between Judges and Samuel in some lists may have been justified by the opening verse of the book, which locates the events recorded in "the days of the judges" (Ruth 1:1). In some Hebrew manuscripts the book of Ruth follows the book of Proverbs, which probably represents an attempt to identify Ruth, called a "virtuous woman" *(ʾēšet ḥayîl)* in Ruth 3:11, with the "virtuous woman" *(ʾēšet ḥayîl)* in Proverbs 31:1-31. The placement of a book within the OT canon was not arbitrary. Its position likely is related to how the book was understood within the context of the whole Bible. It may have been an early "biblical theology," a theological assessment of how the books of the OT were to be connected and fitted together and what central themes they addressed. The order given to the books of the OT played a significant role in what context each book was read. One need not argue that this order was inspired or that it was the only order in which these books could be arranged. It is enough to say that the canonical order of the books of the OT varied in part because the understanding of the meaning of the books of the OT varied from community to community. In each case, the order of the OT books guided the reader through the proper sequence and appropriate context for each book. One naturally would start with Moses and the Pentateuch, moving to the Prophets, and to the Writings and Wisdom books. The same order is followed by Gerhard von Rad's book on OT theology and more recently by that of Rolf Rendtorff. The Tanak thus functions as a kind of theological framework for an early biblical theology of the OT.

In the shape given the Tanak at the time of Jesus, the book of Joshua (the first book of the Prophets section) follows the Pentateuch. When the books are viewed in that order, clear compositional connections emerge between the end of the Pentateuch and the beginning of the book of Joshua. Also, Psalm 1 (the beginning of the first book of the Writings) follows Malachi (the last book of the Prophets). There are compositional connections between these two segments of the OT. Peels calls them "redactional glue."[100]

The end of both the Pentateuch and the Prophets focus on a coming prophet: one like Moses (Deut 34) and one like Elijah (Mal 4). Both Joshua 1 and Psalm 1 speak of "meditating on the law of God" as the means of becoming wise and prosperous. The two canonical links (Josh 1:8; Ps 1:3) appear to be read as cross-citations, each citing the other. This is a common way of linking larger sections of the OT canon. Joshua is admonished to "meditate on [the Torah] day and night in order that you do all that is written in it because then you will make your way successful and then you will become wise" (Josh 1:8). Psalm 1 speaks of the blessed person as "he whose delight is in the law of the Lord, and on his law he meditates day and night. . . . In whatsoever he does, he prospers" (Ps 1:2-3). The verbal identity of these two texts suggests an intentional strategy. It places identical texts at the beginning of the second (the Prophets) and third sections (the Writings) of the Tanak. What gives these two texts their importance within the overall strategy of the Tanak is not only that they introduce the second and third sections of the OT canon, but also that they make explicit reference to the Law, the first section of the Tanak. Both texts consciously address the meaning of the Pentateuch as "law" (Josh 1:7) and as wisdom (Deut 4:6). In these two canonical seams the law becomes an object of meditation and the primary source of wisdom.

These two seams, or "redactional glue," Joshua 1:8 and Psalm 1:2, contrast the role of law as wisdom in the present and as prophecy in the future. In do-

---

[100]"Was there a purposeful final redaction not only of the individual books but also of the books of the Old Testament as a whole? Is it possible to trace the 'redactional glue' between the different sections of the canon?" (Peels, "The Blood 'from Abel to Zechariah,'" p. 601).

ing so, they raise a further question: How does one live in the present while waiting for God's new work in the future? These seams refocus the reader's attention from the present to the future arrival of a great prophet like Moses (Deut 34:10), whose way is prepared by another great prophet, Elijah (Mal 4:5 [3:23 MT]).

A final theme is embedded in these canonical seams. It is the role of Scripture in the lives of those who are called to wait for God's future work. By meditating "day and night" on Scripture (Josh 1:8; Ps 1:3), one finds wisdom and prosperity. Prophecy is a thing of the past. It has ceased and has been replaced, for the moment at least, by Scripture. The Scriptures, as God's prophetic Word, have been given for those who wait for the return of prophecy. The coming of the new prophet and prophecy is a future event.

The note sounded in these canonical seams reflects the concerns as well as the point of view of those who drew up the OT canon. They laid great stress on the role of written Scripture in continuing the office of prophecy. It is not surprising to find such such a plea for Scripture coming from the pen of the one who gave Scripture its final shape. There is a distant echo of these canonical seams in the Protestant "Scripture principle" *(sola Scriptura).* These seams urge us to look to the Scriptures for divine guidance. They also hold much hope for the future. It will be the time for a new work of God accompanied by the renewal of prophecy (Deut 34:10). These central themes are part of the strategy of the "redactional glue" linking the seams connecting the pieces of the Tanak in its present shape. They are also themes that play heavily in the NT. In 2 Peter 1:19 we have a paraphrase of the message of the OT canonical seams: "We have also a more sure word of prophecy; whereunto you do well that you take heed, as unto a light that shines in a dark place, until the day dawn, and the day star arise in your hearts."

# Part Two

# REDISCOVERING THE COMPOSITION OF THE PENTATEUCH WITHIN THE TANAK

*Chapter 5*

# Textual Strategies Within the Tanak

ARE THERE RECOGNIZABLE INTERNAL PATTERNS or cohesive structures at lower levels in the compositional strategy of the Tanak? Do any of these play a recognizable role in giving the Tanak its present shape? An observation made by Ernst Hengstenberg helps frame that question. Hengstenberg notes that "in history the Messianic hopes of the nation always assume the appearance of an echo only," and that "they seem to have been introduced from above into the spirit of the nation, and that each particular element was to be found in a prophetic communication, before it took possession of the mind of the nation."[1] Hengstenberg's idea of the "echo" of divine revelation was a foundational insight of his monumental study of biblical theology, *Christology of the Old Testament*. Hengstenberg saw in the composition of the OT considerable interdependence among the authors of the individual books. Hengstenberg believed that the message of the prophets was grounded in the central themes of the Pentateuch as they played out in the prophetic literature.[2] Although Hengstenberg believed the origin of these seminal prophetic ideas to be solely divine, he understood the interdependence of the OT prophets to consist of a kind of verbal echo of the words of earlier scrip-

---

[1]Ernst W. Hengstenberg, *Christology of the Old Testament* (1854; McLean, Va.: MacDonald, 1972), 2:1352. A similar idea was also understood by C. F. Keil as an echo ("a similar cord") (*The Twelve Minor Prophets*, trans. James Martin [BCOT; Grand Rapids: Eerdmans, 1954], 2:96). Note also Eduard König: "In dieser Zeit wie weiterhin ein lebhaftes Echo finden konnten" (*Theologie des Alten Testaments: Kritisch und vergleichend dargestellt* [Stuttgart: Belser, 1922], p. 115).

[2]For example, Numbers 24:7; 1 Samuel 2:10; cf. Matthew 2:15.

tural texts in the Pentateuch. He understood nearly the whole of the messianic themes in the OT to be a function of this prophetic echo. In the words of the prophets, Hengstenberg thought that he could hear an echo of the words of Moses. He also heard an echo of the words of the prophets in the words of Moses. What held the messages of the prophets together and made them understandable to the reader was the recitation of the words of Moses by the prophetic authors of OT Scripture.

Walter Kaiser has identified a similar innertextual phenomena in the OT Scriptures as "the analogy of antecedent Scripture." Each biblical writer works within the context of a developing canon of Scripture. This developing canon functions as a *regula fidei*, a rule of faith that guides the interpretation of new revelation. The difference between Hengstenberg and Kaiser on this question is that for Kaiser, the prophets played a passive role in shaping their verbal echoes of Moses and the prophets. They did not read back into the earlier OT Scriptures what could be known only from later prophecy. Thus, their primary contribution to the developing meaning of the OT as a whole is to be found in their faithfully recording their own words alongside the chronologically earlier biblical texts. Later Scriptures were not allowed to influence the reading of earlier texts. Implicit in Kaiser's approach is the interpretive role it assigns to the later prophetic words placed alongside earlier texts (Num 24:24). Later prophetic words served as inspired commentary on earlier prophetic texts.

Hengstenberg put the matter differently. He believes that the prophets not only passed the words of Moses back and forth between themselves, but also sent those words back freighted with their own theological notions. In Numbers 24:23, the words of Balaam in the Mosaic Pentateuch, "Woe! Who shall survive when God does this?" are given an inspired prophetic interpretation in the next verse, "And ships shall go around the Kittim and afflict Assyria and afflict Babylon [Eber]" (Num 24:24). These words are linked to the prophetic word in Daniel 11:30, "and Kittim ships will come out against him." The biblical prophets contributed to the sense of earlier Scripture by weaving their interpretations and ideas into the verbal fabric of those texts. Sometimes this is seamless, as in repeating what was said in Genesis 49:9b about the king from Judah, "He lies down, he spreads out like a lion, and like a lioness; who will raise him up?" in a later description of the victorious king in Balaam's vision (Num 24:9). At other times it can appear as an obvious insertion, as when the terse poetry of Deuteronomy 33:2-3 is explained in the next verse as a reference to Sinai and the giving of the law: "Moses commanded the law [Torah] to us" (Deut 33:4). What the reader hears in the words of the Pentateuch are the words of Moses coupled with the prophets' inspired commentary.

Kaiser argues for a more passive understanding of the prophetic word, in part because he understands the prophets as "chronologically later" and wants to guard against any kind of later biblical (e.g., NT) texts adding their meaning to earlier texts. Hengstenberg finds such levels and redirections of biblical interpretation helpful in coming to terms with the NT's reading of the OT, which is his ultimate goal. What Hengstenberg sees in the NT is an inspired and therefore valuable interpretation of the words of Moses and the prophets.

I suggest that Kaiser's insistence on the original author's intent is a proper, even preferred, goal of biblical interpretation. Among other things, it guards against reading the OT in light of the NT. If one seeks to know the meaning of an OT book in terms of its author's original intent, then Kaiser is right in insisting on not overriding the OT meaning with the NT. This does not mean that Hengstenberg's position cannot make a positive contribution to exegesis. Hengstenberg, like Kaiser, wants the OT to interpret itself, apart from, or at least prior to, one's reading the NT. That is the only way, he argues, to interpret the NT properly. Thus, Hengstenberg has a desire, similar to Kaiser's, to read the OT in its original OT context. For Hengstenberg, that means more than the context of the original author. It means the context of the OT and the Bible as a whole, something not brought into the discussion by Kaiser. In taking into account the context of the whole Bible, Hengstenberg is better positioned to move the discussion of the meaning of biblical texts into the NT. In his concept of a prophetic echo, Hengstenberg is able to view OT texts within their original context and within the context of the authorial role of the biblical prophets. Hengstenberg's discussion of the "prophetic echo" raises the question of interbiblical interpretation within the context of a thoroughly evangelical view of biblical authorship, inspiration and canon.[3] Although he largely neglected a truly "innertextual" approach to the books of the OT, Hengstenberg was ahead of his time in viewing the whole OT, and not merely the NT, as the proper context for understanding its parts.

---

[3]In the early days of the nineteenth century, Hengstenberg found that the OT canon was still a safe haven from the storms of biblical criticism.

In his description of the prophetic echo, Hengstenberg shows that he understands the central issue to be the shape and sequence of the books in the OT canon. It was this shape and pattern that he understood as both prophecy and commentary. Unlike most of his contemporaries, Hengstenberg had not succumbed to viewing biblical theology in terms of "prophecy and fulfillment." Biblical prophecy, for Hengstenberg, is in any one instance always an unfinished task. Being an echo, the prophetic word carried with it the context of earlier prophecy, but only in a concrete and limited sense. That sense was always too great for an individual prophet to comprehend in its totality. Hengstenberg believes that not only was one prophet alone unable to comprehend or tell the whole story, but also the actual divine communication of the message to the prophet was so overwhelming that the supernatural prophetic moment of revelation could never be humanly and fully grasped. Only Jesus, the incarnate Son of God, could see the whole picture. Hengstenberg believes that individual prophets had to be content to grasp only a fleeting moment of the total vision and to provide what context they were able to gather from their own immediate circumstances. Hence, a multitude of biblical prophets and contexts were essential for grasping a brief glimpse of the whole prophetic vision. Each could make a verbal contribution to the whole, though the most that an individual prophet could hope for was to utter a fragmentary piece of memory triggered by a biblical word. As prophetic words were passed on and spread about, other prophets recognized them as a part of the vision they had seen and thus added their own fragmentary memories to the description of the complete vision, including any explanations and commentary they could gather from their exegesis of those same biblical texts.

Prophecy, for Hengstenberg, thus can be understood as an echo or, when viewed as a whole, "a conversation with an echo." One prophet's words were heard by another, and then exegeted, explained and returned. Each time the prophet's words were heard and sent back to the text there was an added insight attached to it and a new relevance to the message. The meaning remained the same, but there was a deepening and broadening of its vision. Such a moment, for Hengstenberg, represented a distinct historical step in the progress and unfolding of the meaning of the prophetic literature. Within the hallowed halls of the OT Scriptures Hengstenberg hears the words and commentary of all the prophets from Moses to Malachi.

The "prophet like Moses" in Deuteronomy 18 was identified in Deuteronomy 34 as the "prophet" who was yet to come. Malachi 4 proclaims him as that prophet whose way was to be prepared by the prophet Elijah. The "king," like Moses, will bring his people out of Egypt and defeat an enemy identified by some as "Agag" (in the MT) and by others as "Gog" (Num 24:7-8).[4] Here it is clear that the "echo" of Numbers 24 was sent back twice: once in a scribal gloss, as a picture of Saul and David's defeat of Agag, and a second time by a prophetic word, as the new David foreseen in Ezekiel 34:23, as the messianic defeat of Gog (Ezek 38:18a) (see *BHS* apparatus).

## Compositional and Canonical Echoes

Throughout the whole of the OT are numerous echoes of the poems in the Pentateuch. The poems are part of the macrostructure of the Pentateuch and are introduced with the well-known prophetic expression "in the last days." The poems are about a future king from the tribe of Judah who will reign over Israel and the nations. One of the earliest and most striking echoes of these poems is the additional verse attached to the end of the "psalm of Hannah" in 1 Samuel 2:10. After the miraculous birth of Samuel, the one who would initiate the kingship in Judah (1 Sam 16:13), Hannah, whose name means "gracious," goes to the house of God and sings a hymn to God's grace. Her hymn is not, strictly speaking, a hymn of thanksgiving for what God has done; rather, it is a call for divine help in bringing to pass the promises of the poems of the Pentateuch. At least in its last verse, the psalm is an eschatological hymn like those in the Pentateuch. At the conclusion of the hymn, Hannah addresses God, asking that he "raise the horn of his anointed one [messiah]" (1 Sam 2:10).

The language Hannah uses throughout the psalm suggests that she does not intend to give a prophecy of the rise of the kingship (as is commonly suggested in the English versions). Nor is she proclaiming the "consummation of

---

[4]Compare "Gog" in the earlier versions of Numbers 24:7 (see *BHS* apparatus ad loc.) and in Ezekiel 38:16-17: "And thou shalt come up against my people of Israel, as a cloud to cover the land; it shall be in the latter days, and I will bring thee against my land, that the heathen may know me, when I shall be sanctified in thee, O Gog, before their eyes. Thus saith the Lord God; Art thou he of whom I have spoken in old time by my servants the prophets of Israel, which prophesied in those days many years that I would bring thee against them?" (KJV).

the kingdom of God."[5] The text is clear that Hannah is pleading[6] with God to do what he has promised: "Would you please raise up your anointed one and give strength to your king!" Hannah's hope in a coming king goes far beyond the rise of the throne of David. Her words in 2 Samuel 2:10 are a messianic echo of the poems in the Pentateuch.

Evangelical views of messianic prophecy, like many issues in OT theology, can be traced to two early nineteenth-century OT scholars, Ernst Wilhelm Hengstenberg (1802–1869) and Johann von Hofmann (1810–1877).[7] The views of these two scholars continue to set the agenda for much of evangelical biblical scholarship. In many respects, their views were similar. Both were influenced by the Berlin revivals in the early nineteenth century. For both, the last word on the meaning of messianic prophecy in the OT came from Jesus and the NT. Both believed that the fulfilled prophecy, particularly messianic prophecy, offered essential (apologetic) support for the truth of the gospel. Both also believed that in giving us messianic prophecy, God had intervened in a real *(res)* way into human history. He had made known his will and purpose. Messianic prophecy was not a product of a human yearning for a better life; it was the result of a "supernatural" revelation.

In spite of these basic similarities, each scholar offers a fundamentally different set of answers to essential questions.

***Ernst Hengstenberg and Johann von Hofmann.*** Hengstenberg's understanding of messianic prophecy is shaped by two primary concerns: (1) his own experience of conversion, which for him was supernatural, sudden and undeniable; (2) his desire to use his religious experience as a basis for the defense of the Bible. For Hengstenberg, God's work in the world is accomplished by means of specific divine interventions. These are miraculous events that occur within the arena of ordinary history. The incarnation is a prime example. It marks a new beginning for God's relationship with the world. In the incarnation, the Word has become part of the world. Israel's history is a

---

[5]"Hannah's prayer rises up to a prophetic glance at the consummation of the kingdom of God" (C. F. Keil and F. Delitzsch, *Biblical Commentary on the Books of Samuel*, trans. James Martin [Grand Rapids: Eerdmans, 1950], pp. 33-34).

[6]In those cases in 1 Samuel 2:10 where the form is clear, the verbs Hannah uses are jussive, not imperfect. Hannah asks that that God bring his king. She is not merely announcing that the king will come.

[7]The following discussion of messianic prophecy in the Old Testament draws on John H. Sailhamer, "The Messiah and the Hebrew Bible," *JETS*, 44, no. 1 (2001): 5-23, and is used by permission.

record of the many and diverse instances of that intervention. Although Israel's history is part of ordinary human history, it is also, like his own conversion, punctuated with miraculous exceptions.

That a prophet could foresee the exact name of the future Persian king Cyrus (e.g., Is 45:1) is an exception to ordinary history. But it is an exception that could be expected, given the divine origin of the prophetic word. When God steps into the flow of human history, his actions are direct and clear to anyone who witnessed them or heard them recounted. They are so self-evident and convincing that they could be used as proof of the truth of the gospel.

As Hengstenberg sees it, God's acts in history have an immediate but short-range effect on the rest of history. As miracles, they are not part of the rest of history. They are historical, but not part of history. They are exceptions to ordinary history and, as such, are clear signs of divine activity. God's acts in history are like one's stepping into the current of a river. One's feet make a splash, but there are no ripples made in the river. The ripples are lost in the flow of the river. Hengstenberg's own conversion was a divine splash whose ripples were quickly dissolved by the flow of time. There was nothing left of the event itself for the historian to fix upon and draw conclusions from. It was an "above nature" (supernatural, miraculous) event lost within the course of ordinary history.

For Hengstenberg, the divine revelation of messianic prophecy consists of similar kinds of miraculous events. In this way, his entire understanding of messianic prophecy came to be shaped by his conversion experience.[8] As Hengstenberg understands it, the prophets of old were given sudden, miraculous, panoramic visions of the whole of the messianic future. Those visions were like flashes of supernatural light and insight onto the meaning of the biblical text or its imagery. Often they came so suddenly and faded so quickly the prophet could record only a small portion of the vision—like flashbulbs, which leave one momentarily stunned and unable to see anything but a large blue dot fading slowly before one's eyes. When encountering such a vision, the prophet hurriedly recorded the vision as it faded from sight.

Hengstenberg believed that the prophetic visions came so quickly that in some cases new visions appeared to the prophet in the midst of other visions. The prophet had to stop recording one vision to pick up his description of

---

[8]Hengstenberg, *Christology of the Old Testament*, pp. 1361-96.

another. What the prophet ultimately was able to record were only bits and pieces of the visions he had seen. Hence, for Hengstenberg, to discover Christ in the OT means finding all the bits and pieces of the one grand messianic puzzle and piecing them back together. It is as if the prophetic books were large scrapbooks containing scattered fragments of once-whole paintings by Rembrandt and Michelangelo. A single verse in the Bible might contain fragmented pieces of several visions. Only the trained eye could spot a piece of both a Rembrandt and a Michelangelo in the same verse. Only one who knew the whole vision could piece all the fragments together.

In finding and piecing together such splintered visions, the NT is indispensable. It is like the picture on the cover of a jigsaw puzzle box. For Hengstenberg, little or nothing was left to the prophet; he merely recorded the visionary fragments from which the student of prophecy had to piece together the whole.

Given these assumptions about the nature of prophecy and the books of the Hebrew OT (which were novel and unusual in Hengstenberg's day), it is not hard to understand the approach he took to finding the Messiah in the OT. Following Hengstenberg through the HB is like following a trained geologist through the Black Hills. We watch him pick up a stone here and a rock there and tell us that these once were part of a great prehistoric mountain range or ocean floor. Hengstenberg points to a fragment here and a text there and reconstructs for us the great messianic mountain range and ocean floor that once inhabited the prophet's mind. Without knowing the whole scope of messianic prophecy as well as Hengstenberg does, one would have to follow him and take his word about the messianic remnants of the verses to which he had drawn attention.

Although few evangelicals today would openly adopt Hengstenberg's approach, his legacy continues to influence the contemporary discussion. That legacy consists of three commonly held assumptions.

First, Hengstenberg believed that the meaning of any one messianic prophecy is not immediately transparent on its own. There is a need for some translation of what is said in the OT into what is seen in the NT. For Hengstenberg, the meaning of a text is to be found in its "spiritual" interpretation. One finds that interpretation by looking to the NT for clues to the OT's meaning. Another word for this is *typology*. OT biblical characters and events were "living pictures" (types) of NT realities. In finding the meaning of any event, for Hengstenberg, the NT held the key.

Second, Hengstenberg believed that the messianic meaning and import of the OT consisted of the predictive nature of its prophecy. To be messianic, the OT must have accurately predicted the historical events in the life of Jesus. He thus judges the messianic intent of the OT by indexing it to the picture of Jesus in the Gospels. Once again, the NT holds the key to the meaning of the OT.

Third, the value of the messianic prophecies for Hengstenberg lies in their being largely apologetical in establishing the truth of the NT. To the extent that an OT passage proves to be messianic and thus predictive of the NT life of Jesus, it shows that Christianity, or the gospel, is true. This is the argument from prophecy, and its legacy extends as far back as the church apologists in the early centuries. It is to Hengstenberg, however, that the credit must go for reviving this concern. The fact that this is one of the legacies of Hengstenberg does not mean that it remains, at present, a productive use of messianic prophecy. Hengstenberg's approach attracted few even of his own evangelical colleagues.[9]

Whereas Hengstenberg focused his attention on the messianic prophecies in the OT Scriptures, von Hofmann looked beyond the Scriptures to the historical realities they recorded. According to von Hofmann, it is not the text of Scripture that is messianic. Messianism, for von Hofmann, is a matter of history itself. It is not Israel's historical writings that are messianic, but the history that Israel itself experienced. Von Hofmann believed that history as such was a "living picture" of the coming Messiah. Historical events were a *vaticinium reale*,[10] a "material prophecy" consisting of real events that played out in real time. He believed that the events of Israel's history are an "inspired" messianic picture, just as he believed that the Bible is an "inspired text." To be sure, the HB functions as our primary means of "seeing" the picture in history, but the messianic picture itself and the means of "seeing" that picture are found by looking beyond the Scriptures as such to Israel's history as real events. The full messianic picture can be seen only as one observes Israel's history unfold itself into the first century and the life of Christ. The history becomes clearer, the picture more focused, as it moves

---

[9]His popularity among evangelicals in English translation was probably more because of his strong stand on Reformed orthodoxy and his sustained attack on biblical criticism.

[10]Franz Delitzsch, *Die biblisch-prophetische Theologie: Ihre Fortbildung durch Chr. A. Crusius und ihre neueste Entwickelung seit der Christologie Hengstenbergs* (BAS 1; Leipzig: Gebauer, 1845), p. 175.

closer to the coming redeemer. When it reaches Christ, the picture comes into full focus.

Because it was truly God at work in this history, Israel's history is like no other. It is a "holy history." God himself stands behind it and caused it. God was not merely working in history; history was God at work. Von Hofmann believed that just as God can be seen by a botanist in every leaf of a tree, so God can been seen by the historian in every moment of Israel's history. For von Hofmann, there is not a moment in all of world history in which something divine does not dwell.[11] History is God working out his will in the world. In Israel's history, God was, as it were, submerging himself into human events, making it increasingly more sacred and increasingly more messianic. Ultimately, Israel's sacred history tilts toward Christ in God's final act of stepping into history, the incarnation.

For von Hofmann, God did not momentarily step in and out of history, as Hengstenberg had envisioned. In Israel's history, God was increasingly immersing himself into everyday human events. Thus, the incarnation of Christ was not a unique and new beginning, but a final stage in a long process of God's becoming a part of his world. The boundaries of world history had been breached by a real divine presence with Israel. God, in effect, had carved out his own "sacred history" *(Heilsgeschichte)* in the midst of a secular history of everyday events *(Weltgeschichte)*.

With such a view of the Bible and history, it is not hard to see how nearly everything in the HB could ultimately take on importance as messianic. It does not initially have to look messianic for it to be an early stage of a developing prophecy. An acorn does not yet look like an oak tree, but eventually it will. As von Hofmann says, "It is a long way between the death of an animal whose skin covered [human] nakedness, and the death of the Son of God whose righteousness covers [human] sin. Yet these are like the beginning and the end of the same journey."[12]

In von Hofmann's view, everything in the Bible can be understood in strictly historical terms. Only the one who understands history as moving toward Christ can understand the messianic element in the HB. The mean-

[11]Johann C. K. von Hofmann, *Weissagung und Erfüllung im alten und im neuen Testamente* (Nördlingen: Beck, 1841), 1:7.

[12]Johann C. K. von Hofmann, *Interpreting the Bible*, trans. Christian Preus (Minneapolis: Augsburg, 1959), p. 137.

ing of Israel's history is messianic when God's messianic intentions are seen behind the real events of that history. The task of understanding the OT as messianic lies in recognizing the divine patterns in these early events and pointing to how they replay themselves throughout the remainder of Israel's history. History's meaning becomes typological and finds its ultimate meaning only with the coming of the antitype (fulfillment). The mere historical similarity between the exodus and Christ's sojourn to Egypt in Matthew 2 constitutes, for von Hofmann, a "material prophecy" of the coming Messiah. Once again, in von Hofmann's approach, the NT holds the key to the meaning of the OT.

The meaning of biblical terminology, such as "anointed one" or "king," spoken at a certain moment in Israel's history transcends the meaning of those words when understood solely within the context of the rest of history. Behind all events in Israel's "holy history" lies the mind of God and his effective will. Every word spoken within Israel's history has a horizontal (historical) range of meaning as well as a vertical (messianic) one. Within Israel's own unique salvation history, not only are biblical words fraught with divine intentionality, but so also are the actual historical events that constituted that history. God is the author of both. His will and intention lie behind both. While David may have referred to himself as "the anointed one" in Psalm 18:50, the real historical event *(res)* that lies behind Psalm 18 *(verbum)* carries with it, potentially, the same range of meaning when understood by the believing historian in terms of the real events of "salvation history." Proof of this comes when the historian views Psalm 18 from the perspective of its NT fulfillment.

To appreciate the legacy of von Hofmann, one must know something of how evangelicals viewed "history" and particularly "salvation history" before him. Before von Hofmann, biblical historians were careful to make a clear distinction between an evangelical view of biblical history and a critical one. The growing trend of biblical history, as critical scholarship had come to view it, was not so much to see Israel's history in its own terms as a "history of the world," but increasingly to view it within the context of what was coming to be known as the "ancient world" or "world history." Israel's history was to be viewed not so much on its own terms, but as part of the history of the ancient world and other ancient civilizations. The Bible played an increasingly minor role even in reconstructing its own history of Israel.

For evangelicals before von Hofmann, biblical history referred to that history which could be read off the pages of the Bible. Evangelical biblical scholars had a largely realistic historical understanding of the Bible. What they read in the Bible was what they understood to have happened precisely in those terms. If the Bible says that the Nile turned to blood, they took that to mean that the Nile River turned to real blood.

Von Hofmann marks the turning point of evangelical biblical scholarship away from such biblical realism. Even C. F. Keil, the most conservative evangelical OT scholar of his day, was willing to concede that "the changing of the water into blood is to be interpreted . . . not as a chemical change into real blood, but as a change in the colour, which caused it to assume the appearance of blood."[13] Von Hofmann did not so much alter the newly developing critical attitude toward Israel's history as accept it as such, and he practiced it in a more conservative manner as an important form of divine revelation. Nevertheless, with von Hofmann, the holy history that progressively revealed the will of God and the hope of a coming messiah was no longer merely the history we read in the Bible; it was a revelatory prophetic history *(Heilsgeschichte)* that needed to be reconstructed and augmented from the modern picture of the ancient world.

A second, and important, legacy of von Hofmann is that OT messianic prophecy could no longer be viewed apologetically as a proof of the Christian gospel. Having assigned the meaning of the OT to a history that defines itself in the events of the NT, one could no longer speak of fulfillment in terms of verification or validation of prophecy. In von Hofmann's notion of prophecy, it is the fulfillment that validates the earlier history, not the other way around. Von Hofmann thus was quick to jettison the notion that OT messianic prophecy could be used in any way to defend the truth of Christianity. For von Hofmann, it is history that validates Christianity, not the miracle of fulfilled prophecy.

Von Hofmann's legacy among modern evangelical approaches to the OT can been seen at several levels. Nowhere is it more tangible than in the study of messianic prophecy. My purpose is not to critique modern evangelical approaches for their dependence on von Hofmann,[14] but instead to

[13]C. F. Keil and F. Delitzsch, *The Pentateuch*, trans. James Martin (BCOT; Grand Rapids: Eerdmans, 1971), p. 478.

[14]See John H. Sailhamer, *Introduction to Old Testament Theology: A Canonical Approach* (Grand Rapids: Zondervan, 1995), pp. 36-85.

explore an evangelical alternative to the approaches of both von Hofmann and Hengstenberg.

***An alternative evangelical approach.*** Though differing in detail, Hengstenberg and von Hofmann share three important evangelical assumptions about the messianic focus of the OT. First, Hengstenberg and von Hofmann understand messianic prophecy as a genuinely (supernatural) "vision" of the future. In real terms, prophecy is a "history of the future." Second, Hengstenberg and von Hofmann see the NT as the primary guide for understanding OT messianic prophecy. Without a NT picture of Jesus, one cannot understand the meaning of the OT. The NT serves as a searchlight cast back over the OT. Without the light of the NT, the OT messianic vision is, at best, hazy and uncertain. Third, for both Hengstenberg and von Hofmann, the messianic vision of the OT is not presented in a straightforward, holistic manner. The messianic picture is scattered and strewn throughout most of the OT. For Hengstenberg, this was the result of the rapidity of the prophetic visions as they were received by the prophet. The visions came to the prophets so quickly that they could not write them all down fast enough. The prophetic books were like large scrapbooks containing scattered fragments of once-whole Rembrandts and Michelangelos. To be sure, the prophets saw the whole picture, but they were able to record only a small portion of what they had seen. A single verse in the Bible might contain fragmented pieces of several visions. Only the trained eye can spot a piece of both a Rembrandt and a Michelangelo in the same verse. Only one who knows the whole vision (from the NT) can piece the fragments together.

There is much truth in these assumptions, but also much room for still more work in each of these areas. An evangelical response would focus on three things. First, prophecy is not merely a "history *of* the future"; it is also a "history *for* the future." It is not merely a description of the destination of Israel's history; it is also a road map that shows how to get there. Second, the NT is not so much a guide to understanding the OT as it is the goal of understanding the OT. Unless we understand the OT picture of the Messiah, we will not recognize the NT picture of Jesus. The OT, not the NT, is the messianic searchlight cast upon the NT accounts of Jesus and the gospel. Third, for Hengstenberg (and von Hofmann), viewing the messianic vision in the OT is like seeing the Jesus of the Gospels looking into a mirror that had been shattered into a thousand pieces. To see the Messiah in the OT, one must look at the NT picture of Jesus as it is reflected through the pieces of this shattered mirror. What remains of the OT messianic picture is now only small bits and pieces scattered throughout the OT. These must be regathered and put back together with the aid of the reflected NT picture.

Most would agree, at least in part, with Hengstenberg on this point, especially those who have read the OT prophetic books. It should also be stressed that these bits and pieces (of the messianic vision) are not randomly scattered, as Hengstenberg believed. They fall along a recognizable pattern. They follow an order. A good number of them fall along and are part of the "compositional seams" of the OT books. They are part of the transitional comments writers use to link their texts together. They are the "redactional glue" of the biblical authors. Some of these bits and pieces of prophetic visions also fall along the seams"of the OT as a whole, the Tanak. The shape of the HB as a whole provides a meaningful context for viewing the scattered bits and pieces of prophetic visions.

Although Hengstenberg's view of Christ in the OT has been widely received by evangelical scholarship, there are important points in the view that are in need of adjustment and change. One point is that rather than a shattered mirror reflecting the NT, a better image of the OT is that of a stained-glass window casting the light of its picture on to the pages of the NT. A stained-glass window is made of fragmented pieces of glass; each piece belongs in a pattern with the others and plays a crucial part in the total picture. If this is a valid observation, it suggests new possibilities for viewing the Messiah in the OT. If there is an order and pattern to the distribution of messianic texts, then the time has come to take a closer look at that order. What is the picture in the OT stained-glass window? What is the meaning that lies behind its order, shape and pattern? Does it have its own shape and picture, or is it an OT reflection of a NT picture? Where does the light cast upon the stained glass come from?

I will briefly outline what taking such an approach might entail, since there are many ways to look at the messianic stained-glass window in the HB. The approach that I have in mind begins by looking at the HB in the shape we find it just at the time of the coming of Jesus. That shape looks at the OT's last word about itself. It looks at how the OT was understood by those (prophets) who gave it its final shape as the Tanak: the Law, the Prophets and the Writings. There were other shapes to the HB, but judging from texts such as Luke 24:44, the Tanak is the form of the OT with which Jesus and the NT authors were most familiar.

Viewed from that perspective, the OT has all the appearance of being a single work with a single purpose. It is connected by literary seams linking Deuteronomy 34 and Joshua 1 and similar seams linking Malachi 3 and Psalm 1. These passages are adjacent within the order of books in the Tanak. There are also links within these individual parts and a distinct compositional strategy that extends from the first word in the HB (*bĕrēʾšît* in Gen 1:1) to the last word (*wĕyāʿal* in 2 Chron 36:23). If we follow along the lines of those compositional seams, we will find it to be motivated by a hope in the soon (see Dan 9:25-26) coming of the promised Messiah and several other NT themes. Its perspective on the OT gives one an ideal view of what the OT authors believed about the Messiah. It also provides a perspective that shows the nature of the literary and theological dependency of the NT on the OT. It is a perspective that suggests that the Tanak is an early attempt to formulate a biblical theology that stresses the meaning of the OT as the "new covenant."[15]

My purpose in the remainder of this chapter is to propose an understanding of the Messiah in the HB. I will describe it in outline only and not attempt to argue a complete case for it here.[16] My goal is simply to lay out the main features of a plausible approach to understanding the biblical Jesus in light of the teaching of the Hebrew Scriptures. I will describe my approach in terms of three propositions: (1) the nature of OT messianic prophecy consists of both prediction and identification; (2) the OT messianic vision is a fragmented one that becomes increasingly more cohesive toward the final stages of the formation of the HB; (3) the HB is both text and commentary.

---

[15]Ernst Hengstenberg's phrase "der Aufhebung des A.B.," in *Geschichte des Reiches Gottes unter dem Alten Bunde* (Berlin: Schlawitz, 1869), which is rendered in English translation as "the abrogation of the Old Testament" (*History of the Kingdom of God under the Old Testament* [Eugene, Ore.: Wipf & Stock, 2005]), clearly shows, along with many similar examples, that the translator introduced a fundamentally new and different category into Hengstenberg's argument: the Old Testament is the "old covenant" (*Bund*).

[16]I have argued a case for it in "Biblical Theology and the Composition of the Hebrew Bible," in *Biblical Theology: Retrospect and Prospect*, ed. Scott Hafemann (Downers Grove, Ill.: InterVarsity Press, 2002), pp. 25-37; *Introduction to Old Testament Theology*, pp. 197-252; *The Pentateuch as Narrative: A Biblical-Theological Commentary* (Grand Rapids: Zondervan, 1992), pp. 1-79; *The NIV Compact Bible Commentary* (Grand Rapids: Zondervan, 1994); *How We Got the Bible* (Grand Rapids: Zondervan, 1998), pp. 38-42; "Creation, Genesis 1–11, and the Canon," *BBR* 10 (2000): 89-106; "A Wisdom Composition of the Pentateuch?" in *The Way of Wisdom: Essays in Honor of Bruce K. Waltke*, ed. J. I. Packer and Sven K. Soderlund (Grand Rapids: Zondervan, 2000), pp. 15-35; "Hosea 11:1 and Matthew 2:15," *WTJ* 63 (2001): 87-96.

A central element of my approach is the attempt to clarify the question of predictive messianic prophecy. There is prophetic prediction in the OT. Prediction is a major apologetic theme in passages such as Isaiah 41. There are other features to the notion of prophetic fulfillment. Alongside terms such as *fulfillment* one might also use terms such as *identification* and *exposition.* The OT not only predicts the coming of a Messiah, but also describes and identifies him.

This is an important difference from Hengstenberg's and von Hofmann's idea of prophecy as a "history of the future." As I have suggested earlier, messianic visions in the OT are not only visions of the future but also visions for the future. They explain and prepare for the future as well as reveal it. OT prophecy focuses not only on what the prophets saw, but also on the future the prophets foresaw (and here I have in mind the NT) as well as the fact that it followed, in real *(res)* terms, the plan the prophets had laid out for it. When the future came at a specific time and place, prophets such as Simeon were waiting for it because they had been prepared to receive it: "And it had been revealed to him by the Holy Spirit that he would not see death before he had seen the Lord's Christ" (Lk 2:26). There were those, also like Simeon and Anna, who already understood the future in terms of the OT prophetic vision. In other words, the prophets' vision was such that it preserved and carried with it a people who both understood the prophets and were there waiting for the fulfillment of their vision. By falling in line with that vision, the NT writers show not only that they accepted the OT as preinterpreted, but also that they were in fundamental agreement with its interpretation. That interpretation, we can see, began long before the time of its fulfillment. Already within the OT itself we can discover signs of an ongoing interbiblical discussion or, as one might prefer to say, intertextual interpretation and commentary.

In the Pentateuch the Messiah is a prophetic priest-king modeled after Moses who will reign over God's kingdom, bring salvation to Israel and the nations, and fulfill God's covenants. This messianic vision is part of the compositional strategy of the whole of the Pentateuch. It is the compositional glue that holds it together and gives it a shape. The Prophets and Writings sections of the Tanak are a detailed exposition of the Pentateuch's messianism. It is in that exposition that the OT messianic hope is extended and deepened to the point at which we find it in the NT. Thus, the last word in the HB is as messianic as any passage in the NT. I have in mind, of course, the vision of a "humanlike being coming in the heavenly clouds" in Daniel 7. That vision and the book of Daniel as a whole are equal to the messianic Christology in the NT.

Some view this in terms of a process of "reinterpretation." Earlier, non-messianic sections of the OT are reinterpreted by later authors and eventually understood as messianic. This is very far from what I have in mind. When the OT reads and interprets itself, as often happens in passages such as Daniel 7, it does so by drawing on the real, historical intent of the original OT authors. There was no need to speak of a "reinterpretation" of texts because it is still exegetically possible to show that from its beginning the Pentateuch was already thoroughly messianic, and that the rest of the OT authors of the Prophets and Writings understood its intent and expanded it still further in their textual commentary and exposition. An appreciation of these intertextual links within the Tanak suggests a direct link between the beginning of the OT and its end, as well as between the end of the OT and the beginning of the NT. From a literary and exegetical perspective, there is no intertestamental gap between the Testaments. The last word in the HB, in 2 Chronicles 36:23, can also be understood as the first word in the NT. It is a verb whose subject is not identified in the OT, *wĕyāʿal* ("let him go up"). Its grammatical subject could be gathered from the first chapter of Matthew in the NT. It is a call for the coming of that one "whose God is with him" and who is to build the temple in Jerusalem. In the book of Chronicles (and the postexilic prophets) this one who is to come is identified as the messianic (priestly)[17] son of David. Matthew's Gospel, which follows immediately after this last OT word, begins, like Chronicles, with a genealogy, this one identifying Jesus as the Christ (Messiah), the son of David, who is Emmanuel, "God with us."

Returning to the metaphor of the NT as a "messianic searchlight," we clearly see that a shift in focus is necessary. It is not the NT, but rather the OT, that is a messianic searchlight.[18] It is only when the OT casts its light on the pages of the NT that we see the biblical meaning of the life of Jesus.[19] In

[17]For example, 1 Chronicles 17:14; Psalm 110; Zechariah 6:9-15.

[18]Note 2 Peter 1:19: the "prophetic word" is "a lamp shining in a dark place."

[19]As is said in the Gospel of John, "Jesus did many other signs in the presence of his disciples which are not written in this book. But these are written that you may believe that Jesus is the Messiah, the Son of God" (John 20:30-31). The signs that Jesus performed are like road signs that reflect

such an approach, the OT (without the NT) is not "inadequate and incomplete," as Walther Eichrodt once described it.[20] The messianism of the OT is fully developed and is the context from which we must identify Jesus as the promised one.

The messianic vision of the OT is a fragmented vision that becomes increasingly cohesive toward the final stages of the formation of the HB. No one who has read the prophets will want to disagree with Hengstenberg that the messianic vision of these books lies before us in bits and pieces. As John Calvin once said, "Those who have carefully . . . perused the Prophets will agree with me in thinking that their discourses have not always been arranged in a regular order."[21]

Hengstenberg proposed to piece together this fractured vision by looking at the picture that emerges from the NT. I propose reading the fragmented prophetic visions not in light of the NT, but in light of the picture that emerges from within the OT. The OT has its own messianic light. There is already a coherent picture behind the composition of the prophetic books and the Pentateuch. The pieces fit remarkably well into that picture. If one follows the order of the HB—the Law, the Prophets, the Writings (Tanak)—the messianic picture becomes increasingly transparent. This is because later biblical texts focus on and provide commentary on earlier biblical texts. In this case, "later" does not mean chronologically late. It means the stage at which the biblical author is making a book. As far as one can tell, biblical authors, such as the authors of Kings and Chronicles, used existing written texts in the composition of their books. They organized and presented those texts so that their narratives gave meaning and sense to the events they recorded. The question of how they did this leads to the next proposition: the HB as "text and commentary."

The intertextual relationship between the compositional shape of the Pentateuch, the Prophets and the Writings is one of text and commentary. The Prophets and the Writings are not intent on giving a new vision for the future. Their aim is to help us understand the messianic vision already laid down in the Pentateuch and repeated in the prophetic writings. God com-

---

in the headlights of the OT.

[20]Walter Eichrodt, *Theology of the Old Testament*, trans. J. A. Baker (OTL; Philadelphia: Westminster, 1961), p. 26.

[21]John Calvin, *Commentary on the Book of Isaiah* (Grand Rapids: Baker, 1979), p. xxxii.

manded the prophet Habakkuk to "write the vision" and "to explain it" (Hab 2:2). Like Habakkuk, the prophets recorded their vision along with its explanation. As Abraham Heschel suggests, we view the interpretation of prophecy as "exegesis of exegesis."[22] The words of the prophets are words of explanation and commentary. Our task in understanding the biblical Scriptures is not so much to explain their prophetic vision as to explain the prophets' explanation of their vision. The aim of the biblical authors of the Prophets and the Writings was to provide a full and detailed textual commentary on the messianic vision that begins in the Pentateuch and is carried along through the rest of the Bible.

Like a stained-glass window, the Prophets and the Writings give the important bits and pieces of the prophets' vision. Isaiah 63 draws a glimmer of light from the poem in Genesis 3:15 and passes it on to Daniel 7 through the prism of Genesis 49. From there, it passes into the NT on its way to the vision of the "rider on the white horse" in Revelation 19. Isaiah measures his starting point from the picture of the king in Genesis 49 whose clothes are stained by grapes. He builds that picture into one of a warrior treading in the wine presses of divine wrath. In doing so, Isaiah intentionally links Genesis 49 to one of the first messianic poem in the Pentateuch, Genesis 3:15. Isaiah thus has linked two strategically important poems in the Pentateuch (Gen 3 and Gen 49), allowing one (Gen 49) to interpret the other (Gen 3). In doing that, the author of the book of Isaiah shows that he is reading the Pentateuch along and in view of its compositional seams. As in a stained-glass window, the light he draws from the Pentateuch is given color and texture as it passes through the remainder of the OT and into the NT. But like a stained-glass window, the various points of light converge into a larger picture.

The line of thought reflected in Isaiah and Daniel, and in the book of Revelation, is the same as the historical intention of the Pentateuch itself. When Psalm 72 says of the Davidic king, "All the nations will be blessed in him" (Ps 72:17), it draws from the eschatology of the Pentateuch in Genesis 12:3. When the same psalm says of the king's enemies, "they shall lick the dust" (Ps 72:9b), it holds its vision up to a piece of light first cast across the pages of Genesis 3.[23]

---

[22]Abraham Heschel, *The Prophets* (New York: Harper & Row, 1962), p. xiv.

[23]Just as in Isaiah 65:25b: "the serpent's food will be dust."

In the same way, when speaking of the eschatological future, Hosea says, "Out of Egypt I have called my son" (Hos 11:1). In doing so, Hosea draws directly on the poetic vision of Balaam in the Pentateuch (Num 24). Also, by focusing on the poetic texts in the Pentateuch, Hosea shows that he is reading the Pentateuch along its compositional seams.[24] In the Numbers passage Israel's messianic future (in Num 24) is viewed in terms of their glorious past, that is, the exodus (in Num 23).[25] The compositional strategy within the Pentateuch itself thus has linked the exodus with the messianic future. The exodus is a picture of the coming one. Hosea draws his messianic vision from these same texts. Both Hosea and the Pentateuch see the fulfillment of their visions in terms of the same eschatological future "in the last days" (*bĕʾaḥărît hayyāmîm* [Hos 3:5; Num 24:14]). Hosea's messianic vision is cast as a commentary on the Pentateuch's messianic eschatology. Matthew's application of the Hosea exodus passage to Jesus suggests that he has linked both the Pentateuch and its commentary in Hosea.

A similar example comes from the Emmanuel prophecy in Isaiah 7:14. We tend to look beyond the book of Isaiah and beyond the words of Isaiah 7 to the historically reconstructed location of those words in the prophet's own day. Doing that makes it difficult to see the prophecies of the virgin birth in the same light as Matthew. But, if we look at the passage within the compositional unity of the book of Isaiah, another viewpoint emerges. According to Isaiah 7:15, when Emmanuel is born, he will be eating curds and honey until he comes of age and knows to reject the evil and choose the good. The author of the book of Isaiah intended Isaiah 7:15 as part of the sign given to Ahaz in Isaiah 7:14. The sign is not only that a virgin is pregnant with a son, but also that when the son is born, he (and Israel as a whole) will be eating "curds and honey." In Isaiah's description of the destruction of Judah in the following verses (Is 7:17-25), Israel will be eating "curds and honey" because the land will have been ruined first by the Assyrians (Is 7:17), then by the Babylonians (Is 39), and finally by other foreign invaders after that (Is 40–66). Within the whole of the book of Isaiah, the birth of Emmanuel is located long after the ruin of the northern and southern kingdoms, even after the eschatological events that fill the final chapter of the book (e.g., Is 65:17).

---

[24]See Sailhamer, "Creation, Genesis 1–11, and the Canon"; "A Wisdom Composition of the Pentateuch?"

[25]See Sailhamer, "Hosea 11:1 and Matthew 2:15."

The nineteenth-century critic Berhard Duhm was so struck by the implications of Isaiah 7:15 that he could only image it was a late "messianic gloss"[26] to Isaiah 7:14, 16. Duhm rightly understood the sense of Isaiah 7:15 and its contribution to the meaning of the sign given to Ahaz, even though his suggestion that it was a late gloss is rendered unlikely by the presence of the verse in the Qumran Isaiah manuscript. No one would dispute that the ultimate focus of the book of Isaiah lies far beyond the exile. That would be long after the time of Isaiah and Ahaz. According to Isaiah 7:15, the sign is for that distant future. According to the book of Isaiah, the prophet had a message for Ahaz, but the message was about what was to happen in the "last days." The rest of the book of Isaiah is an exegesis of the prophet's sign in Isaiah 7:14 and Isaiah 7:15. In this case, one must understand not only the vision, but also the prophet's exegesis of that vision as it plays out in the remainder of the book.

The approach to the Messiah and the OT Bible that I am describing raises several questions. One important question is the concept of the "final shape" of the OT Bible. This topic represents largely uncharted waters for evangelicals. It is not an abandonment of the evangelical concern for the meaning of the "original authors." I am suggesting, on the contrary, that as evangelicals pay increasingly more attention to the whole of the OT Bible, they will not run the greater risk of neglecting equally important "original authors" whose aim was to tell us "the rest of the story." They wrote about the death of Moses and that "a prophet like Moses never arose again in Israel." The anonymous, but inspired, author of those important details remains unknown to this day, but he was a biblical author just the same. His contribution to the meaning of the Pentateuch, though brief, implies that the prophet whom Moses foresaw in Deuteronomy 18 was still to come in the future ("last days") and therefore should not be hastily identified with those who later held prophetic office in Israel. He was a prophetic author who carried out his calling by "making books."[27] The "final" words of the Pentateuch are representative of his anonymous contribution. He understood the words of Moses in Deuteronomy 18 to be about the "prophet like Moses," the long-expected messianic figure who had not yet come to his people. The biblical author who attached Deuteron-

[26]Bernhard Duhm, *Das Buch Jesaia* (HKAT 3/1; Göttingen: Vandenhoeck & Ruprecht, 1892), p. 54.

[27]See John H. Sailhamer, "Preaching from the Prophets," in *Preaching the Old Testament*, ed. Scott M. Gibson (Grand Rapids: Baker, 2006), pp. 115-36.

omy 34 to the end of the Pentateuch was just as important as any of the better-known OT authors. An inspired author is no less important for being anonymous as well.

As we will see, an important implication for the Pentateuch of the view of authorship that I am developing is that it assumes that the Pentateuch is a single book with a single purpose.[28] The whole of the Pentateuch (from Genesis to Deuteronomy) was intended to be read as a single book with a distinct purpose, focus and message. The Pentateuch had an author, and that author had a purpose in writing it. The whole of the Pentateuch has a shape that reflects its compositional strategy.

Four lines of argument suggest that the Pentateuch is a unity and has a single, intentional purpose.

First, the Pentateuch recounts a single story that begins with the creation of the world and the preparation of the land and ends with the postponement of the possession of that land. A central theme of the Pentateuch is the inhabitable land that God has prepared for his human creatures.

Second, the blocks of narrative—primeval history, patriarchs, exodus, wilderness, conquest of the land—are linked around a single theme of faith. Whoever the author of the Pentateuch was, he has linked all the events in Israel's early history to the theme of faith.[29]

Third, the arrangement of narrative texts around major, homogeneous poetic texts in Genesis 49, Numbers 24 and Deuteronomy 32 suggests that the Pentateuch's narratives are linked by a single messianic theme (royal imagery) that recurs in these poems. The Pentateuch somewhat resembles a Hollywood musical. Its story is both interrupted and developed by the songs (poems). Also like a musical, the songs (poems) are not randomly spliced into the story. The songs (poems) develop and carry the central theme of the story. They are the primary means for developing what the narratives are about. A

---

[28]I am not raising the question of whether the Pentateuch "points to" Jesus and the NT. To say that the Pentateuch is about the Messiah is not yet to say that it is about Jesus. Those are two separate and equally important questions. We must first ask whether the Pentateuch is about the Messiah, and then ask whether Jesus is the Messiah. The Pentateuch (and the rest of the HB) tells us that there will be a Messiah. The NT tells us that Jesus is the Messiah spoken of in the HB. It does so by identifying Jesus as the one about whom the HB speaks. In my view, this means that there is an important apologetic value to the identity of Jesus as the OT Messiah. By identifying Jesus as the OT Messiah, the NT makes the claim that Jesus is the true Messiah.

[29]See John H. Sailhamer, "The Mosaic Law and the Theology of the Pentateuch," *WTJ* 53 (1991): 24-61; Hans-Christoph Schmitt, "Redaktion des Pentateuch im Geiste der Prophetie," *VT* 32 (1982): 170-89.

careful attention to the details of the songs (poems) clarifies the message of the Pentateuch.[30]

Fourth, there is the arrangement of the various collections of laws within the narratives of the Pentateuch. What Wellhausen and others saw as remnants of earlier law codes prove to be, on closer examination, a carefully laid out textual strategy within the Pentateuch. At its center lies the account of the golden calf. That story shows that something has gone fundamentally wrong at Sinai. It is only at the end of the book, in Deuteronomy 30, that the reader finds the author's answer: the need for a circumcised heart and the promise of a new covenant.[31] This message closely follows the teaching of Jesus and Paul in the NT.

## The Message of the Pentateuch

I have suggested that the Pentateuch has a shape and a central message that conforms to that shape. I must now seek to describe that message. My initial purpose is to explore how the central message of the Pentateuch is linked to its compositional strategy. It is not enough to point to broad themes and ideas in the Pentateuch. As important as that is, I must show how those themes and ideas are specifically tied to the compositional shape the Pentateuch.

I begin with a brief list of the central components of the Pentateuch's compositional themes. Then I will briefly discuss how those themes are tied to its compositional strategies.

***The prophetic critique.*** The story of the Pentateuch takes the reader from God's creation and preparation of "his world" to Israel's failure in the wilderness and their postponed possession of a part of that world. Neither Moses (Num 20:12) nor the Israelites (Num 14:11) are allowed to enter the land. Israel, at best, can expect a rocky future. In a final compositional seam linking the major poems in the Pentateuch (Deut 31:29), Moses, on his deathbed, warns Israel of their impending apostasy: "I know that after I die you will be completely corrupt and turn from the way I have commanded you." His words are echoed throughout the prophetic books.[32] Exile is on the way. The future is at risk. There is little room for hope among God's people.

---

[30]See Sailhamer, *The Pentateuch as Narrative*, pp. 35-37.

[31]Ibid., pp. 46-59.

[32]This is a major weakness of the approach of double or multiple fulfillment. The Torah itself does not see the immediate events in the life of Israel as a positive fulfillment.

Nevertheless, as in the prophetic literature in general, a message of hope can be heard at the heart of the Pentateuch. As in the prophetic books, it is a message centered on a coming king. It is that king who is the center of focus of the poems in the Pentateuch. Each major (and minor) poem in the Pentateuch sets its sights on his coming. He is the king who will arise from the house of Judah (Gen 49:8), rule over the nations (Gen 49:10b), and reign over God's restored world (Gen 49:11). The Pentateuch leaves little doubt that this king will come "in the last days" (*bĕʾaḥărît hayyāmîm* [Gen 49:1]).

The prophetic critique of Israel's faith leads to the second element of the message of the Pentateuch.

***The centrality of faith.*** The unified "faith theme" in the Pentateuch stresses the role of faith and obedience from the heart that lies at the center of the prophetic notion of the new covenant (Jer 31; Ezek 36). According to the narrative logic and timing of the Pentateuch, when Israel arrived at the foot of Mount Sinai, they immediately fashioned an idol of God in the form of a golden calf (Ex 32). This was explicitly prohibited by the commandments in Exodus 20:1-6. In making images of God, Israel disobeyed their covenant with God at Sinai (Ex 32:7-8). Nevertheless, a future blessing awaited them. That blessing was tied to Israel's faith. According to Genesis 26:5, Abraham's faith was reckoned to him as obedience to God's statutes, commandments and laws. Abraham could not have "kept the Sinai law" in a literal sense, as it had not been given until the time of Moses (cf. Ex 15:25b). Abraham lived a life of faith, and God counted that to him as his "keeping the law" (cf. Gen 15:6). This emphasis on the role of faith, so clearly NT in its outlook, is found at key locations in the compositional strategy of the Pentateuch. Often it lies along the compositional seams that tie together the whole of the book.

***The coming eschatological king.*** The central theme of each of the major poems in the Pentateuch is the promise of a coming "king." The phrase "in the last days" is an important part of the introduction to each of the poems. This is terminology known from the messianic eschatology of the prophets (Is 2:2; Dan 10:14). These poems stress the coming of a future king and are set in the context of "the last days."

In the MT this king is said to conquer and rule over the kingdom of Israel's historical adversary Agag (Num 24:7). This has led some to identify this king (in the MT) with David, who conquered Agag (see 1 Sam 15:8; 2 Sam 1:1). Rashi says of this king, *zeh dāwîd* ("this is David"). However, the reading

"Agag" is found only in the MT. In all other ancient texts and versions[33] this king is said to conquer and rule over the kingdom of Gog, apparently the Gog of Ezekiel 38, the only other scriptural reference to Gog.[34] Ezekiel acknowledges a Gog from earlier Scripture (Ezek 38:17).[35] According to Numbers 24:24, this king will come after the defeat of Assyria and Babylon(?) and the rise of the Kittim (Rome?). This could hardly be David. Thus, there is in the textual history of the Pentateuch a running debate over the identity of the king who will defeat Gog in Numbers 24. The MT, along with Rashi, sees the historical David as the focal point of these prophecies. The earlier and more widely represented texts (including Ezekiel's copy of the Pentateuch!) identify the king with an eschatological redeemer who will defeat Gog.

***The Pentateuch and the Prophets.*** These general features of the composition of the Pentateuch are strikingly similar to the central themes of Israel's prophetic literature, especially its messianic focus on a future new covenant and the divine gift of a new heart to those who trust (believe) in God. At the center of that focus is the coming king who will defeat Israel's enemies and establish a perfect kingdom.

To be sure, the Pentateuch is about the Mosaic covenant and the law given at Sinai, but what it says about that law and Sinai anticipates Paul's message in Galatians 3. The law did not produce a living faith in the heart of the individual Israelite. There was nothing inherently wrong with the law, but it is clear that Israel failed to keep it. God gave Israel a future hope and laws to keep them until the arrival of that future. The Pentateuch is a commentary on the laws of the Sinai covenant. It, like the prophetic books, looks for a better covenant than one dependent on written laws and tablets of stone. That "something better" is a new covenant that embraces both Israel and the nations and has as its centerpiece a royal (messianic) redeemer.

***A messianic composition.*** The primary task of a messianic compositional analysis of the Pentateuch is to show the messianic intent in the many details of the narratives and poetry of the Pentateuch, even in the arrangement and composition of the laws and the narratives that frame them. Here we must ask, "What is the relationship of the details in the Pentateuch to the overall themes briefly outlined above?" It is on those details that the prophets (and

[33]Samaritan Pentateuch, LXX, Aquila, Symmachus, Theodotion (see *BHS* apparatus ad loc.).
[34]The Gog in 1 Chronicles 5:4 is one of the sons of Reuben.
[35]"Thus says the Lord GOD, 'Are you the one about whom I spoke in former days?'"

psalmists) in particular have focused their attention. In that sense, the prophetic writings are intended as "commentaries" on the Pentateuch and other prophetic texts. These prophetic commentaries are similar to the stained-glass window analogy mentioned earlier. By means of fragmentary bits and pieces of light, they cast their vision throughout the Pentateuch and refocus it not only on the needs of their own day but also on their hope for the future.

Evangelical approaches to the Messiah in the OT often have focused on reading the NT back into the OT. I am suggesting that one should also move in the other direction. The OT sheds a great deal of light on the NT. Our primary objective should be to read the NT in light of the OT, not vice versa.

Evangelical approaches have spent a good deal of time and attention looking at the earliest stages of the biblical history for the answer to the meaning of the OT. We ask how Eve understood God's promise to her within the real-life events of Genesis 3:15 and fail to ask the more important question of how Moses, the inspired (biblical) author, understood the text he was writing about Eve within the narrative of Genesis 3:15. There is little to go on to discover how Eve might have understood God's first promise. There is, however, much to go on if we read Genesis 3:15 from the perspective of the author of the Pentateuch and its final shape.

The closer we examine the final shape of the HB (Tanak), the clearer it becomes that its shape and structure are intentional and reveal the meaning of the author. There are clear signs of intelligent life behind its formation. If so, we should be asking about the theological message behind that shape. Where is the author taking us? My answer is that the Pentateuch and its compositional strategy are strongly messianic. By this, I do not mean that the earlier forms of the Bible are not also messianic. I mean simply that in the later stages of the formation of the HB its authors were primarily concerned with the task of interpreting and making more explicit the messianic hope already explicit in the earliest parts of the biblical texts. This is what I call "text and commentary." The later stages in the formation of the HB treat the earlier stages much like the NT treats the OT. They build on and develop the messianic vision of those earlier texts still in need of commentary.

Someone recently described the lens of an old lighthouse along the New England coastline, a lighthouse used long before the discovery of electricity. Its light source was a single candle. The lens of its light consisted of thousands of triangular surfaces. Each surface focused and refracted a small portion of the original candlelight. The result was a beam of light cast twenty miles out to sea. The original light was just a small candle. As it passed through the lens, the light of each part of it was reflected off the other parts until it had become a bright beacon composed of thousands of pieces of the original candlelight. This is not unlike the HB. As the original messianic candlelight passes first through the Pentateuch and then the rest of the Tanak, it becomes a bright light that shines on and enlightens the NT. Unfortunately, we have become accustomed to holding only the candlelight (e.g., Gen 3:15) up to the NT instead of reading the NT in the light cast by the lens of the whole of the Tanak.

Several years ago I taught a course titled "The Use of the Old Testament in the Old Testament." The course explored how later biblical authors (such as Ezra and Nehemiah and the prophets) understood the Pentateuch. Every time I offered the course, the registrar changed the title in the class schedule to "The Use of the Old Testament in the New Testament." The registrar always assumed that I had made a typo. The phrase "use of the Old Testament in the Old Testament" was meaningless to him. Nowadays, the expression has meaning. This question is being asked by many today. It is the question I have been trying to clarify above. How do the OT writers understand the early messianism of OT books such as the Pentateuch?

The books of the OT are messianic in the full NT sense of the word. There is a messianic light in the OT. In texts such as Daniel 7 that messianic light reaches the height of the best NT passage. It is a light that points the way to the NT. Not only does the NT cast its messianic light back on the OT, but also the light of the OT also shines onto the NT. The books of the OT were written as the embodiment of a real, messianic hope—a hope in a future redemption and a promised redeemer. This was not an afterthought in the HB. It was not the work of final redactors. The central purpose of the books of the HB from the outset was to serve as the expression of the deep-seated messianic hope of a small group of faithful prophets and their biblically alert followers.

The question of the composition of the OT books is twofold. First, it raises a set of questions about how OT books were "made."[36] What was the nature of the composition of a biblical book? How did they "make" books in the ancient world?

---

[36]See William M. Schniedewind, *How the Bible Became a Book: The Textualization of Ancient Israel* (Cambridge: Cambridge University Press, 2004).

I believe that such questions are best answered by reading the OT and paying close attention to how the various books were "constructed." What are the strategies that link them together, the compositional glue? Did their authors use sources? Did they write their books "from scratch," as modern authors do, or did they piece together fragments of earlier texts, which seems to have been the method in the ancient world? In the following section I will devote considerable attention to the question of the composition of the Pentateuch. It is an essential question that must be resolved by a biblical theology that aims to ground itself in the intent of the OT authors.

The second part of the question of the composition of the OT involves the specific identity of the biblical authors. Do we know who wrote the books of the Bible? Do they identify themselves? Are some books intentionally anonymous?

The answer to the question of the identity of the biblical authors lies under several layers of secondary issues. Close examination of the nature of the composition of biblical books suggests that the identity of most biblical authors was purposefully omitted. This is also true of the names of most authors of ancient works. The OT authors appear to have followed ancient custom in remaining anonymous. There may also have been additional reasons for a book's anonymity. Some of these will be discussed below. In spite of these difficulties, it may still be important to inquire about the identity of some biblical authors.

Even without a knowledge of the identity of a biblical author, one might still ask what kind of image of themselves the biblical authors wished to project in their books. Whose viewpoint did the biblical authors represent? For whom did their books speak? To what level of society or social class did they belong? What was their message, and how did they direct it to those in their world? What was their aim in writing books? To whom and about whom were they writing? These are crucial questions we must ask, even if, in the end, they lie beyond our historical reach and point us to the identity of little more than a handful of biblical authors.

It often is assumed that the biblical authors and the books they wrote represented the views of the official religious leaders and institutions in ancient Israel. The biblical authors were the official spokespersons of the foundational religious institutions. Since the religious leaders in ancient Israel usually were represented by members of the priesthood and the Jerusalem temple, it is further assumed the biblical books represented the priests and those associated with the temple.

I will offer a different scenerio of the identity of the authors of the OT. I will suggest that far from being the voice of Israel's religious authorities, such as the priesthood or the monarchy,[37] the voice that we hear most in the OT books is that of the prophets. It is the prophets who speak not for themselves or on behalf of the wealthy and religiously connected, but rather for "the poor, the ophan and the widow." The OT represents the unrepresented, those who were otherwise unrepresented by the religious institutions and communities.

Who were these prophetic voices that spoke from within the various books of the OT? Simply put, the prophetic authors of the books of the OT were a small group of "unofficial," but divinely called, prophets in ancient Israel. Within the biblical books, as early as the narrative accounts of the prophets Elijah (1 Kings 17) and Elisha (1 Kings 19), we hear of a small number (seven thousand) of those in Israel "who have not bowed the knee, or paid homage, to Baal" (1 Kings 19:18). Whatever the exact identity of these "faithful" in Israel might have been, it is self-evident from many passages in the OT that the authors of the biblical books understood themselves to be uniquely called by God as his spokespersons and thus ready to stand against overwhelming odds to face off those in Israel who had forsaken him to follow other gods. Although these OT authors put considerable distance between themselves and the "official" prophets, they saw themselves as genuine prophets whose primary claim to be heard rested in the fact that they had received a divine call linked to a specific word they had received from Scripture (Is 8:20).

Two important aspects of the OT Scriptures can be traced to these "writing prophets." The first is that groups of prophets such as these and their disciples were responsible for the preservation and guardianship of the Mosaic Pentateuch. A recurring theme in the OT books is the role of the prophets in giving the Mosaic Scriptures to Israel (cf. Dan 9:10). Second, it was likely these prophets who were most responsible for the composition of the OT books and the OT as a whole. They may also have been responsible for the second edited version of the Pentateuch that is now in our HB.

The story of this group of prophets begins with the observation that throughout most of the early period of Israelite history there is little evidence

---

[37]Or even those who belonged to the prophetic office—"the sons of the prophets" (Amos 7:14).

of the use and familiarity of the Bible as we know it today. An awareness of the Bible as a whole appears to have ebbed early in Israel's history only to resurface at a considerably later period. At the beginning of the biblical period, after the death of Joshua and the elders of Israel, "there arose a new generation that knew neither the LORD nor what he had done for Israel" (Judg 2:10). This comment raises the question of the whereabouts of the Pentateuch at that time. At the end of the period, shortly before the fall of the Davidic monarchy and the Babylonian exile, a lost copy of the "book of the law" was discovered during repairs to the temple (2 Kings 22:8). Surprisingly, even the priests and the king did not recognize "the book of the Torah." Only the prophetess Huldah (2 Kings 22:14) recognized the book as Scripture and was familiar enough with its content to interpret it for the king's messengers. This passage and others like it raise the question of the role that the prophets played in the authorship of the biblical books.

The composition of the books of the OT is closely related to two central historical events in ancient Israel: the establishment of the monarchy in Jerusalem (2 Sam 7) and the fall of that monarchy in the Babylonian captivity (2 Kings 25:21). These two events stand at the beginning and end of two central institutions, the Davidic kingship and the Aaronic temple. Both institutions were marked by hereditary office; Judah's kings were limited to descendants of the house of David (2 Sam 7:12-16), and the priests traced their lineage to the house of Aaron (Num 3:10). Alongside these two established institutions arose a third, the office of prophet. Unlike the other two, the identity of a prophet was marked solely by a divine call (Jer 1:5).

The view of the OT is largely negative toward the three groups. According to the "prophetic" authors of the books of the OT, these divinely ordained leaders had progressively turned their backs on the responsibilities (cf. Deut 33:8-11) of their office and had strayed irretrievably off course. Jeremiah, himself the son of a priest (Jer 1:1), and one called by God to be a prophet (Jer 1:5), admonished both priests and prophets for their defiant opposition to God (Jer 2:8). Amos, a true prophet who had received a divine call, found it undesirable even to be identified with the other prophets (Amos 7:14). Amos preferred to be recognized by his occupation as a herdsman and arborist rather than as a prophet (Amos 7:14). Many legitimate prophets, Jeremiah among them, had to contend with opposition from prophets who had not received a genuine divine call (Jer 28).

Ultimately, a true prophet's only line of defense was an appeal to the support of his message from Scripture:

> When they say to you to consult the mediums and the wizards who whisper and mutter, should not a people consult their God? On behalf of the living (should they go) to the dead? (They should go) to the Torah *[tôrâ]* and to the testimony *[tĕʿûdâ]*! If they do not speak according to that word *[dābār]* it is because they have no light *[šāḥar]*. (Is 8:19-20)

It is not surprising to learn that those prophets who remained true to their calling turned increasingly to Scripture as their primary, if not sole, court of appeal. The God who had called them was the God they knew intimately from the Scriptures. He was the God of Moses and the Sinai covenant. Consequently, when the prophets preached to the disobedient nation, the scriptural text to which they appealed was nearly always the (forgotten) Mosaic Pentateuch. It was the Pentateuch that lay forgotten by the nation but carefully preserved and read by those prophets who had received a true call from God. As readers of the Mosaic Pentateuch, these prophets were well aware of the inevitable failure of the Sinai covenant (Deut 29:21-27). They therefore held little hope in that covenant. They also knew that Moses himself had entertained little hope in Sinai and the covenant that God had entered there with his people (Deut 31:29). Moses found his hope in the prophetic word about another covenant, one "not like" the covenant God had made with Israel at Sinai (Horeb [Deut 29:1]). Thus, the message of the prophets was grounded in the biblical hope they had drawn from the writings of Moses. The source of that hope became the prophetic word about a "new covenant" (Jer 31:31). That hope was the centerpiece of the prophetic vision for the future (Deut 30).

Later on, the prophets who had remained true to God's Word increasingly drew their central themes from scriptural books such as the Pentateuch. The prophets became biblical expositors. Themes such as covenant, faith, law and obedience, redemption, and the promised seed were the fabric of the prophetic hope. These themes formed the structural framework of scriptural texts such as the Pentateuch. In proclaiming their words, the prophets brought central pentateuchal themes forcibly to the forefront by applying them to contemporary situations in the life of the nation. At a time in Israel's history when, through neglect and disobedience, much of the Scriptures lay forgotten and in danger of being lost (e.g., 2 Kings 22), the prophets were deeply immersing themselves in the Mosaic Scriptures (Josh 1:8), seeking ways to apply them to ever more complex situations in their day. In doing so, they were following the lead of the prophet Moses himself, who, throughout the pages of Deuteronomy, preached and taught the application of covenant themes to everyday life. Moses, like Ezra and the biblical prophets, devoted much attention to the study of the very Scriptures that he was putting into final form. The book of Deuteronomy opens with Moses' own statement that he, on the banks of the River Jordan, as the nation prepared to enter the land, "began to explain the law [to them]" (Deut 1:5). Moses, like Ezra much later (Ezra 7:10; Neh 8:8), devoted himself to the study and teaching of the Scriptures.

Throughout Deuteronomy one finds examples of Moses' teaching and his exegesis of Scripture. Not surprisingly, it is an exegesis much like that which the prophets and the NT writers later applied to Moses. In Deuteronomy 10 Moses draws a "spiritual" lesson from God's command to possess the land. It is the sort of interpretation we might expect to find in the NT (cf. 1 Cor 10:1-11). Having reminded Israel of what possession of the land would mean to Joshua's generation (Deut 10:11), Moses turns to the readers of the Pentateuch and asks, "And now,[38] O Israel, what does the Lord your God ask of you?" (Deut 10:12). His answer reads like a page out of the prophetic Scriptures: "[You must] fear the Lord your God, to walk in his ways and love him and serve the Lord your God with all your heart and soul" (Deut 10:12). Moses' words are echoed throughout the rest of Scripture. The prophet Micah asks, "What does the Lord require from you but to be just and love mercy and walk humbly with your God?" (Mic 6:8). The prophet Ezekiel draws a similar personal and ethical application from the Genesis story of Sodom: "Behold, this was the iniquity of thy sister Sodom: pride, fullness of bread, and abundance of idleness was in her and in her daughters, and she did not strengthen the hand of the poor and needy. And they were haughty and committed abomination before me; therefore I took them away as I saw good" (Ezek 16:49-50). Ezekiel grounds his ethical lesson in the contrast between the inhabitants of Sodom who failed to "strengthen the hand" *(ḥāzaq yād)* of the poor and the angels who did "strengthen the hand" *(ḥāzaq yād)* of the persecuted Lot and his family in Sodom.

---

[38]S. R. Driver notes that the phrase "and now" introduces "the practical inference to be deduced from the preceding retrospect" (*A Critical and Exegetical Commentary on Deuteronomy* [ICC; Edinburgh: T & T Clark, 1895], p. 124).

Moses, like the prophets Micah and Ezekiel after him, is pictured as one who has studied the law (Torah) and knows how to apply its covenant themes to the lives of his readers. In doing that, Moses does not turn his back on a biblically warranted interpretation that moves the text toward an application. He grounds his lessons in the words of Scripture. Working with the biblical text in this manner presents Moses as a prime exemplar of how to read Scripture. As in Joshua 1:8 and Psalm 1:2, the wise person is one who "meditates on Scripture day and night." Presenting Moses in this way suggests that he, as the author of the Pentateuch, was already seeking ways of linking the Scriptures to the everyday lives of their readers (see also Deut. 4:1). Like the prophets, his message was a result of a careful reading of Scripture, a Scripture that he himself was in the process of making (composition).

***Exegesis and composition.*** The role of the Scriptures in the lives of the prophets raises a further question: How do we know that the prophets were immersing themselves so deeply in the Mosaic Scriptures, even while the very existence of these Scriptures was rapidly fading from the memory of their contemporaries (Judg 2:10; 1 Kings 19:18)? The first part of an answer to that question lies in the broader implication of texts such as Joshua 1:8 and Psalm 1:2, the last stages of the "canonical glue" holding the OT together. These texts present an ideal picture of how the Scriptures in general were to be read. They suggest the nature of the expectation and assumptions of those persons responsible for giving the OT its final form *(Endgestalt).* They show that, ideally, the Scriptures were meant to be read and pondered "day and night." If this was how the ideal was represented to the reader, it suggests that these same biblical authors would have attempted to live up to that ideal (see also Ps 1:2). Though only an ideal, the picture they present is realistic enough in its depiction of Torah piety that they would have had no difficulty recognizing themselves in this ideal.

The other part of the answer lies in the witness of the words of the prophets. It is clear from a comparison of the prophetic literature with the words of Moses in the Pentateuch that the prophets share a considerable amount of the words and ideas of the Pentateuch. In the end, the prophets' vocabulary is essentially the vocabulary of Moses. Among other things, this suggests that they have spent considerable time reflecting and meditating on the words of Moses, as Joshua 1:8 and Psalm 1:2 call for. The central thrust of Hosea's words to Israel and Judah is drawn from his reflection on the Decalogue (Hos

4), the Genesis narratives (Hos 12) and the Balaam narratives (Num 24:7-9), all part of the compositional framework of the Pentateuch.[39]

The biblical narratives also suggest that it was not the prophets alone who had immersed themselves in the Mosaic writings. Hannah's song (1 Sam 2:1-10) shows that she too found grounds for hope in the central compositional message of the Pentateuch. From the picture given by her own words, Hannah speaks as one who has been reading the poems in the Pentateuch "day and night." Breaking into the conclusion to her poem of praise (1 Sam 2:1-9), Hannah calls for the coming of the Lord's king, "his messiah" (1 Sam 2:10). Where would Hannah have learned of this king? Judging from the way these poetic texts are distributed within the Pentateuch, and from Hannah's own words, we surmise that the author of Samuel suggests that Hannah has read and knows the Pentateuch and has drawn her image of the Messiah from the poems of the Pentateuch.

From a purely literary viewpoint, both the prophetic word and the words of the faithful in Israel disclose their preoccupation and close association with the Mosaic Scriptures. The right people (the prophets and lay people) are aware of the right texts (the Mosaic Pentateuch) and draw their hope (spiritual lessons and messianic hope) from just those texts. Their God and his plan of redemption are made known through a message they have come to know from the Mosaic writings of Scripture. It is the words of the prophets that tell the story of the prophets' immersion into the message of the Scriptures. The link between Moses and the prophets is hard to deny. Even in the minute details of their sometimes complex messages the prophets' words echo the words of Moses and bear his literary signature. Anyone who has read the Pentateuch's creation account in Genesis 1 will not fail to recognize the influence of Genesis 1 in Jeremiah 27:5: "I made the land, humankind, and the animals that are upon the land, with my great strength and with my outstreched arm, and I will give it to whomever is upright in my eyes." Listening attentively to the prophets' words tells us much about the Scriptures that they read and the thoughts that filled their minds. These were thoughts and ideas that ultimately have their origin in the Mosaic Torah.

In addition to the influence of Moses on the words and the thematic structures of the prophets' message, the prophetic message bears other marks of

---

[39]See Sailhamer, "Hosea 11:1 and Matthew 2:15."

Mosaic origin. It lies in what I have suggested above: the magnitude of the scope of the prophets' message. The prophets' message and its context are much larger than what was called for by the immediate issues that confronted the prophets. For the most part, the prophets were called to address immediate issues in immediate situations. When, however, we look at their messages alongside the contexts in which they delivered them, it becomes apparent that their words have been linked to a much wider scope, one that likely was drawn from their reading and pondering the world of the Pentateuch. The prophets delivered their messages in response to the news of the day, but they cast those messages within the much larger scope of the Pentateuch and its focus on creation and the "last days." It was for that reason that Jeremiah addressed Israel's impending military defeat in terms of the Pentateuch's prophetic vision of creation. These words of Jeremiah are unmistakably drawn from the creation account in Genesis 1: "I made the land, humankind, and the animals that are upon the land, with my great strength and with my outstreched arm, and I will give it to whomever is upright in my eyes" (Jer 27:5).

Isaiah 45:18 also has links to the Genesis creation account and shows that its author had devoted considerable attention to understanding its meaning: "For thus says the Lord, the creator of the heavens—he is the God who made the land, and he is the one who made it, he himself established it; he did not make it to be uninhabitable, but rather he made it for dwelling—'I am the Lord and there is no one else.'" Prophets such as Isaiah had a vision of a world that was larger than their own world. Where did they get that vision? It came from their reading about the world of the Pentateuch. "(God) is the one who is able to declare the beginning from the end. From the most ancient times, when nothing had yet been made, he is the one who said, 'My counsel will stand, and I will accomplish all I have intended" (Is 46:10).

Hannah speaks for those who stood under the influence of the prophetic message as it was drawn from the Mosaic Scriptures. God's intrusion into her family struggle and her desire for a son (1 Sam 1) are taken up within the context of his faithful word about the coming Messiah (1 Sam 2:10). We may take it for granted that the scope of the prophets' message was as broad as it was, but there is little grounds for explaining that scope without the magnitude of the prophetic writings drawn from the Mosaic Scriptures.

This scope of the prophetic vision leads some to suppose that Israel's prophets were religious geniuses. They saw a world larger and more different from that of their contemporaries. Others attribute the scope of the prophets' vision to divine inspiration. Their viewpoint is the viewpoint given them by divine revelation. Both explanations have a ring of truth to them. The words of the prophets are divinely inspired (2 Tim 3:16) and thus represent a divine point of view. Neither explanation, however, tells the whole story. If we look closely at the writings of the prophets, we see where they found their view of the world. The prophets were living in the world they had discovered and come to appreciate from the Pentateuch. The magnitude of their message was suited to the world of the pentateuchal narratives. Their message could only fit the world laid down for them in the Scriptures, especially the Pentateuch. One might characterize this prophetic vision by what Thomas Mann called "the quoted life."[40] The prophets' world, and with it their lives, were drawn from their reading of Scripture. The world they had come to know was the world of the Bible; its meaning was assigned to it by the Pentateuch. Their prophetic message was woven out of scriptural quotations, and they lived in a world whose meaning was borrowed from the world of the pentateuchal narratives.

When Hosea speaks to the Israel of his day, he does so by addressing them as the Jacob of the book of Genesis: "In the womb he took his brother by the heel, and in his maturity he contended with God. Yes, he wrestled with the angel and prevailed. He wept and sought his favor" (Hos 12:3-4).

When Jeremiah speaks to the nations, he does so within the scope of the creation narrative in Genesis 1: "Thus says the LORD of hosts, the God of Israel, thus you shall say to your masters, 'I made the land, humankind, and the animals that are upon the land, with my great strength and with my outstreched arm, and I will give it to whomever is upright in my eyes'" (Jer 27:5).

The magnitude of the prophets' message betrays the influence of the Pentateuch on their lives. Only the biblical world of the Pentateuch was big enough for the scope of their prophetic message. They measured their words to the scale of the world of the biblical text. It may be partly for that reason that later biblical authors linked the prophets to the composition and preservation of the Pentateuch (2 Kings 17:13; Ezra 9:10; Dan 9:10; Zech 7:12). From the beginning of the proclamation of their message, the prophets openly identified themselves with the words of Moses and the Scriptures.[41]

---

[40]"Zitathaftes Leben" (quoted in Michael Fishbane, *Biblical Interpretation in Ancient Israel* [Oxford: Clarendon Press, 1985], p. 1).

[41]"Law and the Prophets" is a title of the Pentateuch.

## The Literary History of the Old Testament

Having connected Israel's prophets to the origin and development of the message of the Pentateuch, we now address the question of whether it is possible or desirable to trace the literary history of the Tanak from the internal evidence of the Tanak itself. Two aspects of such a history are the notion of biblical composition and the concept of a "book."

We have noted that the establishment and growing importance of the kingship, the temple and the prophetic office provide the most immediate theological context for understanding the development of biblical composition. The stages of compositional activity are defined roughly by those events and institutions:

1. The period before the Davidic monarchy (before 1000 B.C.)
2. The period after the monarchy (before 600 B.C.)
3. The period of the exile (600–500 B.C.)
4. The period after the exile (after 500 B.C.).

***Prior to the Davidic monarchy (before 1000 B.C.).*** An understanding of the composition of biblical books before the reigns of David and Solomon must be gathered principally from the occasional references to "books" and "writings" in the OT itself. The sense of the Hebrew word for "book" *(sēper)* at this early period of Israelite or Canaanite history may refer to any kind of written material, whether papyrus, wood, pottery, stone or leather.[42]

The mention of "the book of the Torah" in Joshua 1:8 raises a question of the state of Scripture at the beginning of Israel's history. Moses gave Joshua a "book" *(sēper).* He was to read it "day and night" and to obey what was written as a way of gaining wisdom *(śākal)* and prosperity *(ṣālaḥ).* This reference to a book raises further questions about the relationship of this "book of law" in Joshua 1:8 to the Pentateuch in our Bible. Also, what was its relationship to "the book of the law of Moses" in Joshua 8:31, and "the law of Moses" cited in Joshua 8:32?[43] A copy of the "law of Moses" was written on the whitewashed stones of a large altar set up by Joshua at Mount Ebal (Josh

[42]On the possible implications of the meaning of "book" in ancient Israel, see John Barton, "What Is a Book? Modern Exegesis and the Literary Conventions of Ancient Israel," *Intertextuality in Ugarit and Israel*, ed. Johannes C. de Moor (OtSt 40; Leiden: Brill, 1998), pp. 1-14.

[43]See also the "book" in Deuteronomy 17:18.

8:30-34). Was that a copy of only part or the whole of the Mosaic law? In Deuteronomy 27:1-8 Moses had commanded the "words of the law" to be written on the stones of the altar, adding that they should be accompanied by a "good commentary."[44] Can we identify this "text" with the "book of the Torah" that was given to Joshua in Joshua 1:8?

Most English translations follow the MT in this passage, rendering Joshua 8:31 as "the book of the law of Moses." The Greek version (LXX) renders this expression as "the law of Moses," with no mention of a "book." The same is true in Joshua 8:34, where the MT reads "the book of the Torah," and the Greek reads only "the law of Moses." The difference in both cases lies in the addition of the word "book" in the MT. The LXX does not have this word in its Hebrew text *(Vorlage)*.[45] The textual question thus turns on the identification of the "book" in Joshua 1:8 with what was written on the stones of the altar in Joshua 8:32. According to the MT, it was the same "book" as Joshua 1:8, but in the LXX the "law" in Joshua 8:32[46] was not identical with the "book" in Joshua 1:8.[47]

*A genealogy book for the family of Adam.* Early in the Pentateuch, a "book" is cited: "this is the book *[sēper]* of the genealogy of Adam" (Gen 5:1). It refers to the list of ten names and their families in Genesis 5. It may have included additional lists under the heading "These are the generations of," which occurs throughout the rest of Genesis. The list concludes with the genealogy of Aaron and Moses in Numbers 3:1: "And these are the generations of Aaron and Moses."

*The book of the wars of Yahweh.* Numbers 21:14 cites a document entitled "The Book *[sēper]* of the Wars of Yahweh" *(sēper milḥămôt yhwh)*. Little is known about this "book," though much was conjectured in earlier periods.[48] For those who hold to the Mosaic authorship of the Pentateuch, this citation raises the question of whether it was a written source for the Mosaic Pentateuch or an early history of Israel that drew from either the Pentateuch itself or sources other than the Pentateuch. The manner of its citation in Numbers

---

[44]Or by means of a "proper interpretation" *(baʾēr hêṭēb)*.

[45]The term *Vorlage* refers to the Hebrew text used by the LXX translator.

[46]The words "which he wrote" in Joshua 8:32 are also not in the Greek version (LXX).

[47]The LXX in Joshua 1:8 also distinguishes between the law given by Moses and the "book of the law" given to Joshua for reading and meditation.

[48]Heinrich A. C. Hävernick, *Handbuch der historisch-kritischen Einleitung in das Alte Testament* (Erlangen: Heyder, 1836–1849), 1/2:504-5.

reflects a surprisingly modern historiography, including an awareness of written sources.[49] Recent evangelical scholarship has rarely, if at all, discussed the implications of this citation for an understanding of either the early history of Israel or the availability of written sources at the time of the composition of the Pentateuch.

Although this "book" is no longer extant, its mention in Numbers suggests the widespread belief that such a book existed, and that the author of the Pentateuch accepted the notion of written sources in biblical composition. If one can judge from the book's title, it was a book about the "wars of Yahweh." What wars were these? Were they those wars we read about in the Bible, or were they wars only similar to the kind of accounts we read in the Bible and may thus have served as prerecorded history for the accounts in some biblical narratives? The context of Numbers 21:13 suggests that these wars were waged against the "Amorites," a term for the early Canaanite populace (Gen 15:16).

According to Numbers 21:27-30, a poetic account of the Amorite defeat of Moab is attributed to "those who speak proverbs." In Genesis 48:22 there is mention of Jacob's struggle or battle with the Amorites, by which he gained possession of Shechem with sword and bow.[50] The "book of the wars of Yahweh" may thus have been an ancient account of the wars between Israel and the Amorites. Genesis 15:16 suggests a reckoning was yet to be completed with the Amorites. There is no mention of such a reckoning with the Amorites in the earlier Genesis narratives, though this verse suggests that in Abraham's day God's land promise to Israel was linked in some way to the historical fate of the Amorites. A war between Amraphel and the Amorites is recounted in Genesis 14:7. In that war Abraham was an ally with the local Amorites (Gen 14:13). Israel's battle with "the five kings of the Amorites" (Josh 10:1-14) was included in a book later cited as "the book *[sēper]* of the upright" (Josh 10:13).

*The book of the upright.* The book *(sēper)* cited in Joshua 10:13 as "the book of the upright"[51] may have included only the poem about the sun standing still (Josh 10:12-13). A book *(sēper)* by the same title is cited in 2 Samuel

---

[49]Hävernick makes much of this (ibid., 1/2:504). C. F. Keil omits Hävernick's discussion (*Manual of Historico-Critical Introduction to the Canonical Scriptures of the Old Testament,* trans. George C. M. Douglas [Edinburgh: T & T Clark, 1869], 1/2:189).

[50]Genesis 48:22 suggests that there were wars in Israel's past not recorded in Scripture.

[51]Sometimes translated "the book of Jashar."

1:18. Since both citations include poems,[52] it has been suggested that this book was a collection of poems. The importance of poems for the composition of the Pentateuch may suggest that this book was a collection of poems such as those used in the composition of the Pentateuch. It would account for the preservation of these ancient poems. Such a collection of poems may also be related to the fact that prophets often presented their messages and visions in poetic form.

*The testimony and Torah.* Although the term "book" *(sēper)* is not mentioned in Isaiah 8:16, 20, the description of the "testimony" *(tĕʿûdâ)* alongside the "law" *(tôrâ)* suggests that it was an ancient "book" like the Torah. According to this passage, the "testimony" was a text or book that could be read or searched, not unlike the "law" (Torah) was to be searched. Like the law, reading it for its meaning was a way of diligently searching *(dāraš)* for divine guidance: "If the word of the prophets does not speak the same message as the word of the law and testimony, they [the prophets] do not have light [dawn, *šāḥar*]."

*The book of Yahweh.* A "book" *(sēper)* that can be "searched diligently" *(dāraš)* for a prophetic word is cited as the "book of Yahweh *[yhwh]*" in Isaiah 34:16. The book contains prophecies that can be checked against their fulfillment.[53] The identity of this "book of Yahweh" is uncertain. It could be a reference to the book of Isaiah[54] or another collection of prophetic words.[55] Some have identified this book with the Pentateuch because Isaiah appears to be citing Numbers 24:18 in this passage. Isaiah's citation of this book in Isaiah 34:16 is similar to Obadiah's citation of Numbers 24:18.[56] Both Oba-

---

[52]See Sailhamer, *NIV Compact Bible Commentary*, p. 191.

[53]"Die beiden letzten Strophen bilden einem eigentümlichen Abschluss dieser Gerichtsdrohung über Edom; denn sie fordern die Leser auf, sich durch genaue Vergleichung dieser Weissagung mit der Erfüllung davon zu überzeugen, dass auch nicht eines von den genannten Tieren und Gespenstern in Edom fehle" (Karl Marti, *Das Buch Jesaja* [KHC 10; Tübingen: Mohr Siebeck, 1900], p. 245).

[54]"The prophet applied the title 'The Book of Jehovah' to his collection of the prophecies with which Jehovah had inspired him, and which He had commanded him to write down" (Franz Delitzsch, *Biblical Commentary on the Prophecies of Isaiah*, vol 2., trans. James Martin [BCOT 20; Grand Rapids: Eerdmans, 1954], p. 75).

[55]"Darum kann auch der Verf. Von Cap. 34 entweder seine niedergeschriebene Prophetie über Edom für sich oder eine grössere Sammlung (etwa Cap. 28-35 resp. selbst Cap. 1-35), welcher er seine eigene Prophetie einverleibte, ein סֵפֶר יְהוָה, Is 34:16), eine *Schrift Jahwes*, nennen" (Marti, *Das Buch Jesaja*, p. 245).

[56]"Those of the Negev shall posses the mountain of Esau [Edom] . . . and the kingdom shall be the LORD's" (Obad 1:19-21).

diah and Isaiah could be citing the Pentateuch. Both appeal to their readers to search (*dāraš*) and read from this "book of the Yahweh" because "not a single word will go unfulfilled." Franz Delitzsch gives the sense of the verse: "Whenever anyone compared the prophecy with the fulfillment, they would be found to coincide."[57] Delitzsch held that the prophecies to be fulfilled were listed in the first part of Isaiah 34, but it seems more likely that Isaiah has in mind the prophecies in Numbers 24:18, where the kingdom of the "star from Jacob" will extend to the possession of Edom. At the beginning of the chapter Isaiah warns all nations of the day when God would bring retribution on them (Is 34:1-17) "to uphold Zion's cause" (Is 34:8). As in Numbers 24:18, the prophet Isaiah singles out Edom as Israel's foe (Is 34:9-15). When judgment comes upon Edom and the nations, the "book of Yahweh" will testify that all these things were foretold and came to pass just as written (Is 34:16).

As in Isaiah 8:20; 30:8, Isaiah is conscious of the effect his work will have on later generations of readers who will know of the events foretold in this book. An important comment within 34:16 identifies the words of this "book of Yahweh" as those commanded "by [God's] mouth" and gathered into this book by "his Spirit." Such words clearly are a claim for the inspiration of the book and suggest its identification with the Pentateuch. Its title, "book of Yahweh," may be explained by the fact that, like the "book of the wars of Yahweh" (Num 21:14), the composition of the Pentateuch often has been credited to the work of a "Yahwist" whose primary intent was to unify the theology of the Pentateuch around the worship of the covenant God, Yahweh.[58] Isaiah 34:16 finds an echo in the "more sure word of prophecy" of 2 Peter 1:19.

*This shall be written.* Psalm 102:18 makes an important comment about the purpose of written texts: "This shall be written for a later generation." Isaiah 8:16-17 makes a similar statement: "Bind up the testimony, seal the law among my disciples. And I will wait upon the LORD, who is hiding his face from the house of Jacob, and I will look for him." Daniel 12:4 also is similar: "And you, Daniel, stop up the words and seal the book until the time of the end arrives" Biblical texts are written because they need to last a long time to

---

[57]Franz Delitzsch, *Biblical Commentary on the Prophecies of Isaiah,* trans. James Martin (Grand Rapids: Eerdmans, 1969), 1:75.

[58]"Das ist eine Auffassung von der Prophetie, wie sie das spätere Judentum und die Schriftgelehrten besassen: ein Prophetenwort ist tale quale ein Jahwewort, eine Prophetenschrift ein Jahwebuch" (Marti, *Das Buch Jesaja*, p. 245).

serve as comfort and strength for the faithful and to be a constant reminder of God's words to the prophets. The viewpoint reflected in these texts is similar to 2 Peter 1:19: "We have also a more sure word of prophecy."

***The Davidic monarchy (before 600 B.C.).*** During the period of the Davidic monarchy religious life centered on the temple and the kingship. Judging from the account of the "discovery" *(māṣāʾ)* of "the book of the law" *(sēper hattôrâ)* during the reign of Josiah (2 Kings 22:8), we deduce a general neglect of the Scriptures throughout much of this period. Biblically, this could be traced to the generation following Joshua, "who knew neither the LORD nor what he had done for Israel" (Judg 2:10). Were it not for the writings of David and Solomon and the later literary activity of some prophets, we would have to suppose that there was little or no composition of Scripture throughout much of this period of Israel's history. The Bible's own account of this period shows scant evidence of an impact of Scripture on the life of the people.[59] Although there is enough evidence to suggest that the Scriptures were existent and being read by some (e.g., Josh 1:8), there is little more than that. Meditating on Scripture "day and night" appears to have been more an ideal than a realizable state of affairs. To be sure, our understanding of the composition of biblical books during this period is limited. Most of it must be gathered from observations of compositional details from the biblical texts themselves. What does the shape, structure and content of the biblical books tell us about the work of their authors?

***The period of the exile (600–500 B.C.).*** Life for Israel after the Babylonian exile was a far cry from life under the Davidic monarchy.[60] Israel's exile to Babylon meant an end of the monarchy and, with that, a potential end to the future hopes that had surrounded it.[61] Israel's exile also meant the end of temple life as it had been known in Jerusalem since the time of David and Solomon. The temple and its priesthood were more than mere symbols of God's presence; they were also the means for the realization of that presence. The temple and its sacrifices were the place and the means by which God met with his people. We read in the psalms,

---

[59]In Samuel's day "the word of the Lord was rare . . . and visions had not broken through" (1 Sam 3:1).

[60]For an eyewitness account of the devastation, see the book of Lamentations; see also Sailhamer, *NIV Compact Bible Commentary*, pp. 385-86.

[61]Note the plaintiff cry of Psalm 89:38-39.

> My tears have been my food day and night, while men say to me continually, "Where is your God?" These things I remember, as I pour out my soul: how I went with the throng, and led them in procession to the house of God, with glad shouts and songs of thanksgiving, a multitude keeping festival. Why are you cast down, O my soul, and why are you disquieted within me? Hope in God; for I shall again praise him, my help and my God. (Ps 42:3-5 RSV)

> But when I thought how to understand this, it seemed to me a wearisome task, until I went into the sanctuary of God; then I perceived their end. (Ps 73:16-17 RSV)

The destruction of the temple and the consequent exile of the priesthood meant a fundamental change in, if not the nature, at least the outward manner of Israel's relationship with God. Where once Israel had sought God's presence at the temple, that temple now lay in ruins (Ps 74). Whereas once they vowed allegiance to the Davidic monarchy, the heir to that throne was an erstwhile prisoner in a Babylonian jail (2 Kings 25:27). Who or what would assume the role of the scattered priesthood? Who would stand before God and speak in their behalf? Where would they look for atonement and sacrifice? Where, and on whom, could they fix their hope for the future? Had it all been for naught (Lam 5:22)?[62]

The answer for those in exile, at least, was to be found in the freshly minted and newly issued Hebrew Scriptures. Those who had once found blessedness and wisdom in trusting God's promises to the Davidic monarchy (Ps 2:12b) could now find that by meditating "day and night" upon God's Word (Ps 1:1-2),[63] even while in Babylon. Where the priesthood had once mediated God's presence at the temple, the Scriptures offered every individual both access to God's grace (Ps 119:11) and a verbal vision of his glory (Is 6). With the tragic events of the exile and the destruction of the Jerusalem temple came a new assessment of Scripture as the focal point of God's promises and presence (Lam 3:25). Hope that once centered collectively in the congregation and in the physical presence of God among the kings and priests at the temple was now mediated to every individual through the "printed page" of Scripture.

The compositional strategy behind the formation of the Pentateuch had already anticipated this state of affairs. Central to the narrative of the giving

---

[62]In Lamentations 5:22 the LXX speaks of Israel's rejection, whereas the MT raises only the possibility of rejection.

[63]The structure of the book of Psalms is a theological answer to the questions of the exile.

of the Sinai law (Ex 19–24) is the ideal of a "kingdom of priests" (Ex 19:6). The priesthood is democratized. Everyone is a priest. That, at least, is how the narrative begins, but not how it ends. The Sinai narrative ends with the establishment of a priesthood of a select few (Ex 19:24).[64] From a "kingdom of priests" they had become a "kingdom with priests."

***The period after the exile (after 500 B.C.).*** The return from exile and the rebuilding of the temple did not alter the central position that Scripture had assumed. When, after the exile, Ezra returned to Jerusalem with the Levites (Ezra 7–10; Neh 8–10), their aim did not appear to be to establish the proper worship of God at the temple (Ezra 8:35).[65] By the time Ezra had arrived (Ezra 7), the temple (and its service) had been restored (Ezra 8:33, 36). Ezra's task was to deliver temple supplies (Ezra 7:12–8:36) and to teach both "the law of the [Persian] king" and "the law of [Ezra's] God" (Ezra 7:25-26). When, later, Ezra (Neh 8) gathered a solemn assembly in Jerusalem, it was not for worship at the temple; rather, it was so that they might stand "in the town square" *(ʾel-hārĕḥôb)* to hear the reading of the Scriptures, "the book of the law of Moses" (Neh 8:1). Reading the law in the streets was placed alongside temple service.[66] Isaiah's vision of the nations gathered in Jerusalem to learn the Torah (Is 2:3) had been realized in the mission of Ezra the scribe.

The expanded role of the Scriptures led to a shift in Israel's religious center of gravity. Where hope once rested in the return to the ancient institutions of the kingship, the temple and the priesthood, that hope was now being increasingly attached to the Scriptures as the words of the prophets. Before the exile, the prophetic words had been all but forgotten. They rested in the hands of a small community of prophetic disciples (Is 8:16; Dan 9:2). With the return from exile, those communities found themselves holding not merely the Scriptures, but Israel's future, in their hands. Their teachers, the "earlier" prophets, had passed from the scene, but their words remained.

---

[64]See Sailhamer, *The Pentateuch as Narrative*, pp. 51-57.

[65]Compare in the LXX, however, in 1 Esdras 9:38, "before the gateway toward the east of the temple" *(tou pros anatolas tou hierou pylōnos)*, which suggests a more temple-oriented view of the return from exile.

[66]"Gegen die Propheten, die bald nach der Rückkehr von Verbannten aus Babylonien eine Wende zum Heil verkündeten (vgl. Hag 2,20-23; Sach 6,9-15), traten drei Generationen später Esra und Nehemia auf. Sie sahen in diesen politischen Träumen eine Gefahr für den Bestand Israel. Darum überließen sie die Ordnung der politischen Verhältnisse den Persern und konzentrierten sich auf den inneren Ausbau der Bundesgemeinde im Sinne Jeremias auf Grund eines heiligen Buches, das—bisher Priesterprivileg—jetzt zum Allgemeinbesitz wurde (vgl. Neh 8)" ("Israel," *TBNT* 2:744).

Their warnings of judgment had been borne out by the nearly insurmountable difficulties of the exile. Now all that remained was the memory of their words "Did not my words and my statutes, which I commanded my servants the prophets, overtake your fathers?" (Zech 1:6).

Thus, a new sense of urgency had found expression in the words of the "later" prophets, that is, those who had returned with the people from exile. Before the exile, the "earlier" prophets had warned of the impending dangers, but that warning had fallen on deaf ears. With the exile came the proof of the prophets' words (Zech 1:6). That proof also raised questions: What else had the prophets' message contained? What else lay in store for those who had neglected their message (Zech 1:6b)? Where, amidst their words of judgment, could one find hope? With the exile, the prophets' words had earned a right to be heard. The exile got everyone's attention, but the words of the prophets still lay hidden away in sealed books. As we saw earlier, on the eve of the exile prophets such as Isaiah sealed their words, instructing their disciples to "bind up the testimony and seal up the Torah. I will wait for the LORD, who has hidden his face from the house of Jacob. I will wait for him" (Is 8:16-17). With the return from exile came a renewed interest in the rest of the prophets' words. Along with that interest came the need for the interpretation of the prophetic word.

The composition of the OT books was the prophetic answer to the renewed hope in the return from exile as well as the urgency to hear the prophetic words again and to ponder their meaning.

## Composition, Canonization and Consolidation

A compositional approach to the OT is concerned not only with how a book was preserved and written, but also with whether and to what extent a biblical book may have been interpreted after its initial composition. The steps by which a biblical book achieved its final form often were complex and followed many different paths. In general, however, the making of a biblical book can be understood roughly in terms of three stages: composition, canonization, consolidation.

The stage of composition is the point at which the individual books of the Bible were given their initial, and essential, shape. The period of canonization was the stage during which the biblical books were selected and arranged into the OT as a whole (Tanak). There may still have been some editing of the individual books at this stage. The stage of consolidation represents an important and frequently overlooked moment in a book's history, the point at which the Bible as a whole became acclimated to both its Jewish and its Christian communities. A compositional approach is concerned primarily with the first stage. These three stages, however, are not easily distinguishable. In some cases, biblical books were still in the process of being written at the time of their canonization and even consolidation.[67]

The invention of writing and the accompanying spread of literacy are the first and most important prerequisites of the composition of a biblical book. Without a high degree of literacy, ancient Israel would not have produced the OT, at least not the one we now have. Books must have readers, and they must have authors. The picture of the intended ("ideal") reader of the OT (Tanak) is given in Joshua 1:8 and Psalm 1:2. The intended reader is cast as a private individual[68] who "meditates day and night" on Scripture. This suggests that the reader not only reads the Scripture, but also reflects on it and applies those reflections to daily living. The result of reading is a skill *(taṣlîaḥ ʾet-dĕrākekā)* that produces wisdom *(wĕʾāz taśkîl)* (Josh 1:8). The Scriptures as a whole thus are cast as one thinks of wisdom literature. They are not so much for governing in the public square as they are a means for individual piety.

The biblical authors rarely focus their attention on the actual task of composing a biblical book. When they do, the terms they use suggest that the process of "making" a book involved more than merely recording one's thoughts in writing. To be sure, the biblical authors "wrote" their books, just as modern authors. But the idea of "writing a book" was more aptly expressed as "making" or "composing" a book. The familiar proverb in Ecclesiastes 12:12 speaks of the "making" *(ʿāśâ)* of many books, not the "writing" of many books. When in the OT someone "writes in a book" (*kĕtōb bassēper* [Ex 17:14]) or "writes upon a book" (*kātab ʿal-sēper* [Deut 17:18]), we should keep in mind that the Hebrew word for "write" *(kātab)* commonly refers to "copying" words (Deut 17:18; 31:19, 24) or "copying down" words in a book (Jer 36:2). It generally did not have the sense of what we would today describe as "writing (composing) a book."[69]

[67]For an example of the continuation of a book's composition during and after the time of canonization and consolidation in the book of Jeremiah, see John H. Sailhamer, "Biblical Theology and the Composition of the Hebrew Bible," in *Biblical Theology: Retrospect and Prospect*, ed. Scott Hafemann (Downers Grove, Ill.: InterVarsity Press, 2002), p. 30.

[68]Which does not rule out public reading as well (cf. Ezra 7:5).

[69]See Marvin H. Pope, *Job* (AB 15; Garden City, N.Y.: Doubleday, 1965), pp. 139-46. "O that my

Regardless of the exact intent of the biblical terminology, there appears to have been a genuine distinction between "writing in a book" and "making a book," a distinction found also outside the Bible.[70] "Making" *(ʿāśâ)* a book, as in Ecclesiastes 12:12, has in view the larger task of shaping and editing pieces of a book into a single work. It is close to the modern task of producing a book. It is similar in meaning also to the notion of composition (cf. Prov 25:1: *heʿtîqû*, "they copied"; עתק = "to remove away, transcribe, move a word from one scroll to another" [BDB]).[71]

The complexity of the task of making a biblical book may also be intimated in Ecclesiastes 12:12. The expression *harbēh*, translated as "many," may be used as an adjective, as in the English translation "many books," or it may be used as an adverb, meaning, roughly, the "constant" process of making books. There is no end to the composition of a book. Thus, it may mean either that an endless number of books can be made or that the process of making a book is endless. The fact that this comment comes at the end of the book of Ecclesiastes, along with a warning against adding more "wise sayings" to the book, suggests that in Ecclesiastes it aims at cutting short the process of making a book. The problem is not making more books, but deciding whether and when to end this one.

Hence, this statement is about the complexity of "making" a book. Part of the complexity of making a book involved the use of "written" records. There are ample traces of such records embedded in many OT books. Such records are known to us only as parts of existing books. No written source presently exists apart from those within OT books. "Making" books such as we have in the OT involved piecing together written sources into a single and complete book. Any attempt to understand the process of making a biblical book must come to terms with such diverse tasks as writing, editing, composing and copying.

As far as we know, the original manuscripts of the OT were written in ancient Hebrew. Hebrew was a language indigenous to Canaan. It had been

---

words were written, were engraved on a stela, with iron stylus and lead, carved in rock forever" (Job 19:23-24).

[70]See Fishbane, *Biblical Interpretation in Ancient Israel*, pp. 29-36.

[71]"What appears certain, at any rate, is that Eccles. 12:9-12 drew from a conventional stock of ancient Near Eastern scribal practices and vocabulary" (ibid., p. 31). "Further information about scribal activities in ancient Israel can be deduced from other contexts. Prov. 25:1, Jer. 8:8, and Ezra 7:10-12 deserve particular mention in this regard" (ibid., p. 32).

in use in Canaan since the time of Abraham. The OT was written in Hebrew presumably because it was the language of the Israelites to whom it was written. By the time Abraham had settled in Canaan, local scribes were already at work inventing and perfecting the alphabet. That alphabet, once developed, spread quickly throughout the ancient world and was the prototype of most later and modern alphabets.

As we know it from biblical manuscripts, the Hebrew alphabet consists of twenty-two letters. The invention of this alphabet was an impressive achievement, far ahead of its time. It suggests a brilliance and resourcefulness unmatched even by modern standards. By reducing the sounds of a spoken language to a small inventory of signs (letters), a scribe was able to record in writing the sound of any word in his own language. It was a far simpler method of writing than the one current in that day, which used graphic signs to denote various words and syllables, requiring an inventory of a minimum of several hundred complicated signs. Only professional scribes could hope to read or write in such a system. The alphabet therefore was a far simpler way to read written texts. It did not require a guild of professional scribes. Thus, the invention of the alphabet meant that Hebrew could be used by common people to record everyday information about local events. It required minimal learning. The only requirement was the memorization of twenty-two letters.

Because of the simplicity of the alphabet, one could write on virtually any surface. The letters were simple and could be accommodated to small and uneven surfaces. Broken pieces of pottery (potsherds) made excellent writing surfaces. The alphabet made the collection and widespread use of written texts not only possible, but also within the reach of nearly anyone. Already in Abraham's day, ordinary citizens were writing their names on personal items such as knives and pottery. That suggests not only that the owners of such items could read, but also that reading was widespread. The identification of personal belongings would be pointless unless others also could read. By the time of Moses, the stage had been set for the writing of Scripture and the making of books.

Written records were a necessary component of the process of making books. Much of what we see in the compositions of OT books consists of the collection and arrangement of ancient written material. The HB is like a scrapbook of newspaper and magazine clippings, along with a family album. Those clippings have been skillfully arranged and woven into a single, coherent book. But viewed close up, a biblical book appears to be "made" of many pieces of written documents much like we would see in a family scrapbook. The book of clippings, arranged a certain way, tells the story of a family.

As a finished product, each book of the HB is a complex, yet coherent, composition. The written records used in these books are known to us only from the biblical books themselves. Biblical scholars have expended much effort attempting to reconstruct the earlier written records that lie behind OT books. The results of those efforts have not met with wide acceptance, especially in recent years. Although general agreement exists that written sources were used, there is little optimism about the possibility of extracting those documents from the present OT books.

It is also possible, though unlikely, that earlier parts of the biblical books were never circulated in written form. They may have been passed along orally and preserved by memory. If so, it would explain the scarcity of extant written sources. Having said that, one must bear in mind that still much of the material in these books gives the appearance of having been preserved in written form. Stories and bits of information attached to oral texts tend to blend together and lose their individual shape. The presence of oral stories can be detected only by tracing the themes and patterns that once governed the shape of their oral form. They no longer reflect much of their original oral shape. Thus, there is little hope in attempting to reconstruct the original forms of oral stories.

Unlike oral sources, the stories and historical notes found in the biblical narratives have retained much of their original written form. They were copied and made part of the biblical books while in written form. Such written texts have been woven remarkably well into the larger narrative fabric of which they are now a part. There are only occasional traces of their original independence. The comment about Abraham's travels in Genesis 20:1, "And Abraham journeyed *from there* toward the land of the Negev," suggests that it was once preceded by a narrative that had specified Abraham's whereabouts, as in Genesis 18:1-33 or Genesis 13:18. As it now stands, the account of Abraham in Genesis 20 is preceded by the account of Lot and the destruction of Sodom in Genesis 19. The words "from there" are thus a reference from an earlier state of the biblical narrative.

As I noted above, a written account of the family of Adam is attached to the Pentateuch at the end of Genesis 4. It is called "the book *[sēper]* of the genealogy/history of Adam" *(zeh sēper tôlĕdōt ʾādām).* This "book," which later became part of the book of Genesis (cf. Gen 5:1-32; 9:28-29), serves as an overall framework for the flood account (Gen 6:5–9:27) and several later narratives (e.g., Gen 6:9; 10:1; 11:10, 27). The way the author has inserted the flood story into the framework of this "book of Adam" can be seen by comparing the symmetry of the list of names and the segments on either side of the flood narrative (Gen 5:32; 9:28-29). We can see from the way the narratives fit together that the flood account as a whole was inserted into the list of names after the introduction of Noah.[72]

The uniformity of the general pattern of this list reveals the following three deviations from the pattern, suggesting that they are the result of an intentional compositional strategy that is the work of its author.

First, at the beginning of the list (Gen 5:3b) an addition names the next son: "and he named him Seth." At the end of the list (Gen 5:29) an identical addition names the next son: "and he named him Noah." The first addition (Gen 5:3b) connects the list in Genesis 5 to the creation account in Genesis 1–4 (cf. Gen 4:25). The second addition (Gen 5:29) prepares the reader for the flood account and its aftermath (Gen 8:21).

Second, there is no mention of the deaths of Enoch and Noah in the list of Genesis 5. For each man, the narrative specifically notes that "he walked with God." Traces of similar formal patterns can be detected:

These observations suggest that the written pieces of the flood account were inserted into a written copy of the "book of Adam" after Genesis 5:32. The remainder of the list continues, without modification of its formal pattern, at the end of the flood story (Gen 9:28-29). The account of the "sons and daughters" in Genesis 6:1-4 provides the missing birth account following Noah's introduction, as well as a transition to the account of the flood. The flood account begins at Genesis 6:5 with an allusion to the creation account in Genesis 1, "and God saw . . ."

The use of written sources is not unique to these chapters of Genesis. It is clear from the Gospel accounts that isolated and independent written accounts of the life and teaching of Jesus circulated at an early period. These

---

[72]See "Genesis–Leviticus," in *The Expositor's Bible Commentary,* ed. John H. Sailhamer, Tremper Longman III and David E. Garland, rev. ed. (Grand Rapids: Zondervan, 2008), pp. 110-11.

were gathered by the Gospel authors and fit together to tell a complete story of Christ's life (see Lk 1:1-4). In a similar way, the book of Kings frequently cites its written sources (e.g., 2 Kings 12:19). From a comparison of the books of Chronicles with the books of Samuel and Kings, it is clear that they were the primary written sources of the book of Chronicles. There were other sources as well (e.g., 2 Chron 9:29).

Keeping written records was widely practiced in the ancient world. The art of writing was a by-product of the need to keep records. Some of the earliest written records are administrative texts written on clay tablets. Graphic signs, which later developed into complex writing systems, originated as marks made in soft clay to denote the number of a farmer's sheep or the quantity of olive oil in a jar.

With the use of the alphabet, the earliest written prose and poetry in the Bible probably once were written on the surface of a fragment of a broken jar. Once the custom was established, words and the ideas associated with them could be etched with a sharp instrument. Such records could remain for hundreds, even thousands, of years. Simple letters scratched onto a smooth stone could preserve a recorded event in the life of an ancestor for a hundred generations. Many such small, written documents are as readable today as they were three thousand years ago.[73]

Job 19:23-24 provides a helpful insight into the purpose of writing. It served two primary purposes. It made one's words sharable and it made them permanent: "O that my words were written down! O that they were inscribed in a book! O that with an iron pen and with lead they were engraved on a rock forever!" (Job 19:23-24 NRSV).

***The making of books.*** When did "books" first begin to be used in the ancient world? At what point were ancient records collected and made into books? The questions are somewhat anachronistic. The English word *book* usually refers to a bound document with pages. Technically, this was called a "codex," and it was a relatively late development in the art of writing. The codex was invented by Christians and eventually taken over as a way of producing copies of the Bible. There were no "books" of that sort in the ancient world.

---

[73]See Hubert Grimme, *Die Altsinaitischen Buchstaben-Inschriften auf Grund einer Untersuchung der Originale* (Berlin: Reuther & Reichard, 1929); William Foxell Albright, *The Proto-Sinaitic Inscriptions and Their Decipherment* (HTS 22; Cambridge, Mass.: Harvard University Press, 1969). Note Job 19:24: "they were engraved in a rock forever" *(lāʿad baṣṣûr yēḥoṣbûn).*

A "book" as it would have appeared at the time of the formation of the OT could sometimes be no larger than a flat surface on a stone or a broken piece of pottery inscribed with a metal stylus or with pen and ink. It could also consist of a wooden tablet or, as in most OT books, pieces of leather or papyrus stitched together and given a smooth surface to receive the pen and ink. Such a scroll could be stored by rolling it onto a stick and sealing it at one end with wax. There are many examples of such "books" from antiquity.[74]

In the broadest sense, any type of literary, or written, document was considered a "book" *(sēper)*. Its size or scope might have been extensive, and its content might have consisted of literary (narrative or poetry) or legal (collections of laws, sayings, names [e.g., Gen 5:1]) material.

Moses appears to be "making" or "copying" *(kātab)* such a "book" in Deuteronomy 31:24. It was to be placed beside (or inside) the ark of the covenant (Deut 31:26). This may have been similar to the document given to the king in Deuteronomy 17 or to Joshua after the death of Moses (Josh 1:8). Joshua was to read the "book" "day and night." It was a religious but practical book, as is evident from the fact that its purpose was to strengthen Joshua's resolve to trust in God and to make him wise (Josh 1:8).

This "book" may have been all or part of the Mosaic Pentateuch. That, at least, is what the author of the book of Joshua seems to assume. As we have noted, its size and extent are unknown from that passage. This may also have been the book in which Moses recorded the account of the battle with the Amalekites (Ex 17:14). It may also have been the "book of the law" that Joshua copied on the stones of the altar he built on Mount Ebal (Josh 8:32) and that he read to the congregation on that occasion (Josh 8:34). From that book "there was not a single word from all that Moses had commanded that Joshua did not read before all the congregation of Israel" (Josh 8:35). The exact object of these references is hard to reconstruct.

Whatever the extent and shape of the book at that time, it seems certain from the biblical account that this was an early Mosaic book, one that he himself had made. As such, this book was a kind of the prototype of subsequent biblical books.[75] Abraham did not write a book, nor did Adam, al-

[74]See James B. Pritchard, *The Ancient Near East in Pictures Relating to the Old Testament*, 2nd ed. (Princeton, N.J.: Princeton University Press, 1969), p. 82.

[75]The exact nature and scope of the "book of the wars of the Lord" in Numbers 21:14 is unknown.

though, as we have noted, there is a reference to a "book" that included a genealogy tracing the lineage of Adam to Noah (Gen 5:1) or perhaps as far as Moses (Num 3:1). This book may have been part of a genealogy of Aaron and Moses.

It may be significant that in the description of the antediluvian civilization in Genesis 4:17-26, which included such skills as "playing the lyre and the pipe" (Gen 4:21), there is no mention of the skill of writing or literature. From the perspective of the biblical writers, the "written book" arrived late on the scene. As a medium of divine revelation, the biblical authors suggest, it originated with Moses. It was the great legacy that Moses passed on to future generations, a written book whose words were the Word of God.

Moses did not invent the art of writing, nor did he discover new forms of writing material. The Egyptians had used papyrus "books" centuries before him. It was the writing of a book as the embodiment of God's acts [Ex 17:14]) and blessings that the Bible attributes to Moses (cf. Josh 1:8). The Bible depicts Moses as the inventor of a book that, in time, came to encompass acts of God amid the everyday lives of Israel and the nations.[76]

According to some early Hebrew texts (MT), the book of Moses at an early stage was called the "law," or *tôrâ*, a Hebrew word meaning "instruction." The law is identified as divine "wisdom" by which Moses instructed Israel in the will of God (Deut 4:6). According to Deuteronomy 1:5, Moses wrote a commentary on the rest of the laws and narratives in the Pentateuch. That commentary was given the name "second law," or "Deuteronomy" (*deutero* = "second"; *nomos* = "law").

The actual process of writing a book in biblical times is described in Jeremiah 36. Jeremiah was told by the Lord to take a "scroll of a book" *(mĕgillat-sēper)* and "write upon" it "all the words which I have spoken to you from the days of Josiah until this day" (Jer 36:2). Jeremiah's ability to carry out the Lord's command makes it likely that he had kept written notes of his messages. He then dictated his words to Baruch either from memory or from

---

[76]In the Pentateuch, there are nineteen (out of 187) occurrences of the word "book" *(sēper)*.

1 <1> Genesis •
4 <2> Exodus •
0 <0> Leviticus
2 <1> Numbers ••
11 <6> Deuteronomy •••••••••••

written notes (Jer 36:18). In carrying out God's instructions, Jeremiah commissioned his scribe, Baruch, "to write the words upon" the scroll as he dictated them (Jer 36:4).

Having written the book, Baruch was instructed to take it to the temple on a day of fasting and read it aloud (Jer 36:6-10).[77] We also see from this chapter that the scroll was portable. Baruch was able to "take it in his hand" as he appeared before the king's scribes (Jer 36:14). After the scribes heard Baruch read the book, they read it to the king (Jer 36:21). Once they had heard the scroll read aloud by Baruch (with the pronunciation of its vowels), they understood the sense of the consonants and could supply the necessary vowels.

***The composition of a biblical book.*** It took the convergence of several important achievements to make the OT a practical reality. The alphabet made it possible to write a book so that nonprofessionals could read it. From texts such as Joshua 1:8 and Psalm 1:2, it is clear that these books were designed for individual reading.

Writing materials, such as a pen and ink, as well as various kinds of writing surfaces (leather, papyrus, wood), were also necessary and apparently in sufficient supply. By this time, the potential of literary works for shaping public opinion had been explored and used successfully.[78]

The biblical authors were willing to take advantage of these possibilities. The concept of a written work's ability to order the world by means of literary strategies such as plot and characterization was entering perhaps for the first time into ancient Israel's social consciousness. The biblical authors not only were quick to explore these new possibilities, but also they were more than ready to carry them to new levels. The lessons of Sinai were cast as narratives, dramas, poems, didactic wisdom and law. These various genres were woven together into a single whole, each contributing in its own way. The biblical books were a product of an intentional effort to recount all that God had accomplished in his calling Israel and to preserve for future generations what he intended to do further.

In the prophetic books, the prophet's words not only are made readily

---

[77]It may have been necessary for Jeremiah to read the book aloud because, in all likelihood, it was written without vowels and would have been unintelligible without an oral recitation.

[78]See "The Tale of Si-nuhe," in James B. Pritchard, *Ancient Near Eastern Texts Relating to the Old Testament* (Princeton, N.J.: Princeton University Press, 1969), p. 22.

available, but also are allowed to speak for themselves within a context provided by the author's arrangement of the material in a book. At times, the authors of these OT books are so successful at presenting the words and acts of the prophets that even today we think of their books as the prophet's own writings. The OT books are similar to the four Gospels. Each Gospel is written about Jesus, each contains his words and accounts of his deeds, but none of them was written by Jesus himself.

Also like the Gospels, the prophetic books cast the prophet's words within a broader interpretive context. The prophets sometimes provide their own interpretation. In Isaiah 46:11 the prophet envisions the Persian king Cyrus as a bird of prey coming from "a far off land" *(merḥāq)* to do the will of God. But in the following verse, Isaiah 46:12, the prophet looks beyond the historical referent of his words to their spiritual meaning. He who is from "afar off" is a picture of "those who are afar off *[hārĕḥôqîm]* from righteousness." The prophet gives the spiritual sense of his own words.

In recent evangelical biblical scholarship, the compositional view provides a viable alternative to the classical Documentary Hypothesis. It differs from the critical view in two important respects. First, the compositional approach views the end product of the Pentateuch, and other biblical books, in light of the intentional design and purpose of its author. The Pentateuch is not the result of a merely historical process; it is also the result of an intelligent design. Its shape makes sense and can be viewed as part of the intention and literary strategy of its author.

Second, the difference between the compositional view and the classic Documentary Hypothesis is that the compositional approach neither assumes the existence of, nor attempts to discover, earlier versions of the Pentateuch lying behind the present Pentateuch. The compositional view assumes only that the present text of the Pentateuch such as a Yahwist Pentateuch or a Deuteronomist Pentateuch was composed of earlier "pieces" of written texts—stories, genealogies, laws, poems. Those written records were woven together to form the larger picture presented in the Pentateuch. The question of what those earlier "pieces" once looked like, or where they came from, is not the concern of the compositional approach. Although it may concede the possibility of isolating and attempting to reconstruct an earlier form of some of those pieces of texts, the compositional view maintains that such an endeavor is not needed to appreciate the textual strategy evidenced in the present shape of the Pentateuch. In a word, the compositional approach is about strategy (authorial design), not strata (earlier documents).

The compositional approach to the OT starts with the notion that the present form of the Pentateuch, or any biblical book, has a literary strategy. There is something in store for the reader of the book. To understand what the Pentateuch is about, one must read it.

Few today doubt that it may be possible to peer beneath the surface of the text to get a clearer sense of where the author is taking readers. There are instances where traces of written documents and records can still be detected. By examining those records in their present shape within the biblical text, one might gain an additional understanding of the author's textual strategy. One might also understand more fully how an author has accomplished his task. It is possible to see why an author uses a poem at one point in the narrative and a genealogy in another. Or one might see why a section of text intentionally repeats a similar story several times throughout a book. Questions about the structure of a narrative are also important. Why, for example, does the Pentateuch begin with an account of creation and conclude with the death of Moses? Such questions can cast light on the underlying strategy of the author.

In seeking answers to such questions, a compositional approach does not aim merely to retrace the history of a book's composition. Its aim is always the structure and message of the present text. Its aim is to understand why a particular book says what it says and why it is written as it is written. What is the meaning of its shape? Such questions are similar to asking why an artist chooses a particular color of paint or paints a landscape rather than a portrait. In the biblical books we see literary artists at work. The aim of a compositional approach is to appreciate more fully their mastery of the art of making a book.

## The Pentateuch as a Whole (Macrostructure)

***The written material in the Pentateuch.*** Judging from what we see in the Pentateuch, we surmise that the author began his work with several parts already intact. There were blocks of narrative texts, collections of laws, genealogical lists and a selection of ancient poems. It is not known how these ancient written texts were originally formed or what purpose they may have fulfilled before they were used in the Pentateuch. Most of the written texts found their way into the Pentateuch with minimal adjustment. Some still bear the marks of their previous literary contexts.[79]

The actual process of making of the Pentateuch appears to have begun with several large blocks of narrative already intact. The author created a single story by weaving those blocks into a literary whole. In "making" the Pentateuch, the author treated these early texts with great respect, preserving them much as he found them or as they had been handed down to him.

The individual blocks of narrative in the Pentateuch are:

1. the primeval history (Gen 1–11)
2. the patriarchal narratives (Gen 12–50)
3. the exodus narratives (Ex 1–19)
4. the wilderness narratives (Num 11–25)
5. the conquest narratives (Deut 1–11)

The initial work of shaping the Pentateuch and weaving these blocks of narrative together was accomplished by a variety of means. The most basic structural pattern was to arrange them in chronological order. Within each of the blocks of narrative there was likely already an implicit chronological ordering. By linking them further, each block was brought into the larger chronological schema lying between the blocks and embracing them as a whole.

The author's use of ancient poetry was another part of the compositional picture. Throughout the Pentateuch the author relies heavily on the interpretive value of poetry in connecting the large blocks of narrative into a single story. From what we can gather from his use of poetry, the author highly valued poems as a way of picturing the broader meaning of the texts he was linking together. To understand the Pentateuch, it is important to pay close attention to its poetry.

The major poems in the Pentateuch are

1. Genesis 3:14-19
2. Genesis 49:2-27

---

[79]See the discussion of Genesis 20:1 under "Composition, Canonization and Consolidation" above.

3. Exodus 15:1-19
4. Numbers 23–24
5. Deuteronomy 32–33

For the most part, these ancient poems are preserved in their original shape. Their archaic character is betrayed by the fact that the author often finds it necessary to add explanatory comments and clarifications to them. The brevity and density of their poetic imagery sometimes obscures the light that the author intended them to cast upon his text. The author frequently supplies his own commentary and explanation to the poems, leaving the reader with little doubt about how he understood them. Also, the poems are placed within a narrative framework that highlights much of what the author wants the reader to see in the poetic imagery. As poems, these texts play an important role in shaping the Pentateuch. They function somewhat like the songs in a Hollywood musical. They give thematic unity to the narratives by focusing on a single theme.

An important feature of these poems is their distribution within the Pentateuch. They do not cluster in one or two places. They are inserted into the narratives at more or less even intervals in every section of the Pentateuch, extending from the early chapters of Genesis to the final chapters of Deuteronomy, and they are positioned at the conclusion of each of the large blocks of narrative noted above. Their distribution suggests that these poems are a comprehensive organizational feature of the entire Pentateuch, not an isolated feature of only some of these texts. The original shape of the Pentateuch has been remarkably stable.

It is a common assumption that the Pentateuch in its present form is the result of a gradual process of literary growth and development. The distribution of these poems, noted above, suggests otherwise. Either its present form is its original shape and there has been little structural development, or its original shape has been preserved despite its many stages of development. The first of these two possibilities is the more probable because redevelopment over a long period surely would have eroded much of the clear structures now noticeable in the Pentateuch's present shape. Either possibility argues for a shorter time period between the present shape of the Pentateuch and its original form.

***Collections of laws.*** The author of the Pentateuch used several collections of written laws:

1. the Ten Commandments in Exodus 20
2. the Covenant Code in Exodus 20–23
3. the laws for priests in Exodus 25–Leviticus 16
4. the Holiness Code in Leviticus 17–27
5. Deuteronomy 12–26

These collections of laws apparently were drawn from law codes that Moses possessed both before and after Sinai. According to Exodus 15:25b-26, God gave Moses laws *(ḥōq ûmišpāṭ),* statutes *(ḥuqqāyw)* and commandments *(miṣwōtāyw) before* Sinai. In Exodus 18:16, 20, *before* Sinai, Moses taught "the statutes of God" *(ḥuqqê hāʾĕlōhîm)* and "his laws" *(tôrōtāyw). At* Sinai, God gave Moses the "ten words" (*ʿăśeret haddĕbārîm* [Ex 34:28; cf. Ex 20:1-17]), the "book of the covenant" (*sēper habbĕrît* [Ex 24:7]), which apparently contained laws (Ex 24:3), and numerous other collections of laws (e.g., Ex 20:22–23:19; 25:1–31:18; Lev 1:1–16:34; 17–27), as well as *after* Sinai (Numbers passim; Deuteronomy passim). A compositional approach asks why these various collections of laws are in the Pentateuch. Why is there not a single, complete and unified collection of laws? Why were various collections inserted at various times?

As we noted, the work of recording and preserving these collections of laws in the Pentateuch often is associated with the priesthood, beginning with Moses and Aaron. Along with their priestly duties (Deut 33:10b), those of the house of Levi were to teach the "judgments and laws" to Israel (Deut 33:10a). Other biblical texts point to close connections between these laws and Israel's prophets (e.g., Dan 9:10). This raises the question of who was responsible for these laws and whose perspective we are now to associate with the collections of laws in the Pentateuch. Do these laws reflect the viewpoint of the priests, the prophets, both, or neither? We will return to that question along with the nature and purpose of these laws within the compositional strategy of the Pentateuch.[80]

***The use of sources in the Pentateuch.*** I have argued that the task of discovering important aspects of the theology of the Pentateuch lies in retracing the author's gathering and shaping of the large blocks of narratives, ancient poems and the collections of laws. By retracing those steps, we can better under-

[80]See Sailhamer, "The Mosaic Law."

stand the author's contribution to the book and thereby gain important clues about its central themes. Once we understand the macrostructure of the Pentateuch and the meaning behind it, the remainder of our task is relatively straightforward. It consists of tracing the line of argument laid down by the varied and sundry details of the text (microstructure). How do they fit into, and contribute to, the sense of the whole?

This approach to the written sources of the Pentateuch is similar, perhaps identical, to the view noted earlier of the classical evangelical scholars Robert Jamieson, A. R. Fausset and David Brown:

> It may be conceded that, in the composition of those parts of the Pentateuch relating to matters which were not within the sphere of his personal knowledge, Moses would and did avail himself of existing records which were of reliable authority; . . . it is evident that, in making use of such literary materials as were generally known in his time, or had been preserved in the repositories of Hebrew families, he interwove them into his narrative conformably with the unity of design which so manifestly pervades the entire Pentateuch.[81]

These venerable nineteenth-century biblical scholars freely acknowledge the use of written sources in "making" the Pentateuch. They also seek to discover the overall plan and argument of the Pentateuch. They expect the Pentateuch to make sense when viewed as a whole, and they understand that "sense of the whole" in terms of the compositional shape that the author has given to his written sources. Their view represents the view of most evangelical scholars throughout the seventeenth and eighteenth centuries. One of the most venerable from that period, Campegius Vitringa,[82] often is cited as representative of the view followed by evangelical scholars prior to the nineteenth century. Regarding the Mosaic composition of the book of Genesis, Vitringa stated, "It is our view that Moses collected, arranged, adorned, and where lacking, filled in, those written pages and records of the patriarchs which were preserved by the Israelites, and from them he composed the first of his books."[83]

---

[81]Robert Jamieson, A. R. Fausset and David Brown, *A Commentary, Critical, Experimental and Practical, on the Old and New Testaments* (Grand Rapids: Eerdmans, 1945), 1:xxxii.

[82]For a helpful assessment of Vitringa, see Brevard S. Childs, "Hermeneutical Reflections on C. Vitringa, Eighteenth-Century Interpreter of Isaiah," in *In Search of True Wisdom: Essays in Old Testament Interpretation in Honour of Ronald E. Clements*, ed. Edward Ball (JSOTSup 300; Sheffield: Sheffield Academic Press, 1999).

[83]"Has vero schedas & scrinia Patrum, apud Israelitas conservata, Mosen opinamur collegisse, di-

Since the rise of biblical and historical criticism in the nineteenth and twentieth centuries, with its focus on the earliest "reconstructed" forms of the biblical material, the evangelical position has, understandably, shied away from talking about "sources" or "written records." Nevertheless, if pressed, most evangelical OT scholars acknowledge the basic validity of the earlier conservative view and its acknowledgment of written sources in the OT. According to Edward Young, "It is perfectly possible that in the compilation of the Pentateuch Moses may have made excerpts from previously existing written documents."[84]

The only variation on this approach among evangelicals is the suggestion sometimes made that the "sources" available to Moses were not in written form. Moses may have relied on oral tradition. The difficulty with that approach to the question is that it fails to deal adequately with the realities of the text itself, which include both the frequent mention of written sources by the biblical authors and evidence of the use of written records in the texts. In addition to that, the supposition that biblical writers used only oral sources introduces an unnecessary level of uncertainty into the process.

If one steps back to view the narratives of the Pentateuch in their entirety, what one begins to see is a kind of web of many narratives woven together into a single story. Those narratives range in size from small, almost anecdotal episodes (e.g., Gen 9:18-27), to large novel-like compositions (Gen 37–50). It is also apparent that the author has further linked these narrative blocks so that they are now a part of a complete, unified narrative that runs, with few interruptions, the full length of the Pentateuch, from Genesis 1 through Deuteronomy 34.[85] Woven into the fabric of these narratives are the ancient poems, genealogies and various collections of laws. The laws gather at the center and toward the end of the Pentateuch (Ex 20–Deut 29). On

---

gessisse, ornasse, &, ubi deficiebant, complesse, atque ex iis primum Librorum suorum confecisse" (Campegius Vitringa, *Sacrarum observationum libri quatuor* [Franeker, 1700], p. 35).

[84]Edward J. Young, *An Introduction to the Old Testament*, rev. ed. (Grand Rapids: Eerdmans, 1984), p. 153. Compare Wilhelm Möller: "Doch liegen auch schriftliche Unterlagen durchaus im Bereich des Möglichen oder sogar Wahrscheinlichen. In Gen. 14 haben wir einen Fall, in dem das von vielen Kritikern selbst angenommen wird. Wann diese begonnen haben möchten, in welcher Sprache, in welcher Schrift, in welchem Ausmaße, darüber zu spiritisieren, ist ziemlich müßig und einstweilen auch aussichtslos. Ob durch Moses eine Redaktion erfolgte, ist gleichfalls schwer zu sagen, wiewohl durchaus wahrscheinlich" (*Biblische Theologie des Alten Testaments in heilsgeschichtlicher Entwicklung* [Zwickau: Herrmann, 1938], p. 42).

[85]See Jean Louis Ska, *"Our Fathers Have Told Us": Introduction to the Analysis of Hebrew Narratives*, 2nd ed. (SubBi 13; Rome: Editrice Pontificio Instituto Biblico, 2000).

close examination, there appear to be not one, but several, independent collections of laws. As has often been observed, the central theological question posed by the Pentateuch is the nature and purpose of these collections of laws. Why are there laws in the Pentateuch? Why is there such diversity in the various collections of laws? Why is there such little effort to overcome that diversity within the pages of the Pentateuch itself?

The task of weaving these literary pieces together into a single composition, a "Pentateuch," was the achievement of a great literary talent. It is the work of the "author" of the Pentateuch. The unity of the book's plan, its design and scope, betray a singularity of purpose that can only be described as that of an author *(mens auctoris).* The aim of a theology of the Pentateuch lies in the discovery of that purpose through careful examination of the author's compositional strategy. Ultimately, our aim is not to deconstruct the Pentateuch, but to let it remain intact and attempt to sort out its various parts, assigning some weight of importance to their pattern of distribution within his book. The goal must always be guided by the hope of catching a glimpse of the author at work, which means seeking to know what he is attempting to say in this work and allowing him, at his leisure, to guide us through the book. For this task, one must become an attentive and sensitive reader.

*Chapter 6*

# The Composition of the Pentateuch

It seems reasonable to suppose that the author of the Pentateuch set out to give readers a single and complete historical story. The Pentateuch is neither an anthology of isolated stories nor a complete collection of laws. It is a book that tells a story that ultimately centers on one's relationship to God. There are diverse kinds of literature in the Pentateuch, but taken as a whole, its thematic structure displays little diversity. The making of the Pentateuch was a great achievement. To understand it, one must know something about how it was made.

An analysis of its literary shape indicates that the making of the Pentateuch consisted primarily of weaving together and connecting these ancient texts into a single historical story or narrative. The work often was complex and involved many intricacies of grammar and style. "Making" the Pentateuch meant deciding when to add a comment to a passage or perhaps when merely to summarize the material from various written sources. Adding comments and commentary to the written text was the kind of activity that lay at the heart of the Pentateuch's composition. Where would we be with a Pentateuch that did not include the author's comment in Genesis 15:6, "And Abraham believed God, and it was reckoned to him for righteousness"? As I will suggest, that comment by the author is not an isolated remark. It is, rather, an essential part of a compositional "faith strategy" that runs the length of the Pentateuch, from beginning to end, and plays a major role in the prophetic literature and, ultimately, the NT.

The use of ancient sources also made explanations or clarifications of details an essential part of the author's work. In accomplishing that task, the inspired author displays a considerable amount of historical and literary knowledge of the written texts that he used. The various written texts were not haphazardly thrown together. The author had a clear idea of how the various written texts should be fit together. Often, the insertion of a comment was necessary, not because of a lack of clarity, but to help the reader understand the importance of a word or written expression in a text and its relationship to the literary surroundings. In such cases, the author's comments were intended to guide the reader in understanding the text. A close examination of the literary results suggests that the author worked with a detailed knowledge of the interrelationships of each of the written texts. In addition, it is apparent that the author adhered rigorously to a single, coherent master plan, a plan outlining in detail how the pieces should be fit together.[1] All this not only suggests the presence of a competent author, but also assumes a level of competence on the part of the reader.

Lying behind the composition of the Pentateuch is a clearly defined theological program rather than raw data in need of explanation.[2] The Pentateuch is a work whose composition required both literary and theological judgment. It is a work that addresses specific issues, and one can only suppose that those issues were of vital importance to its readers. The author surely was aware of the response his work would evoke from some quarters. He surely knew, for example, that his account of the golden calf in Exodus 32 would not be entirely to the liking of some, particularly those in the priesthood (see Ex 32:1-6). The possibility of a negative response to his highlighting of Moses' lapse of faith in the wilderness (Num 20:12) could not have escaped his attention. He must also have known that his explicit (almost Pauline) spiritualization of obedience to the law in the life of Abraham (Gen 26:5)[3] would cast a shadow over

[1]The comment "after he [Moses] sent her away" *(ʾaḥar šillûḥeyhā)* in Exodus 18:2 demonstrates the broad scope within which the author viewed his narrative. With a minimal number of words, the author irons out a major wrinkle in his narratives by linking Exodus 18:2 to Exodus 4:26 chronologically. That this is more than a "harmonistische" (Julius Wellhausen, *Die Composition des Hexateuchs und der historischen Bücher des Alten Testaments*, 4th ed. [Berlin: de Gruyter, 1963], p. 80) gloss can be seen in the fact that with this note the author is able to maintain the strict chronological order of these events, thus ensuring that Jethro's instruction on the administration of law is placed chronologically before the giving of the law at Sinai (Ex 19).

[2]See, for example, A. A. Hodge, *Outlines of Theology* (New York: Carter, 1878), p. 314.

[3]"Abraham obeyed me, and kept my charge *[mĭšmartî]*, my commandments *[miṣwōtay]*, my statutes *[ḥuqqôtay]*, and my laws *[wĕtôrōtāy]*" (Gen 26:5).

the lives of those under the law who did not exhibit that same faith (Num 14:11; 20:12). Clearly, the Pentateuch is not a work that aims at playing to a self-satisfied, largely religious audience, nor can it be construed as a defense of the religious status quo. It is in no respects an attempt at theological compromise. Taken together, these observations support the view of other key OT authors that in the Pentateuch we hear the voice of a prophet or someone sympathetic to viewpoints that later surface in prophetic communities and ultimately the NT (cf. Ezra 9:10; Dan 9:10 LXX).

## The Chronological Framework of the Pentateuch

The first task of the author in shaping the Pentateuchal narratives into a single, coherent story was to arrange its various parts into a chronological framework. Although the Pentateuch often follows an explicit chronological system, down to days and years (e.g., Gen 7:6, 13), there is also an implicit temporal sequence that establishes broader chronological points of reference. The narrative strategy of the Pentateuch involves a "beginning" (*rēʾšît* [Gen 1:1]) and an "end" (*ʾaḥărît* [Gen 49:1; Num 24:14; Deut 4:30; 31:29]), along with a series of chronological reference points around events at Sinai. The Sinai narratives are situated between a "beginning" *(Urzeit)* and an "end" *(Endzeit)* and along a chronological axis ranging from "before Sinai" (Ex 12:40) to "at Sinai" (Ex 19:1) and "after Sinai" (e.g., Deut 4:25-31; 30:1-11). Theocracy (the Sinai covenant) is intersected by eschatology *(Urzeit* and *Endzeit).* The meaning and theology of the Pentateuch are played out along the intersection of these two sets of coordinates.

Within this temporal schematic, chronology supplies important theological reference points. To be situated chronologically "before Sinai" is, theologically, to be removed from accountability to the law (Gen 15:6; 26:5).[4] To live "at Sinai" means to be accountable to the law (Lev 18:5). To live "after Sinai" is to view its covenant in terms of new (spiritual) realities (Deut 10:12-19; 30:1-11).

The Pentateuch's chronological reference points do not so much establish sequential moments within narrative time as prescribe directionality within the Pentateuch and the Bible as a whole. Some of the earliest efforts to view the Bible and the Pentateuch theologically, and apart from dogmatic systems, fixed their attention on this chronological framework. Theological definition

[4]John H. Sailhamer, *Introduction to Old Testament Theology: A Canonical Approach* (Grand Rapids: Zondervan, 1995), p. 186.

and explication were drawn along the sequence of narrative time.

Johann Coccejus, for example, assigned the structure of divine revelation itself to a movement through time *(ordo temporum)*[5] centered on the question of the law given at Sinai. His system was simple and biblically defensible: (1) before the law; (2) under the law; (3) after the law. Following Coccejus's basic schemata, others, such as Johann Bengel, extended the notion of time to the level of a central integrating theme:

> God proceeded gradually in making known the mysteries of his kingdom, whether one has in view the details of the events themselves or merely the times. Initially that which was kept concealed was then understood openly. That which was given in whatever particular state, the saints were to understand, not taking more nor accepting less.[6]

The centrality of an *ordo temporum* for contemporary evangelical biblical theology can be seen in Geerhardus Vos's description of the distinctions between the covenants within special revelation. For Vos, the categorical distinction between the administrations of the covenant of grace were cast in terms of a chronological divide:

> The Old Testament belongs after the fall. It forms the first of the two divisions of the covenant of grace. The Old Testament is that period of the covenant of grace which precedes the coming of the Messiah, the New Testament that period of the covenant of grace which has followed His appearance and under which we still live.[7]

Vos thus drew a temporal distinction between the two central theological covenants (testaments), whereas Calvin had drawn a logical distinction between them:

> The covenant made with all the patriarchs is so much like ours in substance *[substantia]* and reality *[re ipsa]* that the two are actually one *[unum]* and the same *[idem]*. Yet they differ *[variat]* in the mode of dispensation *[administratio]*.[8]

[5]Hans-Joachim Kraus, *Die biblische Theologie: Ihre Geschichte und Problematik* (Neukirchen: Neukirchener Verlag, 1970), pp. 20-24.

[6]Quoted in Sailhamer, *Introduction to Old Testament Theology*, p. 125.

[7]Geerhardus Vos, *Biblical Theology: Old and New Testaments* (Grand Rapids: Eerdmans, 1948), p. 32. Walter Kaiser's chronological ordering of his biblical theology can be seen from the way he structures the notion of "promise" along various chronological "eras": the prepatriarchal era, the patriarchal era, the Mosaic era, the premonarchical era, and so on.

[8]John Calvin *Institutes* 2.10.2 (*Institutes of the Christian Religion,* ed. John T. McNeill, trans. Ford

After Coccejus, few evangelical theologians were willing to follow Calvin's static (scholastic) distinctions between substance and administration. For the most part, evangelical biblical theologians have felt increasingly at home within the chronological framework of the Pentateuch and its use as a central organizing dividing line. Important theological conclusions could be drawn from it, such as a dividing between the biblical covenants. Just as importantly, by means of it central theological categories could be emphasized, such as the apparent discontinuity of the biblical covenants. What had been a central theological tenet of evangelical theology—the unity of Scripture *(unitas scripturae)*—was, by the *ordo temporum*, easily reduced to the chronological idea of "progressive revelation." Few evangelical theologians have understood the chronological framework of the Pentateuch as the work of its author. Rather, it has been assumed to be a natural consequence of the historical events recorded in the biblical narratives themselves. Biblical narrative was identified as biblical history in need of learned historical explanation.

In addition to the global chronology of the Pentateuch, there is within that chronological movement also a "local time" within each of the individual narratives playing itself out within its own specific time zone (e.g., Gen 3:8-10). The events of the individual narratives are not synchronized with the chronology of the Pentateuch as a whole. In that way, the Pentateuch is allowed to follow a single "one way" course of events from the creation of Adam to the death of Moses, while still allowing for considerable movement within the individual time zones of each narrative (e.g., cf. Gen 4:17-26 with Gen 5:1). There is no mechanism in the Pentateuch's global chronology for reversing its directionality. There are, however, many important examples of reversibility within the various narratives—for example, the "flashbacks" in Exodus 19–24. These are often theologically relevant, as when Rashi appeals to the lack of narrative sequence in the Bible as an apologetic for Israel's involvment in making the golden calf in Exodus.[9]

At the end of the Pentateuch the narratives do not return to "the beginning."[10] That would mean reversing the chronological direction of the whole Pentateuch. Hence, at the end of the Pentateuch there is no clear sug-

---

Lewis Battles [LCC 20; Phildelphia: Westminster, 1960], 1:429).

[9]Rashi: "There is no going back and proceding in the Torah."

[10]At the end of the Tanak the Chronicler reverts to Adam (1 Chron 1:1). This, however, is not the same as a return to "the beginning."

gestion of a "return to the garden of Eden" or a "paradise regained." Although that is a frequent theme within the individual Pentateuchal narratives[11] and is an important poetic image (e.g., Gen 49:11-12), it is not set as a goal of the Pentateuch's temporal movement or directionality. The past is left in the past. The future supersedes the past. The direction of the global narrative is thus toward a future envisioned by the Pentateuch not as a return to the past, but as a journey toward what is new.[12] It is a forward movement toward a new work of God (Deut 30:1-6).[13] Ultimately, the new work is linked to the prophetic hope of a new covenant (Jer 31:31-32).

That the author takes this chronology with utmost seriousness is partly seen in the fact that he begins his story with creation, a nonrepeatable (irreversible) temporal event.[14] A return to the past would mean a "new creation" (Is 65:17). Only after compressing the themes of the Pentateuch into two chapters (Gen 1–2),[15] and only after tracing the history of humanity from the garden of Eden to the fall of Babylon (Gen 2–11), does the author turn to a new page and a new chapter where Abraham enters the narrative bringing the twin themes of salvation and redemption into historical[16] perspective (Gen 12). Abraham, who represents God's new work with humanity by forshadowing the return of the exiles, comes into the narrative only after the fall of the kingdom of Babylon (Gen 11). Genesis 11:1-9 is about the rise and fall of the kingdom of Babylon, not merely a city named "Babel."[17]

According to the pattern later canonized in the book of Daniel, after the fall of the human kingdoms represented in Babylon (Gen 11:1-9; Dan 2:34-

---

[11]See John H. Sailhamer, *The Pentateuch as Narrative: A Biblical-Theological Commentary* (Grand Rapids: Zondervan, 1992), pp. 214-15.

[12]The structure of the prophetic books follows this sequence by dealing first with the transgressions of the people (former things) and then looking to the future for something new (new things).

[13]Compare Deuteronomy 30:9, which may contain a "return to paradise" motif.

[14]He could not give an account of creation at the beginning of each narrative, though that happens frequently in the book of Psalms, which is not governed by a global chronological sequence.

[15]Creation (Gen 1:1), blessing (Gen 1:28), relationship (Gen 1:26; 2:18, 23), provision (Gen 1:11-12; 2:8-14), worship (Gen 2:15), obedience (Gen 2:16), dependence (Gen 2:17, 24-25), dominion (Gen 2:19-20).

[16]The themes of salvation and redemption are, of course, globally already in Genesis 1–11—for example, the flood narrative and Noah's burnt offering (Gen 8:20-21)—but it is only with Abraham that the theme(s) are linked to the personal or family history of Abraham.

[17]The city is called "Babel," which is a transliteration of the Hebrew name of the city, בָּבֶל *(bābel)*. Here and in Genesis 10:10 the KJV transliterated the name as "Babel." In Revelation 18:2 בָּבֶל is called βαβυλών *(babylōn)*. The term βαβυλών is not used in the LXX, where בָּבֶל is rendered as Σύγχυσις *(synchysis)*, meaning "confusion."

35), "The God of heaven will set up a kingdom which will never be destroyed" (Dan 2:44). This kingdom is represented in Daniel 2:34 as a kingdom "not made with human hands." After Genesis 11 God's kingdom (located in the "seed" of Abraham [Gen 12:1-3; cf. Gal 3:16]) arises out of the ruins of fallen humanity (Babylon [Gen 9:1-11]). In that kingdom God would make a name for Abraham (Gen 12:2). It would not be a kingdom in which those of Babylon would make their name known (Gen 11:4). The writer of Hebrews understood the narrative strategy in terms of Abraham's quest "for a city which has foundations, whose architect and builder is God" (Heb 11:10; cf. Dan 2:44). From this point on, the Pentateuch offers only rare glimpses of the events narrated in Genesis 1–11. Nevertheless, those events remain the foundation of the rest of the Pentateuch.[18]

Given the anticipation of divine blessing built up in Genesis 1–2, the reader surely would be heading for a surprise ending in the death of Moses, outside the land (Deut 34), were it not for the narratives in Genesis 3–11. The conclusion of the Pentateuch is a surprise only to the reader who has paid insufficient attention along the way to the book's subtext of human failure and divine grace. The only hope that remains for the reader of the Pentateuch lies in God's grace and faithfulness (Deut 30:1-15; 34:10).

One should not underestimate the importance of the Pentateuch's chronology. It is an element of the book's compositional strategy that lies perhaps closest to its basic purpose. Several essential issues of interpretation are tied directly to the sequence of events in the Pentateuch. Chronology inevitably establishes the protocols of action within the biblical narratives. Without a comprehensive chronology in the Pentateuch, the reader could not know the direction of the central movement of the story. Although we often take such things for granted, without a chronological compass one would not know for certain even which way is forward in the book as a whole. Local time frames are unreliable guides for plotting the direction of large narratives or whole texts. Hence, disregard of chronology can lead both to temporal ambiguity and a loss of narrative context. Failure to respect chronology has led some, in effect, to read the Pentateuch "backwards," as if its movement was from its end to the beginning. Under such conditions the ultimate direction of the Pentateuch becomes a return to the theocratic garden of Eden (Gen 2) rather

---

[18]For example, Genesis 14:19 is intended to ground the divine blessing of humanity (Gen 12:1-3) in creation and redemption (Gen 1:28; 9:1) See also Genesis 49:10-12; Numbers 24:6.

than an eschatological release from Babylon (Gen 11:1-9; Deut 30:1-6). The future, not the past, is what lies ahead—not a return to the covenant at Sinai, but preparation for a new covenant and a new heart (Deut 30:11-16).

## Thematic Development through the Pentateuch

The next step in the making of the Pentateuch involved weaving into the various narratives a series of theological motifs and themes (theolegomena). There are, by most counts, at least five such themes:

1. human failure
2. divine grace (blessing)
3. faith
4. law
5. covenant

These themes play off one another within the narratives and ultimately provide the central theological momentum of the Pentateuch. God *graciously* initiates a *blessing* for the patriarchs and the nations. The blessing is grounded in a call for *faith*, but it results in the giving of the *law*. These three themes are further grounded in the concept of *covenant*. Blessing, faith and law become operative (or unoperative) through the making (and breaking) of covenants. Those themes play themselves against a narrative subtext of human failure and divine grace. Finding and assessing the theology of the Pentateuch is largely a matter of locating the points of intersection of these themes.

Later, I will trace the development (compositional strategy) of each of these themes throughout the Pentateuch. For the moment, it is sufficient to acknowledge that the themes of failure, grace, faith, blessing, law and covenants have been carefully woven into the fabric of the pentateuchal narratives by means of a definite literary, or compositional, strategy. So basic are these themes to the message of the Pentateuch that, for the most part, by the simple act of reading they are picked up as the core knowledge necessary for understanding the Pentateuch. The degree to which one reads the Pentateuch more or less with these themes in mind is a measure of the success of the author in communicating them through these narratives. Such truths are not an incidental feature of understanding the message of the Pentateuch; they predetermine how one views the central message of the Pentateuch.

## Legal Strategies (the Shape of the Laws)

A conspicuous compositional technique of the Pentateuch is its inclusion and distribution of several distinct collections of laws. Contrary to a common assumption, the laws in the Pentateuch do not seem to be part of a single collection of laws. The laws fall into various parts of law codes, each distinct from the others. As such, these collections of laws raise interesting questions. Why did the author put laws in the Pentateuch? Why did he include them in their separate collections? Why did he devote so much attention to the laws as part of various collections of laws? Why did he include laws that repeat and differ from other laws? Moses, for example, is commanded to fashion an altar out of dirt (Ex 20:24), but only a few chapters later he is commanded to build an altar made of acacia wood. Why are two different kinds of altars required on Sinai?

The narrative effect of these two sets of laws is striking. With their insertion, beginning at Exodus 20, the narrative movement of the Pentateuch comes to a halt. The central event in Israel's history is frozen in a single moment of narrative time while Israel encamps at Mount Sinai and Moses receives and delivers the laws to the people at the bottom of the mountain. From the summit of the mountain, God delivers the Ten Commandments to all who hear them. After that, God speaks only to Moses, and Moses passes God's laws on to the people. By pausing to listen to God and Moses speaking (cf. Ex 19:19b), the author temporarily puts the story of Israel in the wilderness on hold and concentrates solely on the giving of the law. All other activities come to a halt until the law is given by God and accepted by the people.

The most striking thing about these collections of laws and God's giving them at Mount Sinai is that reading the narratives chronologically suggests that Israel already had a collection of laws by which they were to govern themselves (Ex 15:25b; 18:16-24). They apparently had no need for more laws. Their coming to Sinai was not to receive the law, but to enter a covenant with God (Ex 19:4-5). By the time they had left Sinai, they had many more laws.

A close look at the various collections of laws in the Pentateuch reveals two distinct features. First, the collections of laws as a whole are not exhaustive. There are significant gaps and omissions. In Deuteronomy 24:4 a law concerning divorce is recounted that presupposes other laws about divorce that were not included in the Pentateuch. What, for example, were the grounds for the kind of divorce we see in Deuteronomy 24? Could one remarry? If so, under what conditions? Deuteronomy 24:4 assumes that laws governing such questions exist, but they are not given in the Pentateuch.

Second, the laws in the Pentateuch sometimes repeat laws already given. On the one hand, laws sometimes are accompanied by elaborate details. On the other hand, the law "Do not boil a young goat in its mother's milk" has few details, but it occurs three times (Ex 23:19b; 34:26; Deut 14:21). The Ten Commandments appear twice (Ex 20:1-17; Deut 5:6-21) with minor differences. A second "decalogue" (*ʿăśeret haddĕbārîm* [Ex 34:28]) is recounted in Exodus 34:11-26, in which there are primarily ritual laws.

Collections of laws in the Pentateuch often are incomplete. They have gaps. At the same time, some of those same laws are prescribed with elaborate detail. These two general observations call for further explanation. They suggest that behind the collections of laws in the Pentateuch is a conscious strategy or intelligent design that reflects an intentional selection of certain laws and law codes. Some laws have been included, others excluded. Although that process of selection apparently reflects no attempt to be exhaustive, it does seem to reflect a conscious effort to be comprehensive. It further appears that no attempt was made to avoid duplication and repetition. These various observations suggest that the task of a compositional approach to the Pentateuch is to discover the intentionality that lies behind the kind of selection of laws we have noted in the Pentateuch. Why were some laws included in the Pentateuch, and why were some excluded? What principle of selectivity was employed? What larger purpose lay behind the Pentateuch's selection of laws? A compositional approach to the theology of the Pentateuch attempts to answer these questions and tie them to the author's theological purpose.

## THE FINAL SHAPE (*ENDGESTALT*) OF THE PENTATEUCH

There are numerous approaches to the meaning that lies in the final shape of the Pentateuch. For an approach that focuses on the literary composition of the book, the key questions are these: Whose ideas are given the last word? Whose voice is represented by its final shape? This is more than a matter of who wrote the Pentateuch and why. It is a matter of whether the present shape of the Pentateuch has an authorial intent and whether that intent was theological in nature. Is the Pentateuch merely an early history of a people, or does it have a larger message that includes God's revealed purposes?

The answers lie in the consideration of the compositional shape of the Pentateuch. What are the ideas that lie within the shape and strategy of the Pentateuch, and who was responsible for them?

***A priestly editor.*** Biblical critics often have believed that a priestly editor is responsible for the basic shape of the present Pentateuch, a shape that includes the large amounts of laws in the center of the Pentateuch. This does not mean, however, tthat hey would necessarily see such a work having the last word. A priestly Pentateuch may have been edited by someone who was neither a priest nor a representative of priestly ideas.[19] In either case, a common view of the composition of the Pentateuch is that a final editor recounted the story of the Pentateuch from the viewpoint of the priesthood. The traditional view identified Moses as the final "priestly" author. If Moses is the author of the Pentateuch, it is only natural that he, being of the family of Levi, would show an interest in the priesthood. It is commonly held that the final editor of the Pentateuch was Ezra or one of his priestly associates (see Neh 8:9). Ezra, being a priest, would have an interest in the role of the priesthood. The traditional view is that Moses wrote the Pentateuch and Ezra was its second editor who brought it up to date by adding a few comments such as the details of the death and burial of Moses.

According to most historical-critical views, the editor of the final version of the Pentateuch was an anonymous member of the priestly community who edited the Pentateuch with his priestly interest in mind. A great deal of prominence was thus given to the laws, sacrifices and tabernacle/temple duties of the priests.

***An administrative editor.*** Recent studies in the Pentateuch have rekindled an interest in the possibility of a final priestly version of the Pentateuch. It has again raised the question of Ezra's role in the composition of the Pentateuch. Ezra was a scribe who studied and taught the Torah (Ezra 7:6, 10). There is general agreement that in this passage and others like it "Torah" *(tôrâ)* refers to the Pentateuch. In some Aramaic portions of the Bible (e.g., Ezra 7:25), Ezra's activities appear to have centered on a collection of "the laws *[dātê]* of God." Ezra was commissioned by the Persian authorities to teach "the laws of

---

[19] "Auch wenn wir die Bildung der priesterlichen Hauptkomposition wohl als den entscheidenden formativen Schritt hin zur kanonischen Tora sehen dürfen, ist sie doch keineswegs mit deren 'Endgestalt' gleichzusetzen" (Erhard Blum, *Studien zur Komposition des Pentateuch* [BZAW 189; Berlin: de Gruyter, 1990], p. 361).

[his] God" to "anyone who was ignorant of them." Could this collection of laws have been the ancient Mosaic Pentateuch? Or was it an edited version of the Pentateuch?[20] Was Ezra commissioned by Artaxerxes to "make and teach" the laws of the Pentateuch?

The answer to these questions may be found in the precise meaning of the two terms for *law* used in these two texts. The one term is the Hebrew word for "law" *(tôrâ),* and the other is the Aramaic word "law" *(dāt).* The Hebrew word "Torah" could be identical in meaning to the Aramaic expression "laws of God." The two words also could refer to altogether different sets of laws. According to Ezra 7:25, the Persian king Artaxerxes commissioned Ezra to enforce "the laws *[dātê]* of God" in his province of "Beyond the River." Since this is a portion of the OT written in Aramaic, it would have been natural to refer to the "law" with an Aramaic word. The use of the term "laws" in Ezra 7:25 may refer either to Ezra's teaching the Pentateuch or to his teaching the civil laws of the Persian Empire:

> You, Ezra, according to the wisdom of your God which is in your hand, appoint magistrates *[šāpṭîn]* and judges *[dayyānîn]* that they may judge all the people who are in the province Beyond the River, even all those who know the laws *[dātê]* of your God; and you may teach anyone who is ignorant of them.[21]

A well-accepted view is that this text is a Persian authorization of Ezra to teach his fellow citizens the Pentateuch.[22] If so, an example of Ezra's carrying out that task may be found in Nehemiah 8, where his compatriots gather in the streets of Jerusalem to hear the Pentateuch read and explained. Ezra "was a scribe skilled in the law of Moses *[bětôrat mōšeh],* which the LORD God of

---

[20]"The relation of Pentateuch and the law of Ezra has been a key question for the development of Torah. . . . We must accept the important statement in Ezr 7:25, which equates the laws of God and of the Persian king as both legally applicable and juridically binding. There was a policy of the Persian empire, known today from a whole series of examples, which sanctioned local law through the empire, recognizing it as binding. . . . The same thing is also largely true for Israel: Israelite law, thus the traditional law of the God of Israel, simultaneously became the law of the Persian empire for Jews. . . . The main question remains: how did a law, coming into force in this way, relate to the Pentateuch? . . . If we cannot identify the law of Ezra acccording to the evidence we have, we ought not to speculate" (Frank Crüsemann, *The Torah: Theology and Social History of Old Testament Law*, trans. Allan W. Mahnke [Minneapolis: Fortress, 1996], pp. 334-37).

[21]Note the similarities to Jethro's instructions to Moses in Exodus 18:20-23.

[22]"'All the people on this side the river' is limited to Israelites or Jews by the further particulars, 'who know the law of thy God,' etc." (C. F. Keil, *The Books of Ezra, Nehemiah, and Esther*, trans. Sophia Taylor [Grand Rapids: Eerdmans, 1949], p. 101).

Israel had given" (Ezra 7:6). He had been appointed to administer justice among "all those who know the laws of your God; and you may teach anyone who is ignorant of them" (Ezra 7:25). Given that task and Ezra's skill in the "law of Moses," the natural assumption would be that the "the laws *[dātê]* of God" referred to by Artaxerxes were the same laws as those in the Pentateuch and the collection of those laws was the Pentateuch.

There continues to be a consensus that the Pentateuch was closely related to, if not identical with, the document cited as "the laws of your God" in Ezra 7:25. Given the historical setting of the return from Babylonian exile, a document such as the Pentateuch would have well served the political purpose of unifying the Persian province. This would also explain the theocratic notion reflected in the pentateuchal laws. It was the policy of the Persian Empire to honor the laws and religious customs of the local inhabitants.[23] It would also have been consistent with that policy for Artaxerxes to commission Ezra to teach Judeans the laws of their own Torah. With that task in mind, some have further argued that the compositional shape of the Pentateuch, specifically its diverse collections of laws, well served Ezra's commission to govern the Persian province of "Beyond the River." Since during this period priests such as Ezra provided both religious and political leadership, it is not difficult to envision how the final version of the Pentateuch could have come to reflect the viewpoint of the priesthood and its laws.

***A prophetic editor.*** A convincing case against a priestly, administrative background to the composition of the Pentateuch has been argued by Rolf Rendtorff.[24] According to Rendtorff, the "laws" that Ezra was commissioned to teach in the Persian province referred not to the Pentateuch, but to a unique collection of laws drawn from various sources and approved by the Persian authorities. This would be much like the distinction between the "statutes of God and the laws" in Exodus 18 and the "words and judgments" given at Sinai in Exodus 19–20. Central to Rendtorff's argument are the nature of the relationship between Ezra's teaching "the laws *[dātê]* of [his] God" in Ezra 7:25 and his reading and explaining "the book of the Torah of Moses" in Nehemiah 8. Rendtorff disputes the assumption of many biblical scholars

---

[23]"There was a policy of the Persian empire, known today from a whole series of examples, which sanctitoned local law through the empire, recognizing it as binding. . . . P. Frei categorized the process of recognition of local norms by authorities of the empire as "state authorization" (Crüsemann, *The Torah*, pp. 336-37).

[24]Rolf Rendtorff, "Esra und das 'Gesetz,'" *ZAW* 96 (1984): 165-84.

that these two accounts of Ezra's activities are two versions of a single event. Ezra 7:25 describes Ezra's political role as an official of the Persian government (much like Daniel). Nehemiah 8, on the other hand, describes Ezra's religious role as a priest in following the dictates of Deuteronomy 33:10: "They shall teach your ordinances to Jacob, and your law to Israel."

The basis of Rendtorff's argument is the fact that Ezra 7 and Nehemiah 8 are found in different parts of the book of Ezra-Nehemiah. One cannot assume without clear warrant that the two accounts refer to the same event. There was an entirely different set of circumstances for Ezra's teaching the "laws" in Ezra 7 and his reading the "law of Moses" in Nehemiah 8. In Ezra 7 Artaxerxes commissions Ezra to establish a legal system in his western province. For that, Ezra needed an authorized collection of laws ("the laws of your God"). But in Nehemiah 8 Ezra was summoned by the people in Jerusalem to teach them the "law of Moses." For that, he would have needed the Torah, that is, the Pentateuch. Although in both cases Ezra is called to teach and interpret "the law,"[25] that is where the similarity ends. Everything else stated about the two events suggests that they represent two separate occasions. The drastic measures taken by biblical critics to identify these two passages is evidence of the fact that, as they now stand, the events are not related. The only way one can equate these two events in the life of Ezra is by rearranging the order of the books of Ezra and Nehemiah to fit a critically reconstructed series of historical events. One must take the events of Nehemiah 8 out of their present context and place them alongside the events of Ezra 7–8.[26] To hold this position together, one must further assume that sometime during the literary-textual history of Ezra 7 and Nehemiah 8, which "originally" were placed side by side, the two passages were separated and linked to a distinctly different order of events.

Keep in mind that the critical reshuffling of the parts of the books of Ezra and Nehemiah is not represented in any manuscripts, texts or versions of these books, nor is it consistent with the present narrative sequence of these two books. The order of events as we now have them within the books of Ezra and Nehemiah suggests that the collection of "the laws *[dātê]* of God" by which Ezra governed the Persian satrapy of "Beyond the River" (Ezra 7:25) was not

[25]The Aramaic word for "law" (דָּת, *dāt)* is used in Ezra 7, and the Hebrew word for "law" (תּוֹרָה, *tôrâ)* is used in Nehemiah 8.

[26]Which is the way biblical criticism usually reads these two texts, but without sufficient evidence.

the same as the "book *[sēper]* of the Torah *[tôrâ]* of Moses" that Ezra read and expounded in the solemn convocation of Nehemiah 8. That book, judging from the summary of its content in Nehemiah 9, was the Pentateuch. The collection of "the laws of your God" in Ezra 7:25 was a collection of Israelite laws authorized by Persian officials for use in their provinces.

Rendtorff's demonstration of the fundamental distinction between these two documents has important consequences for understanding the role of the priesthood and Ezra in giving the Pentateuch its final shape. If, as Rendtorff suggests, instead of the Pentateuch Ezra used a collection of diplomatically authorized laws to govern the Persian satrapy, it shows that there was an important difference between the Pentateuch and a collection of civil and religious law as such. Put simply, our model for how the Pentateuch is to be understood would not be that of a legal system designed for a Persian satrapy. Our model, instead, would be the religious gathering in the streets of Jerusalem as recounted in Nehemiah 8. The Pentateuch was understood to be Scripture, not a code of laws. In the streets of Jerusalem it was reverently read with understanding and insight (*śekel* [Neh 8:8]). Such a conclusion finds additional support from the interpretation of the Pentateuch in Nehemiah 9. It is clear from Nehemiah 9 that the Pentateuch was understood not as a collection of laws, but as religious and theological instruction.

The foregoing discussion casts considerable light on the question of the final form of the Pentateuch and its relationship to the priesthood. It suggests that priests such as Ezra probably had a substantial impact on the viewpoint of the final version of the Pentateuch, but not in the way many biblical scholars have envisioned it. The priests did not aim at a political use of the Pentateuch as a legal code of governance. Their aim was personal and devotional. It was to lead the faithful in following the will of God. Nehemiah 8, not Ezra 7:25, is the proper model for the priestly role in the shaping of the Pentateuch. Ezra the priest, as scribe (Ezra 7:6), was an editorial guardian of the Pentateuch in the postexilic era, not its author. As a scribe, his task was to explain the meaning of the Pentateuch that lay before him (*mĕpōrāš wĕśôm śekel* [Neh 8:8]), not to give it additional meaning by being its author. As to the question of who ultimately is to be credited with the preservation and composition of the Pentateuch, Ezra himself acknowledged the central role of the prophets (Ezra 9:10). Others also, more recently, have heard an echo of the prophets in the Pentateuch. Hans-Christoph Schmitt has argued for the presence of a prophetic voice in the final edition of the Pentateuch. John Calvin also associated the selection and arrangement of the laws in the Pentateuch with the work of the prophets: "Of old there was a constant controversy of the Prophets against the Jewish people; because, whilst strenuously devoting themselves to Ceremonies, as if True Religion and Holiness were comprised in them, they neglected real righteousness."[27]

The view of a "prophetic-priestly" Pentateuch is consistent with the understanding of the OT that found expression in the shape of the OT canon (Tanak) as a whole. The seams of the Tanak (Josh 1:8; Ps 1:2) envision the ideal reader of the Torah as one who meditates on Scripture day and night, seeking wisdom and the knowledge of God's will. Such a person finds blessedness (Ps 1:1; 2:12b) in Scripture while waiting for the fulfillment of the prophetic hope (Deut 34:10; Mal 4:1-6).

## THE GENRE OF THE PENTATEUCH

It is possible to seek the meaning of the Pentateuch in its overarching themes by approaching the Pentateuch in terms of its literary genre or macrostructure. Some interpret the Pentateuch by comparing it with the genre of an ancient Near East vassal treaty. Others have looked to form criticism (Rad) or tradition criticism (Rendtorff) for the genre of the Pentateuch. Still others have attempted to understand the Pentateuch in terms of its literary development from the earliest to its final stages. This has resulted in a return to earlier approaches such as the Fragmentary Hypothesis.[28] Such an approach sees nearly every generation of priests and prophets playing a hand in the Pentateuch's long history of composition. It focuses attention both on the assumed ever-changing shape of the Pentateuch and on the initial formation of the blocks of tradition forming its inner core. Such pieces of narrative play an essential role at the intermediate stages of the Pentateuch's composition.[29]

---

[27]John Calvin, "The Preface of John Calvin to the Four Last Books of Moses," in *Commentaries on the Four Last Books of Moses Arranged in the Form of a Harmony*, trans. Charles William Bingham (Grand Rapids: Baker, 1979), p. xvii.

[28]"Nimmt man das Modell der Entstehung des deuteronomistischen Geschichtswerks als Orientierungspunkt für einen neuen Zugang zum literarischen Problem des Pentateuch ernst, so wird man auch beim Pentateuch von den das Gesamtwerk umspannenden Redaktionen ausgehen müssen und erst nach der Klärung der redaktionellen Verhältnisse nach vorgegebenen Quellen und Traditionsblöcken fragen dürfen" (Hans-Christoph Schmitt, "Redaktion des Pentateuch im Geiste der Prophetie," *VT* 32 [1982]: 172).

[29]See Terence Fretheim, *The Pentateuch* (Nashville: Abingdon, 1996).

The view of the Pentateuch that I take here does not seek to uncover a lengthy or complex compositional history. My focus is on the shape of the Pentateuch as we presently have it and the meaning reflected in that shape. Whatever one might say about its early literary history, compositionally, the Pentateuch is now a single work that, as I will attempt to demonstrate, can be traced to the work of a single author. That, of course, is not to deny the Pentateuch may also have been edited to make it fit the OT canon. Such work of canonical editing was of a different sort than the work of an author. The primary focus in this section is the work of the author of the Pentateuch.

***A law book or a book with laws?*** The question of the genre of the Pentateuch centers on the purpose behind its various collections of laws. Were they intended as a code of theocratic laws for Israel under the Sinai covenant, or did they serve a broader theological purpose? The insertion of the laws into the Pentateuch may have been intended to sound a thematic note regarding the nature of the laws as such, or they may have been intended as a statement about the other themes in the Pentateuch, such as faith, promise, obedience, covenant and kingdom. Whatever their specific purpose, the collections of laws in the Pentateuch raise the question of the genre of the Pentateuch. Is it a law book or a book with laws?

Geerhardus Vos moves in the direction of seeing the Pentateuch as a code of laws when he attempts to explain the Pentateuch's concept of law in terms of theocracy and covenant: "From the nature of the theocracy thus defined (as kingdom) we may learn what was the function of the law in which it received its provisional embodiment."[30]

For Vos, the laws in the Pentateuch must be understood in terms of the larger purpose of a "theocracy," or kingdom of God. The laws are Israel's code of behavior under the Sinai covenant. They show Israel how to live as subjects of the divine king. Implicit in Vos's approach is an understanding of the genre of the Pentateuch as a law code for Israel's theocracy. Vos sees the Pentateuch and its laws in terms of a "provisional embodiment" of theocratic law. Such a view of the law and the Pentateuch allows for a shifting of the "function of the law," insofar as the nature of the theocracy and kingdom undergoes change. This shifting function of these theocratic laws becomes,

---

[30]Vos, *Biblical Theology*, pp. 141-42.

for Vos, the key to understanding the changing views of the law between the OT and the NT.

> It is of the utmost importance carefully to distinguish between the purpose for which the law was professedly given to Israel at the time, and the various purposes it actually came to serve in the subsequent course of history. These other ends lay, of course, from the outset in the mind of God. . . . From the theistic standpoint there can be no outcome in history that is not the unfolding of the profound purpose of God. In this sense Paul has been the great teacher of the philosophy of law in the economy of redemption. Most of the Pauline formulas bear a negative character. The law chiefly operated towards bringing about and revealing the failure of certain methods and endeavors. [Paul's negative statements about the law] were made under the stress of a totally different philosophy of the law-purpose, which he felt to be inconsistent with the principles of redemption and grace. . . .[31] Paul's philosophy, though a partial one, and worked out from a retrospective standpoint, had the advantage of being correct within the limited sphere[32] in which he propounded it.[33]

Vos sees the laws in the Pentateuch as part of a theocratic code. Such a view, however, overlooks an important observation. The collections of laws in the Pentateuch clearly play a greater role than merely that of a legal code. The laws and the individual codes of laws are part of the narrative and of the larger story carried by that narrative. It is not enough to view these laws merely as a code. Their meaning ultimately must be found within the context of the narrative strategy of the Pentateuch.[34] Hence, we return to the question of the genre of the Pentateuch. Was the purpose of the collections of law to serve as a theocratic code of conduct, or was their purpose to cast light on important thematic elements in the narratives?

If we are seeking to understand the final shape of the Pentateuch, any explanation of its laws must be drawn from an analysis of their role in shaping the genre and strategy of the whole of the Pentateuch. It is not enough merely to treat them as laws and consequently the Pentateuch as a book of law, or to treat them as laws and isolate them from the rest of the Pentateuch. Whatever

---

[31]Law as event and law as text.

[32]For Vos, Paul is responding to an improper view of the law, not to the view of the law in the Pentateuch.

[33]Vos, *Biblical Theology*, p. 142.

[34]On this proposal, see Gordon Wenham, *Story as Torah: Reading the Old Testament Ethically* (OTS; Edinburgh: T & T Clark, 2000).

view one takes of the purpose of the laws in the Pentateuch, one must first demonstrate the correctness of that view in terms of the genre and narrative, or compositional, strategy of the Pentateuch as a whole.

Such an approach to the overall structure and meaning of the Pentateuch may reverse some time-honored assumptions. If the Pentateuch is to be treated as a book of laws, which Schleiermacher believed to be the case, it is essential to find exegetical support for that view from the Scriptures themselves, which Schleiermacher failed to do. Only then can it be allowed to cast light on the larger theological question of the meaning of law and gospel in the Pentateuch.

***Asking the right questions.*** A compositional approach raises important questions about the structure, and consequently, the genre, meaning and theology of the Pentateuch. One must begin with the right questions, which, in this case, are those that help unlock the compositional strategies of the Pentateuch. We will look at two such questions in the following discussion.

*Genesis 1–11 and the Pentateuch.* An important question that arises from the compositional nature of the Pentateuch involves the interrelationships of the individual blocks of narrative that form its core. Of those blocks, the first, Genesis 1–11 (the primeval history), is the most problematic. What is its relationship to the other blocks of narrative in the Pentateuch?[35] How has Genesis 1–11 been integrated into the narratives and laws in the rest of the Pentateuch? How has it been integrated or connected, compositionally or thematically, to the rest of the Pentateuch?

There are perceptible links connecting some blocks to others—for example, Genesis 12–50 and Exodus 1–15 (cf. Gen 15:14; Ex 2:24b), but similar links are not so apparent between Genesis 1–11 and Genesis 12–50, or between Genesis 1–11 and Exodus 1–15. The narratives of Genesis 12–50 show little relation to Genesis 1–11. This has led some to conclude that the primeval history (Gen 1–11) lies outside the compositional horizon of the Pentateuch. Some have suggested that it was added to the Pentateuch secondarily. This would leave little hope of finding discernible compositional links between Genesis 1–11 and the Pentateuch.

---

[35]Not merely to Genesis 12:1-3, as with David Clines (*The Theme of the Pentateuch* [JSOTSup 10; Sheffield: JSOT Press, 1978], pp. 77-79), but to each of the large blocks of narrative and the collections of laws throughout the Pentateuch.

Such observations sometimes have led to attempts to understand the theology or theme of the Pentateuch without Genesis 1–11.[36] That would mean the whole of the Pentateuch must be viewed without connections to Genesis 1–11. This is an important question that calls for attention.[37] It seems that to consider the meaning of the Pentateuch without taking into account the themes in Genesis 1–11, or its theme as a whole, would have serious consequences for understanding the theology of the Pentateuch.

We will see in what follows that a compositional approach finds considerable evidence of interdependence between Genesis 1–11 and the rest of the Pentateuch. It is, for that reason, an important key to the theology of the Pentateuch.

*Moses: Editor, commentator, author?* A second question raised by a compositional approach is the need it creates for a clearer understanding of two distinct, but related, literary tasks: editorializing[38] and composition. Editorializing, or redaction, is understood as making subtle changes and shifts of meaning in a completed biblical text. Biblical scholars have devoted considerable attention to isolating various levels of editorializing (editorial changes) within a single text. Their aim is to identify the work of an editor and trace it throughout a biblical book or a group of books. Additions and comments enable an editor to update the biblical text and apply it to new situations in his

[36]Clines (ibid., pp. 13, 61) may be taken as an example of such an approach, though it is unclear whether he ultimately intends to read the Pentateuch with Genesis 1–11. "Not only is its material temporally prior to the first statements of what is to be the theme of the rest of the Pentateuch, and therefore hardly capable of being subsumed under that theme, but also the tendency of Genesis 1–11 seems to be in a quite different direction from that of the remainder of the Pentateuch. It seems to me therefore necessary to give close attention to the theme of Genesis 1–11 in itself, and then to examine how these chapters are related to what follows" (ibid., p. 15).

[37]See Rolf Rendtorff, *The Problem of the Process of Transmission in the Pentateuch*, trans. John J. Scullion (JSOTSup 89; Sheffield: JSOT Press, 1990), p. 185. Schmitt, like Rendtorff and others, is unable to find a single homogeneous editorial linkage between Genesis 1–11 and the rest of the "larger blocks" of tradition. Rendtorff starts with Genesis 12–50, Schmitt with Exodus 1–14(15). Rendtorff, and to a lesser extent Schmitt, assume a continuous growth of the tradition from the smallest units through the "larger blocks" to the final redaction. But it is also possible, as Schmitt has suggested, that the final redaction was laid down over these earlier stages in a way that both absorbed their own unique contribution and also fundamentally redirected the focus of the tradition toward that of the later prophetic spirit. An important part of the problem of linking Genesis 1–11 to the other "larger blocks" of tradition has been, according to Rendtorff, the insistence on seeing these chapters solely as "constituent parts of the pentateuchal sources." Consequently, the connection between Genesis 1–11 and the rest of the larger blocks of tradition "is made merely by a few remarks about Gen. 12.1-3, or not at all."

[38]The technical (German) word for "editorializing" is *redaction (Redaktion)*. In English usage, the word *redaction* has another meaning.

day.[39] If one can isolate the work of such an editor, it might shed light on the meaning of the final shape given a book such as the Pentateuch.

The concept of "composition" moves the focus away from an editor and toward the work of an author. An author does not merely introduce comments into a book that already exists; an author makes the book. The kind of comments added to the book by its author must be considered part of the book itself. They are not the result of editing.

A book is the embodiment of its author's intent. An author's intent is not merely expressed in occasional editorializing comments. For an author, the whole of his book is his or her "comment." Editorializing is the attempt to give a text a new direction in meaning or to connect it with other books. It introduces something into the text that was not there, at least explicitly, as part of the original work. Authorship, or composition, results in the making of a meaningful book. It is the work of an author.[40] By means of editorializing, a book is given new meaning. Composition creates a new book, whereas editorializing gives an existing book new meaning.

The attempt to identify and trace editorializing in a book such as the Pentateuch may lead far beyond the book itself. An editor can make additions or comments not merely in a single book, but in many books. Some recent studies have noted signs of editorializing in Joshua 24 that point back beyond the boundaries of that book into the early parts of the Pentateuch. An editor apparently wanted to tie these two books together more closely.

The question of the proper burial place for Joseph's bones is raised both in Genesis 50:24-25 (in the Pentateuch) and Joshua 24:32 (outside the Pentateuch). The comment in Joshua links the two passages. The burial of Joseph (Josh 24:32) is cast as the "fulfillment" of Joseph's last request in Genesis 50:24-25. This brief comment in the book of Joshua connects the end of Joshua to the end of Genesis and assigns a meaning to the two passages that goes beyond the scope of either the Pentateuch or the book of Joshua. The comment in Joshua 24 has the appearance of the work of an editor. Of course, it may have been written by the author of the book of Joshua, but in drawing this kind of connection, he was not acting as an author. He was, instead, doing the work of an editor (redactor). His intent was to draw out explicitly a particular aspect of the narrative that otherwise had only an implicit connection within the two books.

[39]See Sailhamer, *Introduction to Old Testament Theology*, pp. 99-101.

[40]See ibid., pp. 98-99.

Thus, an editorializing approach can lead quickly to the question of the final shape of a much larger section of the Bible. In this sense, the idea of "editorializing" in the Pentateuch may lead us in an entirely different direction than the quest for the "final composition" of the Pentateuch.[41] One may never be able, in practice, to locate the final "editorialized form" of the Pentateuch. As I have suggested, aspects of the editorializing process in the Pentateuch can sometimes extend beyond the Pentateuch to the far ends of the OT canon. At the same time, later editorializing can establish new connections between later books and the Pentateuch. The existence of editorializing in the Pentateuch and other biblical books often is related to the shape of the OT canon and goes even beyond that to include the work of scribes who often attempt to accommodate the Scriptures to their community's understanding. This can be a way of accommodating the Pentateuch to one's own beliefs.

So, if our goal is to discover the composition *of* the Pentateuch, we will need to do more than discover the editorializing *in* the Pentateuch. As important as that process may be, we must focus on the work of the author—that is, the work contained within, and as a part of, the literary boundaries of the Pentateuch. We must look for the compositional links that reach only within the boundaries of Genesis and Deuteronomy. What we are seeking is a view of the Pentateuch that takes seriously the fact that it begins in Genesis 1 and ends in Deuteronomy 34.[42]

*A preliminary report.* I have raised two questions posed by a compositional approach to the Pentateuch. First, what is the relationship of the primeval history (Gen 1–11) to the other blocks of narrative in the Pentateuch, and, second, how can the "composition" of the Pentateuch be distinguished from the "editorializing" in the Pentateuch? I will suggest a preliminary answer to those questions as a way of illustrating the nature of a compositional approach.

### Narrative + Poetry + Epilogue

One way to think about the two questions is to see the answer to the first question as the key to unraveling the second. If we look closely at the compositional pattern linking the small pieces of narrative into the whole of Genesis 1–11, we see that it involves a strategic use of poetry. Each unit of narrative within Genesis 1–11 is concluded by a short poem that is, in turn, followed

---

[41]Blum, *Studien zur Komposition des Pentateuch.*

[42]Or Deuteronomy 32:52.

by a brief epilogue. Within the "narrative world" of the Pentateuch, the poem represents the "last words" of the central character of the narrative. It is a way of viewing the events of the narrative from the viewpoint of someone within the story itself. The author gives the reader his perspective on the events through the eyes of the central character in the narrative.

This same narrative strategy is used to connect the larger blocks of narrative in the Pentateuch. Large blocks of narrative are linked to each other by a poem and an epilogue. At both levels, poetry is used as an interpretive summary and as a connecting link tying together the smaller and larger blocks of narrative. The pattern we have noted shows that the same compositional strategy is present at two levels. The smaller blocks of narrative in Genesis 1–11 are linked by means of poems, just as the larger blocks of narrative are linked in the Pentateuch as a whole. This suggests that the individual "author" who stitched together the smaller blocks of narrative in Genesis 1–11 can be identified with the one who stitched together the larger blocks of narrative to form the whole Pentateuch. What, then, is the relationship of Genesis 1–11 to the rest of the Pentateuch? The similarity of strategy in these two parts of the Pentateuch suggests that both are the work of the same "author." The author of Genesis 1–11 was the author of the whole of the Pentateuch.

How does this observation help us distinguish "composition" and "editorializing"? It does so by giving us a compositional profile, or strategy, that we can trace throughout the Pentateuch. By following the lead of that pattern, we see that its core structure ends at the conclusion of the Pentateuch with the last of the major poems in the Pentateuch, Deuteronomy 33. Using that pattern as a compositional profile, we can look for additional profiles with the same patterns within the Pentateuch. Such patterns connect the levels of strategy in Genesis 1–11 which link the larger narrative blocks. Compositional signs linked to the use of poetry in the Pentateuch can be identified as compositional elements. In other words, it appears to be the kind of work we would expect of the author. They are not signs of editorializing. They extend across major sections of the Pentateuch. An awareness of such a pattern might then also help us identify other patterns of composition not specifically linked to the poetic patterns in Genesis 1–11. Some of these may be related to the larger blocks of narrative and may thus be related to another level, possibly that of the editorializing that extends beyond the Pentateuch and into the rest of the OT canon.

This does not mean, of course, that there are no traces of editorializing within the compositional seams of the Pentateuch. It is probably not without importance that each of the three major poems in the Pentateuch (Gen 49; Num 24; Deut 33) has placed alongside it another poem (Gen 48; Num 23; Deut 32) that in content and form resembles the fourth remaining major poem in the Pentateuch, Exodus 15. It is likely of importance also that the same strategic use of poetry is found both in the primary history (Genesis–2 Kings), Judges 5; 1 Samuel 2; 2 Samuel 22; 2 Kings 19, and in its editorial connections with the "prophetic" books. Of special interest is the use of the phrase "in the last days" *(bĕʾaḥărît hayyāmîm)* in the poem in Isaiah 2:1-4. The distribution of these "editorial" comments throughout the HB suggests a hand at work at a much higher level than the composition of the Pentateuch.

## The Structure of the Pentateuch

***The compositional strategy of Genesis 1–11.*** To understand further the theological role of Genesis 1–11 within the rest of the Pentateuch, we must pursue its compositional strategy at a microlevel.

Genesis 1–11 is a mosaic of small, self-contained narratives. Many have attempted to explain how the pieces of this narrative were linked in their present form. To understand its present shape, we must view the whole in terms of its fragmentary pieces. The following is a list of the individual pieces of narrative in Genesis 1–11. Each of these pieces forms an independent whole, yet each is attached to the others in such a way that they tell a complete story.

1. The creation of the universe (Gen 1)
2. The making of the land (Gen 1)
3. The garden of Eden (Gen 2)
4. The fall (Gen 3)
5. The account of Cain and Abel (Gen 4)
6. The genealogy of Adam (Gen 5)
7. The account of the flood (Gen 6–9)
8. The genealogy of the sons of Noah (Gen 10)
9. The fall of Babylon (Gen 11)
10. The genealogy of Shem (Gen 11)
11. The genealogy of Terah (Gen 11)

There are several ways to view the compositional strategies uniting these various narratives. The most common and intuitive method of linking small pieces of narrative into a single story is by arranging them along a story line. Each segment of narrative is assigned a position and sequence along various functional slots that constitute the design of the story. If a story design calls for the repetition of a specific narrative pattern, then a segment of story that manifests that pattern, or one similar to it, may be assigned to a slot where such a repetition is expected. This appears to be the way the narratives in Genesis 1–11 are linked. They are aligned along a single story line from Adam and his three sons to Noah and his three sons. The repetition of the "father-with-three-sons" pattern is obvious once pointed out, but it is still functionally meaningful even when not a part of the reader's conscious awareness. It is the lives of the sons by which the author attaches the remaining segments of narrative. In the same way, the "chaos-creation-chaos-creation" motif provides the functional slot for both the creation account in Genesis 1 and the flood account in Genesis 6–9. Still further, the "fall narrative" of Genesis 3 is repeated in Genesis 9:18-27. In placing the story of Noah's drunkenness at this point in the story line, the author continues to follow the plan of casting the flood narrative as a recursion of the creation account. In the Genesis creation account God blessed humankind and planted (Gen 2:8) a garden where they could enjoy his fellowship. At the close of the flood account, as the narrative returns to God's "blessing" (Gen 9:1) and Noah's covenant with God (Gen 9:17), the story of Noah turns again to the planting (Gen 9:20) of an orchard.

The outcome of the two narratives is remarkably similar. Noah ate of the fruit of his orchard and became naked (Gen 9:21), just as Adam and Eve ate of the fruit of their garden and came to realize their nakedness. The author, in pointing out the similarities of Noah and Adam, attempts to show that even here, after a miraculous salvation from the flood, Noah's enjoyment of God's good gifts was not sustained. Noah, like Adam, faltered, and the effects were felt in the subsequent generations of sons and daughters. As in Genesis 3, the effect of Noah's sin can be seen in his "nakedness" (Gen 9:22; cf. Gen 2:25; 3:7). When read in the context of the events of the garden of Eden (Gen 3), the allusive details of Noah's drunkenness become remarkably transparent. In what appears to be a subtle parody of humankind's original state ("[They] were both naked, and they felt no shame" [Gen 2:25]), Noah in his drunkenness shamefully "uncovered himself in his tent."[43]

Once a link has been established between creation and the denouement of the flood, a further link is forged identifying the call of Abraham and the new creation. In the same epic style of the description of the entry of the ark,[44] the author depicts the exit. He is careful to show that even here Noah left the ark only at God's command (Gen 8:15-16). The description, though condensed, closely follows the creation pattern in Genesis 1 (e.g., "Let them swarm upon the earth, and let them be fruitful and multiply upon the earth" [Gen 8:17]). The picture given is that of a return to the work of creation "in the beginning." It is significant that right at this point in the narrative the author takes up a lengthy account of the covenant (Gen 8:20–9:17). The restoration of God's creation was founded on the establishment of a covenant (Gen 8:15-19).

There are numerous thematic parallels between the verbal picture of God's calling of Noah out of the ark (Gen 8:15-20) and God's call of Abraham (Gen 12:1-7).

**Table 3.1**

| **Genesis 8:15-20** | **Genesis 12:1-7** |
|---|---|
| Then God said to Noah (8:15) | The LORD said to Abram (12:1) |
| "Come out from the ark" (8:16) | "Leave your country" (12:1) |
| So Noah came out (8:18) | So Abram left (12:4) |
| Then Noah built an altar to the LORD (8:20) | So Abram built an altar there to the LORD (12:7) |
| Then God blessed Noah (9:1) | "And I will bless you" (12:2) |
| "Be fruitful and increase" (9:1) | "I will make you into a great nation" (12:2) |
| "I now establish my covenant with you and with your descendants" (9:9) | "To your offspring I will give this land" (12:7) |

Both Noah and Abraham represent new beginnings within the course of events recorded in Genesis. Both are marked by God's promise of blessing and

[43]See John H. Sailhamer, "Genesis," in *The Expositors Bible Commentary*, ed. Tremper Longman III and David E. Garland, rev. ed. (Grand Rapids: Zondervan, 2008), 1:21-332.

[44]Compare the sentence structure of Genesis 7:7-9 with Genesis 8:18-19. Both are examples of "epic repetition." See Francis Andersen, *The Sentence in Biblical Hebrew* (JLSP 31; The Hague: Mouton, 1974), p. 39.

his gift of the covenant. Humankind's original fellowship with God was grounded in their creation in the image of God. Fellowship with God was part of their nature. After the fall, fellowship with God comes through a covenant. It is a result not of "human nature," but of an act of "divine grace." This theme is played out many times in the pentateuchal narratives. Before the narrator describes Noah as a "righteous" (*ṣaddîq* [Gen 6:9]) and "whole" (*tāmîm* [Gen 6:9]), he states that Noah was already the object of God's grace: "Noah found grace in the eyes of the LORD" (*nōaḥ māṣāʾ ḥēn bĕʿênê yhwh* [Gen 6:8]). Before God calls upon Abraham to be "whole" (*tāmîm* [Gen 17:1]), the narrator says that he was accounted "righteous" (*ṣĕdaqâ* [Gen 15:6]) because of his faith.

In this way, each section of narrative plays itself out within a preprogrammed story line. Each unit of narrative finds its location (functionality) within a single chronological framework that underlies the whole of the primeval history. The chronological context of its story line has so shaped our reading of these narratives that it would be difficult to arrange them in any other order. This is also because, partly, the stories have been shaped by their role within the story line. Such irreversibility and functionality suggest an inherent, if not also a strategic, sequence lying along the small pieces of narrative in Genesis 1–11 making them a single unit. The sequence of the stories presupposes an underlying chronological framework consistent with the order in which they are now arranged.

Genesis 11:1-9, the dispersion of Babylon by means of the confusion of their language, is sometimes considered out of sequence with Genesis 10, the dispersion of the sons of Noah, "each according to their language" (Gen 10:5, 20, 31). How could the populations in Genesis 10 be dispersed according to their various languages if the origin of those languages does not occur until Genesis 11? This suggests that the story of Babylon is not about the origin of the world's languages, but rather about the confusion of the language of Babylon.

*Introductory headings.* Introductory headings are a well-known way to signal compositional strategies. The heading "these are the generations of" is a visible framework marker to which most of the narratives in Genesis 1–11 are attached (Gen 2:4; 5:1; 6:9; 10:1, 32; 11:10, 27). The organization of the narratives by means of this heading is not limited to Genesis 1–11. The pattern appears to include further parts of the Pentateuch (cf. Num 3:1).

There are two serious drawbacks to relying on this heading as a guide to the final shaping of the Pentateuch. The first is that it does not encompass the whole of the Pentateuch. It extends only to Numbers 3:1. The second is that it does not include the Abraham narratives. There is no "genealogy of Abraham" *(tôlĕdōt ᵓabrāhām)* in the Pentateuch. These two observations do not diminish the importance of the phrase "these are the generations of" for compositional shaping of smaller units of narrative. On the contrary, it is all the more important to ask why Abraham is not attached to a "genealogy." He is, of course, included in other genealogies, but why does he not have one of his own as do the other central figures in the book? The answer may lie in the author's desire to exclude any notion of a natural right, or birthright, of Abraham to God's blessing. He is a "son of Adam" like the rest of humanity. The divine blessing comes to Abraham as an expression of divine grace. He stood to inherit nothing. If so, the omission of Abraham's "genealogy" is a signal of his central importance to the narrative.

*Thematic patterns.* David Clines has discussed the organization of Genesis 1–11 along three widely accepted thematic patterns.[45]

*Theme 1: Sin, speech, mitigation, punishment.* The first theme to be investigated is realized in the plot or story pattern of the narratives in Genesis 1–11. Gerhard von Rad has pointed out how each of the narratives of the fall, of Cain and Abel, of the "sons of God," of the flood and of Babel exhibits a movement from human sin, to divine punishment, to divine forgiveness or mitigation. "Whenever man sins, God's response is just, yet gracious; he punishes, yet he forgives."[46]

Clines notes a later observation by Claus Westermann, who suggested that von Rad's thematic structure overlooked an important element of the thematic pattern between the act of sin and the act of punishment: "a divine *speech* announcing or deciding the penalty."[47] Clines observes,

> Neither Westermann nor von Rad has noted that this element of mitigation or grace occupies a significant place in the pattern of these narratives: it is always to be found after the speech of punishment and before the act of punishment. That is to say, God's grace or "forgiving will to save" is not only revealed "in and after the judgement" . . . but even *before* the execution of judgement.[48]

---

[45]Clines, *The Theme of the Pentateuch*, pp. 61-79.
[46]Ibid., pp. 61-62.
[47]Ibid., p. 62.
[48]Ibid., p. 63.

Ultimately, Clines concludes that however much the "sin-speech-mitigation-punishment" theme contributes to the meaning of Genesis 1–11, it is not broad enough to include all the elements that are a part of the narrative. What role, for example, do the creation account (Gen 1), the genealogies (Gen 4; 5; 11) and the Table of Nations (Gen 10) play in this theme?

*Theme 2: Spread of sin, spread of grace.* Clines offers a second, and further, attempt at a more comprehensive theme in Genesis 1–11. It is

> the theme of the "spread of sin," to which there corresponds increasingly severe punishment, and a spread of "grace" on God's part. That is to say: (i) From Eden to Babel by way of sins of Cain, Lamech, the "sons of God," and the generation of the Flood, there is an ever-growing "avalanche" of sin, a "continually widening chasm between man and God." . . . (ii) God responds to the extension of human sin with increasingly severe punishment: from expulsion from the garden to expulsion from the tillable earth, to the limitation of human life, to the near annihilation of mankind, to the "dissolution of mankind's unity." (iii) Nevertheless, these are also stories of divine grace: God not only punishes Adam and Eve, but also withholds the threatened penalty of death; he not only drives out Cain, but also puts his mark of protection upon him; not only sends the Flood, but saves the human race alive in preserving Noah and his family. Only in the case of the Babel narrative does it appear that the element of "grace" is lacking.[49]

To his statement of the theme Clines adds other elements from Genesis 1, the genealogies and the Table of Nations.

> The pattern according to which creation proceeds in ch. 1 is in fact the positive aspect of the sin-judgement motif: here it is a matter of obedience followed by blessing, not sin followed by curse. So, for example, light comes into being in prompt obedience to the word of God (1:3), whereupon the divine judgement is pronounced: God saw that it was good. . . . In the genealogies there is in the monotonous reiteration of the fact of death, which increasingly encroaches upon life, a pessimistic note which corresponds to the narrative theme of the continuing spread of sin. But as in the narratives, history is not simply a matter of sin and punishment; where sin abounds, grace much more abounds. Even though the divine grace is experienced not in dramatic acts of deliverance, as it is in the narratives, but in the steady silent expansion of human life, it is the divine grace all the same. To the grace that

[49]Ibid., pp. 64-65.

> appoints for Eve another child to take the place of the dead Abel is owed also the furtherance of mankind's growth throughout the genealogy of Genesis 5; and to the grace that preserves the human race through the dramatic rescue of Noah and his family from the Flood is due also the repeopling of the earth after the flood (Gen. 10).[50]

Clines adds a comment to Genesis 10 that the "dischronologization" in locating the Table of Nations before the dispersion of Babylon allows it to function as the fulfillment of the divine command of Genesis 9:1, "Be fruitful and multiply, and fill the earth," rather than after Genesis 11, where it would have been read as part of the judgment of Babylon.[51]

> The theme of the spread-of-sin accounts for the vast majority of the content of Genesis 1–11. It is visible, not only in the narratives, but also in other literary types in these chapters. It is more than probable that, even if this suggested theme alone does not adequately express the thrust of Genesis 1–11, its pervasiveness ensures that it will have to be taken into account in any statement of theme in the primeval history.[52]

We should note that the theme of the spread of sin in Genesis 1–11 is found in other parts of the Pentateuch. According to the narrative structure of Leviticus 11–15, for example,

> the purification regulations intentionally followed the sequential pattern established in the early chapters of Genesis. The apparent purpose of that pattern was to show that the spread of ritual defilement retraced the spread of sin in the beginning. Or, from the viewpoint of the Genesis narratives, its purpose was to show that humankind's original sin was a form of cultic contamination. . . . In the further parallels between these levitical laws and the Genesis narratives, the writer sees that the Flood and Noah's sacrifice played an important role in the cleansing of humankind and in the preparation of God's covenant. . . . The author continues to align these Levitical laws with the patterns of the Genesis narratives to reveal God's plan in the covenant stipulations within the context of his larger plan in Creation.[53]

*Theme 3: Creation, uncreation, re-creation.* Clines begins his third thematic pattern with the observation that "the Flood narrative does not function sim-

[50]Ibid., pp. 65-68.
[51]Ibid., p. 68.
[52]Ibid., p. 73.
[53]Sailhamer, *The Pentateuch as Narrative*, pp. 337-38.

ply as yet a further stage in the development of human sin, but imports concepts of 'end' and 're-creation' into the primeval history."[54]

> "The world in which order first arose out of a primeval watery chaos is now reduced to the watery chaos out of which it arose—chaos-come-again" [J. Blenkinsopp]. While Genesis 1 depicts creation as largely a matter of separation and distinction, Genesis 6f. portrays the annihilation of distinctions. . . . Re-creation occurs, in the first place, by the renewed separation of sea and land: the waters recede from and dry up from the earth (8:3, 7, 13). Then comes the renewal of the divine order to living beings to "breed, be fruitful, and multiply" (8:17). . . . Finally, the creation ordinances are re-announced.[55]

Clines remains convinced that the pattern of "creation-uncreation-re-creation" is central to the compositional thematic structure of Genesis 1–11.[56] Others too have pointed to that theme.

*The editorial shape of the primeval history.* The approach taken by Markus Witte illustrates a recent trend in the compositional analysis of the Pentateuch, and particularly Genesis 1–11.[57] Witte's aim is to identify the seams that connect the narratives of Genesis 1–11 and to describe the theological characteristics of those seams. How do they contribute to the overall theology of Genesis 1–11 and the Pentateuch?

To identify the seams, Witte looks for features in the texts that reveal the presence of the author. He looks for texts that establish connections with other texts,[58] and he looks for texts that stand out from their surroundings. Using these criteria, he identifies three compositional passages, Genesis 2:4; 4:25-26; 6:1-4. After identifying those passages,[59] Witte examines each one closely, looking for characteristics or features that might help identify other texts that appear to be part of this same compositional strategy.

> If a close study of these three passages should confirm the hypothesis that they consist of redactional [compositional] additions from the same hand, then criteria can be drawn from them which may enable us to identify further redactional passages in the primeval history and thereby give us a

---

[54]Clines, *The Theme of the Pentateuch*, pp. 73-74.

[55]Ibid., p. 74.

[56]Ibid., p. 76.

[57]Markus Witte, *Die biblische Urgeschichte: Redaktions- und theologiegeschichtliche Beobachtungen zu Genesis 1,1-11,26* (BZAW 265; Berlin: de Gruyter, 1998).

[58]For Witte, these separate texts are the J and P documents.

[59]And a fourth series of texts within the flood story: Genesis 6:7abgb; 7:1b, 3, 8-9, 23aa.

clearer literary and compositional profile of the composer *[Redaktor]* of Genesis 1–11.[60]

At the completion of his study of Genesis 1–11, Witte has identified the following compositional and supplemental texts: Genesis 1:1–2:3; 2:1; 2:4; 4:25-26; 5:1-32; 5:29; 6:1-4 (6:3/2-3 [tree of life]); 6:7abgb; 7:1b, 3, 8-9, 23aa; 3:22; 11:1-9; 9:19, 20-27.[61] Witte concludes that these texts are the direct work of the author of the Pentateuch.

As one might expect, the theology reflected in these compositional seams is complex. Witte suggests that it represents a theological viewpoint found elsewhere in the Pentateuch, particularly in those texts usually associated with the patriarchal narratives in Genesis, the priestly laws in Exodus and Leviticus, and the explication *(baʾēr)* of the Sinai laws in Deuteronomy. The function of this composition of Genesis 1–11 is to present these various theological themes and viewpoints at the beginning of the Pentateuch and thus to provide a context for the development of these themes in the remainder of the book. Witte identifies the perspective of these themes in Genesis 1–11 as that of the biblical wisdom literature. He surmises that these same compositional themes also made their way into the composition of the remainder of the Pentateuch.[62]

*Supplemental additions.* Gordon Wenham has suggested that the original composition of Genesis 1–11 was based on an early creation and flood narrative well known in the ancient world. He draws that conclusion from the observation that Genesis 1–11 follows the basic plot structure of several ancient stories dealing with creation and the flood. He suggests that in the composition of Genesis 1–11 several supplemental stories, drawn from documents of various antiquity, were added to this basic narrative. According to Wenham,

---

[60]"Sollte sich die Hypothese bestätigen, daß es sich bei diesen drei Texten um solche redaktionellen Zusätze handelt, die auf dieselbe Hand zurückgehen, dann dürften sich aus ihnen Kriterien ergeben, die es erlauben, weitere redaktionelle Abschnitte in der Urgeschichte zu bestimmen und so den Redaktor von Gen 1–11 zunächst literarisch und kompositionell genauer zu profilieren" (Witte, *Die biblische Urgeschichte*, p. 53).

[61]This list is abbreviated; for a complete list of the texts, see ibid., p. 334. See also John H. Sailhamer, "A Wisdom Composition of the Pentateuch?" in *The Way of Wisdom: Essays in Honor of Bruce K. Waltke*, ed. J. I. Packer and Sven K. Soderlund (Grand Rapids: Zondervan, 2000), pp. 15-35.

[62]"Legen die Vermutung nahe, daß der $R^{UG}$ auch jenseits des Komplexes von Gen 1,1-11,26 literarisch tätig war" (Witte, *Die biblische Urgeschichte*, p. 329).

> Within Gen 1–11 at least, a case can be made for supposing that both the basic outline of the primeval history and many elements within the stories existed prior to the major editorial work of J. This proto-J material consists not only of many elements conventionally ascribed to P but also parts of J itself. This is most clearly seen in the flood story. If the final form of the story, the P version, and the J version are compared with the Gilgamesh epic's account of the flood, it is apparent that the final form of the narrative is closer to the Gilgamesh version than the latter is to J or P. This implies . . . that the final editor of Gen 6–8 had before him a flood story containing much of J and P. It seems unlikely that he combined J and P himself, as the usual theory maintains, because the basic outline of the flood story in Genesis was already known in the second millennium B.C. in other parts of the ancient orient.
>
> What is true of the flood story is true also of the basic plot of Gen 1–11. Pre-biblical accounts of primeval history include features from both the J and P parts of Gen 1–11.[63]

*Poems as compositional strategy.* Alongside the evidence of composition in Genesis 1–11 discussed above, there are additional indications of authorship. One such sign we have already noted is the strategic use of poetry. Throughout Genesis 1–11 each of the individual narratives has a poem attached at its conclusion. Each poem is followed by an epilogue whose function is to prepare the narrative for the next series of actions. There is a conscious compositional strategy running through the whole of Genesis 1–11.

1. The creation of the universe (Gen 1:1)
2. The making of the land (Gen 1:2–2:3)

   *poem* (Gen 1:27)
3. The garden of Eden (Gen 2)

   *poem* (Gen 2:23)
4. The fall (Gen 3)

   *poem* (Gen 3:14-19)
5. The account of Cain and Abel (Gen 4)

   *poem* (Gen 4:23-24)
6. The genealogy of Adam (Gen 5)

[63]Gordon J. Wenham, *Genesis 1–15* (WBC 1; Waco, Tex.: Word, 1987), p. xxxix.

*poem* (Gen 5:29)

7. The account of the flood (Gen 6–9)

    *poem* (Gen 9:25-27)

8. The genealogy of the sons of Noah (Gen 10)
9. The fall of Babylon (Gen 11)
10. The genealogy of Shem (Gen 11)
11. The genealogy of Terah (Gen 11)

*Creation.* The creation account in Genesis 1 is drawn to a conclusion with the poetic verse in Genesis 1:27:

> God created mankind in his image.
> In the image of God he created him.
> Male and female he created them.

The account of creation in Genesis 2 also concludes with a short poem spoken by Adam after being presented with his newly created wife. He says, "Bone of my bones, flesh of my flesh. This one will be called woman because she was taken from man" (Gen 2:23). Then comes the epilogue (Gen 2:24). The purpose of this poem is, like Genesis 1:27, to stress the creation of the man and the woman in God's image. It suggests that the central meaning of the creation of human beings in God's image is a preset potentiality for fellowship both between God and human creatures and among human creatures themselves. Human beings are created in God's "likeness."

These first two poems provide the grounding for the developing concept of covenant in Genesis 1–11. There is already built into the notion of a created human being the real possibility for personal fellowship with God and with each other.

*Fall.* The account of the fall in Genesis 3 concludes with a poem in Genesis 3:14-19:

> And the LORD God said to the snake,
>   "Because you did this,
> cursed are you from the cattle
> and from the animals of the field.
>   Upon your belly you must walk
> and dust you will eat

—all the days of your life;
    and I will put enmity between you and the woman,
and between your seed and her seed.
He will strike you on the head,
and you will strike him on the heel."

And there follows an epilogue in Genesis 3:20-24.

The lengthy poem in Genesis 3 points to the disruptive effect of Adam's disobedience in the garden.

*Cain and Abel.* The account of Cain and Abel in Genesis 4 concludes with a genealogy giving a short history of the Cainite family (Gen 4:17-26), including Lamech's poem (Gen 4:23), an epilogue (Gen 4:24-26), and a brief continuation of the Caninite genealogy (Gen 4:25-26). The genealogy of Genesis 5 concludes with a poem (Gen 5:29) and an epilogue (Gen 5:30-32).

*The flood.* The story of the flood (Gen 6:1–9:24) concludes with Noah's poem (Gen 9:25-27) and an epilogue (Gen 9:28-29).

Each of these poems plays an important role in the development of the meaning of the individual narratives. The poems guide the reading of the narratives. They help the reader to follow the direction of the central movement of the story.

At the conclusion of Genesis 9 the pattern is suspended. The Table of Nations, which follows in Genesis 10, is not a narrative, and there are no further poetic texts in Genesis 10 and Genesis 11. There are important reasons for inserting Genesis 10 into Genesis 1–11, and particularly for attaching it to the flood account and Noah's poem in Genesis 9:25-27. In its present location, Genesis 10 gives an overview of the outcome of Noah's programatic statement in Genesis 9:27 that the sons of Japheth will dwell in the tents of Shem. It also gives an answer to several questions raised by Noah's poem. It identifies the descendants of Japheth who will dwell in the tents of Shem. It also identifies the descendants of Shem and Ham. Finally, it summarizes what will eventually become of these people, particularly in light of Noah's "prophetic" poem.

Attached to the final lists of the descendants of Shem in Genesis 11 is an account of the interruption of the building of the city of Babylon and the dispersal of its inhabitants (Gen 11:1-9). This is the same Babylon featured prominently in the narrative sections of the Table of Nations (Gen 10:8-12). Not only is the story of Babylon wedged between two genealogies of "Shem" *(šēm)*, but also the central theme of the narrative is built around the quest for a great "name" *(šēm)*. The people of the city of Babylon want to make a great "name" *(šēm)* for themselves, but in Genesis 12:1-3 God promises Abram that he will make him a great "name" *(šēm)*. By means of the theme of "making a name" *(šēm)*, the primeval history of Adam's family is linked to the patriarchal Abraham narratives in Genesis 12–50. The traces of this linkage are found already in Genesis 6:4, where the great men of the past are called "men of name" *(ʾanšê haššēm)*.

To summarize: Genesis 1–11 follows an intentional compositional strategy that links together an otherwise loose collection of minor independent narratives. The strategy largely consists of attaching poems to small units of narrative. The poems play a significant role in thematizing the author's understanding of the meaning of each individual narrative. Noah's pronouncement in Genesis 9:25-27 is an example of how programmatic such poems prove to be within the larger context of the Pentateuch. The poem in this case provides an interpretive context for the Table of Nations and the account of the building of the city of Babylon. It sets the stage and establishes a larger playing field for the remaining narratives in the Pentateuch.

In all of this, the author still has not drawn our attention to the role that Abraham and his descendants are to play in the subsequent narratives. That may be because the author has much yet to say about the "seed" of Abraham, which he will introduce in Genesis 12. That "seed" appears to be a continuation of the promised one of Genesis 3:15. All this leads to a further consideration of the importance of the poems in the compositional structure of the Pentateuch as a whole. As we proceed to follow the compositional seams and strategy of the Pentateuch, it is ultimately to these (and other) poems that we must turn to find the author's identification of Abraham's "seed."

*The role of the poems in Genesis 1–11.* The role of the poems at the conclusion of each story in Genesis 1–11 is to explain or clarify the sense of the narrative. We should take special note of what these poems contribute to the author's strategy. First, the poems are presented as the words of the central character in the narrative. As such, each poem views the events of the narrative not so much through the eyes of the author as from the perspective of one of the central characters in the narrative. At the start, the poem in Genesis 1:27 represents the point of view of the narrator. There are as yet no central characters. In the remainder of Genesis 1–11 the poems open the reader to the point of view of the central characters within the narrative. To be sure, the poems express the author's understanding of the narratives, but they are not put in the author's own words, nor do they give us an interpretation from the author's perspective. Instead, they express the author's understanding of the events of the narratives as they are mediated through the viewpoint of the central character(s). The reader sees the narratives as if he or she were one of the characters in the narrative. Rather than having to rely on didactic comments by the author or the narrator, the reader learns the meaning of the narratives firsthand, just as the characters within the narratives learn it by experiencing it. In the poem in Exodus 15 the meaning of the exodus (expressed by the character Moses) is that God will reign as king in the holy sanctuary built "on the mountain of [his] habitation" (Ex 15:17). In this case, Moses' poem tells the reader that the exodus is God's assurance that his promise in Genesis 49:9-12 will be faithfully fulfilled by a king from the house of Judah in Israel's future theocracy. The Mosaic perspective of the poem in Exodus 15 takes a long-range view into the historical future (the Davidic monarcy) and carries with it the perspective of the other poems introduced by the temporal marker "in the last days" (Gen 49; Num 24; Deut 33).

A second observation about these poems in the Pentateuch is that, as poetry, they reveal to the reader the meaning of the narratives not as narratives, but as poetry. Being poetry, they leave much of their meaning for the readers to discover. The poems serve a didactic purpose without being didactic. They are intended as commentary, although, being poetry, what they add to the narrative is not merely commentary, but also the opportunity of thoughtful reflection. The poems, as such, slow readers down and challenge them to reflect on the narrative through the eyes of a poet. Ultimately, the reader is left not with a narrative meaning, but with a poetic one. The reader joins the narrator in filling in the sense of the story. Although this may challenge the patience of modern readers, it adds an essential feature to the meaning of biblical narrative.

The poems in the Pentateuch add to its narrative a level of ambiguity not commonly encountered in biblical narrative. Ambiguity is a positive literary feature. Technically, it is the deliberate withholding of part of a text's meaning and forcing the reader to take a more active role in understanding. The reader is called upon to bring some personal understanding to the resolution of a poem's meaning. The reader is not free to add whatever he or she wishes. The author is always in control of the meaning of the narratives, but through the poems much of that meaning is left in the hands of the reader. Starting from what the poem itself says through its imagery and metaphor, ambiguity forces the reader to say more. An author will expect a competent reader to know how to fill in a poem's meaning and apply it to the narrative context. The reader cannot make a poem mean what he or she wishes it to mean. The meaning must come from what has already been said poetically in the biblical poem. The reader is expected to supply the right meaning, even though it is never fully revealed in the poem. Figurative meaning and the use of images are examples of this in poetry. The reader is rarely given the meaning of the images that the author uses in a poem. "What a poem means" by its use of an image is almost always left to the reader to decide.

This is not to say that the reader receives no help from the author. A competent biblical reader will take note of the explanatory comments in biblical poetic texts. When Isaiah describes God's future salvation in terms of a surviving tree stump after the forest has been felled (Is 6:12-13), he adds the explanation that the "stump is the holy seed" (Is 6:13b).

A word of caution: although a poem can be ambiguous in some respects, this does not mean that it is "vague" about its meaning. Vagueness in poetry means that a poem may give insufficient grounds or clues to its meaning but still expect the reader to discern the correct meaning. With vagueness, the reader has nothing to go on within the poem itself. A reader may not even know what all the possible meanings of a poem or narrative are. In poetry, one must not confuse poetic ambiguity with literary vagueness. Both are appropriate literary tools for developing meaning in narrative and poetry. Ambiguity can lead to a deeper appreciation for a poem's meaning by leaving that meaning in the hands of the reader. Vagueness, on the other hand, ultimately leaves the missing clues of the meaning of a poem in the hands of the author. The reader must wait for more information from the author. Meir Sternberg calls such missing pieces "gaps." A gap is a piece of the meaning of a text withheld until it is supplied by the author at some point in the text. In dealing with ambiguity, the reader is left with the text to search competently for its meaning as literature. With vagueness, the reader must wait for further help from the author. Often that help comes from an innertextual insertion by the author or a later biblical text. When Isaiah writes of the withering of grass and wilting of flowers (Is 40:7a), the author[64] of the book adds "surely the grass is the people" (Is 40:7b), leaving the reader in no doubt about the meaning of the otherwise vague imagery employed.

This understanding of the nature of poetry is essential for appreciating the central themes of the Pentateuch. If it is true that the poetry has strategic importance, we should expect to find central themes in the Pentateuch explained within its poetry. It may be discovered as part of the ambiguity of its poetry or through the author's own resolution of its poetic vagueness, as in the example above. As we noted, the latter is often accomplished by means of explanatory comments attached to poetic texts.

In the second line of the poem in Genesis 3:15, God says to Eve, "and he shall bruise you on the head." The pronoun "he" *(hûʾ)* is ambiguous. It could mean "he" (as a singular), or it could mean "they" (as referring to a collective noun, "your seed"). It is ambiguous because it could be either "he" or "they." It is not vague, since it cannot mean "you" or "she."[65] The issue is whether the resolution of this question can be found within the poem itself (ambiguity) or whether at this point we must leave either possibility, or even further possibilities, open (vagueness). In other words, is the author using the inherent ambiguity of the Hebrew pronoun "he" *(hûʾ)* to leave the intended referent unexplained until he has been properly identified in the remainder of the Pentateuch? I believe so. While the Hebrew pronoun may be ambiguous within the poem, it may also become vague and have to be resolved by the author within the remainder of the Pentateuch. As it now stands, the reader is forced to remain open to all the possibilities and ranges of meaning within the poem. By tracing the identity of the promised "seed" in Genesis 3:16 through the poems in the remainder of the Pentateuch, we see that the pronoun "he" *(hûʾ)* refers to the singular "seed of Abraham," who is the "king from the tribe of Judah" (Gen 49:9-12) and the one who will reign over Israel and the nations "in the last days" (Num 24; Deut 33). These are the meanings supplied to Genesis 3:15 by the poems in the rest of the Pentateuch. Both the ambiguity and the vagueness of the pronouns in the Genesis 3:15 poem are

[64]This is not to say that Isaiah was not the author of the book of Isaiah, but rather to say that although there is a real distinction in status between a prophet, such as Isaiah, and the author of a book about a prophet, such as the book of Isaiah, it is important to distinguish the two kinds of tasks that one person would be called upon to perform.

[65]Compare the Vulgate: *ipsa*.

resolved by the author by means of the compositional strategy in the remainder of the Pentateuch.

The poems in the Pentateuch thus embody and represent the author's viewpoint on the events of the narratives. Through the words of the central characters the author makes a programmatic statement about where the events of the narrative are taking us. In this sense, the poems serve a purpose not unlike that of the songs in a Hollywood musical. They thematize the meaning that the author intends for the reader to draw from the narratives. The poems are like literary glosses that explain the author's understanding of the narratives. How the poems are to be read within the strategy of the Pentateuch must be worked out in detail for the reader by following the lead of the author. If the author has a specific meaning in mind for these poems, ambiguity and vagueness cannot stand in the way of unmasking that meaning.

Failure to appreciate the author's work of resolving ambiguity or vagueness in the Pentateuch's poems has resulted in some interpreters sensing the need to look beyond the Pentateuch for the meaning of its poems and narrative. Christian theologians often have resorted to the NT for the identity of the "seed" promised in Genesis 3:15. In such an approach there is usually a proper appreciation for the ambiguity or vagueness of this poem, but the approach itself often overlooks the possibility that the ambiguity and vagueness of the poem have already been resolved within the Pentateuch's own poetry. It is unnecessary to look to the NT for a resolution of the meaning of the Pentateuch's poetry. The answer to the question of the identity of the "seed" in Genesis 3:15 is given by the author in the identity of the "seed" of Abraham and the king from Judah in the rest of the poems of the Pentateuch. The author of Genesis, who was at the same time the author of the Pentateuch as a whole, surely knows his own understanding of the identity of the "seed" as he writes Genesis 3:15, but as the author, he leaves the identity of the "seed" ambiguous (or vague) until he supplies the proper answer in the remainder of the Pentateuch. One might be applauded for being careful not to see Christ too quickly in the words of the poem in Genesis 3:15, but in the end, one might also prove shortsighted in failing to find the author's delayed identity of that "seed" within the further compositional strategy of the Pentateuch and its poems. One should not conclude too quickly that if the identity of the "seed" is not given in Genesis 3:15, one must immediately move to the NT to identify the "seed" of which this poem speaks. What we must consider is whether the author of the Pentateuch was merely raising the question of the identity of the "seed" in Genesis 3:15 in order to answer that question throughout the rest of the Pentateuch.

***Further compositional strategies in the Pentateuch.*** I concluded the previous section on the compositional strategies of Genesis 1–11 by calling attention to the strategy of using interpretive poems to blocks of narrative. The importance of this strategy lies in the fact that it is "text immanent."[66] It is focused on the verbal patterns and literary genres of the text. It does not import themes and ideas from outside its immediate compositional context. I also suggested that the thematic and theologically rich elements of Genesis 1–11 follow the contours of this "formal" literary pattern. The content of the poems, for example, focuses the reader's attention on the promised "seed" of Genesis 3:15 and the role that seed will play in bringing about a future divine blessing. I will have more to say about this compositional strategy and its role in the theology of the Pentateuch, but for now, it is necessary only to point out that the pattern of linking interpretive poems to blocks of narratives is also found at a higher level in the Pentateuch. It extends through the whole of the Pentateuch and serves as a connecting framework for each of the major blocks of narrative in the Pentateuch.

We will begin by tracing this compositional pattern briefly through the Pentateuch. Witte's methodology is useful. Once we have established an overall idea of the nature of the compositional links in the Pentateuch, we can go back to look for additional details belonging to the same compositional strategy.

The major blocks of narrative in the Pentateuch are

1. the primeval history (Gen 1–11)
2. the patriarchal narratives (Gen 12–50)
3. the exodus narratives (Ex 1–19)
4. the wilderness narratives (Num 11–25)
5. the conquest narratives (Deut 1–11)

---

[66]See Wolfgang Richter, *Exegese als Literaturwissenschaft: Entwurf einer alttestamentlichen Literaturtheorie und Methodologie* (Göttingen: Vandenhoeck & Ruprecht, 1971), pp. 179-87.

There are four major poems:

1. Genesis 49:1-27
2. Exodus 15:1-21
3. Numbers 23–24
4. Deuteronomy 32–33

Each these poems is attached to one of the major blocks of narrative within the Pentateuch. The attachment of a poem to the end of a narrative is identical to the strategy we observed in Genesis 1–11. That similarity suggests that the placement of the larger poems in the Pentateuch is part of the same compositional strategy in Genesis 1–11.

1. The first poem, Genesis 49:1-27, is positioned at the conclusion of the "patriarchal history" (Gen 12–48). Genesis 49:28-33 is an epilogue.
2. The second poem, Exodus 15:1-18, concludes the narrative which recounts the "exodus from Egypt" (Ex 1–14). Exodus 15:19-21 is the epilogue.
3. The poetic material in Numbers 23–24 concludes the narratives dealing with the wilderness wanderings (Num 10–22). Numbers 24:25 is the epilogue.
4. The poem(s) in Deuteronomy 32–33 conclude the narratives of the conquest of the Transjordan that are part of the book of Deuteronomy (Deut 1–10). Deuteronomy 34:1-4 is the epilogue.

The distribution of these poems within the Pentateuch appears to be part of a conscious strategy that spans the whole of the Pentateuch from Genesis 1 to Deuteronomy 34. This strategy is an extension of the compositional strategy of Genesis 1–11. The same literary patterns (strategies) in Genesis 1–11 are found in the composition of the Pentateuch as a whole, which suggests that the composition of Genesis 1–11 is part of the composition of the whole Pentateuch.

The extent of this compositional strategy ranges from Genesis 1–11 to the end of Deuteronomy. Its aim, apparently, was to give a meaningful shape to the entire Pentateuch. It is a composition that envisions the Pentateuch we now have. That shape suggests not a gradual development in its formation, but rather a conceptualization of the totality of the material.

*The compositional strategy of the major poems.* To appreciate the theological role of the larger poems in the final shape of the Pentateuch, one must pay close attention to the details of these poems, in particular the "authorial activity" (composition) that reflects an understanding of the broader scope of the Pentateuch. Specifically, one must look for material in these poems that appears to have been added in the process of linking the poems to the narratives. In poetry, additional material sometimes can be identified by its failure to conform to the formal patterns of ancient poetry—for example, meter and parallelism. Additional material in poetry can also be identified by its nonpoetic features (e.g., use of the *nota accusativi*)[67] or from its allusions to other texts (e.g., Num 24:9; Gen 49:9). Often, additional authorial material can be detected by its sheer volume (i.e., word count).

Of the four major poems in the Pentateuch, three show considerable signs of composition and authorial shaping.

*Genesis 49:1-28.* Authorial composition, or commentary, in the poem in Genesis 49 is seen in the descriptive material that has been added to the poetic sayings about Judah and Joseph. These sections are considerably more developed in comparison to the rest of the poem. A word count of the poetic sections of Judah (54 words in Gen 49:8-12) and Joseph (60 words in Gen 49:22-26) reveals considerably more descriptive material devoted to these two tribes than the average for the other tribes. The poetic sections devoted to the ten other sons of Jacob average 13 words each. To Judah and Joseph are given 54 and 60 words respectively. Subtract the words to Judah that focus on his supremacy over his brothers (7 words [Gen 49:8a]), the reign of a king from his tribe (20 words [Gen 49:9a, 10]), or allusions to other poems (10 words [Gen 49:8b, 9b]), and Judah has 17 words, the same amount as Reuben (Gen 49:3-4). This suggests that 37 additional words in Judah's segment are devoted to the kingship (e.g., supremacy, allusions, royalty). What remains of the Judah poem after Genesis 49:10—Genesis 49:11-12—is roughly equal to the material for the other ten sons, suggesting that Jacob's words to Judah are of special importance to the author, and that the kingship is the thematic focus of the material added to Judah's poem. This does not, by itself, mean

[67]GKC §117a-b.

that the kingship is not an essential part of all the words to Judah. It does suggest, however, that the images of royalty inherent in Judah's poem may have been additionally expanded to highlight his promise of the kingship. The additional material that focuses on Judah contrasts sharply with the often commonplace and sometimes obscure poetry of the other ten sons.

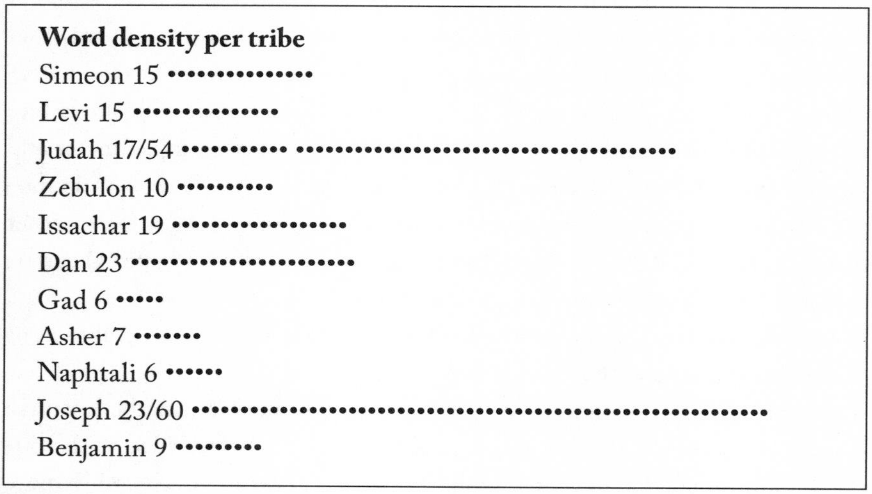

**Word density per tribe**
Simeon 15
Levi 15
Judah 17/54
Zebulon 10
Issachar 19
Dan 23
Gad 6
Asher 7
Naphtali 6
Joseph 23/60
Benjamin 9

**Figure 3.1**

The Joseph segment (Gen 49:22-26) also has unique characteristics and additional material. The noun for "blessing" *(bĕrākâ)* occurs six times in Jacob's words to Joseph and, by contrast, ten times in the rest of Genesis, making over one-third of the occurrences in Genesis part of the Joseph poem. The term for "blessing" *(bĕrākâ)* does not occur elsewhere in Jacob's poem (Gen 49:3-27), though the verb "to bless" *(bārak)* does occur in the Joseph section (Gen 49:25), but not in the rest of the poem. Apart from these occurences, the verb "to bless" is more common throughout the rest of the book of Genesis. There are a total of 7 words for "blessing" or "to bless" in the Joseph segment, with no other use of the terminology in Jacob's poem. The terms for "blessing" occur three times in the epilogue of Jacob's poem: "and he blessed *[wayĕbārek]*, each according to his blessing *[kĕbirkātô]*, he blessed *[bērak]* them" (Gen 49:28). There are 10 words dealing with "blessing" vocabulary in the Joseph poem. Jacob's words to Joseph also contain multiple occurances of the verbs "be fruitful" *(pārâ)* and "multiply" *(rābâ)*, vocabulary clearly linking it with the "blessing" *(bārak)* in Genesis 1:28. If the number of words in the sections linked to Joseph's "blessing" (37 words) are subtracted from the total number of words in the Joseph section (60 words), it leaves 23 words for Joseph. That number is the same as for Dan,[68] for whom there is one of the largest word counts among the twelve brothers, suggesting that some additional prominence besides "blessing" has been allotted to Joseph. Attention to Joseph is not surprising, given that this poem comes as the conclusion of the Joseph narratives in Genesis 37–50. We would expect Joseph to be given a prominent position, even though the Joseph narrative has its own separate (poetic) conclusion in Genesis 48:15-20.

*Judah in the Joseph narratives.* I have been suggesting in the previous discussion that the poem in Genesis 49 gives special treatment to Judah. That is consistent with the special attention given to Judah in the whole of the Joseph narrative (Gen 37–50). As the story of Joseph's journey to Egypt is getting underway (Gen 37), the author interrupts the narration to insert a lengthy story about Judah and his "righteous" (Gen 38:26) descendants (Gen 38). Also, when Joseph's brothers devised a plot to kill him (Gen 37:18), it was Judah, rather than the firstborn, Reuben, who saved Joseph from sudden death. Such "reversals" occur numerous times within the remainder of the Joseph narrative. Judah is singled out from the other brothers as the one through whom the rescue of the family of Jacob was accomplished.[69]

Throughout the Joseph narrative the author makes it clear that his brothers' plans against him were motivated by Joseph's dreams. In one dream, Joseph saw his brothers' sheaves bowing down to him (*wattištaḥăweynā* [Gen 37:7]). In another, the sun, moon and stars were bowing down to him (*mištaḥăwîm* [Gen 37:9]). Joseph's brothers understood his to mean they too would bow down to him (*lĕhištaḥăwōt* [Gen 37:10]). As the narratives unfold, that is exactly what happens. Joseph's brothers come to Egypt, and, through a labyrinth of events, they find themselves bowing down to him (*wayyištaḥăwû* [Gen 42:6]), just as Joseph had dreamed. When they bow to him, Joseph "remembers his dreams" (Gen 42:9), and with him, the reader discovers that this is a work of divine intervention. The point of the narrative is to show that these and similar events are a fulfillment of Joseph's dreams. At the end of the story the narrative takes a turn in a new direction.

---

[68]Whose number is actually 20, since the last three words in the Dan section, "I will wait, O Lord, for your salvation" (Gen 49:18), are likely part of an authorial commentary.

[69]See Sailhamer, *The Pentateuch as Narrative*, pp. 207, 219, 222.

The narratives that focus attention on the fulfillment of Joseph's dreams are not permitted a final word. There are still important parts of the narrative that draw our attention not to Joseph, but to Judah. That focus reaches its fullest expression in Jacob's poem (Gen 49). The last word of the Joseph narrative turns our attention toward the preeminence of the tribe of Judah: "your brothers will bow down to you" (*yištaḥăwwû* [Gen 49:8b]). These words connecting Judah to Joseph's dreams are, strictly speaking, not part of the poetic lines of Jacob's poem. In terms of their literary shape, theses lines fall outside the boundaries of the poem (in Gen 49:8b) and serve as a kind of explanation of the poetic imagery in the first half of the verse (Gen 49:8a). Those additional words in Genesis 49:8b are important in giving us another look at the author's understanding of Jacob's first words to Judah. By means of these words (Gen 49:8b), a larger lesson is drawn from the Joseph narratives. What was once true only of Joseph, that his brothers would bow down to him (Gen 37:7-10), is now to find its fulfillment in the reign of one who holds the scepter from the house of Judah (Gen 49:10). It would be through Judah, not Joseph, that the blessing of creation (Gen 1:28) will be restored to humanity. In drawing a connection between the Joseph narratives and the promise to the house of Judah, Joseph and the events of his life foreshadow what will ultimately happen to the king from the house of Judah, the one spoken of in this poem. The king who was to come from the house of Judah is foreshadowed by the life of Joseph. He will save his people and the nations, just as Joseph saved the families of the sons of Jacob (Gen 50:20) and the nations (Gen 47:19). Joseph, rather than Reuben, will be the firstborn among his brothers, but Judah will reign through the kingship. Note how these passages were read by the author of the book of Chronicles (1 Chron 5:1-2).

We might inquire about the strategy of the writer in inserting the account of Joseph and his brothers (Gen 42–46) in the midst of the narratives dealing with Joseph's rise to power in Egypt (Gen 39–41; 47). The answer may lie in the way in which this final narrative resembles the story of Joseph and his brothers. Throughout those narratives the theme is repeatedly expressed that Joseph's wisdom and administrative skills saved the life of his brothers and father. Thus, at the beginning of the story, Jacob had told his sons to go down to Egypt to buy grain "that we may live and not die" (*wĕniḥyeh wĕlōʾ nāmût* [Gen 42:2]). Then Judah, "in the second year" (*šĕnātayim* [Gen 45:6]), told his father to let them return to Egypt "that we may live and not die" (*wĕniḥyeh wĕlōʾ nāmût*

[Gen 43:8]). Finally, when he revealed himself to them, Joseph told his brothers that God had sent him to Egypt "to save life" (*lĕmiḥyâ* [Gen 45:5]).

In keeping with that emphasis, the present narrative opens with the statement of the Egyptians to Joseph as they seek to buy grain from him: "Why should we die before your eyes?" (*wĕlāmmâ nāmût negdekā* [Gen 47:15]). Then it continues with the account of their return to Joseph "the second year" (*baššānâ haššēnît* [Gen 47:18]), when they again said, "Why should we perish?" (*lāmmâ nāmût* [Gen 47:19]), and then again, "that we may live and not die" (*wĕniḥyeh wĕlōʾ nāmût* [Gen 47:19]). Such repetitions in the surface structure of the narrative suggest that a thematic strategy is at work. First with his brothers and then with the Egyptians, Joseph's wisdom is seen as the source of life for everyone in the land.

A further evidence of a distinct strategy behind the present narrative in Genesis 47 can be seen in the ironic twist given the earlier narratives by the outcome of this chapter. The whole of the story of Joseph and his brothers began with Joseph being sold (*wayyimšĕkû* [Gen 37:28]) into slavery (*ʿebed* [Gen 39:17]) for twenty pieces of silver (*kāsep* [Gen 37:28]). Now, at the conclusion, Joseph is shown selling (*mākĕrû* [Gen 47:20]) the whole of the land of Egypt into slavery (*ʿăbādîm* [Gen 47:19, 25]) and taking his family's "silver" (*hakkesep* [Gen 47:18). In the end, because of the wisdom of Joseph, the offspring of Abraham became "fruitful" *(wayyiprû)*, "increased *[wayyirbû]* greatly in number," and were dwelling safely and prosperously in the "region" *(ʾereṣ)* of Goshen (Gen 47:27). This picture clearly looks like a replication of the intended blessing of the early chapters of Genesis: "Be fruitful *[pĕrû]* and increase *[ûrĕbû]* in number; fill the earth *[hāʾāreṣ]*" (Gen 1:28).[70]

*Jacob's last word on Judah (Gen 49:1-28).* As suggested above, an interbiblical commentary on Jacob's words to Judah and Joseph, 1 Chronicles 5:1-2, reflects a similar interest in these two tribes:

> And the sons of Reuben, the firstborn of Israel—because he was the firstborn—but when he polluted the bed of his father *[ûbĕḥallĕlô yĕṣûʿê ʾābîw;* cf. Gen 49:4: *ḥillaltā yĕṣûʿî]*, his right of the firstborn was given to the sons of Joseph, the son of Israel, and he was not reckoned as the firstborn. Because Judah prevailed *[gābar;* cf. Gen 49:9: *gûr]* over his brothers, one from his family *[mimmennû]* would become prince [*nāgîd*, royal heir], but the right of firstborn belonged to Joseph.[71]

---

[70]See Sailhamer, "Genesis," p. 38.
[71]See ibid., p. 324.

*Joseph and the Genesis narratives.* As also suggested above, the idea of "blessing" is expanded in the Joseph section of the poem. This cluster of select vocabulary (ברכה *[brkh]*, בְּרַךְ *[brk]*, פרה *[prh]*, רבה *[rbh]*) serves as a verbal link to the primeval blessing in Genesis 1:28 and the frequent repetition of that blessing the Pentateuch.

This also conforms to the poem's subscription in Genesis 49:28, which repeats the word "blessing" three times. Clearly, the material in Jacob's words to Joseph and the subscription to the larger poem (Gen 49:28) link the Joseph narrative to the theme of "blessing" in the other parts of the patriarchal narratives. What is said about Judah points in the same direction but with the additional anticipation of a future kingship arising out of the house of Judah (Gen 49:8-12). The focus on a future king and blessing is evident also in other parts of the Pentateuch's compositional strategy involving poems: "This is the blessing *[bĕrākâ]* which Moses the man of God blessed Israel before he died" (Deut 33:1).

*Balaam's poetry (Num 23:5-24; 24:1-24).* The poetry in Numbers 23–24 contains considerable duplication and expansion. The first of the two poems, Numbers 23, is about the history of the people of Israel and their redemption from Egypt. It draws on the narrative account of the exodus in Exodus 14 as well as the poetic version of the event in Exodus 15:1-21. It presents a picture of God as Israel's king (Ex 15:18), who leads them in defeating their enemies and freeing them from captivity. Like the prophetic literature (e.g., Hos 2:2) and the NT (e.g., Mt 2:15), the "exodus" theme is central to the Pentateuch's understanding of salvation and redemption. According to Numbers 23:21-24 (RSV),

> He [the LORD] has not beheld misfortune in Jacob; nor has he seen trouble in Israel. The LORD their God is with them, and the shout of a king is among them. God brings them out of Egypt *[ʾēl môṣîʾām mimmiṣrāyim];* they have as it were the horns of the wild ox. For there is no enchantment against Jacob, no divination against Israel; now it shall be said of Jacob and Israel, "What has God wrought!" Behold, a people *[hen-ʿām]*! As a lioness it rises up and as a lion it lifts itself; it does not lie down till it devours the prey, and drinks the blood of the slain.

The poetry in Numbers 24 looks in a new direction. It is, to some extent, a rewritten version of the poem in Numbers 23. Although it draws its imagery of the exodus from the poem in Numbers 23, the poem in Numbers 24 ultimately is not about the exodus of the past; it is about the reign of a future king. According to Numbers 24:5-9, Balaam speaks to Israel about that king:

> How fair are your tents, O Jacob, your encampments, O Israel! Like valleys that stretch afar, like gardens beside a river, like aloes that the LORD has planted, like cedar trees beside the waters. Water shall flow from his buckets, and his seed *[wĕzarʿô]* is in the many waters, his king shall rise up from Agag, and his kingdom shall be exalted. God brings him out of Egypt *[ʾēl môṣîʾô mimmiṣrayim];* he has as it were the horns of the wild ox, he shall consume the nations his adversaries, and shall shatter their bones, and inflict them with his arrows. He couched, he lay down like a lion, and like a lioness; who will arouse him? Blessed be every one who blesses you, and cursed be every one who curses you.

There is a significant difference between Numbers 23:22 "God brings *them* out of Egypt" *(ʾēl môṣîʾām mimmiṣrāyim)* and Numbers 24:8 "God brings *him* out of Egypt" *(ʾēl môṣîʾô mimmiṣrayim).* What Balaam said about the historical exodus from Egypt in Numbers 23, he here restates and applies to the future king in Numbers 24. The poems in Numbers 23–24 are deliberately linked in a way that foreshadows the future with an image from the past. There is a kind of typological pattern of thinking that links the two poems in Numbers 23–24. The depiction of Israel's past exodus from Egypt (Num 23) is cast as a literary image of a future king (Num 24). The king is identified in Numbers 24:9 as the one promised in Genesis 49.[72] The link is made by a "learned quotation" of Genesis 49:9b in Numbers 24:9: "He laid down, he reclined like a lion, and like a lioness; who will arouse him?"

*Moses' song (Deut 32–33).* The poetry in Deuteronomy 32–33 also shows considerable development of earlier pentateuchal themes.[73] Along with the other poems in the Pentateuch, Deuteronomy 33 looks forward to a future king who, like Moses (Deut 33:4), will, with God's help (Deut 33:26-29), unite the tribes of Israel (Deut 33:4-5, 7) and bring peace, safety (Deut

---

[72]See John H. Sailhamer, "Hosea 11:1 and Matthew 2:15," *WTJ* 63 (2001): 93-95.

[73]"The Song [Deut 32] shows great originality of form, being a presentation of prophetical thoughts in a poetical dress, on a scale which is without parallel in the OT" (S. R. Driver, *A Critical and Exegetical Commentary on Deuteronomy* [ICC; Edinburgh: T & T Clark, 1895], p. 345). Driver also quotes Cornill in characterizing the poem as a "compendium of prophetical theology" (ibid., p. 346).

33:28a), great abundance (Deut 33:28b), salvation (Deut 33:29) and blessing (Deut 33:29).[74]

*The song of the sea (Ex 15:1-17).* The poem in Exodus 15:1-17 does not have the same compositional and thematic development as the others. In character and purpose it is similar to the poem in Numbers 23.[75] Both poems (Ex 15; Num 23) are not part of the compositional strategy of the three other poems (Gen 49; Num 24; Deut 32–33). Nevertheless, they both, along with Genesis 48:15-16 and Genesis 48:20, make an important contribution to the strategy of the Pentateuch.[76] They link the author's poetic images to the historical realities of Israel's past.

*Narrative introductions (Gen 49:1; Num 24:14; Deut 31:29).* An important clue that these three poems are part of a single strategy and the work of the same author lies in the fact that they have a common introduction that identifies them with central themes in the Pentateuch. In the introduction to each poem the central character of the narrative (Jacob, Balaam, Moses) calls an audience together (with imperatives) and advises them (with cohortatives) of what will happen (with imperfects) "in the last days." The audience, in this case, includes the reader. The phrase "in the last days" is found in the introduction to each of these poems but elsewhere in the Pentateuch only in Deuteronomy 4:40.

The phrase occurs fourteen times—thirteen in Hebrew, once in Aramaic (Daniel). Willy Staerk traced the meaning of the phrase to Ezekiel 38:16, where it refers to the fall of Gog at the time of the establishment of the messianic kingdom: "The expression generally is not found in the older prophetic and preexilic literature; it is first found in Ezekiel in the prophecy against Gog and denotes there the inauguration of the messianic kingdom."[77] He viewed the occurrences of the phrase in the Pentateuch as a late prophetic interpolation. However, he paid no attention to the distribution of the phrase within the programatic introductions to each of the poems, which is a serious oversight. Among other things, it means that Staerk and others were unable to appreciate

---

[74]"In general character, it resembles the Blessing of Jacob" (ibid., p. 385).

[75]Compare Exodus 15:18 with Numbers 23:21b.

[76]Compare Exodus 15:2 with Isaiah 12:2.

[77]Läßst sich in den älteren Profetenschriften wie überhaupt in der vorexilischen Literatur nirgens belegen; die Wendung findet sich vielmehr zuerst bei Ezechiel in der Weissagung gegen Gog und bezeichnet daselbst deutlich den Anbruch des messianischen Reiches" (W. Staerk, "Der Begrauch der Wendung בְּאַחֲרִית הַיָּמִים im alttestamentlichen Kanon," *ZAW* 11 [1891]: 247-53).

fully the meaning of the phrase within the context of its own occurrences in the Pentateuch as a whole. Along with that, the attempt to understand the phrase within the immediate context of each individual psalm led to a reference point for the phrase "last days" that was drawn from the immediate historical events depicted in the poem. Whatever might be said about the sense of the phrase "in the last days" or its English translation within the historical horizon of each poem, consideration of its distribution within the Pentateuch (with these three major poems and Deut 4) is crucial to a compositional approach. There is little doubt that the expression is part of the final composition of the Pentateuch. Its repetition within four Pentateuch-level compositional seams, linking the whole of the Pentateuch to its present shape (Gen 49:1; Num 24:14; Deut 4:30; 31:29), serves as an important backup for assigning a single eschatological sense to the phrase in all four instances. That all of them are to be read eschatologically finds further support from the use of the phrase in Deuteronomy 4:30, which looks beyond the return from Jerusalem's Babylonian captivity to a distant "prophetic" future. Since, as we will see, the phrase "in the last days" is also linked to the first word in the Pentateuch, *bĕrēʾšît* ("in the first [days]"), there is good reason to believe that the expression and its use span the length of the canonical Pentateuch. It is the work of the author of the Pentateuch as we now have it.

To guard against overreading the phrase "in the last days," it is imporant to ask why the phrase was omitted before the poem in Exodus 15. It too is a major poem whose scope spans large sections of biblical narrative and law within the Pentateuch, and reaching, some believe, as far as the book of Samuel. One must ask what there is about the poem in Exodus 15 that would have rendered the phrase "in the last days" inappropriate as its introduction. Or, at least, one must consider the possibility that the variation in the subject matter of the poem in Exodus 15 rendered the expression "last days" unsuitable. A preliminary observation might be that the three poems (Gen 49; Num 24; Deut 32–33) actually deal with future events that extend beyond David and his kingdom to a future royal personage from the house of Judah, whereas Exodus 15 clearly is about the historical Davidic kingship. There is nothing in the poem of Exodus 15 that would merit the scope of the phrase "last days" as Staerk saw it.

Hermann Gunkel rejected Staerk's eschatological-messianic interpretation of the phrase "in the last days" in Genesis 49:1, believing that it referred only to the time of David.[78] Gunkel, however, held that the other occurrences of the phrase in the Pentateuch were drawn from the prophetic literature (e.g., Ezekiel and Daniel)[79] and thus are eschatological in intent. Gunkel missed an important implication of his own observations. If the other occurrences of the expression "last days" do refer to an eschatology, then the poem in Genesis 49, being a part of the same single compositional strategy, likely has that same meaning. What is missing in Gunkel's reading of this expression is its global nature in terms of being a part of the composition of the whole Pentateuch. Current scholarship is still not fully sensitive to the distribution of the phrase within the Pentateuch, viewing it as more or less flexible in meaning as judged by its specific historical content. If the phrase is part of a single compositional strategy, then its sense likely is uniform throughout the whole of its uses in the Pentateuch. In any event, it is widely recognized that by the time of the exile, the phrase had taken on a generally eschatological sense, owing to its relatively frequent use in the prophetic literature.

Clearly, too little attention has been given to the importance of the distribution of the phrase "last days" within the Pentateuch. The fact that it occurs within the introductions to the major poems in the Pentateuch, and not in Exodus 15, which relates to the Davidic monarchy, suggests that it has a role to play in the composition of the Pentateuch that cannot not be ignored. Its meaning within each of these introductions to the poems likely was understood by the author in a generally related, if not identical, sense. It is unlikely that an author would repeat such a phrase with a multiple sense. It is also unlikely that the author would overlook the similarity in the content of each poem. Of particular importance is also the sense of the compositional (linking) material within each of the poems, especially if it can be identified with the same level of composition within each introduction. What I have in mind is not merely the central topic of each poem (e.g., the kingship), but also the additional material within the poems that tends to fill out and focus on the central message of the poetry. Much of that material may play itself out in the echo of themes in the rest of the OT Scriptures. An example is the way prophetic texts such as Isaiah 63:1 take up and develop "the rider on the horse" motif begun in Genesis 49:11-12, a poetic image that continues into the NT (Rev 19:11-16).

---

[78]Hermann Gunkel, *Genesis*, 8th ed. (Göttingen: Vandenhoeck & Ruprecht, 1969), p. 478.
[79]Ibid.

As I have suggested, in the poems in the Pentateuch the focus of each poem is on a future king from the house of Judah and the establishment of his kingdom. In Genesis 49 this king is specifically linked to the tribe of Judah and is identified, through quotations and allusions, with the king described in Numbers 24:9 and Deuteronomy 33:7. It is this king whose reign will come "in the last days." Whether these poems envision David's reign, the reign of an historical Davidic king, or the reign of a future messiah, the final verdict must come from a close examination and exegesis of the text of these three poems, their literary connections with each other, and also their links to the Pentateuch as a whole. For now, it is important to leave open both possibilities: the kingdom of the historical David or the kingdom of the one who would follow him (e.g., an eschatological king like David).

As mentioned above, apart from the introductions to these three poems, the phrase "in the last days" is used elsewhere in the Pentateuch only in Deuteronomy 4:30. Since that passage appears to be part of the same (or related) compositional strategy as the three poems, we might expect it to provide additional help in determining the meaning of the phrase in the Pentateuch. In Deuteronomy 4:30 the phrase refers to a distant time, well beyond the postexilic restoration of the nation. It has a similar range to the that of other prophetic contexts in which the phrase is found (e.g., Is 2:2; Ezek 38:16; Dan 10:14). In those texts its eschatological meaning is not in doubt.

*Cross-referencing (innertextuality).* Another feature that calls for attention in the Pentateuch's poems (Gen 49; Num 24; Deut 32–33) is their considerable cross-referencing or innertextuality. Not only do the poems frequently quote each other, but also they quote other parts of the Pentateuch, especially those connected to the compositional seams discussed above. It is clear from reading the seams of the Pentateuch that the poems are the center of the author's attention. What is said of the king in Numbers 24:9a, for example, amounts to nearly a verbatim quotation of Genesis 49:9b: "He crouches down, he lays down like a lion, and like a lioness; who will arouse him?" Texts such as these raise the question of why the author would want to draw such a close link between these two poems. The answer may lie in the author's intention to allow the reader to see that these two poems, and others, are about the same king from the house of Judah, one who is to come in the distant future. He might also have wanted to identify the king in each of these poems with the coming king from the house of Judah.

Other innertextual links, such as that between Deuteronomy 33 and Genesis 49, are well known. Whole phrases have been taken from one poem and recombined within another (cf. Gen 49:25 with Deut 33:13; Gen 49:26 with Deut 33:16).[80] Such intentional cross-referencing and borrowing between these poems suggests the author's conscious appreciation of their strategic importance to the message of the Pentateuch.

*Intextuality.* Each of these poems (Gen 49; Num 24; Deut 32–33) also contains considerable editorializing and commentary. This can been seen especially in those places where ancient poetic features such as meter and parallelism are obscured by comments and commentary. Although features of ancient poetry are not always understood, enough is known to draw our attention to those features when they are missing or have been altered in some way. Even an initial reading of the Pentateuch's poetic texts is enough to reveal additional material of a "thematic" character in those poems. Allusions to typically biblical notions of kingship, dominion and eschatology fill these poems.

The first two lines of the Judah section in Genesis 49:8 read, "Judah, you are the one your brothers will praise; your hand is on the neck of your enemies"; the third line reads, "The sons of your father will bow down to you." It is of no small consequence that these additional lines in the poetry of Genesis 49 allude to crucial aspects of the Joseph narrative, which precedes this poem in Genesis 37–48. In the context of the Joseph narrative (Gen 37:10), Joseph has had two dreams that are taken by the author (and the other characters in the story) to mean that his father, mother and brothers would, at some future time, "bow down" to him. Driven by that expectation, the Joseph narrative works its way decisively to the fulfillment of those dreams in Genesis 42:6. There, as his brothers come to Egypt to buy food, they are ushered into his presence and unwittingly "bow down to him" as the acclaimed leader of Egypt. The sense of the passage is clearly ironic, which serves to drive home the point that God is at work in this story of Joseph.

Irony in the Genesis narratives is the stock and trade of narratives dealing with divine sovereignty. In order to assure a proper reading of the narrative, the narrator tells us that Joseph, upon seeing his brothers bowing before him, "remembered his dreams" (Gen 42:9). This is the narrator's way of saying to

[80]See Stefan Beyerle, *Der Mosesegen im Deuteronomium: Eine texts-, kompositions- und formkritische Studie zu Deuteronomium 33* (BZAW 250; Berlin: de Gruyter, 1997).

the reader, "Are you getting this? Joseph's dreams are being fulfilled!" Also, the reference to Judah's brothers "bowing down before him" in Jacob's poem (Gen 49:8b) is not lost on the alert reader. Such an allusion to Joseph's brothers ties the poem to the surrounding Joseph narrative and injects an important element of the thematic picture of the Joseph story into the picture of the reign of the future king envisioned in the poem. Like Joseph, the brothers of the king of Judah will also "bow down to him" and, like Joseph, will save many lives. By means of the additional line in this poem, the story of Joseph is brought in as a verbal icon of the future reign of the king from Judah. Simply put, that king will be *like* Joseph. A link such as this opens the way for many of the Joseph traits to be read into the promise of the future king from Judah. For the author of the Pentateuch, Joseph has become a "figure" of the future king from Judah.

To summarize: Much of the additional poetic material in the Pentateuch is linked to other sections of text by further cross-referencing and compositional seams growing out of Genesis 1–11. Such links provide further support for the notion that the composition of Genesis 1–11 is closely related to the composition of the Pentateuch as a whole. Many of the same kinds of explanatory details and additional commentary are found in the poems of Numbers 24. They provide an additional look into the meaning and message of the Pentateuch.

*Commentary within poems.* Biblical scholarship has long recognized both the importance and uniqueness of the Balaam pericope (Num 22–24). It offers a rich variety of literary and compositional material from which to trace the thematic strategy of the Pentateuch. Among critical scholars there is little agreement about the exact nature of the literary strata detected in these texts. In Balaam's last oracles (Num 24) many critical scholars detect numerous layers of "glosses," each linked to events in the latest periods of Israel's history. In Numbers 24:23-24 Balaam cries out in poetic verse, "Woe! Who shall live when God has accomplished this?" The verse continues, "And there will be ships from the side of the Kittim, and they will afflict Assur and they will afflict Eber, and also he will be utterly destroyed."

From a literary-historical point of view, these poetic lines appear to modern scholars to represent the "final" layer of "editorializing" *in* the Pentateuch. The unanimous opinion among literary critics is that Numbers 24:24 is a late (second century B.C.) addition to the Balaam oracles and to the Pentateuch itself. According to A. Freiherr von Gall, Numbers 24:24 was added "by a pious soul" living in the first century A.D.[81] Although most evangelical commentators would disagree with critics who date these comments so late in the text's history, they often agree that these verses are about the same events recorded in Daniel 11:30, where the "Kittim ships come against [the king of the North]." According to the *NIV Study Bible*, for example, the Kittim ships in Daniel 11:30 are "Roman vessels under the command of Popilius Laenas," and the king of the North is "Antiochus."[82] As in Numbers 24:14, in the book of Daniel this event was to happen "in the last days" (Dan 10:14).

*Innertextuality*. In the poem(s) in Numbers 24 an interesting pattern occurs in the identification of the names of individuals cited in the poetry. The proper names in the poetic texts of this chapter fall into two groups. In the first group the names refer to Israel's ancient neighbors. They represent those who inhabit the immediately surrounding areas in the narratives. Five are mentioned in Numbers 24: Moab, Edom, Seir, Amalek and the Kenites. These names occur only within the poetic material in Balaam's verse. They are not a part of the comments that have been added to explain the background of the poems.

A second group of names is not drawn from the historical events recounted in the surrounding narratives. They are names of persons and groups specifically mentioned in Genesis 1–11. There are five of these names as well: Seth (Num 24:17), Cain (Num 24:22), Assur (Num 24:24), Eber (Num 24:24) and the Kittim (Num 24:24). Within Numbers 24 these names are part of the comments added to the poems. That they are not part of the poetry is clear because they do not follow the poetic meter and parallelism that typically characterize biblical poetry.

Three of these five names occur in the Table of Nations in Genesis 10. They are Assur (Gen 10:22), Eber (Gen 10:21) and the Kittim (Gen 10:4).

---

[81]"Ohne weitere prosaische Ergänzungen hingen dann noch RV und RVI ihre Sprüche an, die dann durch einen zur Zeit Christi lebenden Frommen in V. 24 ihren Abschluss erhielten" (A. Freiherr von Gall, "Zusammensetzung und Herkunft der Bileam-Periokope in Num. 23-24," in *Festgruss Bernhard Stade: Zur Feier seiner 25 Jährigen Wirksamkeit als Professor* [Giessen: Ricker, 1900], p. 47). What is particularly interesting about this set of glosses (in Num 24:24) is that they form an arch that reaches from the Pentateuch to one of the last books in the Hebrew canon, the book of Daniel. These are, in fact, events that the book of Daniel describes as "the last days" (Dan 10:14). Within the context of the Balaam pericope, the same events are said to happen in "the last days" (Num 24:14).

[82]*The NIV Study Bible*, ed. Kenneth Barker (Grand Rapids: Zondervan, 1985), pp. 1316-17.

Within the editorial work of Genesis 10 these names are in the commentary part of Noah's poem (Gen 9:27). In the poem itself Noah prophesied, "Japeth shall dwell in the tents of Shem" (Gen 9:27). To understand the poem's intention, we must go on to the Table of Nations in the next chapter. There we discover that the Medes (Gen 10:2), the Greeks (Gen 10:2), and the Kittim (Gen 10:4) belong to the family of Japeth, and to the family of Shem belong Eber (Gen 10:21) and Assur (Gen 10:22). When viewed within the context of those details in Genesis 10, Noah's poem in Genesis 9:27 envisions the Medes, the Greeks and the Kittim "dwelling in the tents of" Babylon, Assyria and Eber.[83] That picture is the same one gotten from the commentary attached to Balaam's poem in Numbers 24:23-24. The Kittim will afflict Assur and Eber. The composition of one part of the Pentateuch, Genesis 9:27, is taken up and reinforced by another, Numbers 24:24. The focus and horizon of the argument of these texts and their accompanying commentary suggest that Balaam's poetry may be part of a larger, single, macrocompositional strategy extending through a major part, if not the whole, of the Pentateuch, including at least Genesis 10 and Numbers 24. If so, it calls for further study and a renewed quest for additional clues pointing in that direction.

*Commentary within the Pentateuch at large.* The commentary in the Balaam poem in Numbers 24:23-24 is Numbers 24:24a: "Ships will go out from the side of the Kittim, and they will afflict Assur and they will afflict Eber." Balaam's original oracle (poem) appears to have been Numbers 24:23b: "Woe! Who can survive when God does this work?"[84] Numbers 24:24a is, then, a commentary on Numbers 24:23b. This appears likely from two considerations: (1) Numbers 24:24a is not poetic and thus is not likely a part of the original poem; (2) the text of Numbers 24:23-24 shifts from singular to plural and then back to singular within the scope of a single verse. The grammatical forms that open the line are singular (Num 24:23b: "*Who* can survive?"), and then plural, following the "ships" (plural) in Numbers 24:24a ("And there will be ships from the side of the Kittim, and *they* will subdue Assyria [Assur] and *they* will subdue Eber"), and then back to singular in

[83]"To dwell in the tents of" probably means "to occupy," as in 1 Chronicles 5:10.

[84]There is general agreement among the commentaries and versions on the translation of this line of poetry offered above, though the NASB offers a different translation: "Alas, who can live except God has ordained it?"

Numbers 24:24b ("and also *he*[85] is destined for destruction"). Although it is possible to shift grammatical forms, such as person and number, abruptly within a brief span of text, in this case the singular in Numbers 24:24b ("he also will come to ruin") is unaware of the plurals between it and the singular that it resumes in Numbers 24:23b ("who will survive?"), suggesting that the plurals are secondary. Hebrew does not employ the device of parenthesis, so it must rely on subtle grammatical shifts in person and number to signal a parenthetical comment.

When viewed as commentary on the short poetic line in Numbers 24:23b, the sense of Numbers 24:24a often is explained with reference to related biblical texts and events in Israel's later history. George Gray suggests that the statement "There will be ships from the side of the Kittim" assumes the historical situation of Daniel 11:30, the rise of Antiochus,[86] interpreted prophetically by some (Delitzsch).[87] Carl Steuernagel also takes Numbers 24:24a as a reference to events in the Maccabean period,[88] assuming that the names "Assur" and "Eber" were code names for Assyria and Babylon, and the Kittim are Rome. According to James Montgomery, Numbers 24:24 states that the Romans "shall humble Ashur (i.e., Syria), and shall humble Eber (Abar-naharaim), and he (Antiochus!) shall be unto destruction."[89]

Not always appreciated by the commentators is that these comments on the poetry of Numbers 24, and elsewhere, are connected to earlier references to these people in the Table of Nations in Genesis 10. These brief comments are not isolated notations; they are commentary that in most cases can be traced to a single author and are linked to multiple occurances in the Pentateuch. In his comments in Numbers 24:24 the author of the Pentateuch has intentionally drawn on the lists of names in Genesis 10 and Genesis 4, intending to guide the reader in linking these two texts. The commentary in Numbers 24:24a reaches back to Noah's poem in Genesis 9:27 and the Table

---

[85]Note the plural in the NASB: "So *they* also will come to destruction."

[86]"Both Dan. 11:30 and 1 Macc. 1:1 appear to allude to the present poem, and thus show how it was understood in the 2nd cent. B.C." (George Buchanan Gray, *A Critical and Exegetical Commentary on Numbers* [ICC; Edinburgh: T & T Clark, 1965], p. 378).

[87]Ibid., p. 379.

[88]"Ein ganz später Zusatz dürfte Num 24:23-24 sein, der wohl auf die hellenistische Zeit zu deuten ist, wenn auch das Ereignis, das er im Auge hat, nicht sicher zu bestimmen ist" (Carl Steuernagel, *Lehrbuch der Einleitung in das alte Testament: Mit einem Anhang über die Apokryphen und Pseudepigraphen* [STL; Tübingen: Mohr Siebeck, 1912], p. 224).

[89]James A. Montgomery, *A Critical and Exegetical Commentary on the Book of Daniel* (ICC; Edinburgh: T & T Clark, 1927), p. 455.

of Nations in Genesis 10 for the meaning that it assigns to the ancient poem in Numbers 24:23b. It considerably broadens the context within which the author reads Balaam's oracles. The aim of the author's commentary is to show Balaam's vision on the screen of a future already forecast in Noah's poem in Genesis 9:27. The sense of the two poems is drawn from their intertextuality. The author uses these two (among other) poems to construct a composite picture of persons and events that lie in the future. The sense of these poems is not drawn from Israel's history as such, but from the ongoing intertextual reading of that history within the poems in the Pentateuch. Each poem is set within the context of the development of the other poems and the contributions that they make to the narratives in which they are embedded. The poems provide, as it were, their own historical context by filling in the poetic vision begun in Genesis 3:15 with material drawn from other poems such as Genesis 49, Numbers 24 and Deuteronomy 32–33.

What makes this observation theologically relevant is the fact that these poems already on their own terms are highly developed (density) theologically. By tying them together and linking them to the larger blocks of narrative in the Pentateuch, the author creates a kind of compositional-theological "critical mass" already on its way toward carrying its story into the Pentateuch and its vision of the future. As we will see, the theological vision developed out of the compositional strategy of the Pentateuch has made its own effect on the later prophetic literature. It is the theological vision that underlies the theology of the prophets. In Daniel 9–11 (especially Dan 10:14), which looks back to the poems in Numbers 24, God's promise to send a messianic redeemer is linked specifically to "the last days" (Num 24:14). At that time there will be peace and security for the nations of Genesis 10. Thus, the book of Daniel, along with other prophetic books such as Jeremiah and Isaiah, visualizes the future drawn from the innertextual strategy of the poems in the Pentateuch.

*The "beginning" of the Pentateuch.* I have argued thus far that the compositional strategy of Genesis 1–11 is identical to the larger literary strategy that encompasses the whole of the Pentateuch. That pattern is found in both the smaller units of narrative in Genesis 1–11 and the larger blocks in Genesis 12–Deuteronomy 34. The similarities suggest that those parts of texts had the same author. The literary strategy that now lies behind the Pentateuch aims to find the prophetic "good news" within the poetic speeches that echo in the words of its central characters. It is the message of the new covenant so familiar in the NT (e.g., Gal 3:15-18).

The fact that this compositional strategy covers the entire scope of the Pentateuch and does not extend beyond that range suggests that it is part of the compositional superstructure of the Pentateuch and not merely a layer of editorializing that may or may not be contained within the literary borders of the Pentateuch. This is important if we are seeking the author's intention in reading the Pentateuch.

I also have suggested that the comments in the major poetic texts show an interest in and focus on the same events within Genesis 1–11. This suggests that the comments in the poetic material are related to the same process of composition in Genesis 1–11 and the whole of the Pentateuch. They are not mere editorializing additions to already existing books. The nature of their work is that of an author making a book. Given the distribution of the Pentateuch's poems at the conclusion of its large blocks of narrative, I am suggesting that its compositional strategy follows the line laid down by the placement of those blocks of narrative from Genesis 1 to Deuteronomy 34. It is the work of an author who is viewing the whole of the Pentateuch in terms of its theological vision, which he is attempting to carry out from its beginning to its conclusion. The task of a theology of the Pentateuch is to find and describe that vision in terms laid down by the author.

With that broad purpose in mind, I will continue by making another observation about the extent of the Pentateuch.[90] That observation lies in the connection between the phrase "in the last days" and the first word in the HB, "in the beginning" *(bĕrēšît),* in Genesis 1:1.[91]

Franz Delitzsch was the first to explain the meaning of the term "beginning" *(rēšît)* in Genesis 1:1 in terms of its antonym "end" *(ʾaḥărît).*[92] According to Delitzsch, the author's use of "beginning" in Genesis 1:1 implies that he also had in mind the notion of an "end" *(Endzeit),* an

---

[90]See John H. Sailhamer, "Creation, Genesis 1–11, and the Canon," *BBR* 10 (2000): 89-106.

[91]The use of *rēšît* is unusual in Genesis 1:1 because elsewhere in the Pentateuch the adverbial notion of "beginning" is not expressed with *rēšît* but with *rešōnâ* or *tĕḥillâ* (cf. *Pentateuch with Targum Onkelos, Haphtaroth and Prayers for Sabbath and Rashi's Commentary,* trans. *Morris Rosenbaum* and Abraham M. Silbermann [London: Shapiro, Vallentine, 1929], p. 2).

[92]"Denn alle Geschichte ist ein von der Ewigkeit umschlossener Verlauf von ראשׁית bis zu אחרית; ihre ראשׁית ist der Anfang der Creatur und mit ihr der Zeit, ihre אחרית die Vollendung der Creatur und damit der Uebergang der Zeit in die Ewigkeit" (Franz Delitzsch, *Commentar über die Genesis,* 3rd ed. [Leipzig: Dörffling & Franke, 1860], p. 91).

*ʾaḥărît*. Otto Procksch went a step further by suggesting that *bĕrēšît* in Genesis 1:1 was deliberately chosen to correspond to its antonym *bĕʾaḥărît*, as in Genesis 49:1.[93]

When viewed from the broader perspective of the compositional strategy that we have noted in the whole of the Pentateuch, the phrase "the end of days" in the poetic seams and the "beginning" that leads off the Pentateuch in Genesis 1:1 appear to be related to a larger strategy. They are parts of an author's compositional strategy, which extends the full length of the Pentateuch. They form part of the *Endgestalt* of the Pentateuch. The *bĕrēšît* in Genesis 1:1 corresponds not only to the *bĕʾaḥărît* in Genesis 49:1, but also to the other occurrences of *bĕʾaḥărît* in the remainder of the Pentateuch (Num 24:14; Deut 4:30; 31:29). The Pentateuch's "beginning" already already has an "end" in view. In the use of these terms, the author of the Pentateuch appears to have already developed a specific vocabulary for his understanding of the biblical end. Biblical history has an *Urzeit* and an *Endzeit (rēšît* and *ʾaḥărît).*[94] By the use of these two terms and *bĕʾ*, God's activities are divided into a beginning and an end—that is, a "last days" *(ʾaḥărît hayyāmîm).* By opening the Pentateuch with a statement about the "beginning" *(rēšît),* the author attaches the early chapters of Genesis to the broader eschatological (or apocalyptic) schema in which its events forecast and anticipate those of an *Urzeit*, a "primeval time." As we have seen from the context of the individual poems in the Pentateuch, its "last days" are centered on a hope of a coming king whose reign extends to all the nations: "To him shall be the obedience of the nations" (Gen 49:10).

Within that broad schema further parallels are drawn between the *Urzeit* of Genesis 1–11 and the *Endzeit* described in the later poetry. Those parallels are found not only in the poetic texts but also, and perhaps more importantly, in the explanatory commentary attached to those poetic texts. Such comments are not scattered randomly throughout the Pentateuch; rather, they are

---

[93]Otto Procksch, *Die Genesis: Übersetzt und erklärt* (KAT 1; Leipzig: Dechert, 1913), p. 265. "The antithesis of רֵשִׁית is not שֵׁנִית or שְׁלִשִׁית , but אחרית (Deut 11:12; Is 41:22); also here [in Gen 1:1] [immediately] comes to mind the notion of the אַחֲרִית הַיָּמִים, the absolute end of the present world. In all probability, P has deliberately chosen the expression with a view to the אַחֲרִית of all things" (ibid., p. 425).

[94]Wilhelm Bousset and Hugo Gressmann, *Die Religion des Judentums im späthellenistischen Zeitalter* (HNT 21; Tübingen: Mohr Siebeck, 1966), p. 283.

part of a single distributional pattern, or compositional strata, that extends from Genesis 1 to Deuteronomy 34. This is likely the work of an author. Any reading of the Pentateuch that seeks to take it in its entirety *(Endgestalt)* must reckon with such a conscious overarching design and the meaning that it brings to each of the individual parts of the Pentateuch.

The foregoing discussion suggests that there is a conscious design or pattern behind the composition of the Pentateuch. That design includes the interrelationship of its narratives and key poetic texts. The poems are attached to the end of the narratives and provide the theological context within which we are to read the narratives. An important part of the design includes brief but strategically important additions, or comments, to the poetic texts. These are not isolated or random comments of later scribes; rather, they are part of the final composition of the whole Pentateuch and are the work of an author. They are also, it appears, the result of an exegesis of existing written texts, some of which were already ancient at the time of composition. This conclusion raises the question of whether there are still further traces of other kinds of literary, or compositional, design in the Pentateuch, and if so, how they might relate to the themes in its poetry.

*Focus on faith.* In the preceding section I discussed compositional elements of the Pentateuch that reflect themes and issues prominent in the prophetic literature. The Pentateuch uses poetic texts to highlight and thematize central ideas in its narrative. The narratives, with their poetic commentary, foreshadow events that lie in the future. Past events are forged into images of the prophetic future.

Along similar lines, Hans-Christoph Schmitt has identified a compositional strategy in the Pentateuch that resembles both the prophetic literature and the NT. It is a strategy that, like the prophetic books and the NT in general, focuses attention on the centrality of "faith."[95] Ultimately, Schmitt's concern is to demonstrate how one might approach the theological message of the Pentateuch by means of an analysis of its compositional strategy. We do so, he argues, by paying close attention to the final shape of the Pentateuch. We must come to the text at the point where its historical author has finished his task and laid down his tools. What features of the existing text connect its various parts into that completed whole? The

[95] Schmitt, "Redaktion des Pentateuch."

theological meaning of the Pentateuch is then read off the surface of that final shape. One need not suppose a long process of formation. It is only necessary to aim at the shape of the text that comes most directly from the hands of the author.

Schmitt begins his analysis of the Pentateuch with the large blocks of narrative that we noted earlier: Genesis 1–11; 12–50; Exodus 1–15; 19–24. These blocks of narrative, Schmitt argues, have been woven together by means of an intentional, theologically oriented, literary strategy. The central feature of that strategy is its use of the vocabulary of "faith" *(ʾāman).* At crucial points within these narratives Schmitt identifies a recurring use of the terminology of "faith" *(ʾāman).* He also finds that this "faith" terminology is embedded in narratives that share formal characteristics with the lament psalms in the Psalter. They begin with a description of an emergency situation, then move to a promise that calls for a response of faith, and then move to the description of a response of trust (faith). According to Schmitt, these compositional "seams" linking the larger blocks of narrative provide crucial staging points from which the reader can evaluate the events recounted in the narratives. In whatever emergency that arises they direct the reader's attention to the importance of "faith."

Schmitt's study helps us see the important role that compositional strategies play in discovering the overall theological intention of the author. If Schmitt's argument represents a proper assessment of the text's formation, it suggests that a central part of the message of the Pentateuch is its focus on "faith." What the author intends to say about that theme must be further ironed out alongside other themes that he may also have woven into that same text. As with the nature of composition in general, the starting point is the attempt to retrace the author's work of "making" the Pentateuch.

*The literary strategy of Exodus 1–14.* The starting point of Schmitt's assessment of the Pentateuch's "faith" theme is the internal pattern of the narrative in Exodus 1–14. According to Schmitt, Exodus 1–14 is an internally self-contained literary unit. The introductory segment, Exodus 1–4, reaches its literary climax in a reference to God's remembering his covenant with the patriarchs (Ex 2:23-25). This back-reference *(Nachverweissung)* to the patriarchal narratives in Genesis 12–50 serves to connect events in the lives of the patriarchs to the exodus and the covenant at Sinai.

At the conclusion of the opening segment in Exodus 4 Schmitt isolates a strategic text segment that ties the theme of covenant renewal to "faith." What is initially most significant about these observations is that this segment of text follows the "lament" pattern in the form-critical study of the psalms. It is from within that segment that Schmitt finds a pronounced emphasis on "faith" (Ex 4:31). "Faith" is cast as the necessary response to "lament."

The "lament" pattern exhibits the following elements:

1. *Emergency:* God's people are faced with a dangerous situation in which their leaders are being called before Pharaoh to ask for their release (Ex 3:18-19).
2. *Promise:* In the face of that danger God gives the assurance that he will be there to rescue and to help (Ex 3:20-22).
3. *Faith:* This section is a presentation of a call for faith. Moses asks, "What happens if the people do not believe what I tell them?" (Ex 4:1-5)
4. *Certainty:* Israel's response of faith is anticipated in the "signs" given Moses and Aaron (Ex 4:1-17). The people's faith is realized when the signs are performed (Ex 4:27-31). In both texts are found the same terminology of "faith," the Hiphil verb "to believe" (אמן, *ʾmn*). At the conclusion of this literary segment we again find an emphasis on "faith" (Ex 14:31). As Exodus 4:1 shows, the focus of the narrative is an emphasis on "faith" in the divinely given "sign" *(ʾôt).* Faith in the divine promise of salvation is strengthened by the witness of the "signs."

*Literary links to other text units.* An emphasis on "faith" is found also at strategic points in other literary units in the Pentateuch (e.g., Gen 15:6; Ex 19:9; Num 14:11; 20:12). Exodus 19:9 sits within a text segment containing a reference to a covenant that links the exodus narrative to the Sinai narrative. It is a "bridge" passage. Exodus 19:4 looks back to the exodus from Egypt, and Exodus 19:5 looks forward to the covenant at Sinai. It is within this pericope that we find a pronounced emphasis on faith. The object of Israel's faith is not the Mosaic law, but the promise of their becoming "a kingdom of priests and a holy nation" (Ex 19:6).[96]

*Genesis 15.* Genesis 15 is a text widely acknowledged for its emphasis on faith. The NT gives considerable attention to this chapter, as does the au-

[96]This theme is seen again most clearly in Isaiah 61:6.

thor of the Pentateuch.[97] It also contains a reference to the making of a "covenant" *(bĕrît)*. The purpose of remembering Abraham's faith in Genesis 15:6 is to connect the promise of multiple descendants in Genesis 15:1-5 to the covenant-guaranteed possession of the land in Genesis 15:7-21. Abraham's faith is presented in Genesis 15:6 as a response to God's assurance of his presence. In Genesis 15:7-21 his faith is a prophetic sign of assurance that God will be loyal to the words of his covenant. This is the same sign that God later gives Moses in Exodus 3:12: "And this shall be the sign *[ʾôt]* that I have sent you: when you bring the people out of Egypt, you shall worship God upon this mountain." These are "signs" that call "for faith" and that call "forth faith."

The attachment of a sign as the object of Abraham's faith is identical to the literary strategy of the "faith" theme in Exodus 19. In both texts faith is directed toward a sign. The same lament pattern is found in the Genesis 15 passage:

1. *Emergency:* Abraham is childless (Gen 15:2-3).
2. *Promise:* God promises to give him an heir (Gen 15:4-5).
3. *Faith:* Abraham believes God (Gen 15:6).
4. *Certainty:* Abraham asks for proof and receives a covenant as a sign (Gen 15:7-21).

*Numbers 14.* Numbers 14:11 and Numbers 20:12 also occur at crucial points in the literary structure of the Pentateuch. They answer the question why the whole generation (Num 14:11) and why Moses and Aaron (Num 20:12) were not permitted to enter the land. The answer in both passages is their lack of faith. In Numbers 14 the Israelites followed the advice of the ten spies and refused to take the land. Their lack of faith is characterized as a refusal "to believe" in the divine "signs" (*ʾōtôt* [Num 14:11]) performed in their midst.

An important element included in this account is the theme of the Lord's rejection of his people: "How long will this people provoke me, and how long will it be that they do not believe me, for all the signs *[ʾōtôt]* which I have shown among them? I will smite them with the pestilence, and I will disinherit them" (Num 14:11-12).

[97]On the importance of Genesis 15 for the composition of the Pentateuch, see John Ha, *Genesis 15: A Theological Compendium of Pentateuchal History* (BZAW 181; Berlin: de Gruyter, 1989).

Ultimately, God proved merciful and relented: "And the Lord said, 'I have pardoned according to your word'" (Num 14:20). The reference to this passage in Ezekiel 20 is an example of how its theme found its way to the center of the prophetic retelling of the story. The Pentateuch thus reflects the prophetic hope of God's promised future and his continuous mercy. The lament pattern in Exodus 14 is cast in reverse because the people do not have faith:

1. *Emergency:* Murmuring and rebellion (Num 14:1-10).
2. *Promise:* Threat and intercession (Num 14:12).
3. *Faith:* No faith *(lōʾ-yaʾămînû)* in the divine signs (Num 14:11).
4. *Certainty:* God's forgiveness after intercession (Num 14:13-23).

*Numbers 20.* In the Pentateuch the reasons for divine forgiveness are like those in Ezekiel. It was for the sake of God's holy name, which Israel had profaned among the nations (cf. Ezek 20:8-9, 13-14, 21-22, 44). The "faith" theme in Numbers 20:12 is part of a narrative that aims to lay the responsibility of a lack of faith on the priests and the law. The "faith" theme in these narratives is like Rendtorff's "promise" theme. Both themes are at work in these faith naratives (Num 14:11, 16, 23a).

The lament pattern in the Numbers 20 narratives is focused on the people's lack of faith:

1. *Emergency:* No water (Num 20:3-5).
2. *Promise:* Instructions for water (Num 20:6-8).
3. *Faith:* Moses and Aaron have no faith *(lōʾ-heʾĕmantem)* (Num 20:7-12a).
4. *Certainty:* Moses and Aaron are not allowed to enter the land (Num 20:12b-13).

The final shape of the Pentateuch's narratives is a dynamic collection of sacred texts that reflect the view of the prophetic literature. It is a view that stands waiting in anticipation (Is 40:31) before a new work of God. Within the context of that anticipation it calls for a response of faith that many times translates into the simple idea of "waiting on God" (Is 40:31).

## Legal Strategies in the Pentateuch: A Compositional Approach

We noted above that the exodus and Sinai narratives begin with a back-reference to God's covenant with the patriarchs: "And God heard their groaning, and remembered his covenant with Abraham, with Isaac, and with Jacob" (Ex 2:24). This reference above to the patriarchal narratives in Genesis 12–50 connects events in the patriarchal narratives to the exodus and the Sinai covenant. Within these narratives the Sinai covenant is cast as the central means of realizing the patriarchal blessing. Throughout the remainder of the Pentateuch this picture of Sinai undergoes considerable variation, eventually giving way to a more hopeful and lasting means of enjoying God's blessing. As the strategy proceeds through the blocks of narrative in the Pentateuch, one begins to see taking shape a growing hope for the establishment of a covenant "apart from the covenant at Sinai"—that is, one unlike and distinct from the Sinai (Horeb) covenant. This growing anticipation of a covenant "apart from" or "besides" *(millĕbad)* Sinai is especially true of those texts that reflect the influence of the prophetic literature and Deuteronomy. Indeed, by the time the Pentateuch draws to its conclusion in the final pages of Deuteronomy, the Sinai covenant has already begun to appear as a thing of the past, and the stage has been set for its critical assessment by the prophetic scribes who guarded it and passed it on to future generations. For that reason, it is an assessment that looks very much like the kind of critique given the Sinai covenant in the later prophetic literature. This prophetic critique of Sinai is accompanied by a hope for a new covenant much like Jeremiah's envisioning of the "new covenant" (Jer 31:31).

One of the clearest expressions of this newly developing prophetic hope at the close of the Pentateuch is found in Deuteronomy 29:1: "These are the words of the covenant which the Lord commanded Moses to make with the people of Israel in the land of Moab, besides *[millĕbad]* the covenant which he had made with them at Horeb." A similar hope for a new covenant is found in Jeremiah 31:31-32: "Behold, the days are coming, says the Lord, when I will make a new covenant with the house of Israel and the house of Judah, not like the covenant which I made with their fathers when I took them by the hand to bring them out of the land of Egypt." In both texts the Sinai covenant is cast in the shadow of a future covenant that will eventually overtake and replace it. Like the prophetic "new covenant," the covenant announced in Deuteronomy

29:1 will be distinct from Sinai and will ultimately be the means of fulfilling God's covenanted blessing of the seed of Abraham, "that you may enter into the sworn covenant of the LORD your God, which the LORD your God makes with you this day; that he may establish you this day as his people, and that he may be your God, as he promised you, and as he swore to your fathers, to Abraham, to Isaac, and to Jacob" (Deut 29:12-13).

It is clear from these texts that Deuteronomy 29 is a description of the covenant announced in Deuteronomy 29:1. The following chapter, Deuteronomy 30, sketches a further description of the effect that this covenant will have on the lives of the people of God who enter it. These two chapters form the basis and culmination of a hope expressed throughout the Pentateuch. It is a hope that the Pentateuch shares with other parts of Scripture, both in the OT and the NT. An understanding of the theology of the Pentateuch comes only through seeing the nature and interplay of these two covenants as well as the directions they move us in our further reading of the OT and the NT. This means that understanding the narrative strategy and compositional shape of both the Sinai covenant narratives in Exodus 19–24 and the Moab covenant texts in Deuteronomy 29–30 is essential to an appreciation of both the theology of the Pentateuch and the later prophetic literature, not to mention the NT. Essential to the task of a compositional analysis of the Pentateuch and its view of "covenant" is understanding the narrative strategies of these two sections of the Pentateuch, Exodus 19–24 and Deuteronomy 29:1–31:20.

An important advantage of a compositional approach is its holistic attitude toward the HB. It is an approach that helps us to look at the Bible's parts as well as its whole.[98] It encourages the biblical exegete to view the Bible in its totality, synchronically, and also historically, or diachronically, in terms of its development. The attempt to recreate the strategy of the author can be of service in understanding the meaning of the synchronic shape *(Endgestalt)* of the Pentateuch.

Since such a view of Scripture is similar to the way the Bible was read and understood before the rise of historical criticism, such an approach to the meaning of the Pentateuch can address, and redress, many classical problems in dogmatics and systematic theology. Dogmatic approaches to the Bible arose at a time when the whole of Scripture was considered fair game for

[98]See Georg Fohrer et al., *Exegese des Alten Testaments: Einführung in die Methodik* (Uni-Taschenbücher 267; Heidelberg: Quelle & Meyer), 1983), pp. 116-43.

drafting Christian doctrine. Thus, the questions addressed by dogmatics often presuppose the entirety of biblical revelation the OT and the NT. In the same way, the goal of systematic theology is specifically to provide a synthetic appraisal of all parts of the Bible. A compositional approach has close affinities with these time-honored approaches and is in a position to address many questions of a dogmatic or systematic nature.

An example of the use of composition criticism to address a classical doctrinal question is its contribution to our understanding of the role of the Mosaic law in the Sinai covenant. The topic of the law and the Christian has remained an important question for systematic theology and dogmatics. In the evangelical world it plays out in a number of ways. Understanding the place of the Mosaic law in the two major theological systems of evangelicalism—dispensationalism and covenant theology—is essential to a clear understanding of those systems. This question has been formulated in many ways, but I will put it as follows: When God entered into a covenant with Israel at Sinai and gave them his laws, were those laws to be understood as part of the Sinai covenant as such, or were they to be seen as an addendum to the covenant, something added to the covenant to vouchsafe a covenant way of life? Another way to state the question is to ask if there is any difference between God's covenant with Abraham and the covenant with Israel at Sinai. Is law, as such, an essential or constitutive part the biblical covenants?

Covenant theologians and dispensationalists are in general agreement on the question of the essential role of the Mosaic law in the Sinai covenant. Both systems, however, often have come to different conclusions on important related issues. As it now stands, both theological systems maintain that the Mosaic law was an essential part of the Sinai covenant. For covenant theology, the legal aspects of the covenant are seen as the basis for an emphasis on the role of the law in the life of the Christian. For dispensationalists, the legal aspects of the covenant are seen as the basis for their separation of the Sinai covenant, with its laws, from the life of the Christian.

Historically, the question of the place of the Mosaic law in the Sinai covenant has been the source of considerable debate, not least among covenant theologians.[99] Nor did the problem originate with Reformed theology or dis-

[99]See Gottlob Schrenk, *Gottesreich und Bund im älteren Protestantismus: Vornehmlich bei Johannes Coccejus*, 2nd ed. (Darmstadt: Wissenschaftliche Buchgesellschaft, 1967), pp. 116-23; Hans Heinrich Wolf, *Die Einheit des Bundes: Das Verhältnis von Altem und Neuem Testament bei Calvin*

pensationalism. Already with Justin Martyr one finds the view that the laws given to Moses at Sinai were not original to the Sinai covenant. The covenant, it was argued, was originally intended solely as a covenant of grace, to which secondarily the laws were later attached. The apostle Paul appears to argue the same point in Galatians 3:19: "Why then the law? It was added because of the transgressions."

Justin, in his *Dialogue with Trypho*, attributed the giving of the law to the making of the golden calf: "Thus also God by the mouth of Moses commanded you to abstain from unclean and improper and violent animals: when, moreover, though you were eating manna in the desert, and were seeing all those wondrous acts wrought for you by God, you made and worshipped the golden calf." Irenaeus held a similar view (*Haer.* 4.14.2; 4.15.1). Calvin made a great distinction between the Sinai covenant and the law that was a kind of apendage to it. He held that the external rites and sacrifices in the law, excluding the Ten Commandments, were not intended by God, nor were they "of the substance of the law" or required as "necessary or even as useful."

> Therefore, God protests that he never enjoined anything with respect to the Sacrifices: and he pronounces all External Rites but vain and trifling, if the very least value be assigned to them apart from the Ten Commandments. Whence we more certainly arrive at the conclusion to which I have adverted, viz., that they are not, to speak correctly, of the substance of the law, nor avail of themselves in the Worship of God, nor are required by the Lawgiver himself as necessary, or even as useful, unless they sink into this inferior position [of being an interpretation of the two tablets]. In fine, they are appendages, which add not the smallest completeness to the Law, but whose object is to retain the pious in the Spiritual Worship of God, which consists of Faith and Repentance.[100]

The chief representative of this early Reformed view of the law in the formation of later covenant theology was Johann Coccejus. The central characteristic of the Coccejian view is its dynamic, rather than static, view of the law. Coccejus saw the law in terms of a changing set of (covenant) relationships between God and Israel. God called Israel to a life of faith, much like

---

(BGLRK 10; Neukirchen: Verlag der Buchhandlung des Erziehungsvereins Kreis Moers, 1958), pp. 38-54; Mark W. Karlberg, "Moses and Christ—The Place of Law in Seventeenth-Century Puritanism," *TJ* 10 (1989): 11-32.

[100]Calvin, *Four Last Books of Moses*, p. xvii.

he had called Abraham.[101] When Israel proved unable or unwilling to trust him, God gave them law.[102] Only after each set of laws proved fruitless, did God continue to give them additional laws. Each time Israel failed to trust God, God gave them additional laws until, at last, Israel's covenant was weighted down with an increasingly heavy burden of law.[103] Ultimately, Israel's state as being under the law was intended by God to teach them the need for God's grace. Louis Berkhof summarizes Coccejus's view:

> Coccejus saw in the Decalogue a summary expression of the covenant of grace, particularly applicable to Israel. When the people, after the establishment of this national covenant of grace, became unfaithful and began to worship the golden calf, the legal covenant of the ceremonial service was instituted as a stricter and harsher dispensation of the covenant of grace. Thus the revelation of grace is found particularly in the Decalogue, and that of servitude in the ceremonial law.[104]

Although largely overlooked by Berkhof, it should be noted that Coccejus found exegetical support in Galatians 3:19, where Paul states that the law "was added because of the transgressions, till the offspring should come to whom the promise had been made." Berkhof's critique of Coccejus arises from his assertion that Coccejus's view, and others similar to it, find no support in Scripture. According to Berkhof,

> These views are all objectionable for more than one reason: (1) They are contrary to Scripture in their multiplication of the covenants. It is un-Scriptural to assume that more than one covenant was established at Sinai, though it was a covenant with various aspects. (2) They are mistaken in that they seek to impose undue limitations on the Decalogue and on the ceremonial law.[105]

---

[101]"Porro secundo est in decalogo stipulatio foederalis eadem, qua Deus etiam cum Veteribus antea convenerat & foedus fecerat: nempe fidei, quae per charitatem esset operosa" (Johann Coccejus, *Summa theologiae ex scripturis repetita*, in *Opera omnia* [Amsterdam, 1701], 7:281-90).

[102]"[Transgressio populi occasio graviorum praeceptorum foederi addendorum.] Interim populus vitulum facit: Moses ea causa jubetur descendere, &, quum intercessisset pro populo, descendit, &, viso vitulo, projicit tabulas easque frangit. . . . Deus autem a tabernaculo cum Moses loquens praecepta dat de holocaustis & aliis sacrificiis, & nominatim injungit sacrificium pro peccato & reatu, Levit. 4. & 5. & varia alia dogmaqa imperat. Quae recensere non est opus" (ibid., p. 285).

[103]"Quod Israëlitae transgressione sua meriti sint, ut lex, quae iram operetur, & grave jugum servitutis ipsis imponeretur, & Deo occasionem dederint eam imponendi & ipsis & posteris eorum. Id perspicue dicit Jeremias cap. 31:32" (ibid., p. 287).

[104]Louis Berkhof, *Systematic Theology* (Grand Rapids: Eerdmans, 1941), p. 299.

[105]Ibid.

That Coccejus's view is "un-Scriptural" is a curious objection by Berkhof in view of the fact that Coccejus makes extensive use of Scripture in his argumentation.[106] Even more curious is the fact that Berkhof himself offers no evidence from Scripture to refute Coccejus's exegesis. Regrettably, Berkhof leaves us without a scriptural refutation of Coccejus's otherwise compelling argument.

Contrary to Berkhof's objections, there is ample support in Scripture for Coccejus's view. As we have seen, the overall compositional strategy of the Pentateuch suggests a view of the law similar to that of Coccejus. The written law was not a constitutive part of the Sinai covenant, though the natural law that it embodied was already operative in the hearts of the first human beings. That was because Adam and Eve were created "in God's image" (Gen 1:26-27) and thus enjoyed God's guidance from the beginning. In patriarchal times the faithful, like Abraham (Gen 15:6), obeyed the law (Gen 26:5) from their hearts, but Israel's refusal at Sinai to hear the Decalogue and obey God's call (Ex 19:16) led to the commissioning of Moses as a priest to speak God's words (Ex 20:18-22).

The basis of the Sinai covenant (Ex 19–24) was the same as the patriarchal covenant: obedience from the heart (Ex 19:5) exhibited by faith (Ex 19:9). The general structure of that obedience was put forth by God in "ten words" on Mount Sinai (Ex 19:19). The argument of the Pentateuch, and the way in which the prophets appear to have read it, suggests that, apart from the Decalogue, God's immediate plan for Israel at Sinai had not included the many collections of "laws" in the Pentateuch. They were added to the Sinai covenant as stipulations because of Israel's multiple transgressions, the greatest of which was their participation in making and worshiping the golden calf.

---

[106]Coccejus, *Summa theologiae*, 7:281-90.

Chapter 7

# Exploring the Composition of Legal Material in the Pentateuch

THERE IS LITTLE AGREEMENT AMONG OT SCHOLARS regarding the hypothetical shape and extent of the written pentateuchal material before it found its place in the Pentateuch.[1] On the other hand, there is considerable agreement on the nature of the material in its present shape as part of the Pentateuch. A growing number of OT scholars, for various reasons, have rejected the classical views of source criticism in order, sometimes, to take up in its place the view that the present Pentateuch consists of a mosaic or collage of written sources or sometimes fragments. This is not meant to imply that OT scholars have come over to the other side and now accept Mosaic authorship. That is not the case. What appears to have happened in many cases is an acceptance of the idea that the Pentateuch, when viewed as the product of an intelligent design, has a certain unity and message as a whole. The composition of the Pentateuch may thus have been much like we might expect of the later historical books such as Judges, Samuel and Kings, and also the Gospels.[2]

Among older conservatives and reformed orthodox OT scholars, whose descendants make up the lion's share of evangelical OT scholarship today, the

---

[1]See Rolf Rendtorff, *Das Überlieferungsgeschichtliche Problem des Pentateuch* (BZAW 147; Berlin: de Gruyter, 1977); Hans Heinrich Schmid, *Der sogenannte Jahwist: Beobachtungen und Fragen zur Pentateuchforschung* (Zürich: Theologischer Verlag, 1976); R. N. Whybray, *The Making of the Pentateuch: A Methodological Study* (JSOTSup 53; Sheffield: JSOT Press, 1987).

[2]See Erhard Blum, *Studien zur Komposition des Pentateuch* (BZAW 189; Berlin: de Gruyter, 1990), pp. 1-5.

view was widely held that the Pentateuch was composed of various kinds of ancient written documents from the time of the patriarchs *(schedas et scrinia patrum)*.[3] Some went so far as to describe those ancient written documents as "differing in style, and distinguishable by the primitive formality of their introductions."[4]

Here we will make a general review of what I have already proposed about the literary makeup of the Pentateuch as a whole. I have suggested that the literary material of the Pentateuch consists of at least three types of written sources: collections of laws (legal corpora), narratives and poetry. The focus of the following discussion will center on the arrangement (compositional strategy) of the legal corpora (written laws)[5] within the final shape of the Mosaic Pentateuch.

## COLLECTIONS OF LAWS (LEGAL CORPORA) IN THE PENTATEUCH

Several legal codes make up some of the largest portions of the Pentateuch.

---

[3]Johann Henrich Heidegger: "Quanquam ex traditione Majorum, utpote quartus a Jacobo, neque adeo remotus ab iis temporibus, quibus Adamus ipse superstes fuit, plurima haurire potuit" (*Enchiridion Biblicum* [Jena: Bielckium, 1723], p. 18); Campegius Vitringa: "Schedas et scrinia patrum, apud Israelitas conservata, Mosem collegisse, digessisse, ornasse et ubi deficiebant, complesse et ex iss priorem librorum suorum confecisse" (*Observationum sacrarum libri sex* [Franeker, 1712]); André Rivet: "Multa enim scripserunt, quae aut ipsi viderunt, aut etiam ab alijs hominibus acceperunt" (*Isagoge, seu introductio generalis, ad Scripturam sacram Veteris et Novi Testamenti* [Leiden, 1627] p. 10). Johann Gottlob Carpzov, the leading Lutheran orthodox OT scholar of the early eighteenth century, held to the possibility of sources in the Pentateuch, but his view of the nature of inspiration—dictation—precluded his attaching any importance to them: "Quamvis enim nonnulla de his, quae tradidit in Genesi, habere potuerit ab Amramo patre suo. . . . Rectius tamen soli qeopneustivai omnia tribuimus" (*Introductio ad libros canonicos bibliorum Veteris Testamenti omnes*, 4th ed. [Leipzig, 1757], pp. 62-63). Louis Gaussen writes, "Whether they describe their own emotions, or relate what they remember, or repeat contemporary narratives, or copy over genealogies, or make extracts from uninspired documents—their writing is inspired, their narratives are directed from above" (*The Divine Inspiration of the Bible*, trans. David D. Scott [Grand Rapids: Kregel, 1971], p. 25).

[4]Robert Jamieson, A. R. Fausset and David Brown, *A Commentary, Critical, Experimental and Practical, on the Old and New Testaments* (Grand Rapids: Eerdmans, 1945), 1:xxxv. "Independently of any hypothesis, it may be conceded that, in the composition of those parts of the Pentateuch relating to matters which were not within the sphere of his personal knowledge, Moses would and did avail himself of existing records which were of reliable authority; and while this admission can neither diminish the value nor affect the credibility of his history as an inspired composition, it is evident that, in making use of such literary materials as were generally known in his time, or had been preserved in the repositories of Hebrew families, he interwove them into his narrative conformably with that unity of design which so manifestly pervades the entire Pentateuch" (ibid., 1:xxxii).

[5]There is considerable evidence of nonwritten laws in circulation during period of time before the giving of the law at Sinai. According to Exodus 15:25; 18:16, for example, laws were well known and had become an essential part of the ordering of life in ancient Israel. This was before the giving of the law at Sinai.

Clearly recognizable collections of laws are the Decalogue (Ex 20:1-17), the Covenant Code (Ex 20:22–23:33), the Holiness Code (Lev 17–26) and the Priestly Code (Ex 25–Lev 16). Belonging to this last corpus are the instructions concerning the pattern of the tabernacle (Ex 25–31) and narratives of its construction (Ex 35–40). Although questions regarding the setting and date of such strata often predominate in scholarly discussions, when viewed in terms of the compositional strategy of the Pentateuch, these texts present us with a very different set of questions. The primary question that they pose involves the purpose of these various collections in the final arrangement of the text. Are these collections of Mosaic laws presented to the reader "as law" (qua law), or do they have some other purpose? One way to get at this question is to ask what each collection of laws contributes to the sense of the whole Pentateuch. How and why has the author arranged them in the sequence and shape they now have? What is the purpose that lies behind the often divergent forms of law in each collection? Is there a strategy lying behind the apparent randomness of these laws?

It has long been recognized and considered problematic to many evangelicals that conspicuous differences exist between these various collections of laws. The requirements for the building of an altar in the Covenant Code (Ex 20:24-25), for example, are significantly different from those in the Priestly Code (Ex 27:1-8). According to the Covenant Code, the altar was to be made of earth or stones and could be set up "in every place" that God caused his name to be remembered (Ex 20:24-26). This was a simple form of altar reminiscent of the altars in the patriarchal period (Gen 12:7). Abraham set one up in nearly every place he traveled.

According to the Priestly Code, on the other hand, the altar was to be made of the rare acacia wood overlaid with bronze (Ex 27:12) and was to be placed in the tabernacle where only the priests could have access to it. This appears to be an entirely different altar. Modern biblical criticism has made such differences the centerpoint of their contention that the Pentateuch had various authors, each with his own version of the Pentateuch and its laws. In doing so, however, they have largely failed to take into account the possibility that the biblical author was well aware of these differences and actually intended the reader to take note of them. They are, in other words, not so much evidence of various strata of legal documents as a part of the compositional strategy of the Pentateuch as a whole.

As one might expect, there have been numerous attempts to provide well-intended harmonizations of these two "altar laws." According to one traditional harmonization, there were to be two altars in the tabernacle, one was to be an earthen altar for the burnt offering, and the other a wooden altar for burning incense. Already centuries ago, Michael Walther rejected this harmonization, chiefly on the grounds that in Exodus 38:1 the altar used for the burnt offering was to be made of wood.[6] Another common harmonization is built on the observation that in the narrative itself the bronze altar of Exodus 27 is said to be hollow (Ex 27:8) and was therefore to be filled with dirt or stones to make the earthen altar of Exodus 20.[7] The two legal requirements of the altar thus were merged to form the inside and outside of a single altar. Thus, what appears to be a description of two distinct altars is only a different aspect of the description of a single altar.

Such attempts serve better to demonstrate the literary problem than to provide its solution. Among recent conservative biblical scholars, the two passages usually are allowed to coexist without a harmonization, the earthen altar being taken merely as a temporary measure.[8] Although this explanation may provide a solution to the historical problem of the purpose of the two altars, it fails to see the literary question of why the two types of altars are prescribed in the Pentateuch without an explanation of their differences.

Critical scholarship has been unanimous in seeing the two laws as arising out of different historical settings.[9] It is commonly argued, for example, that along with the other laws in the Covenant Code, the instructions for building an earthen altar come from a more primitive period in Israel's religion, a time when their forms of worship were much like that of the patriarchs in the Genesis narratives. Individuals and groups could provide local centers of worship by building an altar and giving offerings.[10] Critics have argued that in the early stages of their religion, Israel, like Abraham in the Genesis nar-

---

[6]Michael Walther, *Harmonia totius S. Scripturae* (Strasbourg, 1627), p. 176.

[7]H. S. Horovitz, ed., *Mechilta D'Rabbi Ismael* (Jerusalem: Wahrmann), 1970, p. 242. "Alij melius sic conciliant, internam altaris partem fuisse de terra solida et compacta, externam autem de lignis dictis" (Walther, *Harmonia totius S. Scripturae*, p. 176). "The enclosing copper case served merely to keep the earth together" (Jamieson, Fausset and Brown, *Old and New Testaments*, 1:391).

[8]Walter Kaiser Jr., "Exodus," in *The Expositor's Bible Commentary*, ed. Frank E. Gaebelein (Grand Rapids: Zondervan, 1992), 2:428.

[9]See Otto Eissfeldt, *The Old Testament: An Introduction*, trans. Peter R. Ackroyd (New York: Harper, 1965), p. 218.

[10]F. Horst, *RGG*[3], vol. 1, cols. 1523-25.

ratives, built an altar at each new place they settled. It is assumed that the laws dealing with the bronze altar, on the other hand, represent the final stages of Israel's religion, when only a single official worship site was recognized. The question that I am raising here is not whether those assumptions are correct. Those questions, at the moment, are beside the point. The point is what role these two views of the prescribed altar play in the present narrative. As we now have them in the Pentateuch, one view gives us a prescription of a patriarchal earthen altar, while the other is a view of the kind of altar that was secondarily prescribed by Moses at Mount Sinai. In the patriarchal altar every representative member of a household, such as Abraham or Isaac, was considered a priest. The Mosaic altar presupposes a priesthood at the central sanctuary—that is, the tabernacle.

The major weakness of the critical view is its lack of a convincing explanation of why such an obvious dissonance would have been tolerated in the final canonical text. Otto Eissfeldt, clearly sensing the need for an explanation, argued that in the process of editorializing, after the Covenant Code had been replaced by the laws of Deuteronomy, the law regarding the primitive altar could not be removed from the text because it was "already so rooted in the popular mind that such a transformation of it would not be possible." Such a "neutralizing" of the book of the covenant, Eissfeldt argued, "seems to us not merely remarkable, but also impracticable. But we must bear in mind that the attempt has been successful not only in this case but also in many others. . . . Older precepts which are allowed to remain, are now quite naturally understood in the light of the newer, or, where that is not possible or necessary, they simply remain unheeded."[11]

Eissfeldt's explanation is remarkable. While it must be acknowledged as possible that the biblical author intended his readers to ignore the Covenant Code in their reading of the Pentateuch, it is by no means probable. On the contrary, its position alongside the Decalogue and within the Sinai narrative itself suggests that the author intended to call attention to it, or even highlight it, in the overall structure of his work. There is a need to explain its presence in the text. It is not enough merely to explain it away. Unlike literary criticism, which seeks to find the origin of various literary strata, it is the task of compositional criticism to explain the textual strategy in the text that we

[11]Eissfeldt, *The Old Testament*, pp. 222-23.

now have. This means attempting to explain the placement of a text such as this within the final shape of the Pentateuch.

## Narrative and Law in the Pentateuch

Along with the legal codes discussed above, there are numerous other narrative texts of varying lengths and subject matter. These too are found in the central portion of the Pentateuch and often intersect with the laws. These texts not only provide a framework for the legal collections, but also are embedded within the various collections of laws. The framework of the large center section of the Pentateuch is made up of three complex narratives: the exodus narrative (Ex 1–18), the Sinai narrative (Ex 19–34) and the wilderness narrative (Num 10:11–20:29). There are several smaller but strategically important narratives within this larger section, and they are related to this larger framework—for example, the oppression narrative (Ex 1), the call of Moses (Ex 3; 6) and the call of Joshua (Nun 27:12-23), the accounts of the faith of Moses, Aaron and the people (Ex 4; 19) and the accounts of their lack of faith (Num 13–14; 20), the narrative of Aaron's calf idol (Ex 32) and the narrative of Israel's goat idols (Lev 17:1-9),[12] the narrative of Moses and Pharaoh (Ex 7–12) and the narrative of Balaam and Balak (Num 22–24). Each each of these narratives has a discernible internal structure and strategy, but our interest in them at present is their relationship to each other and to the collections of laws discussed above. As Eissfeldt says, "It is one of the tasks of Pentateuchal criticism to explain how this interruption of the narrative by large blocks of law took place."[13] I would add that it is also our task to explain the sense and strategy of the final form of the text produced by the merging of these two kinds of texts.

## The Collections of Laws in the Sinai Narratives

A curious feature of the Sinai narratives[14] is the way they envelop and thus serve to link the Decalogue, the Covenant Code and the Priestly Code, precisely those collections of laws that, at least according to critical theory, differ

[12]The Hebrew word *śāʿîr* usually means simply "goat," but it can also mean "goat idol," as in 2 Chronicles 11:15, where Jeroboam is said to have "made" goat idols along with his calf idols. See *HAL* 4:1250.

[13]Eissfeldt, *The Old Testament*, p. 157.

[14]"This section, more precisely its actual narrative kernel, . . . is exceptionally difficult to analyze" (ibid., p. 193).

most markedly from each other.[15] The Decalogue follows the account of the covenant ceremony in Exodus 19:1-25. This narrative is complex and includes two large segments. The first is an account of the establishment of an initial covenant on Mount Sinai (Ex 19:1-16a). The second is an account of Israel's fearful retreat from God at the foot of the mountain (Ex 19:16b-25). The Decalogue (Ex 20:1-17), in turn, is followed by a short narrative recounting the fear of the people at Sinai (Ex 20:18-21). This is a repeat of their fear in Exodus 19:16, where they refuse to go to the mountain and remain fearfully in the camp. The Covenant Code is embedded in the Sinai narrative between Exodus 20:21 and Exodus 24:1, and this narrative is followed by the Priestly Code (Ex 25–Lev 16). The account of the making of the golden calf (Ex 32) and the reestablishment of the Sinai covenant (Ex 33–34), both parts of the Sinai narrative, break into the Priestly Code just after the instructions for making the tabernacle (Ex 25–31) and before the account of its completion (Ex 35–40). Consequently, the instructions for building the tabernacle are separated from the remainder of the Priestly Code by the account of the making of a golden calf (Ex 32) and the "renewal"[16] of the Sinai covenant (Ex 33–34).

These observations raise important literary questions about the strategy of the author of the Pentateuch. What effect does the arrangement of these laws and the narrative between them have on the meaning of the present shape of the text? Is there a sense to be drawn from the pattern of events and laws reflected in the text as it is? Is the shape of the text semantically relevant, or must we reconstruct it to the earlier shape it might have had before it became a part of the Pentateuch? I will address these questions by attempting to unravel the literary strategy behind the present shape of the Sinai narrative. An important part of my argument is that these texts make good sense as they are now situated in the present shape of the Pentateuch. The author has a story to tell that involves both the interweaving of these events within the narratives and the specific laws to which they are connected.

---

[15]In most critical assessments of these two corpora, the Covenant Code is taken as the earliest of the legal codes, and the Priestly Code is assigned the lastest date. See *RGG*[4], "Ethik," p. 1604: Covenant Code → Deuteronomy → Decalogue → Priestly Code → Holiness Code; which is different from the present order: Decalogue → Covenant Code → Priestly Code → Holiness Code → Deuteronomy.

[16]It is not exactly correct to call this a "renewal" of the covenant, since the covenant was broken, and a new one, rather than a renewal, was necessary.

In the present form of the text, it is clear simply from reading the narratives that the author, by means of the arrangement of the narrative, wants to characterize the Sinai covenant, before the incident of the golden calf, by means of the laws of the Decalogue, the Covenant Code and the instructions for building the tabernacle. Israel is given these rather simple laws before any trouble begins to occur at Sinai. After the Sinai covenant, however, and after the golden calf, the covenant at Sinai begins to be characterized by means of the fundamentally different and more extensively elaborated Priestly Code (Ex 35–Lev 16). After the golden calf, things begin to get quite a bit more complicated at Sinai. After the golden calf, the bulk of the complex priestly laws (Ex 35–Lev 16) begin to take the place earlier occupied by the Decalogue, the Covenant Code and the tabernacle (Ex 19–24). Given its central location within the narrative, it thus appears that the episode of the golden calf is intended to signal a fundamental change in the nature of the Sinai covenant. When viewed within the context of the striking differences between the laws of the Covenant Code and those of the Priestly Code, the arrangement of this material appears to reflect a definite strategy. Rather than wanting to conceal the differences in these codes of law to which I alluded earlier, the author appears to deliberately call them to our attention. Set over against the rather simple patriarchal earthen altar, Israel is now given a large and expensive altar and a priesthood to serve it. Along with both of these, they also receive a tabernacle, a sacred place, where Israel can come before God on a representational basis only. Fellowship with the God of the covenant is now the responsibility of a priesthood.

The association of the original Sinai covenant with the Covenant Code and the renewal of that covenant with the Priestly Code suggests a differing assessment of the two codes. The incident of the golden calf has been strategically positioned between these two codes of law. As such, it is presented as the underlying cause of the changes in law codes. In positioning the texts this way, the author now narratively presents the changes between the laws in the two codes as part of a larger change in the nature of the Sinai covenant itself, a change that has come as a result of the incident of the golden calf. Rather than attempting to render the differences between the two law codes invisible, as modern critical studies suggest, the author appears to be using these very differences as part of his larger strategy. In their present position, it is these very differences that point to a change that had come over Israel's covenant with God owing to the sin of the golden calf. Israel's initial relationship with God at Sinai, characterized by the patriarchal simplicity of the Covenant Code, was now to be characterized by a complex and restrictive code of laws belonging principally to the priests.

What begins to emerge from these observations of the narrative strategy is the notion that the biblical portrayal of the covenant at Sinai was not intended to be read in terms of a static unchangeable set of regulations. The author wants, instead, to show that Israel's relationship with God, established in no uncertain terms at Sinai, almost immediately began to undergo important changes, due principally to Israel's repeated failure to obey God. What began as a covenant between God and Israel, fashioned after that of the patriarchs (the Decalogue and the Covenant Code), had quickly become an increasingly more complex set of restrictions and laws primarily aimed at the priesthood (the Priestly Code). Humanity's well-documented propensity to idolatry and seeking "other gods," as demonstrated in the Genesis narratives and here in these narratives by the transgression of the golden calf, necessitated God's giving them the additional laws found in the Priestly Code. Eissfeldt's argument that the Covenant Code was shaped as a polemic against a more complex form of worship suits rather well the role that the code has assumed within the strategy of the Pentateuch. It is now part of a social and religious apologetic for the necessity of the more complex requirements of the Priestly Code.[17]

The placement of the other law codes throughout this narrative shows further signs of the same strategy. The Priestly Code (Ex 25–Lev 16), for example, is followed by the Holiness Code (Lev 17–26). The specifically unique feature of that particular code of laws is that in its introduction, and throughout its collection of laws, the specific audience that it addresses is not the priests as such, but the whole of the congregation. It therefore addresses the people of God as a whole with the call to holiness. It has long been observed that the Holiness Code is not attached directly to the Priestly Code. Between these two legal codes lies an obscure but alarming reference to Israel's offering sacrifices to goat idols (Lev 17:1-9). This short fragment of narrative—and it

[17]In this light, the view of Adam Welch (*Deuteronomy: The Framework to the Code* [London: Oxford University Press, 1932]), Wilhelm Caspari ("Heimat und Soziale Wirkung des altestamentlichen Bundesbuches," *ZDMG* 83 [1929]: 97-120) and Henri Cazelles ("L'auteur du code de l'alliance," *RB* 52 [1945]: 173-91), that the Covenant Code was compiled in Kadesh or the east Jordan, by Moses or during the time of Moses, is of considerable importance.

is only that—usually is taken to be the work of one of the final editors of the Pentateuch.[18] It portrays the Israelite people as forsaking the tabernacle and sacrificing to goat idols "outside the camp" (Lev 17:3). Gordon Wenham, along with C. F. Keil, suggests that these verses are a prohibition not just of sacrifices, but of any kind of animal slaughter, and that the prohibition was limited only to the time Israel was in the wilderness. However, what is specifically prohibited is not every kind of slaughter, but, specifically, slaughter for sacrifice. This is shown by the fact that Leviticus 17:5 identifies the "slaughter" of Leviticus 17:3-4 specifically and only as sacrifice. It was not a general slaughter for food. It should be noted too that later in this same chapter, Leviticus 17:13-14, provision is made for animals slain in hunting. This would also suggest that slaying animals for food was permissible, and hence only slaughtering for sacrifice was expressly prohibited. Moreover, in Leviticus 17:7 the prohibition is called an "eternal ordinance," which rules out its limitation to the time of the wilderness sojourn. Furthermore, Deuteronomy 12:15, which appears to be a clarification of this law, restates the provision that mere slaughtering of animals could be done anywhere. What was specifically prohibited in Deuteronomy was neglecting the role of the central altar.

Though brief, the content of the narrative is suggestively similar to the incident of the golden calf. There are also literary parallels between this text and the opening sections of the other law codes—for example, the establishment of the proper place of worship in Exodus 20:24-26; 25ff.; Deuteronomy 12; Ezekiel 40–48.[19] The people have forsaken the Lord and his provisions of worship and are now following after other gods, in this case, the "goat idols." Unlike the narrative of the golden calf, which places the blame on the priesthood, in this narrative it is the people, not the priests, who are responsible for the idolatry. Thus, within the overall plan of the text, the incident of the people's sacrificing to the goat idols plays a similar role to that of the priests' involvement with the golden calf. Just as the narrative of the golden calf marked a transition in the nature of the covenant and additions to its laws, so here also the incident of the goat idols marks the transition from the Priestly Code to that of the additional laws in the Holiness Code.

---

[18]Literary critics of the old school of Wellhausen took this composer to be a late redactor, usually associated with the priestly circles. See Alfred Bertholet, *Leviticus* (KHC 3; Tübingen: Mohr Siebeck, 1901), pp. 58-59. Composition criticism, however, attempts to remain neutral on the question of the historical time period of the final composition of the Pentateuch.

[19]Ibid., p. 58.

Three major law collections—the Covenant Code, the Priestly Code, the Holiness Code—are now embedded in the whole of the Sinai narratives, and they are arranged around two similar narratives. Both narratives focus on the Lord's displeasure with Israel's fall into idolatry, the first involving idolatry in the form of calf worship, and the second that of goats. There appear to be intentional compositional links between the golden "calf" erected by the priests (Ex 32:4) and the young "bull" (Lev 9:2) required as sin offering for the priests; both are described by the same Hebrew word, *ʿēgel*. The same holds true for the "goat" idols worshiped by the people (Lev 17:7) and "goats" (Lev 4:23) required for a sin offering of the people, both of which are described by the Hebrew word *śāʿîr*. Such a verbal pattern betrays a strategy at a high level in the Pentateuch. In this arrangement: (1) the laws of the Covenant Code are intentionally connected to the original covenant at Sinai (Ex 19–24); (2) the laws of the Priestly Code are associated with the covenant renewal after the sin of the golden calf (Ex 32–34); (3) the laws of the Holiness Code are placed in the context of the people's offering sacrifices to the goat idols outside the camp (Lev 17) and the covenant renewal in Leviticus 26.

In the following section I will trace the compositional strategy that has become apparent in the detail of the arrangement of the laws and the narrative texts of the Pentateuch. I have given considerable attention to this compositional strategy elsewhere.[20] Here, I will limit the discussion to two central questions raised by the foregoing observations. The first is the internal shape of Exodus 19–24. How does the structure of the initial Sinai narrative (Ex 19–24) fit into the larger scheme of the Pentateuch and its view of the law that I traced above? The second question has to do with the location of the instructions for the tabernacle (Ex 25–31). Why are they placed before the incident of the golden calf (Ex 32) rather than after it? If the addition of the Priestly Code is the result of the sin of the golden calf, why does a significant portion of these instructions appear to be placed before the incident itself?

***The Sinai narrative (Ex 19–24).*** The Sinai narrative is at the center of the compositional strategy of the Pentateuch. It begins in Exodus 1 and extends to at least Numbers 24, and perhaps to the end of the book of Numbers. It falls between two large blocks of narrative, the Exodus narrative (Ex 1–15) and the Balaam narrative (Num 22–24). It also links several collections of

[20]John H. Sailhamer, *The Pentateuch as Narrative: A Biblical-Theological Commentary* (Grand Rapids: Zondervan, 1992).

laws to the covenant-making events at Sinai. The aim of these narratives and their overall structure is to provide an explanation of the purpose and role of the Mosaic law in the Sinai covenant.

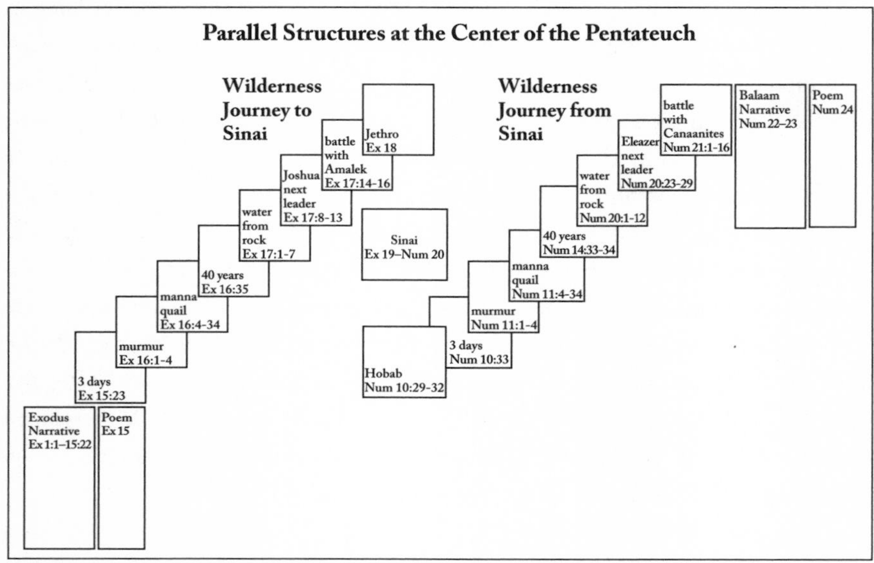


**Figure 4.1**

When viewed in its entirety, the structure of the Sinai narrative is transparent (see figure 5). It has a remarkable symmetry. The events at Sinai are recounted in the center narrative (Ex 19–Num 20). The Sinai pericope, with its laws, is framed on the left by the wilderness journey to Sinai (Ex 15:23–18:27) and on the right by the wilderness journey from Sinai (Num 10:29–21:16). The fact that these various episodes are recounted in symmetrical patterns arranged around the Sinai narrative suggests that its author had a definite purpose in mind. It also suggests that the Jethro narrative (Ex 18) and the Hobab narrative (Num 10:29-32) are intentionally placed on either side of the Sinai narrative. Such careful design and shaping raise the question of the meaning intended by this order. What meaning does this structure intend to contribute to our understanding the covenant at Sinai?

*The compositional role of Exodus 18 and Numbers 11.* The two episodes on either side of the Sinai narrative focus the reader's attention on the Gentile-nations and what they mean for Israel. The nations are represented, before and after Sinai, by Moses' father-in-law, Jethro (Ex 18) or Hobab (Num

10:29-32).[21] In Exodus 18 we find Jethro instructing Moses on how to administer the law among his people. In Numbers 10:19-32 we find him (Hobab) instructing Moses on how to traverse the wilderness terrain and where to set up their evening campgrounds. In both cases Jethro (Hobab), relying on his own wisdom or skills, performs duties that otherwise God would have provided through supernatural means. In the next chapter it is God, not Jethro, who gives Moses instructions about laws at Sinai (Ex 19:19). Many chapters later, as Israel prepares to leave Sinai (Num 10), it is Jethro (Hobab) who leads Israel through the wilderness, not the pillar of cloud and fire (Num 10:11). What can be the intention of the author in setting up these obvious and intentional contrasts between Jethro's experienced advice and the Lord's supernatural help? What point did the author have in mind in arranging his narratives this way? Why are two sets of laws given to Moses, those in Exodus 18 and those in Exodus 19? What is the reader to make of these contrasts? On the face of it, we are asked to understand the Sinai covenant and its laws within the broader context of the laws Israel had obtained (Ex 18) before Moses went to Sinai (Ex 19). In the same way, what could be the intended contrast in Numbers 10 between following the cloud and pillar of fire and following the trusted guidance of Jethro, a man experienced in the ways of the wilderness. Does it not appear that the author has arranged these narratives in such way that the reader must come to understand the Sinai covenant and its laws within the broader context of human experience?

Keil comes close to this understanding, but ultimately falls victim to the simple need to harmonize the two kinds of action, one grounded in human experience and the other supernatural guidance.

> Although Jehovah led the march of the Israelites in the pillar of cloud, not only giving the sign for them to break up and to encamp, but showing generally the direction they were to take; yet Hobab, who was well acquainted with the desert, would be able to render very important service to the Israelites, if he only pointed out, in those places where the sign to encamp was given by the cloud, the springs, oases, and plots of pasture which are often buried quite out of sight in the mountains and valleys that overspread the desert.[22]

---

[21]For a fuller explanation of various names of Jethro and his role within the Sinai narratives, see ibid., p. 382.

[22]C. F. Keil and F. Delitzsch, *The Pentateuch*, trans. James Martin (BCOT; Grand Rapids: Eerdmans, 1971), pp. 60-61.

There may be some value to Keil's suggestion, but surely the author wants us to see not merely two kinds of action, but, as in several of the chapters of Exodus that precede this section, two sides to the Lord's guidance, one that follows a direct and miraculous path, such as the pillar of fire, and another that follows the route of human experience. These two passages (Ex 18; Num 10), like bookends, provide an introduction and conclusion to the narratives of the Sinai covenant. They would have us see, or at least ponder the possibility, that both kinds of action are essential to the nature of the covenant that was granted Israel at Sinai. Ultimately, the divine guidance that the author has in mind will be resolved through the work of God's Spirit indwelling his people, like wisdom, leading them in the right path. That will come in what the Pentateuch sees as a different kind of covenant, unlike the one made at Sinai (cf. Deut 29:1). In anticipation of that covenant (cf. Jer 31:31; Ezek 36:24), Numbers 11:17 points to the role of God's Spirit in guiding the seventy elders who assisted Moses in leading the people. Also as a prelude to the giving of the law in Exodus 19, Jethro (in Ex 18:20) sees the goal of law as making "known the way in which they are to walk, and the work they are to do." Already in the compositional strategy of the Pentateuch, and its treatment of the theme of law, new covenant ideas of the relationship of God's Spirit and human effort are anticipated.

*Contrast of Exodus 17 and Exodus 18.* The symmetry of the structural diagram of the Sinai narratives (see figure 5) suggests that the account of Israel's battle with the Amalekites in Exodus 17 should also play a role in our understanding of the Jethro narrative in the adjacent Exodus 18. Cornelis Houtman, in fact, has drawn attention to the contrast between Exodus 17:8-16 and Exodus 18:

> Ch. 17 relates the coming of non-Israelites, who have in mind to wipe out the people and destroy the work of YHWH. Ch. 18 relates the coming of a non-Israelite, who is deeply sympathetic with Israel and who praises YHWH for his mighty deeds in history. The wonders performed by YHWH prompt quite different responses among the nations.[23]

A similar contrast exists between the narrative of the invasion and capture of Lot's land by the four kings (Gen 14:1-17) and the figure of Melchizedek,

[23]Cornelis Houtman, *Exodus,* trans. Johan Rebel and Sierd Woudstra (HCOT; Kampen: Kok, 1993–2000), 2:401.

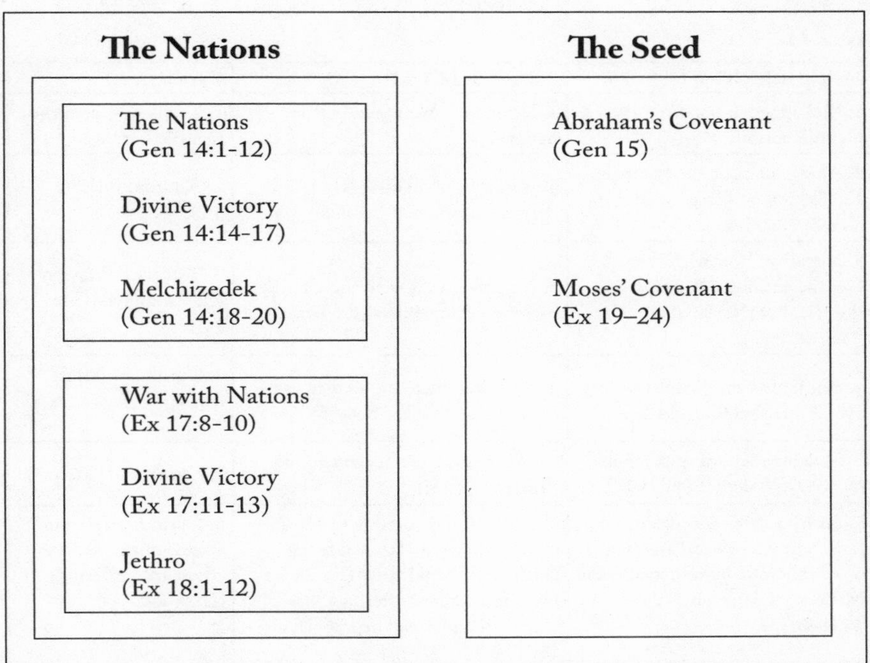


**Figure 4.2**

who arrives on the scene as one favorable to the God of Abraham. Both sets of narrative serve as a prelude to two distinct covenants: the Abrahamic, which reaches out to the nations, and the Mosaic, which draws a line between itself and the nations.

*Melchizedek and Jethro.* The following table lists numerous parallels between the nations and Israel. The nations are represented by Melchizedek, Jethro and Cyrus. Israel is represented by Abraham, Moses and Ezra. Among the three nations—Melchizedek, Jethro, Cyrus—each enters a relationship with one of the three Israelites and then enters a covenant with God in which the nations are to have a part. Abraham meets Melchizedek in Genesis 14, and he enters a covenant with God in Genesis 15. The purpose of Abraham's covenant is that all the nations be blessed in his "seed." This is the Abrahamic covenant, and it is the central covenant of the Pentateuch. Moses meets Jethro in Exodus 18, and he then enters a covenant with God at Sinai in Exodus 19. The purpose of the Mosaic covenant is to be the means of fulfilling the covenant with Abraham (Ex 2:24). In Ezra 1-8 the Persian king Cyrus commissions Ezra. The Persian kings then bring to fulfillment all that Ezra had

**Table 4.1**

| **Melchizedek (Gen 14:18-20)** | **Jethro (Ex 18:1-12)** | **Cyrus (Ezra)** |
|---|---|---|
| 1. Melchizedek was from the Gentile nations. | 1. Jethro was from the Gentile nations. | 1. Cyrus was from the Gentile nations. |
| 2. Abraham built an altar (Gen 13:18b) (cf. building an altar in Gen 8; 12; 13; 22). | 2. Moses built an altar (Ex 17:15) (first occurrence in Exodus). | 2. Altar built (Ezra 3:2). |
| 3. Negative: War with the Gentile nations—Amraphel in the "field of the Amalekites" (Gen 14:1-12). | 3. Negative: War with the Gentile nations—Amalekites (Ex 17:8). | 3. War with Babylon (cf. Amraphel [Gen 14]). |
| 4. Abraham's miraculous victory over Amraphel (Gen 14:15). | 4. Moses' miraculous victory over the Amalekites (Ex 17:8-16). | 4. Cyrus proclaims divine victory (Ezra 1:2). |
| 5. Melchizedek was priest-king *(kōhēn)* of Salem (Gen 14:18). | 5. Jethro was a priest *(kōhēn)* of Midian (Ex 18:1). | 5. Cyrus was a king. |
| 6. Positive: Melchizedek brought *(hôṣîʾ)* bread *(leḥem)* and wine to Abraham as he returned from battle with Amraphel (Gen 14:18-20). | 6. Positive: Jethro came to Moses (Ex 18:5) after his return from battle with Amalekites (Ex 18:1-5). He offered burnt offerings, sacrifices and bread (*leḥem*) (Ex 18:12). | 6. Cyrus brought out vessels of the temple (Ezra 1:8), offerings (Ezra 3:4). |
| 7. Melchizedek was king of "Salem" *(šālēm)* (Gen 14:18). | 7. Jethro asks "peace" *(šālôm)* for Abraham (Ex 18:7). | 7. — |
| 8. The "son of Abraham's house" was Eliezer, whose name means "God is my help" (Gen 15:2). | 8. The "son of Moses" was Eliezer, whose name means "God is my help" (Ex 18:4). | 8. Ezra was a descendant of Eleazar (Ezra 7:5) |
| 9. Back-reference to creation: Melchizedek acknowledges God's deeds in previous narratives, saying, "Blessed is the Most High God, creator of heaven and earth *[qōnēh s] āmayim wāʾāreṣ*" (Gen 14:19). | 9. Back-reference to the exodus: Jethro acknowledges what God did in previous narratives: "The Lord brought Israel out of Egypt" *[hôṣîʾ yhwh ʾetyiśrāʾēl mimmiṣrāyim]* (Ex 18:1). | 9. Back reference to return from exile (Ezra 1:2) |
| 10. Melchizedek blesses God for saving Abraham from his enemies, saying, "Blessed be the Most High God *[ûbārûk ʾēl ʿelyôn]*, who delivered his enemies into his hand" (Gen 14:20). | 10. Jethro blesses God, saying, "Blessed by the Lord (*bārûk yhwh*), who rescued *[hiṣṣîl]* you [Moses] from the hand of Egypt *[miyyad miṣrāyim]*"(Ex (18:10). | 10. Ezra: "Blessed be the Lord (*bārûk yhwh*), the God of our fathers" (Ezra 7:27). |
| 11. Abraham's seed will be "a sojourner *[gēr]* in a foreign land" (Gen 15:13). | 11. Moses' second son is named "Gershom" because he said, "I have become a sojourner *[gēr]* in a foreign land" (Ex 18:3). | 11. Gershom (Ezra 8:2). |

**Table 4.1 continued**

| | | |
|---|---|---|
| 12. Abraham gives a tithe (Gen 14:20b). | 12. Moses has statutes and laws (Ex 18:13-27). | 12. Ezra has the law of God and law of the king. |
| 13. The location of the Melchizedek narrative is Mount Zion (Salem) (Gen 14:18). | 13. The location of Jethro narrative is Mount Sinai (Horeb), "the mountain of God" (Ex 18:5; cf. 3:1). | 13. The location is Jerusalem (Ezra 7:27). |
| 14. The Melchizedek narrative closes with a reference to a meal: "Only that which the young men ate and the portion of men who traveled with me, that is, Aber, Eschol, Mamre, shall take their portion" (Gen 14:24). | 14. The Jethro narrative closes with an account of a communal meal: "And Aaron and all the elders of Israel came to dine before God with the father-in-law of Moses" (Ex 18:12b). | 14. — |
| 15. the Melchizedek narrative (Gen 14) precedes the account of a major new development in the strategy of the Pentateuch: a divine covenant with Abraham (Gen 15). | 15. The Jethro narrative (Ex 18) preceeds the account of a major new development in the strategy of the Pentateuch: the giving of the Mosaic law (Ex 19–24). | 15. Major new development: Torah replaces the temple (Neh 8:1-8). |

hoped for from God's covenants with Abraham and Moses. By authority of the Persian king (Artaxerxes), God's law was to be administered throughout his realm.

These parallels suggest that the author of the Pentateuch has intentionally selected and shaped his material to highlight the similarities between the Abraham/Melchizedek narrative (Gen 14–15) and the Moses/Jethro narrative (Ex 18:1-27). The author shows that Israel's dealings with these nations tell something about the nature of the covenants that they were to enter and their relationship to the nations.

**Table 4.2**

| **Artaxerxes instructed Ezra on the law (Ezra 7)** | **Jethro instructed Moses on the law (Ex 18)** |
|---|---|
| **Artaxerxes/Ezra** | **Jethro/Moses** |
| And thou, Ezra, after the wisdom of thy God that is in thy hand, appoint magistrates and judges, who may judge all the people that are beyond the River, all such as know the laws of thy God; and teach ye him that knoweth them not. And whosoever will not do the law of thy God, and the law of the king, let judgment be executed upon him with all diligence, whether it be unto death, or to banishment, or to confiscation of goods, or to imprisonment (Ezra 7:25-26 KJV). | Moreover thou shalt provide out of all the people able men, such as fear God, men of truth, hating unjust gain; and place such over them, to be rulers of thousands, rulers of hundreds, rulers of fifties, and rulers of tens: and let them judge the people at all seasons: and it shall be, that every great matter they shall bring unto thee, but every small matter they shall judge themselves: so shall it be easier for thyself, and they shall bear the burden with thee (Ex 18:21-22 KJV). |

The similarities with the narratives in the book of Ezra suggest that these parallels were appreciated by the author of that book, and that he, along with the author of the Pentateuch, wanted to point out the same general contrast between God's work with Israel (Abraham and Moses) and his commitment to the "nations" (Melchizedek and Jethro). Melchizedek's reference to "the Most High God" of creation shows that the author of the Pentateuch wants to trace God's plan for the nations back to God's plan for creation. This is the first real link between creation and covenant, or creation and redemption, in the Pentateuch. So, Melchizedek was to Abraham what Jethro was to Moses, and, in a similar way, Cyrus and Artaxerxes were to Ezra. By pointing to these parallels, the author shows that the nations do play an important role in God's plan of blessing. The first blessing in the Pentateuch, Genesis 1:28, includes all of humanity, not merely a select group. It retains that scope throughout the whole of the Pentateuch and the rest of the Scriptures. Part of the way by which the author holds our focus on this early creation blessing is through the words of Melchizedek in Genesis 14. Melchizedek's words to Abraham reveal his understanding of the creation blessing that Abraham is about to inherit. Melchizedek reintroduces into the Pentateuch the notion that God will use the nations of the world to further his plans of blessing through the "seed" of Abraham. In those plans God's intent is to bless "all the nations" (Gen 12:1-3).

*The purpose of Exodus 18.* The uniqueness of Exodus 18 has long been noted. It raises basic questions. For example, how is it that Israel already has laws, civil and cultic, before the laws are given Moses at Sinai? Some look back to Exodus 15:25-26 to show that God had already given Israel laws before Exodus 18 and before Sinai in Exodus 19–Numbers 10:

> There he made for them a statute and an ordinance, and there he proved them, and said, If thou wilt diligently hearken to the voice of the LORD thy God, and wilt do that which is right in his sight, and wilt give ear to his commandments, and keep all his statutes, I will put none of these diseases upon thee, which I have brought upon the Egyptians: for I am the LORD that healeth thee. (Ex 15:25-26 KJV)[24]

But Exodus 15:25-26 does not tell the whole story, nor does it answer the question of why God gives Israel laws at Sinai. If they already have laws and

[24]I cite the KJV here and in other places because it best represents the early English versions of the MT.

judges who administer those laws (Ex 15; 18), why does God continue to give them laws at Sinai?

*A retrospective vision.* One explanation of the purpose of the narrative in Exodus 18 comes from Jethro's rehearsal of God's great deeds for Israel:

> And Jethro said, Blessed be Jehovah, who hath delivered you out of the hand of the Egyptians, and out of the hand of Pharaoh; who hath delivered the people from under the hand of the Egyptians. Now I know that Jehovah is greater than all gods; yea, in the thing wherein they dealt proudly against them. (Ex 18:10-11 KJV)

By providing the occasion for Jethro's retrospective view of God's actions, the Jethro narrative in Exodus 18 provides a fitting context for the covenant that was about to be established at Sinai. Houtman's observation is helpful: "With the introduction of Jethro into the account, the writer offers a retrospect on the mighty deeds of YHWH (Ex 18:1-12) and prepares for the acknowledgment of YHWH as Lord at the Sinai."[25]

In a similar way, the introduction of Melchizedek into the Abraham narratives provides the author an occasion for a similar retrospect on the mighty deeds of God in creation:

> And he blessed him, and said, Blessed be Abram of God Most High, possessor of heaven and earth: and blessed be God Most High, who hath delivered thine enemies into thy hand. (Gen 14:19-20 KJV)

Melchizedek, along with Abraham, identifies God as "the creator of the heavens and earth" (Gen 14:19, 22). By means of the Melchizedek narrative, the author links the blessings of the Abrahamic covenant to the biblical creation account.

*Exodus 18 as a context for the law in Exodus 19.* As the Melchizedek narrative (Gen 14) set the context for the unique work that God was about to do through his covenant with Abraham (Gen 15), the Jethro narratives (Ex 18) show that he is already working in a similar way among the nations. Melchizedek's words in Genesis 14:19-20 point out that God's work among the Gentiles is grounded in God's work and purpose in creation. The Melchizedek narrative speaks for the importance of creation (nature); the Jethro narrative speaks for the importance of the exodus

---

[25]Ibid.

(grace). The covenant that God was about to initiate with Abraham is cast, in Genesis 14, as a continuation of his work of creation. In Exodus 18 it is cast as a continuation of his work of redemption—that is, the exodus from Egypt:

> And Jethro said, Blessed be the LORD, who hath delivered you out of the hand of the Egyptians, and out of the hand of Pharaoh, who hath delivered the people from under the hand of the Egyptians. (Ex 18:10)

These two important pentateuchal narratives, Genesis 14–15 and Exodus 18–24, link creation and redemption blessings to God's covenants with the "seed" of Abraham. Genesis 14–15 links the creation blessing (Gen 14) to covenant blessing (Gen 15), and primeval law (Ex 18) to Mosaic law (Ex 19–24). God's work of redemption is grounded in creation and covenant.

***Why was the Mosaic law given at Sinai (Ex 19–20)?*** If Israel already had laws (Ex 18:13-23), why were they given additional laws at Sinai? Houtman offers a helpful answer:

> The impression is given that from the start of its sojourn in the wilderness Israel was initiated into a life with YHWH and attendant rules. It should be kept in mind that also after the theophany at Sinai that initiation did not stop. Further instructions were forthcoming after that (Num. 9:8ff. et al. . . . ). Consequently, in the Pentateuch in its current form, Israel's encounter with YHWH at the Sinai is "only" culmination and focus of the giving of the Law.[26]

What Houtman means is that the giving of the law at Sinai was the last step in a series of encounters that led to giving Israel their laws. Houtman raises a further point dealing with the strategy behind these multiple sets of laws:

> An exegetically more promising question is why the writer has put the meeting between Moses and Jethro at this particular place in Exodus, and why it is here that he brings up an aspect of Moses' work not touched on before as well as the new legal system put in place by Moses at the suggestion of his father-in-law.[27]

Houtman's question is helpful because it rightly focuses our attention on the purpose of the arrangement of the narratives in their present sequence. It

---

[26]Ibid., 2:400-401.
[27]Ibid., 2:399.

is a question of textual strategy and narrative meaning. The purpose question that Houtman raises could be answered in several ways. The narrative strategy that Houtman asks about may have been intended to show that the giving of law at Sinai, though necessary, given Israel's chronic failure to trust God, was not essential, since Israel already had laws (Ex 15:25) and their administration (Ex 18). This could be a decisive point to emerge within these narratives, and Houtman appears to be moving in that direction. The difference implied by Houtman seems to have been that the law before Sinai was written on each Israelite's heart and not on tablets of stone (Gen 26:5). The narrative does cast them much in the same way it does Abraham in the earlier stories.[28] Their need was not to know more laws, but to be shown how more of their law could be applied in individual cases. The scene with Jethro in Exodus 18 is much like Nehemiah 8, where it is clear that the reading of the "law" was to be accompanied by discerning interpretation and application within specific situations. Houtman once more:

> Looking ahead, one can say that the author, by describing the revamping of the system of delivering justice, indicates that just before the revelation at the Sinai the conditions were created for insuring an effective communication between YHWH and Israel.[29]

Within its present context, the giving of the Mosaic law in Exodus 19 thus is cast as a special occasion marked by a new need for law and its application to life. Specifically, that new context is the Mosaic covenant at Sinai. This view of the "addition" of law to the Mosaic covenant conforms to the apostle Paul's view of the Mosaic law in Galatians 3:19. Paul asks, "Why then the law?" and he answers, "It was added because of transgressions, till the offspring should come to whom the promise had been made."

We should note that these parallels come only from Exodus 18:1-12 and not from the sections dealing with the restructuring of the law within the covenant in Exodus 19–24. These observations lead to the question of what meaning we are to gather from the interbiblical parallels noted above between Melchizedek, Jethro and Cyrus. In general, one can say that these texts (Gen 14; Ex 18; Ezra 7) demonstrate that apart from God's specific work with his chosen people, God's work of creation (Melchizedek [Gen

---

[28]See Sailhamer, *The Pentateuch as Narrative*, pp. 147-48.

[29]Houtman, *Exodus*, 2:395-96.

14:18-20), redemption (Jethro [Ex 18:1]) and restoration (Cyrus [Ezra 7]) are already known to the nations. The purpose of these parallels is to cast Jethro (and Cyrus) as another Melchizedek, the paradigm of the righteous Gentile. It is important that in this setting Jethro has such credentials[30] because he plays a major role in the events of Exodus 18. He overshadows Moses the lawgiver by showing Moses how to carry out the administration of God's law with Israel. In this, he anticipates the role that Cyrus is to play in the postexilic literature (Ezra 7:25).[31]

Jethro is a precursor to the covenant about to be established. Just as Abraham was met by Melchizedek the priest (Gen 14) before God made a covenant with him in Genesis 15, so Moses is met by Jethro the priest (Ex 18) before God enters a covenant with him at Sinai (Ex 19). Cyrus plays the same role within the new covenant of the prophetic literature (Is 45–55).

Some (e.g., Rashi) have suggested that the whole of Exodus 18 recounts events that occurred after the time at Sinai. This would explain why the Israelites appear already to have "statutes and laws" (Ex 18:16) before God's giving Moses the law at Sinai (Ex 19). That interpretation is unnecessary, however, since, as I have shown, the assumption of other "laws" can be explained by the fact that the Lord has already given them "commandments and statutes" at Marah (Ex 15:25-26). The author has paved the way (Ex 15:25) for what happens in Exodus 18, and he expects the reader to know that Israel already had "statutes and laws"[32] as they approached Sinai.

The fact that the additional "Mosaic law" is given to Israel at Mount Sinai in Exodus 19, when there are already "Mosaic" laws functioning in Exodus 18, suggests that the law given to Moses in Exodus 19 has a different purpose than the laws of Exodus 18. The narrative in Exodus 18 suggests that the purpose of the laws in that chapter is the administration of justice: "Moses sat down to judge *[lišpōṭ]* the people" (Ex 18:13). The purpose of the additional Mosaic law in Exodus 19 is reflected in the compositional strategy of Exodus 19 (cf. Gal 3:19). The Mosaic law (Ex 19) may also have been given as a sum-

---

[30]"Remarkable in Exod. 18 is that it is not divine intervention that does the validating (cf. Num. 11:16ff., 24ff.), but that it rests on the advice of a non-Israelite" (Houtman, *Exodus*, 3:402).

[31]"You, Ezra, according to the wisdom of your God which is in your hand, appoint magistrates *[šāpṭîn]* and judges *[dayyānîn]* that they may judge all the people who are in the province Beyond the River, even all those who know the laws *[dātê]* of your God; and you may teach anyone who is ignorant of them" (Ezra 7:25).

[32]There is little to be made from the observation that the terms "commandment(s)" and "statute(s)" in Exodus 15:25 are singular, since we can read them as collectives, as the plurals in Ex 15:26.

mary of the laws given to Moses and the judges in Exodus 18. They were to carry out their duties along the lines laid down by the advice of Jethro (Ex 15:25; 18:13-26).

The system developed by Moses (on Jethro's recommendations) is a refinement of what appears to have been the accepted procedure for both the development and the administration of law. There is every reason to believe that it was intended to continue in effect after Moses. The Mosaic law that is unfolded in passages such as Exodus 19–24 was intended as a summation of God's purposes in giving laws to Israel. As such, it was to remain static, with no additional elements. The laws generated by Moses and the judges in Exodus 18, however, were intended to continue their development and administration after Moses. That they are two distinct kinds of laws, with entirely different purposes, may be discerned from the fact that both sets of laws are given under entirely new and different circumstances.

The comment in Exodus 19 that "Moses was speaking and God was answering out loud" (Ex 19:19b) suggests that the giving of law at Sinai continued to follow the pattern in Exodus 18. When Moses describes his role in administering the law, it sounds very much like his role on Mount Sinai. He told his father-in-law, Jethro, "When the people come to me to seek God on a matter, I judge between them and make known the divine statutes and laws" (Ex 18:16). For the sake of the people's administration of law, Moses spoke to God, and God answered him, much like Exodus 19:19b: "Moses was speaking, and God was answering out loud." God's answer is known through the statutes and judgments given by Moses. Moses' role as lawgiver and teacher in Exodus 18–19 is similar to Isaiah's picture of the lawgiver in Isaiah 2:3-4, where, again, it is the nations who seek to know God's laws:

> And many peoples shall come, and say: "Come, let us go up to the mountain of the Lord, to the house of the God of Jacob; that he may teach us his ways and that we may walk in his paths." For out of Zion shall go forth the law, and the word of the Lord from Jerusalem. He shall judge between the nations, and shall decide for many peoples.

This pattern suggests a primarily compositional motive behind the placement of the Jethro narrative (Ex 18) before the Moses Sinai narrative (Ex 19) and the giving of the Mosaic law.

**Table 4.3**

| Exodus | Isaiah |
|---|---|
| The aim of Exodus 18:16 is to bring one's legal dispute *(dābār)* to Moses *(ʾēlay)*. Moses would then judge *(wĕšāpaṭtî)* between the plaintifs *(bên ʾîš ûbên rēʿēhû)* and accordingly make known *(wĕhôdaʿtî)* the word from God *(ʾe-tḥuqqê hāʾĕlōhîm wĕʾet-tôrōtāyw)*. | Similarly in Isaiah 2:2-4, the aim is to teach *(wĕyōrēnû middĕrākāyw)* the Torah *(tôrâ)* and judging *(wĕšāpaṭ)* the nations *(bên haggôyīm)* on the "mountain of the LORD" *(har-yhwh)*. |

*God on the mountain (Ex 19:1-25).* It has long been recognized that within Exodus 19 there are two conceptualizations of Israel's covenant with God at Mount Sinai. In one version of the account (Ex 19:1-16a) the focus is on a covenant between God and Israel that results in a "kingdom of priests and a holy nation" (Ex 19:6). The only requirement of that covenant is Israel's "faith" (*yaʾămînû* [Ex 19:9]) and "obedience" (Ex 19:5). Unlike the Mosaic covenant, there appear to be no "laws" in this covenant. Later biblical writers also seem aware of such a covenant. In Jeremiah 7:22-23 the Lord says,

> In the day that I brought them out of the land of Egypt I did not speak to your fathers or command them concerning burnt offerings and sacrifices. But this command I gave them, "Obey my voice, and I will be your God, and you will be my people, and you will walk in the way I will command you so that it would be well to you."[33]

To ratify this covenant, Moses and the people were to meet with God on Mount Sinai. They were to wait three days and then "go up" into the mountain to meet with God. They were not merely to go up "to the mountain"; they were to go "upon the mountain" and there be with God. The original intention of going up the mountain was that the people were to go up upon the mountain with Moses. Although this is not always reflected in the English translations, there is little doubt that it is the view of the Hebrew text: "they may go up on the mountain *[bāhār]*" (Ex 19:13b NJPS).[34] This view of the Sinai covenant is anticipated in Exodus 3:12: "When you [sg.] bring the people out of Egypt, you [pl.] shall worship God on this mountain *[hāhār*

[33]The translation above follows the RSV, NASB, KJV, NJPS. The NIV translation, "I did not just give them commands about burnt offerings and sacrifices," appears to be a harmonistic attempt of the translators to remove an obvious problem.

[34]The NJPS has correctly rendered the Hebrew text of this verse: "When the ram's horn sounds a long blast, they may go up on the mountain." See the discussion of this verse below.

*hazzeh].*" According to this verse, Moses and the people were to worship God on the mountain (cf. Ex 4:27b; 5:3, and later biblical texts that refer back to this chapter).

In another version of the Sinai covenant in Exodus 19 (Ex 19:16b-25) there is a different viewpoint. Instead of a kingdom *of* priests, there is now a distinction between the people and the priests: it is to be a kingdom *with* priests (Ex 19:22-24). Instead of the people being called to come upon the mountain, the people were to "be kept from going up" the mountain. Only Moses and Aaron were to go up the mountain to be with God (Ex 19:12, 13a, 21-23). Finally, instead of simple faith and obedience, the Decalogue and the Covenant Code are the basis of Israel's keeping the covenant. A similar view of the Sinai covenant is expressed in Ezekiel 20:19-25:

> "I am the LORD your God; walk in my statutes and keep my judgments and do them; keep my sabbaths holy, and it will be a sign between you and me to know that I am the LORD your God." But they rebelled against me. . . . And I gave them statutes that did not result in good [for them] and judgments in which they could not live.[35]

When these two covenant narratives are read together, it appears that God's initial intention at Mount Sinai was a relationship with Israel much like his covenant with Abraham, based on faith and having no laws. Subsequently, laws were added to the covenant.

According to literary-critical theory, these two versions of the Sinai covenant are a reflection of the composite nature of the present text. It was the view of the E source that both Moses and the people were to "go up" to the mountain to meet with God (Ex 19:13b). As conceived by the E source, the

---

[35]The NIV and New Scofield Reference Bible's translation of *nātattî lāhem* to come up with "I also gave them over to statutes" is an unfortunate harmonization of this difficult passage (cf. RSV, NASB, NJPS, KJV, which render it as above). The same is to be said of the addition of "in fire" (Ezek 20:26) in some English versions, making it appear that the "statutes" in Ezekiel 20:25 relate to offering their firstborn "in the fire." The words "in fire" do not occur in the Hebrew text and are not implied. The text is rendered correctly in NJPS: "when they set aside every first issue of the womb." As the identical phraseology shows, the statement "when they set aside every first issue of the womb" *(bhʿbyr kl-pṭr-rhm)* is a reference to God's claim of the firstborn in Exodus 13:12: "You are to give over to the LORD the first offspring of every womb" *(hʾbrt kl-pṭr-rḥm),* not to child sacrifice (cf. Ex 34:19; Num 3:12-13). Moreover, "causing one's children to pass through the fire" is expressly forbidden in Deuteronomy 18:10. The collocation *hʾbyr pṭr rḥm* does not occur in the OT with *bʾš,* but, as in Exodus 13:12, with reference to the firstborn. When *hʾbyr* occurs with *bʾš*, the object is not *pṭr rḥm,* but rather *bn* (Deut 18:10; 2 Kings 17:17; 21:6; 23:10; 2 Chron 33:6; Ezek 20:31 [omitted in the LXX]).

covenant was like that in Exodus 19:2b-8. It was a renewal of the patriarchal covenant of faith and obedience. Owing to their fear of God's presence (Ex 19:16b), however, they appointed Moses to go up the mountain and speak with God on their behalf. Fearing God, they remained behind at the foot of the mountain (Ex 19:17, 19b).[36] In the J source's account of the Sinai covenant, the people, from the start, were forbidden to go up the mountain (Ex 19:12-13a). They were to watch the fiery display of God's powerful presence at a safe distance (Ex 19:18, 20-25).[37]

Before the rise of literary criticism, the tensions within this narrative were already apparent, and various harmonizations had been offered. A strictly chronological reading of Exodus 19 and Exodus 24 suggests to some that there were two covenants made at Sinai: the original covenant (Ex 19:3-8), and a second one (Ex 24:1-8). Rashi attempted to refute that view by arguing that these two narratives (Ex 19; 24) were not to be read in a chronological sequence. As Rashi understood it, the covenant recounted in Exodus 19 was the same covenant as in Exodus 24. Rashi supported his argument by means of an important observation of the word order of Exodus 24:1. The verb comes second in the opening clause, and thus, Rashi argued, it must be read as a pluperfect: "And to Moses [the LORD] *had said*, 'Come up . . . ,'" making it refer back to Exodus 19:3, "And Moses went up to God [on the mountain]." That reading of this text moves the narrative of Exodus 24 back to the events of Exodus 19:3-8, the original covenant.[38] Rashi's explanation of this difficulty has had little influence on Christian interpretation.[39] C. F. Keil, however, may be dependent on Rashi in suggesting that Exodus 19:3-8 is as an initial statement of the covenant and hence associated with the proclamation of the "fundamental law of the covenant in the presence of the whole nation (chap. xix. 16-xx. 18)."[40] The problem with Rashi's view is that it overlooks

---

[36]See Otto Eissfeldt, *Hexateuch-Synopse: Die Erzählung der fünf Bücher Mose und des Buches Josua mit dem Anfange des Richterbuches*, 2nd ed. (Darmstadt: Wissenschaftliche Buchgesellschaft, 1973), pp. 146-47.

[37]Ibid., pp. 146-48.

[38]"This section [24:1ff] was spoken before the Ten Commandments were given; it was the fourth of Sivan when 'Come up' was said to him" (*Pentateuch with Targum Onkelos, Haphtaroth, Prayers for Sabbath and Rashi's Commentary, Exodus*, trans. M. Rosenbaum and A. M. Silbermann [New York: Hebrew Publishing Company, 1930], 2:128).

[39]Neither does NJPS follow Rashi in Exodus 24:1: "Then He said to Moses, 'Come up. . . .'"

[40]C. F. Keil and F. Delitzsch, *Biblical Commentary on the Old Testament* (Grand Rapids: Eerdmans, 1968-1971), 2:101. Recently, Rashi's view apparently has been adopted by G. C. Chirichigno: "We have argued that the awkward surface structure of the narrative, which results in the non-linear

the grammatical (and compositional) link between Exodus 24:1 and Exodus 19:21.[41] That link ties the covenant in Exodus 24 (Ex 24:1-2) not to Exodus 19:3-8, but to the texts that link the Covenant Code (Ex 20:23–23:23) to the original covenant in Exodus 19–20 (Ex 20:22).

The usual explanation among Christians is that in Exodus 19:3-8 God begins to expound on the nature of the Sinai covenant, but before he can fully explain it, the people all too quickly agree to its terms. According to John Calvin, the people "were carried away by a kind of headlong zeal, and deceived themselves"[42] into thinking they could keep the laws of the Sinai covenant. "Yet soon after they relapsed into their natural mind, and kept not their promise even in the smallest degree."[43] Rather than see these texts in a dynamic transition from a covenant like Abraham's to one like Sinai, Christian interpreters have read Exodus 19 and Exodus 24 as two parts of the same unchanging covenant intended from the outset to be operative through the laws promulgated subsequently at Sinai. One of the key unanswered questions arising out of this view of the Sinai covenant involves the uneven nature of the laws of this covenant. The variety and repetition of various versions of the laws given at Sinai raise questions about its fundamental unity.[44]

Another lingering question arising from the attempt to read Exodus 19–24 as a homogeneous narrative is the identity of those who were to go up into the mountain in Exodus 19:13b: "When the horn blows a long blast, they shall go up the mountain." This is taken by some to be at variance with the prohibition in Exodus 19:12 against the people going up the mountain. Rashi believed that the key to the unity of the narrative lay in the stated purpose of the "blast" to signal for Israel's move up the mountain. Rashi

---

temporal ordering of events, can be explained when one takes into account the sequence structure of the narrative, particularly the use of the literary device called resumptive repetition" ("The Narrative Structure of Exod 19–24," *Bib* 68 [1987]: 479).

[41]The *wayyiqtol* clause in Exodus 19:21, *wayyōʾmer yhwh ʾel-mōšeh*, is linked to the w + x + *qatal* clause, *wĕʾel-mōšeh ʾāmar*, in Exodus 24:1.

[42]John Calvin, *Commentaries on the Four Last Books of Moses Arranged in the Form of a Harmony*, trans. Charles William Bingham (Grand Rapids: Baker, 1979, p. 320). Compare the comment of Henry Ainsworth: "The people not yet knowing the unpossibility of the Law, which is weak through the flesh, Rom. 8:3, make promise of more than they were able to performe. After, when the Law was pronounced, they feare and flee away, Exod. 20. 18,19" (*Annotations upon the Five Bookes of Moses* [London, 1639], p. 68).

[43]Calvin, *Four Last Books of Moses*, p. 320.

[44]See Sailhamer, *The Pentateuch as Narrative*, pp. 44-46.

reasoned that the long blast of the ram's horn was a signal of God's departure from the mountain and a call for all the people to move up the mountain.[45] Although the people were warned in Exodus 19:12 not to go up into the mountain, in Exodus 19:13 they were called to go up into the mountain when the horn sounded. Rashi's interpretation has found its way into early scholarly translations[46] and can be found as early as the LXX. The LXX translated only the sense of the phrase, not the words: "Whenever the sounds and the trumpets and the cloud depart from the mountain, they may go up the mountain *[epi to oros]*."[47]

Nicholas von Lyra, who usually follows Rashi, departed from Rashi's explanation in this case by suggesting that "to go up the mountain" meant that the people could go only so far as the limits that had been established by Moses (Ex 19:12).[48] This appears to be the sense taken by many modern English versions: "When the horn blasts, they shall come up to the mountain."[49] The obvious difficulty with this view is that the text says not "up *to* the mountain," but "up *in* the mountain," just as in Exodus 19:12.[50]

---

[45]Rashi's interpretation is represented in several Christian commentaries—for example, Münster: "Cum prolixius buccina sonuerit; prolixior enim sonus signum erat Dominum majestatis montem deseruisse"; Fagius: "Sensus est, Dum satis protractus adeoque finitus est sonitus tubarum, tum ascendere potest populus; at praesente Domino nequaquam. Neque enim veto ut in perpetuum non ascendatis. Dum ergo sonitus cornu cessaverit, potestis ascendere. Prolixior sonus signum erat, Dominum majestatis montem deseruisse." According to Eben Ezra, Rashi's explanation was inadequate because the Lord's glory was always on the mountain until the completion of the tabernacle.

[46]Calvin, *Commentary* (1563): "Quum protraxerit buccina, ipsi ascendent in montem"; Münster, *Biblia sacra* (1534): "Cum prolixius buccina insonuerit, tunc poterunt ascendere montem"; Tyndale, *The Seconde Boke of Moses* (1530): "When the horne bloweth: than let them come up in to the mounten"; *Geneva Bible* (1599): "When the horne bloweth long, they shall come up into the mountaine"; Junius and Tremellius, *Biblia sacra* (1575): "Cum tractim sonabit cornu, ea ascendere poterunt in ipsum montem"; cf. NJPS: "When the ram's horn sounds a long blast, they may go up on the mountain."

[47]Compare the Vulgate: "Cum coeperit clangere bucina tunc ascendant in montem"; *Targum Onqelos:* "When the horn blast is protracted, they may go up into the mountain."

[48]"In montem hic est versus montem, usque ad terminos a Mose Dei jussu praefixos" (in Matthew Poole, *Synopsis criticorum aliorumque S. Scripturae interpretum* [London, 1669-1676], 1:398). Lyra apparently followed Eben Ezra on Exodus 19:17: "[Under the mountain] means outside the borders set by Moses." A similar interpretation may already be present in the Samaritan Pentateuch's reading in Exodus 19:12a rather than as in the MT.

[49]This translation is represented in the NIV, NASB, KJV. That it is a harmonistic attempt to avoid the problem of the Hebrew text is suggested by the fact that these same versions render the identical expression (עלה בהר, *ʿlh bhr*) in the preceding verse not with "go up to the mountain," but with "go up/into the mountain" (Ex 19:12). The NJPS renders עלה בהר in Exodus 19:12, 13b as to "go up (on) the mountain."

[50]A third explanation was offered by Drusius. Following Eben Ezra, Drusius identified the pronoun

Another problem within the narrative is the statement in Exodus 19:12: "Beware of going up the mountain" (NJPS). This statement often is taken as an absolute prohibition of the people's going up the mountain. It does not, however, have that sense. It is a warning: "Watch yourselves going up into the mountain," or "Watch yourselves as you go up into the mountain." It does not say, "Watch yourselves lest you go up the mountain," or "Do not go up the mountain." If it were a prohibition such as "Beware not to go up," it would require the preposition "from" (מִן, *min*) before the infinitive, as in the textual variant reflected in the Targumim,[51] or the negative particle "lest" (פֶּן, *pen*) before the imperfect (תעלה, *tʿlh*). In any case, when read in the context of Israel's waiting three days (Ex 19:11) until "the horn is blown" (Ex 19:13b), the warning in Exodus 19:12 is a warning not to come up into the mountain until the signal is given. According to this narrative, there is an expectation that the people are eventually, in three days, to go up the mountain with Moses, and there they were to meet with God on the mountain.

To understand the sense of the passage further, one must see what each of the smaller units of narratives[52] contributes to the sense of the whole. We will begin that task by looking briefly at the compositional strategy of each of these pieces of narrative and what they contribute to the sense of the whole of the account in Exodus 19–20.

*The people's refusal (Ex 19:10-19).* Grammatically and syntactically, it is clear that in the Sinai narratives God's intention was to meet with all the people *on* the mountain. This is not merely the viewpoint of a hypothetical source, such as the E source; it is the consistent view of the entire narrative. The problem, of course, is that this did not happen. At the blast of the horn, signaling that they should come up the mountain (Ex 19:13b), the people remained "fearfully" in the camp. Although Moses brought them out of the camp to meet with God at the mountain (Ex 19:17a), they went only "to the foot" *(bĕtaḥtît)* of the mountain (Ex 19:17b). Although it is not yet explicitly

---

"they" (Ex 19:13b) with Moses, Aaron, Abihu and the elders and thus avoided the suggestion that the people were allowed to go up the mountain. This is also the position of *Targum Neofiti 1:* "When the trumpet is sounded, Moses and Aaron are authorized to come up into the mountain." That it was the people rather than Moses and the elders, however, is seen from Exodus 19:12, 17, where "the people" are expressly in view.

[51]The variant suggested in *BHS* apparatus shows what would be expected for an unequivocal negative sense.

[52]The various smaller passages that make up Exodus 19–20 are Exodus 19:20-25; 20:1-17; 20:18-21.

stated, the people refused to go up the mountain because they were afraid of God and the great display of his glory and power on the mountain (Ex 19:18). As we will see, their fear will be further described in a later section (Ex 20:18-21) that serves as a commentary to this part of the story. Here we are told only that they remained in the camp, and that they were terrified by what they saw on the mountain.

As the display of God's glorious power on the mountain grows stronger and louder, the people are able to listen as Moses converses with God. Moses speaks from the foot of the mountain, and God answers him from the top (Ex 19:19). Given the importance of this narrative, we might expect their conversation to center on the Ten Commandments. That was not the case, however. The Ten Commandments come into view several verses later, but they come only after Moses has ascended the mountain again and only after a further conversation between God and Moses on an entirely different subject than the Decalogue. The conversation here centers on access to God on the mountain. It is a conversation that lays the groundwork for the priesthood and the tabernacle (Ex 19:20-24).

*The priesthood and tabernacle (Ex 19:20-25).* Although the sound of the horn continued to increase (Ex 19:19a), the people remained silent while Moses alone went up to speak with God. It is important to note that the nature of Moses' continuing conversation with God is cast as a response to the people's refusal to come up the mountain. It was when the people refused that God called Moses to the top of the mountain (Ex 19:20). Curiously, as we noted above, the conversation that ensued between Moses and God (Ex 19:20-24) was not about the Ten Commandments, even though it ends with the recitation of those commandments as foundational to the Sinai covenant. Although not about law, the conversation in Exodus 19:20-24 is about another feature of the covenant at Sinai, the priesthood.

God begins the conversation by admonishing Moses to warn the people not to "break through to look upon Yahweh," in effect barring them from going up the mountain at all: "And the LORD said to Moses, 'Go down and warn the people, lest they break through to the LORD to gaze and many of them perish" (Ex 19:21). All the people had been expected to go up the mountain (Ex 19:13b). When they refused, they became subject to stricter requirements and were restricted from "breaking through to gaze upon the LORD" (Ex 19:21). The Lord, however, continued to speak with Moses, turning his attention to Aaron and the priesthood (Ex 19:22, 24), who have not yet been mentioned in these texts. The priests were those who were "to go near to God" (Ex 19:22). This meant they must have the means to maintain their holiness. They were called to "make themselves holy" (*yitqaddāšû* [Ex 19:22]). Finally, this passage makes clear that God himself established barriers to the mountain to safeguard against the people's ever going up the mountain. As we will see below, the laws regarding the tabernacle (Ex 25–31) are intended to fill this need. Mount Sinai has become a prototype of the tabernacle and eventually the temple.[53]

The result of these new requirements was threefold: (1) as with the tabernacle, the people were warned against an improper entry into God's presence (Ex 19:21); (2) the priests were made responsible for maintaining their holiness (Ex 19:22); (3) God assumed the ultimate role of sanctifying (*wĕqiddaštô* [Ex 19:23]) the mountain or the place of his holy presence. This section closes with a summary of the new divisions now laid out among the people: Moses and Aaron, the high priest, the priests, the rest of the people: "And the LORD said to him, 'Go down, and come up bringing Aaron with you; but do not let the priests and the people break through to come up to the LORD, lest he break out against them" (Ex 19:24).

In Exodus 19:12 the people are called upon to go up the mountain when the horn was sounded.[54] In Exodus 19:16 the people, in fear, refused to obey. Consequently, in Exodus 19:21 the people are forbidden to go up the mountain at all. They can only send their priestly representatives. The initial expectation of these narratives was that the horn would blast, and the people would go up into the mountain. However, when the horn was sounded, the people remained in the camp and refused to go up the mountain. Their refusal is a narrative signal of a changed relationship to God's holy presence.

The sense of this passage, as I have developed it from within its larger context (Ex 19–20), is that the people's refusal to come up the mountain

---

[53]See Sailhamer, *the Pentateuch as Narrative*, pp. 296-98.

[54]Exodus 19:12 did not prohibit going up the mountain. It was a temporary precaution about not going up the mountain until the blast of the ram's horn is heard. This is clear from the express statements of the two verses (Ex 19:21, 23), as well as from the use of the same terminology in both. The use of הָעֵד in Exodus 19:12 and Exodus 19:23 is sometimes taken as the grounds for seeing Exodus 19:23 as a harmonization of Exodus 19:12 and Exodus 19:13b. However, the phrase "set limits for the people" (Ex 19:12) is not the same as "set limits for the mountain" (Ex 19:23). The reading of the Samaritan Pentateuch in Exodus 19:12, ההר rather than העם, points to the difficulty of making Exodus 19:23-24. Refer to Exodus 19:12.

brought about a fundamental reshaping of the Sinai covenant. The Sinai covenant began as a call to remain faithful to the Abrahamic covenant. With the people's fear and failure came a shift in that covenant. It was a sign of the people's lack of faith. Something more was needed to keep them loyal to the covenant. There was a need for law. Beginning with the Ten Commandments, laws were added to the divine promises to Abraham.

The same adjustment of the Sinai covenant can be seen in Deuteronomy 5:2-5:

> The LORD our God made a covenant with us in Horeb. . . . The LORD spoke with you face to face on the mountain out of the midst of the fire, while I stood between the LORD and you at that time, to show you the word of the LORD; for you were afraid because of the fire, and you did not go up into the mountain.

The same view of the Sinai covenant is found in the book of Hebrews. In a lengthy commentary on this passage the writer of Hebrews explains the failure of the Sinai covenant in terms of the people's refusal to go up to meet God on the mountain.

> For ye are not come unto the mount that might be touched, and that burned with fire, nor unto blackness, and darkness, and tempest, and the sound of a trumpet, and the voice of words; which voice they that heard intreated that the word should not be spoken to them any more. . . . But you are come unto mount Sion. . . . and to Jesus the mediator of the new covenant, and to the blood of sprinkling, that speaketh better things than that of Abel. See that you refuse not him that speaketh. For if they escaped not who refused him that spake on earth, much more shall not we escape, if we turn away from him that speaketh from heaven. (Heb 12:18-25 KJV)

Hebrews describes the failure of the people at Sinai as a refusal to obey the word of God on the mountain.

*The law was added (Ex 20:1-17).* Having received God's warnings of the necessity of the priesthood and the sanctuary, Moses returned to the foot of the mountain to deliver the Ten Commandments to the people: "Moses went down unto the people and spoke to them" (Ex 19:25). In this way, the Decalogue became an integral part of the Sinai covenant.

Several problems are raised by Exodus 19:25 and its position immediately prior to the account of Moses' presenting the Ten Commandments (Ex 20:1-17). The most important matter is how to understand the verb "to say" (אמר, *ʾmr*).

Normally, this verb requires one or more object clauses specifying the content of what was said. In Exodus 19:25 the object of the verb is not explicitly stated. Translators either treat the verb "to say" as an intransitive, "So Moses went down to the people and spoke *[wayyōʾmer]* to them" (NKJV), or they understand it to mean that Moses came down the mountain to the people and told them what God had said to him in the preceding verses, "So Moses went down to the people and told *[wayyōʾmer]* them" (RSV).

Although such translations are, in themselves, an acknowledgment of the difficulties the verse presents, it is possible to arrive at a grammatically correct understanding of the verse. It is likely that the whole of the section on the Ten Commandments, which follow in Exodus 20:1-17, is the object of the verb אמר. Read in that way, the text says that when Moses descended to the bottom of the mountain, he enumerated the Ten Commandments to the people. That *Targum Neofiti 1* understood the verse in that way is shown by its translation: "And Moses went down from the mountain unto the people and he said to them: Draw near (and) receive the ten words!"[55]

If the Decalogue is what Moses "said" to the people in Exodus 19:25, then the sense of the verse may be described as follows. When Moses came down the mountain, he spoke the Ten Commandments to all the people at the foot of the mountain. Those commandments were that which God had spoken to him on the mountain. The grammatical form of the first verse, Exodus 20:1, shows that it is a narrative. This suggests that Moses rendered these commandments in the form of a restatement of what had actually occurred in Exodus 19:19. Moses "narrated" to the people at the foot of the mountain what God had said to him in the mountain. Rather than directing his words specifically to the people, Moses narrated the account of God's speaking the commandments to him, even quoting God's words to Moses in the second person:

> I am the LORD your God *[ʾĕlōheykā]*, who has brought you *[hôṣēʾtîkā]* out of the land of Egypt, out of the house of bondage. You shall have no *[lōʾ yihyeh-lĕkā]* other gods before me. (Ex 20:2-3)

Judging from the sense of Exodus 19:19—"and God answered aloud"—

---

[55] ואמר להון קרובו קבילו עשירתא דביריא (Alejandro Díez Macho, *Neophyti 1: Targum Palestinese ms de la Biblioteca Vaticana* (Textos y Estudios 8; Madrid: Consejo Superior de Investigaciones Científicas, 1970), 2:125. *Targum Psuedo-Jonathan* renders this verse with the addition "Draw near and receive the Torah with the ten (words) of the covenant."

the people had already heard the commandments spoken out loud by God on Mount Sinai. Moses spoke to God, and God's reply to Moses was the Ten Commandments. In Exodus 19:25 Moses now speaks these same words, or commandments, to the people. In doing so, Moses states the Ten Commandments in a form more suitable for their role as covenant stipulations.

The picture of Moses that emerges from these texts is identical to that of Deuteronomy 33:10,[56] Exodus 18:20[57] and Deuteronomy 4:45.[58] In three passages the priests are given the covenant responsibility to give the law to Israel and to teach it in order to safeguard the covenant. In this picture of Moses as the lawgiver one can detect the influence of the picture of Moses and the priesthood in Deuteronomy 33:8-11.

*The fear of the people (Ex 20:18-21).* Our understanding of the compositional meaning of the Sinai narrative (Ex 19–20) becomes clearer as we further probe the interrelationships of the individual narratives within the account. The smaller individual texts are laid alongside and attached to the larger, completed narratives. This is consistent with the way many biblical narratives are composed. The technique, called דרישׁת סמוכים ("explanation by attachment"), was described in the early postbiblical era. It was an early form of exegesis by which individual biblical texts were linked to form larger contexts of interpretation. Wilhelm Bacher described the technique thus: "Placing two texts together can function as a way of explaining one text by another: one text, so to speak, 'learns' from the other."[59]

The biblical authors were careful to preserve their written sources intact, as close to how they had received them. Careful preservation of original texts in composition made it necessary on occasion to provide explanations and commentary without adding to texts or rewriting them. This often meant that commentary on biblical texts could come only by attaching additional written documents that speak, sometimes only in an abbreviated way, to specific questions. In the case of Exodus 19–24, the question of the people's fear of God at Sinai was an important aspect of the various Sinai narratives. The

[56]Deuteronomy 33:10: "[The priests] shall teach Jacob your judgments, and Israel your law."

[57]Exodus 18:20: "And you [Moses] shall teach them ordinances and laws, and shall show them the way wherein they must walk, and the work they must do."

[58]Deuteronomy 4:45: "These are the testimonies, and the statutes, and the judgments, which Moses spoke to the children of Israel after they came forth out of Egypt."

[59]"Das Nebeneinander zweier Abschnitte kann dazu benützt werden, den einen mit Hilfe des andern zu erklären: der eine der beiden Abschnitte 'lernt' von dem andern" (Wilhelm Bacher, *Die exegetische Terminologie der jüdischen Traditionsliteratur* [Hildesheim: Olms, 1969], p. 133).

author clearly was concerned with clarifying the nature of that fear and how it ultimately contributed to a process of refinement and clarification of the nature of the Sinai covenant. This aspect of the Sinai covenant, along with other features, has rarely been dealt with by biblical theologians. Why or what did the people fear? Why did they not go up into the mountain? Why did Moses have to face God alone? Did he take the people's place by representing them before God? Did Israel's fear result in a changed relationship with God? These are important biblical-theological questions that lie behind the present shape of the Sinai narrative. Answers to these questions can help us better understand the nature of the Sinai covenant and, ultimately, the new covenant. Our concern here, however, is that these questions are the very ones that the author is attempting to answer by attaching brief narratives such as Exodus 20:18-21 to the Sinai pericope.

The attachment of Exodus 20:18-21, which refocuses on and clarifies the nature of the people's fear, is accomplished grammatically by the circumstantial clause in Exodus 20:18. The clause is a back-reference to Exodus 19:16, the display of the thunder and lightning at Sinai: "And all the people were witnessing the thunderings and the lightnings and the noise of the trumpet and the mountain smoking" (Ex 20:18).

The grammatical and exegetical role of the circumstantial clause in Exodus 20:18 is to return the reader to the first, and somewhat problematic, account of the people's fear at Sinai (Ex 19:16): "All the people that were in the camp trembled." What kind of fear was this? Was it even fear, in a real sense, at all? Could it simply mean that they "trembled" in the camp and no more? To the brief and almost passing mention of "trembling" in this narrative the author adds[60] a more detailed and comprehensive explanation of the same event. This addition considerably clarifies the reader's understanding of the situation: "And when the people saw it, they removed, and stood afar off. And they said to Moses, 'Speak with us, and we will hear; but let not God speak with us, lest we die'" (Ex 20:18b-19).

In this additional account, which is attached to the original statement of the people's "trembling in the camp," the reader learns considerably more about the nature of the people's fear of going up the mountain. It was fear that caused the people to run from God at Sinai. They were afraid of what they

[60]Attaches as commentary (דרישת סמוכים).

saw and heard. It was fear that caused them to remove themselves "afar off" from the mountain. It was fear that caused them to refuse to hear God speak on the mountain. They wanted Moses to speak to God for them. They were afraid to go near to God. They wanted to remain at a distance while Moses carried their words to God.

Within the immediate context it is not difficult to see the direction in which these individual texts are moving the narrative as a whole. In effect, the addition of Exodus 20:18-21 serves to bring into focus a question that has long plagued these narratives. That question is the role of a priesthood—that is, the necessity of a priesthood to serve at the tabernacle. Viewed within the larger context of Exodus 19–Numbers 10, when the people ask Moses to go before God, they appear to be asking for a priesthood to represent them, to teach them, and to stand before God in their place. They want priests, like Moses, to go in their place, to receive God's words and to come back, like Moses, to teach them the law. Curiously, this is the same interest that we saw in the advice given Moses by Jethro in the narrative leading up to Sinai (Ex 18). It is here again confronting us in this additional narrative that has been attached to the Sinai pericope. Clearly, the purpose of this small segment of narrative is to alert the reader to the coming discussion of the importance and place of the priesthood in the Sinai covenant, and with it, the tabernacle-sanctuary. The laws regulating the priesthood and tabernacle worship, which are immediately enumerated in the following section (Ex 25:1–30:17), are given an appropriate historical context by this narrative.[61]

*Signs of "intelligent life" in the narrative shape?* The foregoing overview of the compositional strategy of the Sinai narratives raises important questions. Why does the divine viewpoint reflected in the narrative change so radically after the episode of the people remaining, trembling, in the camp? Why is Moses then given a new command that prohibits the people's coming up the mountain altogether? Is it that two conflicting accounts have been preserved intact in this chapter, as literary-critical theory would have us believe? Or is this sudden shift in God's commands a signal of a changing relationship brought on by the people's refusal to obey God, as the author of the book of Hebrews apparently believed? If the latter, how does it change our understanding of the overall intention of the author of the Pentateuch? Are the

---

[61]See Sailhamer, *The Pentateuch as Narrative*, p. 58.

tensions, which are so transparent in the Hebrew text of this pericope, merely the result of conflicting sources, or are these tensions also semantically and theologically relevant? Do they reflect an author's intent? The only way to answer these questions is to ask whether there is evidence of "intelligent design" behind the specific shape of the narrative. Does the present shape of the narrative follow a recognizable "logic" that conforms to the overall purposes of the Pentateuch? If so, how does that purpose play itself out in the theology of the Pentateuch?

Fortunately, as I have suggested, the narrative and its compositional strategy do not leave us without an answer to these questions. As I have suggested in the questions asked, the sense of this passage appears to hinge on the failure of the people to come up the mountain when they heard the blast of the horn. According to Exodus 19:16, on the third day, when the people were to be ready to "go up the mountain," the horn was sounded. However, when the people saw the fearsome display of God's power and when they heard his voice (*qōlōt* [literally, "thunders"]) coming out of the fire and lightning, they were "terrified" *(wayyeḥĕrad)* in the camp. In the immediate context (Ex 19:17-19) it is not exactly clear what this text intends to say about the people's experience at Sinai. Moses appears to move quickly to bring the people out of the camp to meet God. They stood at the foot of the mountain (Ex 19:17), watching the display of God's presence on the mountain. The mountain itself shook with terror as the people watched and listened to the conversation between God and Moses (Ex 19:19). Moses spoke, and God answered. Moses then ascended the mountain, there to meet with God. It was then that he, at God's behest, warned the people not to "break through to look upon God" (Ex 19:21). It was also at that time that the priests were admonished to consecrate themselves "lest the LORD break out upon them" (Ex 19:22). This divine word was by no means merely a repetition of the warning early given to Moses in Exodus 19:12. It is presented here as a new prohibition involving both the people and the priests. In Moses' own words (Ex 19:23), God was "testifying against his people" (Ex 19:21), warning them not to go up the mountain.

The general flow of events is not hard to follow in these verses, but there is much that appears to be without immediate explanation. Ultimately, for answers to such questions we must turn to the author's own work of shaping and linking these various narratives. We must look for the author's own composition strategy of linking these narratives into a larger whole. The key to the meaning of this section is to be found in the "further reflection" on this Sinai narrative in texts such as Exodus 20:18-21. We have noted that the account in Exodus 20:18-21 does not immediately follow the events of Exodus 19:16-19. In that text the author returns the reader to those same events by means of a "flashback," or back-reference, a technique that G. C. Chirichigno calls "resumptive repetition."[62] Once there, the story is retold with additional details. Hence, at the conclusion of the Decalogue the author brings us back for one final look at the people's fear at Sinai, clearly an important moment in the actions covered by these narratives. The author accomplishes his purpose by rewinding[63] the narrative back to the original divine display on the mountain and the effect it had on the people: "Now when all the people witnessed the thunderings and the lightnings and the sound of the trumpet and the mountain smoking, the people were afraid and trembled; and they stood afar off" (Ex 20:18).

In this last time around, the author gives helpful additional information about the people's fear and Moses' explanation of it: "And (they) said to Moses, 'You speak to us, and we will hear; but let not God speak to us, lest we die" (Ex 20:19). The people's fear of God's presence finds its explanation in their response to Moses. They were unwilling to stand before God to receive his words. Their solution was to appoint Moses to stand for them and to speak with God on their behalf. In turn, Moses would speak to them for God. Their view of the role of Moses is much like that of Jethro's plan in Exodus 18. Let Moses go before God in the difficult questions, and the people will take his words as authoritative. With that kind of credentialing, Moses entered into the dark cloud to meet with God and there to receive God's words for the people (Ex 20:21).

In light of these compositional clarifications in Exodus 20:18-21, what we learn about Exodus 19 is that God's original intention to meet with the people on the mountain (Ex 19:13b; cf. Ex 3:12) was fundamentally altered by the people's fear of approaching God (Ex 19:16b). In their fear, the people traded a personal, face-to-face relationship with God for a priesthood.

*Further compositional details.* At this point, we must consider again the compositional framework and its role in the strategy of the Pentateuch. The important question continues to be the relationship of the smaller units of

---

[62]Chirichigno, "The Narrative Structure of Exod 19–24," p. 479.

[63]Circumstantial clause.

narrative to the larger whole of Exodus 19–24. The narratives that we will look at, and their sequence within the Sinai narratives, are Exodus 19:1-19, 20-25; 20:1-17, 18-21. The problems of the literary relationship of these individual narratives to each other seem at times insurmountable. Critical scholars take these difficulties as evidence of multiple sources or the strata of various levels of texts. I have suggested that whatever might be said about text strata in these narratives, the present shape of the narratives demonstrates sufficient evidence of compositional purpose and text strategy.

It is clear from a close reading of Exodus 19:1-19 that the author understands it to be an account of the continuing covenant relationship between God and Abraham's descendants. The events at Sinai are recounted as both the beginning of a new episode in that relationship and a continuation of the past. The clue to the identity of the Abrahamic covenant in this passage is the fact that, at least initially, the narrative focuses on an existing covenant that, like Abraham's covenant, calls only for faith and obedience (Ex 19:1-9). Within the larger context of the Pentateuch and particularly Genesis, that covenant can only be the covenant with Abraham (Gen 12–50). In support of that conclusion, it can be noted that precisely what is missing in this account of the covenant in Exodus 19:1-9 is any mention of "stipulations" or "laws" that govern this covenant. All that is necessary to keep the covenant in Exodus 19:8 is an obedient heart and trust, or faith *(yaʾămînû),* in God.

Initially in Exodus 19 all appears to be going well, until suddenly and unexpectedly the people refuse to go up the mountain to meet God when he appears there. God had assured them that when they heard the blast of the horn, they could safely ascend the mountain, but instead, the people remained in the camp, terrified at the prospect of a face-to-face meeting with this awesome God (Ex 19:16). In response to their refusal to go up the mountain, Moses led those remaining in the camp to the foot of the mountain (Ex 19:17), and then he alone went back up the mountain to speak with God. God's answer to Moses came from the flames of fire that he encountered upon the mountain. From the foot of the mountain, the people watched and listened to the terrifying display of God's power and glory on the mountain.

In the midst of the exhibition of God's power on Sinai the people at the foot of the mountain could see and hear as Moses spoke and God "answered him aloud" (Ex 19:19). The assumption of the narrative is that Moses spoke with God on the mountain, and God "answered him" from the summit (Ex 19:19). All the people with Moses at the foot of the mountain heard God speak. As the text makes sufficiently clear, the reader is not told what Moses and God were speaking about. If the narrative that ends at Exodus 19:19 had been placed immediately before the Decalogue in Exodus 20:1-17, we might conjecture that their conversation was about the Decalogue.

The Decalogue does not follow Exodus 19:19 in the present order of the text. A short narrative (Ex 19:20-25) is positioned between Moses' "conversation" with God (Ex 19:19) and the Decalogue (Ex 20:1-17). The author appears to want the reader to see Exodus 19:20-25 as a continuation of the conversation between Moses and God in Exodus 19:19, as well as a prelude to Moses' speaking the Ten Commandments at the foot of the mountain in Exodus 20:1-17. The shape of these narratives suggests that the Ten Commandments were spoken twice, once by God to Moses on the mountain (Ex 19:19?), and a second time by Moses, several verses later, at the foot of the mountain (Ex 20:1-17).

The position of the narrative (Ex 19:20-25) that follows Exodus 19:19 may provide a clue to the content and sequence of events in these two chapters. Since Exodus 19:20-25 immediately follows the conversation between Moses and God (Ex 19:19), it is reasonable to conclude that the author wants us to identify the content of that conversation with what was said in Exodus 19:20-25. By simply noting the details of that narrative, we are expected to surmise that it was about the need to establish a clear distance between God's presence on the mountain and the people and the priests who represent them. In those few verses one breathes the air of the priesthood for the first time in these two chapters.

What is most striking about the narrative in 19:20-24 is that, even granting that the Decalogue had been given to Moses on the mountain, there is in this narrative no mention of it. There is only the mention of the need for separation from God at Sinai and the priesthood. Since the narrative in Exodus 20:20-25 focuses on the physical separation of the people from God, the purpose of this narrative may be to demonstrate the necessity of the priesthood and the tabernacle in light of that separation. The fundamental failures recorded in Exodus 19:19 and Exodus 20:18-21 thus lead to and give an occasion for the need of a priesthood and a temple (Ex 19:20-25). These short narratives call for a priesthood and temple.

Following the intervening narrative (Ex 19:20-24), and having spoken with God in that narrative about the necessity of separation, the priesthood and holiness, Moses now descends the mountain and proclaims to all who hear his voice the Decalogue (Ex 24:3), the Covenant Code (Ex 24:3) and the instructions for the tabernacle (Ex 25:1–31:18). For the most part, these commands were understood by the author as stipulations to the Sinai covenant (Ex 19:25).

Much has transpired in these few verses. The people have heard God's voice on the mountain and have fled in fear. God has responded by sealing off Israel's access to Sinai. Although it may have made for a smoother reading of these events to see the Ten Commandments recounted just after the account of God's conversation with Moses in Exodus 19:19 and the people's hearing his voice, the text does not now allow for that reading, and there are good reasons to believe that the author had important reasons for this view of the events at Sinai. In effect, the shape of the present narratives serves to delay the reading of the Decalogue until, at least, after Exodus 19:20-25. If the conversation between Moses and God on Mount Sinai (Ex 19:19) also included the Decalogue, as seems to be the case based on our look at some of the details of these narratives, then it was God who first spoke the Ten Commandments to the people (Ex 19:19) and Moses who repeated them at the foot of the mountain (Ex 20:1-17). But if God originally spoke these words to the people standing at the foot of the mountain, why did Moses need to repeat them when he came down from the mountain? The answer comes from Exodus 20:18-23. As I have suggested, the purpose of that narrative is to give the readers a second look at the people huddled in fear as they watched the awesome display of God's presence on the mountain. By arranging and attaching these small but semantically dense narratives alongside the central Sinai narrative, the author has given an added opportunity to hear in their own words the fear of the people cowed trembling in the camp (Ex 19:16).

> Now when all the people witnessed the thunder and lightning and the sound of the trumpet and the mountain smoking, they were afraid and trembled; and they stood afar off and said to Moses, "You speak to us, and we will hear; but let not God speak to us, lest we die." (Ex 20:18-19)

It is clear from reading it that Exodus 20:18-21 is a more reflective version of the same incident recorded in Exodus 19:16. As such, it gives the reader considerably more details of the catastrophic nature of the people's failure to draw near to God. It also gives the narrative an inside look at the people's thoughts. Its similarity of viewpoint raises the larger question of the relationship of Exodus 19 to Exodus 20. It is frequently argued that the narrative about Israel's retreat from the mountain in Exodus 20:18-21 should have followed Exodus 19:25 rather than the Decalogue (Ex 20:1-17), as it is presently in the text.[64] The Decalogue as it now occurs in the larger narrative begins with the narration of a divine discourse ("And God said all the words, saying . . ." [Ex 20:1]) rather than a word directly from Moses. Anything following Exodus 19:25 ("And Moses said to them . . .") should have been cast as a spoken word, not a narrative. Critical scholarship argues that the narrative in its present state is a rearrangement of an earlier narrative. The Decalogue now comes before Exodus 20:18-21 and not after it, as might have been expected, given the fact of its being a back-reference to Exodus 19:16-19. In giving the Exodus narrative that sequence of events, the passage now conforms to the sequence of narrative in Deuteronomy (cf. Deut 5:5-6). Hence, it is argued that this new arrangement of the narratives reflects some editorializing within the chapter. If so, its purpose appears to have been to include the Covenant Code along with the Decalogue as part of the "word" that God spoke to Israel in the Sinai covenant. Originally, the Decalogue was the only "word" God spoke at Sinai. But in its present shape, God's "word" at Sinai includes the Covenant Code. Hence, Exodus 24:3a, "and all the judgments" *(wĕʾēt kol̇hammišpāṭîm),* is taken as a harmonistic gloss.

Although there are little grounds for evaluating such a proposal, the basic structural observation on which it rests is sound. As the narrative now stands, the Decalogue (Ex 20:1-17) is presented not as the word that God spoke to the people, but rather as the word that Moses spoke in Exodus 19:25 (cf. Ex 19:19). To be sure, Moses' words, spoken to the people in Exodus 19:25, recounted what God had spoken to him earlier on the mountain (Ex 19:19). However, these words are presented in the narratives as first given to Moses by God (Ex 19:19) and then given to the people by Moses (Ex 19:25–20:17). In other words, the narratives show a growing distance between God and the people, one that was not intended at the outset of the Sinai narrative (Ex 19:12-15) but that follows on some of the events recounted in these narratives themselves.

---

[64]See Eissfeldt, *Hexateuch-Synopse*, pp. 145-49.

The important role of Exodus 20:18-21 within the larger narrative merits closer scrutiny. There are marked similarities, and differences, between the two narratives on either side of the Decalogue (Ex 19:16-24; 20:18-21). Both narratives explain why Moses went up to the mountain alone (Ex 19:16b; 20:19). According to Exodus 19:21, the Lord instructed Moses to keep the people away from the mountain "lest they break through to see the LORD and many of them fall (dead)." In Exodus 20:18-19, however, the people flee "a great distance" from the presence of the Lord on the mountain, telling Moses, "You speak to us, and we will hearken, so that the Lord not speak to us, lest we die." In addition, according to Exodus 19:19, the Lord spoke only to Moses, whereas in Exodus 20:19 the narrative infers that God spoke with all the people as well as Moses.

Without raising the question of whether such variations can be related to hypothetical literary documents, we turn directly to the question of the role these variations play in the composition of this segment of the Pentateuch. Here we must ask, "How do the similarities and differences in the two narratives advance the author's purpose?"

It can be argued that in the present shape of the Pentateuch, the Decalogue (Ex 20:1-17) is intended to be read as the content of what Moses spoke to the people upon his return from the mountain in Exodus 19:25. By the time Moses spoke those words—the Decalogue—to the people (Ex 19:25–20:17), the narrative has already made it clear that he had received the Covenant Code along with the Decalogue. This is because God's further communication of his laws to Moses in Exodus 20:22–24:2 is cast as a back-reference to Exodus 19:20b. It thus makes sense that when Moses speaks the Decalogue (Ex 20:1-17) to the people in Exodus 19:25, it is introduced as "and God said" (Ex 20:1). Moses tells the people what God had said to him in Exodus 20:23–24:2. The clause structure *(wayyiqtol)* of Exodus 20:1 suggests the sense of narration.[65]

As we have noted, two further syntactical features link Exodus 20:18 to its surrounding context. In returning to the incident in Exodus 19:16-19, the second narrative (Ex 20:22–24:2) fills in important "gaps" in the reader's understanding of the first. Whereas Exodus 19:16-19 looks at the people's fear from a divine perspective, Exodus 20:18-21 views it from the

[65]See Wolfgang Schneider, *Grammatik des biblischen Hebräisch: Ein Lehrbuch* (Munich: Claudius, 2001), pp. 177-97.

viewpoint of the people themselves.[66]

The syntax of Exodus 20:22 and Exodus 24:1 also suggests that the events at Sinai, which began in Exodus 19, continue in Exodus 24:1, on the other side of God's giving the Covenant Code. The narrative link is established syntactically in Exodus 24:1 by means of a "chiastic coordination" with Exodus 20:22.[67] Thus, in Exodus 24 we find Moses still on the mountain receiving God's "word." In Exodus 24:3, when God had finished speaking, Moses went down the mountain to bring God's words to the people. The expression "all the words of the Lord and all of the judgments" in this section shows an intentional linking of the Decalogue and the Covenant Code to the final ceremony of Exodus 24:3-8. The mention of Moses, Aaron and the priests in Exodus 24:1 anticipates the role of Moses, Aaron and priest in Exodus 24:9 and is a carryover from Exodus 20:21, where the people's "fear" necessitated a mediator and priesthood.

We learn from these narrative connections that there was a growing need for a mediator and a priesthood in the Sinai covenant. Because of their fear of God's presence, the people stand "afar off" (Ex 19:16-24; 20:21; 24:2). It is not hard to see that a narrative platform is being constructed plank by plank within these texts. What lies ahead in the logic of this narrative is a new view of the covenant relationship between God and his people. It has moved from a relationship based on faith and simple obedience to one centered in the requirements of the tabernacle (Ex 25–31). The role of Moses has shifted from that of a prophet of God to a priest at the tabernacle. The people who are "afar off" must be brought near to God by a priesthood, which was to play a role similar to Moses and Aaron. This is the purpose of the instructions for the tabernacle that follow these narratives in Exodus 25–31.

***The place of the tabernacle instructions (Ex 25–31).*** We can now turn briefly to the question of why the instructions for the tabernacle were recorded before the account of the sin of the golden calf. If it was the golden

---

[66]The position taken here, though arrived at independently, is in some respects similar to the view of Chirichigno, that the two passages reflect two different perspectives on the covenant: Exodus 19:16-25 represents the Lord's perspective, and Exodus 20:18-21 represents the perspective of the people. Also for Chirichigno, Exodus 20:18-21 "elaborates in detail the fear of the people" ("The Narrative Structure of Exod 19–24," p. 479). I also agree with Chirichigno that Exodus 20:18-21 "acts as a causal link between the fear of the people and their sinful acts below the mountain in Exod 32" (ibid.).

[67]*Wayyiqtol* (20:22) is continued by x + *qatal*. See Francis Andersen, *The Sentence in Biblical Hebrew* (JLSP 31; The Hague: Mouton, 1974), pp. 122-26.

calf that led to the priestly laws, why does the tabernacle precede the golden calf? Rashi maintained that the sequential arrangement in the Pentateuch does not reflect the chronological order of the events. In actual fact, says Rashi, "the incident of the golden calf happened much earlier than the instructions for the building of the Tabernacle."[68] For Rashi, the priestly laws, including those for the tabernacle, came after the sin of the golden calf and subsequent to the Day of Atonement (Lev 16).

The narrative strategy of Exodus 19–24, as outlined above, suggests another reason for the position of the tabernacle instructions in the present narrative. We have seen in the depiction of the Sinai covenant that an emphasis was placed on the need for a mediator and for an office of priesthood. The people, in their fear of God, stood "afar off." Just as they could no longer go up into the mountain to meet with God (Ex 19:21-23), they also could not go into the tabernacle to meet with him. Thus, according to the logic of the narrative, it was Israel's fear that lay behind their need for a safe approach to God. It was for that reason that the tabernacle was given to Israel. The golden calf was an important part of God's motive for giving Israel the tabernacle, but that was not the only reason. There were multiple "transgressions" of the people recorded in these texts. There were stages of transgressions that led up to the golden calf and also followed it.

***The covenant in Deuteronomy 29:1-29 (28:69–29:28 MT).*** There has been considerable discussion of the exact nature of the covenant alluded to in Deuteronomy 29–30. Some have questioned whether there is a covenant form at all in these chapters. Is it a covenant, as actually stated in Deuteronomy 29:1, or is it a collection of sermons based on a presumed covenant found elsewhere in Deuteronomy? The chief problem with seeing Deuteronomy 29 as a covenant is that it is missing a list of stipulations or covenant laws. Such stipulations were an essential part of ancient covenants (see chart below). The lack of stipulations in Deuteronomy 29 has led some to suppose that Deuteronomy 29:1 is not a covenant, but an introduction to one or more of the many references to the Sinai covenant elsewhere in Deuteronomy.

The chart shows that whatever may be said about the "covenant" form of Deuteronomy 29–30, it clearly is lacking a stipulations section. Loren Fisher states, "Chapters 29–30 clearly contain elements that are found in the treaty

---

[68]Chaim Dov Shual, ed., *Rashi's Commentary on the Torah* [Hebrew] (Jerusalem: Mosad Harav Kook, 1988), p. 303.

**Table 4.4**

| **Ancient Treaty** | **Deuteronomy 29–30** |
|---|---|
| 1. Title: states name/titles of the king | 1. Mise en scène (Deut 29:1) |
| 2. History: recounting of past events leading up to the present | 2. Historical prologue (Deut 29:1b-8) |
| 3. Stipulations: laws, rules, instructions constituting the body of the treaty | 3. — |
| 4. Tablet clause: provides for the deposit of the treaty tablet | 4. — |
| 5. Witnesses to the treaty | 5. Witnesses (Deut 30:19a) |
| 6. Curses and blessings | 6. Curse (Deut 29:19-27); blessing (Deut 30:1-10) |

schema, as has been indicated. However, the one essential element of a treaty, the stipulations, are missing."[69] This poses a unique problem for the covenant *(bĕrît)* in Deuteronomy 29–30. How do we identify the right covenant in this section, and how do we explain its missing stipulations?

Whatever one might say about the absence of stipulations in Deuteronomy 29, two things are certain from Deuteronomy 29:1. First, it is a covenant *(bĕrît)*, and second it is not the Sinai covenant. The covenant identified by Deuteronomy 29:1 cannot be the Sinai (Horeb) covenant, since it is a "covenant that God commanded Moses to make *[likrōt]* with Israel in Moab besides *[millĕbad]* the covenant *[habbĕrît]* which [God] had made with [Israel] at Horeb" (Deut 29:1 [28:69 MT]). If it is a covenant that is distinguished from the Sinai covenant, it must therefore not refer to any covenant that precedes Deuteronomy 29, since all such references to a covenant prior to Deuteronomy 29 are clearly identified in the narrative with the Sinai (Horeb) covenant. No one disputes that. Thus, the point of the explanatory note in Deuteronomy 29:1 must be to identify Deuteronomy 29–30 as a covenant and to distinguish it from the Sinai covenant. Its intention must also be to identify Deuteronomy 29 as a covenant without "stipulations." Can it be a "covenant" if there are no stipulations? Before looking at the details of Deuteronomy 29, we must be clear about what its introduction (Deut 29:1) understands it to be.

*Introduction to the covenant (Deut 29:1 [28:69 MT]).* As noted above, the passage begins with the identification of a "covenant" *(bĕrît)* that is con-

[69]Loren R. Fisher, ed., *Ras Shamra Parallels: The Texts from Ugarit and the Hebrew Bible* (AnOr 50; Rome: Pontificium Institutum Biblicum, 1975), 2:170.

trasted with the Sinai covenant. The introductory nature of this verse suggests that its focus is on the further details of Deuteronomy, though that has often been disputed.

> These *[ʾēlleh]* are the words of the covenant *[habbĕrît]* which the LORD commanded Moses to make with the children of Israel in the land of Moab, besides *[millĕbad]* the covenant which he made with them in Horeb. (Deut 29:1 [28:69 MT])

On the analogy of some ancient treaties from Ugarit, Fisher suggests that the word "covenant" in Deuteronomy 29:1 is a title for a covenant found "somewhere" in Deuteronomy, but not in Deuteronomy 29.[70] Ancient covenants, he argues, always contain "stipulations"—that is, rules and regulations that govern the parties of the covenant. As we have also noted, such elements are not found in Deuteronomy 29. Fisher concludes from this that when Moses states that "these are the words of the covenant," he cannot be referring to the "words" in Deuteronomy 29, because there are no "words," in the technical sense of "stipulations," in that chapter.

In most English Bibles this verse is numbered as Deuteronomy 29:1. By beginning the chapter with this verse, the English versions lead us to identify the "covenant" in this verse with the covenant outlined in Deuteronony 29:2-29. Moving in a different direction is the versification of the HB. That reading interprets this verse, numbered as Deuteronomy 28:69, as a summary conclusion to Deuteronomy 28. Thus, as the Hebrew text was understood, the reference to "these *[ʾēlleh]* words of the covenant" is to the Sinai (Horeb) covenant described in the previous sections of Deuteronomy (1:6-43; 4:44–28:68).

There is one insurmountable obstacle to understanding "the words" in Deuteronomy 28:69 [29:1 ET] to refer to the covenant at Sinai (or Horeb). According to this verse, this covenant is explicitly contrasted with the covenant that "God made with them at Horeb (Sinai)." This verse therefore speaks undeniably of another covenant that will be "made" *(likrōt)* with Israel "besides" *(millĕbad)* the one God made with them at Horeb (Sinai).

The seemingly insurmountable difficulty of identifying the covenant in Deuteronomy 28:69 [29:1 ET] with the Sinai covenant has not kept some from attempting to do so. Calvin held the view that this covenant mentioned

---

[70]Ibid., p. 165.

in this verse was not another covenant, but one and the same with the Sinai covenant, identical to it in all points "except" *(millĕbad)* for additional, and necessary, explanations in the final version of Deuteronomy. These additions were necessary, Calvin argued, because the human weaknesses of the people necessitated further explanations of the laws in Deuteronomy.[71] Similarly, S. R. Driver understood the reference to a "covenant" at Moab to be a reference to the whole of the book of Deuteronomy (Deut 5–26), and thus "the two covenants are accordingly distinguished" by the word "except" *(millĕbad),* which refers not to a different covenant, but to the "many entirely new regulations" appended to the end of the book.[72]

Neither of these two explanations has much exegetical support to commend it. As is well known, Calvin was theologically precommitted to a view of the biblical covenants in which there were many covenant administrations but always of one and the same covenant.[73]

Driver, though granting the sense given the verse by the word "besides" *(millĕbad),* insists that this reference to a "covenant" *(bĕrît)* in Deuteronomy 29:1 (28:69 MT) cannot be related to the events that follow in Deuteronomy 29–30, because those events contain no specific statement respecting what the "words" mentioned in that verse comprise.[74] Carl Steuernagel, however, points out that these "words" are not laws as such, but comprise, rather, the spoken words of the covenant ceremony.[75] Steuernagel's observations are generally discounted by modern scholars in view of the lack of examples of such ceremonies in ancient literature. Hence, many assume that since there are no stipulations in Deuteronomy 29–30, Deuteronomy 29:1 (28:69 MT) cannot be a superscription for a covenant in those chapters.[76]

---

[71]Calvin believed that after the forty years in the wilderness Moses added a second explanation of the Decalogue because "it was necessary that the Decalogue should be more fully explained, lest its brevity should render it obscure to an ignorant and slow-hearted people" (*Four Last Books of Moses*, p. 416).

[72]S. R. Driver, *A Critical and Exegetical Commentary on Deuteronomy* [ICC; Edinburgh: T & T Clark, 1895], p. 319.

[73]Calvin (*Institutes* 2.10.2) maintained, "The covenant made with all the patriarchs is so much like ours in substance and reality that the two are actually one and the same. Yet they differ in the mode of dispensation" (*Institutes of the Christian Religion,* ed. John T. McNeill, trans. Ford Lewis Battles [LCC 20; Phildelphia: Westminster Press, 1960], 1:429).

[74]Driver, *Deuteronomy*, p. 319.

[75]"Nicht das Gesetz, sondern die beim Abschluss der ברית gesprochenen Worte, die Bundesschluss-Predigt" (Carl Steuernagel, *Übersetzung und Erklärung der Bücher Deuteronomium und Josua* [HKAT 1/3; Göttingen: Vandenhoeck & Ruprecht, 1900], p. 105).

[76]"Since chapters 29–30 describe covenant-making ceremonies, and not the 'words' of the covenant,

These various attempts to deal with the biblical narratives in light of the historical realities of ancient treaty forms put far too little emphasis on the fact that Deuteronomy 28:69 (29:1 ET) actually uses the word "covenant" *(bĕrît)* and that it contrasts ("besides" *[millĕbad]*) this covenant with the Sinai (Horeb) covenant. Whether or not this covenant fits the ancient pattern, there is little doubt it is considered a covenant by the author of the Pentateuch, and it is a covenant without stipulations. Moreover, since this covenant is contrasted with the covenant at Sinai, it cannot at the same time be equated with the Sinai covenant spoken of elsewhere in Deuteronomy 1:5–28:68. This leads to the conclusion that Deuteronomy 28:69 (29:1 ET) would have us believe that the author of the Pentateuch meant the reader to understand Deuteronomy 29–30 as a covenant of a different kind than Sinai. That being the case, the lack of stipulations in the Deuteronomy 28:69 (29:1 ET) covenant may be the very feature that in the author's strategy contrasts the two covenants. This may be especially so, given the fact that the Sinai covenant is noted for its numerous stipulations (613 laws). It may well be that the lack of stipulations is the very feature that the author believed distinguished ("besides" *[millĕbad]*) it from the Sinai covenant.

In light of the contrast in covenants in Deuteronomy 28:69 (29:1 ET), it is instructive to recall the other covenant in the Pentateuch that has no stipulations or laws. I am referring to the covenant introduced in Exodus 19:5: "And now, if you obey me and keep my covenant. . . ." We have already noted the curious fact that this initial covenant in Exodus does not specifically list the stipulations or laws that must be obeyed. In that regard, it is similar to, if not identical with, the covenant in Deuteronomy 29.

These two "covenants" (Ex 19:1-9; Deut 29), neither of which has a list of stipulations in their covenant formula, serve as a frame around the Sinai covenant, which itself has an abundance of stipulations and laws. Both of these covenants make reference to "the words" (Ex 19:7; Deut 28:69 [29:1 ET]) of the covenant, but in neither case is there a description or elaboration of what those "words" are.

What is especially interesting about these types of covenants in Exodus 19:1-9 and Deuteronomy 29 is that their lack of actual stipulations and laws is later noted by prophets such as Jeremiah and Ezekiel. Jeremiah sees this

28:69 cannot be a title for 29–30; hence it must refer to what precedes it" (Fisher, *Ras Shamra Parallels*, p. 165).

lack of stipulations as a mark of a different kind of covenant from that which God originally set his sights on at Sinai. This was a type of covenant much like the one God had made with Abraham. It was a covenant for which there were no stipulations or laws intended. In Jeremiah 7 the prophet outlines God's original covenant intentions at Sinai in a way that recalls the covenant in Exodus 19:1-9. It is a covenant without stipulations or laws.

> For in the day that I brought them out of the land of Egypt, I did not speak to your fathers or command them concerning burnt offerings and sacrifices. But this command I gave them, "Obey my voice, and I will be your God, and you shall be my people; and walk in all the way that I command you, that it may be well with you." (Jer 7:22-23)

This passage is clear in showing that later prophetic authors were aware of a lack of stipulations in the initial covenant established at Sinai (Ex 19:5-9), and that they interpreted such an omission in terms of the type of covenant God first offered to Israel at Sinai. It was a covenant like that given to Abraham. It was a covenant with no explicit stipulations. The prophets also saw that covenant to be short-lived. Almost immediately, when Israel failed to trust God and not "obey him," God added stipulations (laws) to this covenant, and it became a different kind of covenant, one like that which we now see at Sinai, a covenant with hundreds of minute stipulations.

We have seen, as noted above, that in Jeremiah 7:22-23 the prophet saw the absence of stipulations as intentional on God's part and something quickly lost at Sinai. Shortly after Jeremiah's comments on the shift in the type of covenant in Exodus 19, he offers another look at this covenant, this time specifying the cause for the shift in covenant type. Why was the offer of a covenant like that with Abraham so quickly changed into an offer of the Sinai covenant with Moses? Jeremiah 11:7-8 clarifies the prophet's earlier statements in Jeremiah 7:22-23 and makes additional comments on the shift in covenant type after Exodus 19:1-9. There are several important statements in this passage in Jeremiah, and we must progress carefully with an eye to detail.

The first observation, to which we will return below, is that the "historical reminiscence"[77] in Jeremiah 11:7-8 is not in the LXX version. This crucial "omission" deserves special attention because it may not be an "omission" of the LXX

[77]William McKane, *A Critical and Exegetical Commentary on Jeremiah* (ICC; Edinburgh: T & T Clark, 1986), 1:238.

as such, but rather a scribal "addition" in the MT. In either case, we will have to explain why they were "omitted" or "added" to Jeremiah's message.

The second observation about these verses is the meaning of the verb וָאָבִיא (*wāʾābîʾ*, "I have brought" [NJPS]) in Jeremiah 11:8. Ernst Rosenmüller has correctly noted that this verb, as vocalized by the MT, is a narrative tense *(wayyiqtol)* that looks back to the earlier events at Mount Sinai: *wāʾābîʾ ʿălêhem ʾet-kol-dibrê habbĕrît-hazzōʾt* ("And I brought upon them all the words of this covenant").[78]

The NRSV follows Rosenmüller in rendering this verb as past:[79] "So I brought upon them all the words of this covenant, which I commanded them to do, but they did not."[80] Despite the clear indication of a past reference in Jeremiah 11:8, the meaning and tense of the verb וָאָבִיא *(wāʾābîʾ)* is taken by some translations as a future, something that would require a change in the vowel pointing of the verb (*weyiqtol*: וְאָבִיא), *wĕʾābîʾ*—for example, "Therefore I will bring upon them all the words of this covenant, which I commanded them to do, but which they have not done" (NKJV).

A third observation involves the sense and reference of the phrase "all the words of the covenant" *(ʾet-kol-dibrê habbĕrît-hazzōʾt)* in Jeremiah 11:8. To what do these "words" refer? Some understand them to be the stipulations of the Sinai covenant, its laws. Others take them to be the curses and judgments that came through disobedience to the covenant laws and stipulations. Bernhard Duhm believed that the additional "words" of the covenant were the punishments listed at the close of Deuteronomy.[81]

Judging from the meaning of the Hebrew terms and the immediate context, I think it more likely that the "words" in Jeremiah 11:8 are the "words" in Jeremiah 11:6. They were the "words" that Israel was to "obey" (שׁמע, *šmʿ*), the

---

[78]Ernst F. C. Rosenmüller, *Scholia in Vetus Testamentum*, part 8 (Leipzig: Barth, 1826), 1:336.

[79]The *wayyiqtol* "tense" is a narrative, and as often is the case, it is used to recount a past event. The verbal form itself is not "past tense," though the English "past tense" is the most common way it is translated. See Schneider, *Grammatik des biblischen Hebräisch*, p. 179.

[80]Other English versions following Rosenmüller are ASV: "Therefore I brought upon them all the words of this covenant, which I commanded them to do, but they did them not"; RSV: "Therefore I brought upon them all the words of this covenant, which I commanded them to do, but they did not"; NIV: "So I brought on them all the curses of the covenant I had commanded them to follow but that they did not keep." Compare NJPS: "So I have brought upon them all the terms of this covenant, because they did not do what I commanded them to do."

[81]"Die Worte des Bundes, die Jahwe über die ungehorsamen Väter gebracht hat, sind die Drohungen, die das Deuteron. besonders in 27 28-30 über die Nichtbefolgung des Gestzes ausspricht" (Bernhard Duhm, *Das Buch Jeremia* [HKAT 11; Tübingen: Mohr Siebeck, 1901], p. 109).

stipulations or laws of the covenant. The covenant that Jeremiah had in mind was the Sinai covenant with its laws and stipulations that must be obeyed.

In Jeremiah 11:8 the prophet looks back to Sinai and recounts how the laws or stipulations of Jeremish 11:6 came to be part of the Sinai covenant. Israel at Sinai did not obey God. They went their own way, so God brought upon them the "words of the covenant." He added laws and stipulations to the original covenant that had to be obeyed. God brought upon Israel "words" that they were to obey *(laʿăśôt)*, but they did not obey them *(wĕlōʾ ʿāśû)* (Jer 11:8), and so God gave them the "words" of Jeremiah 11:8 which were the laws or stipulations they must now obey in Jeremiah 11:6.

According to some commentators the, "words" in Jeremiah 11:8 are the punishments and judgments Israel must endure if they do not obey the covenant in Jeremiah 11:6. Such a reading of these verses proves to be contradictory. According to verse Jeremiah 11:6, Israel must obey "the words of the covenant," but the "words of the covenant" were subsequently added as punishment in Jeremiah 11:8 because of Israel's disobedience.

Most English translations follow Rashi[82] on this verse, taking the phrase "the words of the covenant" to mean two things. In Jeremiah 11:6 the "words" are the stipulations of the covenant that must be obeyed, but in Jeremiah 11:8 they are "the threats and curses of the covenant" that were the result of Israel's disobedience. Within two verses the phrase "words of the covenant" is given two meanings. The NIV renders Jeremiah 11:8b as "So I brought on them all the curses of the covenant I had commanded them to follow" The NIV's rendering of the last clause points to the difficulty of this translation. How could God have commanded them to follow "all the curses of the covenant"? How could God bring curses and punishment on Israel because "they did not do *[wĕlōʾ ʿāśû]* the curses and punishments of the covenant"? How can anyone "do" curses? One can only be called upon to "do stipulations and laws," not to "do curses."

Rosenmüller, who is responsible for introducing Rashi's interpretation of Jeremiah 11:8 into the English versions, gives the following explanation of this interpretation of Jeremiah 11:7-8.

> (God says) I brought about all those judgments which I had threatened those who violated the covenant would experience. The Targum explained this fairly

---

[82] האלות האמורות בברית על הדברים אשׁר צויתי לעשׂות ולא עשׂו.

well: I sent punishment upon them because they did not accept the words of the covenant. Rashi said, 'I brought curses upon them which were proclaimed in the covenant by means of the words which I imposed upon them to observe, and which they by no means obeyed.'—for וָאָבִיא "I brought" I wish to read as וְאָבִיא, a future tense, "I will bring," "I will fulfill the threat" which the events horribly demonstrated. VENEMA believed the same, though not seeing that this interpretation was impossible without a change of vowels. But recognizing that, I see verses 9, 10, and 11 as suiting this interpretation better.[83]

Rosenmüller's interpretation, which, as he acknowledges, follows Rashi and the Targumim, clearly is motivated by his failure to accept the notion of the secondary nature of the laws of the Sinai covenant. The Hebrew text, however, states as a matter of fact that when Israel came out of Egypt, God called upon them to "obey him" (*šimʿû bĕqôlî* [Jer 11:7]), which is what Exodus 19:4 states, but Israel refused to obey (*wĕlōʾ šāmʿû* [Jer 11:8]), and so God "brought *[wāʾābîʾ]* upon them" the "words of the covenant" that he commanded them to do and that they did not obey (Jer 11:8). These "words of the covenant" must be the "laws and stipulations" that Jeremiah is now calling on them to obey and to do: "Obey *[šimʿû]* the words of this covenant *[ʾet-dibrê habbĕrît hazzōʾt]* and do them *[waʿăśîtem ʾōtām]*" (Jer 11:6). Jeremiah 11:6-8 follows the compositional strategy of Exodus 19–24 in seeing the addition of laws to the Sinai covenant as a result of Israel's disobedience.

What the omission of Jeremiah 11:7-8 in the Hebrew *Vorlage*[84] to the LXX means for the interpretation of these verses and their role within Jeremiah and the Pentateuch must now be explored. Is this an omission by the LXX (i.e., its Hebrew *Vorlage*),[85] or have these verses been added by the MT? The fact

---

[83]"וָאָבִיא עֲלֵיהֶם אֶת כָּל דִּבְרֵי הַבְּרִית הַזֹּאת *Et duxi contra eos omnia verba huijus foederis*, i.e. effeci, ut omnia illa mala, quae iis, qui foedus cum iis initum violaverint, minatus sum, in eos irruerent. Chaldaeus haud male sic exposuit: *immisi eis poenam propterea quod non susceperunt verba foederis*. JARCHI: 'Induxi in eos exsecrationes, quae pronuntiatae sunt in foedere propterea, quae iis observanda injunxi, quae vero non observarunt.'—Pro וָאָבִיא venire feci, mallem legere וְאָבִיא, in Futuro, *venere faciam*, implebo minas, diris constabit eventus. Idem sensit VENEMA, non tamen videns, Punctis mutatis tantum hance interpretationem posse locum habere. Sed recogitans, video Versum 9. 10. 11. Aptiorem esse consuetae interpretationi" (Rosenmüller, *Scholia in Vetus Testamentum*, p. 336).

[84]The term *Vorlage* refers to the Hebrew text of the translator of the LXX.

[85]"The explanation which is nearest to hand is, perhaps, the best one, namely, that the translator had a Hebrew text in which vv. 7-8 (except for ולא עשו) were not represented (so Streane, Duhm)" (McKane, *Jeremiah*, p. 238). "On the other hand, it may be argued that LXX does attest an earlier stage of the text, and that verses 7-8 are secondary from 7.22-24 and Deuteronomic language elsewhere (note the parallels between chapters 7 and 11, expecially 7.22-24 and 11.1-5)."

## *EXCURSUS*

## THE INTERPRETATION OF JEREMIAH 11:6-8

Rosenmüller's interpretation has serious difficulties. The chief difficulty among them is the meaning that he assigns to the phrase "words of the covenant" in Jeremiah 11:8. First, there is universal agreement that this same expression, "words of the covenant," in Jeremiah 11:6 refers to the stipulations of the Sinai covenant. Jeremiah calls out, saying, "Hear the words of this covenant and do them" (Jer 11:6). The same expression is used two verses later in Jeremiah 11:8. There, it is explained that when Israel at Sinai did not obey God, he brought upon them the "words of the covenant." The same expression just two verses apart should have the same meaning unless there are compelling reasons to change their meaning. Second, the "words of the covenant" in Jeremiah 11:8 cannot be "the penalties and curses" of the Sinai covenant, because they are given Israel as something they must do, stipulations, not as something that will happen to them, curses. Simply put, in Jeremiah 11:6 the "words of the covenant" are given Israel to "do" *(šimʿû ʾet-dibrê habbĕrît hazzōʾt waʿăśîtem ʾôtām).* Also, in Jeremiah 11:8 these "words of the covenant" are something that God commanded them "to do but they did not do them" *(ʾet-kol-dibrê habbĕrît-hazzōʾt ʾăšer-ṣiwwîtî laʿăśôt wĕlōʾ ʿāśû).*

Some English translations render these words differently with little attempt at exegetical justification.[a] This raises the question of what issues are at stake. Why is the same phrase rendered so differently? The answer lies in the overall sense of the passage. If the phrase "words of the covenant" is to be understood as the stipulations and laws of the covenant, then Jeremiah 11:8 would state that the stipulations of the Sinai covenant—that is, the "words of the covenant"—were something later added to the covenant after Israel's disobedience:

> And they did not obey and did not incline their ear, and they walked, each one of them, in the stubbornness of their heart, and I brought upon

[a]Compare, in Jeremiah 11:6, "words" of the covenant (KJV, NKJV, RSV, NRSV) and "terms" of the covenant (NIV, NJPS).

> them the words [stipulations] of this covenant which I commanded them to do. (Jer 11:8)

The underlying issue is the sense of God's assigning law to the Sinai covenant only after and because of Israel's disobedience. The text as it now reads is sufficiently clear that initially at Sinai Israel was called upon to "obey" God, but with no laws specified, as in Exodus 19:5: "If you obey me and keep my covenant, you will be a prized possession" But, when the people disobeyed God by their fear and unbelief, God brought upon them not punishments to obey, but "the words of the covenant"—that is, the stipulations of the Sinai covenant that they must obey. Jeremiah is reading the Pentateuch along the lines of the compositional strategy I have pointed to in the Sinai narratives. The law was added to the covenant because of Israel's transgressions.

Those English translations that follow Rosenmüller and Rashi render the term "words" *(dibrê)* as "curses" and give a sense to the verse that is focused more on the idea of God's sending punishment as the result of Israel's disobedience rather than his giving them laws. In that reading of these verses, God does not say, "I brought laws upon them for their disobedience," but, "I brought curses upon them." That was clearly Rashi's intention in explaining "words" as "curses" in this verse. The notion that God brought "the curses of the covenant" upon his disobedient people is fundamentally different from the notion that God brought stipulations—that is, "words (laws) of the covenant" upon the people in response to their disobedience.

The foregoing discussion of the verse is clear enough to show that the "words" which God brought upon Israel were not the "curses," but rather the "laws" that were added to the Sinai covenant.

Jeremiah 11:8 thus further clarifies the sense of Jeremiah 7:21-28. God entered a covenant with his people at Sinai. As suggested already in Exodus 19:1-9, originally there were no stipulations or collections of laws associated with that covenant. It was cast as a continuation of the Abrahamic covenant, which also had no laws, but rather was based on the call to faith, as Exodus 19:9 *(yaʾămînû)* clearly states. Then the people disobeyed God, and God brought stipulations/laws upon them to govern their relationship within the covenant. Law was given not as a punishment, but as a way to curb Israel's disobedience and lead them in following God's will. It was a good thing for Israel and was an act of divine grace on their behalf. According to both texts, Jeremiah 7:22-23 and Jeremiah 11:7-8, God added laws to the Sinai covenant from the time he brought them out of Egypt, and he continued to do so by means of his prophets right up to Jeremiah's own day:

> For I solemnly warned your ancestors when I brought them up out of the land of Egypt, warning them persistently, even[b] to this day, saying, Obey my voice. Yet they did not obey or incline their ear, but everyone walked in the stubbornness of an evil will. So I brought upon them all the words of this covenant, which I commanded them to do, but they did not. (Jer 11:7-8)

> From the day that your ancestors came out of the land of Egypt until this day, I have persistently sent all my servants the prophets to them, day after day. (Jer 7:25)

[b]The conjunction *waw* in וְעַד (*wĕʿad*, "even to") divides God's actions between his bringing the "words of the covenant" against the people at Sinai "and even to" the prophet Jeremiah's own day. In the parallel text, Jeremiah 7:25, the use of the preposition מִן (*min*, "from") and the lack of a similar *waw* with עַד (*ʿad*, "until") shows that Jeremiah 7:25 looks primarily to the giving of the law by the prophets throughout Israel's history and not principally at Sinai. Thus, "From *[min]* the day your fathers came out of the land of Egypt until *[ʿad]* this day" shows that the verse looks to the giving of the law by the prophets (Jer 7:25) throughout Israel's history and not specifically at Sinai.

that Jeremiah 11:6 and Jeremiah 11:9 join together seamlessly if Jeremiah 11:7-8 is extracted suggests that the latter two verses were added to the MT. If so, why? Duhm and most others offer little help beyond generally recognizing these two verses as an addition to the MT.[86] Shorter readings like this are common in the LXX of Jeremiah.

*Israel in Egypt and the wilderness (Deut 29:2-8 [29:1-7 MT]).* The description of the covenant begins with a summary of God's faithful provisions for Israel and contrasts them with Israel's ongoing faithlessness:

And Moses summoned all Israel and said to them: "You have seen all that the

[86]"Warum v. 7f. in der LXX fehlt, das ist schwer zu sagen" (Duhm, *Das Buch Jeremia*, p. 109).

LORD did before your eyes in the land of Egypt, to Pharaoh and to all his servants and to all his land, the great trials which your eyes saw, the signs, and those great wonders; but to this day the LORD has not given you a mind to understand, or eyes to see, or ears to hear. I have led you forty years in the wilderness; your clothes have not worn out upon you, and your sandals have not worn off your feet; you have not eaten bread, and you have not drunk wine or strong drink; that you may know that I am the LORD your God. And when you came to this place, Sihon the king of Heshbon and Og the king of Bashan came out against us to battle, but we defeated them; we took their land, and gave it for an inheritance to the Reubenites, the Gadites, and the half-tribe of the Manassites. (Deut 29:2-8 [29:1-7 MT])

*Call for spiritual obedience (Deut 29:9 [29:8 MT]).* Deuteronomy 29:9 (29:8 MT) is a call for obedience to the new covenant announced in Deuteronomy 29:1 (28:69 MT). The point of this section is essential to understanding the nature of this covenant. Moses states that obedience to "the words of this covenant" leads to wisdom:

You shall obey the words of this covenant and do them so that you will be wise *[taśkîlû]* in all you do. (Deut 29:9 [29:8 MT])

These words are a spiritualization of the obedience called for in the Sinai covenant. As such, the passage follows the line of thought of Joshua 1:8: meditation on the Torah results in "being wise" *(taśkîl).* This text from Joshua is an important canonical seam in the Tanak. Knowing and obeying God leads to wisdom.

*Fulfillment of the Abrahamic covenant (Deut 29:10-13 [29:9-12 MT]).* The nature of the obedience called for in this covenant anticipates the notion of the circumcised heart expressed in Deuteronomy 30:6. It also raises the expectation that this covenant will bring about the fulfillment of God's oath to Abraham, the Abrahamic covenant. What was once the role of the Sinai covenant (Ex 2:24) has now been assumed by the covenant in Deuteronomy 29:

You stand this day all of you before the LORD your God; the heads of your tribes, your elders, and your officers, all the men of Israel, your little ones, your wives, and the sojourner who is in your camp, both he who hews your wood and he who draws your water, that you may enter into the sworn covenant of the LORD your God, which the LORD your God makes with you this day; that he may establish you this day as his people, and that he may be your God, as

> he promised you, and as he swore to your fathers, to Abraham, to Isaac, and to Jacob. (Deut 29:10-13 [29:9-12 MT])

*Warning to those in future exile (Deut 29:14-18 [29:13-17 MT]).* The past exile in Egypt and the future exile among the idolatrous nations call for a warning to remain faithful to the Lord:

> Nor is it with you only that I make this sworn covenant, but with him who is not here with us this day as well as with him who stands here with us this day before the LORD our God. You know how we dwelt in the land of Egypt, and how we came through the midst of the nations through which you passed; and you have seen their detestable things, their idols of wood and stone, of silver and gold, which were among them. Beware lest there be among you a man or woman or family or tribe, whose heart turns away this day from the LORD our God to go and serve the gods of those nations; lest there be among you a root bearing poisonous and bitter fruit. (Deut 29:14-18 [29:13-17 MT])

*Example of those for whom the covenant will be fulfilled (Deut 29:19-28 [29:18-27 MT]).* The universal aspects of the fulfillment of this (new) covenant are unfolded in three stages for the people of God: (1) the fulfillment includes those Israelites who will find themselves in the future wandering among the nations; (2) those Israelites in exile; (3) those who failed to keep the Sinai covenant.

Fulfillment includes those tribes of Israel who are wandering among the nations:

> One who, when he hears the words of this sworn covenant, blesses himself in his heart, saying, "I shall be safe, though I walk in the stubbornness of my heart." This would lead to the sweeping away of moist and dry alike. The LORD would not pardon him, but rather the anger of the LORD and his jealousy would smoke against that man, and the curses written in this book would settle upon him, and the LORD would blot out his name from under heaven. And the LORD would single him out from all the tribes of Israel for calamity, in accordance with all the curses of the covenant written in this book of the law. (Deut 29:19-21 [29:18-20 MT])

Fulfillment will find those Israelites in exile:

> And the generation to come, your children who rise up after you, and the foreigner who comes from a far land, would say, when they see the afflictions of that land and the sicknesses with which the LORD has made it sick—the whole land brimstone and salt, and a burnt-out waste, unsown, and growing nothing,

> where no grass can sprout, an overthrow like that of Sodom and Gomorrah, Admah and Zeboiim, which the Lord overthrew in his anger and wrath. (Deut 29:22-23 [29:21-22 MT])

Fulfillment includes even those future generations who disregard the Sinai covenant and its laws:

> Yea, all the nations would say, "Why has the Lord done thus to this land? What means the heat of this great anger?" Then men would say, "It is because they forsook the covenant of the Lord, the God of their fathers, which he made with them when he brought them out of the land of Egypt, and went and served other gods and worshiped them, gods whom they had not known and whom he had not allotted to them; therefore the anger of the Lord was kindled against this land, bringing upon it all the curses written in this book; and the Lord uprooted them from their land in anger and fury and great wrath, and cast them into another land, as at this day." (Deut 29:24-28 [29:23-27 MT])

*Waiting for further revelation (Deut 29:29 [29:28 MT]).* Moses acknowledges that much remains to be revealed about this future covenant that he has here introduced for the first time in Deuteronomy 29:1 [28:69 MT]). He calls on his readers to wait patiently and expectantly for God to reveal more about this covenant:

> The secret things belong unto the Lord our God; but those things which are revealed belong unto us and to our children for ever, that we may do all the words of this law.

In these last words, Moses shows that he is aware of the limitations of his message and of the further message of the prophets who will follow in his steps (e.g., Jer 31:31-32). Moses acknowledges that what God had revealed about this (new) covenant was to be recorded for future generations, and that much more was to be expected. It is clear in this passage that Moses reflects an awareness of future fulfillment and further revelation much like the prophet Isaiah saw the limits of his own vision and the need to wait for further revelation (Is 6; 8). Midway in his prophetic ministry, Isaiah came to the end of his vision. He must await further word from God and further messengers through whom God will reveal his plans. Aware of this limitation, he confides in his disciples: "Bind up the testimony, seal the law among my disciples. And I will wait upon the Lord, who hides his face from the house of Jacob, and I will look for him" (Is 8:16-17).

The compositional role of this last programmatic statement of Moses in Deuteronomy 29:29 (29:28 MT), and its position at the end of the book, suggest that it has in view the further words about the future in Deuteronomy 30, which is the next chapter in the book. The "secret things" hinted at in Deuteronomy 30 are yet to be revealed in the writings of Israel's prophets. Moses records what has been revealed to him about the new covenant (Deut 30:1-14) and then calls on those present to put their trust in the future fulfillment of God's word (Deut 30:15-20) as they await further revelation from the prophets (Deut 34:10?).

Although the Sinai covenant began as an extension of God's covenant with Abraham, the Pentateuch is clear that Sinai was to be replaced by another covenant and assigned a new purpose as law for a people tainted by the sin of the golden calf. To be sure, the Pentateuch was not assigned the status of being Israel's law code. That was a role to be taken over by the laws of the Sinai covenant. The Pentateuch, itself an expression of the hope for a new covenant, was set over against the Mosaic law of the Sinai covenant. This shifting role of the Sinai covenant in the theology of the Pentateuch can be seen already in the beginning stages of the Sinai covenant (Ex 19–24).[87]

When viewed from the perspective of the strategy of its composition and its treatment of the various collections of laws, such as the Decalogue, the pentateuchal narratives present themselves as an extended treatise on the nature and purpose of the Sinai covenant. The author of the Pentateuch is intent on showing that Israel's immediate fall into idolatry with the golden calf brought with it a fundamental shift in the nature of their covenant with God. At the outset of the covenant, the text portrays the nature of the covenant in much the same light as that of the religion of the patriarchs. Like Abraham, Israel was to obey God (Ex 19:5; cf. Gen 26:5), keep his covenant (Ex 19:5; cf. Gen 17:1-14) and exercise faith (Ex 19:9; cf. Gen 15:6). Though they immediately agreed to the terms of this covenant (Ex 19:8), Israel quickly proved unable to keep it (Ex 19:16-17). In fear, they pleaded with Moses to go into God's presence for them while they themselves stood "afar off" (Ex 19:18-20; 20:18-21). In response to the people's fear and disobedience, God wrote out for them the Decalogue, as well as the Covenant Code and the plans for building a tabernacle. As depicted in the Decalogue and Covenant Code,

[87]See John H. Sailhamer, "The Mosaic Law and the Theology of the Pentateuch," *WTJ* 53 (1991): 24-61.

Israel's relationship with God was based on the absolute prohibition of idolatry and the simple offering of praise and sacrifice. The covenant was still very much like that of the patriarchal period, except that now it had clearly defined stipulations ("the ten words").

The people of Israel, led by the priests of the house of Aaron, quickly fell into idolatry in the incident of the golden calf. Even while the laws were being given to Moses on Mount Sinai, Aaron the priest was making the golden calf at the base of the mountain. Hence, the covenant was broken almost before it began (Ex 32). The golden calf marks a decisive moment in the course of the narrative. God, in his grace and compassion (Ex 33), did not cast off Israel. The covenant was renewed (Ex 34), but in its renewal, additional laws were given the Sinai covenant. These are represented in the remainder of the code of priestly laws (Ex 35–Lev 16). Although these laws appeared to keep the priests in check, it became apparent in the people's later sacrifices to goat idols (Lev 17:1-9) that the formulation of even laws was needed. To that end, God gave them the Holiness Code (Lev 17–25) and again renewed the covenant (Lev 26). With Deuteronomy comes the final addition of laws to the covenant, and eventually talk of a different covenant, not like that made at Sinai (Deut 28–30).

The narrative strategy of the Pentateuch that I have outlined is similar to the view discussed earlier that began with Justin Martyr and was subsequently developed by Johann Coccejus in his treatment of the place of law in the covenant of grace. It also reflects the argument that the apostle Paul makes in Galatians 3:19 and that Jesus makes in Matthew 19:8. God added the law to the covenant as stipulations on account of the transgressions ("hardness of heart") of his people.

# Part Three

# INTERPRETING THE THEOLOGY OF THE PENTATEUCH

*Chapter 8*

# The Nature of Covenant and Blessing in the Pentateuch

SEVERAL OF THE THEMES AND IDEAS THAT I WILL DISCUSS under the heading of "covenant blessings" are commonly discussed as aspects of "promise theology." There are, however, important differences between the two approaches.

## PROMISE AND FULFILLMENT (PROMISE THEOLOGY)

"Promise theology" is an approach to biblical theology that focuses on the NT concept of "promise" as the central integrating theme of the Old and New Testaments. The OT is understood as an embodiment of a "promise" of a new work or future act of God, and the NT is viewed as the "fulfillment" or realization of that promise. The use of the NT concept of "promise" as a central theme in biblical theology has deep roots in nineteenth-century evangelicalism, particularly in the works of Johann von Hofmann[1] and Willis Judson Beecher.[2]

NT scholars have conveniently used the concept of "promise" *(epangelia)* as a way of framing the message of Jesus and the NT, though they are not always clear on how it should be understood. The NT is seen as the fulfillment or realization of what was formerly promised in the OT. A complicating factor is that the English word *promise* can translate no fewer than three Ger-

[1]Johann C. K. von Hofmann, *Weissagung und Erfüllung im alten und im neuen Testamente* (Nördlingen: Beck, 1841).
[2]Willis Judson Beecher, *The Prophets and the Promise* (Grand Rapids: Baker, 1963).

man words: *Zusage, Verheissung, Weissagung.*[3] Whereas theologians may entertain real distinctions in the use of these German words, most others are limited by the meaning of the one term *promise* in English.

## DEVALUATION OF THE OLD TESTAMENT

In the approach to the unity of the OT and NT, serious inequities have been created by the use of the English term *promise.* Although it is not always intentional, viewing the OT as "promise" and the NT as "fulfillment" unavoidably relegates the OT to a lower status. The OT is a preparatory stage awaiting something greater and more complete to happen. The NT represents the arrival or realization of something that until now was only promised. What is "promised" is what is "not yet" or what has been only "partially" realized in the OT. What is "fulfilled" is here now, complete. Far from uniting the OT and the NT, the end result of the many forms of promise theology is a reduction of the value of the OT as Scripture.

The attempt to lessen the devaluation of the OT by speaking of "multiple fulfillments" in the OT alongside a "final fulfillment" in the NT does little to correct the overall imbalance of the picture of the OT in promise theology. The concept of "promise," at least in English, has not yet overcome the view of itself as merely a step, or even multiple steps, that fall short of a final "fulfillment" in the NT. Nor does the notion of a "progressive revelation," beginning in the OT and leading through the OT to the NT, relieve the problem. The problem lies in the concept in the English phrase "promise and fulfillment" and its use as a grid through which a biblical theology of the OT and the NT is assessed. This grid is not a neutral vantage point from which to view the inherent relationship between the OT and the NT; rather, it is a precommitted assessment of the inherent value or worth of both parts of the Christian canon. Whatever else one may say about such a grid, a view of the NT as "fulfillment" carries with it a corresponding devaluation of the OT as "unfulfilled." It is difficult to see "promise and fulfillment" as anything but "unfulfillment and fulfillment." Labeling the OT as "promise," at least in terms of the NT idea of "fulfillment," necessarily carries with it a devaluation

---

[3]The notion of "promise" in the literature is divided over the best English word to express this idea. See Werner Georg Kümmel, *Promise and Fulfilment: The Eschatological Message of Jesus*, trans. Dorothea M. Barton (SBT 23; London: SCM Press, 1957), a translation of *Verheissung und Erfüllung* (1945).

of the message of the OT and, to a considerable degree, its importance in the life of the Christian and the church.

Recognition of this problem is, of course, not the same as a solution. The further fact that the NT writers themselves use the idea of "promise" as a way of describing the relationship of the OT to their new situation obliges us to raise the question of the ultimate value of "promise" in biblical theology. Can we still speak of the OT as "promise," as the NT writers did, that is, without devaluing the OT in the life of the contemporary Christian?

## Biblical Terminology for "Promise" Themes

A more difficult problem raised by the attempt to make the NT idea of "promise" the integration point of a biblical theology of the OT and the NT is the observation, acknowledged by all, that the OT itself does not have a word or expression for the NT idea of "promise."[4] The difficulty does not lie merely in the absence of terminology. The difficulty moves in two directions. First, if the idea of "promise" is important enough to serve as the central element in a biblical theology, why has it not risen to the level of verbal expression within the vocabulary of the OT itself? Why must one wait until the NT to find a truly verbal equivalent to the idea of "promise"? This is a serious problem because it lays open the possibility, if not probability, that the "promise" theme is not central or important enough in the OT to merit its own "promise" terminology.

The way to address this problem is not merely to intensify one's search for "promise" terms and words that can be construed as expressing, if only secondarily or by inference, the idea of "promise." As important as such a search may be, a more important solution lies in the quest for other forms of linguistic expression, such as compositional strategy and narrative structure or technique that may carry the idea of "promise" without express OT terminology. I will attempt to move in that direction with the twin themes of "covenant" and "blessing." Although neither of these terms could be adequately identified with the NT idea of "promise," both appear to carry much of the same semantic weight, at least in terms of the promise terminology found in the NT.

[4]"Eine alttestamentliche Vorgeschichte unseres Wortes gibt es nicht" (*TWNT* 2:575). Nor is the LXX of any help: "Die wenigen Stellen, an denen ἐπαγγελία oder ἐπαγγέλλεσθαι in der LXX vorkommen, sind für das nt.liche Verständnis der Wörter bedeuntungslos. Es liegen zT Mißverständnisse des hbr Textes vor" (ibid.).

Second, given the possibility of "promise" themes lying behind numerous OT words and expressions, as Walter Kaiser and others contend,[5] it is essential to raise the further question of whether we are justified in assuming that the OT idea of "promise" is in any way similar to the NT terminology. Assuming that it is possible to find a "promise" theme in the OT, are we justified in expecting it to have the same meaning as the NT "promise" texts? Another way to put it is to ask whether the NT theme of "promise and fulfillment" is already operative in the OT and whether it has developed its own terminology in isolation to the NT. Are there, in a NT sense, already OT promises *(epangelia)* that were fully fulfilled in the OT? Ultimately, this may be the only way one can escape the charge of reading NT ideas back into the OT. The meaning of important terms such as *promise*, especially when it is claimed that they, like the NT promises, are to be drawn from the OT, must be fully established already within the OT apart from the precommitted idea of "multiple fulfillment" noted above. In the absence of a more thorough study of "promise" terminology, we must heed the warning of Friedrich Baumgärtel, who has demonstrated that although the OT has a concept of "promise," as we noted above, it does not have the NT sense of that word. The OT has a range of ideas and terminology that express the concept of "promise," but those ideas do not usually conform to sense of "promise" in the NT.

Thus, the OT has its own sense of "promise" and thus its own terminology that it has developed to describe it. We should not expect the OT, viewed on its own, to have exactly the same ideas as the NT. We should not be surprised when the NT uses OT terminology to express its ideas, and we should not be surprised when it develops its own or gives its own terms an OT sense. Certainly, the idea of "promise" exists throughout the OT, but that does not mean that its terminology would have the same meaning as the NT terms. One must ask what there is in the terminology and thematic structure of the OT that would assure us that its concept of "promise" has the same meaning as the NT term *epangelia*. If that meaning is not the same, as Baumgärtel contends, then we should ask what the OT's meaning is and how it is expressed in the OT texts. Only then can we expect to understand its relationship to the NT idea of *epangelia*, and only then can we attempt to use it, along with NT words, as an integration point linking both the OT and the NT.

[5]Walter C. Kaiser Jr., *Toward an Old Testament Theology* (Grand Rapids: Zondervan, 1978).

Among other things, this means that to provide a genuine OT warrant for the NT's use of promise themes, we should look for genuine fulfillments of OT "promises" already within the OT. This raises the importance of the concept of "intertextuality" within the OT canon. Do the prophets, for example, understand their day in terms of "fulfillment" of a "promise"? Does the Pentateuch understand its narratives as "fulfillment" narratives, not merely in the sense of a "partial" or "multiple" fulfillments? Are the events of the Pentateuch, such as Sinai, to be read as a fulfillment of an earlier divine promise (e.g., Gen 15:15-16)? Does the author of the Pentateuch have an idea of "fulfillment" that would match the statement of Jesus in John 8:56: "Your father Abraham rejoiced to see my day; and he saw it, and was glad"?

In spite of the many difficulties posed by the lack of promise terminology in the OT, the use of the NT concept of "promise" within an OT theology has become a permanent, though largely unsuccessful, fixture in evangelical biblical theology. The primary reason is that the idea of "fulfillment" that accompanies the NT concept of "promise" can be used, at least superficially, to draw the two Testaments together without having to overlap them in any sense of a genuine continuity. However, if one is to understand the NT use of the term *promise* in relationship to the OT, it is essential to clarify the OT terminology. What, if any, are the terms used in the OT for the NT concept of "promise"? What semantic effect does linking the OT and the NT concepts of "promise" have on the OT or the NT notion of fulfillment? Only after such questions are addressed can one expect to profit from the use of both terms in a promise theology. In other words, we must seek to decipher the difference between a promise theology in which the idea of "promise" is grounded in the NT and one in which its idea of "promise" is grounded in the OT.

## Evangelical Promise Theologians

Among contemporary evangelical OT scholars who have aggressively pursued the NT concept of "promise" as a center point in biblical theology are Geerhardus Vos and Walter Kaiser. Because of the difficulties of terminology noted above, neither theologian has been able to produce a biblical theology that assigns equal weight to both the OT and the NT. Both leave us with an OT theology that for the most part looks only to the NT future for the meaning that it assigns to the OT books and, to the extent that either addresses the question, the OT canon as a whole. Consequently, the focal point of the OT's theology is drawn not around the OT as such, but within a future hope centered largely on NT texts. An important result of such a repositioning of focus is that it overlooks almost entirely the present use of the OT as Christian Scripture. After the NT fulfillment of the OT promises has been unwrapped, little is left of the OT other than the packaging.

***Geerhardus Vos.*** Geerhardus Vos's understanding of "promise" is drawn directly from the NT. He understands "promise" as a divine offer that was not fulfilled (realized) at the time it was made (e.g., Abraham), but was to find fulfillment in the future. The theological purpose of withholding the fulfillment until the future was to teach OT saints the importance of faith in God's promises: "God not only reserved to Himself the fulfillment, but also refrained from giving the promises their divine fulfillment during the lives of the patriarchs. Thus Abraham learned to possess the promises of God, in the promising God, alone."[6]

Without going into further details, we should note how different such a view of "promise" is not only from that of John Calvin, who clearly held that God's "promises" to Abraham were fulfilled in him, and also from that of Jesus, whose understanding of the OT promises we have already noted: "Your father Abraham rejoiced to see my day; and he saw it, and was glad" (John 8:56). But, as one can see in the quotation above, Vos believed that God deliberately and intentionally withheld the fulfillment of the promises from Abraham to teach him a lesson in faith and to force him to relate to God as a God who promises. By not immediately receiving the fulfillment of the divine promises, Abraham was taught to trust God as the one who gives the promises rather than to look only for the promises themselves. The ultimate promise given to Abraham was far more valuable than the immediate fulfillment of what God had promised him. According to Vos, the promises "are like an ethereal garment, more precious than the body of the promised thing over which it is thrown."[7] The unfulfilled promises were the means by which God produced a future hope for something more than mere material possessions and blessing. The divine promises as objects of faith in God were more important than their objective fulfillment because "from the earthly, pos-

---

[6]Geerhardus Vos, *Biblical Theology: Old and New Testaments* (Grand Rapids: Eerdmans, 1948), p. 101.

[7]Ibid.

sessed or not-yet-possessed, they had learned to look upward to a form of possession of the promise identifying it more closely with God Himself."[8] The lack of fulfillment of the OT promises was the primary means of teaching God's people to look for the spiritual and future dimensions of God's promises. Vos spiritualizes the OT's lack of fulfillment.

Vos's NT concept of "promise," seen here in his looking forward to the NT fulfillment as something greater and more spiritual, clearly has influenced his understanding of biblical theology and the relationship between the Testaments. Everything in the OT is put on hold, awaiting the arrival of the NT fulfillment, overlooking what may be only "earthly," and awaiting the arrival of "a form of possession of the promise identifying it more closely with God Himself."[9] In Vos's understanding, the OT "promise" is something that must be fulfilled or realized in a future time.

***Walter Kaiser.*** Kaiser also has pressed the NT notion of promise into service as a center *(Mitte)* for his popular OT theology.[10] Although he readily acknowledges that no exact biblical terminology for the NT concept of "promise" exists in the OT, he is nonetheless confident that the NT concept of "promise" is a central part of the theology of the OT and can be found there under the guise of numerous related terms and images. According to Kaiser, "what the NT eventually was to call the 'promise' *(epangelia),* was known in the OT under a constellation of terms."[11]

With this premise as his starting point, the central thrust of Kaiser's biblical theology becomes the exegetical isolation of various promise themes throughout the OT, always with a watchful eye for the NT "fulfillment." For Kaiser, and for most others who take this position, OT fulfillments, such as they are, must be seen as part of a series of initial, or "not yet," fulfillments that serve not as ultimate and final fulfillments in their own right, but rather to heighten the hope and faith of OT believers for the eventual fulfillment noted in the NT.

Since Kaiser acknowledges that there are no specific terms for "promise" in the OT, exegetically his task consists primarily of demonstrating that in spite of the lack of promise terminology in the OT, the idea of "promise"[12] is

---

[8]Ibid.

[9]Ibid.

[10]Kaiser, *Toward an Old Testament Theology.*

[11]Ibid., p. 33.

[12]Ibid., pp. 33-40.

everywhere equally present in all parts of the Bible. Even though Kaiser's efforts lead to numerous fruitful results in linking the OT and the NT, the lack of precision within the OT's own "promise" terminology inevitably leads him into an increasingly complex ambiguity. In the end, in spite of his genuine efforts, Kaiser's central thesis, that the NT concept of "promise" is the only, or even the most important, road to move us from the OT into the NT, is unconvincing. There are too many verbal road signs even still within the OT itself that point in other directions. Although "promise" clearly is an essential idea from the point of view of the NT and the patriarchal narratives of Genesis, Kaiser's notion of a central OT promise that moves throughout the Bible as a whole wears increasingly thin as he seeks to follow its lead through the rest of Scripture.

The lack of a specific OT terminology for "promise" is too serious a problem to ignore, especially when attempting to treat it as a central theme in a biblical theology, particularly one that seeks to deal with the OT on its own terms and to comprehend it along with the whole of the NT. Most contemporary biblical theologians will concede the point that traces of a "promise" theme are to be found in the words and formulas of some, or most, parts of the OT.[13] The problem is that such traces are only slight and require a great deal of NT imagination to uncover. Even when found, they rarely rate being treated as central ideas even in their specific contexts, let alone within the OT as a whole. In putting an emphasis on such rare traces of a "promise" theme, one runs the risk of overemphasizing valid, but secondary, issues. In those cases, a relatively minor OT theme, as the NT concept of "promise" appears to be in the OT, can overwrite the central message of other, more important, themes and terminology. Insisting on finding the NT equivalent of "promise" within the OT may appear to be a worthy, and even necessary, task, but in doing so, one may easily turn a blind eye to more prominent and central OT themes that, on closer examination, do link up with the NT concept of "promise." It is not that the NT has followed a theme not present in the OT; rather, the NT seems to have fixed on and taken up a less prominent OT theme for its particular purposes. One should not assume that in using a

[13]"Wenn auch im Alten Testament ein Wort Verheissung im Sinne des neutestamentlichen Begriffs (epaggelia) fehlt. . . . Die sprachlich Umschreibungen des Begriffs im Alten Testament sind: Wort, Gnadenerweisung, Satzung, Bund, sagen, zuschwören" (Friedrich Baumgärtel, *Verheissung: Zur Frage des evangelischen Verständnisses des Alten Testaments* [Gütersloh: Bertelsmann, 1952], p. 16).

less prominent OT theme such as "promise" to bring the OT together with the NT, the NT authors understood it to be the central theme in the OT. The NT has linked its idea of "fulfillment" to its own understanding of OT prediction. In doing so, it has not attempted to link its NT concept of "promise" to whatever sense of "promise" is resident in the OT. To insist on that would come close to tampering with the evidence.

This pitfall appears to lie behind Kaiser's frequent attempts to uncover the NT "promise" theme in the OT. Kaiser, to begin with, leads off his OT search for the NT concept of "promise" by setting his sights not on the idea of "promise" itself, but on the Hebrew word for "blessing." He does not suggest that "blessing" actually means "promise" in these OT texts; rather, his working model is that the terminology of "blessing" in the OT is one of the earliest of "the constellation of terms" used for the idea of "promise" by the OT authors. Here Kaiser assumes that the idea of "blessing" is correlative to that of "promise." Why he believes that to be the case is not clearly, or exegetically, spelled out, though it is evident that the NT sense of "promise" weighs heavily in his mind. Starting from the assumption that the NT's understanding of the concept of "promise" truly can be found in the OT, Kaiser sets out to identify many examples of such NT "promises" in the OT. Kaiser, of course, is not alone in drawing these kinds of conclusions. It is standard procedure for most forms of promise theology.[14]

Ironically, it is the attempt to use OT terminology that draws attention to one of the major weaknesses of promise theology. In his search for promise-related "blessing" terminology in the OT, Kaiser is forced almost immediately to sidestep the first occurrence of the word "blessing" in the OT (Gen 1:22). He must do so because this use of "blessing" terminology clearly is not an expression of the kind of NT "promise" that he has in mind; rather, it is a reference to the creator's "blessing" of the fish and fowl on the fifth day of creation. That can scarcely be taken as a feature of the NT theme of "promise."[15] Without doubt, "blessing" is a central term in the OT, and its first use here in Genesis 1:22 is exegetically important, but there are no ties in its use here to the concept of "promise" that one finds in the NT. Kaiser as much as acknowledges that this first occurrence of the term "blessing"

---

[14]Again, note Baumgärtel: "Die sprachlichen Umschreibungen des Begriffs im Alten Testament sind: Wort, Gnadenerweisung, Satzung, Bund, sagen, zuschwören" (ibid.).

[15]Kaiser, *Toward an Old Testament Theology*, p. 33.

has little or nothing to do with the NT "promise" theme, though he suggests that other occurrences of the term "blessing" in Genesis 1 are related to that theme.[16] Those other uses of "blessing," he argues, are "the first to signify the plan of God."[17] "Blessing" signifies "a plan," which suggests a "promise." Suffice it to say that a major weakness of Kaiser's approach is that even if he is right about some uses of the term "blessing," which seem to him to signal promise-related themes in Genesis 1, the matter of how one might actually arrive at such a conclusion here and elsewhere is hard to demonstrate exegetically, since it begins by disconnecting the meaning of the words in the text from the text itself—never a good exegetical move. A far better procedure is to concentrate on the idea of "blessing" in this text (Gen 1) and how that fits within the overall meaning of the Pentateuch. At least from that perspective one could tie an interpretation of the text to the actual meaning of its words.

Another series of references to which Kaiser appeals as "promise" texts further reveals the ambiguity of the evidence for a fully developed "promise" theme in the OT. It is the "over thirty examples where the verb *dibber* (usually translated 'to speak') meant 'to promise.'"[18] This argument surely begs the question of whether the idea of "promise" is in these texts. To say that these instances of the verb "to speak" actually mean "to promise" may be correct as far as an appropriate translation is concerned, but it misses the point that the Hebrew verb for "promise" was not chosen by the author in these instances. If the "promise" theme is central to the theology of the OT, which it may well be, it is not unreasonable to expect it to be demonstrable by something more than an English translation of the word "to speak."

Kaiser further argues that there are additional words, phrases, images and formulas that grew "as time went on around a fixed core that contributed vitality and meaning to the whole emerging mass."[19] Verbal reference to such an "emerging mass" of terms can be detected, Kaiser argues, in "a divine 'blessing,' a 'given word,' a 'declaration,' a 'pledge,' or 'oath' that God Himself would

---

[16]Kaiser's statement that the blessing "for men" in Genesis 1:28 "involved more than the divine gift of proliferation and 'dominion-having'" implies that he believes that the "blessing" of the fish and fowl involved only that (ibid.).

[17]Ibid.

[18]Ibid.

[19]Ibid., p. 34.

freely do or be something to all men, nations, and nature, generally."[20]

Kaiser may be right to read these texts as evidence of a "promise" theme, but one must not lose sight of the fact that merely stating that to be so is not the same as demonstrating it exegetically from relevant OT texts. What would keep one from drawing the more likely conclusion that these terms and vocabulary are linked not to a "promise" theme, but to the idea of "covenant" that is abundantly represented by a range of terms and formulas in these texts? What is immediately apparent in Kaiser's lists of the evidence for a "promise" theme in the OT is the growing distance between terms that he links to the idea of "promise" and the actual exegetical evidence for a concept of "promise and fulfillment" in the OT examples he cites. On Kaiser's own reckoning, what one should look for in these texts is the presence of "promise" terminology and concepts in those parts of the text that are important, not to the mind of the modern scholar, but to the intention of the biblical author. If such a theme as "promise" exists in the OT texts that Kaiser cites, one should be able to link that theme to a demonstrable compositional strategy that in some way was an expression of the NT concept of "promise." Only in that way can the idea of "promise" in the OT be exegetically linked to the historical author's intention. Without such links, the evidence is in danger of unraveling under the weight of a growing list of other, equally legitimate, biblical images such as "seed," "branch," "servant," "stone," "root" and "lion," with little or no semantic or exegetical ties to the theme of "promise."

As I have suggested above, an equally serious pitfall in Kaiser's notion of the role of promise in OT theology is one that is common to most "promise" approaches. It rests on a hidden assumption about the nature of the promise that Kaiser and others ultimately attempt to find in the OT. Kaiser's point that "promise" *(epangelia)* terminology plays a central role in NT thought (e.g., Eph 3:6: *tēs epangelias en Christō Iēsou*)—is widely and rightfully acknowledged as true. So also is his idea that there are measurable traces of "promise" themes in various OT terms and formulas. Ultimately, Kaiser's position that the idea of "promise" was also not fully developed until the time of the NT and hence must, necessarily, be borrowed from the NT as the center of an OT theology may prove to be correct.

Nevertheless, the stubborn fact remains that throughout his discussion of

---

[20]Ibid., pp. 34-35.

the "promise" theme in the OT, Kaiser never raises the question of the basic-nature and kind of promise that he expects to find at the center of the OT.[21] He merely assumes, along with most others, that the promise of which he finds traces throughout the OT carries the same notion of "promise" that he finds at the heart of the NT. Kaiser assumes that the OT is shaped around a "promise" theme that is identical to that of the NT. He does not raise the question, as does Baumgärtel, of whether the OT promise is the same kind of promise as that of the NT. For Kaiser, making that assumption is necessary because the promise that one finds in the NT, he suggests, had not yet fully developed in the OT. It is only the final stage of the promise found after the fulfillment that one can rightly use as the center of the OT. Such a completed view of promise, Kaiser assumes, could not have developed within the OT itself because by nature it is a promise that anticipates a fulfillment that came only at the end of the OT or, more accurately, at the beginning of the NT. Such a promise could not have been fully developed until the fulfillment had arrived. Kaiser thus assumes that all biblical promises are the same in that they look forward to a future fulfillment as in the NT. In other words, the "promise" *(epangelia)* that Kaiser has in mind, as in most other promise theologies, is a kind of "prediction" or future-oriented "prophecy" that must be understood and formulated in terms of its fulfillment. It is a promise with an eschatology—that is, a time of fulfillment—as well as a hermeneutic, a basic shape that gives it a meaning. For Kaiser, a promise theology sees the NT as the fulfillment of a particular kind of OT promise, one that anticipates a specific NT fulfillment. Consequently, the promise that Kaiser has read from the NT back into the OT and of which he has found traces in the OT is one that leads to a (NT) fulfillment—a sort of time bomb set to go off at a particular time. Kaiser does not consider, as Baumgärtel does, the possibility of other kinds of biblical promises. Hence he, unlike Baumgärtel, finds none.

The purpose of the foregoing critique of promise theology is to clear some of the ground for my own understanding of these same "promise" texts. My approach to this study of the theology of the Pentateuch shares a great deal of common ground and purpose with Kaiser and other promise theologies. There are, however, fundamental differences, and I have attempted to focus on those rather than the similarities. Where Kaiser and I share a great deal of common ground is

---

[21]See Beecher, *The Prophets and the Promise.*

in the expectation of the NT authors to have properly read their OT texts.

***Friedrich Baumgärtel.*** I have argued above that in working through their various approaches to promise theology, promise theologians often have failed to address the deeper question of whether the kind of promise that plays a central role in the NT *(Weissagung)* is the same kind of promise that Kaiser and others have found traces of in the OT. Kaiser has assumed, maybe wrongly, that the kind of promise of which there are genuine traces in the OT *(Weissagung* or *Verheissung)* is the true counterpart to the NT concept of "fulfillment." Kaiser and most promise theologians have neither raised nor dealt with the question of whether the promise that one might find traces of in the OT could be an altogether different kind of promise than that found in the NT.[22] Such an omission calls for a further examination of the idea of "promise" in the OT and a reassessment of its role in the compositional strategy and theology of OT books such as the Pentateuch. To do that, we must turn to the promise theology of Friedrich Baumgärtel.

It is important to begin with the observation that Baumgärtel has argued, as also has Kaiser, that the NT "promise" *(epangelia)* that seeks its "fulfillment" in Christ is eschatological and focused on a new, future work of God, much the same as the kind of promise we find on the pages of the NT. For Baumgärtel, the kind of promise we find in the OT is quite different. The promise we find in the OT is not the same kind of promise we find in of the NT. Baumgärtel means to say that the idea of "promise" in the OT is not of the nature of a prediction that seeks out a future fulfillment. The OT promise is, instead, of the nature of an affirmation of present assurance that God pledges on the basis of his own faithfulness and covenant loyalty. The kind of promise we find in the OT is much like what we might find in marriage vows. The promises in marriage vows do not assure a future fulfillment. They are not promises of something in the future, an action that can be registered as a fulfillment. A bride and groom take vows that immediately commit them to each other. They are "pledges" more than "promises." They are not vows about what lies ahead, but pledges about present commitment of marriage. The marriage promise has the present moment in mind, but it also entails the whole of the future. The future, however, is not cast in terms of a fulfillment, as if the marriage promise would be fulfilled in some future event. The intent of marriage vows is not to predict

[22]See Baumgärtel, *Verheissung*, pp. 16-27.

a state of affairs in the future, though they may entail that; rather, their intent is to assure and pledge the certainty of the continuing existence of present loyalty and relationship between the married couple. The future that finds expression in marriage vows is that which begins "from this day forward." That, argues Baumgärtel, is the kind of promise one finds in the OT, especially in contexts that involve making covenants and giving out blessings.

Baumgärtel argues that, given this perspective of the OT concept of "promise," the kind of promise recorded in biblical narratives such as Genesis was such that was fulfilled at the moment of its expression in those same narratives. Like marriage vows, they require no time period before one can speak of their fulfillment. They are immediately fulfilled and can be immediately broken. They do not have to wait for their verification. When God "blesses" the animals and humanity, it is not for the sake of a future event, but for the present. The "divine blessing" (Gen 1:28) is a present gift to be enjoyed by God's creatures.

Given Baumgärtel's notion of the OT promise, he argues that the promise as such cannot be the center of the conceptual world of the OT, but rather must be understood as an essential feature of a larger set of themes whose integrity and persistence within the OT are dependent on the kind of divine assurances given in the promise. In other words, "promise" cannot lie at the center of OT thought, though it must always be found close to the center, being an essential part of those elements that are at the center—ideas such as "covenant" and "blessing." In the OT, unlike the NT, the covenant is the central promissory grounds for the security of the divine-human relationship that is realized in the lives of faithful biblical characters. It is a divine pledge of presence and an assurance of help and blessing. In the NT the promissory grounds of one's relationship to God are expressed in the idea of "fulfillment" or "hope." In the OT it is not a promise as such that assures one's relationship to God, but a covenant. Within that context, a "promise" *(Verheissung)*, being of the nature of a divine pledge, bears the stamp of divine faithfulness and is not necessarily oriented toward a future fulfillment. It is, instead, like a vow, to be actualized the moment it has been established through a covenant rite. Hence, blessing and promise-fulfillment are, throughout the OT, expressed more in "covenant-blessing" terminology than in the specific "promise" terminology of the NT. It is along that path that we should find our way from the OT into the NT.[23] That is why one finds "covenant-blessing" terminology most often in the OT. This is not to say that "covenant blessing" and "promise" are semantically identical or even similar in meaning. They are not. However, whereas the NT finds its promissory grounds in the idea of "fulfilled" prophecy, the OT finds it in concepts and terminology such as "covenant" and "blessing."[24]

## Promise as *Weissagung* and *Verheissung*

To be sure, there is a close semantic connection between the two types of "promise," that of the NT and that of OT, but as I have suggested, they do not have the same meaning. The aim of the one (NT) is to be "fulfilled" in the future; the aim of the other (OT) is to be actualized, or established, in the present. This is why there is a great lack of "promise" terminology as such in the OT. In the OT the NT concept of "promise" is realized and actualized by means of covenants. The link between the two types of "promise" is thus to be found in the covenantal notion of "actualization." The making of a covenant is not a future event, nor is it a promise or hope of a future event. The making of a covenant is a present reality in the life of the parties of the covenant. There may be a future aspect to the covenant, but the covenant itself is not future. It is an actualization of a present commitment: "I will be your God, and you will be my people." As such, it is a promise about the present, not a promise about the future. Both types of "promise" could, of course, find their proper expression in a full-orbed promise theology, but so far that has not been the case within evangelical promise theologies. The NT concept of "promise" has provided the essential structures of such theologies.

The NT concept of "promise" (*Weissagung*, "prophecy") is a statement about a future that is grounded in a divine "promise" (*Verheissung*, "pledge") about the present. The divine promise (in the OT), "I will be your God, and you will be my people," is realized (actualized) in the present as a divine-human relationship. It is not merely a prophetic word about the future that must be fulfilled. The fulfillment of such a promise looks not

---

[23]"At that time ye were without Christ, being aliens from the commonwealth of Israel, and strangers from the covenants of promise, having no hope, and without God in the world: But now in Christ Jesus ye who sometimes were far off are made nigh by the blood of Christ" (Eph 2:12-13 KJV).

[24]Is this why covenants and blessings keep getting "renewed" in the OT? Once broken, a covenant, being a pledge, cannot be relied on. One cannot go back to a broken pledge and start over. There must be a new covenant or pledge of blessing—a new commitment.

toward a future event but toward an assurance of a present relationship. The fulfillment of such a promise is not a future event, but an assurance or commitment in the present. In regard to an OT promise, one would not think of an unfulfilled prediction. There is only a statement of assurance that is presently realized by many factors such as prophecy *(Weissagung)* and covenant. This does not mean that the OT may not also contain elements of a NT promise, namely, prophecies that await a future fulfillment. The OT is full of such prophecies (e.g., Dan 9:25). Although the NT has focused on one aspect of the OT promise, it has not done so at the expense of the others, but in light of the whole of what "promise" means in the OT. It is the OT concept of "promise"—commitment and pledge—that governs the use of "promise" terminology in the NT and "covenant" terminology in the OT.

When considering the various differences in promise theology among evangelicals, one must bear in mind that the discovery of "traces" of a promise theme in the OT is not the same as a demonstration of a compositional strategy built around such a theme. As helpful as Kaiser's arguments are in the pursuit of "promise" themes in the OT, the exegetical task is not complete until one has demonstrated that such a promise theme rest in the author's own work of "making" an OT book, and that also includes the task of "making" the OT canon (Tanak). The most important themes would be, of course, those that prove to be an essential part of the biblical authors' work in producing the OT. The first line of approach must be the author's intent. The fact that there is little or no NT "promise" terminology (e.g., *epangelia*) in the OT is as exegetically important as the fact that the NT has a clear and precise "promise" terminology. The exegetical task for an OT-oriented biblical theology is not to search for terms that are not in the OT, but rather to search for reasons why there are so few traces in the NT of the kind of "promise" themes that loom so large in the terminology of the OT. Why is there so little "promise" terminology in the OT to which we can attach a NT fulfillment? The NT concept of "promise," as Baumgärtel and others have shown, and which is easily seen in the NT uses of the term *epangelia*, is a kind of "promise" *(epangelia)* made at a point in time and, as I have stated, awaits a future fulfillment.[25] Where is such a promise in the OT, and what would be its rela-

[25]The title of Kümmel's book on NT eschatology, *Promise and Fulfilment*, states the matter precisely.

tionship to the other major themes found along the compositional seams of the OT? The real issue, as Baumgärtel has stated, is not that there is no specific terminology for the theme of "promise" in the OT. Instead, it lies in the fact that the notion of "promise" found in the OT is of a different sort than that found in the NT. The OT promise is an assurance of a relationship rather than an expectation of a fulfillment. Both are present in the OT and the NT, but neither plays the same role or occupies the same realm of thought as the other.

## The Covenant Blessing

Central to the theological formation of the Pentateuch is the "prophetic" word spoken to Abraham and introduced in Genesis 15:1 by the words "And after those things the word of the Lord came to Abraham, saying, . . ." This expression of the coming of God's word to Abraham is echoed throughout the prophetic literature. Clearly, it casts Abraham as a prophet. One to whom the "word of the Lord" comes is a prophet. Abraham is thus later identified as a prophet in Genesis 20:7. Theologians have been quick to identify the prophetic "word" given to Abraham as a word of "promise." Throughout Genesis 12–50 God "promises" to Abraham, "In your seed all the nations of the earth will be blessed" (Gen 22:18: *wĕhitbārăkû bĕzarʿăka kōl gôyê hāʾāreṣ*). Although the Hebrew word for "promise" is not used in these OT contexts, the notion expressed is much like that of a promise.

Perhaps for that reason, the NT understanding of the OT prophetic word as "promise" may be grounded in the understanding of Christ as the "fulfillment" of OT prophecy. "Promise and fulfillment" thus has become the semantic framework for understanding the overall relationships between the OT and the NT, the law and gospel, the old covenant and the new covenant. The OT prophetic word is cast as "promise," and the NT word is its "fulfillment."

Although the notion of "promise" as a word that awaits its "fulfillment" is primarily a NT idea, it is also an important aspect of the covenanted promise made to Abraham. Nevertheless, as I have argued above, the nature of the prophetic word in Genesis goes beyond the NT concept of "promise" and includes the divine assurance of present fellowship between God and Abraham. God said to Abraham, "I will be your God, and you will be my people"

(Gen 17:7). In the OT view of "promise" God commits himself to be Abraham's helper, provider and protector—all features of the OT idea of "covenant." It is for this reason that in these OT "promise" texts the central focus is on the idea of "covenant." Covenant denotes relationship. God's promise is a covenant promise. In this sense, the promise is a present experience rather than a future hope. It is a word that has been confirmed rather than a word that seeks confirmation.

In reading the OT in light of the idea of "fulfillment," the NT writers have focused on legitimate aspects of the OT prophetic word, even though their understanding of the OT promise does not tell the whole story. The writer of the book of Hebrews understood the OT promises not only as objects of faith still to be realized (Heb 11:1, 13), but also as blessings "already received," even before the coming of Christ (Heb 11:11). Abel received the promise of righteousness by faith when he "offered unto God a more excellent sacrifice than did Cain. It was by that faith that he obtained witness that he was righteous" (Heb 11:4); but he, along with Abraham and others, "died in faith, not having received the promises, but having seen them afar off, and were persuaded of them, and embraced them, and confessed that they were strangers and pilgrims on the earth" (Heb 11:13).

Texts such as these suggest that the writer of Hebrews has an understanding of the OT prophetic word that includes, but goes beyond, the NT understanding of "promise and fulfillment." It is that understanding that we will explore in this section. My thesis is that the prophetic word given to Abraham in the Genesis narratives is an expression of a divine commitment to Abraham. That commitment is to share a relationship with Abraham, to bless him, help him, and, through his seed, bring blessing to all humanity. The NT knows this commitment as a promise that has been fulfilled in Christ. It is not, however, known in the OT as a promise. It is, rather, expressed under several headings, the most important being "covenant." The means of realizing God's commitment to Abraham was known widely in the OT in terms of covenant-making. Fellowship between God and Abraham in the Genesis narratives is effected and secured by covenant. The two central narratives that feature Abraham's covenant with God are Genesis 15 and Genesis 17. Both chapters represent major compositional staging points in the overall literary and theological strategy of the Pentateuch. However, Genesis 15 surpasses all other chapters in the Pentateuch in presenting the nature and purpose of the Abrahamic covenant and blessing.[26] An understanding of covenants and the relationship of promise that they entail must begin with an exegesis of this central covenant narrative.

The sense of "covenant promise" as I am using it here is twofold. First, viewed from the perspective of the NT, it is a promise spoken in the OT that was fulfilled in Christ or is yet to be fulfilled in Christ. Such a prophetic word involved a prediction that was realized—that is, fulfilled—in Christ's earthly ministry, including his death and resurrection, but that was not its main focus in the OT. Second, viewed from the perspective of the OT, the covenant promise is a relationship established between God and Abraham's descendants that was grounded in the making of a covenant. The covenant was an ancient means for establishing a promissory agreement. In the case of the OT covenants, the relationship established by the covenant promise was guaranteed by God's faithfulness and mediated through the OT Scriptures.

My focus on the written nature of the covenant promise—that is, as Scripture—makes my view similar to the classical model of "prophecy." In the classical model, the prophets foretold events and persons whose coming was to be anticipated in hope. In many ways, the view that I am developing is "prophetic" in that classical sense. The difference lies in the notion of prophecy as "prediction." The classical view of the prophetic word, as represented by Franz Delitzsch, focused on specific "prophecies" scattered here and there in the prophetic literature. By piecing together those various texts, biblical scholars sought a kind of composite picture of the one who was to come. My view here, though sympathetic to the classical approach, moves in a different direction. Although the OT and the NT acknowledge that an element of prediction in the prophetic word, the center of focus for the prophets was their trust in God's faithfulness and the assurances granted them in the covenant. Consequently, the prophets spent most of their time writing about the hopes and dreams engendered by their relationship with God and much less time predicting future persons and events in exact historical detail.

Franz Delitzsch is representative of the older classical notion of prophecy and fulfillment. Claus Westermann says of Delitzsch and others,

[26]"Gen. 15, even on first reading, strikes one as a theological composition. Thus, it is not to be taken as a mere compendium of Pentateuchal history but a theological one. The theology reflects the basic theological thrust of the Pentateuch itself" (John Ha, *Genesis 15: A Theological Compendium of Pentateuchal History* [BZAW 181; Berlin: de Gruyter, 1989], p. 6).

> Formerly those who inquired into this relationship within the Old Testament concentrated only on specific utterances (Worte) *[sic]*; which utterances of the Old Testament have the character of promise or prophecy and therefore can be brought into relation with the act of fulfillment reported in the New Testament.[27]

Over against the classical model represented by Delitzsch, Westermann offers a historically oriented understanding of "promise" that is not unlike the view of many evangelicals. He defines "promise" within the context of God's speaking and acting in the historical events recounted in the OT:

> We see today that the promissory or prophetic utterances of the Old Testament are not to be understood apart from a series of acts of God reported there; that is, they are a constituent part of a history reported in the Old Testament and can be brought into connection with the final fulfillment in the New Testament only in the totality of this history.[28]

Such a historical view of prophecy leads Westermann to an understanding of "promise" in terms of "that correspondence of God's speaking and acting which is designated by promise and fulfillment." To arrive at that understanding, Westermann went back to the Yahwist's depiction of the event of the exodus "as the fulfillment of a promise (in other words, the keeping of a pledge or a vow)" (Ex 3:7-8). The account of the exodus begins with a divine "word promising deliverance." However, in limiting his view of the exodus event to that of the Yahwist, Westermann is unable to consider the fact that Genesis 15:13-18 views the exodus in exactly the same terms as he himself has characterized Delitzsch (see above), namely, as a specific utterance that has the character of promise or prophecy in a strict sense. In Genesis 15:13 God tells Abraham in precise words *(Wörter)* the details of the four hundred years of slavery they will suffer at the hands of the Egyptians. Such a view, for Westermann, is later than Exodus 3; but if we are looking for the view with the largest composition range—that is, one that views the whole of the Pentateuch—Genesis 15 is the perspective we should most value. As we will see, however, Exodus 2 and Exodus 3 also play an important role in shaping the Pentateuch's notion of covenant promise.

---

[27]Claus Westermann, "The Way of the Promise through the Old Testament," in *The Old Testament and Christian Faith: Essays by Rudolf Bultmann and Others*, ed. Bernhard W. Anderson (London: SCM Press, 1964), p. 201.

[28]Ibid., p. 202.

## The "Seed" of the Covenant Blessing

In Genesis 22:18 Abraham is told, "In your seed all the nations of the earth will be blessed." The prophetic word about a "seed of Abraham" in the Genesis narratives (Gen 12–50) is well known. The identity of the "seed" is of crucial importance to the meaning of the covenant blessing.

In Galatians 3:16 Paul identifies the "seed of Abraham" with an individual descendant of Abraham. That descendant, Paul says, is Christ. For Paul, the individual seed of Abraham is the foundation of all the promises God made to Abraham. The implication of Paul's argument is that Christ is the mediator of a divine promise of blessing, both to Israel and to the nations. Much in Paul's argument rests on the identification of the "seed" with Christ.

Although contemporary exegetes have been reluctant to concede Paul's reading of Genesis, earlier biblical scholars such as Calvin were far more generous. Many are content merely to overlook Calvin's (and Paul's) focus on Christ as the "seed of Abraham," but it is clear that Calvin fully appreciated the extent to which Paul's argument rested on the identification of Christ as the "seed." He was also well aware of the exegetical difficulties that Paul's argument raised. Nevertheless, Calvin followed Paul's exegesis of Genesis closely, making Christ the center of the divine blessing promised to Abraham. On Galatians 3:16, Calvin wrote, "It is therefore clear that Abraham's seed is to be accounted chiefly in one Head, and that the promised salvation was not realized until Christ appeared."[29]

That Calvin had some reservations with Paul's exegesis of the Genesis narratives is suggested by the qualifications he attached to Paul's argument. Having explained the implications of that argument, he added the proviso "even if in Moses' writings this was not yet expressed in clear words."[30] Calvin most likely had in mind the contrast between Paul's singular reading of the "seed" in Galatians 3 and the more natural plural sense of "seed" in Genesis (e.g., Gen 15:5).

Recent evangelical studies in these Galatians texts have acknowledged that Paul's argument is based on a possible reading of the Hebrew word "seed" as a singular in the Genesis texts, but they have distanced themselves considerably from Paul's understanding of the expression "seed of Abra-

---

[29]John Calvin *Institutes* 2.6.2 (*Institutes of the Christian Religion*, ed. John T. McNeill, trans. Ford Lewis Battles [LCC 20; Phildelphia: Westminster Press, 1960], 1:343).

[30]"Quod etsi non adeo claris verbis exprimitur apud Mosen" (Calvin *Institutes* 2.6.2 [ibid.]).

ham" in Galatians 3. They prefer to understand Paul's position as a rare and exceptional part of his interpretation of the Genesis narratives and thus not an essential part of his argument. Genesis, as they understand it, identifies the "seed of Abraham" not as an individual descendant of Abraham, but as the people of Israel, a chosen people. Rather than an individual "seed," they note that Genesis 15:5 promises Abraham a "seed" as numerous as the stars of the heavens.

Even though Paul's line of thought is difficult to follow through the Genesis narratives, it is hard to get around his clear statement in Galatians that the "seed" is Christ (Gal 3:16). Since the Greek and Hebrew words for "seed" are collective nouns, in most biblical contexts the terms are capable of having a singular or a plural meaning. There is little doubt that Galatians 3:16 identifies the "seed" as Christ, and thus as a singular, but many argue that Paul's identification of the "seed" in that passage does not tell the whole story. Most see Paul's language here as exceptional, even for him. Thus, they marginalize its importance over against the notion that the "seed" is Israel and hence for many may still apply to the church, as in what Paul appears to be saying in Galatians 3:29.[31]

Albertus Pieters, the author of a classic, but not definitive, study of the expression "seed of Abraham" in the NT, correctly points out that in the NT "seed" commonly refers collectively to Israel. Pieters argues that by the time of the NT, "seed" had come to refer specifically to the church. Paul's use of "seed" to refer to Christ in Galatians 3:16 is therefore already an exceptional use of that term, even in his own use of the terminology elsewhere. Hence, Pieters concludes, Galatians 3 cannot be taken, or at least should not be taken, as the only guide to the biblical meaning of the expression "seed of Abraham."

> In the highest sense, according to St. Paul, the "Seed" is the Lord Jesus Christ (Galatians 3:16), which evidently means that in Him the promise culminates. He is, so to speak, the center and core of what is meant by "the Seed of Abraham"; but the circumference lies far from the center, and within the area enclosed by the circle other meanings may be distinguished.[32]

---

[31]In Galatians 3:29 Paul does not identify the "seed" with the "church"; rather, he identifies the church with those who are "Christ's" *(Christou)* and "therefore" *(ara)* the "seed" of Abraham *(tou Abraam sperma este)*.

[32]Albertus Pieters, *The Seed of Abraham: A Biblical Study of Israel, the Church, and the Jew* (Grand Rapids: Eerdmans, 1950), p. 13.

Pieters's use of Paul's language is not commendable here. While admitting that Galatians 3:16 lies at the center of Paul's understanding of the term "the seed of Abraham," he suggests that without further demonstration, this meaning is largely marginal for Paul. Pieters would have us believe that for Paul, Galatians 3:16 expresses a valid, though rare and uncharacteristic, use of the biblical phrase "seed of Abraham." In the sense that Paul has in mind here, one can say, with Paul, that Christ is the "seed of Abraham." But, Pieters continues, Paul's use of the expression in Galatians 3:16 is not normative or exemplary of the uses of the expression elsewhere in the NT. In the Galatians passage Paul momentarily takes up a unique metaphor to express his exalted view of Christ, but having once used it, he lays it aside for the sake of its more common collective meaning. Hence the "seed," properly speaking, is Israel and, along with that, is capable of assuming the place of the church.

Having positioned Galatians 3:16 as an exception to Paul's usual meaning of the expression "seed" of Abraham, Pieters argues in the remainder of the book that the "seed" of Abraham is a collective, referring to either or both Israel and the church.

Pieters thus begins the argumentation of his book under the theological assumption that in spite of Paul's clear statement in Galatians 3:16, the expression "seed of Abraham" must be taken to refer, as a collective, to the people of God. Having dismissed Galatians 3:16 as an exception to Paul's understanding of the "seed" of Abraham, Pieters proceeds to the further conclusion that the Abrahamic "promise" in Genesis "is referred to in the New Testament as 'THE PROMISE' (Acts 2:39; 26:6; Romans 4:13; Ephesians 2:12). All other promises to Abraham and his seed are no more than details, working out the central thought that he and his people should be a source of blessing to the whole world."[33] It is clear from this statement that Paul's christological understanding of the phrase "seed of Abraham" is already far from Pieter's mind. He has identified the "seed" of Abraham with "the whole of [Abraham's] descendants." Apart from Galatians 3:16, and in all other occurrences of the expression, Pieters understands the biblical writers to use the expression "seed of Abraham" to refer to "a community of men, women and children to be called by His name and dedicated to His service."[34]

[33]Ibid., p. 12.
[34]Ibid., p. 14.

Pieters is, of course, on his way to identifying the "seed of Abraham" with the church as a replacement of Israel. There is little room in his system for anything but a marginal interest in Christ as the seed. Biblically and exegetically, however, Paul's argument in Galatians 3:16 (that Christ is the "seed" of Abraham) cannot be dismissed so easily. To begin with, it is clear in Galatians 3 that the "seed" of Abraham does not have a collective meaning. A collective seed would undermine Paul's entire argument in Galatians 3. Not only does Paul assert in Galatians 3:16 that "the seed is Christ," but also he is quite clear in Galatians 3:29 that only those who belong to Christ *(Christou)* are the "seed" of Abraham. The argument cannot be turned around to say that those who are the "seed" of Abraham belong to Christ. The premise of Paul's argument is that the "seed" (singular) of Abraham is Christ (singular). On the basis of that understanding, Paul concludes that if the Galatians belong to Christ, they are (plural) descendants[35] of Abraham.

Paul's argument raises the question of the biblical-theological consequences of his christological identification of the "seed." It also raises the question of Paul's exegesis of the Genesis narratives to which he refers. In the discussion that follows, my aim is to trace the exegetical consequences of Paul's argument in Galatians 3:16 and its relevance for a biblical theology of the Pentateuch. Whether or not Pieters's theological argument is valid is not our concern here.

## The Covenant Blessing in the Genesis Narratives

***Genesis 15.*** Genesis 15 in its present form is a unity. It arrived at that state by means of a complex compositional strategy. That strategy included an internal shaping and weaving together of very old written records. The starting point was likely a short narrative of Abraham's call (Gen 15:1-2, 5-6). To this was attached Genesis 15:3-4, which serves to clarify the central ideas of the earlier narrative. Gordon Wenham says of Genesis 15:3, "This verse is widely regarded as a gloss explaining the obscurities of the previous one."[36] C. F.

[35]The neuter noun *sperma* could be read as singular ("seed") or plural ("seeds"). That the clause *sperma este* (Gal 3:29) should be read "you [plural] are seeds," contrary to the English versions, is suggested by the plural verb *este* and by the nature of Paul's argument in Galatians 3:16 that the scriptural reference is not to the plural ("seeds"), but the singular ("seed"). Although the noun *sperma* could be read grammatically as a singular or plural, it would considerably weaken Paul's argument if he were to suggest that the noun "seed" was both not a plural in Galatians 3:16 while also a plural in Galatians 3:29.

[36]Gordon J. Wenham, *Genesis 1–15* (WBC 1; Waco, Tex.: Word, 1987), p. 328.

Keil understands the verses similarly by suggesting that Abram himself(!) added the verse "to give still more distinct utterance [noch deutlicher auszusprechen] to his grief."[37] Franz Delitzsch, in one of the several early editions of his Genesis commentary, states that "perhaps verse two was drawn from a source adapted to its own particular use and then verse 3 was placed alongside it as a sort of commentary."[38]

The guiding theme brought together by these two pieces of narrative is similar to the larger compositional strategies of the Pentateuch: their purpose is to identify the "seed" of Abraham mentioned throughout Genesis 12–50. Genesis 15 is the author's attempt to clarify an ongoing question of the identity of the "seed" of Abraham. Is the "seed" an individual descendant of Abraham or a collective people of God? In the central core of the narrative (Gen 15:1-2, 5) the "seed" of Abraham is clearly identified as Abraham's descendants, and the term "seed" is understood as a plural. The supplementary narrative (Gen 15:3-4) has been woven into the central core in order to expand, and add to, the notion of the collective "seed" of Abraham. Its purpose is to show that viewed in terms of the Pentateuch in its entirety, the "seed" of Abraham should be understood as both Abraham's descendants and his individual heir. The purpose of highlighting both aspects of the "seed" is to insure the proper range of the identification of the "seed. The author leaves open before the reader both meanings of the term "seed," the collective (plural) and the individual (singular) meaning. It is not that the author wants us to read it both ways each time the word "seed" occurs, but rather that the author wants his readers to be sensitive and open to both possibilities and thus to understand the term as the context suggests. The author thus treats the term "seed" like a homonym, a word with two distinct meanings, except that it does not actually have two meanings, but two grammatical ways to mark plurality.

Understood in terms of the phenomenon of homonym, the dual use of the word "seed" fits comfortably into a common linguistic feature of most known languages. The author treats the word "seed" as a homonym because within the broader compositional shaping of the Pentateuch, he wants us to read

[37]C. F. Keil and F. Delitzsch, *The Pentateuch*, trans. James Martin (BCOT; Grand Rapids: Eerdmans, 1971), p. 211.

[38]"Vielleicht ist v. 2 einer eignen Quelle entnommen, denn v. 3 ist ihm wie zur Verdeutlichung beigegeben" (Franz Delitzsch, *Commentar über die Genesis*, 3rd ed. [Leipzig: Dörffling & Franke, 1860], p. 367).

these texts with both aspects of the meaning of the "seed of Abraham" in mind, plurality and singular. It being a collective noun, the author cannot pluralize the word "seed" to get only the plural sense, "seeds," because the Hebrew plural of collective nouns often does not denote only a plural state, but also the unnatural state of the plural noun such as in "spilt seeds."[39] Oddly enough, the use of a "collective plural" is the only gramatical option the author has to render simply a plural noun. In Hebrew the plural noun "seeds" would mean "seeds in their unnatural 'spilled' state." In the poems of the Pentateuch the singular "seed" of Abraham is identified as a future (individual) king. In Deuteronomy 17:15 the king is to be one "from among his own brethren" *(miqqereb ʾaḥeykā)*—that is, his brethren who are among the collective "seed" of Abraham. Both aspects of the meaning of the term "seed" are important to the message of the Pentateuch and have their own specific contribution to make to that message. The coming king of the Pentateuch's poems is an individual king from the descendants of Abraham. Both aspects of the "seed" form part of the larger compositional strategy.

A close look at the two sets of verses in Genesis 15:1-6 reveals a carefully wrought narrative strategy.

*Intextuality of Genesis 15.*

Genesis 15:1: Prophetic Introduction

Genesis 15:2, 5

Genesis 15:3-4

Genesis 15:1: See "Covenant Blessing."

Genesis 15:2: According to John Skinner, and most commentators, Genesis 15:2b ("and the son of the *mešeq* of my house, he is *damme*ś*eq*, Eliezer") is "absolutely unintelligible."[40] An early (e.g., Rashi) and continuing tendency of commentators has been to explain Genesis 15:2 by means of comparative philology (related Semitic languages and early versions) or by assuming copyist errors (textual criticism). In such attempts, Genesis 15:3 plays a commanding role.[41] What many fail to note, but tacitly assume, is that Genesis 15:3-4 restates and clarifies the difficulties posed by Genesis 15:2. This was argued

---

[39]GKC 400.

[40]John Skinner, *A Critical and Exegetical Commentary on Genesis* (ICC; Edinburgh: T & T Clark, 1910), p. 279. Heinrich Holzinger: "Der Satz bei MT ist unübersetzbar; die Verss. Helfen auch nicht weiter" (*Genesis* [KHC 1; Freiburg: Mohr Siebeck, 1898], p. 148).

[41]Franciscus Vatablus: "Sic (בן ביתי, 3b) vocat vernaculum Eliezerum" (in Edward Leigh, *Critica sacra* [London, 1641], 1:395).

already by Friedrich Tuch.[42] It suggests that Genesis 15:2b was difficult, or "unintelligible," even to the original audience of the Pentateuch. Ferdinand Hitzig noted that within Genesis 15:2 itself there is an early "commentary" on the meaning of the expression וּבֶן-מֶשֶׁק בֵּיתִי (*ûben-mešeq bêtî*, "son of acquisition") in the words following it: הוּא דַּמֶּשֶׂק *(hû᾽ dammeśeq)*—that is, "this is Damascus."[43]

Such observations suggest that even at the time of the writing of Genesis 15 the second verse might already have been in need of an explanatory comment. Even Keil acknowledges as much by suggesting Abraham might have added Genesis 15:3 to explain the earlier and more difficult Genesis 15:2.[44] The nature of the repetitions between Genesis 15:2 and Genesis 15:3-4 further suggests that the latter verses are comments that interpret the obscure former verse. They appear to be part of the composition of, at least, Genesis 15. When put together with similar comments in the Pentateuch, they take us to the broadest possible horizons of the Pentateuch.[45]

"Authorial comments" such as this are common in the Pentateuch. They are often "glosses" that are intended to explain obscure texts by bringing them more in line with the major themes of the Pentateuch. Some of these "authorial comments" are little more than the work of scribes or of the author, whose intent was merely to update an early document. The notation that the town of Bethel was once called "Luz" (Gen 28:19) is such a comment. It deals with issues of minor interest to the meaning of the whole Pentateuch, and its range extends only to the limited horizons of those specific passages or written

---

[42]Friedrich Tuch: "Die Wiederholung des Gedankens ist aber keinesweges überflüssig, sondern hebt ihn stark hervor, wobei das doppelte Ansetzen mit: *und Abram sprach* (vgl. C. 16,9-11), wozwischen eine Pause zu denken, nicht unwirksam ist. Beide Verse erläuern sich dahin, dass עֲרִירִי *nackt* Lev. 20,20. S., *verlassen* (vgl. עַרְעָר bestimmt vom *kinderlosen* ἄγονος Aq. ἄτεκνος Sept.), dem Gott keinen Nachkommen verliehen hat v. 3. Jer. 22,30. Vgl. עָרֹם Hiob 1,21., zu verstehen hat; ferner, dass אֱלִיעזר ein בֵּן בֵּית אַבְרָם d. i. *verna Abrahae s.* C. 14:14. war, der ihn in Ermangelung eines eigenen Kindes beerben soll. Daher muss בֵּן מֹשֶׁק בֵּיתִי v. 2. Dem Sinne nach · יוֹרֵשׁ אֹתִי sein, wodurch die Richtigkeit der Combination des alt. leg. מֹשֶׁק Besitzthum (Simonis, Gesenius, v. Bohlen u.a.) gesichert wird" (*Kommentar über die Genesis* [Halle: Waisenhaus, 1838], pp. 321-22); Franz Delitzsch: "Vielleicht is v. 2 einer eignen Quelle entnommen, denn v. 3 ist ihm wie zur Verdeutlichung beigegeben" (*Commentar über die Genesis*, p. 367); Heinrich Holzinger: "Was im Satz 2b gestanden haben muss, zeigt die Dublette 3b" (*Genesis*, p. 148).

[43]"1 Mos. 15,2. erklärt die Glosse הוּא דמשק das mit מֶשֶׁךְ gleich bedeutende משק durch *Damarskus*" (Ferdinand Hitzig, *Die Psalmen, Historischer und kritischer Commentar nebst Uebersetzung*, part 2 [Heidelberg: Winter, 1835], p. 193).

[44]Keil and Delitzsch, *The Pentateuch*, p. 211. See Wenham, *Genesis 1–15*, p. 328.

[45]See Ha, *Genesis 15*.

sources that relate to the town of Bethel or Luz.[46] Some of these ostensibly minor glosses can also assume a secondarily more important role (cf. 1 Kings 8:8). There are many of these kinds of comments in the biblical narratives. They shed considerable light on the author's, or later scribe's, understanding of the narratives he is constructing as well as his intimate knowledge of the written material he is using as sources. We see the author himself at work, and we can trace his exegetical movement as he works through his text.

Whether the work of a scribe ("scribal gloss") or of the author himself ("authorial comment"), these kind of comments show us the close attention given by scribes and authors to their texts and written sources. No detail was too small or too insignificant to escape the critical eye of the biblical author. Coming across one of these comments in the text is like finding the author's fingerprints in the text.[47]

The presence of an "authorial comment" in Genesis 15:3-4 raises further the question of the extent of the compositional strategy represented in that comment. Is it an isolated remark by a later scribe (such as the former name of the town of Bethel)? Or is the comment in Genesis 15:3-4 part of a larger compositional framework or strategy? The answer lies in our understanding of the range and subject matter of a comment. It is a matter of the textual horizon of the comment. Does the comment reflect an awareness of other parts of a larger narrative? How far afield does the reference of a comment go? Does it refer only to immediate issues or events covered in a text, or does it refer to events and places at considerable distances from the immediate passage?[48] Does it play a larger role within the whole of a narrative or even

[46]It is, of course, always possible that such apparently limited comments may at some point prove to be of a much broader concern.

[47]As a practical matter, it is helpful to distinguish a "scribal comment" from a comment by the author. We can do this by following the textual history of the comment. How far back in the history of the text does the comment go? If it is not fully represented in the textual history of the HB, we should think of it as the remark of a scribe. If there are no significant textual variants to the comment, there is little reason to regard it as the work of a scribe, and thus we should assign it to the author—for example, whether or not it is represented in the most valuable ancient versions, such as the LXX.

[48]Otto Eissfeldt's notion of a "literary unit" ("die kleinste literarische Einheit") must quide our search for the extent of the compositional range of the references contained in these authorial comments: "Die Grenzen einer selbständigen Erzählungs-Einheit sind darnach so weit zu stekken, wie der Horizont der jeweiligen Erzählung reicht. Reicht dieser über eine 'Einzel-Erzählung' hinaus und sind ihre nach rückwärts und nach vorwärts weisenden Elemente integrierencer Bestandteil von ihr, so ist sie keine selbständige literarische Einheit, sondern Teil einer grösseren. Fällt aber der Horizont einer Einzel-Erzählung mit ihrem Anfang und ihrem Ende zusammen,

with the whole of the book? The expression "after these things" in Genesis 15:1 shows its author's awareness of the narrative events that preceded Genesis 15.[49] We are able to identify the particular "things" narrated prior to Genesis 15 by going back a few columns of texts and reading. In the same way, we know that the person who used the expression "after these things" was aware of such events and could, like us, go back and read them. His comment and its scope show that the author intends us, the readers, to understand the events of Genesis 15 in light of those things narrated prior to that point. Genesis 15 assumes the presence of a specific context into which it has been inserted. It is as if the author were watching us read his narrative, and just at the time when he senses that we need some small piece of additional information or help in resolving the text's meaning, he gives it to us in the form of a comment or commentary. The author keeps us on track and helps us understand the details of a passage in light of the whole.[50]

Here, as we will see below, the links between Genesis 15 and Deuteronomy 33[51] are of crucial importance. If the traces of a compositional strategy in Genesis 15 are linked to a similar kind of strategy in Deuteronomy 33, it suggests that the range of this compositional level extends to the boundaries of the present canonical Pentateuch. That is because the poem in Deuteronomy 33 is part of a compositional strategy that extends from the first word in the Pentateuch (*rē᾽šît*, "beginning" [Gen 1:1]) to the last poem (Deut 33) and the epilogue (Deut 34) that follows it. A close study of these two passages, Genesis 15 and Deuteronomy 33, shows that the author of the Pentateuch devoted considerable attention to them. There are, of course, many other passages related to this level of composition, but it is clear that the author has paid considerable attention to these two specific texts in putting together the whole of the Pentateuch. They are a significant part of the compositional structure of the whole of the Pentateuch. The heart of the theology of the

---

so ist sie eine selbständige Einheit" (*Kleine Schriften,* ed. Rudolf Sellheim and Fritz Maass [Tübingen: Mohr Siebeck, 1962], 1:144).

[49]The formula "after these things" "presupposes an already coherent Abraham narrative. It can belong, therefore, only to a later redactional stage when there was no longer any awareness that the Abraham story had grown out of individual narratives" (Claus Westermann, *Genesis 12–36*, trans. John J. Scullion [CC; Minneapolis: Fortress, 1995], p. 217).

[50]One must be careful also to look for the possibility that such links were part of an earlier shape of the text, as in Genesis 20:1, where the narrative begins, "And from there Abraham traveled to the land of the Negev." There is no "there" in the preceding narrative. It appears to refer to a previous segment of text.

[51]See Ha, *Genesis 15*.

Pentateuch must find its way along these strategic seams.

The notion that the horizons of the compositional activity in Genesis 15 extend to the whole of the Pentateuch has found additional confirmation from the observations of John Ha. Ha notes several additional features of Genesis 15 that indicate its horizons extend to the level of composition of the whole of the Pentateuch. Since a similar kind of compositional linkage can be demonstrated between two other widely different narratives, Genesis 14 and Genesis 15,[52] it might also be possible to extend the final range or extent of this compositional strategy to both the beginning of the canonical Pentateuch in Genesis 1 to its conclusion in Deuteronomy 33–34. This could then be linked to the final level of composition for the whole of the canonical Pentateuch.

When seen in this light, it becomes apparent that the comments in Genesis 15:3-4 may be part of the author's larger purpose in writing, not just a theology of a part of the Pentateuch, but the whole of the Pentateuch. Though small and appearing to be of relatively minor importance, these brief comments on Genesis 15:2 in Genesis 15:3-4 may hold an important key to the Pentateuch's theology: the singular identification of the "seed of Abraham" as an individual.

As a way of approaching the meaning of the author's comments in Genesis 15:3-4, we begin with the observation that God's word about Abraham's numerous descendants in Genesis 15:5 does not speak to the question Abraham raises in Genesis 15:3-4, that of him having no heir. There was no individual who would inherit his wealth. In the face of that problem, Genesis 15:5 assures Abraham not that he will have an heir, but that his descendants will be numerous. While it is true that if his descendants will be numerous, he might see this as an assurance of eventually receiving an heir, Genesis 15:5 speaks to a different concern. It speaks to the question raised by God's prophetic word to Abraham in Genesis 15:1 (a great reward) and Abraham's response in Genesis 15:2 (a great reward). Abraham's concern about his great reward in Genesis 15:2 finds its divine response in Genesis 15:5: "Thus will your seed be"—that is, as numerous as the stars in the sky. Genesis 15:5 answers Genesis 15:2 in light of the divine word spoken in Genesis 15:1. The narrative is of one piece, without any help from Genesis 15:3-4. It flows seamlessly

[52]John H. Sailhamer, *Introduction to Old Testament Theology: A Canonical Approach* (Grand Rapids: Zondervan, 1995), p. 309.

from Genesis 15:1 to Genesis 15:6, dealing only with the question of Abraham's "great reward" in the first verse.

The addition of Genesis 15:3-4 takes the narrative in a decidedly new direction. On the one hand, it refocuses God's assurances to Abraham in Genesis 15:1 and Abraham's concerns about an heir in Genesis 15:2 on the promise of an individual "seed" (singular) who will inherit Abraham's blessing. On the other hand, it adds important detail to the sequence of questions and answers that emerge out of Genesis 15:2.

Although these observations do not require us to read Genesis 15:3-4 as an additional comment on Genesis 15:2, or even as part of another source, they suggest that the additional explanation of Genesis 15:2 in Genesis 15:3-4 may have a larger purpose to be worked out within the narrative and possibly within the compositional structure of the Pentateuch as a whole. In these verses two explanations are given for God's statement in Genesis 15:1 that Abraham's "reward will be great." Both are valid explanations, and both play an important role in the author's larger plan in the Pentateuch. In Genesis 15:5 the "great reward" is identified with Abraham's multiple descendants ("so shall your descendants be"). In Genesis 15:3-4 the "great reward" is linked to an individual descendant who will "inherit" (ירשׁ, *yrš*) Abraham's blessing ("the one who comes from your loins, he will be your heir"). The line of interpretation drawn along these two answers to Abraham's question is the same as that which divides the Pentateuch's view of the "seed" of Abraham at several other places. One line of interpretation identifies the "seed" collectively with the descendants of Abraham who are traced by a series of genealogies throughout the remainder of the book. The other line of interpretation can be found in the major poems of the Pentateuch and their focus on the identification of the "seed" of Abraham as an individual king from the tribe of Judah.

Before looking further into the compositional strategy of Genesis 15, we need to make a few more observations. Westermann has noted that the prophetic expression "the word of the Lord came to Abraham" is used only twice in the Pentateuch: Genesis 15:1, 4.[53] In Genesis 15:4 "God's word to Abraham" is deliberately cast as a prophetic utterance (as in Gen 15:1), and so the notion of the "seed" of Abraham as an individual, which is part

---

[53]Westermann, *Genesis 12–36*, p. 218.

of the message of this chapter, is thereby given the mantel of prophetic legitimacy.

The use of the rare term "childless" *(ʿărîrî)* in Genesis 15:2 calls for additional explanation. As is commonly the case in interbiblical interpretation (cf. Gen 29:31–30:24), the explanation of Genesis 15:2 given in Genesis 15:3 rests on a wordplay between "childless" or "seedless" *(ʿărîrî)* and "seed" *(zeraʾ)*. By means of a wordplay that emphasizes "no seed" (in Gen 15:2) versus "seed" (in Gen 15:3), the collective sense of the term "seed" in Genesis 15:2 is effectively removed and replaced by singular reading of this important term. The contrast is not "no seed" (Gen 15:2) versus "many seeds" (Gen 15:3), but "no seed" (Gen 15:2) versus "a seed" (Gen 15:3). That focus on the singular meaning of the term "seed" of Abraham (Gen 15:3) is followed by a similar and even more direct focus on an individual who will inherit Abraham in Genesis 15:4. As we noted above, that understanding of the referent of the term "seed" is given further warrant by being introduced as a prophetic word in Genesis 15:4. The word in Genesis 15:4 identifies the "seed" as "the one who will inherit you" and the one "who comes from your own loins." The "seed" in Genesis 15:3 is identified with an individual son in Genesis 15:4 rather than as a nation as in Genesis 15:5. Wordplay links between Genesis 15:2 and Genesis 15:3 that support a similar focus on an individual "seed" are these:

1. *ʿărîrî* ("seedless") is explained as *zeraʾ* ("a seed")
2. *ûben-mešeq bêtî* is explained as *ben-bêtî* ("one's own son")
3. *elîʿezer* ("Eliezer") is explained as *ʾelî ʿezer* ("my God is my help") explained as *zeraʿ* ("seed")

If Genesis 15:3-4 is intended to clarify Abraham's understanding of the promised "seed" in Genesis 15:2, its purpose must also include a focus on an individual, much along the same lines as the poetic texts in the Pentateuch. The interweaving and shaping of this important narrative in Genesis 15 has joined the ranks of the compositional strategy that forges links with the whole of the Pentateuch.

*Innertextual links between Genesis 14 and Genesis 15.* There are several innertextual links to Genesis 15 within the Pentateuch. The most immediate signs of composition and forged links with Genesis 15 can be seen in the connections it shares with the previous chapter, Genesis 14. The use of unique and key terminology in the narratives of both chapters signals the basic theme expressed in the two narratives. The various connecting terms listed below signal compositional links between the two chapters. The terms themselves are not common in the Pentateuch. In most cases they occur only here in the Pentateuch. Their occurrence is therefore not likely coincidental.

There are numerous verbal links between Genesis 14 and Genesis 15:

**Table 5.1**

| **Genesis 14** | **Genesis 15** |
|---|---|
| v. 13a: הָאֱמֹרִי *(hāʾĕmōrî)* | v. 16: הָאֱמֹרִי *(hāʾĕmōrî)* |
| v. 13b: בְרִית *(bĕrît)* | v. 18: בְּרִית *(bĕrît)* |
| v. 14b: 318 men | v. 2b: 318 = אֱלִיעֶזֶר *(ʾĕlîʿezer)* |
| v. 14c: דָּן *(dān)* | v. 14: דָּן *(dān)* |
| v. 15: לְדַמָּשֶׂק *(lĕdammāśeq)* | v. 2: דַּמֶּשֶׂק *(dammeśeq)* |
| v. 16a: הָרְכֻשׁ *(hārĕkūš)* | v. 14: בִּרְכֻשׁ *(birkūš)* |
| v. 18a: צֶדֶק *(ṣedek)* | v. 6: צְדָקָה *(ṣĕdākâ)* |
| v. 18a: שָׁלֵם *(šālēm)* | v. 15: בְּשָׁלוֹם *(bĕšālôm)* |
| v. 19b: שָׁמַיִם *(šāmayim)* | v. 5: הַשָּׁמַיְמָה *(haššāmaymâ)* |
| v. 20a: מִגֵּן *(miggēn)* | v. 1: מָגֵן *(māgēn)* |
| v. 21: הָרְכֻשׁ *(hārĕkūš)* | v. 1: שְׂכָרְךָ *(śĕkārkā)* (reverse order of consonants) |

The primary compositional purpose of these links between Genesis 14 and Genesis 15 seems to be to widen the thematic structure of Genesis 15 in the direction of Genesis 1–11. This strategy accomplishes that purpose by, first, threading the two chapters together so closely that they can speak with one voice within the context of all the variables these two chapters put before the reader; and second, by leading off with a focus on the nations warring against the family of Abraham in Genesis 14:1-12, the broad universal perspective of Genesis 1–11 is brought over into the narrowly focused attention given to Abraham and his "seed" in Genesis 15. Of the four kings who invade Abraham's homeland, two (Shinar, Elam) are identified in the Table of Nations (Gen 10:10, 22); two are presented, apparently, to augment that lists of nations. God's appearance to Abraham in Genesis 15 thus is placed within the widening context of the nations of the world and their warring against Abraham. In that context, we watch God give assurances to Abraham about his "seed," the very "seed" through whom "the nations" are to be blessed. Finally, the entrance of Melchizedek on this scene and his immediate appeal to the Most High God, the creator (Gen 14:19), effectively brings Abraham into the thematic world of Genesis 1–11 and identifies God as the Lord (YHWH) who has called Abraham to be a blessing to the nations. By thus linking these narratives, the notion of the "seed" of Abraham is given an open line to the original word of assurance that the "seed" of the woman in Genesis 3:15 will crush the head of the serpent.

*Intertextual links between Genesis 15 and Deuteronomy 33.* A far-reaching intertextual link with Genesis 15 is the "blessing of Moses" in Deuteronomy 33. Several observations point to the importance of this connection.

First, as shown in the chart below, these two passages share several key terms. These terms are not common elsewhere in the Pentateuch. Their clustering in these two passages is indicative of an authorial intention and the work of a single hand. These terms also bear considerable theological weight. Some of these terms, such as "shield" *(māgēn)* in Genesis 15:1 and Deuteronomy 33:29, occur in strategic compositional locations throughout the remainder of Scripture. There are several terms in these two passages, such as "righteousness," "covenant" and "shield," that are part of the highest level of theological reflection in both the OT and the NT. The fact that these terms fall along the compositional seams of the Pentateuch as a whole suggests that the author of the Pentateuch saw the events of these narratives through the lenses of these terms.

**Table 5.2**

| **Genesis 15** | **Deuteronomy 33** | **Translation** |
|---|---|---|
| v. 1: מגן *(mgn)* | v. 29: מגן *(mgn)* | shield |
| v. 2: אל יעזר *(ʾlyʿzr)* | v. 7: עזר *(ʿzr)* | help |
| v. 4: ירשׁ *(yrš)* | v. 23: ירשׁ *(yrš)* | possess |
| v. 6: צדקה *(ṣdqh)* | v. 21: צדקה *(ṣdqh)* | righteousness |
| vv. 7, 18: ארץ *(ʾrṣ)* | v. 28: ארץ *(ʾrṣ)* | land |
| v. 14: דן *(dn)* | v. 22: דן *(dn)* | judge |
| v. 18: ברית *(bryt)* | v. 9: ברית *(bryt)* | covenant |

A second observation about these two pentateuchal texts, Genesis 15 and Deuteronomy 33, has to do with the form-critical shape of Genesis 15. When compared to some of the psalms, Genesis 15 follows the pattern (form) of a lament psalm. The pattern begins with a description of an emergency situation *(Not)*, then a promise *(Verheissung)* is made, and it concludes with a call for faith *(Glauben)*. This pattern also occurs in those passages in the Pentateuch that reflect the "faith" theme. Hans-Christoph Schmitt has identified this pattern and compositional strategy as a *Glaubens Thematik* ("faith theme"). It represents a recurring focus on the centrality of faith. According to Schmitt, these narratives contain the links to the largest units of narrative making up the main body of the Pentateuch. The scope of this pattern or type (form) of narrative and the use of the notion of "faith" extend from the beginning of the Pentateuch to its conclusion. It thus represents a textual strategy that spans the entire length of the Pentateuch. The fact that Genesis 15 is a part of this strategy suggests that the meaning reflected in its own compositional strategy (e.g., justification by faith [Gen 15:6]) plays a central role in the meaning of the Pentateuch. Two such elements of meaning stand out in Genesis 15. First, as we have noted above, is its focus on an individual "seed" of Abraham, and second, its focus on faith as the means of being reckoned righteous.

A third observation about Genesis 15 has to do with the textual horizons of its "faith" theme that extend to each of the major blocks of narratives within the Pentateuch, except Genesis 1–11. Genesis 1–11 has little or no signs of belonging to a "faith" composition. If, however, we take into consideration the links between Genesis 15 and Genesis 14 (noted above), a reference to creation (Gen 1) in Genesis 14 brings it and the "faith" theme of Genesis 15 into the structure of Genesis 1–11.

*Intertextual links between Genesis 15 and Exodus 2–3.* There are other sets of links between Genesis 15 and compositionally important narratives. Exodus 2–3, the introductory call narrative for Moses, along with Genesis 15, the prophetic call narrative of Abraham, portray both Abraham and Moses as prophets called to announce the deliverance of their people.

### *Summary Remarks.*

*Composition.* Genesis 15 is a central piece of the pentateuchal puzzle. Its scope is the entire Pentateuch. It is linked to most other central narratives in the Pentateuch both internally, as in its ties to Genesis 14 and Exodus 2–3, and externally, as in its links to Deuteronomy 33.

**Table 5.3**

| | Genesis | Exodus |
|---|---|---|
| God speaks | 15:1 | 3:7 |
| Sinai theophany | 15:12<br>15:17 | 3:1b<br>3:2 |
| Sojourn in a foreign land | 15:13a | 2:22 |
| Bondage, work, affliction | 15:13b | 2:23b<br>3:7<br>3:9 |
| Chronology | 15:13c<br>15:16a | 2:23 |
| Judgment of the nations | 15:14a<br>15:16b | 2:23<br>2:24 |
| Salvation/divine reward of Abraham's descendants | 15:14b<br>15:15<br>15:16a | 3:8a<br>3:10<br>2:25 |
| Covenant | 15:18<br>15:19-21 | 2:24b<br>3:8b |

Genesis 15 seems to be part of a single compositional network that moves from Creation (Gen 1–2) to the last events of the book of Deuteronomy (Deut 33–34) by establishing parallel events at key moments in the pentateuchal narratives. The center of events is located at two points: the call of Abraham and the call of Moses. This strategy incorporates several key terms, some of which find their way into the rest of the Tanak and the NT—for example, "shield," "faith," "covenant," "salvation."

*Purpose of the strategy.* The purpose of this specific compositional strategy is to cast the events of the pentateuchal narratives as players in the plot of salvation, faith and covenant.

*Theological implications of strategy for the theology of the Pentateuch/Tanak.* The Pentateuch is a central part of Scripture. All the themes of the NT and the Bible as a whole are a crucial element of the compositional strategy of the Pentateuch. The clear signs of the work of the author of the Pentateuch suggest that he was aware of this strategy and relied on it to carry the main themes of this book. In the remainder of this book I will continue to follow the authorial signs of this composition and attempt to piece together the theological vision of the author.

## A Profile of the "Promise Narratives" in Genesis

Although no presumption of scientific methodology is made in drawing attention to the following profile of "covenant-blessing" terminology in Genesis, it is noteworthy that the distribution of the term בְּרִית (*bĕrît*, "covenant") in Genesis is remarkably similar to the distribution of the term ברך (*brk*, "blessing") in the same texts. The distribution of these two terms suggests that they share a real commonality beyond mere randomness within Genesis 12–35. Attention should be given to the frequency of these terms in Genesis and, just as importantly, not only the places where the terms occur but also where they do not occur. Finally, it should be acknowledged that the chapter divisions are arbitrary and serve here only to point out those areas of occurrence.

***Fore-reference (Gen 46:1-4).*** This small narrative is an important fore-reference *(Vorverweise)* of the exodus. As such, it is a part of the larger links within the Pentateuch and addresses the question of the nature of the "seed" of Abraham.

> Then he said, "I am God, the God of your father; do not be afraid to go down to Egypt; for I will there make of you a great nation. I will go down with you to Egypt, and I will also bring you up again; and Joseph's hand shall close your eyes. (Gen 46:3-4)

God will go down to Egypt with Israel to bring them out as a great nation (Gen 28:15-16).

***A company of peoples (qĕhal ʿammîm/gôyīm).*** The central element in these series of links is the conceptualization of the "seed" of Abraham as a "congregation of peoples" *(qĕhal ʿammîm).* This is a new departure for the notion of "Abraham's seed," going beyond earlier covenant statements.

> And Jacob said to Joseph, "God Almighty appeared to me at Luz in the land of Canaan and blessed me, and said to me *[wayyōʾmer ʾēlay],* 'Behold, I will make you fruitful *[hinnî maprĕkā],* and multiply you *[wĕhirbîtīkā],* and I will make of you a company of peoples *[ûnĕtattîkā liqhal ʿammîm],* and will give this land to your descendants after you for an everlasting possession.' And now your two sons, who were born to you in the land of Egypt before I came to you in Egypt, are mine; Ephraim and Manasseh shall be mine, as Reuben and Simeon are. And the offspring born to you after them shall be yours; they shall be called by the name of their brothers in their inheritance. (Gen 48:3-6 RSV)

Compare Genesis 28:3; 35:11; 48:4: *qĕhal ʿammîm/gôyīm*; Genesis 49:10: *yiqqĕhat ʿammîm.*

*History of interpretation.* "And thou shalt become gatherings of nations" *(kai esē eis synagōgas ethnōn)* (Gen 28:3 LXX).

*Rashi.* Rashi on Genesis 35:11: "A nation—referring to Benjamin. Nations—referring to Manasseh and Ephraim who would come from Joseph—these actually were counted as tribes."[54]

Rashi on Genesis 48:4:

> He announced to me that there were yet to issue from me an assembly of peoples (i.e. at least two more tribes). Now, it is true that He then said to me, (XXXV. 11) "A nation and an assembly of nations [shall be of thee]," but when He said "a nation" He intended it to refer to Benjamin who was not yet born, and this promise of "a nation" has been fulfilled by the birth of Benjamin, and for that reason I do not mention it now. "An assembly of nations [shall be of thee]," however, presupposes that two more would descend from me besides Benjamin. Consequently, since no other son besides Benjamin was born to me, He was really telling me that one of my tribes (i.e. the tribe formed by one of my sons) would be divided so as to constitute at least two tribes, thus giving that son more importance, and that privilege I confer upon you.[55]

*John Calvin.* Calvin on Genesis 35:11:

> God . . . then promises that he will cause Jacob to increase and multiply, not only into one nation, but into a multitude of nations. When he speaks of "a nation," he no doubt means that the offspring of Jacob should become sufficiently numerous to acquire the body and the name of one great people. But what follows concerning "nations" may appear absurd; for if we wish it to refer to the nations which, by gratuitous adoption, are inserted into the race of Abraham, the form of expression is improper: but if it be understood of sons by natural descent, then it would be a curse rather than a blessing, that the church, the safety of which depends on its unity, should be divided into many distinct nations. But to me it appears that the Lord, in these words, comprehended both these benefits; for when, under Joshua, the people was apportioned into tribes, as if the seed of Abraham was propagated into so many distinct nations; yet the body was not thereby divided; it is called an assembly of nations, for this reason, because in connection with that distinction a sacred unity yet flourished. The language also is not improperly extended to the Gentiles, who, having been before dispersed, are collected into one congregation by the bond

---

[54] *Pentateuch with Rashi's Commentary: Genesis*, trans. M. Rosenbaum and A. M. Silbermann (London: Shapiro, Vallentine, 1929), p. 170.

[55] Ibid., p. 239.

of faith [Hoc quoque ad Gentes non male extenditur: quae quum prius dispersae forent, in unam congregationem fidei vinculo collectae sunt];[56] and although they were not born of Jacob according to the flesh; yet, because faith was to them the commencement of a new birth, and the covenant of salvation, which is the seed of spiritual birth, flowed from Jacob, all believers are rightly reckoned among his sons, according to the declaration, "I have constituted thee a father of many nations."[57]

Calvin on Genesis 48:4:

Jacob regards himself as blessed, because he, having embraced the grace promised to him, does not doubt of its effect. And therefore, I take what immediately follows; namely, I will make thee fruitful, &c., as explanatory of what precedes. Now the Lord promised that he would cause an assembly of nations to descend from him: because thirteen tribes, of which the whole body of the nation consisted, were, in a sense, so many nations. But since this was nothing more than a prelude to that greatness which should afterwards follow, when God, having scattered seed over the whole world, should gather together a church for himself, out of all nations [Is 66:14-24]; we may, while we recognize the accomplishment of the benediction under the old dispensation, yet allow that it refers to something greater. When therefore the people increased to so great a multitude, and thirteen populous tribes flowed from the twelve patriarchs, Jacob began already to grow to an assembly of nations. But from the time that the spiritual Israel was diffused through all quarters of the world, and various nations were congregated into one church [& variae gentes in unam Ecclesiam aggregatae sunt],[58] this multiplication tended towards its completion.[59]

*Johann Mercerius*. "Indicat imperans de propagatione & augmento prolis, ut sequitur declaratio, quia iam 11. Aut 12. susceperat, sed promittit hos latius deincep propagandos, gens & congregatio gentium erit. i. nascetur ex te, & reges ex lumbis seu renibus tuis exibunt, prodibunt, orientur."[60]

---

[56]John Calvin, *Joannis Calvini commentarii in primum librum Mosis, vulgo Genesin* (Amsterdam, 1671), p. 183.

[57]John Calvin, *Commentaries on the First Book of Moses Called Genesis*, trans. John King (Grand Rapids: Baker, 1979), pp. 241-42.

[58]Calvin, *Primum librum Mosis*, p. 229.

[59]Calvin, *First Book of Moses*, p. 423.

[60]Johannes Mercerius, *In Genesin primum Mosis librum, sic a Graecis appellatum, commentarius* (Geneva, 1598), p. 583. "Et sis, id est, vt sis in coetum populorum, id est, euadas in populos multos, sicut & Abrahamo promissum est, vt ex te sc. exeat semen illud benedictum Abrahamo promissum, in quo sunt omnes gentes benedicendae. Hic est effectus benedictionis ipsi datae, vt quod ad

*Cornelius Lapida.* "Duodecim enim tribus ex te proseminandae ita crescent, ut ultis gentibus et populis aequentur."[61]

*Henry Ainsworth.* Ainsworth on Genesis 35:11: "[an assembly] or company, church of nations: the Chaldee saith, an assembly of tribes. Here God confirmeth the blessing given to Iakob by his father Isaak: and amplifieth it, see Gen. 28:3. And 48.3.4."[62]

Ainsworth on Genesis 28:3: "[an assembly] or, Church, congregation, companie, that is, a multitude of peoples, as Ezek. 23:24. The Greek translateth it Synagogues (or assemblies) of nations, and the Chaldee, an assembly of tribes: respecting the twelve tribes that came of Iakob, Exo. 24."[63]

On Genesis 48:3, Ainsworth understands the LXX to refer to "synagogue" (or assembly) of nations.[64]

*Johann Drusius.* "(notae majores): לקהל עמים in ecclesiam populorum . . . [quoting *Targum Onqelos* and *Targum Jonathan*, which interpret as שבטין לכנשת]. Certum est tribus utroque nomine designari. Quanquam gentes proprie גוים dicantur."[65]

*Robert Jamieson, A. R. Fausset and David Brown.* Jamieson, Fausset and Brown on Genesis 28:4:

> The word *[ʿammîm]* uniformly employed in the renewal of the promise to Jacob; whereas the expression used twice to Abraham is, that he should be a father of many nations *[gôyīm]*. The invariable use of these different terms in the two cases indicates an essential difference in the substance of the promise as made to the two patriarchs.[66]

Jamieson, Fausset and Brown on Genesis 35:11:

> A company of nations. This is considered by some as pointing to the Twelve tribes, by others to the spiritual Israel. But neither interpretation is admissible.

---

Abr. dictum fuerat, In Isaac vocabitur tibi semen, ad Iacob referatur, & in ipso sit implendum non in Esau, ex vi benedictionis" (ibid., p. 487).

[61]Cornelius a Lapide, *Commentaria in scripturam sacram* (Paris, 1768), p. 330. "Crescere te faciat multa prole et familia, ut multae tribus et turbae populorum ex te nascantur. Ita reipsa populosae fuerunt tribus duodecim, descendentes ex Jacob."

[62]Henry Ainsworth, *Annotations upon the Five Bookes of Moses* (London, 1639), p. 128.

[63]Ibid., p. 105.

[64]Ibid., p. 62.

[65]Johann Drusius, *Critica sacra sive annotata doctissimorum virorum in Vetus ac Novum Testamentum* (Amsterdam, 1698), p. 1035.

[66]Robert Jamieson, A. R. Fausset and David Brown, *A Commentary, Critical, Experimental and Practical, on the Old and New Testaments* (Grand Rapids: Eerdmans, 1945), 1:198.

> The word which in these promises to Jacob is rendered by "multitude," or "company," in our English Bibles, takes its origin and its meaning from a root which properly signifies "to assemble," or to "call an assembly"; and the force of it in these passages seems more properly expressed in the Greek translation of the LXX than by any later interpreter. Their translation of this passage is, "the gathering together of nations shall be from thee"; and the gathering together which is intended, can be no other than the gathering of all nations into one in Christ. But, if I mistake not, this great event is much more expressly mentioned in these passages than it appears to be even in the version of the LXX—the Messiah being personally mentioned under the character of "the Gatherer of nations."[67]

*John Skinner.* "In spite of Dt. 33:3 (Di.), the phrase cannot well denote the tribes of Israel. It seems to correspond to J's 'In thee shall all nations,' etc. (23:3 etc.), and probably expresses some sort of Messianic outlook."[68]

*Heinrich Holzinger.* "קְהַל עַמִּים hier und 48:4 ist nach 35:11 (קְהַל גּוֹיִם), auch 17:5f. Ein Haufen von Völkern, nicht eine Gemeinde von Volksgenossen."[69] The קְהַל עַמִּים *(qĕhal ʿammîm)* is the way the plural "seed" is linked to the singular "seed." The "seed" (singular) is a gathering (singular) of peoples (plural) (cf. Eph 3:6).

[67]Ibid., 1:223-34.

[68]John Skinner, *A Critical and Exegetical Commentary on Genesis* (ICC; Edinburgh: T & T Clark, 1910), p. 375.

[69]Heinrich Holzinger, *Genesis* (KHC 1; Freiburg: Mohr Siebeck, 1898), pp. 174-75.

*Chapter 9*

# Is There a "Biblical Jesus" of the Pentateuch?

At the heart of evangelical discussions of biblical theology is the question "Who is Jesus?" Historical criticism began its answer to that question with a quest for the historical Jesus. Evangelicalism has taken up a similar quest and continues to contribute much to the debate. For evangelicals, however, there is another part to the question. It is what one might call the quest for "the biblical Jesus." There are at least two ways one might understand a quest for the biblical Jesus.

## The Quest for the Biblical Jesus

***The biblical Jesus as the Jesus of the Gospels.*** In one sense, the biblical Jesus is the one whom Martin Kähler viewed as the "Jesus of the Gospels."[1] Ultimately, Kähler's quest for the Jesus of the Gospels was and is still a kind of historical quest intended as a response to the various historically reconstructed lives of Jesus. As important as that quest is, it is not the one I have in mind.

***The biblical Jesus in a second sense.*** There is yet another sense in which we can, and should, speak of a biblical Jesus. It is the sense in which we seek to know the Jesus of the whole Bible. It is the Jesus we come to know from reading both the OT and the NT.

In this sense, I am using the word *biblical* as it is used in "biblical theology." Just as biblical theology is a theology of the OT and the NT, the biblical Jesus

[1]For a helpful summary of the importance of Martin Kähler in biblical theology, see "Kähler, Martin," *RGG*[4], vol. 4, col. 734.

is the Jesus of the OT and the NT. Biblical theology is more than the combination of an OT theology and a NT theology. A biblical theology is what comes out of viewing the two Testaments as a whole. So too the "biblical Jesus" is more than the combination of an OT Messiah and a NT Jesus. The biblical Jesus is the Jesus who comes out of one's learning of him in both the OT and the NT.

The quest for the biblical Jesus is part of a historical quest for Jesus as a real person, but it is also more than that. Although it is framed as a quest for Jesus as the historical referent of the biblical texts, the biblical Jesus is not a mere historical or literary reconstruction. Just as the historical Jesus may be the historical referent pointed to by this or that isolated passage, the biblical Jesus is the historical person pointed to by the whole Bible. In this sense, Jesus is just as much a product of OT theology as he is of NT theology. Hence, along with being a historical question about Jesus, the quest for the biblical Jesus is also a biblical theological question that asks, "What does the whole Bible tell us about the identity of the historical Jesus we come to know from reading the whole Bible?" The circularity of this quest is an essential part of its statement of the question. We are asking, "What do the Old and New Testament Scriptures, in their totality, tell us about the historical referent we know from reading both the Old and New Testament Scriptures, in their totality?"[2] This is not merely the Jesus we know from reading the NT, nor the Jesus of the OT unfolded (or fulfilled) in the NT. It is the Jesus we know from reading the OT and the NT as a single book. It is the Jesus we know from reading all the biblical texts, and since evangelicals hold those texts to be

[2]The validity of Jesus as the canonical integrating element within the whole of the OT and the NT is established by the prominence given to his death within the canonical seams (Dan 9, the Gospels and Revelation), his resurrection (Dan 12, the Gospels and Revelation) and his ascension (Dan 7, the Gospels and Revelation). Only about Jesus can it be said that as a "messiah" he died, rose again, and ascended to sit at the right hand of the Father. Thus he alone meets the canonical qualifications of "messiah" in one of the only true uses of the term in the OT (Dan 9:24, 26). Christopher Seitz fails to appreciate this feature of the OT canon when he remarks, "The problem for the early church was not what to do with the OT. Rather, in the light of a Scripture whose authority and privileged status were everywhere acknowledged, what was one to make of a crucified messiah and a parting of the ways? . . . The challenge of our day is how to see in Jesus' death and raising actions truly in accordance with the Scriptures of Israel" ("Two Testaments and the Failure of One Tradition History," in *Biblical Theology: Retrospect and Prospect*, ed. Scott Hafemann [Downers Grove, Ill.: InterVarsity Press, 2002], p. 211). In reality, it is just these features of the biblical Jesus that warrant our taking messianic claims about him seriously from the perspective of the OT canon and the Christ of the NT (see Dan 9:25-26).

the Word of God, it is this Jesus whom they stand behind as the one and only historical Jesus.[3]

A major component of the quest for the biblical Jesus is, then, the quest for the theology of the final shape of the Hebrew/Greek OT (plus or minus textual variants) and how the earliest Christian writers (Paul, Acts, the Gospels) integrated that theology in the writings that came to be the NT.

One last word on my approach. My goal in seeking the biblical Jesus is not to look for what is commonly called "the Messiah in the Old Testament." Although it entails some of the same issues, it does not pose the same questions.[4] So, as important as that quest is, it is not the question I am attempting to address here. At this point, I want to focus on the biblical Jesus, not the OT Messiah.

In this section we will examine three central questions: (1) What does the Pentateuch tell us about the identity of the "biblical" Jesus? (2) How have the prophets and psalmists integrated the Pentateuch's Jesus into their central message? (3) How have the NT and biblical theology (OT/NT) integrated the Tanak's biblical Jesus into their understanding of the meaning of the Bible?

Speaking about "Jesus in the Pentateuch and the prophets" sounds anachronistic, and for the most part it is. What I mean by speaking about Jesus this way is not that the OT authors foresaw the historical Jesus of the Gospels. That the NT writers understood the OT authors to have "foreseen" Jesus is, of course, clear from their exposition of such terms as *prooraō* in passages such as Acts 2, where the term is used of David's foresight in Psalm 16 (Acts 2:31). We should not, however, draw the conclusion from such texts that the

[3]A telling historical fact about Jesus, Paul and the early church in Acts is the lack of their own version or interpretive edition of the OT (Tanak). Even if some have attempted to reconstruct a different Christian Bible, the earliest church does not seem to have relied at all on an annotated version of the OT, as was, however, the case with the pesher at Qumran. They accepted, seemingly without question, the Hebrew (and/or Greek) Bible of their day. Note the attitude about the Scriptures reflected in 2 Peter 3:15-16. The NT books as such are, of course, evidence of a growing need for more Scripture. What this statement of the question helps us see more clearly is the historically problematic practice of beginning a biblical theology of Jesus with the NT rather than with both the NT and the OT. It is historically problematic, among other things, because it overlooks the fact that before it was set down in writing in the NT Scriptures, the NT's theology was already in its last stages of being formed on the basis of the OT. In that sense, the biblical Jesus is already the Jesus of the Gospels. The only Bible of the early church was the OT, and there is little or no indication from the NT that the early church felt shorthanded without the NT.

[4]The question of the Messiah in the OT/HB first has to establish the meaning of the OT messianic idea and its proper context and from there to demonstrate its origin and development within the HB. Its range of study is limited to the OT/HB.

Jesus whom they "foresaw" was seen by them as he is now presented in the NT, as if the prophets and authors of the OT were given a preview of the NT writings. That is an unwarranted anachronism. I am using the name "Jesus" more as a pointer to a central literary figure found in both the OT and the NT Scriptures. As biblical historians, we understand this figure to be a real person and the biblical account to be historically trustworthy. As readers of the Bible, we come to know this historical figure from various literary stratagems and compositional strategies used by the biblical authors. In the OT texts this literary figure is realized primarily in a series of poetic images and metaphors, such as "the seed," "a king," "a lion," "the branch"—the list goes on. In the NT we see this historical person in the Gospel narratives in terms of a single literary persona, Jesus. In the Epistles we see him refracted through various theologomena, such as "the Son of God" and "the Christ."

Viewed as a whole, it is by means of this biblical figure that we hope to arrive at what Harmut Gese calls a biblical "Christology"—that is, not just a messianism, but a "logos of the Christ" in both the OT and the NT. The fact that the name "Jesus" is anachronistic in the OT ironically enhances its usefulness within the context of the whole of the Scriptures. As an anachronism, it can be used to pull together texts that, though genuinely belonging together in terms of a literary or narrative construct, have no single or uniform compositional strategy connecting them to the whole Bible. We could, of course, take the route of using the term "Messiah," which can also be anachronistic, but its value here is, ironically, diminished by the fact that it is not anachronistic in at least two instances in the OT (Dan 9:25, 26). So, neither the name "Jesus" nor the term "Messiah," nor any other term I know of, is free of the charge of being anachronistic. Thus, I am inclined to prefer the use of the name "Jesus" throughout because it serves the important function of uniting genuinely related texts and because its anachronistic properties are transparent. In spite of my inclinations, however, I will use such terminology sparingly throughout the following study of the "biblical Jesus." That is partly because, in the long run, I suspect that few will find this solution to be adequate to the task I am assigning it. It will always look as if I am reading the NT Jesus back into the OT, and that is precisely what I am trying not to do. Nevertheless, the problem of appropriate and functional biblical terminology for working with the OT and the NT holistically is a real one and should be addressed, if only in this preliminary way.

***What does the Pentateuch tell us about the identity of the biblical Jesus?*** To begin with, I want to recall our original question about the composition of the Pentateuch. How did Moses write the Pentateuch, or better, how did he "make" the Pentateuch? What materials did he use? How did he use his materials? What kind of literary work is the Pentateuch? What is its genre? Such questions tell us much about the meaning of the Pentateuch and how the author understood it. They take us to the author's intention. By doing so, they help us understand something about the biblical Jesus. The only way we can expect to understand the author's view of the biblical Jesus, if he has one, is to identify and collect his thoughts carefully as they are reflected in the text he has made.

*The materials in the Pentateuch.* To appreciate how the Pentateuch was "made," we have to begin with the materials used by its author. What did the author of this book have to work with? Where did he start? Was it with a blank sheet of paper, or was he an editor of written sources?

Judging from what we see in the Pentateuch, he likely began with several pieces of the book already intact. First, one thing appears to be certain. As he began his work he had several large blocks of narrative already before him: the primeval history (Gen 1–11), the patriarchal narratives (Gen 12–50), the exodus narrative (Ex 1–19), the wilderness narrative (Num 11–25) and the conquest narrative (Deut 1–11). Many of these texts he himself may have also "made." Much of the author's work in making the Pentateuch, however, consisted compositionally of linking these blocks of narratives into the book (the Pentateuch) as a whole. I think that we are on safe ground in suggesting that his work of making the Pentateuch began by attaching and linking the written narratives in a theologically meaningful way.[5]

---

[5]What I am proposing is quite similar to the view of Jamieson, Fausset and Brown in their commentary on the OT. They say in their discussion of the Pentateuch, "Independently of any hypothesis, it may be conceded that, in the composition of those parts of the Pentateuch relating to matters which were not within the sphere of his personal knowledge, Moses would and did avail himself of existing records which were of reliable authority. . . . It is evident that, in making use of such literary materials as were generally known in his time, or had been preserved in the repositories of Hebrew families, he interwove them into his narrative conformably with the unity of design which so manifestly pervades the entire Pentateuch" (*Old and New Testaments*, 1:xxxii). In this they represent the conservative position in the seventeenth and eighteenth centuries. Campegius Vitringa: "Has vero schedas & scrinia Patrum, apud Israelitas conservata, Mosen opinamur collegisse, digessisse, ornasse, &, ubi deficiebant, complesse, atque ex iis primum Librorum suorum confecisse" (*Sacrarum observationum libri quatuor* [Franeker, 1700], p. 35). Since the rise of biblical and historical criticism in the nineteenth and twentieth centuries, the conservative position has

Second, the author also used numerous, sometimes lengthy, poems (Gen 49; Ex 15; Num 23–24; Deut 32–33). These poems also played an important role in giving the Pentateuch its final shape. They were used like glue to hold the large pieces of narrative in place. They also made a major contribution to the theological understanding of the rest of the Pentateuch.

Finally, the author had numerous collections of written laws: the Decalogue (Ex 20), the Covenant Code (Ex 20–23), laws for priests (Ex 25–Lev 16), the Holiness Code (Lev 17–27), the book of Deuteronomy (Deut 12–26). These laws form the major content of the final two-thirds of the Pentateuch.

*The composition of the Pentateuch.* If the author had all these pieces—narratives, poems, laws—how did he put them together? How did he go about "making" the Pentateuch? From what we can gather from looking at its final shape, "making" the Pentateuch consisted primarily of connecting these various pieces of texts into a single story. This part of the process we can rightly call "composition" or "authorship." Needless to say, it required a considerable knowledge of how the pieces should be fit together and knowledge of the relationship of the pieces to each other.[6] It was like following the picture on the cover of a jigsaw puzzle box. The author of the Pentateuch put his jigsaw puzzle together by following his own mental picture of the whole. Here I want to mention three aspects of the Pentateuch's compositional strategy.

*The Pentateuch is arranged in chronological order.* From reading the Pentateuch, we can see that its author brought his narratives together into a simple story by arranging them in chronological order. He begins with creation and then moves to Abraham's entry into the land. He ends with Moses' farewell address outside the land. This may sound obvious, but we should not underestimate the importance of such frameworks. It is clearly the work of the author of the Pentateuch, and in many ways it reflects his point of view on many of the issues raised in the narratives. Many question of interpretation are

---

understandably shied away from talking about "sources" or "written records." But, if pressed, this remains the view of most evangelical OT scholars today. The only variation on this is that many hold that the "sources" available to Moses were not yet written. Moses relied on oral tradition. I find that this not only fails to deal adequately with the realities of the text itself, but also introduces an unnecessary level of uncertainty into the process. Where would we be today in NT studies if we believed that the Gospels were written from "oral sources"?

[6]Some texts within the Pentateuch, such as Genesis 14:22 and Exodus 2:24; 3:6-18, suggest that at the time such knowledge was shared by many. It was a knowledge of God's dealings with "the fathers" and his work of creation. Other texts, such as Genesis 48:22 and Numbers 21:14, suggest that there was more knowledge of the past than was utilized.

linked to the question of whether or not the series of events in the Pentateuch are arranged in chronological order.

Some chronological questions are directly related to the biblical notion of redemption and other central theological themes. It has sometimes been argued, for example, that Genesis 4 (the account of the conception and birth of Adam's sons) preceded (rather than followed) the events of Genesis 3 and the fall of Adam. In that way, Adam's fall (Gen 3) would have occurred chronologically after the birth (or, at least, conception) of his sons (Gen 4). This would mean that they and their descendants were not directly (by conception) linked to Adam's fall. If Adam's fall had no effect on his descendants, there would be no need for redemption or a redeemer. Humanity as a whole would still be in its pristine form, having no direct relationship to fallen Adam. This would also mean that the pledge in Genesis 3:15 would apply only to the lives of Adam and Eve as individuals. It would have no bearing on their descendants. So, for Moses, putting these texts in a chronological framework was an essential and perhaps the most important step in "making" the Pentateuch. In approaching his narratives chronologically, the author laid a theological foundation for his understanding of the pledge in Genesis 3:15. By arranging the events of the Pentateuch chronologically, he places Genesis 3:15 at the beginning of a long history of a fallen humanity. Also, in that way, the pledge of a "seed" in Genesis 3:15 is given a universal scope.

*The Pentateuch is arranged around central themes.* The next aspect of the making of the Pentateuch involved weaving into these various narratives a series of theological motifs or themes (theolegomena). There are three such themes: pledge, faith, law. These three themes play off one another within the narratives and ultimately provide the central movement of the narratives. God makes a pledge to the early fathers, the patriarchs, that is grounded in a call for faith but ultimately results in the giving of the law. All three themes are further linked by means of the concept of "covenant." Pledge, faith and law become operative (or unoperative) only through the making (and breaking) of covenants. The themes of faith, pledge, law and covenants have been woven into the fabric of the biblical narratives. These and other themes are part of the common discussion of the Pentateuch, and we need only mention them here.

It is important to stress, however, that these compositional themes (or motifs) are not themselves necessarily about the biblical Jesus. Nevertheless, they are important to the present discussion because they form the theological backdrop for the next compositional feature of the Pentateuch that is about the biblical Jesus: the insertion of poems at strategic locations within the pentateuchal narratives.[7] These poems then provide a kind of final framework to the whole of the Pentateuch.

*The Pentateuch employs a poetic framework.* I have argued in a number of places that the "making" of the Pentateuch involved, among other things, the insertion of several key poems at the close of the central narratives of the book. These poems focus the reader on God's future work "in the last days" and his promise to send a king from the tribe of Judah. Here I want to suggest that this poetic focus on a coming king is what connects Jesus to the theology of the Pentateuch. It does so, I will suggest, in a very Pauline way.

I have also argued elsewhere that these poems were not inserted into the Pentateuch in an isolated and haphazard way. There is a strategic plan to the whole. Each poem is linked to the others by a network of cross-referencing. The "young lion" from the tribe of Judah in Genesis 49 is identified as the victorious king whom Balaam saw arising "in the last days" (Num 24:9a).

The intent of this cross-referencing to other poems in the Pentateuch is to connect each of the images in these poems to the single picture of a future king. Ultimately, it is along the seams of such strategies that we encounter the theology of the Pentateuch. We know that it extends to the "whole Pentateuch" when the scope and distribution of the strategy lies along the final boundaries of the Pentateuch viewed as a whole—that is, from Genesis to Deuteronomy. This is larger than the compositional shape of the book of Genesis or other sections in the Pentateuch. It is a strategy that encompasses the whole book. This strategy, as I have argued, focuses on a coming king from the house of Judah.[8]

---

[7]I want to emphasize the importance of the comprehensive thematic focus on faith, promise and law noted above. They are not merely the theological substratum of the Pentateuch's messianic hope. They form the basis of the later prophetic dependence on the Pentateuch for its central themes. They are, as well, a major link into the NT.

[8]One has only to read the Pentateuch to see that its narratives are framed by several key poems. These poems are the primary means of introducing the biblical Jesus into the Pentateuch. Unlike the other themes that are woven into the narratives, these poetic texts are like interludes that repeatedly break into the text—something like the songs in a Hollywood musical. They are road signs telling the readers where they are and where they are going. Their distribution within the Pentateuch represents the most comprehensive element of the book's composition. Their range is from the first chapter of Genesis to the last chapter of Deuteronomy. This kind of insertion of highly interpretive material is an ancient literary technique. Shemaryahu Talmon calls this "inli-

Here I want here to make a few observations on three of the four major poems in the Pentateuch (Gen 49; Num 24; Deut 33). These observations, I believe, move us closer to what the Pentateuch has to say about the biblical Jesus.

*"In the last days."* The first observation about these three poems is that each has an identical introduction linking it to events of "the last days." The expression "in the last days" *(bĕʾ aḥărît hayyāmîm)* is common in the prophetic literature, but it occurs in the Pentateuch only in these three introductions and in Deuteronomy 4:30 (in Deut 4 referring to the time of the exile). In the prophetic books it consistently refers to the future messianic age.[9]

The strategic placement of this phrase in the introduction to the poems suggests that it is part of the larger compositional framework of the Pentateuch to which Deuteronomy 4:30 also belongs. In that context, according to C. F. Keil and Franz Delitzsch, the phrase "in the last days" refers at the least to the time of the return from Babylonian captivity and probably beyond.[10] Whatever one might say about the various translations of the phrase "in the last days," it is clear that the author of the Pentateuch saw in it a key to his understanding of the poems and to the Pentateuch as a whole. The poems, and consequently the Pentateuch itself, were about the events of the "last days."

*Announcement of a "coming King."* A second observation about these three poems in the Pentateuch is their common reference point. Each one focuses the reader on a coming king who will bring peace and prosperity to the nations.

---

bration." It is the joining together of diverse "sources," or a secondary stitching together of additional material into the basic fabric of a text. ("The Presentation of Synchroneity and Simultaneity in Biblical Narrative," *Scripta Hierosolymitana* 27 [1978]: 13-14). We have already noted that the individual narratives in the Pentateuch occur in large blocks: the patriarchal narratives in Genesis, the exodus from Egypt narratives in Exodus, the wilderness narratives in Numbers, and finally the early conquest narratives in Deuteronomy. After each of these large blocks of narrative the author has placed a lengthy (and theologically rich) poem: Genesis 49, Numbers 23–24, Deuteronomy 32–33. These poems thematize for the reader a recurring topic: the coming of a royal redeemer. It is there that we can begin to see traces of the biblical Jesus. The same pattern occurs in the compositional seams of Genesis 1–11. Throughout the primeval history the author attaches poems to the conclusions of each segment of narrative. Viewed compositionally, Genesis 1–11 is a kind of patchwork of narratives and poems. As such, it is a microcosm of the rest of the Pentateuch—narratives followed by interpretive poems. To understand the meaning of the Pentateuch, one has to listen closely to these poems.

[9]W. Staerk, "Der Begrauch der Wendung בְּאַחֲרִית הַיָּמִים im alttestamentlichen Kanon," *ZAW* 11 (1891): 247-53.

[10]C. F. Keil and F. Delitzsch, *The Pentateuch*, trans. James Martin (BCOT; Grand Rapids: Eerdmans, 1971), p. 313.

1. The King in Genesis 49:8-12. The poem in Genesis 49 recounts Jacob's last words to each of his sons. The Judah segment (Gen 49:8-12), along with Joseph's (Gen 49:22-26),[11] clearly are the center of the author's attention. These two sections alone make up nearly half the poem (114 words [Judah/Joseph] and 127 words [for the rest of the sons]). Judah's "saying" stresses the ideal kingship promised to his house. It is a vision of a victorious king whose reign encompasses all the nations. His coming will be accompanied by a restoration of the abundance of the garden of Eden.

2. The King in Numbers 24:5-9. The second major poem, Numbers 24, begins with a vision of the restoration of the Lord's garden and the rise of a future king (Num 24:5-9). Its content is similar to Genesis 49. The king in Numbers 24, for example, is identified with the king in Genesis 49 by means of an extended quotation from Genesis 49:9: "He lies down and stretches out *[rābaṣ]* like a lion, and like a lioness; who will awaken him?" *(kāraʿ rābaṣ kĕʾaryeh ûkĕlābîʾ mî yĕqîmennû).* In Numbers 24:9 Balaam quotes these words to describe the king of his vision: "He lies down and stretches out *[šākab]* like a lion, and like a lioness; who will awaken him?" *(kāraʿ šākab kaʾărî ûkĕlābî mî yĕqîmennû).* Keil observes that Balaam closes this utterance, as he had the previous one, with a quotation from Jacob's blessing "which he introduces to show to Balak, that, according to words addressed by Jehovah to the Israelites through their own tribe-father, they were to overcome their foes so thoroughly, that none of them should venture to rise up against them again."[12]

3. The King in Deuteronomy 33:4-7. Like Genesis 49, Deuteronomy 33 describes the future in store for Israel's tribes. In its prologue Moses depicts God's appearing to Israel at Mount Sinai and their establishment there as a people *(ʿam).* In Deuteronomy 33:5 Moses speaks of a king surrounded by his loyal subjects, the tribes of Israel. Then, addressing Judah (Deut 33:7), Moses calls on God to fulfill his promise of a king from Judah. In Deuteronomy 33:7 Moses envisions the king's reuniting God's people and pleads earnestly for his arrival: "O that you would bring him to his people." These features demonstrate a close link between Deuteronomy 33 and the other poems in the Pentateuch.

---

[11]The extra material in the Joseph segment deals with his inheritance of the blessing of the firstborn, as is later explained in 1 Chronicles 5:1-2.

[12]Keil and Delitzsch, *The Pentateuch*, p. 191.

In its opening verse (Deut 33:1) the poem is identified as a "blessing." It is the blessing with which Moses blessed Israel "before he died." This is one of a long list of "blessings" in the Pentateuch that begins in Genesis 1:28 and ends in Deuteronomy 33. According to Keil, the editor of the poem in Deuteronomy has clearly distinguished himself from Moses. This editor, says Keil, made similar additions to the poem when he inserted the blessing of Moses in the Pentateuch.

Deuteronomy 33:4 may be one of those editorial additions Keil had in mind. Moses, as the one speaking (Deut 33:1), would not likely say, "Moses gave us the law." The problem is not whether Moses, as the author or narrator, would refer to himself in the third person as "Moses"— that is, "Moses gave the law." He frequently does that. The difficultly is that if this were Moses speaking in the dialogue, he would not at the same time refer to himself in the third person (as "Moses") and in the first-person plural ("us") as "Israel" *(lānû mōšeh).* The resulting meaning of Deuteronomy 33:4-5 is not difficult. It says that Moses gave Israel the law *(tôrâ)* as their own possession, and that God, as their "king," gathered together the tribes of Israel to make them a people *(ʿam).*

In Deuteronomy 33:7 the speaker turns to the tribe of Judah and calls on God's help for them. He says, "Hear, O LORD, the voice of Judah *[yĕhûdâ]* and bring *[tĕbîʾĕnnû]* to his people *[ʿammô]* the one who contends with his own hands for what belongs to him *[lô].* Be a help [to him] from his enemies *[miṣṣārāyw]!*" Most attempts to explain this obscure saying are unconvincing. The reason lies not so much in the obscurity of the saying itself as in the unlikely attempts to tie it to the actual historical circumstances of the tribe of Judah. The sense of the saying is fairly straightforward. It expresses the hope that God will bring Judah to his own people and help him contend for that which rightly belongs to him. There are no known historical events that can be identified with a hope such as that, apart perhaps from the hope that surrounded the return from Babylonian exile. That, however, is too much of a stretch because in exile Judah was not separated from "his people." There was no need for him to "be brought back to his people."

There is, however, another possibility for the meaning of this verse. The frequent innertextual connections between the other poems in the Pentateuch raise the possibility that the brief remark about Judah in Deuteronomy 33:7 is an allusion to, or "learned quotation" (see the next section below) from, the Judah poem in Genesis 49. There are, in fact, several verbal links between the two poems.

It is commonly recognized, for example, that the whole of Deuteronomy 33 is a patchwork of borrowed bits and pieces of expressions and themes from Genesis 49. Deuteronomy 33:7 is likely one of them, and these pieces have been used by the author to link the two poems.

In Genesis 49:10 Jacob says of Judah, "The scepter will not depart from Judah . . . until the one to whom it belongs *[šîlōh / sîlô]* comes *[yābōʾ];* and to him *[wĕlô]* will be the obedience of the peoples *[ʿammîm].*" Judah must wait for the "coming one" *(yābōʾ)* to whom the kingship (scepter) belongs *(šîlōh / sîlô).* When he comes to the peoples *(ʿammîm),* they will submit to his authority—that is, his reign *(wĕlô).*

From reading Deuteronomy 33:7 as a learned quotation of, and commentary on, Genesis 49, we see that here Moses is praying for the coming of the one promised to Judah in Genesis 49. Moses, like Hannah (1 Sam 2:10) many years later, prays for the fulfillment of the Lord's word in these poems. Moses asks that God will bring *(tĕbîʾennû)* the royal scepter from the house of Judah to his people *(ʿammô).* He is the one who "with his own hands, contends for what is rightfully his *[lô]*" and for the "obedience of the peoples/nations *[yiqqĕhat ʿammîm].*" Deuteronomy 33:7 is thus a summary and reiteration of the hope expressed in Genesis 49:10. Hannah's psalm demonstrates that later readers of the Pentateuch were aware of the prophetic meaning of these early poems in the Pentateuch. She sees these poems as visions of a coming "messianic" king: "And may [the Lord] give strength to his kind, and may he raise[13] the horn of his anointed one [messiah])" *(wĕyitten-ʿōz lĕmalkô wĕyārēm qeren mĕšîḥô).* Hannah is not prophesying the coming of a king, the Messiah; rather, she is praying for the fulfillment of the poetic visions of the king in the Pentateuch's own poems. Hannah's reference to "king" and "messiah" suggest that she is citing the poems of the Pentateuch as a learned quotation.

*"Learned quotations" in poetry.* The third observation on the poems in the Pentateuch takes up further the Henricus Ewald's notion of a "learned quotation." As I have suggested, the poems in the Pentateuch often contain com-

[13]The verb form in the second half of the verse (jussive: וְיָרֵם, *wĕyārēm*) shows that Hannah is not predicting a future event, but is requesting the coming of a king about whom she is well versed. This suggests that she is familiar with the Pentateuch's poems.

ments and allusions that manifest a compositional awareness of other poems and strategic texts in the Pentateuch. The point of such quotations is to highlight the role these poems play within the compositional strategy of the book as a whole. We have noted the quotation from Genesis 49:9 in Numbers 24:9 and also the reference to Genesis 49:10 in Deuteronomy 33:7 (recall too what was said in the preceding section about Hannah's psalm in 1 Sam 2:10). Taken together, these poems function as a kind of compositional switchboard of innerbiblical (or innertextual) connections. They contribute to the mutual clarification and identification of the poetic images. Their primary focus is innertextual; that is, they tie together and clarify important themes within the Pentateuch. That they can also function "intertextually" (between books) is clear from from the example of 2 Samuel 2:10 and many other parts of the OT.

Now I want to go a step further and point to some additional cross-referencing in these poems. What I have in mind are the links between these poems and the patriarchal promise narratives in Genesis.[14] Poems are intentionally linked to narratives. These links are a network of cross-references that connect the poems to the patriarchal promise narratives and the themes developed in them. Genesis 49 cross-references the promise narrative in Genesis 27. Numbers 24 also cross-references that narrative. Genesis 27 in turn cross-references Genesis 12.

Although these cross-references have long been recognized, little importance has been attached to them in light of the whole of the Pentateuch and its compositional strategy. The reason for this oversight is a failure to appreciate the role of these poems and promise texts within the composition of the Pentateuch. If one understands that the poems and promise texts are major constituents of the compositional strategy of the Pentateuch, the importance of the connections between them becomes obvious.

In that light, we must reexamine the connections between the poems and the promise narratives in the Pentateuch and raise the question of what those connections tell us about the coming king forecast in the Pentateuch's poetry. The answer to that question, if I am right about the nature of the composition of the Pentateuch, is that the poems in the Pentateuch (Gen 49; Num 24;

---

[14]I am using the expression "promise narrative" as a general reference to a series of narratives in Genesis 12–50 that stress the importance of a divine covenant as the basis of a blessing bestowed on Abraham and his descendants. For a more specific sense of the "promise" terminology, see pp. 419-20.

Deut 33) identify the promised seed of Abraham (Gen 12–13) as the coming king from Judah. The "seed" in the Genesis narratives is the "king" of the poems. There is an almost "Pauline" aspect to the argument in the Pentateuch that its focus is on an individual "seed" of Abraham to whom the promise was made (Gal 3:16; cf. Mt 1:1).

*The poems and the Genesis promise narratives.* A close reading of the Pentateuch's poetry shows that its poems not only cross-reference themselves, as has been illustrated above, but they also cross-reference the promise narratives in Genesis (Gen 12–50). This is a very revealing aspect of the composition of the Pentateuch. It is here that we see the important role these texts play in the theology of the Pentateuch.

The Genesis promise narratives center on the making of a divine promise to the "seed" of Abraham. God says to Abraham, "In your seed all the nations of the earth will be blessed" (Gen 22:18). The question is whether that "seed" is identified as the people of Israel, the plural descendants of Abraham, or a specific descendant of Abraham, a future promised one. Viewed from the perspective of Moses, the author of the Pentateuch, is the "seed" Israel (collective) or Jesus (singular)?

The Genesis promise narratives focus on the making of a divine promise to the "seed" of Abraham. Also well known is the question of whether that "seed" is the whole of Abraham's descendants, the people of Israel, or more simply, an individual descendant of Abraham, the biblical Jesus. Biblically and exegetically, the issue comes into focus with Paul's statement in Galatians 3:16: "Now the promises were spoken to Abraham and to his seed. It does not say, 'And to his seeds,' referring to many; but, referring to one, 'And to your seed,' which is Christ."

Ernest Burton's assessment of Paul's meaning in Galatians is characteristic of many expositions of this passage:

> This is, of course, not the meaning of the original passage referred to. . . . [Paul] is well aware of the collective sense of the word σπέρμα in the Gen[esis] passage (see v. 29 and Rom. 4:13-18). He doubtless arrived at his thought, not by exegesis of scripture, but from an interpretation of history, and then availed himself of the singular noun to express his thought briefly.[15]

[15]Ernest De Witt Burton, *A Critical and Exegetical Commentary on the Epistle to the Galatians* (ICC; Edinburgh: T & T Clark, 1921), p. 182.

To some extent, one can sympathize with Burton's comments. It is difficult to see where Paul's exegesis might have originated. It is just here, however, that the cross-referencing between the poetry and promise narratives in the Pentateuch may provide some exegetical help. Paul's point is very close to the ideas that lie behind the distribution and interrelationship of the poems and the promises narratives in the Pentateuch. Paul may have been guided by these poems in his own reading of the promise narratives in Genesis. If so, Paul may have had more exegetical grounds for his views than Burton has allowed. In any event, in light of the conclusions that Paul seems to draw from the Pentateuch, the relationship between the poems and the promise narratives in the Pentateuch merits further study. Here I want to make a couple observations toward that end.[16]

1. Genesis 27:29 Quotes Genesis 12:3. Before discussing the links between the poetry and the patriarchal promise narratives, I want to point to some cross-referencing within the promise narratives themselves. Genesis 27:29, for example, specifically quotes Genesis 12:3. This is the same kind of cross-referencing we have noted in the poems, though here it connects two promise narrative texts. Ewald characterizes such cross-references as "learned quotations." They are the kinds of references that a well-informed "scholar" would make in citing a specific passage in a book.

Genesis 27:29, a patriarchal promise text, cites another promise text in Genesis 12:3: "Let peoples serve you, and nations bow down to you. Be lord over your brothers, and may your mother's sons bow down to you. Cursed be every one who curses you, and blessed be every one who blesses you *[ʾōrĕreykā ʾārûr ûmĕbārăkeykā bārûk]*" (Gen 27:29). The citation of Genesis 12 within the promise narrative in Genesis 27–28 is an important connecting link between the Abrahamic promise and Jacob's blessing. It reminds the reader that in Abraham's seed (*zeraʿ* [Gen 28:4]) the nations will obtain God's blessing to Abraham.

It is widely conceded that the poem in Genesis 27:29 is a quotation of the Abrahamic promise in Genesis 12:3: "I will bless those who bless you, those who curse you, I will curse" (*waʾăbārăkâ mĕbārkeykā ûmĕqallelkā ʾāʾōr* [Gen

[16]John Calvin: "I have often been astonished that Christians, when they saw this passage so perversely tortured, . . . did not make a more determined resistance; for all pass it slightly as if it were an indisputed territory. And yet there is much plausibility to their objection" (*Commentaries on the Epistles of Paul to the Galatians and Ephesians* [Grand Rapids: Baker, 1979], p. 94).

12:3]). The quotation in Genesis 27:29 of the promise to Abraham in Genesis 12:3 establishes a direct link between the Abrahamic promise (Gen 12:3, 7) and Jacob's blessing in Genesis 27:29. In Abraham's seed (*zeraʿ* [Gen 28:4]) the nations will obtain God's blessing.

Still, the important question for biblical theology (and the quest for the biblical Jesus) is the identity of this "seed." Is the "seed" an individual redeemer, or is it the nation as a whole? The collective nature of the Hebrew word "seed" *(zeraʿ)* makes either sense possible. Here is where we must again turn to the poetic links in the Pentateuch. I have in mind, to begin with, the cross-referencing between Genesis 49 and Genesis 27.

2. Genesis 49:8 Quotes Genesis 27:29. In the poem in Genesis 49 Jacob tells Judah, "The sons of your father will bow down to you" (*yištaḥăwwû lĕkā bĕnê ʾābîkā* [Gen 49:8]). This is a well-known cross-reference to the promise narrative in Genesis 27:29: "And may the sons of your mother bow down to you." Here again a compositionally important poem (Gen 49) is linked to a key patriarchal promise narrative, Genesis 27. The link noted above between Genesis 27:29 and the Abrahamic blessing in Genesis 12 is here extended to the royal figure in Genesis 49:10. The "seed" of Abraham is thus linked directly to the king from Judah.

3. Numbers 24:9a Quotes Genesis 49:9. As we have just seen, the connection between Genesis 27 and Genesis 49 has serious consequences for the identity of the biblical Jesus. A similar learned quotation in the poem in Numbers 24:7-9 provides a further connection between the king of Balaam's vision and the king from Judah in Genesis 49:10. What Genesis 49:9 says about the lion of the tribe of Judah, Balaam, in Numbers 24:9a applies to his own vision of a victorious monarch. He "lies down and spreads out like a lion, and like a lioness; who will arouse him?"[17] Thus, by means of the cross-referencing within these poems and between the poems and the promise narratives, the king of the Pentateuch's poems is identified as the "seed" of Abraham.[18]

[17]In Genesis 49:9 the lion of Judah "lies down and stretches out *[rābaṣ]* like a lion, and like a lioness; who will awaken him?" In Numbers 24:9 Balaam uses those same words to describe the king of his vision: "He lies down and stretches out *[šākab]* out like a lion, and like a lioness; who will awaken him?"

[18]This is an important example because it shows that the author has intentionally linked these poems at the verbal, narrative and thematic levels. See Shimon Bar-Efrat, "Some Observations on the Analysis of Structure in Biblical Narrative," *VT* 30 (1980): 154-73.

It seems clear that these learned quotations of the promise narratives within the Pentateuch's poems are intentional. Their intent is to identify the "seed" promised to Abraham (Gen 12) with the "scepter from the tribe of Judah" (Gen 49) and Balaam's victorious "king" (Num 24). The "king" in each of these poems is thus linked directly to the promise of the "seed" of Abraham.

This brings us to a further link between the poems and the promise narratives. Numbers 24:9b is a learned quotation of the promise narrative in Genesis 27:29.

4. Numbers 24:9b Quotes Genesis 27:29. In his description of the coming king in the poem in Numbers 24:5-9[19] Balaam concludes by citing Genesis 27:29b: "Those who bless you will be blessed, those who curse you will be cursed" (*mĕbārăkeykā bārûk wĕʾōrĕreykā ʾārûr* [Num 24:9b]). Commentaries generally agree that the purpose of citing Genesis 27 in Numbers 24 is to identify the king in Numbers 24:7 as the promised seed of the Abrahamic blessing. However, since the "king" in Numbers 24 is commonly but wrongly identified with Israel,[20] the "seed" in the Genesis promise narratives is also sometimes understood as a collective for Israel. I will argue below that the king of Numbers 24 is not a collective, but is an individual king who is, in fact, contrasted with Israel. Numbers 24 is thus positioned to play a major role in the identification of the "seed" of Abraham as an individual king.

Regardless of the sense of the details in these texts, everyone seems to agree that the citation of Genesis 27 in Numbers 24 establishes an intentional connection between all the major poems and the promise narratives in the Pentateuch. That connection lies at the highest thematic level within the Pentateuch—that is, the composition of the whole. At that level this link identifies Abraham's "seed" in the promise narratives with the king of Numbers 24. In addition, since the king in Numbers 24 is also identified here with the king in Genesis 49, that king (Num 24) cannot be a collective figure for Israel. According to Genesis 49, he can only be the promised king from the tribe of Judah.

The fact that Numbers 24 quotes Genesis 27:29 much like a modern author would quote from a printed book suggests a sophisticated level of inner-

---

[19]Although in the MT this king is said to defeat Agag (something that may identify him with David), in all the earlier texts the king rises from defeating Gog. This is not David, but a future eschatological king known from Ezekiel's vision in Ezekiel 38. It is Numbers 24 that Ezekiel surely has in mind when he identifies Gog with the one spoken of "in former days."

[20]Numbers 24:8: "God brought *them* out of Egypt" (NIV); "God brings *him* out of Egypt" (NASB).

textuality within the compositional strategy of the Pentateuch. Keil accepted the notion that the quotation of Genesis 27 in Numbers 24 was part of a larger strategy linking Jacob's blessing in Genesis 27 to the blessing of Abraham's seed in Genesis 12:3.[21] For much the same reason, Procksch also acknowledged that the individual addressed in Genesis 27:29 was intentionally identified as the future recipient of the blessing of Abraham in Genesis 12:3.[22] In each case, these scholars identified the individual in these texts as the future king of Balaam's vision.

The larger functionality of Numbers 24:9b and its relationship to Genesis 27:29 is thus clearly understood in the commentaries. Yet, in spite of their general awareness of such innertextual connections, commentaries have been reluctant to move on to a further conclusion about the individual in these texts whom I am calling the "biblical Jesus." They have readily acknowledged that the cross-referencing in these texts is a sign of advanced literary (or compositional) activity, and they have acknowledged that these features represent intelligent design and authorial intent. Nobody explains them as coincidental. They are the work of the author of the Pentateuch. What they fail to see is the larger purpose of these connections.

Westermann, although he acknowledges the textual relationships between Genesis 27 and the poems in Genesis 49, Numbers 24 and Deuteronomy 33, draws no significance from these parallels. For him, the parallels suggest only an historical proximity of the various sources in which these texts are found.[23] There is no consideration of any meaningful connection between these texts within the Pentateuch as a whole. Westermann clearly focuses on strata versus strategy.

But clearly what is important about these innertextual connections is that they are evidence of a larger compositional stratagem. The author of the Pentateuch is going somewhere with these texts. Clearly, the connections between the poems and the promise narratives in Genesis tell us much about

---

[21]According to Keil, the author in Numbers 24 has attached to Balaam's oracle the word by which Isaac had transferred the blessing of Abraham (Gen 12:3) to Jacob (Keil and Delitzsch, *The Pentateuch*, p. 191). Keil clearly is aware of a conscious effort within the Pentateuch to link the poems in Numbers 24 and Genesis 49 with Genesis 27 and Genesis 12. He does not appear to be aware, however, of the further implications of these connections, which are that these poems envision an individual, promised "seed."

[22]"Mit v. 29b klingt das Hauptthema 12,3 wieder auf" (Otto Procksch, *Die Genesis: Übersetzt und erklärt* [KAT 1; Leipzig: Deichert, 1913], p. 162).

[23]Westermann, *Genesis 12–36*.

the author's understanding of the "seed" of Abraham in texts such as Genesis 12:3-7; 22:18. The textual links between the patriarchal promise narratives and the focus on an individual "king" in the poems suggest a compositional strategy that intentionally identifies the "seed" of Abraham *(zeraʿ)* with an individual king from the tribe of Judah.

To be sure, at numerous points within the promise narratives, the identity of the "seed" of Abraham is clearly understood collectively. But, as true as that observation is, it is not the whole story. By connecting the poetic texts to the promise narratives, the author of the Pentateuch moves decisively away from a collective reading of the promise narratives and toward an individual understanding of Abraham's "seed" (Gen 12:3-7). It is hard to avoid the implication that in the quotation of Genesis 27:29 in Numbers 24:9b, the author identifies the individual "king" of Balaam's oracle (Num 24:7-9) with the "seed" of Abraham in the Genesis promise narratives. The king[24] whom Balaam foresaw is the individual "seed" of Abraham through whom the nations will be blessed (Num 24:9b).[25]

The obvious question raised by these widely recognized innertextual connections in the Pentateuch is why their full implications have so long escaped the attention of biblical scholars. The answer, I believe, is that biblical scholarship continues to read both the poems in the Pentateuch and the promise narratives in isolation. For most commentators, the clear focus on an "individual" king in the poems of the Pentateuch has little effect on their understanding of the meaning of the promise narratives.[26]

---

[24]What is unusual about the notion of a king in these poems is that otherwise the idea of a king and kingship is relatively uncommon in the Pentateuch. It has been traditionally held that the primary focus of the Pentateuch is on a priestly theocracy (see Vos, *Biblical Theology*, pp. 140-41). These poems carry much of the weight of whatever hope exists for a royal messiah in the Pentateuch, or elsewhere.

[25]The king in the poem in Deuteronomy 33 is one who gathers Israel as Moses once did and leads them in fulfilling God's plan as laid out in the earlier poems. In a direct reference to the promise of a king in Genesis 49, Moses (in Deut 33:7) prays that God would fulfill his promise to Judah and send the promised king.

[26]Genesis 15:5 is a typical example of the collective nature of the promise narratives: "And he brought him outside and said, 'Look toward heaven, and number the stars, if you are able to number them.' Then he said to him, 'So shall your descendants [seed] be'" (RSV). Here the "seed" is clearly a collective. If such a text were all we had, the notion of the "seed of Abraham" in the patriarchal promise texts would almost certainly be understood as a collective, though even here there are important exceptions. But if the promise texts and the poems in the Pentateuch are extended to be read together by the author, a quite different (individual) meaning emerges. These compositional connections among the pentateuchal texts are thus of central importance, even though they have been largely overlooked by the commentaries and biblical scholarship in general.

George Gray, for example, is well-aware of the similarities between Numbers 24:9b and Genesis 27:29, but he gives little or no thought to the possibility of a compositional connection between those texts. Consequently, he fails even to consider the possibility of a semantic link between the poems and the promise texts. For Gray, Numbers 24:9b ("Those who bless you will be blessed, and those who curse you will be cursed") is merely a current saying in Balaam's day.[27] It served as Balaam's personal motive for blessing Israel instead of cursing them (i.e., he merely wanted to get rich).

August Dillmann recognized the implication of the singular pronouns ("you") in Numbers 24:9b, but he explained them without reference to the king in Numbers 24:9a. He thus read even the singular pronouns as collectives. In taking that position, Dillmann was forced to the unlikely conclusion that the singular pronouns in Number 24:9b were a collective reversion to the beginning of the oracle in Numbers 24:5. There, Dillmann argued, Israel and Jacob are addressed as collectives—for example, "your tents, O Jacob." According to Dillman, the attachment of Numbers 24:9b to Balaam's oracle was merely Balaam's warning to Balak lest he continue to mistreat Israel.[28]

So, neither Gray nor Dillmann provides a broader textual explanation for the cross-referencing between these passages (Numbers 24 and Genesis 27).[29]

In our day, with its increasing awareness of composition and textual strategies, the learned quotations and literary connections to which I have pointed cannot be ignored. Within the structure of the Pentateuch, the poems are the author's last and most important word regarding the message of the Penta-

---

[27]Numbers 24:9b is "perhaps a current saying in Israel: cp. Gn. 27:29 (also 12:3). But even if so, it is effectively introduced here as the climax of the blessing. So far from cursing, Balaam will, as he values his own welfare, bless Israel" (George Buchanan Gray, *A Critical and Exegetical Commentary on Numbers* [ICC; Edinburgh: T & T Clark, 1965], p. 366).

[28]"V$^{b}$: seine dominirende Stellung unter den Völkern, wornach ihr Segen u. Fluch davon abhängt, wie sie sich zu Isr. verhalten, wie Gen. 27, 29. 12,3 bei C. . . . Zu bemerken ist, dass die Anrede Israels, womit der Spruch begonnen hat V. 5, hier am Schluss wiederkehrt, so wie dass in יארור וארר ein deutlicher Fingerzeig für Balaq, wenn er seine Versuche fortsetzt, liegt" (August Dillmann, *Die Bücher Numeri, Deuteronomium und Josua* [KEHAT 13; Leipzig: Hirzel, 1886], p. 159). Apart from the questionable identification of "Jacob" and "Israel" as collectives in Numbers 24:5, Dillmann's reading of these poems necessitates an ackward skipping over of Balaam's entire oracle in search of a desired "collective" antecedent. The simple rule of preferring the nearest antecedent would have immediately connected Number 24:9b, "those who bless you, I will bless," to the individual king in Numbers 24:7-9a. The "seed" *(zeraʿ)* of Abraham (Gen 12:3, 7) would then be identified as the individual king linked directly to the "seed" *(lĕzarʿăkā)* of Jacob's blessing (Gen 27:29; 28:4) and to the one who holds the scepter from the house of Judah in Genesis 49:10.

[29]See Sailhamer, *Introduction to Old Testament Theology*, pp. 36-85.

teuch. If we are seeking the author's intent, these texts are of primary importance. The texts and connections that we have examined clearly envision an individual king as the recipient of the patriarchal promise. The "seed of Abraham" is an individual king. In terms of the whole of the Bible, this is part of the picture of the biblical Jesus.

A final word is in order here. In at least one promise narrative, Genesis 15:3-4, an individual meaning of the Abrahamic promise is already in place within the narrative itself. According to Genesis 15:3-4, "Abram said, 'Behold, you have not given me a seed; and behold a household steward will possess me.' And behold, the word of the LORD came to him, 'This *[zeh]* one shall not possess you; one from your own loins shall possess you.'" Clearly, in this promise text the "seed" of Abraham is already viewed as an individual descendant of Abraham. Hence, the move toward an individual reading of the promise texts, which we see within the learned quotations of the poetry, has already made its way into the promise narratives.[30] In the case of Genesis 15:3-4, its individualistic reading of the Abrahamic promised "seed" (as in Gen 4:25) is placed alongside a manifestly collective reading of the same promise (Gen 15:5). Abraham's "seed" will be as numerous as the stars in the heavens, and he will be an individual son of Abraham, such as Isaac. It is hard to avoid the conclusion that Genesis 15 intentionally envisions both an individual and a collective "seed" of Abraham,[31] just as the apostle Paul's treatment of these texts in Galatians 3:16, 29.

*Summary.* The interpretation of the meaning of the expression "seed of Abraham" is grounded in an understanding of the compositional strategy of the Pentateuch. The poems represent the author's final assessment of the details of the promise narratives. If the promise narratives are read in isolation from the Pentateuch's poems, the meaning of "seed of Abraham" can easily be understood in a collective sense as Israel. If, however, the promise texts are understood in terms of the poems in the Pentateuch, they are unmistakably individual. Hence, in terms of the final compositional strategy of the Pentateuch, the primary identity of the "seed of Abraham" is an individual king from the tribe of Judah.[32]

---

[30]Or was already part of those narratives at the time of the composition of the Pentateuch.

[31]In such a case, Burton's judgment of Paul's exegesis as not in "the original passage" needs to be qualified.

[32]See further M. Daniel Carroll R., "New Lenses to Establish Messiah's Identity?" in Richard S. Hess and M. Daniel Carroll R., *Israel's Messiah in the Bible and the Dead Sea Scrolls* (Grand Rapids:

The citation of promise narratives within poetic texts such as Numbers 24:9 demonstrates that an individual reading of those texts was fully intended to play itself out within the Pentateuch at the time of its composition.

Explanatory commentary in promise narratives such Genesis 15:3-4 suggests that an individual understanding of these texts played an early and productive role in the composition of the Pentateuch. This is an interpretation that lies along the compositional shaping of the entire Pentateuch. It is not the sort of strategy that could be loosely introduced into the Pentateuch by a later scribe.

***The covenant-blessing narratives and the prophets.*** We turn now to the question of how the prophets and psalmists understood the Pentateuch's promise texts and how they integrated its picture of the biblical Jesus into their own writings. To answer that question, we must look to the prophets themselves for similar learned quotations of the Pentateuch's promise narratives. Do the prophets quote the Pentateuch (intertextuality) as the Pentateuch quotes itself (innertextuality)? Do the prophets read the Pentateuch's promise narratives as I have suggested that they were intended by the author of the Pentateuch—that is, innertextually? Have they seen the connection between the "seed" of Abraham and the individual king in the Pentateuch's poems?

A likely place to begin in the prophetic literature is the citation of the Genesis promise narratives in Jeremiah 4:1-2:

> If you return, O Israel, says the LORD, to me you should return. If you remove your abominations from my presence, and do not waver, and if you swear, 'As the LORD lives,' in truth, in justice *[bĕmišpāṭ],* and in uprightness *[ûbiṣdāqâ],* then the nations shall be blessed in him, and in him shall they glory.

Since Jerome's day, this text has been recognized as a citation[33] of one or more of the patriarchal promise narratives (e.g., Gen 18:18; 22:18).[34] The

Baker, 2003), pp. 80-81. Carroll suggests, in the case of the "servant" in Isaiah, that the individual servant is not one who is disconnected from his people. The purpose of the ambiguity (collective versus individual) is to insure the identity of the individual servant from within the historical dimensions of the people of Abraham.

[33]Henricus Ewald called it "a learned quotation from a book."

[34]The literary identity between the text of Jeremiah 4:2 and Genesis 22:18 suggests that Jeremiah is quoting, or at least is literarily dependent on, Genesis 22:18. The only notable difference between the two texts is the exchange of "in him" *(bô)* for "in your [Abraham's] seed" *(bĕzarʿăkā).* "Perhaps there is an allusion to the promise to Abraham (cf. Gen xviii 18 and similar passages)" (John Bright, *Jeremiah* [AB 21; Garden City, N.Y.: Doubleday, 1965], p. 34).

similarity of Jeremiah's words to the promise narratives in Genesis is unmistakable.[35] Recent commentaries generally follow Bernhard Duhm in reading Jeremiah 4:2b as "a verbatim quotation" of Genesis 22:18, 26:4 or 18:18.[36] As such, it serves as an index of Jeremiah's understanding of the Pentateuch. If our goal is to understand the prophetic meaning of the Genesis blessing narratives, Jeremiah 4:2 is the place to start.

*Jeremiah 4:2 and the Pentateuch's covenant-blessing narratives.* I have argued above that in the interelationship of the Genesis covenant narratives and the poems in the Pentateuch, the "seed" of Abraham is identified as an individual king from the house of Judah. That king is the central focus of the Pentateuch's poems. According to the poems in the Pentateuch, this king will reign over the nations "in the last days." The original blessings of creation (Gen 1:28) are pledged to him and are fulfilled in the Abrahamic covenant. He comes very close to being the "biblical Jesus" Paul speaks of in Galatians 3:16.

Jeremiah's citation of the Pentateuch in Jeremiah 4:2 suggests that he also saw important ties between these covenant narratives in the Pentateuch and several of his own prophecies. As we will see, those prophecies link the "seed" foretold in the Pentateuch to the "seed of David" who was the center of the Davidic covenant (2 Sam 7). A well-known example of Jeremiah's prophetic vision of this king is the "righteous branch" prophecy in Jeremiah 23:5-8. We will explore that passage and others below.

---

[35]Genesis 18:18 differs from Jeremiah 4:2 only in its use of the Niphal rather than the Hitpael. So similar is Jeremiah 4:2 to Genesis 22:18 that C. F. Keil and, more recently, Wilhelm Rudolph read and interpreted the Jeremiah text as if it were still part of Genesis. To move in that direction, however, it is necessary for them to make minor, but significant, alterations in the Hebrew text. This entails reading the Hebrew "then the nations shall be blessed in *him*" as if it were "then the nations shall be blessed in *you*"—that is "in you, Israel." They then conclude that Jeremiah's text was not a "direct citation" because the "in him" could not refer to Israel, who elsewhere is addressed in the second person. As it stands, the antecedent of the Jeremiah text and the Genesis 22:18 text is expressed in the third person *(bĕzarʿăkā* or *bô).* The "in your seed" of Genesis 22:18 is rendered "in him" in the Jeremiah text. Changing the Hebrew text to suit their interpretation is a bold step on the part of Keil and Rudolph, and it amounts to an admission on their part that the third-person pronoun in the Jeremiah text does not refer to Israel. Only after changing its pronouns to make it refer to Israel is Keil ready to say that "the words stand in manifest relation to the patriarchal blessing" (C. F. Keil, *The Prophecies of Jeremiah* [BCOT; Grand Rapids: Eerdmans, 1968, p. 102]). Keil rejects Jerome's view that Jeremiah's reference to Genesis is a citation, preferring to call it an allusion. His reason, however, is based on the assumption that the third-person pronoun *bô*, in an actual citation, would have to be the second-person *bĕka* to correspond to *wĕhitbārăkû bĕzarʿăkā* in Genesis 22:18.

[36]"Zu dem Citat, das v. 2b aus der späten Stelle Gen 22:18 oder 26:4 beibringt und zwar als wörtliches Citat" (Bernhard Duhm, *Das Buch Jeremia* [HKAT 11; Tübingen: Mohr Siebeck, 1901], p. 45).

A comparison of Jeremiah 4:2 with specific Pentateuchal promise texts (e.g., Gen 18:18; 22:18; 26:4) suggests considerable literary dependency of Jeremiah on Genesis:

> וְהִתְבָּרְכוּ בוֹ גּוֹיִם
> [The] nations in him will be blessed. (Jer 4:2)
> וְנִבְרְכוּ בוֹ כֹּל גּוֹיֵי הָאָרֶץ
> All the nations of the earth in him will be blessed. (Gen 18:18)
> וְהִתְבָּרֲכוּ בְזַרְעֲךָ כֹּל גּוֹיֵי הָאָרֶץ
> All the nations of the earth in your seed will be blessed. (Gen 22:18)
> וְהִתְבָּרֲכוּ בְזַרְעֲךָ כֹּל גּוֹיֵי הָאָרֶץ
> All the nations of the earth in your seed will be blessed. (Gen 26:4)

There can be little doubt that Jeremiah 4:2 is citing one or more of these covenant narratives in Genesis. Such citations raise numerous exegetical and biblical theological questions, but they also cast considerable light on how the Pentateuch was read and understood by other biblical writers, such as the prophets. What is most interesting about this particular example in Jeremiah 4:2 is that Jeremiah does not cite any one of these expressions exactly as it occurs in Genesis. There is in each instance an interpretive element brought over from Genesis and the Pentateuch. Thus, the purpose of Jeremiah's citation of the expressions in Genesis lies not in a mere redundancy or repetition of the key phrase, but in supplying some insight, or interpretation, into the meaning of these phrases in the Pentateuch. As such, they shed considerable light on Jeremiah's understanding of the covenant blessings.

In Jeremiah 4:2 the question turns on the fact that the phrase "in your seed" (*bĕzarʿăkā* [Gen 22:18; 26:4]) is rendered by "in him" *(bô)*. Jeremiah has replaced the word "seed" with the singular pronoun "him," giving the sense that "the nations of the earth will be blessed in him *[bô]*." The noun "seed" can, of course, have a collective or individual meaning. It depends on whether the pronoun that resumes it is plural, "with them" *(bām)*, or singular, "in him" *(bô)*. According to standard Hebrew grammars, if Jeremiah had understood the "seed" to be plural, he would have used a plural pronoun to refer to the collective "seed,"[37] giving the sense "the nations of the earth will be blessed in *them [bām]*." This is shown by other examples, such as "your seed will be in a land not belonging *to them [lāhem]*" (*zarʿăkā bĕʾereṣ lōʾ lāhem* [Gen 15:13]),

[37] "Plural suffixes refer to collective singulars" (GKC 441).

and "because *they [hēm]* are descendants" (*kî hēm zeraʿ* [Is 61:9]).[38] Thus, in Jeremiah 4:2 the singular pronoun "in him" *(bô)* shows that Jeremiah understood the "seed" in Genesis to be singular. The "seed" of Abraham was to be an individual. This suggests that Jeremiah had read the Genesis narratives with the sense that it was about an individual "seed" through whom the nations would be blessed. That reading follows closely the compositional strategy and the interpretation of the covenant blessings of Abraham that lie behind the use of poetry in the Pentateuch. It suggests that Jeremiah was guided by a similar reading of the Pentateuch.

Jeremiah's dependence on the Pentateuch's strategy in his identification of the "seed" as an individual raises the question of how closely he followed that strategy in his reading of the Pentateuch as a whole and in the writing of his book. As we have seen in the case of the compositional strategy behind the Pentateuch's use of poetry, the individual "seed" is identified as a king from the tribe of Judah (Gen 49:8-12). Does Jeremiah's "him" refer to that same individual? Is Jeremiah's understanding of the identity of Abraham's "seed" further developed in the book of Jeremiah, or does Jeremiah know him only from the poems in the Pentateuch?

To answer such questions, we must return for a closer look at Jeremiah 4:2 and its meaning within the book of Jeremiah. That will also take us to a consideration of the overall structure and compositional strategy of the book of Jeremiah. When viewed in that context, it is clear that Jeremiah has much to add to the Pentateuch's understanding of the "seed" of Abraham as a coming king who will be righteous and just and who will bring blessing to the nations. Throughout the book of Jeremiah this notion of the "seed" of Abraham is developed primarily through a careful reading of the pentateuchal poems.

*The contextual meaning of Jeremiah 4:2.* The general sense of Jeremiah 4:2 is clear from its context within the book of Jeremiah. The premise of the book is found in the first three chapters. Israel had strayed far from God and was now faced with the alternative of either repenting or facing the consequences of divine punishment. God's gracious alternative is wrapped up in the prophet's plea for Israel's repentance (Jer 4:1-2). Jeremiah 4 thus sets the stage for the prophet's call for repentance. It does so by returning to the prophetic hope of blessing in the patriarchal narratives of the Pentateuch. It is in these Gen-

[38]See further, ibid.

esis narratives, and the Abrahamic covenant pledged there, that Jeremiah finds his hope for Israel and blessings for the nations.

Jeremiah's citation of the Pentateuch's patriarchal narratives discloses his intimate knowledge and understanding of the Pentateuch and its compositional strategy. The nations could expect divine blessing only if Israel proved obedient. God's blessings for the nations would come only if and when Israel obeyed God. If the nations were to be blessed, as was the aim of God's covenant with Abraham (Gen 12:3), Israel must live justly and righteously (Gen 18:19; 22:16-18). Only on those terms could one expect the experience of God's blessing to be enjoyed by the nations.[39]

The theme embraced in these words is recognizable from three covenant narratives in the Pentateuch, Genesis 18:17-19; 22:15-18; 25:3-5. Both in Genesis and Jeremiah the sense is that if Israel obeys God and lives "justly and righteously" *(bĕmišpāṭ ûbiṣdāqâ),* the nations would receive Abraham's blessing through his "seed" (cf. Gen 18:18-19). As Keil puts it, the repentance of Israel "will have for its outcome the blessing of the nations."[40]

Keil, like many before him, understood the "seed" of Abraham in these texts in a collective sense—that is, as a reference to "Israel," a people. He thus understood Jeremiah 4:2 to say that "the nations will be blessed in them [i.e., Israel])." That reading of this verse, however, is not immediately clear from Jeremiah 4:2. As we have seen above, the Hebrew text is "in him" (*bô*), not "in them" *(bām).* Those who take a plural interpretation, "in them," almost invariably must resort to adjusting the text to suit that interpretation. To arrive at a collective reading, "in them," from the clearly singular pronoun "him" *(bô)* in Jeremiah 4:2, Keil was forced to read his own collective interpretation of the term "seed" in the Pentateuch back into Jeremiah's statement of the Abrahamic blessing. Keil could not, or at least did not, argue a case for the collective meaning of "seed" from the Jeremiah passage alone. Since Keil believed that the Pentateuch understood the "seed" as a plural collective and as a reference to Israel, he believed that it was also the case that Jeremiah had a similar plural meaning. Keil thus believed that what was true of the Genesis narratives was also true of the Jeremiah passage, even though he could not see

[39]"*If* you return, O Israel, says the LORD, to me you should return. *If* you remove your abominations from my presence, and do not waver, and if you swear, 'As the LORD lives,' in truth, in justice, and in uprightness, *then* the nations shall be blessed 'in him'" (Jer 4:1-2).

[40]Keil, *The Prophecies of Jeremiah*, p. 103.

how the Jeremiah passage could alone be read as a plural, "in them."

It would have been better, however, if Keil had gathered the meaning of the term "seed" from the passage in Jeremiah 4:2 before assuming that it had the same meaning for the term "seed" as Genesis. Keil's plural understanding of the covenant-blessing narratives in Genesis is what determined his understanding of the Jeremiah text as plural, "in them."

The singular sense of Jeremiah's citation of the Genesis "seed" passages moves in a different direction. It also appears to follow the compositional strategy of the Pentateuch, but it is a strategy that, as we have seen, reads the term "seed" as a singular and, hence, as an individual. According to the Pentateuch's own compositional strategy, not the one supposed by Keil, the "seed" of Abraham is understood as an individual king from the house of Judah. I will show in what follows that here in the book of Jeremiah the "seed" is also identified as an individual king from the house of Judah and is identified in the course of the book's compositional strategy as the Davidic "righteous branch" *(lĕdāwīd ṣemaḥ ṣaddîq)* whose name is "the LORD is our righteousness" *(yhwh ṣidqēnû)*. He is a royal personage, just as in the Pentateuch's poems. Jeremiah thus appears to be guided in his reading of the Pentateuch by the same kind of compositional strategy that we have previously uncovered in the Pentateuch. I will argue in the following pages that a central thesis of the book of Jeremiah is the demonstration that the "seed" of Abraham is to be understood as an individual king from the house of David who is the focus of Jeremiah's hope in the Lord.

What becomes apparent in Jeremiah's "quotations" from the Pentateuch is that he reads the Genesis texts in light of two central strategies: the blessing of the nations in Abraham's "seed"—that is, the Abrahamic covenant—and a hope for a future king from the house of David, which is the focal point of the Davidic covenant. As we will soon discover, both of these themes come together in Jeremiah's vision of a "new covenant" (Jer 31:31). He carefully weaves these two themes throughout the fabric of the first half of his book, Jeremiah 1–36.

*Crux interpretum.* The crucial question facing a thorough exegesis of this passage is, of course, the identification and grammatical sense of Jeremiah's use of the third-person pronoun "him" *(bô)*. I have suggested above that Jeremiah renders the Genesis covenant narratives in terms of an individual "seed." I should also make it clear that in the Genesis covenant-blessing narratives there is certainly a place for a collective understanding of the "seed" of Abraham as Israel, Abraham's physical descendants, but that is a reading that runs alongside the identity of an individual "seed." When Jeremiah renders the Genesis texts as singulars, "the nations will be blessed in him," he means that they are about an individual. But that raises the question of the identity of this individual "in whom" the nations are to be blessed. Is it Jeremiah's understanding that the singular meaning of the pronoun "him" is a reference to the "king" known from the Pentateuch's poetic texts? Has Jeremiah refracted the Genesis narratives through the lenses of the Pentateuch's theological poetry?

This question remains a *crux interpretum* of Jeremiah 4:2 and the Genesis texts that he cites. It has been so since the time of the LXX, and it is reflected in the apostle Paul's argumentation from this same passage. Both Paul and the LXX read the Hebrew masculine singular pronoun (*bô*) as a singular, "in him" *(en autē).* Paul applies it to Jesus *(hos estin Christos),* though the referent of the LXX is uncertain.[41]

There are four possible identifications of the pronoun "him" in Jeremiah 4:2.

1. The "Him" Is Israel. Commentaries commonly identify Jeremiah's "him" *(bô)* with Israel.[42] Their rationale is usually linked to their understanding the "seed" as Israel in the Pentateuch's covenant narratives. The difficulty posed by this view of Jeremiah 4:2 is that Israel is being addressed and is consistently referenced by the second person throughout this context.[43] As Keil and Rudolph have shown, the interpretation of the pronoun as Israel requires changing the third-person pronoun "him" *(bô)* to the second-person pronoun "you" *(bĕkā).*[44] Several English translations do that, as the NJPS

[41]Paul's view is expressed in Galatians 3:16. The LXX's reading of the pronoun as a masculine singular is found in Jeremiah 4:2b: "and by him [Israel] they [the nations] shall praise God in Jerusalem." To arive at that interpretation, the LXX must read the second-person masculine singular verbs in Jeremiah 4:2a as third-person masculine singular or third-person feminine singular. The LXX's reading of the verbal forms as third person suggests a deeper motivation for their translation, since the second-person masculine singular pronoun in Jeremiah 4:1a MT, *šiqqûṣeykā* (LXX: *ta bdelygmata autou*), identifies the verb forms in the MT as second-person masculine singular. The *autou* in the LXX is consistent with its interpretation.

[42]Already in Jerome: "Cumque, ait, hoc fecerit Israel, et per Apostolos magister fuerit gentium, tunc benedicent sive benedicentur in eo omnes gentes, et ipsum laudabunt quod solus processerit ex Israel" (*Commentariorum in Jeremiam prophetam* 1.4 [PL 24:706]).

[43]For example, *wĕnišbaʿtā* (Jer 4:2a); Rashi, Kimchi: מצודת דוד.

[44]"בְּךָ und וּבְךָ, da sich 2b nicht als wörtliches Zitat aus Gn (12,3 18,18 22,18 26,4) nachweisen lässt

translation shows: "Nations shall bless themselves by you *[bĕkā]*." Since there is no textual evidence for this solution, it can hardly be taken as a serious suggestion if our goal is to make sense of the text before us.[45]

2. The "Him" Is God. An older interpretation, still reflected in some English versions, understands the third-person pronoun "him" *(bô)* to refer to God.[46] The NASB reflects this reading of the singular pronoun: "Then the nations will bless themselves in Him." The unlikelihood of such a reading can be seen in the fact that God is speaking in this passage. If the pronoun referred to God, it would require the first person, "me" *(bî)*.[47]

3. The "Him" Is the Collective "Seed" Israel. A second-person pronoun, "you," would be required if the Jeremiah 4:2 passage referred to Israel, but the third-person singular pronoun "him" *(bô)* could be a reference to a collective, "seed," understood in the Genesis passage. Hence, the meaning of "him" might still be collective, "them,"[48] but referring not to Israel in Jeremiah's context, which would have to be in the second person, but to Israel at the time of Abraham or Israel in a gnomic sense. Jeremiah 4:2 would then have this meaning: "the nations will be blessed in them [the collective seed, Israel, in Genesis]."

Admittedly, such a reading is complex and involves several difficulties. The antecedent of "him" would not be found in the Jeremiah passage at all and would thus be identifiable only by an intertextual reference to the Pentateuch (e.g., Gen 22:18). If, as we have noted above, the pronoun "him" referred to Israel collectively here in Jeremiah 4:1-2, one would expect a second-person pronoun, rather than a third-person pronoun, since Israel is addressed throughout this passage in the second person. Although such an interpreta-

---

(gegen H. Schmidt)" (Wilhelm Rudolph, *Jeremia*, 3rd ed. [HAT 1/12; Tübingen: Mohr Siebeck, 1968], p. 28).

45 *BHS* apparatus suggests emending the text to read the second-person pronouns but cites no textual witnesses.

46 Franciscus Vatablus: "Doctus inter Hebraeos aliam affert expositionem, nempe, Adhuc veniet tempus quo etiam reliquae Gentes benedicentur in eo (scilicet Deo) & gloriabuntur in eo, & non in idolis" (in John Pearson and Anthony Scattergood, *Critica sacra* [London, 1698], 4:777).

47 To be sure, in Jeremiah's citation of the oath "As the LORD lives" in 4:2a, the reference to God is in the third person and thus could be referenced by the third-person pronoun, "in Him." But such an understanding is unlikely, given God's use of the first person elsewhere in this section *(ʾēlay, mipānay)*.

48 A similar example is the *hûʾ* in Genesis 3:15b, read as a collective: "*they* [collective] will bruise you on the head." Such an interpretation appears to be grammatically possible, although in the example from Genesis 3:15 the referent, "seed," is within the same context and not derived from the quoted text.

tion of the collective as "them" is grammatically feasible, it raises the question of why the term "seed" was pronominalized at all. If Jeremiah's quotation is a citation of Genesis 22:18, why did he not simply render it verbatim as "the nations will be blessed in your seed." Why pronominalize the collective "seed" as a third person, and, for that matter, why a third-person singular rather than a collective "in them" *(bām)?*[49]

4. The "Him" Is a Reference to the Future King of the Pentateuchal Poems. Jeremiah 4:2 is a learned quotation of the Genesis blessing narratives. The use of the singular pronoun "him" is intended to identify the "seed" of Abraham with one of his individual descendants. He is the one through whom the nations will be blessed. The use of the pronoun "him" (*bô*) to refer to the noun "seed" in the Genesis narratives suggests an awareness of the compositional strategy of the Pentateuch much like I have described above. The "seed" of Abraham is identified as an individual from the royal house of Judah (cf. Jer 23:5-6). Jeremiah's citation of the Genesis narratives and his identification of the "seed" with the singular pronoun "him" provide a contemporary witness to the Pentateuch's own understanding of the "seed" of Abraham. This citation of Genesis follows the logic of the compositional links between the poems and the covenant narratives in the Pentateuch. Jeremiah cites the covenant narratives, but he does so within the context of the theology he has drawn from the Pentateuch as a whole and, specifically, its poetry. Jeremiah thus cites Genesis 22:18 as a way of saying that when Israel lives justly and righteously, God will bless both them and the nations through the promised king from the house of David.

This interpretation of Jeremiah 4:2 is the only one that makes grammatical and exegetical sense of the pronoun "him." It is consistent with what we know of the compositional strategy of the Pentateuch, and, as I will attempt to demonstrate below, it follows the same line of argument that lies behind the compositional shape of the book of Jeremiah. The prophet Jeremiah has thus followed the innertextual logic of the compositional strategy connecting the Genesis narratives to the Pentateuch's poetic framework. Jeremiah appears to be consciously guided by the kind of connections that the author of the Pentateuch had in mind for his readers. If my understanding of this citation of Genesis is correct, we should expect

---

[49]As in Isaiah 61:9: *kî hēm zeraʿ*.

to find further references to this same strategy in the remainder of the book of Jeremiah.

We cannot, of course, expect Jeremiah to have been critically aware of the compositional strategy and the seams that help tie the Pentateuch together, at least in the way we might be aware of such things today. We can, however, expect him to have read the Pentateuch carefully, and if such compositional strategies do exist in the Pentateuch, it is reasonable to assume that they would have had their effect on any serious reader such as Jeremiah.[50] One does not have to be critically aware of a textual strategy to come under its influence or to follow its logic. One has only to be an alert and competent reader. Texts such as Joshua 1:8, Psalm 1:2 and Nehemiah 8:8, demonstrate that from its earliest beginnings, the Pentateuch has been the object of much careful study, at least by the time of the prophets and probably much earlier.[51] Jeremiah surely was one of its most avid readers. Those who handled the Tanak admonished its readers to "meditate on it day and night" (Josh 1:8; Ps 1:2). According to Nehemiah 8:7b, the priests "explained the Torah to the people who listened attentively." These texts show that exegetical explanations were possible, and at times necessary, at the textual and verbal levels. Having had the Torah explained to them, those who had listened to the public reading in Nehemiah 8 had "insight and understood the Scriptures" (Neh 8:8).

Ultimately, the question of the meaning of this particular text, or any other, rests on one's exegetical judgment regarding both the nature of the composition of the Pentateuch and Jeremiah's understanding of it.[52] Such a judgment could be made only on the basis of those texts in Jeremiah that clearly rest on or are drawn from the compositional shape of the Pentateuch.

We therefore may inquire as to what extent Jeremiah's learned quotation of Genesis 22:18 and Genesis 18:18 is a reflection of his understanding of the Pentateuch and its narratives. Would he have expected his readers to draw the same inferences from their reading of the Pentateuch? Or from their reading of the book of Jeremiah? Is it probable, or even possible, that Jeremiah and his readers would have read the patriarchal blessing narratives against the background of the prophetic vision of a coming king that is expressed in the poems?[53]

[50]Note the Pentateuch's *Glaubens Thematik* ("faith theme") reflected in Psalm 78.

[51]See John H. Sailhamer, "Hosea 11:1 and Matthew 2:15," *WTJ* 63 (2001): 87-96.

[52]Ultimately, it is a question of Jeremiah's understanding of the statement he draws from the Pentateuch: *wěhitbārăkû bězarʿăkā kōl gôyê hāʿāreṣ* (Gen 22:18; 26:4; cf. Ps 72:17; Gal 3:16).

[53]These questions are not unlike those we must ask of the NT's use of the OT. Does a NT quotation

The way to resolve such questions is, of course, to follow the path taken by these learned quotations within the compositional strategy of the remainder of the book of Jeremiah. Where does the book of Jeremiah go with these texts? How are they cited, and what is the basis of their interpretation within the book itself. As is often the case in the composition of biblical books, if the author has something specifically in mind with citations and learned quotations, it is reasonable to expect them to find exegetical support from the grammatical-syntactical sense of the book as a whole. The meaning of the biblical texts lies primarily in the structure and composition of the books themselves. Authors make meaningful texts by shaping and fashioning those texts into a whole. It is the whole that gives meaning to the parts. We come to discover the meaning of a text by relating its parts to the whole. No part is too small to contribute to the meaning of the whole, not even the pronoun "him." We should not expect the author's intent to remain hidden or exist merely as hints or allusions awaiting ingenious discovery. If they are a part of the biblical author's specific intention, we should expect them to come out into the light, grammatically, lexically and syntactically, while still within the book of Jeremiah. If they are genuinely part of the author's intention, their discovery should also pave the way to our understanding of the book and its theological message. We should also look for ways these strategies might continue to influence individual biblical books and the OT canon as a whole. This means that we should expect to find sufficient exegetical clues already within the book itself and within later biblical books to support its intertextual relationship to the Pentateuch and beyond.[54]

*Jeremiah's reading of the Pentateuch.* We have noted that one of the things that make Jeremiah's understanding of the Pentateuch's convenant texts of considerable importance is the light it sheds on how the Pentateuch was understood in his day. As the biblical texts make clear, it was prophets such as Jeremiah who preserved early biblical books such as the Pentateuch.[55] It was likely also those same prophets who were responsible for the final editions of

---

reflect a careful reading of an earlier OT text? Is that reading a real part of the earlier text?

[54]The author could, of course, have quoted Genesis 22:18 verbatim as "In *your* seed all the nations will be blessed," but that would have left unresolved all the ambiguities of the term "seed." The use of the pronoun "him" (not as a reference to a collective, but as an independent pronoun within the Jeremiah passage) suggests that Jeremiah had an individual king in mind as the "seed" in Genesis 22.

[55]For example, "Neither have we obeyed the voice of the Lord our God, to walk in his laws, which he set before us by his servants the prophets" (Dan 9:10).

the biblical books that often accompanied their own works. It is thus not an idle question to ask whether Jeremiah understood the expression "seed of Abraham" along the same lines as the Pentateuch's poems. If we could uncover Jeremiah's understanding of the Pentateuch, we would have a valuable witness to the meaning of the Pentateuch itself.

The attempt to clarify the meaning of Jeremiah's learned quotation in Jeremiah 4:2 thus points us in the direction of three further sets of exegetical questions: (1) Within its broader literary context, who or what is the further reference of the pronoun "him" in Jeremiah 4:2 (intextuality)? Does Jeremiah have someone specifically in mind? (2) Within the compositional strategy of the book of Jeremiah, what meaning is assigned to this quotation from the Pentateuch (innertextuality)? What is the book's relationship to the Pentateuch? (3) Is the meaning of Jeremiah 4:2 expanded and clarified within the remainder of the canonical context of the OT (e.g., the book of Psalms) or within the further biblical context of the NT (intertextuality)?

*Intextuality: A future king (Jer 4:2)?* Our first observation about Jeremiah's citation of the Pentateuch in Jeremiah 4:2 is that if it is read in isolation from the Pentateuch and within its immediate context, the intended reference of the pronoun "him" *(bô)* is not clearly given. It appears that Jeremiah has someone in mind, but it is not clear who that might be. There is only a hint of his identity in the fact that it is a singular pronoun. There is another hint in the use of the terms "justice and righteousness" (Jer 4:2a). Throughout the book of Jeremiah these terms are consistently associated with the Davidic kingship.[56] If they are used here for a similar purpose, these terms sound a kind of distant echo of the Davidic covenant that becomes increasingly audible throughout the rest of the book.

There is otherwise little in the passage to suggest the kind of royal ideology found in the Pentateuch's poems. We are thus largely dependent on the book of Jeremiah (innertextuality) for an understanding of his citation from the Pentateuch and the all-important identification of the pronoun "him" in the citation.

*Innertextuality: Jeremiah 4:2 in the book of Jeremiah?* Here we must raise the question of the kind of help the author of the book of Jeremiah may give us in identifying the singular pronoun "him" in Jeremiah's quotation. Are we given

[56]William McKane, *A Critical and Exegetical Commentary on Jeremiah* (ICC; Edinburgh: T & T Clark, 1986), 1:562.

(by the author) innertextual clues to its meaning? If so, the most likely place to find them appears to be along the compositional seams of the book. That is where we might most readily find the work of the author. So, how does Jeremiah 4:2 fit into the structure of the book? What location does it occupy, and what compositional role does the author assign to it? Can we discover similar texts or terminology within the book's literary strategy? What light do they shed on the meaning of the quotation? Our quest for the identity of the "him" in Jeremiah 4:2 leads us initially to a consideration of the innertextual meaning of the learned quotations and how they play out within the book of Jeremiah.

If we view the compositional (innertextual) role of Jeremiah 4:1-2 within the book of Jeremiah, it is apparent that this short saying occupies an important strategic position at the opening of the book. It is a position much like that of Genesis 3:15 ("he will bruise you" *[hûʾ yĕšûpkā]*) in the Pentateuch. Both texts are used to inject important themes into the book. They are themes that eventually rise to the level of a critical mass in the remainder of the book. Both texts also provide only a hint of the identity of "one" who is to come. In both texts that "one" is identified only by an ambiguous masculine singular pronoun "he/him" *(hûʾ)*. Also in both texts this pronoun refers to the equally ambiguous collective term "seed." This hint of things to come, along with the deliberate withholding of key information, leaves the reader of both texts with many questions. With these texts, the reader is given not so much an answer as a question, or more precisely, the question "Who is this 'seed'?" Is he an individual or a group (collective)?

So, within the compositional strategy of both the Pentateuch and the book of Jeremiah the purpose of both texts is not so much to answer questions about the book's narrative future as it is to raise questions for further reading of the book. The kind of questions raised are those that can find answers only by continued reading. Both Genesis 3:15 and Jeremiah 4:2 focus the attention of the reader on the identity of the "one" who is to come. To find that identity, the reader is obliged to follow the author by continuing to read the book. Little room is allowed for second-guessing the outcome. The authors of both the Pentateuch and the book of Jeremiah leave the readers to ponder what Meir Sternberg calls a "gap." The author of the Pentateuch will eventually fill the gap with an assortment of poetic images, all pointing to a future king who is to come in the "last days."

Thus, the role of Jeremiah 4:2 within the book as a whole is much like that of Genesis 3:15. The author uses the very ambiguity that we, as readers, find so troublesome. Ambiguity in these texts is a mechanism for sharpening the reader's focus. It is a central part of the authors's strategy in both texts.

*The compositional structure of the book of Jeremiah.* Locating Jeremiah 4:2 within the structure of the compositional strategy of the book of Jeremiah involves several steps. First, in a preliminary way, one must look for the shape and strategy of the book as reflected in its overall composition. Then one must look for verbal links between Jeremiah 4:2 and other like-minded texts. These also should fall primarily along the compositional seams of the book. Are there noteworthy terms in Jeremiah 4:2 that also fall along, and are a part of, the compositional seams of the book? Such questions often disclose genuine signs of intelligent design (authorial intent) behind the making of a biblical book. We should look for the same kinds of compositional clues in the prophetic books that we have uncovered in the Pentateuch. Only then can we speak of the author's intent in concrete, exegetical terms.

*The shape and strategy of Jeremiah 1–25.* We begin with the compositional shape of the book of Jeremiah. The first section is Jeremiah 1–25.[57] A major breakout section is Jeremiah 1–10.[58] Jeremiah 4:2 and Jeremiah 9:23 define its subsections. Those are the two passages in this section where the terms "justice and righteousness" occur.[59] Those terms are consistently associated with the Davidic kingship in Jeremiah.

The next section, Jeremiah 11–20, begins with a focus on the Mosaic covenant and links it to the Abrahamic covenant (Jer 11:1-5). Its argument is that the Mosaic covenant was initially intended as the means of granting God's blessings to Abraham (11:1-5). That section is followed by an explanation of the failure and revision of the Mosaic covenant (Jer 11:6-8). The last subsection is Jeremiah 21–24. These chapters "stand out as an independent

[57]"In chs. 1–25, there are not only numerous texts in the 'poetic' language characteristic of prophetic saying but others written in a broad prose style which shows a clear affinity to the language of Deuteronomy. . . . The collection of the sayings of Jeremiah (chs. 1–25) is a composition with many strata which was presumably based on short subsidiary collections" (Rolf Rendtorff, *The Old Testament: An Introduction*, trans. John Bowden [Philadelphia: Fortress, 1983], p. 201).

[58]"These chapters "clearly stand out from what follows by virtue of the fact that here prophetic words with a poetic formulation are dominant . . . whereas later the prose language emerges more strongly." Ibid.

[59]Ibid. (following William L. Holladay, *The Architecture of Jeremiah 1–20* [Lewisburg, Penn.: Bucknell University Press, 1976]).

composition" that contains "sayings against various kings and ends with a composition consisting of messianic sayings (23:1-8)."[60] Here too the expression "justice and righteousness" occurs three times.[61]

*Israel's failure (Jer 1–3).* The book of Jeremiah begins by focusing on Israel's failure to keep the Sinai covenant. Hence, they now face the consequences of divine judgment (Jer 1–3). Although God continues to call for their repentance and issues assurances that anticipate the "new covenant" (cf. Jer 3:14-18 and Jer 31:31-32), little hope remains that Israel will turn back to God (Jer 3:19-25). Judgment is on the way in the form of a mighty nation "from the north" (Jer 1:13-15).

*Hope centered in the kingship (Jer 4:1–23:8).* Having announced Israel's failure and the consequent dissolution of the Sinai covenant (Jer 3:16), Jeremiah is left to seek a new basis for his continuing hope for Israel and the blessing of the nations. He finds that hope in the Abrahamic covenant. Jeremiah sees the proper basis for that hope in a realignment of God's covenant blessings to Abraham (Jer 4:1-2) with his covenant blessings to the house of David (Jer 23:5-8). We have already noted that such an alignment was implicit in the Pentateuch's assignment of the Abrahamic covenant to the royal seed from the house of Judah.

Thus, in Jeremiah 4:1-2 the author opens with a restatement of his central thesis: Israel's only hope for the future lies in God's eternal covenant with Abraham (cf. Mic 7:20). In Jeremiah 4:2 he introduces the Abrahamic covenant with a quotation from the Pentateuch's covenant-blessing narratives. As we have noted, in this quotation he renders "seed" of the Abrahamic covenant[62] with the ambiguous pronoun "him." He says, "In him shall the nations be blessed." In rendering the Genesis covenant texts with an indefinite pronoun, Jeremiah extends its application and moves a step beyond a merely collective view of Israel. The door is opened to a singular royal "seed." In moving in that direction, Jeremiah demonstrates an awareness of, and agreement with, the Pentateuch's own reading of these same texts.

As we will see, this section of the book closes, in Jeremiah 23:5-8, by establishing a link between the covenant blessings of Abraham (Gen 12:1-3) and God's covenant with David (2 Sam 7). When God finally raises up the

---

[60]Rendtorff, *The Old Testament*, p. 201.

[61]The only further occurance of the phrase is the paraphrase of Jeremiah 23:5-6 in Jeremiah 33.

[62]For example, Genesis 22:18: "In your seed shall all the nations be blessed."

"righteous branch" from the house of David (Jer 23:5a), there will be "justice and righteousness" in his kingdom (Jer 23:5b). Only then can one look for the fulfillment of the Abrahamic covenant blessings. Compare these thoughts with the sentiments of Genesis 18:18-19:

> In *him* all the nations of the earth will be blessed. For I have known *him* in order that he might command his sons and his house after him, so that they might keep the way of the LORD to do *righteousness and justice*, so that the LORD will bring upon Abraham that which he has spoken to him.

God's covenant with Abraham will be fulfilled only when Abraham's sons and daughters live "righteously and justly." Jeremiah's allusions to Abraham (Jer 4:1-2) and David (Jer 23:5-8) thus frame his words of judgment upon the disobedient nation (Jer 4:5–23:4). By means of these texts, the hope embodied in God's covenant with the "seed" of Abraham is securely established in God's covenant with the royal house of David.

*Verbal links in Jeremiah: "Justice and righteousness." "Justice and Righteousness" (mišpāṭ ûṣĕdākâ) in Jeremiah 4:2.* In describing the compositional shape of the first half of the book of Jeremiah, I have suggested that Jeremiah 4:2 plays a central role in the author's purpose. The quotation in Jeremiah 4:2 begins the process of linking the king of the Davidic covenant (Jer 23:5-6) to the blessing narratives in the Pentateuch. I have suggested that this was accomplished by means of what Ewald calls a "learned quotation." The same argument can be seen in the use of the expression "justice and righteousness" (מִשְׁפָּט וּצְדָקָה, *mišpāṭ ûṣĕdākâ*) in both the book of Jeremiah and the Pentateuch.

*"Justice and righteousness" (mišpāṭ ûṣĕdākâ) in Genesis 18:19.* The expression "justice and righteousness" occurs once in the Pentateuch (Gen 18:19). That text is one of the covenant-blessing texts quoted in Jeremiah 4:2. In both Genesis 18:19 and Jeremiah 4:2 the expression "justice and righteousness" is linked to the blessing of "the nations" *(wĕnībrĕkû bô kōl gôyê hāʾāreṣ)* in the Abrahamic covenant. Jeremiah 4:2 thus is part of an important intertextual seam (verbal and thematic) attached to a key Pentateuchal covenant-blessing narrative (Gen 18:19). As in Jeremiah 4:2, the blessing of the nations in Genesis 18:19 is tied directly to the ethical demand for Israel's "justice and righteousness."

*"Justice and righteousness" (mišpāṭ ûṣĕdākâ) elsewhere in Jeremiah.* Apart from Jeremiah 4:2, the expression "justice and righteousness" occurs infre-

quently, though always in compositionally important texts. The expression is known for its special association with the Davidic kingship. According to William McKane, the collocation "justice and righteousness" denotes "the king's responsibility to oversee the processes of justice and to ensure that fair trials take place."[63] The expression "justice and righteousness" in Jeremiah 4:2 thus represents a not-so-subtle introduction of the concept of Davidic kingship into the "prophetic" hope that is grounded in the Abrahamic Ccovenant. Where does the notion originate within the book of Jeremiah? One likely source is Jeremiah's dependence on the royal theme in the Pentateuch's poems. Those very themes are introduced into the book of Jeremiah by its learned quotation of Genesis blessing narratives such as Genesis 18:19. An understanding of the compositional strategy behind these interconnected texts helps clear the way for an identification of the third-person pronoun "in him" *(bô)* in Jeremiah 4:2.

*"Justice and Righteousness" (mišpāṭ ûṣĕdākâ) in Jeremiah 9:24 (9:23* MT*).* Along with the use of "justice and righteousness," the "boasting" *(yithallālû)* of the nations in Jeremiah 4:2 is an intentional link to the "boasting" *(yithallēl)* of those who know the Lord in Jeremiah 9:24 (9:23 MT): "Let him who boasts, boast in this: that I am the LORD who works grace, justice and righteousness *[mišpāṭ ûṣĕdākâ]* in the land."[64]

It is noteworthy that in the LXX of Samuel, Jeremiah 9:23-24 (9:22-23 MT) is inserted into the final verse of Hannah's psalm (1 Sam 2:10). As such, these verses link Hannah's prayer for the Lord's "messiah" and "his king" to the "seed" identified as "him" in Jeremiah 4:2 and the Pentateuch's covenant narratives.[65]

*"Justice and righteousness" (mišpāṭ ûṣĕdākâ) in Jeremiah 23:5-6.* Elsewhere the expression "justice and righteousness" occurs three times in Jeremiah 22–23 (Jer 22:3; 22:15; 23:5). Again in these texts, the theme of Davidic kingship is prominent. In each occurrence there is a noticeable association of these terms with the reign of a "just and righteous" king. In Jeremiah 23:5-6 the king is called the "righteous branch" *(ṣemaḥ ṣaddîq)* because he "does justice and righteousness" *(mišpāṭ ûṣĕdākâ).* Consequently, he bears the name

---

[63]McKane, *Jeremiah*, p. 562.

[64]"Boasting" in the Lord is found only in these two passages in Jeremiah.

[65]In *Targum Onqelos* the king in Hannah's prayer is noted for his defeat of "Gog," as in all the versions of Numbers 24:7.

"the LORD is our righteousness" *(yhwh ṣidqēnû).* The close verbal and thematic ties between Jeremiah 23:5-8 and Jeremiah 4:1-2 are evident.

In Jeremiah 22:3, 15 the terms "justice and righteousness" occur along with a rebuke of the reigning king. The king lacked the qualities of justice and righteousness and thus was not a proper king. In Jeremiah 23:5 the reign of the future "righteous branch" is characterized by "justice and righteousness" *(mišpāṭ ûṣĕdākâ).* This is stated again in a parallel text, Jeremiah 33:15.

The terms "justice and righteousness" thus appear at the beginning of the book of Jeremiah and serve as a verbal link between texts within Jeremiah that envision the reign of a future Davidic king. The expression occurs in Jeremiah 4:2 even though there is otherwise little direct royal imagery associated with that passage. Its occurrence there supports the suggestion that Jeremiah intended an echo of the Davidic covenant to be heard in his use of the anonymous "him." It also suggests that Jeremiah understood the Genesis covenant-blessing narratives in light of the royal personage in the poems of the Pentateuch.

*Jeremiah 23:5-6 and the Septuagint.* In considering the importance of the compositional shape of the first part of the book of Jeremiah (Jer 1–25), commentators generally agree that the prophetic word about a "righteous branch" *(ṣemaḥ ṣaddîq)* in Jeremiah 23:5 is a focal point of the book. So important to the book is this passage that it has, in fact, been duplicated almost verbatim in Jeremiah 33:14-26. The significance of this duplication lies in the fact that Jeremiah 33:14-26 is not in the LXX. McKane, and most other commentators, consider Jeremiah 33:14-26 "a secondary, prose paraphrase of 23:5-6."[66]

This "variant" of Jeremiah 23:5-6 in Jeremiah 33 is more important than McKane's comment suggests. Its effect is to reverse the argument and central thrust of the prophecy in Jeremiah 23:5-6. In Jeremiah 23:5-6 the (individual) king is given the name "The LORD is our righteousness." In Jeremiah 33:16 that name is reserved for the (collective) city of Jerusalem. The individual interpretation of the "seed" of Abraham in Jeremiah 23:5-6 is thus given a collective meaning in the Masoretic variant in Jeremiah 33:14-26. The role of Jeremiah 33:14-26 and its effect on 23:5-6 is a direct testimony to the importance of 23:5f. to the book as a whole.

---

[66]McKane, *Jeremiah*, p. 563.

*Conclusion.* When viewed within the whole of the book of Jeremiah, the distribution of the phrase "justice and righteousness" suggests that it is part of a compositional seam tying the book together. The convergence of terminology and compositional structure suggests the presence of an intentional link between the quotation from the Pentateuch in Jeremiah 4:2 and the passages in Jeremiah that focus on the reign of a future king from the house of Judah. Jeremiah 23:8 and its relationship to Jeremiah 4:2 help identify the royal figure whom Jeremiah appears to have had in mind in his learned quotation of the Pentateuch's covenant-blessing narratives.

***The covenant-blessing narratives and the Psalter.*** I have argued above that the prophetic books and the Pentateuch follow a similar kind of compositional strategy. The Pentateuch links the Abrahamic covenant narratives (Gen 22:18) to its own poetic texts that focus on a coming king (Num 24:7-9). In the composition of the prophetic books there is a similar focus on the Davidic (Judaic) kingship (Jer 4:2). This raises the question of whether a similar compositional activity exists in the third section of the OT canon, the Writings. For reasons that will later become apparent, I will take Psalm 72 as our starting point. Not only does this psalm serve as a central compositional seam within the Psalter, but also it quotes directly from the pentateuchal covenant-blessing narratives discussed above.

A comparison of Psalm 72:17 with texts we have examined in the Pentateuch and the Prophets underscores the extent of their literary dependency:

וְהִתְבָּרֲכוּ בְזַרְעֲךָ כֹּל גּוֹיֵי הָאָרֶץ
And in your seed all the nations of the earth will be blessed. (Gen 22:18)
וְהִתְבָּרְכוּ בוֹ גוֹיִם
And in him the nations will be blessed. (Jer 4:2)
וְיִתְבָּרְכוּ בוֹ כָּל־גּוֹיִם
And in him all nations will be blessed. (Ps 72:17)

It cannot be denied that Psalm 72:17 is citing these earlier texts. If a genuine literary dependency[67] exists between Psalm 72 and texts in the Pentateuch (Gen 22:18) and the Prophets (Jer 4:2), it raises the question of the contribution that Psalm 72 makes to our understanding of those texts. To answer that question, first I will explore the internal structure (intextuality) of Psalm 72 and, in particular, the role of the quotation of the Pentateuch and Prophets in

[67]See "intertextual" in Sailhamer, *Introduction to Old Testament Theology*, pp. 212-13.

Psalm 72:17. Next, I will attempt to map the location and functionality of Psalm 72 within the Psalter. Finally, having decided those questions, I will attempt to summarize the meaning of Psalm 72 from within its literary and compositional relationship to the Tanak.

*The compositional shape of Psalm 72.* Psalm 72 is attributed to Solomon *(lišlōmōh),* but it has been placed within the prayers of David (Ps 72:20). Psalm 72 closes Book II of the Psalter (cf. Ps 72:18-19) and is a royal psalm.

*Intertextuality in Psalm 72.* The psalm opens with a call for a king who exhibits "justice" *(mišpāṭ)* and "righteousness" *(ṣĕdāqâ).* It clearly draws on terminology and themes of the Davidic covenant psalms. Compare Psalm 72:5 and Psalm 89:37-38a:

> יִירָאוּךָ עִם־שָׁמֶשׁ וְלִפְנֵי יָרֵחַ דּוֹר דּוֹרִים
> They shall fear you with the sun and before the moon from generation to generations. (Ps 72:5)
> זַרְעוֹ לְעוֹלָם יִהְיֶה וְכִסְאוֹ כַשֶּׁמֶשׁ נֶגְדִּי כְּיָרֵחַ יִכּוֹן עוֹלָם
> His seed will be forever and his throne as the sun before me, as the moon he will be established forever. (Ps 89:37-38a)

Formally, Psalm 72 is both a royal psalm and a linear acrostic. Each poetic line begins with the same two letters of the Hebrew alphabet. Line *a* begins with *yod*, line *b* with *waw.*[68] This pattern is broken at the center of the psalm (Ps 72:8-12) and at places where texts have been inserted that are drawn from other parts of Scripture.

> (1) יֵרֵד כְּמָטָר עַל־גֵּז כִּרְבִיבִים זַרְזִיף אָרֶץ
> He will come down like the rain upon mown grass, like rain showers on the land. (Ps 72:6)
> וּכְאוֹר בֹּקֶר יִזְרַח־שָׁמֶשׁ בֹּקֶר לֹא עָבוֹת מִנֹּגַהּ מִמָּטָר דֶּשֶׁא מֵאָרֶץ
> As the light of day in the morning when the sun shines, a morning with no clouds, from the bright light on the grass after a rain on the land. (2 Sam 23:4)
> (2) וְיֵרְדְּ מִיָּם עַד־יָם וּמִנָּהָר עַד־אַפְסֵי־אָרֶץ
> He will reign from sea to sea and from the river to the ends of the earth. (Ps 72:8)
> וּמָשְׁלוֹ מִיָּם עַד־יָם וּמִנָּהָר עַד־אַפְסֵי־אָרֶץ
> He reigns from sea to sea and from the river to the ends of the earth. (Zech 9:10)
> וְאֶתְּנָה גוֹיִם נַחֲלָתֶךָ וַאֲחֻזָּתְךָ אַפְסֵי־אָרֶץ

[68]Klaus Seybold, *Die Psalmen* (HAT 1/15; Tübingen: Mohr Siebeck, 1996), p. 277.

And I will give you nations for your inheritance and your possessin the ends of the earth. (Ps 2:8)

By means of such allusions, the king in Psalm 72 is identified as the eschatological, Davidic monarch of Psalm 2 and Zechariah 9.

(3) לְפָנָיו יִכְרְעוּ צִיִּים וְאֹיְבָיו עָפָר יְלַחֵכוּ

Before him the islands will crouch down, and his enemies will lick the dirt (Ps 72:9)

עַל־גְּחֹנְךָ תֵלֵךְ וְעָפָר תֹּאכַל כָּל־יְמֵי חַיֶּיךָ

Upon your belly you will crawl, and dirt you will eat all the days of your life (Gen 3:14)

By means of this allusion to Genesis 3:14, the king in Psalm 72 is identified as the one who will defeat the serpent of Genesis 3.

(4) מַלְכֵי תַרְשִׁישׁ וְאִיִּים מִנְחָה יָשִׁיבוּ מַלְכֵי שְׁבָא וּסְבָא אֶשְׁכָּר יַקְרִיבוּ

The kings of Tarshish and the islands will return a gift, the kings of Sheva and Seba will bring a gift. (Ps 72:10)

יְקַוּוּ וָאֳנִיּוֹת תַּרְשִׁישׁ בָּרִאשֹׁנָה לְהָבִיא בָנַיִךְ מֵרָחוֹק כַּסְפָּם וּזְהָבָם אִתָּם כִּי־לִי אִיִּים

Islands will wait and ships of Tarshish are first to bring your sons from afar, their silver and their gold with them—because it is mine. (Is 60:9)

The king in Psalm 72 is further identified from the description of the coming redeemer in Isaiah 60.

(5) וְיִשְׁתַּחֲווּ־לוֹ כָל־מְלָכִים כָּל־גּוֹיִם יַעַבְדוּהוּ

All kings will bow down to him, all nations will serve him. (Ps 72:11)

וְכֹל שָׁלְטָנַיָּא לֵהּ יִפְלְחוּן וְיִשְׁתַּמְּעוּן

And all authorities will worship and obey him. (Dan 7:27)

Here the king in Psalm 72 is identified from Daniel 7.

(6) כִּי־יַצִּיל אֶבְיוֹן מְשַׁוֵּעַ וְעָנִי וְאֵין־עֹזֵר לוֹ

Because he delivers the one who is needy when he calls the afflicted who has no one to help. (Ps 72:12)

כִּי־אֲמַלֵּט עָנִי מְשַׁוֵּעַ וְיָתוֹם וְלֹא־עֹזֵר לוֹ

Because I delivered the afflicted who calls him, and the orphan who has no one to help him. (Job 29:12)

In this allusion to Job, the king in Psalm 72 is identified as the perfectly wise man in Job 29.

*The role of Psalm 72:17 within the Psalm.* Psalm 72:17 is attached as the conclusion to the psalm. This means that compositionally, the psalm concludes with a quotation from a central compositional seam from both the Pentateuch and the Prophets:

> וְיִתְבָּרְכוּ בוֹ כָּל־גּוֹיִם
> And in him all the nations will be blessed. (Ps 72:17b)
> וְנִבְרְכוּ בְךָ כֹּל מִשְׁפְּחֹת הָאֲדָמָה
> And in you all the families of the earth will be blessed. (Gen 12:3)
> וְהִתְבָּרֲכוּ בְזַרְעֲךָ כֹּל גּוֹיֵי הָאָרֶץ
> In your seed all the nations of the earth will be blessed. (Gen 22:18)
> וְהִתְבָּרְכוּ בוֹ גּוֹיִם
> And in him the nations will be blessed. (Jer 4:2)

The king in Psalm 72 is the seed in which all the nations are blessed in the covenant with Abraham in Genesis 12:3.

*Conclusion.* The composition of Psalm 72 appears to be part of the composition of the Psalter as a whole. Its own compositional material (Ps 72:8-12) gathers quotations from wisdom and prophetic texts in order to identify the "king" of Psalm 72:1 with the eschatological messiah of the prophetic texts and the typically wise man of the wisdom literature.

*Psalm 72 and the compositional shape of the Psalter.* We begin by asking some questions. Does the Psalter have a shape? Is there a design to its collection of psalms? What purpose, if any, did the book of Psalms perform within ancient Israel? Why is there a Psalter at all? Until recently, such questions received little attention. Now they are being asked from every corner.

The first modern exegete to see in the Psalter "the imprint of an organising mind"[69] was Franz Delitzsch. Delitzsch believed and attempted to prove that the psalms were arranged in a meaningful order. He argued that the psalms often were linked to each other both by keywords and general themes. Consequently, he attempted to trace certain themes and keywords throughout the Psalter and often understood the individual psalms in light of the context that provided. His explanation of the shape of the Psalter, however, was not carried out by means of a systematic assessment of the structure of the entire book. It was, rather, drawn along the lines of his own

---

[69]Matthias Millard, *Die Komposition des Psalters: Ein formgeschichtlicher Ansatz* (FAT 9; Tübingen: Mohr Siebeck, 1994), p. 23.

historical reconstruction of Israel's early temple worship. Only in a general way did Delitzsch attempt to trace the development of the Psalter from individual psalms and collections to the present canonical Psalter.[70]

Delitzsch's thesis was not taken up enthusiastically by the majority of biblical scholars in his day. According to Christoph Barth, only Bertholet and Böhl received Delitzsch's ideas positively. There were more, however, than those whom Barth has noted. Delitzsch's theory of order and structure in the Psalter was received favorably by his evangelical colleagues. Most notable is the important commentary on Psalms by Ernst Hengstenberg and its translation by A. Alexander. Both Hengstenberg and Alexander followed in Delitzsch's footsteps and went on to view the psalms in light of the comprehensive structure of the Psalter. Heinrich Hävernick, a loyal student of Hengstenberg and a genuinely learned scholar in his own right, followed Delitzsch and Hengstenberg. The noted evangelical OT scholar C. F. Keil in turn followed Hävernick closely.[71] Keil noted, "Our collection of the Psalms has been made at one time, and it would seem under the charge of one man, on account of the principle which is easily recognised running through it, of internal and real [not formal] affinity of the Psalms, of resemblance in their subject-matter, and of identity in tendency and destination."[72] On close examination, it becomes apparent that a wholistic and compositional approach to the Psalter was a characteristic feature of many early evangelical interpretations of the psalms.

Matthias Millard points to Christoph Barth as the first modern scholar to call for a redaction-critical approach to the Psalter.[73] Barth identified structural order in the Psalter.[74] He argued for many keyword links within

---

[70]Franz Delitzsch, *Biblical Commentary on the Psalms*, trans. Francis Bolton (BCOT; Grand Rapids: Eerdmans, 1970), 1:18-19 (German original, 1867).

[71]"Nicht blos die Eintheilung der ganzen Sammlung in mehrere Bücher, sondern auch die Vertheilung der einzelnen Psalmen innerhalb dieser Bücher ist nach der inneren, sachlichen Verwandtschaft der Lieder, nach der Aehnlichkeit ihres Inhalts, der Gleichheit ihrer Tendenz und Bestimmmung gemacht worden. Diesem sachlichen Prinzipe der Aehnlichkeit und Analogie der verschiedenen Psalmen ist der chronologische Gesichtspunkt untergeordnet" (Heinrich A. C. Hävernick, *Handbuch der historisch-kritischen Einleitung in das Alte Testament* [Erlangen: Heyder, 1836–1849], 3:275-76).

[72]C. F. Keil, *Introduction to the Old Testament*, trans. G. C. M. Douglas (Peabody, Mass.: Hendrickson, 1988), 1:464-65.

[73]Millard, *Die Komposition des Psalters*, p. 23

[74]Christoph Barth, "Concatenatio im ersten Buch des Psalters," in *Wort und Wirklichkeit: Studien zur Afrikanistik und Orientalistik*, ed. Brigitta Benzing, Otto Böcher and Günter Mayer (Meisenheim am Glan: Hain, 1976–1977), 1:30-40.

Psalms 3–41. Millard has rightly stressed that Barth made no attempt at a thoroughgoing thematic reconstruction of the literary context of the psalms in the Psalter. Barth understood the work of the psalms collector to consist only in an editorial shaping of the psalms texts. He thus called only for a context-sensitive psalms exegesis, one that proceeded along redaction-critical lines. Numerous other psalms studies have followed in a similar vein.[75]

An important and exemplary recent study of the shape of the Psalter is that of Matthiaas Millard.[76] Millard argues that the Psalter, as such, originated in the Persian period. It was conceived as a collection of prayers for the Diaspora and functioned as a replacement for temple worship. In reading the Psalter, one was both oriented to the temple and, at the same time, absolved from actually having to worship there. The Psalter thus was intended to promote the importance of the temple pilgrimage while at the same time being a substitution for the temple itself. It was a private surrogate for the pilgrimage to the postexilic temple in Jerusalem.

Millard suggests that the *Sitz im Leben*, or purpose, of the Psalter was not to be a collection of prayers for reading in public worship, as it later became in early Christian monasteries. The Psalter would have been much too large and too sparsely available to be read in a pilgrimage context. It is more likely that the Psalter was intended to be a collection of individual prayers from which one could make specific selections for reading in daily life. That is what is actually put forth as the purpose of the psalter in its introductory psalm, Psalm 1. Its "ideal reader" is one who meditates on its words day and night (Ps 1:2). In that sense, the psalms have come to serve as a kind of surogate for the Torah and temple in the daily life of postexilic Judaism.

In such a context, the meaning of each psalm would have been derived as

---

[75]Structural approach: Pierre Auffret, on the basis of several keywords, argues for a chiastic structure of Palms 15–24 (*La sagesse a bâti sa maison: Études de structures littéraires dans l'Ancien Testament et spécialement dans les Psaumes* [OBO 49; Fribourg: Editions Universitaires; Göttingen: Vandenhoeck & Ruprecht, 1982]). Redactional approaches: Erich Zenger; Joseph Reindl. Canonical approach: Brevard Childs. Compositional approaches: Gerald Henry Wilson (*The Editing of the Hebrew Psalter* [SBLDS 76; Chico, Calif.: Scholars Press, 1985]); Frank-Lothar Hossfeld and Erich Zenger (*Die Psalmen*, 2 vols. [NEchtB 29, 40; Würzburg: Echter, 1993–2002]); Millard, *Die Komposition des Psalters*; David C. Mitchell (*The Message of the Psalter: An Eschatological Programme in the Book of Psalms* [JSOTSup 252; Sheffield: Sheffield Academic Press, 1997]); Claus Westermann; Rolf Rendtorff.

[76]Millard, *Die Komposition des Psalters*.

much from the context of the Psalter as from the original setting of each individual psalm. That setting, of course, was not abandoned in the process of reading. The setting was intentionally preserved for the reader in numerous "superscriptions" attached to the individual psalms. By means of such settings and markers, the reader could meditate on a psalm both within the context of the Psalter and within the context the Pentateuch and the prophetic books. The superscription of Psalm 3, for example, locates its original context in the life of David, as is true of most of other superscriptions. Within the Psalter as a whole, that context is expanded to include the other psalms, such as the "son of man" psalm, Psalm 8.

The Psalter thus preserved a variety of prayers and praises and thereby assured a kind of spontaneity in the individual's selection of prayers and praises. By making a daily selection of such prayers and praises from the Psalter, one could readily identify personal particular misfortunes or blessings with those who had gone before in their walk with God and in the context of past acts of God on Israel's behalf. The individual thereby wass given hope in God's help for daily conflicts in life but, in the end, was also pointed back to the worshiping community as the most appropriate context for praise.

It therefore is reasonable to suggest that the Psalter, as a book, was written primarily for individual use. It was not, for example, intended principally as a "hymnbook for the postexilic temple." It was instead a kind of poetic Torah that could be read and meditated on along with the daily duties of life, as is suggested in its introductory first psalm. In such cases, the Psalter may have been written for those still in exile or experiencing present tribulation and, as such, was intended as a source book for hope and divine comfort.

It may have been for those reasons, as Millard suggests, that the framework of the Psalter is noticeably centered on such developed messianic themes as the Davidic covenant and its corresponding hope in a future kingdom of God. Viewed in this light, the individual psalms that are placed within its compositional framework consists of a intentional collection of the prayers and praises of Israel's great leaders, intended to provide a means for those in the present to identify with God's help of those in the past.

A proper understanding of Psalm 72 and its use of earlier biblical material must be carried out in terms of its compositional role within the Psalter.

Psalm 72 has a clear, but often overlooked, role to play within the Psalter. It is a central psalm within the compositional strategy of the present Psalter. It stands, that is, at the center of the Psalter.

*Key Psalms: Psalms 2; 72; 145.* Whatever might be said about the final shape of the Psalter and its overall theology, it is fairly safe to say that it centers on three strategically important psalms: Psalms 2; 72; 145. After the introductory Psalm 1, Psalm 2 has been placed at the beginning of the Psalter. The Hallel psalms, Psalms 146–150, are placed at the conclusion of the Psalter. Before those psalms, Psalm 145 is placed at the end of the Psalter per se. Psalm 72 is halfway between the other two psalms, Psalms 2 and Psalm 145. It has been positioned at the structural center point of the Psalter.

The similarities between these psalms and the suitability of the positions they occupy within the Psalter make it probable that they were composed with a view to their present position and function within the Psalter.

1. Psalm 2. It is generally recognized that Psalm 2, along with Psalm 1, is a programmatic introduction to the Psalter as a whole. It serves to counterbalance the Torah themes in Psalm 1 with the messianic themes of Psalm 2. This probably is related to the later practice elsewhere in the Psalter to counter Torah psalms (e.g., Ps 19), with royal-messianic psalms (e.g., Ps 20). Following the same compositional strategy, Psalm 119 is counterbalanced by the so-called Songs of Ascent, which follow in Psalms 120–134 and center on Psalm 132, a psalm of the Davidic covenant. Psalm 2, Psalm 20 and Psalms 120–124 are centered on the Davidic kingship and the royal descendant. Such a strategy suggests a conscious design of the Psalter.

Four formal observations on Psalm 2 suggest that psalm was composed, or edited, specifically as a "messianic" introduction to the main body of psalms in the Psalter, Psalms 2–145.

The first observation involves the insertion of the phrase "against the LORD and against his anointed" *(ʿal-yhwh wĕʿal-mĕšîḥô)* in Psalm 2:2b. This is judged to be an intrusion because it breaks into the parallelism and meter of the verse. *BHS* takes this to be a late gloss. It is better to view it as a part of the composition of the book of Psalms. The contribution of this brief statement is not difficult to comprehend. It identifies the whole of the psalm as "messianic" regardless of the exact meaning one might assign to the term "anointed one."

A second observation on Psalm 2 involves the insertion of the metacommunicative statement "I will recount the statute of the LORD" *(ʾăsappĕrâ ʾel ḥōq yĕhwâ)* in Psalm 2:7a. This too breaks into the parallelism and meter of the poetic lines that surround it and shifts the identity of the speaker away from the narrator. While in Psalm 2:6, 7b the Lord is speaking, in Psalm 2:7a the discourse shifts suddenly to the king mentioned in Psalm 2:6. The effect of this insertion is to identify the Lord's words in Psalm 2:7-8 as the divine covenant to the house of David recorded in 2 Samuel 7, as well as in several later psalms (e.g., Ps 45; 89; 110; 132).

The third and fourth observations involve what appear to be a literary dependency of Psalm 2:9 and Psalm 2:12 on the Aramaic sections of the book of Daniel:

> תְּרֹעֵם בְּשֵׁבֶט בַּרְזֶל כִּכְלִי יוֹצֵר תְּנַפְּצֵם
> You will break them with an iron rod, you will smash them like pottery (Ps 2:9 [Hebrew])
> תַּדִּק וְתָסֵיף כָּל אִלֵּין מַלְכְוָתָא
> It will crush and wipe out all these kingdoms (Dan 2:44b [Aramaic])
> נַשְּׁקוּ בַר
> Kiss the son (Ps 2:12 [Hebrew])
> כְּבַר אֱנָשׁ
> As the son of man (Dan 7:13 [Aramaic])

To summarize: Psalm 2 introduces a central theme of the Psalter, the hope of the coming Messiah. That hope is grounded intertextually in the Davidic covenant sections of 2 Samuel 7 and the Aramaic portions of the book of Daniel.

2. Psalm 145. Within the Psalter, Psalm 145 is the last of the group of "David psalms," which are introduced by the expression *lĕdāwīd* (Ps 138–145). Psalm 145 begins by introducing "the king" (הַמֶּלֶךְ, *hammelek* [Ps 145:1]). Since the psalm is an acrostic, the author avails himself of the opportunity to use the first letters of the middle lines (כ, ל, מ), which, in reverse order (מ, ל, כ), can be rendered as "king" (מלך, *mlk*). It may thus be significant that the word "kingdom" (מַלְכוּת, *malkût* [from מלך]) occurs four times (out of six in the Psalter) and "dominion" (מֶמְשָׁלָה, *memšālâ*) once in these middle lines (Ps 145:11-13). These are the lines that begin with the letters כ, ל, מ.

The psalm closes on the note of God's protection for "all those who love him" (Ps 145:20). It is worthy of note that it is only the acrostic lines of this psalm that make up the quotations from other parts of Scripture. These psalms also noticeably cluster at the center of the psalm (Ps 145:13-16).

The intertextual cross-referencing within Psalm 145 is noted here:

גָּדוֹל יְהוָה וּמְהֻלָּל מְאֹד וְלִגְדֻלָּתוֹ אֵין חֵקֶר (1)
Great is Yahweh and to be praised exceedingly. Of his greatness there is no measure. (Ps 145:3)
גָּדוֹל יְהוָה וּמְהֻלָּל מְאֹד בְּעִיר אֱלֹהֵינוּ הַר־קָדְשׁוֹ
Great is Yahweh and to be praised exceedingly in the city of our God—his holy mountain. (Ps 48:2 [48:1 ET])
כִּי גָדוֹל יְהוָה וּמְהֻלָּל מְאֹד נוֹרָא הוּא עַל־כָּל־אֱלֹהִים
Because great is Yahweh and to be praised exceedingly. He is fearful over all gods. (Ps 96:4)
כִּי גָדוֹל יְהוָה וּמְהֻלָּל מְאֹד וְנוֹרָא הוּא עַל־כָּל־אֱלֹהִים
Because great is Yahweh and to be praised exceedingly. He is fearful over all gods. (1 Chron 16:25)
חַנּוּן וְרַחוּם יְהוָה אֶרֶךְ אַפַּיִם וּגְדָל־חָסֶד (2)
Gracious and compassionate is Yahweh, patient and great in faithfulness. (Ps 145:8)
וְאַתָּה אֲדֹנָי אֵל־רַחוּם וְחַנּוּן אֶרֶךְ אַפַּיִם וְרַב־חֶסֶד וֶאֱמֶת
You Lord are a God of compassion and graciousness, patient, great in mercy and faithfulness. (Ps 86:15)
רַחוּם וְחַנּוּן יְהוָה אֶרֶךְ אַפַּיִם וְרַב־חָסֶד
Compassionate and gracious is Yahweh, patient and much mercy. (Ps 103:8)
חַנּוּן יְהוָה וְצַדִּיק וֵאלֹהֵינוּ מְרַחֵם
Compassionate and gracious is Yahweh, patient [and great in faithfulness]. (Ps 116:5)
מַלְכוּתְךָ מַלְכוּת כָּל־עֹלָמִים וּמֶמְשַׁלְתְּךָ בְּכָל־דּוֹר וָדוֹר (3)
Your kingdom is a kingdom of all eternity and your rulership is all generation and generation. (Ps 145:13)
מַלְכוּתֵהּ מַלְכוּת עָלַם וְשָׁלְטָנֵהּ עִם־דָּר וְדָר
His kingdom is an eternal kingdom, his authority is with all generation and generation. (Dan 3:33 [4:3 ET] [Aramaic])
שָׁלְטָנֵהּ שָׁלְטָן עָלַם וּמַלְכוּתֵהּ עִם־דָּר וְדָר
His authority rules forever, and his kingdom is with generation and generation (Dan 4:31 [4:34 ET] [Aramaic])
סוֹמֵךְ יְהוָה לְכָל־הַנֹּפְלִים וְזוֹקֵף לְכָל־הַכְּפוּפִים (4)
The Lord is the one who lifts up all the fallen and who straightens all the ones

who are bent over. (Ps 145:14)

יְהוָה פֹּקֵחַ עִוְרִים יְהוָה זֹקֵף כְּפוּפִים

The Lord opens the eyes of the blind, the Lord straightens the bent over. (Ps 146:8a)

עֵינֵי־כֹל אֵלֶיךָ יְשַׂבֵּרוּ וְאַתָּה נוֹתֵן־לָהֶם אֶת־אָכְלָם בְּעִתּוֹ (5)

The eyes of all wait for you, and you give to them their food in its time (Ps 145:15)[77]

כֻּלָּם אֵלֶיךָ יְשַׂבֵּרוּן לָתֵת אָכְלָם בְּעִתּוֹ

They all wait for you to give them their food in its time. (Ps 104:27)

פּוֹתֵחַ אֶת־יָדֶךָ וּמַשְׂבִּיעַ לְכָל־חַי רָצוֹן (6)

You open your hand and satisfy the desire of all living. (Ps 145:16)

תִּפְתַּח יָדְךָ יִשְׂבְּעוּן טוֹב

You open your hand and they are satisfied with good. (Ps 104:28)

Note that only the *nun* strophe of this acrostic is missing in the MT and from Qumran (see *BHS*). A single medieval manuscript (K142), the LXX and the Syriac, however, have the missing stophe. It can be reconstructed as follows:

נֶאֱמָן יְהוָה בְּכָל־דְּבָרָיו וְחָסִיד בְּכָל־מַעֲשָׂיו

The LORD is faithful in all his words and sure in all his works.

The similarity of this line to Psalm 145:17 is noted in *BHS:*

נֶאֱמָן יְהוָה בְּכָל־דְּבָרָיו וְחָסִיד בְּכָל־מַעֲשָׂיו

The Lord is faithful in all his words and gracious in all his deeds. (Ps 145:13/14)

צַדִּיק יְהוָה בְּכָל־דְּרָכָיו וְחָסִיד בְּכָל־מַעֲשָׂיו

The Lord is righteous in all his ways and gracious in all his deeds. (Ps 145:17)

The difference lies in the use of the word נֶאֱמָן *(neʾĕmān)* in the missing line. Does the author of this psalm want us to conclude that the Lord is "faithful" (נֶאֱמָן, *neʾĕmān*) in regard to the Davidic covenant or "righteousness" (צַדִּיק, *ṣaddîq*). Clearly, some discussion of these differences must have accompanied this important psalm. It is also important to note that the term "faithful" (נֶאֱמָן, *neʾĕmān*) links the psalm to the divine covenant with David in 2 Samuel 7:16:

וְנֶאְמַן בֵּיתְךָ וּמַמְלַכְתְּךָ עַד־עוֹלָם לְפָנֶיךָ כִּסְאֲךָ יִהְיֶה נָכוֹן עַד־עוֹלָם

And your house will be faithful, and your kingdom forever before you. Your throne will be established till forever.

---

[77]Note that the use of אכל marks the key difference.

The omission of the *nun* stophe may have intended to expand the psalm's notion of the "kingdom" here celebrated beyond the limits of the Davidic covenant, thus moving the psalm in a less messianic direction. Such a strategy might also be linked to the unusually frequent occurrences of the word "all" (כֹּל, *kōl*) in the second half of the psalm. The word *kōl* is highlighted in the psalms in two ways: (1) it is conspicuously added to those texts taken from other scriptural texts, thus expanding their scope; (2) it occurs with high frequency in the second half of the psalm.[78]

To summarize: Psalm 145 appears to be written to serve its location within the Psalter. It therefore would likely preserve the central theological themes of the Psalter as a whole: Davidic covenant and the kingdom.

3. Psalm 72. Psalm 72 is the middle psalm of Psalms 2–145.[79] Psalm 2 introduces the Davidic king. Psalm 72 makes intertextual links to prophetic eschatology. Psalm 145 shows the result: kingdom of God. In each of these psalms (Pss 2; 72; 145) the beginning introduces the king, the center/middle makes intertextual links to prophetic eschatology, and the end shows the result: the kingdom of God.

***The covenant-blessing narratives and the New Testament.*** All agree that Matthew's understanding of Hosea 11:1 is eschatological and messianic.[80] He applies Hosea's words to Jesus literally and realistically. Jesus was taken to Egypt as a child (Mt 2:14) so that the prophet's words might be fulfilled, "Out of Egypt I called my son" (Mt 2:15).[81]

*History of the problem: Old Testament/New Testament.* The chief difficulty lies in Matthew's application of Hosea's words to an individual eschatological "son of God" figure rather than to Israel in the historical exodus. Erasmus cites Julian the Apostate as the first to take issue against Christianity with Matthew's use of Hosea. But already in the LXX, the Targumim and the com-

[78]Psalm 145:9 (2x), 10, 13 (2x), 14 (2x), 15, 16, 17 (2x), 18 (2x), 20 (2x), 21. On one occasion, early in the psalm, it even occurs in a stereotyped formula (Ps 145:2).

[79]In the MT, Psalm 72 is the middle psalm in Psalms 1–144 (= 145)

[80]The following discussion of Matthew's use of Hosea 11:1 draws extensively from John H. Sailhamer, "Hosea 11:1 and Matthew 2:15," *Westminster Theological Journal* 63 (2001): 87-96, and is used by permission.

[81]The quotation comes directly from the Hebrew text of Hosea 11:1; Numbers 23:22; 24:8, as noted in the margin of NA[27]. The LXX of Hosea 11:1 pluralizes "my sons," making the verse refer explicitly to Israel as a people and making it conform to the plurals of verses 11:2-4. Aquila, Symmachus and Theodotion, as well as the first column of the Hexapla, follow the Hebrew text in reading "my son" as singular (so also Coptic, Ethiopic, Armenian).

mentaries of Rashi and Kimchi it is possible to see a line of interpretation that goes counter to Matthew's eschatological-messianic view.

Modern commentaries take Hosea 11:1 to be referring to Israel and the historical exodus. The most common approach to the meaning of the verse in Hosea is to view the fragmented sayings of the book in light of a reconstructed life and message of the prophet. Such an approach has led to an even deepening of the division between the OT and NT.

The common evangelical solution has been to adopt the earlier view of Wilhelm Surenhuis,[82] that Matthew's understanding of Hosea 11:1 was grounded in a typological or *sensus plenior* reading that was characteristic of the first century. D. A. Carson offers a mediating position in seeing Hosea's use of the term "son" as part of a larger "messianic matrix" of images in previous revelation that pointed to Jesus.[83]

A quite different kind of solution is offered by Brevard Childs. Childs seeks "to do justice to the logic of the material in its canonical context."[84] His focus is on how Hosea's words were preserved and shaped to serve as Scripture. "Hosea's words were recorded in some form and gathered into a collection. This process of collection in itself involved a critical activity of selecting, shaping, and ordering of the material."[85] The guiding principle behind this selection and ordering of material, according to Childs, was a metaphorical application to Judah of Hosea's prophetic words to the northern kingdom. The express statement of this principle is found in Hosea 12:10, where the Lord says, "By means of the prophets, I spoke in parables."

For Childs, of course, such a metaphorical understanding of Hosea's words represented a new direction in meaning. Originally, Hosea would not have intended to speak of Judah, nor would he have understood his words meta-

[82]Wilhelm Surenhuis, *Sefer humash, sive, Biblios katallages in quo secundum veterum theologorum Hebraeorum formulas allegandi & modos interpretandi conciliantur loca ex V. in N.T. allegata* (Amsterdam, 1713).

[83]According to Carson, Hosea understood the exodus in Hosea 11:1 as "a pictorial representative of divine, redeeming love," but, "building on existing revelation, [Hosea] grasped the messianic nuances of the 'son' language already applied to Israel and David's promised heir in previous revelation so that had he been able to see Matthew's use of 11:1, he would not have dispproved, even if messianic nuances were not in his mind when he wrote that verse" ("Matthew," in *The Expositor's Bible Commentary,* ed. Frank E. Gaebelein [Grand Rapids: Zondervan, 1992], 8:92).

[84]Brevard S. Childs, *Introduction to the Old Testament as Scripture* (Philadelphia: Fortress, 1979), p. 377.

[85]Ibid., p. 378.

phorically. Such a reading of Hosea's words is found only in a later stage in the composition history of the book.[86] Crucial to the message of the book as we now have it, says Childs, is the promise of Hosea 3:5: "[After many days] the sons of Israel will seek Yahweh their God and David, their king, and they will fear the LORD and his goodness in the last days." Hosea 1–3 thus provides the necessary context for understanding Hosea's words of judgment in Hosea 4–14. Although Israel has acted the harlot, Yahweh will remain faithful and return to her in the eschatological future.

The canonical interpretation by Childs of the book of Hosea bears directly on our question of Matthew's use of Hosea 11:1. If Childs is correct in his reading of Hosea, then the *sensus literalis (historicus)* of Hosea 11:1 is precisely that of Matthew's Gospel. Hosea 11:1 speaks of the future, not the past. The book, in fact, provides its own clue to the meaning of Hosea 11:1 in Hosea 11:5: "[Israel] will not return to Egypt, but Assyria will be their king because they have refused to repent." In Hosea 11:1-4, then, the historical exodus is understood as a metaphor. It is an image of future redemption. Egypt is Assyria, the enemy oppressor. Matthew was simply following the compositional (canonical) clues within the book itself by applying the picture of the exodus in Hosea 11:1 to the eschatological salvation in Matthew 2:15. The messianic sense that Matthew saw in the words of Hosea 11:1, "out of Egypt I have called my son," was already there in the book of Hosea. Matthew did not invent it. He, better than we, understood the *sensus literalis* intended by the historical author of the book of Hosea.

The approach of Brevard Childs is, by now, well known. It has not, however, been widely accepted within critical OT studies because its focus is on an authoritative canonical text. There is little place for such a text in critical scholarship. Ironically, the approach by Childs has also not been widely accepted within the evangelical community, largely, I think, for a similar reason: his exclusive focus is on the authoritative text and not on reconstructed historical events. I say "ironically" because, of all people, evangelicals have a major stake in the meaning of the canonical text. It is that text which evan-

---

[86]According to Childs, there is at least one additional compositional stage to reckon with in the book of Hosea. At that level, the book of Hosea contains additional material that is decidedly positive, not negative, toward Judah. In the first three chapters, for example, "Judah is the recipient of promise, Israel of judgment (1:7; 2:2; 3:5)" (ibid., p. 380). It is by means of these new words of hope for Judah that the negative message of Hosea can, and should, be read as the backdrop for a new divine promise to Israel. It is a promise grounded in the Davidic covenant.

gelicals hold to be the inspired Word of God. One would think that evangelicals would by now have warmed up to Childs and his canonical approach. That, of course, has not happened.

What troubles evangelicals about Childs is the fact that he shows so little interest in the apologetic task of demonstrating the historical reliability of the canonical text. It is not enough for the evangelical to say, with Childs, that the canonical meaning of the text is the meaning that the NT writers understood. Evangelical apologetics, rightfully, insists that the canonical meaning also conform to the original meaning of Hosea's words. There must be a connection between what Hosea's words mean in the book of Hosea and what Hosea originally intended by those words. If we could find that connection, there would, in my judgment, be no real objection to the way Childs approaches Hosea. It would, in fact, provide a helpful step in linking the OT and the NT.

It is to that question I now want to turn. In doing so, I want to make it clear that I accept Childs' exegesis of the *sensus literalis* of the book of Hosea and its implication for Hosea 11:1. My intent is to pick up the thread laid down by Childs and to push the question further back to Hosea himself. Is it possible to establish the historical point that the eighth-century prophet Hosea himself already understood his words in Hosea 11:1 metaphorically and messianically?

Since at least the eighteenth century, the historical meaning of the prophetic Scriptures has been identified by many with the meaning intended by the individual prophet within his own particular historical context. In our case, the historical meaning of the expression "out of Egypt I have called my son" is that sense which the prophet Hosea would likely have attached to it within his particular historical context. Thus, our question is "How would Hosea have understood the event of the exodus?"

It is axiomatic among most OT scholars that the metaphorical meaning of the exodus, as an event, would not likely be a part of the historical prophet Hosea's understanding. I believe that I am right in saying that such a view holds true for both evangelical and nonevangelical biblical scholars. It is, in fact, precisely for that reason that Matthew's use of Hosea 11:1 is problematic.[87]

[87]Commenting on Hosea 11:1, Leon Wood writes, "Once more Hosea reverted to the earlier hisory of Israel" ("Hosea," in *The Expositor's Bible Commentary,* ed. Frank E. Gaebelein [Grand Rapids, Zondervan, 1992], 7:212). Wood saw no other purpose in Hosea's prophecy than to point to a past event, the exodus. Although Wood mentions Matthew's use of this verse, he does not even hint at an explanation.

Franz Delitzsch, obviously aware of Matthew's use of this verse, provides the brief but complicated explanation that by pointing to a past event in Israel's history, the prophet was acknowledging that it was through that history that a way was paved for the incarnation of God's Son.[88] Israel's history, rather than Hosea's words, was a "material prophecy" of the coming Christ.[89] Hosea's words point not to Christ, but to a historical event that contained within itself the same significance as the life of Christ.[90]

What seems clear from Delitzsch's comments is that considerable common ground is shared by evangelicals and nonevangelicals when it comes to understanding what the historical prophet Hosea meant by the words in Hosea 11:1. He was, clearly and simply, referring to Israel's historical exodus, and he did not likely have any directly messianic sense in mind. What messianic significance may ultimately have been attached to his words is grounded in a larger understanding of the meaning of Israel's own unique history.

One is immediately struck by how similar such approaches also are to the canonical criticism by Childs. What Childs attributes to a later redactional stage in the composition of the book of Hosea, evangelicals see in the work of Matthew and the broader process of *sensus plenior.* What few, on any side of the question, are willing to concede is that *Hosea himself may have actually understood his reference to the historical exodus as a metaphor or symbol of the coming messianic kingdom.*

There is a second area of commonality in these various approaches to Hosea's words. Evangelical and nonevangelicals alike have addressed the question of the historical meaning of Hosea in a way that is entirely exterior to the meaning of the exodus as portrayed in the Pentateuch itself. *The exodus that they see Hosea making reference to is the historical event itself, apart from its narrative construal within the Pentateuch.* It is hard to see Hosea's words as messianic because we see him referring only to the "brute (uninterpreted) fact" of the exodus event. We too easily fail to see, or appreciate, the obvious: *in referring to the exodus event, Hosea was making a reference not to the event itself, but to the historical event as construed in the Pentateuch.* Hosea ap-

[88]Franz Delitzsch, *The Twelve Minor Prophets*, trans. James Martin (BCOT; Grand Rapids: Eerdmans, 1971), 1:137.
[89]Ibid.
[90]Ibid.

proached the exodus as an exegete. Hosea was engaged in what we today call "intertextuality." He referred to the meaning of the exodus not from his own historical understanding of that event, but rather from the viewpoint of the canonical Pentateuch. Hosea's words in Hosea 11:1 are grounded in an exegesis of Scripture. They are grounded in a studied interpretation of the Pentateuch.

Nonevangelicals, of course, do not believe that there was a Pentateuch in Hosea's day, so the question for them simply does not exist. For an evangelical, however, a key to the meaning of Hosea 11:1 must lie in two important and related questions: Are Hosea's words, in fact, grounded in an exegesis of Scripture, the Pentateuch? What is the meaning of the exodus event within the compositional strategy of the Pentateuch?

To those questions we now turn. I will attempt to make the following five points:

1. Hosea's entire message throughout the book of Hosea is grounded in a careful and conscious exegesis of the pentateuchal text.
2. Within the compositional strategy of the Pentateuch, the exodus event is used as a key messianic metaphor or image.
3. When Hosea recalled the exodus event in the words we find in Hosea 11:1, he likely did so because of its central messianic meaning within the Pentateuch.
4. The meaning that Childs describes in the final canonical text conforms to both the Pentateuch's own understanding of the exodus and the sense that Hosea himself would have likely held if he read the Pentateuch.
5. When Matthew quoted Hosea 11:1 as fulfilled in the life of Christ, he was not resorting to a typological interpretation of OT events. He was, rather, drawing the *sensus literalis* of the OT description of the exodus from the book of Hosea, and it in turn was drawn from Hosea's exegesis of the *sensus literalis* of the Pentateuch. As Hosea himself put it, God speaks through his prophets in parables (Hos 12:10). If a messianic eschatology is already thematized by the exodus event in the Pentateuch, then in drawing on that image, the prophet Hosea most likely had a future event in mind much like that of Matthew 2. Crucial to this line of thought is the notion that lying behind the composition of the ca-

nonical Pentateuch is a fully developed messianic eschatology in which the exodus is an intentional and deliberate metaphor.

*Are Hosea's words grounded in an exegesis of the Pentateuch?* There are two parts to this question. The first is whether there was a Pentateuch already in the eighth century and whether it looked like the one we now have. For the sake of time, and within the present context, I will assume that this part of the question needs no further discussion within our present context.[91] The second part of the question is whether Hosea's prophecies were, in fact, grounded in an exegesis of earlier biblical texts. While most would readily concede that the prophets were informed by the theology of the Torah, for our purposes we need to take a closer look at that unique fact.

As I have already mentioned, a recurring feature of Hosea's prophecies (in Hos 4–12) is his constant and continual reference to earlier biblical texts. In today's technical jargon this is called "intertextuality."[92] Put in terms of the prophet Hosea, intertextuality means that Hosea's message assumes an informed knowledge of the Pentateuch on the part of his hearers.

The frequent dependence of Hosea's prophecies (in Hos 4–14) on the exegesis of earlier texts can hardly be disputed. For example, all would agree that Hosea 12:4-5 is based on a careful reading and verbal exegesis of Genesis 32:23-32. In Hosea 12:4, for example, Hosea draws on the verbal root of the names "Jacob" and "Israel" to describe Jacob's wrestling with his brothers and God. In Hosea 12:5 he interprets Genesis 32:29, "you [Jacob] strove with God" to mean "he [Jacob] ruled over an angel." One can easily see that Hosea has pondered the words of the Genesis text and from those words themselves

---

[91]The line of argument I would take to defend this view is as follows. The most revealing feature of Hosea's prophecies is the way he continually refers to past and present events. He opens the book, for example, with a reference to the "bloodshed of Jezreel" that God will visit "upon the house of Jehu." Similar to such historical references, Hosea also grounds his words in references to pentateuchal material. What is striking about these various kinds of references is that only the ones that relate to the pentateuchal material are otherwise known to us biblically. The others, such as the reference to the "bloodshed of Jezreel" (Hos 1:4) or Shalman's destruction of Beth-Arbel (Hos 10:14), are not known in any previous biblical texts. This suggests that in Hosea's day, the book of Kings had not yet been written, but Hosea did have a copy of the Pentateuch much like ours today, at least in those texts that he cites.

[92]Wolfgang Dressler defines "intertextuality" as a factor of textuality that makes "the utilization of one text dependent upon knowledge of one or more previously encountered texts" (Robert de Beaugrande and Wolfgang Dressler, *Introduction to Text Linguistics* [London: Longman, 1981], p. 10).

has derived a specific meaning. He even appears to have employed the technique of *gezera shewa*.

What we see in this one example is repeated throughout Hosea 4–14 and provides the structural framework for the whole of his prophecies. In his opening words of judgment against Israel in 4:2, for example, Hosea summarizes nearly the whole of the Ten Commandments in a series of five infinitive absolutes. Since Hosea 1–3 has focused on Israel's violation of the first (or first two) commandment(s), Hosea 4 begins with the enumeration of the other commandments. His treatment reveals a careful exegesis of Exodus 20. The word *ʾālâ* ("swearing"), for example, commonly refers to calling down a curse on someone. Hence it is a particular application of the second (or third) commandment, which prohibits the misuse of God's name: "Thou shalt not curse." The word means to "lie and deceive." Hence, it is an exegetical extension of the eighth commandment, which appears to speak only of bearing a false testimony in court. The next three infinitives summarize the fifth, seventh and sixth commandments but rearrange their order so as to express more clearly the protection of life and property.[93] The rearrangement also allows Hosea to conclude with "adultery," which was the theme of the first three chapters. Both the attempt to summarize by means of the infinitive absolutes and to interpret by choosing new vocabulary are evidence that behind Hosea's words lies a careful and profound exegesis of earlier biblical (pentateuchal) texts.

One of the most striking examples of Hosea's exegesis of the Pentateuch is found in Hosea 6:7. Hosea says that Israel has broken God's covenant "like Adam." Hosea has identified the fall in Genesis 3 as a breach of God's covenant. Since there is no specific mention of such a covenant in the Pentateuch, Hosea's argument appears to rest on a broadly based exegesis of the Genesis narratives. The history of biblical interpretation provides ample witness to the many ways the notion of covenant can be derived from the Genesis narratives. It is even possible that Hosea himself resorted to the use of the expression in Genesis 6:18 to establish his point. It is hard to reconstruct Hosea's exact exegesis because apparently it rested on a much broader line of argument. The central role of the "covenant" in the final composition of the Pentateuch lends exegetical support to Hosea's conclusion, particularly the

[93]Wilhelm Rudolph, *Hosea* (KAT 13/1; Gütersloh: Mohn, 1966), p. 100.

role of Genesis 15 within the overall structure of the Pentateuch.[94] It suggests that Hosea did read the Pentateuch with larger theological questions in mind, and that he sought a basis for those questions within what we today would call the compositional seams. This leads us to raise the question of Hosea's possible messianic understanding of the exodus. Within the compositional strategy of the Pentateuch, the exodus event is used as a key messianic metaphor or image.

Elsewhere I have suggested that an intentional compositional strategy lies behind the Pentateuch.[95] One way to see this is to look at the way poetic texts have been fitted into the continuous narrative texts. At three macrostructural junctures in the Pentateuch the author has attached an important poetic discourse onto the end of a large unit of narrative (Gen 49; Num 24; Deut 32). A close look at the seams of these junctures reveals a good deal of homogeneous composition. In each of these seams the central narrative figure (Jacob, Balaam, Moses) calls together God's people (imperatives) and proclaims (cohortatives) "what will happen" "in the last days." At the heart of each of these poems lies a clearly defined messianic hope, centered on the promise of a king from the tribe of Judah.

For the sake of time, I will go immediately to the poetic texts of the Balaam oracles (Num 24). I want to emphasize that, in my opinion, Numbers 24 is a central part of the major compositional links uniting the whole of the Pentateuch. It represents the "last word" of the author of the canonical Pentateuch, and it represents his view of the "last days."

The Balaam oracles as a whole offer a complex view of the composition of the Pentateuch.[96] In Numbers 24:5 Balaam begins his oracle with a vision of the restoration of the garden planted by God (Num 24:5-7a) and the rise of a future king in Israel (Num 24:7b-9). The poems continue in Numbers 24:17-20 to speak of Israel's future defeat of their historical enemies. Balaam's oracles conclude by casting a broad vision of the future in which the later prophetic events of Daniel and Ezekiel are portrayed. In these oracles are many examples of innertextuality between Numbers 24 and earlier parts of the Pentateuch, particularly Genesis 1–11. For our purposes, I want to look at one such

[94]See Ha, *Genesis 15*.

[95]See John H. Sailhamer, *The Pentateuch as Narrative: A Biblical-Theological Commentary* (Grand Rapids: Zondervan, 1992), pp. 34-59.

[96]The poems in Numbers 24 are introduced as divinely inspired oracles.

example that sheds light on Hosea's reference to Numbers 24, namely, the way Balaam's oracles in Numbers 24 look back to his oracle in Numbers 23.

The most conspicuous link between Balaam's oracles in Numbers 23 and Numbers 24 is the reference to the exodus in both Numbers 23:22 and Numbers 24:8. So clearly are these two texts related that they are the basis for most source-critical analyses of these chapters. According to Karl Marti, the similarities between these two texts can be adequately explained only as literary "doublets."[97] Most interpreters and translators have followed a similar logic. They have rendered both as virtually identical references to the exodus event. That event, Marti argues, is taken as the grounds for hope in the future: "The God who delivered His people out of Egypt, will himself bring about the great act of salvation in the future."[98] In my opinion, Marti is correct about the meaning only of Numbers 23:22. Not only does the participle have a plural suffix that denotes the nation of Israel, but also in Numbers 23:24 the addition of the words "behold the people" makes it unmistakable that the plural suffix in Numbers 23:22 refers not to an individual, but to the people of Israel.

Where commentaries such as Marti's and modern English translations have gone astray is in treating the similar text in Numbers 24:8 as if it were identical in meaning to Numbers 23:22. Clearly, the two texts are not grammatically identical. Not only are they not identical, but also their differences are semantically dense and clearly intentional. In the reference to the exodus in Numbers 24:8 the singular suffix is used, not the plural (as in Num 23:22). In Numbers 24:8 Balaam says, "God brings *him* out of Egypt," whereas in Numbers 23:22 he says, "God brings *them* out of Egypt." In the context of Numbers 24, the singular clearly refers to the "king" of the preceding verse (Num 24:7). It is that "king" who will rise up to defeat Agag (MT) or Gog (the early versions) in the "last days." God will bring him out of Egypt. Thus, within the context of Numbers 24, that king will come in the eschatological future—"the last days."

There is a further indication within the texts of these two passages that Numbers 24 was meant to be read differently than Numbers 23. As many

---

[97]"Solche Dubletten zu produzieren, wird man der gewiss nicht geistlosen Erweiterungsarbeit in diesem Abschnitt nicht wohl zutrauen; sie sind als etwas quellenmässig Gegebenes verständlicher" (Karl Marti, *Numeri* [KHC 4; Tübingen: Mohr Siebeck, 1903], p. 111).

[98]Ibid., p. 117.

commentaries have noted, all other pronouns in Numbers 23:21-22 are singular. Balaam's oracle in Numbers 23 thus takes up the lead of the narrative framework in Numbers 22:5 by treating the people as a collective singular. The plural in Numbers 23:8 uniquely renders the image *ad sensum*, making it explicit that the oracle has the whole of the people of Israel in view. As a further clarification, an additional עָם has been inserted into Numbers 23:24a. The meaning of the plural in Numbers 23:8 ("God brought *them* out of Egypt") is therefore beyond doubt not a collective. It is about the whole people and their exodus from Egypt.

The fact that so much care was taken to mark Balaam's words in Numbers 23 as a reference to Israel's exodus in the past has important implications for the singulars in Numbers 24:8-9. The fact that they are left as singulars and are not, as in the preceding chapter, intentionally identified as plurals implies that they were not intended as collectives. Rather, they were understood to refer to the eschatological "king" in the immediate context of Numbers 24. It is therefore in the contrast between these two texts, not in their similarity, that the meaning of the author of the Pentateuch can best be seen.

What do such contrasts between Balaam's oracles in Numbers 23 and Numbers 24 suggest about the larger meaning of the Balaam oracles? Are they merely the accidental result of two variant sources? Or, whatever their origin, are they to be read as two aspects of Balaam's future vision? Taking the text as we have it, it appears that Numbers 23 and Numbers 24 were intended to be read as two distinct parts of Balaam's vision. In the first, Numbers 23, Balaam looked back at the exodus as the grounds for God's future salvation of his people Israel. In the second, Numbers 24, Balaam viewed the coming of a future "king" as a new exodus: "God will bring him up from Egypt." The later vision, Numbers 24, is patterned after the earlier, Numbers 23. Unlike Numbers 23, the singulars that follow in Numbers 24:9 refer to the victorious work of a coming king. The past exodus is presented as a picture of the exodus of the future. Internally, within the Pentateuch, Numbers 24 is deliberately linked to Genesis 49 in the statement "He crouches down, he lies down like a lion, and like a lioness; who will raise him?" (cf. Gen 49:9b and Num 24:9a). This further establishes the notion that the singulars in Numbers 24 refer to an individual. It is the future king from the tribe of Judah, whom God will call out of Egypt.

*Hosea's use of the Pentateuch.* This leads me to the third point. How would Hosea have understood the exodus from within the pentateuchal texts that we have been considering? From what I have just suggested, it is clear that there would have been ample grounds for him to draw a messianic meaning. In contrast to Numbers 23, Numbers 24 isolates and focuses on an individual king from Judah and specifically identifies him as a "new Moses" (Hos 2:2) whom God will bring up out of Egypt. A particularly interesting feature of the Balaam oracles is their identification as "parables," hence "images" by which God speaks through the prophets. This fits the expectation of Hosea 12:10, that God speaks in parables through the prophets.[99]

The foregoing observations lead to the conclusion that the meaning that Childs ascribes to the final canonical text conforms both to the Pentateuch's own understanding of the exodus and to the sense that Hosea himself likely would have derived from the Pentateuch. If the Pentateuch existed in Hosea's day, which is likely, there was ample reason for him to understand the exodus in the Pentateuch as an eschatological image of a future messiah.

When Matthew quotes Hosea 11:1 as fulfilled in the life of Christ, we need not understand him to be resorting to a typological interpretation. He is, rather, as Childs has suggested, drawing the *sensus literalis* from the book of Hosea. That sense itself could have been drawn from Hosea's exegesis of the *sensus literalis* of the Pentateuch. As Hosea himself recognized, God speaks through his prophets in parables (Hos 12:10).[100]

## Theological Conclusions and Implications

The implications of this chapter can be stated in light of the positions of both those who allow the NT to interpret the OT and those who insist on allowing the OT to speak for itself.

For the first group, those who allow the NT to interpret the OT, the sug-

---

[99]It is also possible that the expression had its influence on Hosea's own exodus language.

[100]Several features of Matthew 2 support the conclusion that he was reading Hosea in light of the Balaam oracles in the Pentateuch. It is well known that Matthew patterned his portrayal of the magi seeking the messianic star in the heavens (Mt 2:1-12) after Balaam's vision of "the star" in Numbers 24:17. The magi themselves are patterned after Balaam. The story of Herod and the slaying of Jewish children at Christ's birth (Mt 2:16-18) is modeled after the story of Pharaoh slaying the Jewish children in Egypt at the birth of Moses. Viewing Christ as a "new Moses" therefore builds directly on Numbers 24:8. Ernst Lohmeyer suggests that the unusual repetition of the Greek word *paralambanō* throughout Matthew 2 "mag diesen Zusammenhang andeuten wollen" (*Das Evangelium des Matthäus*, 3rd ed. [KEK; Göttingen: Vandenhoeck & Ruprecht, 1962], p. 28).

gestion that the OT itself puts the biblical Jesus at the center of its promise of blessing removes Paul's identification of the "seed" as the Christ from its marginal position in evangelical theology and onto the center stage of biblical theology. Granted that one may allow the NT to interpret the OT—in the case of Galatians 3:16, Christ is the seed of Abraham; Galatians 3:29, those who are Christ's are the seed of Abraham; Acts 3:25-26, the "seed" is God's servant whom he sent first to bless Israel—one then should not pursue that lead and work out its implications, but rather should put it aside and work with the more general thesis that the seed is Israel. Hence, one's central thesis would be that Israel, not Christ, is the seed of Abraham. This would mean that Israel rather than Christ is the "seed," insofar as they are "Christ's."

It is common to identify the "seed," with the help of Galatians 3:16, 29, as Christ, but then to move on to a treatment of the "seed" as the people of Israel.

Oswald Allis suggests that Paul's reference to Jesus as the "seed of Abraham" assigns to Jesus a "preeminent" and "unique" status and implies that Paul's understanding of the "seed" is an exception to the biblical pattern. He says, "[Jesus] is the pre-eminent and unique seed, as Paul makes plain in his comment on the promise to Abraham (Gal. iii. 16)."[101] Allis's reference to Galatians 3:16 as Paul's "comment on the promise to Abraham" implies that Paul's notion of the "seed" is merely an incidental remark and thus not to be taken at face value. Throughout the remainder of his book Allis takes the position that the "seed of Abraham" is the visible church. He does not take into consideration again the notion or the implication of Paul's statement that Jesus is the "seed of Abraham."

As we saw earlier, Albertus Pieters treats Galatians 3:16 in the same manner:

> In the highest sense, according to St. Paul, the "Seed" is the Lord Jesus Christ (Galatians 3:16), which evidently means that in Him the promise culminates. He is, so to speak, the center and core of what is meant by "the Seed of Abraham"; but the circumference lies far from the center, and within the area enclosed by the circle other meanings may be distinguished.[102]

The "other meanings" Pieters has in mind are those that identify the "seed

[101]Oswald T. Allis, *Prophecy and the Church: An Examination of the Claim of Dispensationalists That the Christian Church is a Mystery Parenthesis Which Interrupts the Fulfilment to Israel of the Kingdom Prophecies of the Old Testament* (Phillipsburg, N.J.: Presbyterian & Reformed, 1978), p. 56.

[102]Pieters, *The Seed of Abraham*, p. 13.

of Abraham" as the church, Israel, or the believing remnant of Israel. It is remarkable that throughout the remainder of his book Pieters, like Allis, does not consider further the identification of the "seed" as Jesus. Pieters states his case early in the book. He says, "All other promises to Abraham and his seed are no more than details, working out the central thought that he [Abraham] and his people should be a source of blessing to the whole world."[103] He does not say, "Abraham and his seed, Christ, should be a source of blessing to the whole world." That, it seems to me, would be more in keeping with what Paul states in Galatians 3:16.

The second group is those who insist on the OT interpreting itself and carrying that interpretation back into the NT. It thus takes into consideration the notion that in the composition of the Pentateuch and its subsequent interpretation by the Prophets and the Writings, both the individual biblical Jesus and the collective people of Israel are the "seed" of Abraham. This comes to the heart of one's hermeneutical and theological beliefs.

George Peters formulates the foundation of his concept of the "kingdom" on the premise that the "seed" of Abraham is exclusively the people of Israel. He says, "This Theocracy or Kingdom is exclusively given to the natural descendants of Abraham, in their corporate capacity."[104] However, after quoting Galatians 3:16, Peters says, "If language has any definite meaning, then, without doubt we have here the simple declaration that when God promised 'Unto thy seed will I give this land,' He meant that the land of Canaan should be inherited by a single Person—pre-eminently the Seed—descended from Abraham, even Jesus the Christ."[105] Throughout most of the remainder of his book Peters identifies the "seed of Abraham" with the people of Israel.

The turning point for Peters in the conceptualization of the "seed" comes at the point when the natural "seed" rejects the offer of the kingdom to them and God "raises up a seed unto Abraham out of the Gentiles by engrafting them through faith in the Christ, and accounting them as the children of Abraham by virtue of their Abrahamic justifying faith."[106] Just as Abraham had faith in Christ (the seed), so the Gentiles "who believe in the promised

---

[103]Ibid., p. 12.

[104]George N. H. Peters, *The Theocratic Kingdom of our Lord Jesus, the Christ, as Covenanted in the Old Testament and Presented in the New Testament* (Grand Rapids: Kregel, 1978 [1884]), 1:230.

[105]Ibid., 1:302.

[106]Ibid., 1:396.

seed being also justified by faith, are brought into living union with Christ ('the King of the Jews'), and through Him become the adopted children of Abraham who was of like faith."[107] Peters is careful to distinguish the "seed of Abraham" in Galatians 3:16 from the "seed of Abraham" in Galatians 3:29. The former is the object of Abraham's faith, the Christ; the latter are those Gentiles who participate in the Abrahamic promises and inheritance, which "are given through [Abraham]" by enjoying a "very essential relationship [that] is established in and through Jesus Christ."[108] Gentiles thus receive the adoption as children "because [they are] united and identified with Christ, who is the chief inheritor under the Abrahamic covenant."[109] They are thus "co-heirs" with Christ (Gal 2:5). Gentiles thus become inheritors along with Christ of the promises to Abraham by being grafted into him—that is, into his seed as descendants. Peters has a difficult time seeing Christ as the "seed" in whom the Gentiles are engrafted. Ultimately, he maintains his view that the Gentiles are engrafted into the family of Abraham and thereby inherit his blessings as adopted children.

The Gentile believer must become an adopted member of the elected nation (Eph 2–3), being grafted "into that elected Jewish nation to which was covenanted the promises"[110] "Gentile believers, in virtue of our union with Christ, are grafted in and become members of the Jewish elect nation, virtually becoming believing Jews."[111]

To summarize: The position taken by Peters is that Gentiles are grafted into the Jewish elect nation rather than into Christ, thus they inherit the promises given to Abraham and his sons (and adopted sons). Gentiles are grafted by Christ into the "Jewish elect nation (as the seed of Abraham to whom the promises are given)." "This necessarily becoming 'a child of Abraham' in order to inherit the promises, is unaccountable to those who overlook the covenants by which it is demanded."[112]

Dwight Pentecost states, "Any relationship which the church sustains to the promises is based, not on physical birth, but on a new birth, and is hers

---

[107]Ibid.
[108]Ibid.
[109]Ibid.
[110]Ibid., 1:398.
[111]Ibid.
[112]Ibid., 1:400.

because the individuals are 'in Christ.'"[113] He then affirmingly quotes the above cited passage from Peters, "If language has any definite meaning, then, without doubt we have here the simple declaration that when God promised 'Unto thy seed will I give this land,' He meant that the land of Canaan should be inherited by a single Person—pre-eminently the Seed—descended from Abraham, even Jesus the Christ,"[114] adding, "The church receives of the promises solely because of relationship to the One in whom the promises find fulfillment." [115] Curiously in the following discussion, and throughout the rest of his book, Pentecost's understanding of the "seed of Abraham" is solely that of the nation of Israel.

By overlooking the role of the individual biblical Jesus as the mediator of the Abrahamic blessing covenant, the Gentiles' inclusion in that blessing remains problematic for Peters. This ultimately leads him to identify the Gentiles' role in the Abrahamic blessing as the "mystery" Paul speaks of in Ephesians 3. He says, "The Prophets, however, without specifying the manner of introduction, predict that the Gentiles shall participate in the blessings of this Theocracy or Kingdom."[116] If he were simply to follow the compositional strategy of the Pentateuch and thus see the biblical Jesus as the one in whom all the nations will be blessed (e.g., Gen 22:18), then he would see that the manner of fulfillment is already in the OT (by means of the biblical Jesus), and thus he would have no reason to see the Gentiles' inclusion in the blessing as problematic or not already revealed in the OT, as Paul says in both Romans 1:2; 15:26.

It is clear from Galatians 3:16 that Paul believed that the "seed" of Abraham in the Genesis promise narratives was Christ.[117] Whether or not I have adequately described Paul's exegesis, it is clear what he meant to say in Galatians. Christ is the "seed of Abraham." In him the nations will be blessed (Gal 3:8). If one belongs to Christ (Gal 3:29a *[Christou]*), one is a "seed of Abraham" (*tou abraam sperma* [Gal 3:29b]), but that is only because Christ himself is the "seed" (Gal 3:16). Christians are the "seed" of

---

[113]J. Dwight Pentecost, *Things to Come: A Study in Biblical Eschatology* (Grand Rapids: Zondervan, 1965), p. 89.

[114]Peters, *The Theocratic Kingdom*, 1:302.

[115]Pentecost, *Things to Come*, p. 90.

[116]Peters, *The Theocratic Kingdom*, 1:232.

[117]A focus on Paul's reading of the OT does not exclude other NT writers and how they might have understood the "seed of Abraham." Compare Acts 3:25-26; 7:5; Luke 1:55 (2 Sam 22:51).

Abraham because they are, by faith, in Christ, the "seed" (Gal 3:8-9). For Paul, the term "seed" sometimes should be rendered singular because sometimes it represents "Christ," as in Galatians 3:16, as an individual. But it should also be rendered plural because it stands for those who belong to Christ (Gal 3:29).

The point of this section has been to demonstrate that, if viewed from within the compositional strategy of the Pentateuch and the remainder of the Tanak, Paul's argument is exegetically sound.[118]

***Jesus is the "true Israel."*** I have demonstrated above that Paul's teaching on Christ and the "seed of Abraham" in Galatians is frequently ignored or, what amounts to the same, treated as an isolated variation of the theme that the "seed" of Abraham is Israel or the church. As a result, the passage has received little substantive consideration. If, as I have argued, Paul's argument finds genuine exegetical support in the OT, more attention should be given to it and its theological implications for the whole Bible. How, for example, are we to understand Paul's belief that Jesus, not the church or OT Israel, is the "seed of Abraham"?[119]

An initial response to that question is the suggestion that Jesus is the "true Israel." That appears to be the viewpoint of Paul and the OT writers. The biblical Jesus is the "seed of Abraham" and hence the heir to the Abrahamic blessing. In him both the church and Israel participate in God's promised blessings to Abraham.[120]

***The example of John Calvin.*** The theology of John Calvin builds specifically and intentionally on the identification of Jesus as the "seed of Abraham." For that reason, Calvin's theology provides a concrete example of how such a theme can shape a biblical theology.

As has often been noted, Calvin's *Institutes* are not so much a system of doctrine as a guide to an understanding of the Bible. Calvin himself is clear that the work was meant as a guide to Bible readers. In the preface he writes,

---

[118]"The fulfilment is explained to take place under the promised 'seed,' who is David's Son, and will come again to bring in its realization" (Peters, *The Theocratic Kingdom*, 1:298).

[119]Not only does Paul identify the "seed" with Christ, but also he contrasts that identication with approaches that take the term as a plural: "It does not say 'seeds,' as of many; but it says 'and to your seed,' that is, to one person, who is Christ" (Gal 3:16).

[120]Along with such a reason, it could be added that seeing Jesus as the "seed of Abraham" would make impossible the fulfillment of the Abrahamic covenant during OT times. The Abrahamic covenant could be fulfilled only with the coming the promised "seed," Jesus.

It has been my purpose in this labor to prepare and instruct candidates in sacred theology for the reading of the divine Word, in order that they may be able both to have easy access to it and to advance in it without stumbling. For I believe I have so embraced the sum of religion in all its parts, and have arranged it in such an order, that if anyone rightly grasps it, it will not be difficult for him to determine what he ought especially to seek in Scripture, and to what end he ought to relate its contents.[121]

As intended by Calvin, the *Institutes* were a (confessional) biblical theology and addendum to his commentaries. He writes,

If, after this road has, as it were, been paved, I shall publish any interpretations of Scripture, I shall always condense them, because I shall have no need to undertake long doctrinal discussions, and to digress into commonplaces. In this way the godly reader will be spared great annoyance and boredom, provided he approach Scripture armed with a knowledge of the present work, as a necessary tool.[122]

The *Institutes* are divided into four books. The division is drawn along two central lines in Calvin's thought, the knowledge of God as creator (book 1), and the knowledge of God as redeemer in Christ (books 2–4).[123] Calvin's views of the Abrahamic covenant are found in book 2, which treats of sin, the covenant, and the mediator (Christ).[124]

For Calvin, revelation and theology are grounded in the knowledge of God in creation. Because that knowledge was distorted by the fall, God the

---

[121]John Calvin *Institutes* "To the Reader" (*Institutes of the Christian Religion*, p. 4). "Porro hoc mihi in isto labore propositum fuit, sacrae Theologiae candidatos ad divini verbi lectionem ita praeparare et instruere, ut et facilem ad eam aditum habere, et inoffenso in ea gradu pergere queant: siquidem religionis summam omnibus partibus sic mihi complexus esse videor, et eo pquopue ordine digessisse, ut si puis eam recte tenuerit, ei non sit difficile statuere et quid potissimum quaerere in Scriptura, et quem in scopum quicquid in ea continetur, referre debeat" (John Calvin, *Joannis Calvini Institutio Christianae Religionis*, ed. August Tholuck [Edinburgh: T & T Clark, 1874], 1:20). *RGG*[4], vol. 2, cols. 23-26.

[122]Calvin *Institutes* "To the Reader" (*Institutes of the Christian Religion*, pp. 4-5). "Itaque hac veluti strata via, si quas posthac Scripturae enarrationes edidero, quia non necesse habebo de dogmatibus longas disputationes instituere, et in locos communes evagari, eas compendio semper astringam. Ea ratione, magna molestia et fastidio pius lector sublevabitur: modo praesentis operis cognitione, quasi necessario instrumento praemunitus accedat" (Calvin, *Institutio Christianae Religionis*, 1:20).

[123]*RGG*[4], vol. 2, cols. 23-27.

[124]Book III treats faith, grace and election; book IV treats the church, the sacraments and civil law.

Father sent God the Son to be the redeemer and mediator of an eternal covenant. His aim was to restore humankind's relationship with God. In that, Christ's role as mediator was grounded in two central biblical themes: the incarnation and the unity of the covenant. If the Son was to be the mediator between the Father and humanity, he himself must be both God and human. Those conditions were met by the incarnate Christ. Moreover, if the redemption was to be eternal, there could be only one covenant. If there was only one covenant, there could be only one mediator.

Hence, for Calvin, the *scopus* of the one covenant must be Christ. He is the only possible mediator because only he is incarnate and therefore eternal. The biblical covenant that first laid down the conditions of incarnation and eternality was the Abrahamic covenant in Genesis 12. The incarnation was asserted in the mediator's being the "seed" of Abraham. He was both *a* descendant of Abraham and *the* descendant of Abraham.

The eternality of the Abrahamic covenant was to be found in its mediator being Christ—the same yesterday, today, forever. Calvin therefore clearly understood the necessity of Paul's reading of the Genesis promise narratives in Galatians 3:16. There is no doubt that he understood Paul's reading as the simple meaning of the Genesis promise narratives. Paul's exegesis in Galatians 3 gave the simple meaning, though Calvin believed that it "was not yet expressed in clear words." To demonstrate that Paul's reading of Moses was in accord with the actual intent of Moses, Calvin pointed to the fact that the message was clear enough for the early readers of those texts to see Christ. Calvin's example is Hannah, who saw in those early pentateuchal promises the central role of Christ as mediator and redeemer. Thus, Calvin argued that "before a king had been established over the people, Hannah, the mother of Samuel, describing the happiness of the godly, already says in her song: 'God will give strength to his king and exalt the horn of his Messiah'" (1 Sam 2:10).

*The covenant framework in Calvin's thought.* In book 2, chapter 6, Calvin introduces his discussion of redemption with a consideration of what it means to be "in Christ." He does so at the exclusion of two alternatives: natural revelation (a work of God the Father) and conscience (a work of law). Neither natural revelation nor law was a suitable avenue to reach the heart of fallen humanity. Since God the Father could not recognize fallen humanity, if he were to meet them as Savior, he must come to them "as Redeemer in the person of his only-begotten Son."[125] As for law, it could stand only as judge over fallen humanity. The law could not produce the necessary obedience to restore the lost.

> Consequently that original excellence and nobility which we have recounted [chapters 1–3] would be of no profit to us but would rather redound to our greater shame, until God, who does not recognize as his handiwork men defiled and corrupted by sin, appeared as Redeemer in the person of his only-begotten Son. Therefore, since we have fallen from life into death, the whole knowledge of God the Creator that we have discussed [book I] would be useless unless faith also followed, setting forth for us God our Father in Christ.[126]

It should be clear from this that for Calvin, redemption of fallen humanity necessitated a mediator who was both God and man. Thus, the incarnation was essential to redemption. Neither natural revelation nor law alone per se could restore fallen humanity's relationship with God. Natural revelation could not get beyond humankind's sinful nature. The sacrifices required by the OT law were themselves only able to teach believers "to seek salvation nowhere else than in the atonement that Christ alone carries out."[127] Calvin argued from the book of Hebrews that the OT sacrifices were never efficacious, and that Christ was the only possible mediator of our salvation.[128]

On the question of obedience to the law, Calvin turned the discussion to the biblical notion of covenant.[129] The covenant that Calvin had in mind was neither a "covenant of works" nor a "covenant of grace," as both came later to be known. For his concept of the covenant, Calvin turned directly and immediately to the Bible and, specifically, the Abrahamic covenant of the Genesis promise narratives. Calvin saw in the biblical notion of the "seed of Abraham" a covenant that contained the necessary prerequisites of the Reformation focus on justification by faith *(sola fide)*. It was a covenant that included the incarnation and was grounded in the idea of a mediator. Like Paul in the NT, Calvin saw Christ as the individual "seed of Abraham," the mediator of an eternal covenant. Also like Paul, Calvin held that "Christ was properly that

---

[125]Calvin *Institutes* 2.6.1 (Calvin, *Institutes of the Christian Religion*, p. 341).
[126]Calvin *Institutes* 2.6.1 (ibid.).
[127]Calvin *Institutes* 2.6.1 (ibid., p. 343).
[128]Calvin *Institutes* 2.6.1 (ibid., pp. 342-43).
[129]*RGG*$^4$, col. 27.

seed in whom all the nations were to be blessed" (Gal 3:14).[130]

Although there are signs that Calvin was not entirely satisfied with Paul's exegesis in the OT promise narratives, there is little doubt that he understood and fully appreciated Paul's reasons for identifying Christ as "the seed" and its essential bearing on the biblical presentation of the gospel.[131] To Calvin, Paul and Moses were in complete agreement on the identity of the "seed" of Abraham as Christ (Gal 3:16). The concept of a mediatorial "seed of Abraham" was central to Calvin's understanding of biblical redemption and the Christian's security in Christ. Since Christ is the "seed" of Abraham, his mediation of the Abrahamic covenant is grounded both in the doctrine of the incarnation and the overall scriptural teaching on the Abrahamic covenant. Christ, as the "seed" of Abraham, carried out his work as mediator from within the physical family of descendants of Abraham. The Son of God was also a son of Abraham. Christ was a member of the human line of descent that traced back to Adam, and he was the eternal Son of God who became the eternal surety of humanity's redemption. Calvin's biblical theology of redemption in Christ therefore was grounded in two central doctrines: (1) the scriptural idea of covenant as a relationship between God and Abraham's descendants; (2) the biblical notion of the incarnation.

To understand Calvin's view of the OT, it is essential to know certain aspects of his idea of covenant, which are different from typical notions of covenant that became common after Calvin. There are, first, several important features of Calvin's understanding of covenant derived from the nature of the mediator "seed."

1. In Calvin's understanding, Christ as mediator is always the object of saving faith in the biblical covenant—"the hope of all the godly has ever reposed in Christ alone."

---

[130]Calvin *Institutes* 2.6.1 (Calvin, *Institutes of the Christian Religion*, p. 343).

[131]That Calvin was not completely satisfied with the exegetical basis of Paul's identification of Christ as the "seed" of Abraham is clear from his unsolicited remark on the OT promise texts that Paul uses. After driving home the point that "it is therefore *clear* that Abraham's seed is to be accounted chiefly in one Head, and that the promised salvation was not realized until Christ appeared," Calvin added the comment that "in Moses' writings *this was not yet expressed in clear words*" (italics mine). Paul was clear about the "seed of Abraham," but Moses was not. In any event, Calvin was sufficiently convinced from Paul's writings that the OT taught that the "seed" of Abraham was the incarnate mediator of God's blessing to the nations. It thus became a central theme in Calvin's understanding of redemption and the covenantal structure of biblical theology.

2. Since Christ is the mediator of this covenant, it is an eternal covenant. Christ never changes, and his role as mediator never changes.
3. Since with Calvin, Christ is the mediator of this covenant, there can only be one covenant. Christ never ceases to be mediator of this covenant, nor does he ever become mediator of another covenant.
4. All biblical covenants are one and the same covenant. Any differences between the biblical covenants such are purely "accidental" and nonessential.
5. Since with Moses the law became part of the covenant, Christians cannot dismiss it as a nonessential part of their covenant. The purpose of the law was to present Christ as the object of faith. Through the law "Christ was always set before the holy fathers as the end to which they should direct their faith."[132]

Calvin's stress on the centrality of faith in the biblical covenant led him into a careful consideration of the role of faith in the OT and the old covenant. If there is only one covenant and Christ is its mediator, then the terms of every covenant in the OT are the same: faith in Christ. "From the beginning of the world he had consequently been set before all the elect that they should look unto him and put their trust in him."[133]

Since there is only one covenant (Abrahamic covenant), Calvin insisted that the Mosaic covenant at Mount Sinai was to be understood as a renewal of the Abrahamic covenant. That brings up the question of the law that was added by Moses ("about four hundred years after the death of Abraham [cf. Gal. 3:17]").[134] Because all the biblical covenants are the same, Calvin was opposed to the notion of a "new" covenant per se.

*Calvin's view of the law.* Calvin's view of the nature of the law is found in his commentary on the Pentateuch.

1. The law consists of the Ten Commandments and "the form of religion handed down by God through Moses."[135]
2. The Mosaic covenant was intended as a renewal of the Abrahamic cov-

[132]Calvin *Institutes* 2.6.2 (Calvin, *Institutes of the Christian Religion*, pp. 344-45).
[133]Calvin *Institutes* 2.6.4 (ibid., p. 347).
[134]Calvin *Institutes* 2.7.1 (ibid., p. 348).
[135]Calvin *Institutes* 2.7.1 (ibid.).

> enant. Both are the same covenant with the added "law" given by Moses. Why was the law added by Moses? It was because of Israel's transgressions; that is, their fallen nature required law to show its fundamental shortcomings. The only real law in the OT is the Ten Commandments. They are divided into two parts: ceremonial (commandments 1-5) and civil (commandments 6-10). The ceremonial laws are given to serve as examples of commandments 1-5, and they reveal Christ in types; the civil laws are examples of commandments 6-10, and they serve as models for the application of commandments 6-10 in various situations.

The ceremonial laws, such as sacrifices and orders of the priesthood, are no longer operative, according to Hebrews 4–11. Calvin takes his clues about the ceremonial laws and priesthood from the NT: "In short, the whole cultus of the law, taken literally and not as shadows and figures correspoinding to the truth, will be utterly ridiculous."[136]

For Calvin, the whole of the law was given "according to the pattern Moses saw in heaven." That is why he could understand the law in terms of the spiritual pattern it was modeled after.[137]

Calvin's understanding of the law throughout the Pentateuch is dicussed in his introduction to volume 2 of his commentaries.[138]

1. Apart from the book of Genesis, which is primarily narrative, the four books of Exodus–Deuteronomy contain both narrative and doctrine. This is a distinction not maintained in the books themselves, where the two types of laws are interspersed.

2. The Ten Commandments are given to regulate personal conduct for covenant members.

3. Use of narrative: (a) teaches the mercy of God; (b) teaches the justice of God.

4. Doctrine in the Pentateuch is contained in four parts: (a) the preface to the law; (b) the Ten Commandments, which are a summary of a just

---

[136]Calvin *Institutes* 2.7.1 (ibid., p. 349).

[137]Calvin *Institutes* 2.7.1 (ibid.).

[138]John Calvin, *Commentaries on the Four Last Books of Moses Arranged in the Form of a Harmony*, trans. Charles William Bingham (Grand Rapids: Baker, 1979).

and holy life; (c) supplements to aid in observing the moral law (see ceremonial and civil law below); (d) the end and use of the law.

i. Ceremonial law: examples of ceremonies and exercises of worship. "Therefore, God protests that he never enjoined anything with respect to the Sacrifices: and he pronounces all External Rites but vain and trifling, if the very least value be assigned to them apart from the Ten Commandments. Whence we more certainly arrive at the conclusion to which I have adverted, viz., that they are not, to speak correctly, of the substance of the law, nor avail of themselves in the Worship of God, nor are required by the Lawgiver himself as necessary, or even as useful, unless they sink into this inferior position. In fine, they are appendages, which add not the smallest completeness to the Law, but whose object is to retain the pious in Spiritual Worship of God, which consists of Faith and Repentance, of Praises whereby their gratitude is proclaimed, and even of the endurance of the Cross.[139]

ii. Civil law: examples of political laws. "As to all the Political Ordinances, nothing will obviously be found in them, which at all adds to the perfection of The Second Table: therefore it follows, that nothing can be wanted as the rule of a good and upright life beyond the Ten Commandments."[140]

***Israel's ideal: Patriarchal religion.*** The Pentateuch presents its religious ideal in terms of the faith of a single individual, Abraham. The apostle Paul's use of the Pentateuch in Romans and Galatians follows closely the intent of the author of the Pentateuch. He presents Abraham as an exemplary model of faith (Gen 15:6) and works (Gen 18:19). The life of faith apart from the law is portrayed in the example of Abraham and is counterbalanced by the example of Moses, who lived under the law (Num 12:7).[141] Abraham lived an exemplary life of faith. He trusted God and was counted righteous (Gen 15:6), whereas Moses died in the wilderness, unable to enter the "land" because of a lack of faith (Num 20:12). This is more than a Pauline moment in the Pentateuch's theology; it is a foundational confession of the Pentateuch's own biblical theology. Abraham's faith (Gen 15:6) was grounded in the work

[139]Ibid., pp. 16-17.
[140]Ibid., p. 17.
[141]See Sailhamer, *The Pentateuch as Narrative*, pp. 62-66.

of an individual (singular) descendant ("seed" [Gen 22:18]) of Abraham, through whom God's primeval blessing (Gen 1:28) and eternal life (Gen 3:24) would be restored to all humanity (Gen 49:10). In the patriarchal narratives and poetry, religion of the patriarchs is cast as essentially a pre-Christian version of NT faith—a faith in an individual "seed" of Abraham who is identified as a coming king from the house of Judah who was the mediator of the Abrahamic covenant. This was the king from Judah who is the focus of the Pentateuch's poetry and narrative symbolism.

***Faith and a personal relationship with God.*** Biblically, Israel's relationship with God was not viewed collectively in terms of one's membership in a covenant community as such (contra Pieters and Pentecost).[142] As far as Abraham's example is concerned (Gen 22:18), his personal faith in God's covenantal blessing, mediated by one of his own "seed," included his partaking in an eternal blessing through a personal relationship with God. A central theme in the Pentateuch is Abraham's experience of blessing. There are exegetical grounds in the Pentateuch itself that suggest this notion of faith and redemption was already understood in a NT sense as the gift of eternal life. Abraham's land covenant (Gen 12:1-3), for example, was interpreted in the Pentateuch already as access to spiritual blessings (Deut 11:12) and eternal life in the "tree of life" (Gen 3:23-24). These early Genesis texts were read along a similar line by the OT prophets (Dan 7:13-14) and sages (Ps 133:3). They looked toward a personal relationship with the "seed of Abraham" as mediator of a covenant blessing.[143] Hence, Abraham was instructed by God, "Walk before me and be whole" (Gen 17:1), much the same way Paul enjoins his readers, "Walk in a manner worthy of your calling" (Eph 4:1). These are not merely verbal echoes from the NT; they are fundamental expressions of what it meant to be an OT believer.

***Israel as the collective "seed."*** As we noted in the Genesis narratives, the collective nature of the "seed" of Abraham—that is, Israel as a people—is not portrayed as a "whole" of which each individual member becomes a part. Although Israel as a collective whole is envisioned for the future descendants

---

[142]Contra Pieters: "What that covenant was, and who were in it, we may learn from the seventeenth chapter of Genesis. It was a contract between God and the family of Abraham, whereby they became His people and He became their God" (*The Seed of Abraham*, p. 14). The lack of mention of "Israel" in the Table of Nations (Gen 10), along with a missing *tôldōt* for Abraham, serve to narratively individualize him and his "seed."

[143]See the role of "the nations" in the blessing formulas in the Pentateuch.

of Abraham, the Abrahamic covenant is cast within the context of the individual Abraham and those individuals who follow in his way of faith. Viewed as such, even the collective Israel of the future is understood in terms of the individual Israelite's relationship to the whole, either by means of the external rite of circumcision (Gen 17) or an internal act of faith (Gen 15). The collective nature of the "seed" (Israel) consists in its identification as a gathering of believers not merely for the purpose of fellowship, but more importantly, with a view to personal relationship with the "seed" and the outworking of that in each one's individual life (Gen 18:19). It is thus in a secondary but essential sense that each individual, as an individual, becomes a member of the collective and physical seed, Israel. External factors such as circumcision and Sabbath rest are given as signs (*wĕhāyâ lĕʾôt bĕrît bênî ûbênêkem* [Gen 17:11]) of the fellowship already established by the individual believer's faith in the "seed of Abraham"

***The "seed of Abraham" (Christ) is the true Israel.*** In the NT understanding of the Abrahamic covenant, Christ, not the church, is the "true Israel." Christ, as an individual mediator of the covenant, is the "seed of Abraham." Like Abraham in the promise narratives (Gen 15:6), Christians are individually and by faith placed "in Christ" (the "seed of Abraham") (Gal 3:16). Those who are "Christ's" (*Christou* [Gal 3:29]) by faith (Gal 3:7) are included as members of the fellowship of believers mediated by Christ. In the Genesis patriarchal narratives individual believers are made members of the collective people of God. God is the "God of Abraham, Isaac and Jacob." That personal relationship with the God of the fathers is mediated in the "seed of Abraham" and grounded in each member's personal faith (Gen 15:6; Ex 19:9). In Genesis the people of God are individual believers who, by faith, have a personal relationship with God through the (individual) mediatorial "seed of Abraham." They are called to "walk before God" and to be "whole" ("perfect" [Gen 17:1]). This is restated in Paul's writings, where he says that the individual believer is grafted into Christ, the (individual) "seed of Abraham" (Rom 11). Each member is related individually to Christ. In the NT, the believer becomes a member of the church, the collective "seed of Abraham" (Gal 3:29). In the OT, membership in the collective "seed" is not established by being engrafted into the collective "seed," the church as a new Israel, or by being engrafted into biblical Israel. The church does not replace Israel, but joins alongside Israel as the physical and visible community of those who have put their faith in the individual "seed of Abraham." The two entities, Israel and the church, are distinct from each other, yet they are united in the one individual "seed of Abraham" (Gal 3:28) by virtue of their common experience of faith and blessing "in him" (cf. Jer 4:2). Abraham, as an example of all believers, "trusted in the Lord, and he counted it to him as righteousness" (Gen 15:6).

*Chapter 10*

# The Purpose of the Mosaic Law in the Pentateuch

THE MOSAIC LAW WAS GIVEN BY GOD to Moses on Mount Sinai. Our primary question is "What is the Christian's relationship to the Mosaic law?" That is, is the Christian obliged to follow, as law, the stipulations of the Mosaic law? This is not the same question of whether the Christian is subject to any law (antinomianism).[1] We take it for certain that the Christian is subject to the "law of Christ" (e.g., Gal 6:2) and the "commandments" of Christ (e.g., Jn 15:12: "This is my commandment, that you love one another as I have loved you"). Also not under consideration in the following discussion is whether, or in what way, the Mosaic law can be identified with what philosophers have called "natural law."[2]

## CRITICAL SCHOLARSHIP AND THE LAW

Critical scholarship believes that the Pentateuch originally contained little

[1]Some would use the term *antinomianism* with reference to the Mosaic law only rather than any form of law. Historically, the term has been taken to refer to any form of law. *Antinomianism* is defined as "A general name for the view that Christians are by grace set free from the need of observing any moral law" (F. L. Cross and E. A. Livingstone, eds., *The Oxford Dictionary of the Christian Church*, 3rd ed. [Oxford: Oxford University Press, 1997], p. 78).

[2]"An expression used with a wide variety of meanings, but in a theological context the law implanted in nature by the Creator which rational creatures can discern by the light of natural reason. It has been contrasted with the revealed law, though it was commonly held that the Commandments revealed in the Decalogue (except that about Sabbath observance) were also precepts of the Natural Law" (ibid., p. 1132). Johann Coccejus: "The foedus operum is a foedus naturae not in the sense that it is based on man's essential human nature but in the sense that God has made him upright. This uprightness given man at creation *(imago Dei)* is the natural basis of the foedus naturae (*Summa doctrinae de foedere et testamento Dei*, in *Opera omnia* [Amsterdam, 1701], 7:48-49).

or no collections of laws. Its earliest form was a book of ancient stories. Its laws were added in stages, over time. Among the various strata of laws in the Pentateuch, critics believe, the first to be added was the Decalogue (Ex 20) and, after that, the Covenant Code (Ex 21–23). The book of Deuteronomy and its laws were added during the reign of Josiah (seventh century B.C.). The rest of its laws were added by priests in the postexilic period. Thus, according to many critical scholars, the law, as such, is secondary to the Pentateuch and is, consequently for the most part, not a central issue to the theology of the Pentateuch.

***The Mosaic law in classical theological systems.*** The classical systems of covenant theology[3] and dispensationalism appropriate the Sinai laws in various but consistent ways. As a rule, both systems approach the Mosaic law referentially, with a view to the events that lie behind the biblical narratives rather than to the depiction of those events in the narratives themselves. There is little or no attempt in their thinking to distinguish the Pentateuch from the laws it contains. What is said about the Mosaic law is applied equally to the Pentateuch as a whole. The question of the Christian and the Mosaic law is thus construed in terms of the larger question of the role of the Pentateuch (and OT) in the life of a Christian. The failure to make a distinction between the Mosaic law and the Pentateuch (see p. 235 n. 15) is a fundamental problem for both theological systems, one to which neither has adequately responded (cf. the role of Friedrich Schleiermacher in establishing the notion that the Pentateuch teaches a religion of legalism).

***Does the Pentateuch teach "the Mosaic law"?*** Both covenant theology and dispensationalism share important assumptions about the nature and purpose of the "Mosaic law" in the Pentateuch. First, they recognize that the Mosaic law was given to Israel in the context of the establishment of the Sinai covenant. They also assume that the purpose of the Pentateuch was to teach or inculcate the Sinai covenant and the Mosaic law that accompanied it. The Pentateuch, as they understand it, is the written record of the Sinai covenant and its laws. Hence, the Mosaic law and the Pentateuch are identical.[4] As

---

[3]See Oswald T. Allis, *Prophecy and the Church: An Examination of the Claim of Dispensationalists That the Christian Church Is a Mystery Parenthesis Which Interrupts the Fulfilment to Israel of the Kingdom Prophecies of the Old Testament* (Phillipsburg, N.J.: Presbyterian & Reformed, 1978), p. 37.

[4]The quotations that follow here show that among most evangelical theologians the OT (Pentateuch) is identified as the Mosaic law. Most evangelical biblical scholars freely admit to this identification of the OT with the Sinai law. Dispensationalists, as a matter of course, identify the

they understand it, when Moses gave Israel the law on Mount Sinai, he was, in effect, beginning a process that would eventually culminate in his giving them the Pentateuch.[5]

***Critique of the common assumption about the Mosaic law.*** In the earlier part of this book I argued that the central purpose of the Pentateuch is to teach the importance of a life of faith. As such, there is quite a lot of theological similarity between the Pentateuch and the NT books, especially those of the apostle Paul. Both stress the failure of the Mosaic law and also God's merciful offer of grace in the face of a heartfelt faith.

A major part of the understanding of the Pentateuch in this book is derived from tracing its compositional strategy and paying close attention to the role that the Mosaic law plays in that strategy. The approach involves a holistic reading of the Pentateuch itself, focusing on those textual features that link its many smaller pieces into a larger meaningful whole. It involves asking "textual" questions such as how the author wants us to view the Mosaic law within the context of the Sinai events he is recounting. Why, for example, does he recount the story of the golden calf just before inserting the largest collection of laws relating to the priests? Is there a text strategy at work here? It involves identifying the work of the author himself as the central locus of meaning and thus not attempting to find its meaning outside the Pentateuch's own unique perspective.

---

OT with the law given at Sinai. "The author of Hebrews states plainly that a drastic change has occurred because a different priesthood has been placed into operation. Jesus is a priest, but not according to the Mosaic law (Heb. 7:12). Many other differences have been inaugurated by the new covenant, such as greater glory, greater power, and greater finality; these call into question the continuity between Old and New Testaments" (Wayne G. Strickland, "The Inauguration of the Law of Christ with the Gospel of Christ: A Dispensational View," in Greg L. Bahnsen et al., *Five Views on Law and Gospel* [Grand Rapids: Zondervan, 1996], p. 262). One finds among covenant theologians the same identification of the OT with the "old covenant" at Sinai: "What then is the relationship of the Old Testament to the New Testament or the Law to the Gospel?" (Willem A. VanGemeren, "Response to Douglas Moo," in ibid., p. 377). "Yet it is important to stress again that the Law of the Old Testament is not against the Gospel. It is an expression of God's care. In the interest of teaching his children how they should relate to him and how they should develop wholesome relations with one another, he detailed for them his expectations in laws, statutes, and ordinances" (Willem A. VanGemeren, "The Law Is the Perfection of Righteousness in Jesus Christ: A Reformed Perspective," in ibid., p. 29). "How, then, should the Christian read the law of Moses? In what way is it 'profitable' to us (cf. 2 Tim. 3:16)?" (Douglas J. Moo, "The Law of Christ as the Fulfillment of the Law of Moses: A Modified Lutheran View," in ibid., p. 376).

[5]Hans Frei has documented this subtle process in biblical interpretation, which I discussed earlier in this book. See John H. Sailhamer, *Introduction to Old Testament Theology: A Canonical Approach* (Grand Rapids: Zondervan, 1995), pp. 36-85.

To be sure, we believe that the events recounted in the Pentateuch are real, and the Bible has accurately depicted them. Our task, however, does not involve the reconstruction of those historical events apart from the biblical narratives. Our task is the exegesis of the biblical narratives in which those historical events are recounted. When one speaks of "the law" in the sense of those laws included in the Pentateuch, one must take care to distinguish them as laws given to Israel at Sinai (historical events) and laws now incorporated in the compositional strategy of the Pentateuch (an inspired text). They are, of course, the same laws, but they may not have the same purpose and application for us as readers of the Pentateuch. It is one thing to ask why God gave ancient Israel the Mosaic law, but quite another to ask why the author of the Pentateuch inserted selected collections of those laws in the Pentateuch. Even though we are talking about the same laws, recording them for Israel at Mount Sinai may not have had the same purpose as recording them within the context of the Pentateuch and its literary strategy.[6]

The Pentateuch is a book that contains several collections of laws, but one must be cautious in evaluating their purpose within its overall compositional strategy. There may be several reasons why God gave Israel the "Mosaic law." There may also be several reasons why the author of the Pentateuch included these laws in the Pentateuch. Some of those reasons may overlap, but some may differ considerably. The author may, for example, have wanted to teach the law to his readers, or his intent may have been to educate his readers about the law. He might have intended to accomplish either task, or both tasks, in writing the Pentateuch. The conclusions that we draw regarding these questions will ultimately have to be drawn from our understanding of the author's compositional strategy.

***Covenant theology and the Mosaic law.*** According to covenant theology, God entered a "covenant of grace" *(foedus gratiae)* with Adam after the fall. Adam previously had failed to obey the stipulations of the "covenant of works" (*foedus operum*). Had he succeeded, he and his descendants would have been granted eternal life. With Adam's failure, the covenant of works was replaced by a covenant of grace. All subsequent covenants in the Bible are specific realizations (administrations) of the one covenant of grace. Calvin's view of a single covenant we noted earlier: "The covenant made with all the patriarchs is so much like ours in substance *[substantia]* and reality *[re ipsa]* that the two

[6]For a further discussion of this point, see John H. Sailhamer, *The Pentateuch as Narrative: A Biblical-Theological Commentary* (Grand Rapids: Zondervan, 1992), p. 63.

are actually one *[unum]* and the same *[idem]*. Yet they differ *[variat]* in the mode of dispensation *[administratio]*."[7]

In the covenant of grace God promised eternal life to those who put their trust in the promised redeemer. At different times and within distinct contexts, the covenant of grace was administered in a variety of ways. God's covenant with Israel at Mount Sinai was one way in which the covenant of grace was administered. The new covenant that Christ initiated by his death and resurrection is another distinct administration of the one covenant of grace. The Sinai covenant and the new covenant are thus the same covenant with different administrations.

The question of the Christian's relationship to the Mosaic law is central to covenant theology. Covenant theology represents the view of theological continuity between the Mosaic law and the Christian. However, it does so, as we have seen, by identifying the written Pentateuch in our Bible with the Mosaic law embedded in the Pentateuch. According to covenant theology, the OT (e.g., the Pentateuch) was Israel's Bible and continues to be the Bible of the Christian church, the "new Israel." The Christian therefore is obliged to keep the Mosaic law, which, they believe, it is the purpose of the Pentateuch to teach.

The covenant view of the law is represented by the Westminster Confession of Faith (1647):

> Chapter VII: Of God's Covenant with Man
>
> II: The first covenant made with man was a covenant of works [*foedus operum*] (Gal 3:12), wherein life was promised to Adam, and in him to his posterity, upon condition of perfect and personal obedience.
>
> III: Man by his fall having made himself incapable of life by that covenant, the Lord was pleased to make a second, commonly called the covenant of grace [*foedus gratiae*]: wherein he freely offered unto sinners life and salvation by Jesus Christ, requiring of them faith in him that they may be saved, and promising to give unto all those that are ordained unto life his Holy Spirit, to make them willing and able to believe. . . .
>
> V: This covenant was differently administered in the time of the law and in the time of the gospel: under the law it was administered by promises, prophecies, sacrifices, circumcision, the paschal lamb, and other types and ordinances

[7]John Calvin *Institutes* 2.10.2 (*Institutes of the Christian Religion,* ed. John T. McNeill, trans. Ford Lewis Battles [LCC 20; Phildelphia: Westminster, 1960], 1:429).

delivered to the people of the Jews, all fore-signifying Christ to come: . . . by whom they had full remission of sins and eternal salvation; and is called the Old Testament. . . .

Chapter XIX: Of the Law of God

I: God gave to Adam a law, as a covenant of works, by which he bound him and all his posterity to personal, entire, exact, and perpetual obedience; promised life upon the fulfilling, and threatened death upon the breach of it; and endued him with power and ability to keep it.

II: This law, after his fall, continued to be a perfect rule of righteousness; and, as such, was delivered by God upon mount Sinai in ten commandments, and written in two tables. . . .

III: Beside this law, commonly called moral, God was pleased to give to the people of Israel, as a church under age [*minorenni*], ceremonial laws. . . . All which ceremonial laws are now abrogated under the New Testament.

IV: To them also, as a body politic, he gave sundry judicial laws, which expired together with the state of that people, not obliging any other, now, further than the general equity thereof may require.

V: The moral law doth forever bind all, as well justified persons as others, to the obedience thereof. . . .

VI: Although true believers be not under the law as a covenant of works, to be thereby justified or condemned; yet is it of great use to them, as well as to others; in that, as a rule of life, informing them of the will of God and their duty, it directs and binds them to walk accordingly. . . .

***The threefold use of the law.***

1. The civil use of the law *(usus politicus):* The function of the law is to restrain sin and promote righteousness. It is a part of God's common grace and is not a means of special grace.
2. The pedagogical use of the law *(usus pedagogicus):* The function of the law is to bring men and women under conviction of sin and of their inability to meet the demands of the law. The law is a tutor that leads to Christ and his grace.
3. The normative use of the law *(usus didacticus):* The "third use of the law" *(tertius usus legis)* is as a rule of life for believers, "reminding them of their duties and leading them in the way of life and salvation."[8]

[8]Louis Berkhof, *Systematic Theology* (Grand Rapids: Eerdmans, 1941), p. 615. Lutherans, though they stress the second use of the law, hold that the third use applies to believers only insofar as

***Three questions.*** Within the system of covenant theology, the continuing meaning of the Mosaic law raises three important questions: (1) Is the Sinai covenant an administration of the original covenant of works *(foedus operum)* or the covenant of grace *(foedus gratiae)?* (2) Is the Mosaic law an essential part of the Sinai covenant, or was it added to the covenant? (3) Is the Christian obligated to keep all the Mosaic law or only a part of it?

The first question is whether the Sinai covenant is an administration of the original covenant of works *(foedus operum)* or the covenant of grace *(foedus gratiae).* Covenant theologians generally acknowledge the necessity of Christ fulfilling the covenant of works on our behalf. Christ was the obedient second Adam, who earned our righteousness through his obedience to the first Adam's covenant of works. This was Christ's work of "active" obedience. He lived a righteous life under the law. Just as in his "passive" obedience it was necessary for him to die to the law, so it was also necessary for him first to live a sinless life under the law. For some covenant theologians, this implied that the covenant of works was, in some way, still operative in Christ's day: "[The covenant of works] having been broken by Adam . . . and Christ having fulfilled all of its conditions in behalf of all his own people, salvation is offered now on the condition of faith. In this sense the Covenant of Works having been fulfilled by the second Adam is henceforth abrogated under the gospel."[9]

There has been much discussion within covenant theology regarding whether and in what way the covenant of works might have been preserved under the administration of the covenant of grace.[10] Was the covenant of works abrogated with the establishment of the covenant of grace, or did the two covenants exist simultaneously until it was finally abrogated in Christ's death?[11]

---

they are still sinners (*simul justus et peccator, homo carnalis*). "It is not surprising therefore that this third use of the law occupies no important place in their [Lutheran] system. . . . The Reformed . . . stand strong in the conviction that believers are still under the law as a rule of life and of gratitude" (ibid., p. 615).

[9]A. A. Hodge, *Outlines of Theology* (New York: Carter, 1878), p. 314.

[10]See Mark W. Karlberg, "Reformed Interpretation of the Mosaic Covenant," *WTJ* 43 (1980): 1-57.

[11]Karlberg: "It is our contention that within the historic Reformed tradition the hermeneutical key to [the interpretation of the Mosaic covenant] is the proper biblical assessment of the symbolic-typical aspect of Old Testament revelation, and the recognition of the dual principles of law and grace operative in the Mosaic Covenant administration. The Mosaic Covenant is to be viewed *in some sense* as a covenant of works" (ibid., p. 3).

Covenant theologians have stressed the point that the Sinai covenant itself was not a covenant of works, but an administration of the covenant of grace. Nevertheless, some have sought to identify elements of a covenant of works in the Mosaic law:

> What was the true nature of the covenant made by God with the Israelites through Moses? . . . It was in one aspect a legal covenant, because the moral law, obedience to which was the condition of the covenant of works, was prominently set forth, and conformity to this law was made the condition of God's favor, and of all national blessings. Even the ceremonial system in its merely literal, and apart from its symbolical aspect, was also a rule of works, for cursed was he that confirmeth not all the words of this law to do them. Deut. xxvii. 26.[12]

This aspect of the Mosaic law is difficult to harmonize with the notion of a covenant of grace. A central text is Leviticus 18:5: "You shall keep my statutes and my judgments which, if a man does them, he will live by them." This text appears to say that obedience to the law brings the reward of "life." An important discussion within covenant theology centers on its understanding of the "life" that is awarded under the Mosaic law. Covenant theologians generally acknowledge that this is not the eternal life that Adam and Eve forfeited in the fall. Eternal life comes only to those who are members of the covenant of grace. The life that comes to those who keep the Mosaic law is thus variously understood (1) in terms of the temporal enjoyments of this life; (2) as a hypothetical offer of life that was never obtained under the Sinai covenant; (3) by a "keeping of the law" that also entailed repentance and sacrifice for sin. Thus, in this last sense, life could be obtained under the Mosaic law through the continued practice of the sacrificial system and its forgiveness of sin. Ultimately, only Christ was able to obey the Mosaic law and hence be rewarded with eternal life.

Covenant theology also believes that the practice of the Mosaic law contained within it the promise of Christ's atoning work. Each element in the Mosaic law was understood as a picture or a type of Christ's redemption. Therefore, in the very requirements of the Mosaic law the promise of redemption was spelled out pictorially (typologically) to the believer.

An important part of covenant theology for many is the notion that in preserving the covenant of works, the Sinai covenant made it possible for

---

[12]Hodge, *Outlines of Theology*, pp. 376-77.

Christ to fulfill the righteous works that Adam failed to accomplished. He lived under the law and thus could fulfill it in every way ("But when the fullness of the time came, God sent forth his Son, born of a woman, born under the law, so that he might redeem those who were under the law, that we might receive the adoption as sons" [Gal 4:4-5]).

Along with the covenant of works, individual Israelites could also enjoy the eternal blessings of the covenant of grace by faith in the coming Christ. In that context, the purpose of the law was to point to the need for Christ's sacrifice.

The second question is whether the Mosaic law is an essential part of the Sinai covenant or was it added secondarily to the covenant. The discussion has centered on Paul's statement in Galatians 3:19 that the law "was added because of transgressions, until the offspring would come to whom the promise had been made; and it was ordained through angels by a mediator."[13]

Johann Coccejus, the seventeenth-century "father" of contemporary covenant theology, understood the Ten Commandments to be an original part of the covenant of grace. The rest of the laws in the Pentateuch were added to the covenant after Israel proved unfaithful in worshiping the golden calf: "The legal covenant of the ceremonial service was instituted as a stricter and harsher dispensation of the covenant of grace. Thus the revelation of grace is found particularly in the decalogue, and that of servitude in the ceremonial law."[14]

Many contemporary covenant theologians have rejected the view of Coccejus. They hold that the whole of the Mosaic law was an integral part of the covenant of grace. Support for that view is commonly found in analogies drawn between the Sinai covenant and ancient Near Eastern treaty documents. An essential part of the ancient treaty formula was a section of stipulations prescribed for expressing loyalty to the treaty agreements. These stipulations are taken as proof of the role of laws in keeping the Sinai covenant.

The third question is whether the Christian is obligated to keep all the Mosaic law or only a part of it. Most Christian theologians accept the notion

---

[13]See Gottlob Schrenk, *Gottesreich und Bund im älteren Protestantismus: Vornehmlich bei Johannes Coccejus*, 2nd ed. (Darmstadt: Wissenschaftliche Buchgesellschaft, 1967), pp. 116-23; Hans Heinrich Wolf, *Die Einheit des Bundes: Das Verhältnis von Altem und Neuem Testament bei Calvin* (BGLRK 10; Neukirchen: Verlag der Buchhandlung des Erziehungsvereins Kreis Moers, 1958), pp. 38-54; Mark W. Karlberg, "Moses and Christ—The Place of Law in Seventeenth-Century Puritanism," *TJ* 10 (1989): 11-32.

[14]Berkhof, *Systematic Theology*, p. 299.

that at least part of the Mosaic law has been abrogated with the death of Christ (Heb 7:12). The remaining question is how much of the law has been abrogated and how much the Christian must still keep under the new covenant. One of the most common approaches to that question is to divide the Mosaic law into distinct categories and to conclude that certain of those categories are no longer applicable to the Christian. There are three categories, as follows.

*The ceremonial laws.* These laws governed Israel's tabernacle and temple ceremonies. They include laws for carrying out sacrifices and offerings and those that regulate the activities of the priests. Before the coming of Christ and his death on the cross, there was a continual need to atone for sin through these various ceremonies. That was the purpose of the ceremonial laws. They were the basis and focus of the religion of the Sinai covenant. With the atoning death of Christ, there was no longer a need for the sacrifices. The Levitical priesthood and, ultimately, the temple were replaced. Since the ceremonial laws are no longer necessary, the Christian is not obligated to keep them.

*The civil laws.* These law governed the everyday affairs of ancient Israel. They showed how Israel was to live as a people of God (theocracy). After the Babylonian captivity, when the kingship had ceased, the notion of a theocracy was no longer applicable. Thus, there were no further occasions for the application of the civil laws. Hence, according to covenant theology, the Christian is not obligated to keep them.

*The moral law.* According to covenant theology, the moral law (or natural law) is a basic notion of right and wrong divinely implanted in the human soul at creation. By the time covenant theology had established itself in Europe (seventeenth century), a strong connection between the notion of moral law and the Ten Commandments had already been affirmed. The Ten Commandments were understood as a written summary of the basic dictates of the human conscience. Such dictates, being of divine origin, would never change. They were true before being formulated in the Mosaic law, and they continue to be true. The moral law is what makes up the basic principles of right and wrong that lie behind the Mosaic law. Hence, the Mosaic law is an application of the moral law to a specific historical situation in ancient Israel. Although the Mosaic law, as a temporary expression of the moral law, might be abrogated, the moral law itself could never be abrogated. Thus, covenant theologians believe that Christians, as participants of the covenant of grace, are obligated to obey the moral law as it is expressed in the Ten Commandments.

***The New Testament view of the Mosaic law.*** Covenant theology's largely positive view of the Mosaic law raises questions about the sometimes negative view of law in the NT. Romans 6:14: "For sin will have no dominion over you, since you are not under law but under grace." Galatians 3:12: "But the law does not rest on faith; on the contrary, 'Whoever does the works of the law will live by them.'" How does covenant theology respond to negative expressions such as these about the Mosaic law?

A common response of covenant theology to the negative view of the law in the NT is that when Paul speaks of the law in these texts, he has in mind not the original meaning of the Mosaic law as understood within the Pentateuch, but a later, first-century misunderstanding of the Mosaic law by his Jewish contemporaries. Geerhardus Vos believed that, being a part of the "provisional" nature of the theocracy, the original understanding of the Mosaic laws in the Pentateuch changed along with the fluctuating ideas of "theocracy." Thus, in Paul's day both the theocracy and the nature of the law within it had changed from what they had been at Sinai and in the Pentateuch. With those changes, the law came to be viewed by his contemporaries as "a powerless ministry of the letter." The changes in the conditions under which Paul viewed the Mosaic law changed his understanding of the role of the law for Christians. According to Vos, in Christ's day the theocratic view of the law "asserted that the law was intended, on the principle of meritoriousness, to enable Israel to earn the blessedness of the world to come. . . . Paul's philosophy, though a partial one, and worked out from a retrospective standpoint, had the advantage of being correct within the limited sphere in which he propounded it."[15]

Despite the changes in the understanding of the law by Paul's contemporaries, his own view of the law must be gathered from texts such as Romans 7:12: "So the law is holy, and the commandment is holy and just and good."

***Evangelical options.***

*A central problem for covenant theology.* A basic problem for covenant theology is how the Christian should respond to the demands of the Mosaic law.

[15]Geerhardus Vos, *Biblical Theology: Old and New Testaments* (Grand Rapids: Eerdmans, 1948), p. 142.

If the Pentateuch (OT) was written to those under the Mosaic law, how do its laws apply to the Christian today? There are two common responses to this problem among covenant theologians.

First, there is the Coccejian response. Johann Coccejus believed that the Mosaic law was not an essential part of the covenant of grace, which included the Sinai covenant. The Mosaic law was added to the Sinai covenant because of Israel's numerous transgressions (e.g., the golden calf). Hence, in the new administration of the covenant of grace in the NT Christians were not under the whole of the Mosaic law. Coccejus believed that only the Ten Commandments were part of the covenant of grace, and Christians were obligated to obey only them as law.

Second, there is the Kuyperian response (Abraham Kuyper, Hermann Bavinck, Louis Berkhof). Most covenant theologians today believe the Mosaic law cannot be approached as a totality. In its essential nature it is a threefold set of laws: ceremonial, civil, moral. Both the ceremonial and civil portions have been abrogated and are not applicable, as law, to the Christian today. Any remaining value that they might have for the Christian lies in their teaching, typologically, the truths of the gospel. Only the moral law, as represented in the Ten Commandments, continues to be applicable to the Christian. Its statutes, as law, are universal and timeless. Since nine of the Ten Commandments are repeated in the NT, this reduces the disputed territory to the question of whether Christians should keep the Sabbath, the only commandment not reiterated in the NT.

One should remember that these theological systems usually operate on both a popular and a technical level. At the popular level, there is considerable blurring of many technical distinctions.

*A central problem for dispensationalism.* The dispensational system is characterized by theological discontinuity. The Pentateuch (OT), which dispensationalists, just as covenant theologians, understand to be a statement of the Mosaic law, is identified as the Bible of the Sinai covenant. The NT, on the other hand, is the part of the Bible that is specifically for the church. The Pentateuch (OT) is part of the Bible, but its message is not for the church; it is for Israel.

A basic feature of dispensationalism is the distinction that it makes between Israel and the church. That same distinction carries for the Bible. The OT is for Israel, and the NT is for the church. Whereas covenant theology equates Israel and the church, dispensationalism makes a clear, though not always complete, distinction between the "two peoples of God." The Mosaic law was given to Israel under an earlier dispensation ("administration"). The church was not a part of that earlier dispensation. That dispensation was administered for Israel under the Sinai covenant, and the Mosaic law played a central role in the process. The church now is not obligated to keep the Sinai covenant, since it is not under the Mosaic law. As Paul said to the Roman church, "You are not under law, but under grace" (Rom 6:14); and to the Galatian churches, "But the law does not rest on faith; on the contrary, 'Whoever does the works of the law will live by them'" (Gal 3:12). Such texts form the basis of the dispensationalist understanding of the church, its relationship to the Mosaic law, and ultimately its relationship to the OT.

A basic question that dispensationalism raises for the church is "What are Christians to do with the Old Testament?" Does the whole Bible (OT/NT) belong to the church? Is that not the implication of NT texts such as 2 Timothy 3:16, which speaks of the value of the OT to all Christians today: "All [OT] Scripture is given by inspiration of God, and is profitable for doctrine, for reproof, for correction, for instruction in righteousness, that the man of God may be perfect, thoroughly furnished unto all good works"?

The Mosaic law as such is not essentially problematic in dispensationalism as it is in covenant theology. That is because, as the dispensationalist sees it, the Christian is not part of the Sinai covenant and thus is not under obligation to keep the Mosaic law. Since the NT has confirmed most of the Ten Commandments, there are still ample divine guidelines for living out the Christian life. There are, as it were, nine NT commandments rather than ten. Moreover, dispensationalists believe that the NT is clear that the Christian is to live according to the law of Christ (Gal 6:2) and Christ's commandments (Jn 15:12). Thus, the charge that dispensationalists are antinomian is not a fair assessment of their position.[16] They have their laws, but they are not the same laws as the Mosaic law given at Sinai.

The problem that besets dispensationalism is of another kind. As we have seen, the Mosaic law is almost universally identified by dispensationalists with the Pentateuch (and the OT in general). As we have also seen, covenant theology holds to the same belief about the Pentateuch. What, then, can one

[16]Antinomianism is the belief that the Christian is not obligated to any law in living out the Christian life.

say about the role of the OT in the Christian's life? If, as the dispensationalist believes, the Sinai covenant and the Mosaic law have been abrogated, and if one identifies the Mosaic law with the Pentateuch, where does that leave the Pentateuch in the life of the Christian? Is it also abrogated, or, at least, not an essential part of Scripture for Christian living today? The Pentateuch, and the OT in general, having been identified by dispensationalists with the abrogated Sinai covenant, would seem to have little claim in the lives of those living under the new covenant. Those in the church, it would appear, seem to have little use for the OT, especially the Pentateuch, whose purpose, most dispensationalists believe, is to teach the Mosaic law.

The task of dispensationalists is to explain more clearly the role they assign to the Pentateuch (and the OT) as Scripture for the church. By identifying the Pentateuch with teaching the Mosaic law, they seem to be left with little of the OT that is aimed at the life of today's Christian.

*A central problem for biblical (promise) theology.* As we have noted often in this book, contemporary evangelical biblical theology has focused not so much on the text of the OT as on the historical events pointed to in that text. This theology thus is built around a series of historical events and institutions that it seeks to link up in continuity with the church. In that schema, the Pentateuch (OT) is understood in anticipation (promise) to the NT (fulfillment). Biblical theology consists of laying out various lines of historical and theological continuity between OT events and institutions and NT events and institutions. The meaning of the OT is drawn from its role within a chain of historical events that point to and ultimately culminate in the coming of Jesus Christ. The meaning of the OT lies in its anticipation (promise) of the events of the NT (fulfillment).

The nagging problem confronting most evangelical biblical theologies is their lack of success in identifying the central message of the Pentateuch and the OT as a whole. What remains constant within the historical movement and development of revelation? What is the central theme that draws all the other themes together and links the whole of the OT to the whole of the NT? There has been little agreement on what this center point might be. Many have suggested that the center of the Pentateuch and OT is the notion of a divine promise. For others, it is a more loosely defined set of beliefs and themes. The problem boils down to the question of how a Christian today can read the Pentateuch in its own way as a Christian. Ultimately, as I have suggested earlier in this book, treating the OT as promise and not fulfillment amounts to a devaluation of the scriptural status of the Pentateuch and the OT. They become signposts, witnesses, to a future fulfillment, while the OT itself remains only a promise, not the fulfillment.

Evangelical biblical theologians have devoted considerable time and effort in attempting to deal with this basic lack of clarity in their understanding of the role of the OT in the life of the Christian. They recognize that they must see the OT as Scripture, but how can one do that without merely assigning the OT, as promise, to the past? Contemporary evangelical biblical theologians have taken three approaches.

*The analogy of faith* (analogia fidei). The general meaning of the whole of Scripture is taken together is a guide to what is constant throughout. This was the approach of the early church. The difficulty is that this approach can too easily slip into a dependence on creeds. The "general meaning of the whole" can be too easily identified with a specific creed.

*The analogy of antecedent Scripture* (analogia scripturae). The accumulated meaning of Scripture up to a specific moment in the progress of revelation becomes the rule by which subsequent revelation is judged. Although this approach has many benefits, it can easily get snagged in the need to address the question of priority. What does the notion of "antecedent Scripture" mean within the context of OT biblical history? Does it require our determining what Scriptures were written before and after other Scriptures? If so, this approach quickly gets mired in the enormity of the task of deciding the relative chronological order of the composition of the OT books. One cannot merely arrange the OT books in the same order as the events they contain. The fact that the book of Joshua precedes the book of Judges in the OT canon does not mean that historically Joshua is antecedent Scripture with respect to Judges. The book of Joshua may have been written long after Judges, but written to be read before the book of Judges. The notion of antecedent Scripture as it is described must arrange the OT books in the order in which they were written. What is common practice in seeking antecedent Scripture is to take the order of the OT books as they are arranged in the OT canon. That, however, raises the issue of the canonical shape of the OT and its relevance for biblical theology. Thus, some evangelical biblical theologians, in part at a loss to arrange the order of OT books historically, have turned to the question of the canonical order or shape of the OT canon.

*The Old Testament canon as hermeneutical and theological construct.* The shape of the OT canon, the Tanak (Law, Prophets, Writings), provides the most appropriate context for understanding the whole of Scripture.[17]

## Israel's Faith and the Old Testament

Neither dispensationalism nor covenant theology has satisfactorily distinguished between the Pentateuch (as a text) and the religion of ancient Israel (as a historical event).[18] Israel's religion was the religion of the Sinai covenant. The Pentateuch is a book that arose out of the failures of that covenant and from the prophetic vision of a new covenant. The nature of Israel's religion under the Sinai covenant is expressed in the biblical passage that describes the making of that covenant:

> Then [Moses] took the book of the covenant, and read it in the hearing of the people; and they said, "All that the Lord has spoken we will do, and we will obey." Moses then took the blood and threw it on the people, and said, "See the blood of the covenant that the Lord has made with you in accordance with all these words." (Ex 24:7-8)

This passage raises several questions. What, for example, was the "book of the covenant" *(sēfer habbĕrît)* from which Moses read? Although, as some have suggested, this book may have been preserved as part of the Pentateuch, the "book of the covenant" was neither our present Pentateuch nor an early version of it. The Pentateuch, as a book, came after and later than the making of the Sinai covenant. As such, the Pentateuch is not called a "book of the covenant." It is a book that tells the story *of* the covenant at Sinai and its failure. The Pentateuch is about Sinai and its covenant, but it is not written on behalf of that covenant. It is written from the perspective of one whose eyes are fixed not on Sinai, but on "the covenant" *(habbĕrît)* that lies beyond Sinai:

> These are the words of the covenant, which the Lord commanded Moses to make with the children of Israel in the land of Moab, besides the covenant which he made with them in Horeb. (Deut 29:1 [28:69 MT])

---

[17]See Sailhamer, *Introduction to Old Testament Theology*.

[18]This question continues to be a central problem of biblical theology. See Martin Ebner, Irmgard Fischer and Jörg Frey, eds., *Religionsgeschichte Israels oder Theologies des Alten Testaments?* (JBTh 10; Neukirchen-Vluyn: Neukirchener Verlag, 1995).

This passage makes it clear that the covenant God has in mind in the last chapters of Deuteronomy was not the one Moses made at Sinai. It was a covenant made "besides the covenant which he made with them in Horeb [Sinai]." It therefore refers to the covenant we see envisioned in Jeremiah 31:31-32, which also is "not like the covenant that [God] made with their ancestors when [he] took them by the hand to bring them out of the land of Egypt." Hence Jeremiah says,

> The days are surely coming, says the LORD, when I will make a new covenant with the house of Israel and the house of Judah. It will not be like the covenant that I made with their ancestors when I took them by the hand to bring them out of the land of Egypt—a covenant that they broke, though I was their husband, says the LORD. (Jer 31:31-33)

## Israel's Hope and the Old Testament

What kind of hope was to arise out of the Sinai covenant and make its way into the Pentateuch and, from there, into the remainder of the OT? How did it then find its way into the pages of the NT and attach itself ultimately to Jesus and the Gospel narratives? How did that hope become the basis for the NT, the church and its gospel message? To answer those questions properly, I have sought to demonstrate that the first impulse to envision this hope came in the attempt to enshrine it in a book, the Pentateuch. It was not enshrined so as to become a faith *in* a book. It was, rather, enshrined so as to be a faith that sought expression *by means of* a book. This means, among other things, that it had an author and was shaped along the lines of a distinct compositional strategy. One can understand the biblical hope by reading the Pentateuch.

The aim of the Pentateuch is to be a textual expression of the prophetic hope grounded in the words of Moses. It is a hope that echoed throughout the OT (Tanak) and could be heard as far away as the NT and the church. At the center of that hope is a king whose reign is described in the three large poems in the Pentateuch (Gen 49; Num 24; Deut 32/33). The Christian faith is in large measure an expression of the belief that Jesus is this king. The Pentateuch itself, however, does not raise questions of whether Jesus can be identified with this king. Although it later came to be used for that purpose, its focus was the more basic question of the nature of that king's rule. He was to be a king from the house of Judah who would reign over Israel and all the nations. He was to be a redeemer who would defeat and destroy all evil and in the process restore God's original blessing to humankind. The Pentateuch is not about the identity of Jesus; it is about the identity of this universal king, the "seed of Abraham." It was those who read the Pentateuch who eventually came to identify Jesus as the king and the "seed" (Gal 3:16). The first attempt at this was made by a group of outsiders, Israel's own prophets.

Here, I can give only a brief sketch of my understanding of how the Pentateuch expresses its hope in a coming king. The author of the Pentateuch does not portray its hope by looking into the future. The Pentateuch is not a prediction of one to come. It also does not occupy itself primarily with typological images. The images in the Pentateuch are directed not at Jesus, but to a coming king who in the NT is identified with Jesus. The author of the Pentateuch understood and trusted in God's covenant pledges to his forefathers (Abraham, Isaac, Jacob). In light of those pledges, and based on God's faithfulness, the author lays into full view a new future for ancient Israel. The Pentateuch is not about a light coming from the future, cast back upon the past, nor does its meaning depend on our reading the NT back onto its verbal images. The Pentateuch is not a light from the future; it is a light from the past that discloses to its readers a way of viewing the future. Its light shines in such a way that when the future arrives, its meaning will already have been contained within that light. The Pentateuch is not so much a searchlight from the future as it is a slideshow of the past.

Understanding the Pentateuch's slideshow is not so much a question of how one might have recognized Jesus when he came as it is a question of how, after Jesus has now departed, we might still recognize him as the "one who is to come." Jesus understood his life and knew himself in terms of the hope he found expressed in the Pentateuch. When Jesus came, those who understood the OT may or may not have recognized him as the "coming one." But, by the time he had departed—after his death, resurrection and ascension—who could not have seen him as the "one who was to come"? The "son of man" of Daniel 7, the "cut off" messiah of Daniel 9, and the redeemer bruised on the heel by the ancient serpent (Gen 3:15)—in the Gospels, Jesus bore all these accrediting signs and images in his own person and life. For many, they came to full light only after his resurrection (Rom 16:25-26). But when the light came and those signs and images were identified in their OT setting, it was clear that they had always been there in the words of the prophets. Jesus could not be recognized without the OT. Like the disciples in Galilee, one only knew Jesus when one saw him as "he about whom Moses in the law and also the prophets wrote" (Jn 1:45; cf. Lk 24:44). Still, they knew him only when "he opened their minds to understand the scriptures" (Lk 24:45). This did not mean that he was not there to be known or recognized in the OT; rather, it meant that the "proclamation of Jesus Christ was kept hidden for long ages and could only now be disclosed in the prophetic writings" (Rom 16:25-26).

We must remember that those who first saw Jesus did not have a NT version of Jesus to compare with the OT. They had only the Jesus they knew, or knew about, to compare with the OT. Their comparison was later enshrined textually as the NT against the background of the OT. It was the end result of much reflection on the meaning of the OT Scriptures not the NT. As Jesus had said in Matthew 13:52, "Therefore every scribe who has been trained for the kingdom of heaven is like the master of a household who brings out of his treasure what is new and what is old." Seeing Jesus in Scripture was a function of understanding him in old and new terms. Surely, the clearest example of such a "master of a household" was the apostle Paul, who knew of the "coming one" from the OT Scriptures but did not recognize him on that basis. It was only after the resurrection, when his eyes were opened by the risen Christ (Gal 1:15-16), that he recognized Jesus as the "coming one" (cf. Mt 16:28; 21:5; 24:3, 27, 30, 37, 39, 42, 43, 44; 26:64). Once he saw Jesus for who he was, Paul had no trouble understanding the gospel, for he already knew his gospel "according to the Scriptures" (Rom 1:2-6; Gal 1). The same can be said for Simeon (Lk 2:25-35).

## The Atonement

In light of their views of the Mosaic law, the theological systems of covenant theology and dispensationalism also have their own way of expressing the accomplished work of Christ. In covenant theology, atonement is a legal transaction. Christ fulfilled the covenant of works and thus was legally rewarded with a meritorious righteousness on our behalf (active obedience). Dispensationalists, however, view the atonement in terms of Christ's sacrificial death. Christ died as a sacrificial offering on our behalf. The two conceptualizations of the atonement are not contradictory, but are two complimentary sets of categories for explaining the efficacy of Christ's death. Both are grounded in central ideas drawn from the OT, and specifically, the Pentateuch.

## The Mosaic Law

According to Galatians 3:19, the Mosaic law was added to the Sinai covenant because of Israel's transgressions. Jesus also said that the law (of divorce) was given "because of the hardness" of Israel's heart.[19] In that way, the Mosaic law became essential to the Sinai covenant. When that covenant passed away, so did the law that had become a part of it (cf. Heb 7:12: "For when there is a change in the priesthood, there is necessarily a change in the law as well"). The establishment of the new covenant meant the disappearance of the old covenant. According to Hebrews 8:13, "In speaking of 'a new covenant,' he has made the first one obsolete. And what is obsolete and growing old will soon disappear."

It is important to note that those texts are about the Mosaic law and the Sinai covenant. They are not about the Pentateuch. They tell us that the Sinai law and covenant were temporary. Both were given to Israel under the Sinai covenant. They were not intended for those living under the new covenant. They also do not imply that the Pentateuch was temporary and was abrogated along with the Mosaic law. The Pentateuch (OT) was written to Israel when they were under the Sinai covenant, but its purpose was to teach them the new covenant, not the old covenant. The author of the Pentateuch understood this well. That is why he, like the apostle Paul, illustrates the nature of faith with stories from the life of Abraham (Gen 26:5) rather than of Moses (Num 20:12). That is also why he looks not into the past, but into the future ("in the last days" [Deut 31:29]), to find the fulfillment of his hope in a new covenant (Deut 30:1-16). It is in this sense that the Pentateuch is about Christ (cf. Jn 5:46).

Whether, or to what extent, Christians today must abide by the Mosaic law is a question that covenant theologians and dispensationalists will continue to debate. This, however, should not be taken to mean that there is any doubt about our being under the authority of the Pentateuch as Scripture. The central question for the Christian who reads the Pentateuch

---

[19] "He said unto them, 'Moses because of the hardness of your hearts suffered you to put away your wives, but from the beginning it was not so'" (Mt 19:8).

should be why the author of the Pentateuch has put these laws in the Pentateuch and what lesson is to be drawn from them.[20]

## The Laws in the Pentateuch

The question of why the author of the Pentateuch put the Mosaic law in the Pentateuch is a literary question. We are not asking why God gave the Mosaic law to Israel at Mount Sinai. That is a historical question. One is free to raise such an historical question, and, in fact, it is important to do so. The question being raised here, however, is the altogether different one of literary strategy. Why did the author of the Pentateuch choose to devote so much attention to the laws that God gave Israel?

***The insertion of laws in the Pentateuch.*** The Mosaic law is a large collection of laws inserted into the wilderness narratives of the Pentateuch. With the insertion of these laws, beginning at Exodus 19, the Pentateuch's story comes to a standstill and only occasionally reappears as bits and pieces of narrative that move the story along. It is as if the author wants the readers to put the events of the wilderness narrative aside for a moment and concentrate on the nature and purpose of these laws.

***What is in the Pentateuch's collections of laws?*** A close look at the collections of laws in the Pentateuch reveals two important features of the law in the Pentateuch.

First, the collections of laws, as a whole, are not exhaustive. There are major gaps in what we might expect to find in these collections. In Deuteronomy 24:4, for example, there is a law concerning divorce that implies many other laws not recorded in the Pentateuch. This law appears to be only a part of a series of laws about divorce. What, for example, are the grounds for divorce? How does one get a divorce? Can one remarry after divorcing another? The one law on divorce in the Pentateuch clearly assumes many other laws covering these topics not presently found in the Pentateuch.

There is also a law in Deuteronomy 25:1-3 that assumes various cases for which flogging was the punishment. In the Pentateuch, however, there is

---

[20]This is similar to what David Puckett says about Calvin's reading of the OT: "The task of biblical interpretation involves asking what God's purpose may have been in giving the information recorded in scripture. In his interpretation of Leviticus 11:13 Calvin indicates that the exegete must always consider the intention of God *(Dei consilium)*. By this he means that the interpreter must keep in mind God's purpose in giving the law to his people" (*John Calvin's Exegesis of the Old Testament* [Louisville: Westminster John Knox, 1995], p. 33).

only one such (questionable?) case (Deut 22:18).

Second, the laws in the Pentateuch often are repetitive and contain elaborate detail. The law "Do not boil a young goat in its mother's milk," for example, occurs three times in the Pentateuch (Ex 23:19b; 34:26; Deut 14:21). The Ten Commandments appear twice (Ex 20; Deut 5). There are two sets of laws that describe the making of an altar (Ex 20:24; 27:1-3).

These two observations suggest that an intentional selection lies behind the collections of laws in the Pentateuch. In that selection no apparent attempt was made to be exhaustive, and in many cases, no attempt was made to avoid repetition of some laws. Can we discover the intent that lies behind such selections of laws in the Pentateuch? Can we explain why these laws were put in the Pentateuch, and why only these laws were selected?

***Why is the Mosaic law in the Pentateuch?*** The question of why the Mosaic law is in the Pentateuch is a literary and compositional question. It is a question about the intent *(mens auctoris)* of the author of the Pentateuch. If the Pentateuch is not a "law code" in the strict sense of the term—that is, if the Pentateuch is not a book *of* law, but a book *about* the law—why is the Mosaic law in the Pentateuch? Because the Pentateuch has been commonly understood as a "book of law," little attention has been given to this question. The assumption has been that the laws are there as part of the code of laws to be followed by those in the theocracy.[21] Often the question of why the Mosaic law is in the Pentateuch is treated as a question about why the Mosaic law was given to Israel within the context of the Sinai covenant.[22] Consideration of that question can cast some light on the question being raised here, but one must bear in mind that the two questions are very different. Why God gave Israel the Mosaic law is a historical question. Why the author of the Pentateuch included the Mosaic law in his book is a literary question.

There are at least four answers to the question of why the Mosaic law was inserted into the Pentateuch.

*The laws are part of the narrative technique.* The laws in the Pentateuch are part of the narrative technique used to disclose the nature of Israel's relationship to God under the Sinai covenant. The laws give the reader a realistic picture of the nature of Israel's worship and fellowship with God. The collec-

---

[21]"From the nature of the theocracy thus defined we may learn what was the function of the law in which it received its provisional embodiment" (Vos, *Biblical Theology*, pp. 141-42).

[22]Ibid., p. 142.

tions of laws give the readers an insider's view of what God required of Israel. The sacrifices help demonstrate the nature of sin as a barrier to humankind's relationship with God and what must be done about it. Hence, as can be seen by reading the various collections of laws, the notion of sacrifice and the analogous problem of sin are of central importance to the author.

The prescriptive laws regulating the building and maintenance of the tabernacle show that a genuine, tangible relationship with God was fully possible. God could meet with Israel in a specific location and a predetermined moment of time. Although God is not a physical being, the tabernacle was God's physical dwelling place. His presence dwelt there and was manifest in a number of holy objects and actions. The holiness laws show that Israel was to take God's presence in the tabernacle seriously. One could come into God's presence only after careful and proper preparation for holiness. The purpose of the tabernacle was not to keep Israel from God, but to provide a way for the holy God to be with his people.

Why are many laws omitted from the various collections? Why are others seemingly arbitrarily listed? It has long been believed that the purpose of the selective listing of laws in the Pentateuch was to show its readers that the will of God, which was reflected by these laws, demanded its place in every area of life. There was no area of life excluded from God's care and scrutiny. Hence, in the arrangement of laws in the Pentateuch the various laws are purposely selected from every area of life. Not every law is included, but every area of life is accounted for. Regardless of one's station in life or one's position, there were laws in the Pentateuch that addressed it in detail.

Why, then, were some laws given in extended detail while others were omitted altogether? The author's purpose in listing laws in great detail was to show that God was deeply concerned about every detail of life. There is no area of life that is not a direct concern of the will of God. God peers into our most private moments and says, "Do this!" or "Do not do that!" One need only survey the topics covered and the personal details to see how present God appears in these texts. Nothing escapes God's notice in prescribing how Israel should live in God's presence.

*The laws are a sign of Israel's failure.* The laws in the Pentateuch are a graphic picture of Israel's failure to obey God. There is little question for anyone who has read the Pentateuch that a major part of its purpose was to show that Israel failed to keep the law properly—that is, by faith. The story of the Pentateuch is, for the most part, a story of failure. The whole of the generation that left Egypt and received the law at Mount Sinai died in the wilderness. They were disobedient and failed to trust God (Num 14:11). There were only two exceptions, Joshua and Caleb. Beyond that, even Moses had little hope for better things ahead: "For I know that after my death you will surely act corruptly, and turn aside from the way which I have commanded you; and in the days to come evil will befall you, because you will do what is evil in the sight of the LORD, provoking him to anger through the work of your hands" (Deut 31:29 RSV).

When we view the Pentateuch in light of the need of obedience and faith, we see that the author lays great stress on the contrast between two key individuals, Abraham and Moses. Simply put, its narrative strategy was to show that Abraham lived a life of faith long before the law was given. His faith was reckoned to him as the righteousness of keeping the law (Gen 15:6; 26:5). Moses, on the other hand, lived under the law. He died in the wilderness because of lack of faith (Num 20:12). The author of the Pentateuch speaks of Moses and his lack of faith because he, of all people, would most likely have kept the law. In Numbers 12:7 Moses is said to have been faithful in the things relating to the house (the temple) of God. Apparently, this means that he kept the requirements of the priestly laws. Nevertheless, Moses, and Aaron his brother were not allowed to go into the land, because they "did not believe" (Num 20:12).

The Pentateuch thus presents an astonishing paradox: Moses, who lived under the law, did not have the requisite faith to enter the land; on the other hand, Abraham, who lived by faith, is said to have "kept the law." The laws of the Pentateuch thus show Israel's failure under the law to trust and obey God.

*The laws show why God gave the law to Israel.* The laws in the Pentateuch also are intended to show why God gave the Mosaic law to Israel. It was to keep them from straying from God until he sent the Messiah.[23] The Pentateuch is a treatise on Israel's experiences under the law. The author of the Pentateuch is concerned with the same question Paul raises in Galatians 3:19: if the law could not save Israel, why did God give them the law? The answer given by the Pentateuch is that the law was meant not to save Israel, but to preserve them until the time when their hearts would be renewed and they

[23]This is the same as Paul's argument in Galatians 3:19, though I am suggesting that it was also the view of the author of the Pentateuch.

could obey God out of love for him. By means of the Mosaic law Israel was preserved until the days of the new covenant. Without the law to guide them and to set them apart, Israel would have quickly joined the ranks of their neighbors and abandoned their worship of God.

Paul says in Galatians 3:19 that God gave Israel the law "because of transgressions" *(tōn parabaseōn charin).* Biblical scholars have puzzled over Paul's use of the plural "transgressions." It is sometimes understood as a reference to Adam's sin in the garden of Eden, but that was only one "transgression." Why the plural? If we look at the various sets of laws edited into the Pentateuch, we can see that there were several "transgressions." Throughout the narratives of Exodus 19–Deuteronomy there are numerous examples of Israel's failure to follow God's will. Here we can see the hand of the author at work. After each episode of disobedience we see that God gave Israel a new and more complete set of laws. As Israel continued to transgress the laws given to them, God continued to give them more. God did not give up on his people. When they sinned, he added laws to keep them from sinning further. The laws were not added to keep them from sinning; the laws were added to keep them from disappearing into the world of sin around them. It thus was the transgressions of the people that provided the motivation for God's giving the Mosaic law. As the transgressions increased, more laws were added.

*The laws are a collection of "just" decisions.* The laws in the Pentateuch provide an exemplary collection of "just" decisions to help inculcate a spirit of justice in the reader's heart. Perhaps the most important reason for the Mosaic law in the Pentateuch is to serve as a textbook on justice. By reading and reflecting on these examples of "just" decisions in particular and specific contexts, one gains a sense of that justice as it occurs in specific cases. To be sure, the laws in the Pentateuch are only particular and specific examples within actual ancient contexts. They are not mere abstractions that can be applied to everyday, or contemporary, settings. They are actual examples of God's specific decisions in the past. As such, the laws in the Pentateuch show what divine justice looked like in actual situations. The goal of reading such laws was likely not to strip them of their context in order to uncover an embedded principle. Although there may be a place for that, the goal was to allow the narrative context to disclose an insight into the way God sees our tangled lives. The laws do not answer the question "What should we do in cases like this?" but rather the question "What did God think about specific cases like these and how, or what, can we learn about justice from him?" In some ways, what Walther Eichrodt once said about Israelite law in general applies here to the Mosaic law:

> If we are seeking to define the distinctive character of the Mosaic law . . . then attention must first be drawn to the emphasis with which the entire law is referred to God. . . . Israelite law on the whole contents itself with applying a few basic dicta fairly freely over and over again. These dicta are, however, inculcated as the divine will and thus impressed on the heart and conscience. Application to individual concrete instances is then left in many cases to a healthy feeling for justice.[24]

Thus, the Pentateuch is intended to be the object of meditation and reflection (cf. Josh 1:8; Ps 1:2; Mal 4:4). It teaches, by concrete example, what justice *(mišpāṭ)* and righteousness *(ṣĕdāqâ)* are. Hence, the Pentateuch is written not for the Sinai covenant, but for the new covenant (Jer 31:31-32; cf. Deut 4:6). Unlike the Sinai covenant, in the new covenant the law was to be written on the heart. God's people were to have a new heart (Ezek 36:26). The Spirit of God was to remove their heart of stone and give them a new heart, one that would obey and seek to follow God's will. The law was to be written on the heart in the same way it was written on the pages of the Pentateuch: example by example. The Spirit of God was to use the Word of God to write his will on the heart of the reader. The Pentateuch therefore is a book much like Proverbs. One can read it and find there a healthy sense of what is right and good as well as what is not good. Justice is imprinted on the heart by reading and meditating on its words. This is illustrated in the admonitions of Joshua 1:8 and Psalm 1:2. The source of wisdom is meditation on the Scriptures, which includes its laws.

The way to gain wisdom and a sense of what is right and just from the Pentateuch is to read it as wisdom, looking for an accumulation of the sense of what justice looks like in concrete and qualified situations. Just as one becomes wise by reflecting on the examples of wisdom in Proverbs, so one becomes good and just by reflecting on the laws in the Pentateuch.

---

[24]Walther Eichrodt, *Theology of the Old Testament*, trans. J. A. Baker (OTL; Philadelphia: Westminster, 1961), pp. 74-77.

*Chapter 11*

# The Theme of Salvation in the Pentateuch

The aim of this chapter is to describe the Pentateuch's understanding of salvation. By "salvation" is meant the establishment of an eternal relationship with God and the participation in his blessings. My aim is not to describe the salvation and religion of Israel as such nor their relationship with God as Israelites; rather, I wish to describe the teaching of the Pentateuch regarding the gift of salvation from God. That may sound like a NT idea, and it is, but in this section I will discuss it only within the OT.

Although evangelicals often have understood the question of salvation in the OT in terms of the beliefs of particular individuals in the OT, such an aim is not the focus of a textually based biblical theology. Rather than seeking to uncover the religious beliefs of OT saints, I wish to focus on the Pentateuch and its message. To what extent are the religious beliefs and practices of OT saints a model of the nature of the Pentateuch's understanding of salvation? What does one learn about God and salvation from reading the Pentateuch? What does the Pentateuch tell its readers about their relationship with God? To what extent does it offer its readers an understanding of salvation like that of Moses and the Sinai covenant? Or, to what extent does it offer them an alternative covenant, a "new covenant" like that of the prophetic literature (cf. Jer 31:31-32)?

This concern for the meaning of Scripture and its understanding of salvation raises several questions. Two are particularly important here. First, what is the role of the law, the priesthood, the tabernacle and the sacrifices in the

Pentateuch's understanding of salvation? Second, what is the role of Scripture and biblical revelation in the Pentateuch's understanding of salvation? The religion of ancient Israel largely centered on the tabernacle and temple. OT saints such as Adam, Eve, Noah and Abraham built altars and sacrificed much like the Israelites, though they had no written Scripture. Even at a later period there appears to have been little emphasis on written Scripture for long periods of time (cf. 2 Kings 22:8). Does the Pentateuch endorse that kind of "unwritten" religion? Or does it set out to establish a religion grounded in written revelation—*sola scriptura?* What is the Pentateuch's view of the relationship between the temple and the Scriptures?

## Preliminary Questions

Before entering into a discussion of salvation in the OT, we must turn briefly to certain aspects of evangelical approaches to this question. Salvation in the OT has been of central interest to evangelical biblical theologians. The focus of that interest has almost always been the nature of the salvation experienced by individual biblical characters such as Adam and Eve, Abraham and Moses. What was their experience of salvation, and how does it compare with our own in the NT? The answers given to these questions have largely fallen along predetermined theological lines. Covenant theologians view the salvation of early biblical saints such as Abraham as essentially the same as those under the NT. They do so because covenant theology recognizes only one covenant as operative from the beginning: the covenant of grace. All who are saved in the OT are saved through that covenant. Dispensationalists see the salvation of OT saints as, in some important ways, distinct from the NT. Both theological positions share common assumptions and goals in approaching this subject, giving the impression of considerable agreement on basic points. Both believe that Abraham's salvation was grounded in the finished work of Christ and received individually through his faith. Salvation was the same with Adam and Eve as it is with NT believers.

Further discussion of this question by evangelicals has tended to center on how the details work out within their respective theological systems. Covenant theologians, who stress the identity of the NT (new covenant) faith with the OT (which they equate with the Sinai covenant), seek to discover ways in which OT believers "saw Christ" and thus actually were able to put their faith in him. In doing that, covenant theologians often have resorted to hermeneutical approaches that allowed them to see beyond a strict literalism in interpreting biblical texts. Dispensationalists believe that the faith of early biblical saints need not have had Christ specifically in view. Thus, they have tended to see salvation along the same lines as Israel's covenant responsibilities. Their task therefore has been to show the relationship between "keeping the law" and "faith," since they believe that those are the two undeniable factors of the OT religion, at least when it is understood as the religion of Sinai.

What both sides have failed to note is that *they have focused their attention on the notion of salvation as it might have been understood by the biblical characters* within their own world *rather than as it might be viewed by the biblical authors and their books.* This has been a particularly difficult question to frame because evangelicals often view the authorship of the biblical books in terms of the central characters in those books. It has been all too easy to identify the authorship of the OT with the central characters in the OT, as if they wrote the sections in which they appear. It thus is easy to assume that the biblical character's view of salvation is identical with the author's view of salvation, though that would involve a misunderstanding of the nature of narrative texts. If, as evangelicals hold, Moses wrote the Pentateuch, Abraham could not have written the book of Genesis. Nevertheless, evangelicals tend to treat Abraham's faith as if it were grounded in the message of Genesis 1–11. They are guided by the assumption that Genesis 1–11 reflects the theology of Abraham, or those who proceeded him, rather than Moses, who most evangelicals believe was the author of Genesis. The issue is complicated but is essential to understanding the evangelical view of salvation in the OT.

It is a truism in biblical studies that we know very little about the religious views of Adam and Eve or of Abraham. We see these biblical characters within the context of the Pentateuch as a whole and the intention of its author. It is clear that the author wants us to see that these early believers were like us in their faith. This does not mean that the author of the Pentateuch wants us to discover "on our own," without his help, the various facets of their faith in God and understanding of salvation. It was of considerable importance to the author to show what these early saints believed and how they lived. To us who now read the Pentateuch, it is important to see that its author wants us to understand from this book what our own faith should be. Abraham's faith is a lesson to us about our faith. In the narratives of the Pentateuch these early saints are put before our eyes to illustrate our faith, not so that we can emulate their faith, even though we share a common faith. The assumption of the author of the Pentateuch is that Adam and Eve and Abraham and the other patriarchs believed what he, the author, believed, and that is why he has included them in his book. Whatever their outward form of religion might have been, the author of the Pentateuch wants us, the readers, to have faith like that of Adam, Eve and Abraham. In telling us what it is that we should believe, he does not leave it up to us, his readers, to second-guess what they might have believed. He expends considerable literary effort showing us how and what we are to believe and how we are to act, always assuming that the early biblical characters such as Adam, Eve, Abraham and the others believed and acted that same way. Thus, the aim of the Pentateuch is not to tell its readers what the saints of old believed, but what, and how, we, the readers, should believe. Our concern should be what the author of the Pentateuch intends to teach us *in the Pentateuch* about our faith.

Evangelical attitudes about the question of OT salvation have thus been shaped by fundamental assumptions about the nature and the object of the task itself. Although I can give only a summary description of some of those assumptions, it is important to do so, if only to clear the air of misconceptions. These aspects of evangelical approaches to salvation in the OT have not always been clearly understood or articulated, if at all. Evangelical approaches to OT salvation often overlap and lack precision in laying out their claims. It is therefore important that we look briefly at three frequently overlooked aspects of evangelical approaches to salvation in the OT.

***Primeval revelation* (Uroffenbarung).** The classical orthodox understanding of salvation in the OT begins with the idea of "primeval revelation" *(Uroffenbarung)*. Primeval revelation is the idea of an early (primeval) and ongoing constant access to divine revelation on the part of the earliest biblical characters. Before the fall, this special kind of revelation was found in an unbroken chain of communication from God to humanity. This stream of revelation between God and biblical saints, such as Adam and Eve in the garden of Eden, was initially "unobjectified" and in nonwritten form.[1] It con-

[1]"The most important function of Special Revelation, however, under the regime of sin, does not lie in the correction and renewal of the faculty of perception of natural verities; it consists in the introduction of an altogether new world of truth, that relating to the redemption of man. The newness here, as compared with the supernatural rerevelation in the state of rectitude, relates to both the form and content, and further also affects the manner in which the supernatural approach

tinued in an unwritten form until the pressing need arose for stabilizing it in written form as Scripture.

Furthermore, according to the notion of a primeval revelation, human beings enjoyed a nearly perfect relationship and fellowship with God, their creator. Their "religion" was based on the primeval revelation available to them. This was not a form of "natural revelation," because unlike natural revelation, it was grounded in a genuine supernatural work. The only difference between primeval revelation and the special revelation we have today in Scripture is that it was in a nonwritten form. Geerhardus Vos describes his understanding of primeval revelation, which forms the basis of his understanding of biblical theology:

> Previously (before the Fall) there was the most direct spiritual fellowship [between God and human creatures]; the stream of revelation flowed uninterruptedly, and there was no need of storing up the waters in any reservoir wherefrom to draw subsequently. Under the rule of redemption (after the Fall) an external embodiment is created to which the divine intercourse with man attaches itself. Where an ever-flowing stream of revelation was always accessible, there existed no need of providing for the future remembrance of past intercourse.[2]

According to Vos, before the fall there was so much divine special revelation available to humanity by virtue of the ongoing immediate relationship between the creator and his creatures that there was no need to preserve it for future use. There would always be plenty. There was a continuous and abundant supply of immediate supernatural revelation.

By means of this direct special communication from God, humanity (Adam and Eve) was able to know God's will at all times. Humanity therefore could be held culpable whenever they disobeyed this divine revelation, and they could enjoy direct fellowship with God without the need of written (or unwritten) Scripture. This abundant supply of special revelation came to an end, however, when the relationship between God and his creatures was broken by the fall. As human beings became increasingly distant and alien-

---

of God to man is received. As to the form of direct intercourse, this is objectified. . . . Under the rule of redemption an external embodiment is created to which the divine intercourse with man attaches itself" (Geerhardus Vos, *Biblical Theology: Old and New Testaments* [Grand Rapids: Eerdmans, 1948], p. 30).

[2]Ibid.

ated from God in their sin and rebellion, the channels of this special primeval revelation became mired and increasingly scarce. Orthodox theologians believed that with the impending loss and the eventual disappearance of the divine source of special revelation, an effort was made to replace this spontaneous, immediate revelation with an "objective," still unwritten, version of the same revelation as Scripture. What we now have as the Bible is the inscripturated version of what at one time was the full and complete unwritten revelation of God's will along with his acts to make his will known to fallen humanity. The Bible is thus a kind of repository of the religious beliefs and practices of those early saints to whom the original primeval revelation was given. The Bible consists of the remnants of the true religion as it existed before the fall and in unwritten form after the fall. To understand the nature of salvation in the OT, one must attempt to find it in the remaining traces of primeval revelation still embedded in the pages of the Pentateuch. Remnants of early pentateuchal religion and revelation had thus to be "discovered" in what is left of it in the Pentateuch. The Pentateuch itself did not teach those beliefs. It was merely a cache, where the remnants of primeval revelation had been stored.

Unfortunately, as the orthodox theologians believed, every bit and piece of this early revelation had not been preserved in the written Scriptures. There were many parts of it not preserved or recorded, and consequently, much that the early saints understood about God and their own salvation has not been fully preserved. We may never know all that the early saints knew about God and their own salvation, nor will we likely know all that biblical characters such as Abraham and Isaac once knew about their salvation. Although in their time it was a rich and pure source of divine revelation, primeval revelation is now only sparsely preserved here and there in scattered corners of Scripture. Today, by reading the Bible, one can gain a fairly clear, if only partial, understanding of the religion of early biblical saints such as Adam, Abraham and Moses. According to the orthodox view, the Bible is our only repository of the religious faith of ancient biblical saints such as Melchizedek and Jethro, but the Bible has not presented the scattered remains of this early nonwritten revelation in a comprehensive and organized way. Much of what these biblical characters believed may never be fully known. What we can know, however, serves us today as a model for our own religious faith in the biblical God. Their primeval understanding of salvation, though expressed differently from ours today, was the same as ours and can be used as a model to strengthen the common faith that ties our two ages together.

This view of OT salvation has enjoyed a continuing influence in the thinking of evangelical biblical theologians. It is considered the task of much contemporary evangelical theology to attempt to find, uncover, or, if need be, reconstruct this ancient "biblical faith," thinking that in doing so, one is discovering an early form of true "biblical religion." Vos saw this as the primary goal of a biblical theology. He begins his own biblical theology with the attempt to describe "the content of preredemptive Special Revelation."[3] By "preredemptive" Vos means that it was known as far back as the garden of Eden. He even defines "biblical theology" as "seeking to exhibit the organic growth or development of the truths of Special Revelation from the primitive preredemptive Special Revelation given in Eden to the close of the New Testament canon."[4] Vos's view of primeval revelation is typical of the classical orthodox view, though he added to it a central role to be played by the historical method. According to Vos, one need not look only to the written Scriptures for remnants of the primeval revelation; one could also scour the historical records of early Israelites in the attempt to discover other aspects of what was once believed and accepted as special revelation *(Uroffenbarung).* Thus, for Vos, history plays a central role in biblical theology and is a primary tool for reconstructing the primeval understanding of salvation in the OT. In this, Vos moved in a direction different from most of those evangelical biblical theologians of the nineteenth century who had preceded him at Princeton (e.g., Charles Hodge and Benjamin Warfield). For them, the Bible was to remain the only source of revelation, even if it had to be reconstructed along lines that paralleled one's understanding of historical events.

The task of a biblical theology constructed along the lines of the present book is considerably at odds with Vos and other evangelicals who have retained much of the classical concept of "primeval revelation" under the rubric of "salvation history." My aim is not to discover the beliefs of biblical characters such as Adam and Eve, nor to retrieve the various components of the religious beliefs of biblical characters such as Abraham and Jacob. Such beliefs lie largely outside the boundaries of the biblical texts. My aim is to discover the view of salvation that is taught by the Pentateuch in its role as

[3]Ibid., p. 37.
[4]Ibid., p. 5.

Scripture. What does the Pentateuch tell its readers about salvation? It may indeed be important to pursue the religious beliefs of early biblical characters such as Adam and Abraham, but we must acknowledge that Abraham and Sarah did not have the Pentateuch as we do. They had no Scripture at all. Thus, if our goal is the theology of the Pentateuch and its understanding of the nature of salvation, we must understand their beliefs only as the Pentateuch describes them to us.

***The covenant of grace* (foedus gratiae).** The notion of a "covenant of grace" *(foedus gratiae)* is a theological construct that attempts to explain the common links between the religion of Israel in OT times and later NT beliefs. From the earliest stages of human-divine communion, as recorded or implied in the OT, it is believed that the true revealed religion was grounded in a single covenant of grace experienced through faith in God's promised redeemer. In various times and places that covenant took on different characteristics and external features, but it always remained the same covenant of divine grace grounded in God's promise of a redeemer. Biblical religion, in whatever time period one may wish to view it, is an expression of a covenant of grace established by God with Adam and Eve after the fall. That covenant continued throughout the period of the OT and into the present day, where it is known as the new covenant. As part of the same covenant of grace, OT salvation was the same salvation we know today as the NT salvation that all believers enjoy. For those who hold to the idea of a covenant of grace, understanding the OT view of salvation consists largely of finding evidence of the covenant of grace in the lives of the early OT saints. Where various approaches to this issue part company is in their attempts to explain how much and to what extent an understanding of Jesus, or a coming messianic king, was known by these early biblical characters. Consequently, in convenant theology messianism (reference to Christ in the OT) plays an essential role in understanding the nature of OT salvation.

***Progressive revelation.*** For many evangelical theologians, the idea of "progressive revelation" provides the only adequate answer to the question of salvation in OT times. "Progressive revelation" is the belief that divine revelation comes to human beings under the conditions and limitations of their fallen natures. As we have noted above, before the fall, human beings enjoyed an uninterrupted revelatory communion with their creator ("primeval revelation"). It was a steady and unmediated stream of divine revelation. The fall, however, meant an end to that discourse, and along with that a fundamental inability to comprehend spiritual realities. Humanity, in effect, had to start over and relearn divine truth from the beginning. God, in his grace, patiently and gently set about the task of "reeducating" humanity so that they would be increasingly able to comprehend divine truth. Gotthold Lessing captured the essence of the idea in his much quoted aphorism "What education is to the individual person, revelation is to the whole of humanity."[5]

To meet human limitations in understanding revelation, salvation in the OT was presented in the simplest possible terms. That often meant that it was viewed in terms of simple physical realities such as the priesthood, sacrifice, tabernacle, land and earthly treasures. The religion of the OT therefore was a kind of picture lesson for the higher levels of spiritual realities usually found in the NT. The physical realities of OT religion were to be understood not as God's intended way of salvation, but as lessons in spiritual truth cast in terms of everyday life in the ancient world. To understand the nature of the salvation of the faithful in OT times, one had to see through the temporal, physical aspects of their religion to the eternal truths they embodied. Human beings by nature were capable of understanding full spiritual reality only if it was presented to them in ways they currently understood the world. Full maturity came only with the appearance of the NT and the gospel.

***Summary.*** Understanding salvation in the Pentateuch does not lie in a critique of various approaches to the OT I have outlined above. Nor is my aim to describe the religion of the people we read about in the OT. My aim is to describe the nature of salvation as taught by the Pentateuch itself. What did its author want us to understand about God and our salvation? The Pentateuch, as written Scripture and as divine revelation, presents a view of God and salvation that is essential to the Christian faith. Paul saw Abraham as one who shared his basic faith in Christ. He thus used the example of Abraham to teach the NT idea of salvation. The author of the book of Hebrews sees almost the whole cast of OT characters as men and women of "Christian" faith. My aim in this section is to describe the various elements of the Pentateuch's view of salvation, beginning with its notion of the "kingdom of God." My thesis, which I hope to demonstrate exegetically from within the

---

[5]"Was die Erziehung bei dem einzeln Menschen ist, ist die Offenbarung bei dem ganzen Menschengeschlechte" (Gotthold E. Lessing, *Die Erziehung des Menschengeschlechts* [Stuttgart, 1780], p. 7).

Pentateuch itself, is that the Pentateuch contains the sort of ideas and themes that the NT writers saw in it.

## THE KINGDOM OF GOD

The relationship between God and his creation is commonly described by biblical theologians as a "kingdom" *(regnum)* or the "kingdom of God" *(regnum dei)*.[6] The idea of "kingdom" can describe God's relationship to all of creation *(regi a Deo)* or his relationship to part of creation *(regnare cum Deo)*. The centrality of the idea of the "kingdom of God" in biblical theology is undisputed (cf. Mk 1:15). The question is whether the concept is part of the theology of the Pentateuch, and if so, what its nature and purpose are.

To be sure, kingdom ideas and terminology are present in the pentateuchal narratives (Gen 17:6; 35:11; 36:31; 37:8), but most occurrences of the vocabulary and concept of "kingdom"[7] (e.g., *malkût*, *melek*, *mālak*, *mamlākâ*) occur, as I have shown, in its poetry (Gen 49; Num 23:21; 24:7).

***The kingdom in Exodus 15.*** The centrality of the notions of "king" and "kingdom" reflected throughout the Pentateuch's poetry finds its fullest expression in Exodus 15:1-18,[8] one of the four major poems in the Pentateuch. Compositionally, the focus on the notion of kingdom in this poem falls in its concluding statement: "The LORD shall reign *[yhwh yimlōk]* forever and ever" (Ex 15:18). This is the final note of the poem, and as such, it becomes an essential part of the message of the poem in its present shape and central location within the Pentateuch. Unlike the other poems, the notion of kingship in this poem focuses on God as king rather than on an individual of the house of David. The poem's focus on the eternal aspects of the reign of Yahweh is perhaps the reason why Exodus 15 is the only poem among the Pentateuch's major poems that does not have the introductory heading "in the last days" *(bĕʾaḥărît hayyāmîm)*. The kingdom that this poem has in mind is not an eschatological, or future, kingdom of "the last days," but an eternal kingdom, for all time, including the present. It is a divine kingdom much like that

---

[6]See Gottlob Schrenk, *Gottesreich und Bund im älteren Protestantismus: Vornehmlich bei Johannes Coccejus*, 2nd ed. (Darmstadt: Wissenschaftliche Buchgesellschaft, 1967).

[7]Specifically for Israel and the nations, as opposed to the various "kings" and "kingdom" in the ancient world.

[8]Numbers 23:21b, "The LORD their God is with them, acclaimed as a king among them" (NRSV), is a reference to Exodus 15:18, "The LORD will reign forever and ever" (NRSV).

"kingdom of YHWH" *(malkût yhwh)*[9] in 1 Chronicles 28:5. The lack of the introductory heading of "last days" probably is linked to the poem's subject matter in the same way as the use of "last days" as an introduction to the other poems is related to their focus on an individual king from the house of Judah. So the heading "in the last days" *(bĕʾaḥărît hayyāmîm)* is related to the individual subject matter, or message, of each of each poem. Given its lack of a "last days" heading, Exodus 15 is not about a future kingdom in the sense of its coming in "the last days." It is, rather, about the present reign of God centered in his "holy sanctuary" *(miqqĕdāš).* According to the message of this poem, God himself at creation prepared and "planted" his own sanctuary "in the mountain of his inheritance" (Jerusalem?) (Ex 15:17). Unlike the other poems in the Pentateuch (Gen 49; Num 24; Deut 32), there would have been little reason for attaching the introductory phrase "in the last days" to Exodus 15. It is about the eternal reign of God—the present, past and future king.

Apart from its move away from an eschatological kingdom *(regnare cum Deo)* to an eternal king *(regi a Deo),* the poem in Exodus 15:1-18 also takes a decided turn toward an individualized identity of its speaker. Although the poem comes from the lips of Moses and the people of Israel (Ex 15:1), in the poem itself it is an individual, Moses, who speaks and praises God. The poem celebrates the redemption of the nation at the Red Sea; the event is identified in the poem as an act of individual salvation, but it does so by personifying the exodus of the nation as a personal work of Moses (cf. Num 23:22; 24:8). In its opening statements Exodus 15 acknowledges just such a personalization: "[The Lord] has become my salvation" *(wayĕhî-lî lîšûʿâ)* [Ex 15:2]). "My salvation" is not a statement of national redemption, but rather it has its sights set clearly on the individual who acknowledges God's salvation. The individual application is further strengthened at the end of the poem by identifying the speaker as the prophet Miriam (Ex 15:20).

An almost identical confession of hope in a personal salvation is found in Jacob's poem in Genesis 49:18: "For your salvation I wait, O LORD" *(lîšûʿātkā qiwwîtî yhwh).* This individual "confession of faith" stands out distinctly from the other poetic lines. Its voice is heard above the collective voice of the rest of the poem. It is likely that these individualizing elements and the commentary they contain were inserted into the poetry by the au-

[9]The expression *malkût yhwh* ("kingdom of YHWH") occurs once in the OT (1 Chron 28:5). See also Deuteronomy 33:5.

thor in the final stages of composition. As such, they reflect the central interests of the final shape of the Pentateuch and the Tanak. I have already argued that this final stage of composition is one in which these poems in the Pentateuch (Gen 49; Num 24; Deut 33) play a central role. It is likely that such expressions of individual spirituality within the poems were central to the author's view of the role of the Pentateuch and the rest of Scripture at this final stage. They either are directly the work of the author or are a part of the author's later reflection on the final shape he was giving to the Pentateuch. They also appear to have been part of the final shaping of the literary context that was to become the OT canon (Tanak). It is of considerable interest to a proper theological evaluation of the Pentateuch and the OT as a whole (Tanak) to note that the two most comprehensive compositional links between the sections of the Tanak, Joshua 1:8 (connecting the Law and the Prophets) and Psalm 1:2 (connecting the Prophets and the Writings), reflect this same interest in the individual and his or her book-centered spirituality[10] by connecting the quest for wisdom and understanding to an individual daily reading and meditation on Scripture:

> This book of the law shall not depart out of thy mouth, but thou shalt meditate there on day and night, that thou mayest observe to do according to all that is written therein: for then thou shalt make thy way prosperous, and then thou shalt have good success. (Josh 1:8 ASV)

Clearly, what these macrocompositional seams envision is a direct link between seeking divine wisdom *(wĕʾāz taśkîl)* and success *(taṣlîaḥ)* and private Scripture reading. The distribution of these seams, along with their content, suggests that they were part of an intentional design of the whole of Scripture for a specific purpose (functionality).[11] Judging from what

---

[10]"The historical truth which in its own way biblical scholarship does have to mediate is the true meaning and context of the biblical texts as such. . . . What [this] does mean is a radical re-orientation concerning the goal to be pursued, on the basis of the recognition that the biblical texts must be investigated for their own sake to the extent that the revelation which they attest does not stand or occur, and is not to be sought, behind or above them but in them. If in reply it is asked whether Christianity is really a book-religion, the answer is that strangely enough Christianity has always been and only been a living religion when it is not ashamed to be actually and seriously a book-religion" (Karl Barth, *Church Dogmatics* 1/2 [Edinburgh: T & T Clark, 1958], pp. 494-95).

[11]I am using the word *functionality* in the sense of a purposeful design. Scripture has been given a design and shape that enables it to fulfill a specific purpose. For an example of the functionality of the Psalter, see my comments on Matthias Millard, *Die Komposition des Psalters: Ein formgeschichtlicher Ansatz* (FAT 9; Tübingen: Mohr Siebeck, 1994) in chapter 5.

these seams have to say about Scripture, we see that they appear to assert that its purpose is for private spiritual edification. Reading and meditation on Scripture makes one wise and successful (capable). Expressing a similar view of the Scriptures centuries later, Peter said, "Wherefore laying aside all malice, and all guile, and hypocrisies, and envies, and all evil speakings, as newborn babes, desire the sincere milk of the word, that ye may grow thereby" (1 Pet 2:1 KJV).

What strikes one immediately as unique, and even provocative, given the importance of the temple and public worship throughout this period, is that within these final compositional seams in the Pentateuch and the Tanak there is no mention of, or call for, a public, congregational reading of Scripture as is found in, for example, biblical texts such as Deuteronomy 31:10-13:

> And Moses commanded them, "At the end of every seven years, at the set time of the year of release, at the feast of booths, when all Israel comes to appear before the LORD your God at the place which he will choose, you shall read this law before all Israel in their hearing. Assemble the people, men, women, and little ones, and the sojourner within your towns, that they may hear and learn to fear the LORD your God, and be careful to do all the words of this law, and that their children, who have not known it, may hear and learn to fear the LORD your God, as long as you live in the land which you are going over the Jordan to possess.

Although this passage in Deuteronomy does not rule out private scriptural reading, the comments inserted into Genesis 49:18 and Exodus 15:2, along with the seams of the Tanak (Josh 1:8; Ps 1:2), call for another kind of reading of Scripture. They call the individual to a daily reading and meditating on Scripture. These comments are part not only of the final compositional shape of the Pentateuch, but also the whole of the Tanak. They represent a high level of concern for daily reading and meditation on the Scriptures. It is this concern that lies so strongly behind the author's molding and shaping of these texts in their present form as the Pentateuch and Tanak. It is as if the author is speaking directly to the reader with a word of advice that the correct use of the Scriptures is intended to give wisdom and success to the one who reads and meditates on them "day and night." This is a long way from reading these texts every seven years. The ideal thus fits the very kind of text that it endorses. By means of their final shaping and organization, the Scriptures are presented as a written text that can be read and meditated on and hence is, at least theoretically, available to all in an understandable and enjoyable form (Neh 8:10). It is a canonical text in the fullest sense of the word.

A historical setting similar to what may lie behind the development of this kind of canonical text is recounted in Nehemiah 8. When Ezra gathered the people of Israel at the Water Gate to read publicly to explain the Scriptures, the similarities between his public gathering and those gathered for worship at the nearby temple appear to represent a striking contrast between the temple as a house of worship and a congregation gathered for reading the Scriptures in the streets. The reading and explaining of Scripture was not guided by Ezra, a priest from the temple, as would have been appropriate (Deut 33:10), but, as the author of the book of Ezra continually stresses, by Ezra, the scribe, in the streets of Jerusalem (Ezra 7:6-7).

The numerous interpretive comments within the Pentateuch and the Tanak as a whole are intended to guide the reader in the meaning of these texts as a whole. They are not mere glosses added by a well-meaning scribe. Their scope, which extends far beyond the immediate literary context of these poems, suggests that they are part of a shaping and compositional process that had in view the whole OT as a unity. They reflect a shift of focus toward a daily reading of the Scriptures that reflects the calling of Ezra the scribe. It is one in which the focus is on the individualized application of Scripture to everyday life. A similar point of view is found in other key pentateuchal texts such as Deuteronomy 10:11-12. There, in a straightforward and remarkable way, the admonitions relating to the historical details of the conquest of the land and its possession (Deut 10:11) are applied to the ethical and religious obligations of the individual reader of Deuteronomy (note the second-person singulars in the Hebrew, which the KJV makes apparent):

> And now, Israel, what doth the LORD thy God *[ĕlōheykā]* require of thee *[mēʿimmāk]*, but to fear the LORD thy God *[ĕlōheykā]*, to walk in all his ways, and to love him, and to serve the LORD thy God *[ĕlōheykā]* with all thy heart *[lĕbābkā]* and with all thy soul *[napšekā]*? (Deut 10:12 KJV)

The tendency to individualize collective commands and exhortations is, in addition to the composition of the Tanak as a whole (Josh 1:8; Ps 1:2), part and parcel of the compositional seams of other individual biblical books. These seams, and texts such as Ezra 7 and Nehemiah 9, also demonstrate the important role of the prophets in giving the Scriptures their final shape and the importance of the priests and Levites as those who were to teach the Scriptures to the people (Deut 33:10; Ezra 7:10; Neh 8:7).

Along with the individualizing tendency of the comments in Exodus 15, its interpretation of the exodus and conquest narratives also follows conceptual and terminological lines that stress the eternality of the kingdom—for example, "The LORD will reign forever and ever" (Ex 15:18). This emphasis stands in marked contrast to the "this worldly" view of the Lord's sanctuary (temple) elsewhere in the Exodus 15 poem, but it suits the focus of this poem on individual spirituality. Having described the exodus and God's deliverance through the Red Sea (Ex 15:1-13a), the poem takes up the theme of God's leading his redeemed into his "holy abode" (*nĕwēh qodšekā* [Ex 15:13b]). There, God is enthroned (*lĕšibtĕkā* [Ex 15:17a]) "on the mountain of his possession" (*bĕhar naḥălātkā* [Ex 15:17a]). The topography expressed in Exodus 15 is important for a proper identification in Exodus 15:17a of the "possession" and of the "foundation" *(mākôn)* that the Lord "made" *(pāʿaltā).* The terms used suggest that this poem is speaking of the foundation of the Lord's "sanctuary" (*miqqĕdāš* [Ex 15:17b]) that "his own hands built" (*kônĕnû yādeykā* [Ex 15:17b]). The allusions to God's "making" and "building" the place of his habitation and sanctuary in Exodus 15:17 point to Genesis 2, if not also the whole of the creation narrative in Genesis 1:2–2:23. This, among other things, shows the focus of Psalm 1 on salvation in "this worldly" and collective terms. The temple is the location of the nation's abiding with God. Clearly, a national salvation is in view.

> You guided them by your strength to your holy abode. . . . You brought them in and planted them on the mountain of your own possession, the foundation, O LORD, that you made your abode, the sanctuary, O LORD, that your hands have established. (Ex 15:13b-17)

The poem in Exodus 15 comes to its conclusion by returning to the view of God that highlights the individualism of the earlier parts of the poem. The author accomplishes this shift by moving our attention away from God's dwelling at the sanctuary of his making "in the mountain of his inheritance" and redirecting it toward God's eternality and transcendence: "the LORD reigns *[yimlōk]* for ever and ever" (Ex 15:18).

At the conclusion of the Tanak, this statement, "the LORD reigns for ever and ever," is echoed in the Aramaic portions of Daniel. These Aramaic texts appear to be some of the most recent parts of the "Hebrew" Bible:

> And in the days of those kings shall the God of heaven set up a kingdom which shall never be destroyed, nor shall the sovereignty thereof be left to another people; but it shall break in pieces and consume all these kingdoms, and it shall stand for ever. (Dan 2:44)
>
> How great are his signs! How mighty are his wonders! His kingdom is an everlasting kingdom, and his dominion is from generation to generation. (Dan 4:3 [3:33 MT])
>
> And the kingdom and the dominion, and the greatness of the kingdoms under the whole heaven, shall be given to the people of the saints of the Most High. His kingdom is an everlasting kingdom, and all dominions shall serve and obey him. (Dan 7:27)

To summarize: The compositional shaping of the poems in the Pentateuch serves to advance its central theological themes that are reinforced by brief explanatory comments throughout the text. These themes are echoed back through the rest of the OT Scriptures. The numerous interpretive comments in the poems further serve to align themselves with specific NT theolegomena, such as the importance of daily private reading of Scripture as the source of wisdom and understanding the will of God and the functionality of Scripture as a replacement of the divine presence at the temple.[12] Thus, in the Pentateuch the themes of salvation and the eternal reign of God are cast along lines that stress the NT hope of an individual believer—for example, "This is my God" (Ex 15:2).[13] The innertextual allusions to the Genesis narratives in Exodus 15 point unmistakably to God's work of creation as depicted in the Genesis narratives (Gen 2). The creation account of the Genesis narratives is further recast in terms of God's building a place for his sanctuary *(miqqĕdāš)* in Jerusalem.

***Creation and salvation.*** In the Pentateuch, as elsewhere in the Bible, the twin ideas of creation and salvation are inseparably linked. This is expressed compositionally at the macrolevel in the fact that the Pentateuch begins with an account of creation (Gen 1:1) and reaches its culmination point in the

[12]"For now we see in a mirror dimly, but then face to face; now I know in part, but then I will know fully just as I also have been fully known" (1 Cor 13:12).

[13]The same tendency can be seen in Hannah's psalm in 1 Samuel 2:10.

salvation story of the exodus (Ex 14). We have seen that the poem in Exodus 15 summarizes God's acts of creation and redemption by grounding its view of salvation in creation. I also have argued that creation and "this-worldliness" as such do not express the last word about salvation in the poem. Ultimately, the author elevates our view of God and salvation by shifting his attention to the notion of God as the eternal king (Ex 15:18). The meaning of salvation expressed in Exodus 15 is that of the individual's relationship to the eternal God. The compositional macrostructure of the Pentateuch (Gen 1–Ex 15) therefore is a witness to the centrality of creation in the biblical notion of salvation, but it is also left open to another theme that is also deeply embedded in the early narratives of Genesis: the blessing of eternal life. The Genesis narratives are clear that what was lost in the fall was not only access to the garden, but also, more importantly, access to the tree of life "in the midst of the garden" (Gen 2:9). The cherubim were placed to guard access to the "tree of life" (Gen 3:24), not merely access to the garden. It is thus not without purpose that the earliest biblical "salvation history" (Gen 1–Ex 15) concludes by returning to the hope of eternal life that lies in the idea of God as the eternal king.

A similar reading strategy of Genesis 1–Exodus 15 is reflected in Psalm 133. God's commands and blessings have as their aim the gift of eternal life (Ps 133:3).

An additional early interpretation of the Pentateuch's view of creation and salvation can be found in Psalm 136. It is clear from the similarities that Psalm 136 is an early reflection on the theological intent of the Pentateuch. Its author clearly has read portions of the Pentateuch and by means of this psalm provides a selective account of its meaning. It is therefore a witness to how portions of the Pentateuch were understood by one of its earliest audiences.

Like the Pentateuch itself, Psalm 136 begins with God as creator. The psalm is a praise of God as creator, as seen in Psalm 136:5-9:

> to him who by understanding made the heavens . . .
> to him who spread out the earth upon the waters . . .
> to him who made the great lights . . .
> the sun to rule over the day . . .
> the moon and stars to rule over the night . . .

There is little doubt that Psalm 136 is dependent on the creation narrative in Genesis 1. Also clear is that the psalm focuses only on two places in Genesis: Genesis 1:1, 14-17. Both places focus on the "heavens and earth" and the "great lights and stars." Unlike Psalm 33, which also draws from its understanding of the creation account in Genesis 1, Psalm 136 does not mention the role of divine speech, which is a central theme in Genesis 1:3–2:3. Psalm 136 thus gives a selective reading of the creation account in Genesis 1:1–2:4. It points the readers to those elements of creation that are cosmic in scope: the sky, land, celestial bodies.

After the praise of God as creator, Psalm 136:10-16 continues with a focus on God as redeemer.

> to him who smote the firstborn of Egypt . . .
> and brought Israel out from among them . . .
> with a strong hand and an outstretched arm . . .
> to him who divided the Red Sea in sunder . . .
> and made Israel pass through the midst of it . . .
> but overthrew Pharaoh and his host in the Red Sea . . .
> to him who led his people through the wilderness . . .

Psalm 136:10 moves immediately from creation to events of the exodus and the Pentateuch's account of it in Exodus 12–14. There is no mention of the patriarchal narratives (Gen 12–50).

Like Psalm 136, Nehemiah 9:6-8 is dependent on the canonical Pentateuch, but it moves from creation (Neh 9:6) to the patriarchal narratives (Neh 9:7-8), and then the text goes on to the exodus (Neh 9:9-12) and Sinai (Neh 9:13a) along with the giving of the law (Neh 9:13b). Nehemiah 9 thus gives a full account of the Pentateuch's narratives with no substantial omissions. When compared with Psalm 136, Nehemiah clearly follows the whole of the Pentateuch in its present compositional shape. Psalm 136, on the other hand, follows Exodus 15 and its selective reflection on creation and redemption, linking them in an immediate sequence.

The selectivity and shape of Psalm 136 suggests that it has followed Exodus 15 as its Pentateuch, omitting the patriarchal narratives and moving immediately from creation to the exodus.

Psalm 136 concludes with a focus on God as protector (Ps 136:17-20),

to him who smote great kings . . .
and slew famous kings . . .
Sihon, king of the Amorites . . .
and Og, king of Bashan . . .

and God as provider (Ps 136:21-26),

and gave their land as a heritage . . .
a heritage to Israel his servant . . .
It is he who remembered us in our low estate . . .
and rescued us from our foes . . .
he who gives food to all flesh . . .
O give thanks to the God of heaven . . .

***Intertextuality: Exodus 15 and Psalm 136.*** Looking back at our observations on the poem in Exodus 15, particularly its focus on the land as the place God built for his sanctuary (Ex 15:17), it is possible to view the Pentateuch's notion of salvation in much narrower terms than the creation of the "universe" of Genesis 1:1. If I have correctly described Exodus 15 as reaching back at least to Genesis 2 or possibly Genesis 1:2–2:3, then its purpose may be to ground its message of salvation in a creation not merely consisting of "the heavens and earth," but including God's laying the foundation of his sanctuary on "the mountain of his inheritance," apparently a reference to the preparation of the land in Genesis 2. Thus, the poem in Exodus 15 would intentionally link the scope of its understanding of salvation to the creation narrative in Genesis 2, that is the "creation" to which Exodus 15 links its understanding of the exodus redemption. Such a scope and selectivity, if I have accurately interpreted the intent of the textual evidence in Exodus 15, would be consistent with the Pentateuch's view of the salvation experienced in the exodus (עַם־זוּ גָּאָלְתָּ, Ex 15:13). What is at stake in the redemption portrayed by the exodus narrative is not the condition, or eventual outcome, of the universe, but the place of God's abode on earth. Like many modern commentators, the author of Exodus 15 understands the garden of Eden in Genesis 2 in terms that anticipate the tabernacle sanctuary (Ex 25–31).

In terms of what can be said of the reign of God described in Exodus 15:18, its focus is also limited to the realm depicted in Genesis 2, approximating that of the realm of the dynasty of Judah—just as Psalm 136:22 and Psalm 78:68-72, both of which present themselves as commentary on Exodus 15.

If I have correctly pointed to the compositional intent of the various noted links, particularly those between the creation and exodus narratives and poems, such as Exodus 15, which serve to interpret them, then it may be possible to say that Exodus 15 provides an additional answer to the question raised earlier by these creation texts. Put simply, what is the relationship between salvation (covenant) and the kingdom of God (kingdom)? The opening of the Pentateuch, along with its echo in Exodus 15, moves us in two directions, suggesting an answer to the problem of the relationship between kingdom ideas and covenants. If we view the notions of covenant and kingdom together with the biblical idea of universal (Gen 1:1) and local creation (Gen 2), one might say that the creation and preparation of "the earth" (Gen 2) is recounted as the proper context within which one must view the covenant blessings; that is, obedience is required of those who live in the land (Gen 2:16-17; 3:24), and at the same time all creation (Gen 1:1) is subject to God's dominion—that is, kingship. We have seen that the kingdom anticipated in the various poems of the Pentateuch is located within the inheritance of the tribe of Judah. It is that kingdom which is to be identified with God's sanctuary on earth. Although David is never mentioned in the Pentateuch, the king in its poetry clearly anticipates and is later identified as the king who was to come from the house of David (2 Sam 7:12-16).

***A biblical theological understanding of "kingdom."*** We noted above that classical evangelical theology holds a twofold view of the kingdom of God. On the one hand, there is a kingdom of God in which all creation is subject to God as king *(regi a Deo),* and on the other hand, there is a kingdom of God consisting only of those who willingly submit to God as king *(regnare cum Deo).* These find expression in the notions of God's eternal kingdom and his temporal kingdom.

The problem that these two ideas of "kingdom" present to biblical theology is that the "kingdom" concept within the Bible almost always is linked by biblical theologians to the notion of "covenant."[14] While linking the idea of "kingdom" to that of "covenant" may suit one's concept of "kingdom" in its narrower sense as those who submit to God's will *(regnare cum Deo),* the idea of a covenant is far too narrow to suit its identification with the universal reign of God *(regi a Deo).* How can the concept of "covenant," which consists

[14]Schrenk, *Gottesreich und Bund im älteren Protestantismus*, pp. 116-23.

only of those who voluntarily submit to the will of God, be identified with the notion of a universal kingdom of God that consists of God's rule over all of creation? The solution offered by biblical theology has almost always been to exchange the notion of an eternal kingdom with that of an eschatological kingdom.[15] An eschatological kingdom removes the universal kingdom of God *(regi a Deo)* from the present sphere to a future realm.

The foregoing observations and discussion suggest that there are indications within the compositional strategy of the Pentateuch that the author has attempted to deal with this problem compositionally by refusing to link the creation of the universe (Gen 1) with a covenant of any kind.[16] Although many attempts have been made to recover a covenant somewhere in the creation account (e.g., Julius Wellhausen), the fact remains that in the present shape of the text (cf. Hos 6:7) there is no mention of a covenant involving creation (Johann Coccejus's *foedus naturae*). Covenants begin to appear in the Genesis narratives only after the account of the fall and in connection with redemption. That may be why the poem in Exodus 15, in the development of its view of the kingdom (Ex 15:18), goes back only to Genesis 2 with its linkage of fellowship and divine presence in a sanctuary. Those are the features of the temporal kingdom that are stressed in Exodus 15.[17]

## Exodus 15 and the Patriarchal Narratives

Unlike other texts such as Nehemiah 9:6-8, which make frequent reference to the Genesis patriarchal narratives, Exodus 15 omits any mention of the patriarchs. A compositional approach must ask whether such an omission is intentional. What might it mean? How does it affect our understanding of the rest of the Pentateuch? Broadly speaking, what has been omitted is the idea of "faith-righteousness" or "covenant loyalty,"[18] which pervades the patriarchal narratives.

In Exodus 15 those whom God brings out of Egypt are not so much the "righteous" as the "redeemed." But how are we to understand such a linkage?

---

[15]Note Rudolf Bultmann's explanation of the origin of OT eschatology in the incomplete identity of the kingdom ideal and the covenant reality.

[16]The first mention of a "covenant" in the Pentateuch is in Genesis 6:18.

[17]In Gen 1:1 the scope of the kingdom is the universe, "heavens and earth," and in Gen 1:2–2:4 the scope of the covenant is "the land." Genesis 1:1 attached to Genesis 1:2–2:4 in order to widen the scope of the kingdom to all creation. This is not a redactional step, but a compositional one.

[18]Compare the twofold conception of land as world and as land.

The focus of Genesis 1 is God's creation of the world and his preparation of the "land." In Genesis 2 fellowship between human beings and God is demonstrated by the garden. Though it was short-lived, Adam walked with God in the garden. The underlying idea of this strategy is that the fellowship, reestablished between God and humanity, which is the ultimate goal of salvation, will be realized within this same primeval realm. Hence, in Genesis 1–2 one finds the essential features of the "kingdom" concept still under development. To be sure, there are missing pieces, such as the explicit identification of God as king.

Earlier in the discussion I suggested that there are compositional connections between "the beginning" in Genesis 1:1 and the poems that speak of a coming king in the "last days" (Gen 49; Num 24; Deut 33). By means of such connections and other compositional strategies, we can see that the notion of a king and a kingdom had already begun to make its way into Genesis 1–2, and from there to other key passages.

What is missing, however, is a further textual link between creation, redemption and kingship, the kind of link that can be established by exegesis—one that reflects an author's specific choice of words and strategy. With such an important theme as "the kingdom of God," our expectation level ought to be high. Here, general themes and nuances are not enough.

With that expectation in mind, we turn again to the passage that has stood out from the others in all these discussions of the poems in the Pentateuch: Exodus 15:1-18. The poem begins with a lengthy and noteworthy poetic account of the exodus from Egypt (Ex 15:1-11). It then covers most of the ground of the Pentateuch's own exodus narrative. At the conclusion to this segment there is a poetic summary of the exodus in which it is cast as a divine act of redemption. The exodus was God's redemption of his people: "In your steadfast love you led the people whom you redeemed" (*ʿam-zû gāʾāltā* [Ex 15:13a]). It is difficult to deny that this is an intentional, verbal, theological commentary identifying and establishing the exodus as a divine act of redemption.

The poem then turns to the conquest of Canaan and portays the nations as standing silently, in trepidation, as the Lord brings his people into their land (Ex 15:14-17).

Finally, in an allusion to Genesis 1, the poem concludes with the identification of the Lord's abode as the "mountain of [God's] dwelling place" which he has made *(pāʿaltā* [Ex 15:17a]).

***The Fall.*** The early chapters of Genesis move quickly from creation to the fall. We hear no more of the garden of Eden. These narratives make the point that the commonplace reality within which the biblical ideas of the kingdom and salvation are worked out is under the curse. God's world is no longer "very good" (Gen 1:31). Instead of the formulaic expression "and God saw that it was good" (Gen 1:10, 12, 18, 21, 25), we read only that "the LORD saw that the calamity of mankind was great in the land" (Gen 6:5), and "God saw the land, and behold, it was corrupted *[nišḥātâ],* because all flesh had corrupted *[hišḥît]* his way" (Gen 6:12). From this point on, the events of the Pentateuch will play themselves out in a fallen world in need of redemption. The description of this world hints at Moses' last words in Deuteronomy 31:29:

> For I know that after my death you surely will act corruptly *[hašḥēt tašḥitûn]* and turn aside from the way which I have commanded you; and in the days to come evil will befall you, because you will do what is evil in the sight of the LORD, provoking him to anger through the work of your hands.

Since it is the world of Genesis 1 that is under a curse, and not humankind alone, the goal of salvation must reach beyond fallen humanity. Ultimately, the scope of salvation in the Pentateuch is the fallen universe of the "heavens and earth." Hence, God's covenant with Noah (Gen 9:8-17) is an essential reminder for the author of the Pentateuch that redemption must extend to the salvation of "all flesh"—that is, the fallen universe: "God said to Noah, 'This is the sign of the covenant which I have established between me and all flesh that is upon the earth'" (Gen 9:17).

As in the prophetic promises of a new covenant, salvation in the OT expands in scope to the broad horizons of the Noahic covenant.

*Intertextuality: Isaiah 24:4-6.* The prophet Isaiah grounds all of God's future actions in both creation and his covenant with Noah:

> The earth mourneth and fadeth away, the world languisheth and fadeth away, the haughty people of the earth do languish. The earth also is defiled under the inhabitants thereof; because they have transgressed the laws, changed the ordinance, broken the everlasting covenant [cf. "everlasting covenant" in Gen 9:16]. Therefore hath the curse devoured the earth, and they that dwell therein are desolate: therefore the inhabitants of the earth are burned, and few men left. (Is 24:4-6)

*Innertextuality: The flood (Gen 6–9).* It is important to bear in mind that from the author of the Pentateuch's perspective, the world is still under God's curse. Creation's redemption is not yet complete. The world is still not "very good" apart from salvation and redemption. The road from nature, and creation, will not lead back to God. Noah's vineyard results in drunkenness, nakedness and a curse, just as God's good garden was the scene of the fall.

***The will of God.*** Salvation in the Pentateuch is not restricted to the physical world. The world, as creation, is grounded in a free divine act. It owes its purpose to the creator's will. Neither creation nor salvation is rooted in the natural processes. Neither seeks its end in a glorification of nature. The highest goal of both creation and salvation is the will of God and his glorification. This means that the salvation (i.e., relationship with God) that is to work itself out in God's creation is ultimately to be realized within an ethical kingdom whose highest ideal is obedience to the will of God.

Thus, the biblical notion of salvation is not merely a blissful future life. The anticipated future life is devoted not to fulfilling human desires, but to doing the will of God. Humankind is to trust and obey God, who knows and desires what is "good."

***The Word of God.*** Salvation in the OT is not a mere ideal or doctrine. It is a verbal act, an object of hope, rooted in creation and destined to be worked out in history. It is grounded in a series of divine acts that cannot be explained as the mere product of human invention or natural development.[19]

The Pentateuch's concentration on divine acts should not divert our attention from the fact that all of those "acts" come to us as words. God's acts are subordinated to his words. We cannot, or should not, attempt to draw our own meaning from divine acts. Actions are capable of multiple explanations. In Genesis 1 God talks as he does his work. His work of creation does not remain a mystery. He explains everything he does.

The role of the Pentateuch is to explain the meaning of the divine acts it records. The way that the Pentateuch explains God's actions is by presenting them within the context of a meaningful story—a narrative. God's acts in history come to us as part of his story. His word accompanies his work and is

---

[19]See Heinrich A. Hävernick, *Vorlesungen über die Theologie des Alten Testaments*, ed. H. A. Hahn (Erlangen: Heyder, 1848), pp. 112-17.

that which gives it meaning. Creation is not only something God has done; it is also something God has said.[20]

## Salvation in the Primeval History (Gen 1–11)

The biblical meaning of salvation is played out in summary form as a connected series of historical events aimed at the establishment of a renewed relationship between God and humanity. The first human event in the story is an account of the loss of that relationship in the primeval period. That is the story of the fall (Gen 3). Evangelical biblical theology has, from its beginning, viewed this early story of salvation as the prototype of all subsequent versions of the biblical notion of redemption. It is sometimes called the "proto-gospel" and is associated with Genesis 3:15. The earliest theological outline of the story, in modern biblical theological terms, was published by Heinrich Hävernick in his lectures on the theology of the OT.[21] This was the first truly biblical-theological account of the history. Hävernick's account of this early "primeval" story of salvation is worth reviewing. It has been adopted almost intact by numerous subsequent evangelical biblical theologies.

***Narrative Strategy (Story) of Genesis 1–11.*** *The battle.* With the entry of sin into the world, the whole of humanity was divided into two peoples (seed), each locked in mortal combat with the other in an intense struggle of good and evil.

*The victory.* The battle will result in a decisive victory of one "seed" over the other (Gen 3:15). God and the forces of good (the "seed" of the woman) will mount a victorious campaign against the forces of evil and those aligned with them (the "seed" of the serpent).

*The seed.* The campaign is not waged in general terms, but is linked directly to a chosen seed. The ultimate victory envisioned in the campaign is not the result of human achievement; it is grounded solely in the sovereign will of God, which will achieve its purpose only by means of the chosen "seed." In Genesis 1–11 the "seed" is both a select individual and a line from which that individual will come. It is a line of descendants identified with Noah, Shem and Abraham. In the remainder of the Pentateuch the "seed" is identified as a future king who will arise from the house of Judah (Gen 49:8-12).

---

[20]"In a mystical action something happens, in a prophetic action something is said" (Abraham Heschel).

[21]See Hävernick, *Theologie des Alten Testaments*, pp. 115-18.

> At the close of the book [of Genesis], a curtain on the future is drawn back and a glimpse of the future seed of Abraham is briefly allowed (49:8-12). This one "seed" who is to come, to whom the right of kingship belongs, will be the "lion of the tribe of Judah" and "to him will be the obedience of the nations" (49:10). . . . The interest of the author in this king who is to come does not stop here. The future reign of this king and the blessing that is to ensue is the focus of other poetic texts in the Pentateuch [cf. Num 24; Deut 33].[22]

*The promise.* What has been called the "first gospel" *(protevangelium)* in Genesis 3 often is misunderstood on two sides: one can find there too much or too little.[23] Some find in Genesis 3:15 a direct reference to a single individual, the person of the Messiah: "I will put enmity between you [the serpent] and the woman, between your seed and her seed." According to Hävernick, and others, such a reading of the "promise" is unwarranted. The Hebrew term "seed" *(zeraʿ)* is a collective and often has that sense in the book of Genesis and the Pentateuch.

Hävernick suggests the term "seed" *(zeraʿ)* is used in Genesis 3:15 to refer to those individuals who, in the remainder of the Pentateuch (and beyond), are identified and set apart by God for his work of redemption. Genesis 3:15 is, then, about the origin of that group of individuals.[24] In that sense, a strictly messianic reading of Genesis 3:15 would too quickly detach this passage from the important subsequent literary contexts within the Pentateuch and would result in its being read in an entirely spiritual (unhistorical) sense. The term "seed" would be little more than a figure of speech, a picture of a messianic redeemer. What would be lost in such a transaction is the physical, concrete character of the promise in Genesis 3:15 and the possibility of its further development within a family (Gen 12:1-3) and a royal dynasty (Gen 49:8-12), just as happens throughout the remainder of the book of Genesis. It can thus be a costly mistake to read too much into the text. It can empty the passage

[22]John H. Sailhamer, *The Pentateuch as Narrative* (Grand Rapids: Zondervan, 1992), p. 140.

[23]Hävernick, *Theologie des Alten Testaments*, p. 117.

[24]Hävernick's view finds some support from recent grammars. "With collective nouns the singular is used to refer to *a group*. . . . The plural form of a singular collective noun indicates *a disruption or processing of the collective*. With nouns referring to crops it often indicates the processed state. . . . שְׂעֹרָה barley (in the fields) . . . שְׂעֹרִים *cooked* barley" (Christo H. J. Van der Merwe, Jackie A. Naudé and Jan H. Kroeze, *A Biblical Hebrew Reference Grammar* [BL 3; Sheffield: Sheffield Academic Press], pp. 183-85). Compare זַרְעֵיכֶם (*zarʿêkem*, "planted seed") in 1 Samuel 8:15; "eine Fülle von Einzelmomenten in sich schlossen" (Eduard König, *Historisch-comparative Syntax der hebräischen Sprache: Schlussteil des historisch-kritischen Lehrgebäudes des Hebräischen* [Leipzig: Hinrichs, 1897], p. 181).

of just the kind of meaning one seeks to find already there. Genesis 3:15 is not so much a picture of the messianic redeemer as it is a hint and an affirmation that such a redeemer will come. By identifying the "seed" as Christ in Genesis 3:15, one forfeits a real identification of the seed with the royal personage in Genesis 49:10.

It is equally wrong, argues Hävernick, to see nothing of real importance in the words of Genesis 3:15. There are those who understand it to be only about the struggle between human beings and snakes. Such a purely physical sense would be unlike the OT (Pentateuch). It would also find little or no support from the remainder of the Pentateuch. Where else in the Pentateuch, besides Numbers 21:6-9, is the theme of conflict between snakes and humans taken up? Is not humankind given dominion over all the animals in Genesis 9:3? In Genesis, and the remainder of the Pentateuch, not only is conflict a central theme, but also the specific struggle between human families takes center stage. It therefore is likely that Genesis 3:15 is about that conflict, and if so, the "seed of the woman" would not refer to all humanity. It would refer, argues Hävernick, to only a segment of the family of humankind. The "seed of the serpent" would refer to the rest of humanity. The distinction between the seed of the woman and the seed of the serpent is, then, a matter that awaits further elaboration in the subsequent narratives in the Pentateuch. One thing, however, is abundantly clear: there is to be a struggle within the family of Adam between two warring parties, those who identify with the rebellion of the serpent and those who, like Eve, will bear the seed of the coming redeemer.

Hävernick's "text sensitive" reading of Genesis 3:15 has many points in its favor. Its critique of the rush to identify all the NT elements in this early saying is important in the face of many Christian readings of the poem. Literarily, it is to be expected that some, if not most, elements of meaning in the brief saying would be left unsaid, only to be filled in later by the author.

Meir Sternberg suggests that biblical narratives, as all narratives, leave much to be filled in, either by the reader or by the author. Sometimes the reader is required to fill in material from personal experience. Sternberg calls such omissions "blanks." At other times such apparent "omissions," or missing story material, are left for the author to fill in for us at a later point in the story. Sternberg calls these "gaps." Only the author can, or should, fill in a gap. That is part of the *mens auctoris* (author's intent). In those cases, the reader is to watch every move of the author to see when and how the author fills in the gap. The only way to distinguish a blank from a gap is to catch the author in the act of filling in a gap in the story at some later moment in the narrative. If an author takes up an element of a story and gives it additional focus, it is a gap.

In the case of Genesis 3:15, the many references to the "seed" in the subsequent narratives strongly suggest that the identity of the seed is a gap. Since it is a gap, we must let the author, not ourselves, fill in the identity. Our only question is how the author is going to fill the gap as we read on. The answer to that question, at least initially, is to look around in the narrative to see how the word "seed" is picked up and used by the author. In other words, we should look for texts such as Genesis 12:7: "Then the LORD appeared to Abram, and said, 'To your seed *[zeraʿ]* I will give this land.'"

So, the answer appears to lie somewhere in the numerous occurrences of the divine word concerning the "seed of Abraham" in Genesis 12–50. As I have shown, in the poetic texts the "seed" is further identified as a king from the house of Judah, suggesting that the "seed of Abraham" is being understood as a singular. The collective "seed of Abraham" in the Genesis narratives is thus further defined in individual terms by the poetry in the Pentateuch. Whether one of the historical Davidic kings or a future messianic king is meant is a question that can be answered only within the context of the compositional strategy of the rest of the Pentateuch. Certainly, such indicators as the introductory phrase "in the last days," as well as the actual content of the individual poems, argue strongly for a messianic reading of the poems. When these poems are again taken up in the prophetic and poetry literature, the "seed" is identified as the future king from the house of David (Ps 72:17; Jer 4:2).

***The compositional strategy of salvation in Genesis 1–11.*** How has the author of the Pentateuch woven the theme of salvation and redemption into the narratives in Genesis 1–11? To answer that question, we must note several key statements that reveal the author's theological intentions. These statements turn the focus of the reader toward the curse of the ground and the role of Noah's sacrifice in removing that curse.

*The curse of the ground (Gen 3:17; 4:11; 5:29; 8:21).* According to the narratives in Genesis 1–11, the primary obstacle to the enjoyment of creation was the curse of the ground after the fall.

Thorns also and thistles shall it bring forth to thee; and thou shalt eat the herb of the field; in the sweat of thy face shalt thou eat bread, till thou return unto the ground; for out of it wast thou taken: for dust thou art, and unto dust shalt thou return. (Gen 3:18-19 ASV)

The ground had been cursed because of human disobedience. The compositional strategy of Genesis 1–11 drives home just that point. Throughout these narratives one hears literary echoes of the divine curse, each leading up to the account of the flood. The task of understanding the strategy of salvation in Genesis 1–11 consists of asking how these various echoes are related, both to the narratives as a whole and to each other. Here is a list of literary echoes of the curse on the ground:

1. Genesis 1:31: "And God saw all that he had made *[ʿāśâ]*."
2. Genesis 3:17: "And to the man [God] said, '. . . cursed is the ground *[ʾădāmâ]* on account of you.'"
3. Genesis 4:10-11: "And [the LORD] said, '. . . now cursed are you from the ground *[ʾădāmâ]*.'"
4. Genesis 5:29: "He will give comfort from our work and from the toil of our hands, from the ground *[ʾădāmâ]* which the LORD cursed."
5. Genesis 6:12: "And God looked at the land *[ʾereṣ]*, and behold, it was ruined."
6. Genesis 8:21a: "And the LORD . . . said to himself, 'I will not constantly curse the ground *[ʾădāmâ]* again because of man."
7. Genesis 8:21b: "I will not continue further to smite all living creatures."
8. Genesis 9:11: "Never again will a flood destroy the land *[ʾereṣ]*."

These combined snipets are intentionally linked to connect the events in Genesis 1–11. They represent the most clearly marked layer of composition throughout the primeval history. By means of these (mostly poetic) texts, the reader is shown that God's "very good land" quickly became corrupt and ruined through human disobedience. Those who inhabited the land also became corrupt and were destroyed by the flood (Gen 6:5-8). Only Noah was saved (Gen 6:8). After the flood, God altered the curse on the land and vowed never again to destroy the land with a flood. In the process, a new way of life was initiated through the making of a covenant.

Within this compositional layer the account of Noah's sacrifice (Gen 8:20-22) occupies the central position. It was only after God's acceptance of Noah's sacrifice (not merely after the flood) that the curse on the ground *(ʾădāmâ)* was altered and order was returned to the land *(ʾereṣ).*

*Sacrifice (Gen 8:20-22).* What kind of offering or sacrifice did Noah bring after the flood? A common tendency among interpreters of Genesis 1–11 is to view Noah's sacrifice in Genesis 8:20 as a "thanksgiving offering." To be sure, Noah was grateful for God's rescuing him and would have had ample reason to give a thanksgiving offering to God. That would be what one might expect of Noah after being rescued from the flood. Also, in ancient Near Eastern flood accounts, the surviving hero dutifully offers a gift of thanksgiving. In the terminology used in this section, Noah's first act after leaving the ark was to offer sacrifices from the clean animals and birds—that is, burnt offerings for sin *(ʿōlōt).* The terminology in Genesis 8:20 indicates that the sacrifice was not merely a thanksgiving offering (e.g, *šelem* or *tôdâ*), but an offering for sin (*ʿōlâ* [Lev 1:4). After the flood, Noah built an altar and offered a sacrifice (Gen 8:20). God accepted the sacrifice ("smelled the soothing aroma"),[25] and on that basis God vowed never again to curse the ground (Gen 8:21).[26] God also vowed never again to destroy all humankind as he had in the flood (Gen 8:21). In Genesis 9 God vowed never again to send a flood (Gen 9:11). Each of these acts represents a distinct divine action. Noah's sacrifice initiated multiple divine actions that ultimately secured order and restoration in the fallen world.

Although it is common to see each of these actions as aspects of a single divine vow never again to send a devastating flood, a close look at these texts suggests otherwise. They speak of three distinct divine responses, each seen as a result of Noah's sacrifice. What God vows in Genesis 8:21 is grounded in his acceptance of Noah's sacrifice: "Then Noah built an altar to the Lord, and took of every clean animal and of every clean bird, and offered burnt offerings on the altar. And when the Lord smelled the pleasing odor, the Lord said. . . ." (Gen 8:20-21a).

---

[25]"That God's anger at sin is appeased by sacrifice is the clear implication of this phrase" (Gordon J. Wenham, *Genesis 1–15* [WBC 1; Waco, Tex.: Word, 1987], p. 189).

[26]"The obvious implication of the sequence of verbs 'the Lord smelt . . . said' is that God's thoughts about mankind were prompted by his appreciation of the sacrifice" (ibid.).

The message of this passage is that God was deeply moved by the offering of a sacrifice. Given the role of sacrifices and offerings in the rest of the Pentateuch, it would be hard to overstate the importance of this first demonstration of the premise of all sacrifice, that God was genuinely moved by the sacrifice. God accepted the sacrifice, and it reversed all the toil and futility of the curse. This is the first mention in the Pentateuch of a sacrifice (burnt offering). The "offering" of Cain and Abel was not a sacrificial one; it was a gift *(minḥâ),* not a burnt offering *(ʿōlâ).* As these narratives play out, all the sacrificial offerings *(ʿōlâ)* in the "laws" of the Pentateuch are grounded in this first instance of divine acceptance. In this brief narrative the author of the Pentateuch raises a fundamental question: "How does one know that God accepts the sacrificial offerings prescribed in the Mosaic law?" He then answers that question with a narrative that shows God accepting Noah's sacrifice. The author does not simply tell us that God accepts sacrificial offerings and is moved to compassion by them; he shows us an indisputable example of God's response. He then drives home the point by showing that the order of God's creation is still grounded in God's acceptance of the first sacrificial offering by this one righteous man. What evil had destroyed could be restored by the sacrifice of a single righteous one: "As long as the earth endures, seedtime and harvest, cold and heat, summer and winter, day and night, shall not cease" (Gen 8:22).

The author's point is that some things are true and work in the world because that is how they were made to be. God made the world that way. It is a part of what makes the world we live in work as it should. The Pentateuch's use of narrative shows how fundamental the truth of God's acceptance of a sacrifice is in the biblical world. It is a truth woven into the fabric of God's world. All that need be done by the Pentateuch is to point to it, showing that it has always been there and that it works. It is a more basic part of the world than even the power that gives creation its order and endurance. To question it would mean to call the universe itself into question. In Genesis 8:20-22 we are shown a law at work. We see it happening, and so we know that it is still there and has been there from the beginning.

*Genesis 8:21: A* Crux Interpretum. Genesis 8:21 is a *crux interpetum* for a major segment of the primeval history. The question turns on what God means when he says, "I will never again curse the ground because of man." What is the scope of God's statement? Is he vowing never again to send a worldwide flood? Or is he removing from the ground the curse of Genesis 3:17-19? Do we now live in a world in which the "curse of the ground" has been lifted?

If we read Genesis 8:21a to refer to God's cursing the ground in Genesis 3:17, these questions inevitably arise. At the center of the questions that arise out of these verses is the meaning of Genesis 8:21. The following observations and discussion of this verse are intended only to move us in the direction of an answer.

The first question that must be raised is whether Genesis 8:21 is to be viewed merely as a concluding statement to the flood account (Westermann) or as a statement intended to embrace and conclude the entire primeval history in Genesis 1–11. In other words, does Genesis 8:21 refer back only to Genesis 6:5 (Westermann), or does it also refer back to Genesis 3:17; 4:11; 5:29 (Rendtorff)?

*Three views of Genesis 8:21a.* Here we look at the views of Rolf Rendtorff and Claus Westermann and then my own view regarding Genesis 8:21a.

According to Rendtorff, God's vow never to curse the ground again (Gen 8:21a) refers to God's original curse of the ground in Genesis 3:17. After the fall, God cursed the ground (Gen 3:17), but now, in Genesis 8:21a, he has removed or altered that curse so that it is not effective in the same way it had been. Rendtorff bases his argument on the fact that two Hebrew words are used to describe the notion of "cursing" the ground in Genesis 3:17; 8:21. Rendtorff argues that since the word for "curse" (ארר, *ʾrr*) in Genesis 3:17 is different from that for "curse" (קלל, *qll*) in Genesis 8:21 they are not semantically equivalent. In Genesis 3:17 God "cursed" *(ʾrr)* the ground, and it remained cursed; that is, God continued to treat it as "cursed" *(ʾrr)*. After the flood and Noah's sacrifice (Gen 8:21a), God was deeply moved and vowed never again "to consider the ground as cursed" *(qll)*. In other words, although the ground would always remain under God's curse—that is, thorns and thistles will continue to plague *(ʾrr)* his creation—God will no longer "consider the ground cursed." He will no longer treat it as cursed *(qll)*. As far as God is concerned, he has taken the power out of the curse of Genesis 3:17 by no longer actively carrying out its curse. Seeing Noah's sacrifice moved God to relent to that extent.

The value of Rendtorff's view is that takes seriously the author's use of the two words for "curse" in this passage. The main objection raised against

Rendtorff is something that he readily acknowledges: after the flood and after Noah's sacrifice, the world was still plagued by thorns and thistles, painful birth and arduous labor—all those things brought on by the curse in Genesis 3:17. How can he say that the curse on the ground was lifted? Surely, the description of the curse in Genesis 3:17-19 is intended as a description of the author's experience in the present world.

According to Westermann, God's vow in Genesis 8:21a refers not to the original curse of the ground in Genesis 3:17, but to God's sending the flood in Genesis 6:7. God had sent the flood because of the wickedness of the human heart (Gen 6:7), and now, after the flood, God vowed never again to send another flood for that same reason (Gen 8:21). Since the human heart was unchanged by the flood, God, in an act of grace, henceforth would tolerate humankind's wicked state and never again send such a destructive flood (cf. Mt 5:45). According to Westermann, this is a form of "common grace."

The main objection to Westermann's view is that the terminology in Genesis 8:21a suggests that it does not refer to God's sending the flood in Genesis 6:7. The flood, in Genesis 6:7, is not called a "curse," yet in Genesis 8:21 God vows never to "curse" the ground again. He must be speaking not of the flood, but of the "curse" on the ground in Genesis 3:17; 4:22; 5:29. God does bring the flood into the picture in the next chapter (Gen 9:11), where he establishes a covenant with all the earth not to send a flood again. But that is not the "curse" we see in Genesis 8:21.

In my own view, Genesis 8:21a ("I will never again curse the ground because of man") refers to all those places in Genesis 1–8 that speak of God's "curse" on the ground *(ʾădāmâ):* Genesis 3:17; 4:22; 5:29. In Genesis 8:21 God vows never again to "curse" the ground as he had in Genesis 3:17 and as he continued to do in Genesis 4:22; 5:29. In the remainder of our verse, Genesis 8:21b, God picks up another topic, the flood, and says, "I will never again destroy all life," referring to his decision to send the flood in Genesis 6:7. If the ground is cursed more than once in these narratives, as appears to be the case in Genesis 4, then the sense of Genesis 8:21a would be "I will not again *[ʾōsīp . . . ʿôd ]* curse *[lĕqallēl]* the ground [as I have already cursed it twice]." God then adds this comment in Genesis 8:21b: "I will not any further *[ʾōsīp ʿôd]* strike *[lĕhakkôt]* all life as I have done."

Evaluation: Although the terminology is inexact, it seems clear that Genesis 8:21b refers to God's decision to send the flood in Genesis 6:5-7.

God had said, "I will blot out *[ʾemḥeh]* from the earth the human beings I have created" (Gen 6:7), and in Genesis 8:21b, "I will never again destroy *[lĕhakkôt]* every living creature as I have done." God's devastating resolve to end all life (Gen 6:5-7) is ended in Genesis 8:21b by the sacrifice offered in Genesis 8:20.

The first part of Genesis 8:21 appears to have a scope that reaches far beyond God's sending the flood. Here the verse introduces the broader issue of God's cursing the ground in Genesis 3:17. What will become of that curse in light of Noah's sacrifice and God's consequent resolve to "never again curse the ground because of man"? As I said earlier, it is not enough merely to link this statement to the beginning of the flood story (Gen 6:5-7), because the flood in Genesis 6–8 is not called a "curse," nor is it treated as a curse in these narratives. It was a judgment upon human wickedness, but not a curse. A curse cannot be a single event, such as the flood; it is a continuous condition imposed upon the ground, as the allusion to it in Genesis 5:29 demonstrates. Noah's name is derived from the fact that he brought comfort "from the ground that the Lord had cursed *[ʾērĕrâ],*" not from the flood (Gen 5:29). Thus, God's statement in Genesis 8:21a must refer to his curse of the ground in Genesis 3:17: "Cursed *[ʾărûrâ]* is the ground because of you [man]."

We can thus draw from this discussion that Genesis 8:21 is not merely the conclusion of the flood story, but is the conclusion of the whole of the earlier narratives of Gen 2–5 and thus concludes the primeval history from the garden of Eden to the flood. The fallen state of one man, Adam, which began with the curse on the ground (Gen 3:17), is extended to the whole of humankind and leads to God's decision to wipe out all life (Gen 6:5-17). At the conclusion of the flood, God makes a new beginning by removing the curse on the land and replacing it with blessing (Gen 8:22).

That the author of the Pentateuch sees Genesis 8:21a as a new beginning for the "ground" *(ʾădāmâ)* and consequently for humanity *(ʾādām)* is shown by the comment in Genesis 5:29. There, the author identifies "Noah" (נח, *nḥ*) with the "comfort" (נחם, *nḥm*) he brought to humanity by releasing them from their labor and toil upon "the ground which the Lord cursed." Noah brought comfort from the toil of the cursed ground. That comfort consisted in Noah's sacrifice having removed the power of the curse on the ground.

The logic of the narrative in Genesis 2–8 is this:

1. The Lord cursed the ground (Gen 3:17).
2. A removal of the curse on the ground is envisioned (Gen 5:29).
3. Noah offers a sacrifice (Gen 8:20).
4. The power of the curse on the ground is removed by Noah's sacrifice (Gen 8:21).

*The translation of Genesis 8:21a.* An important part of the solution that I have offered to Genesis 8:21a is its exact translation. Gordon Wenham translates the verse as God saying, "I shall not curse the soil any further," meaning that the ground had been cursed in Genesis 3:17 and will not be cursed any further. This is not so much a promise about the future as it is a statement about the status quo. What God, in effect, is saying is "It is not going to get any worse than this." Wenham's translation raises the question of why God would make such a statement at this point in the narrative. Having just witnessed the devastating effects of the flood, Noah and company would receive little consolation from learning that it will not get any worse.

In my view, God says, "I shall not constantly curse the ground again." I take this to mean that the ground has been constantly cursed since Genesis 3:17, but God will not continue doing so in the future. The curse will not be unremitting. There will be times when the ground will not be cursed. In the past, as a result of the curse of Genesis 3:17, the ground was unremittingly cursed. God's vow in Genesis 8:21 suggests that a way may be opened to avert the curse on the ground in the future. Or, to say it another way, Noah's sacrifice has opened a way to break the power of the curse on the ground *(ʾădāmâ).*

If this is the sense of Genesis 8:21a, then in this brief narrative the author is laying the foundation for an important lesson on the power of the rite of sacrifice. Through it, if even partially, God's primeval curse on the ground *(ʾădāmâ)* can be remitted. Such a statement at this early stage in the narratives of the Pentateuch suggests considerable reflection on the part of the author about the role of sacrificial offerings and the possibilities of a future enjoyment of the land ("ground," *ʾădāmâ*). The way back to the enjoyment of God's good land and its blessings is through the sacrificial offering for sin. It can hardly be accidental that Abraham's first act upon entering the land was to build an altar and call upon God. This is, in fact, the common practice of all the patriarchs. In keeping with this focus on the centrality of sacrifice and blessing, it is important to note that at the close of the Pentateuch, in one of the book's last poetic statements the author returns to the theme of "making atonement" (sacrifice) for the ground *(ʾădāmâ)* upon which God will again bring salvation and blessing to his people and the nations. The poem ends with the statement that God "will atone *[wĕkipper]* for his land *[ʾadmātô]* and his people" (Deut 32:43).

These texts show how closely in the Pentateuch the idea of salvation is tied to that of sacrifice.

*The translation of Genesis 8:21b.* In Genesis 8:21b, when reference is made to the destruction of the flood, there is a slight but significant difference in the translation. The sense is "I will not continue any further to smite all living creatures." God does not say in Genesis 8:21b that he will never again smite all living creatures. That is what he will say in Genesis 9:11, in conjunction with the Noahic covenant. In Genesis 8:21b, however, he states only that the destructive force of the flood is over. God is finished smiting all living creatures by the flood. Hence, in his next statement, he reestablishes the order of creation: "While the land remains, seedtime and harvest, and cold and heat, and summer and winter, and day and night shall not cease" (Gen 8:22).

Genesis 8:21b thus marks a major turning point in the narrative. In the flood, God had been "destroying all life." Now, as a result of Noah's sacrifice, he has ceased. God calls off his decree to "destroy all life" in Genesis 6:5-7. He relents. Here it is important to note that God's statements in Genesis 6:5-7 and Genesis 8:21b do not mention the flood. Their coming at the end of the flood (Gen 8:1-19) does not mark the end of God's decree in Genesis 6:5-7. That decree comes to an end only after (and because of) Noah's sacrifice in Genesis 8:21b. God's promise never again to send a flood comes only in Genesis 9:11.

My translation of Genesis 8:21 suggests two initial conclusions about the meaning of the verse. First, in Genesis 8:21a Noah's sacrifice marks a new turning point in God's dealings with humankind and the world. As a result of Noah's sacrifice, God made a new decree about the ground he had cursed in Genesis 3:17. It does not merely limit any further addition to the curse, leaving the original curse intact (Wenham), nor does it in some sense actually remove the curse (Rendtorff). The syntax of Genesis 8:21 suggests God's decree in Genesis 8:21a does significantly alter the nature of the curse made in Genesis 3:17. God says that he will no longer continuously curse the ground. The curse on the ground (in Gen 3:17) is not God's final word about creation and his world. Through Noah's sacrifice the curse has been not so much removed as overcome. Humankind's relationship with the cursed ground is therefore linked to the need for a sacrificial offering. Humankind's relationship to God's original blessing of the land *(ʾădāmâ)* now depends on his building altars and offering sacrifices in the land *(ʾădāmâ).* A way is provided for enjoying God's original gift of the land (cf. Deut 32:43). It is significant to note that although after Genesis 8:21 the narratives in the Pentateuch do not again mention God's curse of the ground *(ʾădāmâ),* those same narratives do seem to be preoccupied with the need for building altars and offering sacrifices in the land *(ʾădāmâ).*

The second conclusion to be drawn from my translation of Genesis 8:21 is that Genesis 8:21b is a reference to the decree to destroy all life in Genesis 6:5-7. It is not a decree never again to send a flood, a decree that comes only in Genesis 9:11. The author of the Pentateuch takes God's decree in Genesis 6:5-7 seriously. When God said, in Genesis 6:7, that he would destroy all life, the assumption of the narrative is that God would have continued to do so until his decree had been rescinded. Hence, as Noah leaves the ark, his life was still threatened by God's statement in Genesis 6:7. According to Genesis 8:21b, it was only after Noah's sacrificial offering that God rescinded the decree made in Genesis 6:7. His own words are "I will not continue any further to smite all living creatures." It was God's grace that ended the flood (Gen 8:1), but Noah's sacrifice was necessary to end God's decree of judgment.

The close relationship of Genesis 8:21b and Genesis 6:5-7 alerts us to the possibility that Genesis 8:21a may have a similar function. It may be intended to rescind, or significantly alter, an earlier decree, namely, the curse of the ground *(ʾădāmâ)* in Genesis 3:17. If God has cursed the ground, there would be no possibility for blessing unless that curse was rescinded. When it is rescinded, in Genesis 8:21a, a way is opened for the blessing that follows in Genesis 9:1. That blessing restores humankind to its place in nature, laid out in Genesis 1:28, God's original blessing of creation. The renewed blessing in Genesis 9:1 is then also grounded in Noah's sacrifice.

By means of this complex narrative, the author has established a close and necessary link between humankind's blessing and the curse of the ground *(ʾădāmâ)* in Genesis 3:17. Both the blessing and the curse are tied to the ground *(ʾădāmâ)*. Man *(ʿādām)* was created from the ground (*ʾădāmâ* [Gen 2:7]). The ground *(ʾădāmâ)* was cursed because of humanity's disobedience (Gen 3:17). For humans, the curse meant that one must "work the ground" (*ʾădāmâ* [Gen 3:23]) and ultimately return to the ground *(ʾădāmâ)* in death (Gen 3:19). The very name of humankind, "Adam" *(ʾādām)*, was drawn from its origin, "the ground" (*ʾădāmâ* [Gen 2:7]). When murder polluted the ground *(ʾădāmâ)* upon which they lived, humankind *(ʾādām)* was forced to wander aimlessly away from this cursed ground (*ʾădāmâ* [Gen 4:13]). It is the ground *(ʾădāmâ)* that is the ultimate source of humankind's curse (Gen 4:11). For the author of the Pentateuch, there was no possibility for blessing as long as a curse remained on the ground *(ʾădāmâ)*. Before the account of the covenant and the renewal of the divine blessing (Gen 9:1-17), God must remedy the curse of the ground *(ʾădāmâ)*, and that required a sacrifice.

*Noah's sacrifice (Gen 8:20).* If we take into account what I have said about the meaning of Genesis 8:21, a sin offering would not only be appropriate for Noah after the flood, but also essential to the well-being of those who would live on the ground after the flood. The flood itself was not an atonement for the wickedness of humankind. The flood was punishment, judgment (Gen 6:5-7). After the flood, God's decree of judgment to destroy all the living was still in force. There was still the need for an atonement sacrifice, and the first thing Noah did after leaving the ark was to offer that sacrifice (Gen 8:20), which God accepted (Gen 8:21a).

A central part of the compositional purpose of Genesis 8:20-22 is to show the efficacy of Noah's offering. It is only after he acknowledged and accepted Noah's sacrifice that God rescinded the curse on the ground and his decree to destroy all life (Gen 8:21). The author's purpose is to place these three elements (sacrifice, forgiveness, the reestablishment of order) as closely together as possible. His point is that sacrifice is essential to forgiveness of sin. It is also important to see that the efficacy of Noah's offering is immediately linked to the central importance the author of the Pentateuch gives to the notion of the ground *(ʾădāmâ)*. Only after God accepted Noah's offering was order restored and life again possible on the ground *(ʾădāmâ)*.

*Summary*. An interesting picture of the curse in Genesis 3:17 emerges from Genesis 8:20-22. Although only the "ground" *(ʾădāmâ)* was cursed in Genesis 3:17, its effects were universal. The curse on the "ground" continued in force until the time of the flood, but it was significantly altered after Noah's sacrificial offering. In that sacrifice, a way was made for a new life "on earth [ground]." In spite of the curse on the ground, it could again be subject to God's blessing (Gen 9:1).

# Conclusion

The aim of the studies in this book has been to find the compositional strategy of the Pentateuch and what it says about the Pentateuch's theological and normative claims as Scripture. Throughout this book I have sought to encourage serious discussion among those who hold an evangelical view of Scripture as God's Word.

I have drawn several conclusions about the Pentateuch and its theology. I am well aware that other conclusions could be drawn and other observations made. There is room for flexibility. Evangelicalism has a large umbrella.[1] In terms of the history of biblical theology, the view argued in this book follows most closely in the footsteps of John Calvin and Johann Coccejus, without itself being Calvinistic or Reformed. Representative of the sixteenth and seventeenth centuries are Calvin and Coccejus, and of the eighteenth and nineteenth centuries, Franz Buddeus and Johann von Hofmann.

I have attempted to clarify and defend my own view, not specifically that of Calvin or Coccejus. I mention them here in passing only because in my exegesis and theological reflection on the Pentateuch I most often find myself gravitating toward the views of those two men. This is true not only at the level of theological systems, such as the role of the Mosaic law in the new covenant, but also in practical questions, such as the Pentateuch and the nature of Christian faith.

## Theology and the Old Testament

I opened these studies with a general discussion of the nature of theology

[1]See John H. Sailhamer, *Introduction to the Old Testament* (Grand Rapids: Zondervan), pp. 115-83.

and the OT. I suggested that the term "Old" is not a statement about the relevance of the "Old Testament," but rather is an affirmation of the continued value and importance of all parts of the Christian Bible, especially the "older" parts. My general conclusion was that the message of the Pentateuch is not so much about the Mosaic law and Sinai covenant as it is about the prophetic hope of a new covenant. At the center of that hope, and extending to the whole of the Pentateuch, is the role of the king from the house of Judah who will reign over Israel and the nations. I found that focus particularly in the poems that accompany the narratives. The compositional strategy reflected in the shaping of the poems within the Pentateuch embraces the whole of that book. For that reason, it can be taken as from the author of the original work ("Pentateuch 1.0"). I further argued that in the present Pentateuch each of these poems has been given additional interrelated commentary in the form of narrative insertions (glosses) and comments. These additions, and their focus on "the last days" and a coming king, suggest that the present Pentateuch was a final *(Endgestalt)* messianic edition of the original ("Pentateuch 2.0").

The unique feature of the OT is that it is considered to be authoritative Scripture by both Christianity and Judaism. Both faiths claim to understand it as singularly authoritative for themselves only, creating enormous hermeneutical problems that cannot be ignored. It is not enough merely to read the HB from a NT vantage point. Christians are obliged to read the OT as the OT writers understood it and only then ask how it relates to the NT and the church. That is why I have extensively addressed hermeneutical questions dealing with ancient texts such as the Pentateuch.

I have in mind particularly the attention given in this book to Hans Frei's discussion of Friedrich Schleiermacher and others who, to one degree or another, followed or identified with him. I have devoted considerable attention to both Frei and Schleiermacher primarily to get a sense of the unintended, though considerable, influence of Schleiermacher on the evangelicalism of his day. With Schleiermacher came the view of the OT as teaching the Mosaic law. That said, I also felt obliged to chart, at least in summary form, the complex history of Schleiermacher's influence on the interpretation of the OT by evangelical theologians in his day. With Schleiermacher, the question of history comes into full view, making it the sine qua non of a modern, scientific approach to the OT.

My treatment of evangelical theologians and biblical scholars, and their views of history and the Bible, stands at the center of the argument of this book. Simply put, real (historical) biblical events such as the exodus, though rightly accepted and studied as history, came to replace the biblical version of that history found on the pages of the OT. Hans Frei calls the shift away from the historical narratives of Scripture to the "raw facts" pointed to by those narratives an "eclipse" of biblical narrative. Real "historical" events rather than written Scripture came to be the primary locus of divine revelation.

Another task that I take up in this book is the proper evangelical approach to biblical theology. Given evangelicalism's commitment to the inspiration of the Bible and its value as the primary (or only) source of special revelation, I have argued for a more intentional focus on the biblical text itself as the locus of divine revelation and hence the object of a biblical theology. I also argued that such a focus on the biblical text necessitates the identification of the meaning of the text with the "author's" intent. This means not what the author may have been thinking or feeling when he wrote the biblical text, but rather what his written words actually say. The author's intent *(mens auctoris)* is the "verbal meaning" of his words. Since they are instruments of divine revelation, we take them at their word. The biblical authors knew what they wanted to say, and they said it.

We arrive at the author's verbal meaning by taking note of two questions. First, we seek to know the words that the author has written, which is the task of textual criticism. There is an important difference between what was written by the author and what may have been inserted into the text by a well-meaning scribe. Next, we need to know the lexical meaning of each of his words and how they fit together in the written text. A good philologist[2] seeks to know what the words mean, not merely what they point to outside the text. The philologist also needs to know the syntax of the biblical text. The Bible does not merely strew words on a page. The biblical authors knew what they wanted to say, and they followed the rules of their language to say it.

The second question that we may use to discover the verbal meaning or the author's intent is the compositional strategy of the author who "made" the text. How does the author arrange and shape the text to convey his intended meaning? Does he, like the author of the Pentateuch, mix poems and narra-

[2]A philologist studies ancient texts and their language.

tive? Is there a strategy behind what he has written? Does he comment on his finished text to make sure that the reader gets the point? The meaning of the author of a text is found just as much in the shape and reading strategy he gives to it as in the words he chooses.

The question I raised to give sense to the discussion of meaning was whether the message of the Pentateuch included any messianic hope. My conclusion is that it does, and that it could be discovered in the text by looking at the words, their syntax, and the composition of the whole Pentateuch.

What this means to the readers of Scripture is that God's words revealed to them as readers often are mediated through the biblical narratives as historical events fashioned into stories of real "things." In such cases, we are called to understand the meaning of the story before we can apply God's words to real events in our lives. That is why we are advised in the OT to meditate on the Scriptures "day and night" (Josh 1:8; Ps 1:2). Understanding the OT is complex and cannot be accomplished "overnight." Only with much effort ("day and night") will one prosper through reading the Scriptures. The admonition to read the Bible earnestly is a part of the final composition of the whole OT (Josh 1:8; Ps 1:2).

Finally, there is something everyone must do to get a better understanding of the Bible: look for the big picture in the OT and Pentateuch. The details of the Bible make sense when we view them in light of the big picture. Like the picture on the cover of a jigsaw box, the pieces of the puzzle make more sense if we see them as parts of the whole puzzle shown on the front cover.

1. Make sure that the big picture comes from the OT itself. That is, make sure that you get it from reading the OT rather than reading the Bible backwards from the NT to the OT or from the top down by reading it in light of a theological system.

2. Do not let the details of your own life determine the big picture of the Pentateuch. This means that you should not read the details of the biblical story as if they were part of your story. As tempting as that may be, you should, rather, read the details of your own personal story as parts of the biblical story. The Pentateuch and the Bible as a whole have a world far more meaningful than your own individual story. As important as that world is to you, the Bible works by giving its readers an even greater picture of the real world. In 1 Samuel 2:10 Hannah did not say to God, "Use your kingdom power to give me a son." Her prayer was, "Use the son you have given me to

establish your kingdom." As much as having a son meant to Hannah, her prayer of thanksgiving shows not only that she had been reading the Pentateuch, but also that she had come to be absorbed not so much in the details of her own life as in the details of God's plan of redemption and how her son would fit into that.

3. Both the OT and the NT are parts of one Bible (cf. Lk 24:44-49; Acts 28:23). The Christian canon listed the OT before the NT, perhaps to show the foundational nature of the OT. It may also have been to show that the OT is the narrative beginning of the NT. The church has reversed the order by reading the OT in light of the NT (typology and allegory). The Reformation restored the order from OT to NT but kept the sequence of the Vulgate rather than the Tanak of the HB.

4. However one might construe the order of the OT books within the Hebrew OT canon (Tanak), the central implication has been given little attention until recently: the OT's view of itself.[3] Many have asked, "What is the NT's understanding of the OT?" but few have also asked, "What is the OT's understanding of itself?" There has been no end to the question of the NT's citation of the OT, but very little attention has been given to how the OT cites itself. How, for example, does the book of Hosea (Hos 11:1) cite Numbers 24:8?[4] And how does Numbers 24:9a cite Genesis 49:9b? Only when we have answered those questions can we address questions such as Matthew's citation of Hosea 11:1.

5. The Tanak was, for the most part, the only Bible that Jesus and the early church acknowledged as Scripture (cf. 2 Tim 3:15). The early first-century church, as we know it in the book of Acts, did not yet have the completed NT, but they did have the OT, and it was their NT. There is no indication in their literature that they felt a need for more Scripture in their teaching and evangelism. The only Bible they knew was the OT Tanak, which they considered their "New Testament," not their "Old Testament" (cf. 2 Tim 3:15-16). As they themselves understood their Bible, the early church had no "Old Testament." The only Bible they had was what we today call the "Old Testament," which they considered their "New Testament."

---

[3]See John H. Sailhamer, "Biblical Theology and the Composition of the Hebrew Bible," in *Biblical Theology: Retrospect and Prospect*, ed. Scott Hafemann (Downers Grove, Ill.: InterVarsity Press, 2002), pp. 25-37.

[4]See John H. Sailhamer, "Hosea 11:1 and Matthew 2:15," *WTJ* 63 (2001): 87-96.

6. There is a unity (continuity) of the OT and the NT.[5] In due time, the early church produced its own NT rather than an "edited" version of the OT such as we find among the Dead Sea pesher scrolls. They left the OT intact as their "New Testament Scriptures," not changing anything. They simply added the NT to it as a continuation, not a replacement. The NT authors were in complete agreement with the prophetic authors of the OT that the Hebrew OT canon (Tanak) was Scripture to the same extent that it was valued in first-century Judaism. According to Paul, through the OT Scriptures "the person of God is complete and equipped for every good work" (2 Tim 3:17). This is an astonishing statement. The NT tells us important new details about Jesus, his birth and death, but then it reminds us that all these things happened "according to the OT Scriptures."

## Theology of the Pentateuch

There are two ways to understand the nature, and ultimately the task, of a theology of the Pentateuch. The point of departure is the question of the nature of the Bible (OT) itself. Is the Bible—that is, the Pentateuch—divine revelation, or is it merely an account of the religion of ancient Israel and God's revelation of himself to them alone? I have argued in this book that the Pentateuch is divine revelation. To the extent that we understand the author's verbal meaning, we can be assured that we understand the mind of God *(mens dei)* in the words of the Pentateuch.

***The "big idea" of the Pentateuch.*** My focus has been the importance of reading the biblical text in light of its "big idea." Although many have insisted that the big idea of the Pentateuch is focused on the centrality of obedience to the Mosaic law, my reading of the Pentateuch has taken us along a different path. I have argued that the big idea of the Pentateuch is about both obedience to the Mosaic law and living by faith. Admittedly, my reading of the Pentateuch within the context of "faith" has not initially pointed us to most of what is in the book. Most of what is in the Pentateuch consists of law or discussions of law that must be obeyed. From Exodus 12 on, it is almost entirely about the laws given Israel at Sinai.

We will see that the big idea of "faith" helps us see what is most important to the author. As I have located and isolated and ultimately described the

---

[5]Note 2 Timothy 4:13: scrolls (books) and parchments (OT?).

work of the author, it has become increasingly clear that his interest lies in developing an understanding of faith and trusting God. The law, as such, takes on a secondary importance, even though the author has devoted a considerable amount of time and attention to it.

Throughout this book I have attempted to feel a way along a path laid out by the author of the Pentateuch, and I have attempted to formulate a big idea that includes both the notion of obedience to the Mosaic law and the concept of living by faith. Ultimately, these two themes of law and faith have found their place alongside each other as a juxtaposition of law and gospel. The gospel—that is, the notion of justification by faith—is God's means for our fulfilling the law.[6] This immediately strikes one as "Pauline," but not in the sense of reading Paul's theology back into the Pentateuch. The theology of the Pentateuch is "Pauline" in the sense that we must read the Pentateuch's theology into Paul. Paul's line of thought about the law and faith is drawn from the theology of the Pentateuch and the prophetic authors of Scripture who read the Scriptures "day and night," not the other way around. To be sure, an exegetical validation of the Pauline notion of "faith" must be demonstrated exegetically in the Pentateuch itself. Throughout this book my concern has been to introduce the concept of a big idea and to demonstrate the way one must shape an understanding of it in the Pentateuch. However one may eventually formulate an understanding of the Pentateuch, its warrant or validity must be sought exegetically, beginning with a statement of its big idea.

*Warrant (verbal meaning linked to the biblical text).* The importance of formulating an understanding of the central message of the Pentateuch, obliges us to think about proper warrants for doing so. Although this is not the place to give a detailed explication of the various means for validating my understanding of the Pentateuch's big idea, I must explain some of the general principles I have followed in this book.

Shimon Bar-Efrat suggests four textually based levels from which our understanding of the meaning of biblical narratives can be assessed and validated: verbal, narrative technique, narrative world, thematic structure. Each level of structure in biblical narrative provides a perspective for viewing the author's shaping of the biblical material. This will give us what Wolfgang

[6]As in Romans 8:4: "in order that the requirement of the Law might be fulfilled in us, who do not walk according to the flesh but according to the Spirit" (NASB).

Richter has called a "text immanent"[7] warrant for the meaning we assign to the biblical text. Richter has in mind grounding the textual meaning in the text itself as it has been constructed "from the ground up"; starting with the most basic level, the words of the text, one moves to the syntax of those words and the narrative world depicted by those words. Only then can one speak of "themes" or "ideas" being grounded in the text. It is an exegetical attempt to understand the text in terms of its own range of meaning without importing ideas and meanings from outside sources. The various levels of structure in narrative must be exegetically anchored to each other and to the text as a whole. By "exegetically anchored" Richter means how the authors of biblical texts connect the meaning at each level to the one below. That can be done on the verbal level by showing an author's linking of two pieces of similar thematic texts by the use of the same or similar words.[8] Tracing the author's work at each level is essential for finding the proper warrant for an interpretation of narrative. The poems in the Pentateuch are linked by the fact that they share the same thematic focus on the kingship.

*Verbal level.* The starting point in approaching the meaning of biblical narrative is located in the words themselves. This is the level that Bar-Efrat designated as the verbal level. At this level, meaning is a function of the grammar and syntax of the original language of the text (Hebrew) or a translation (e.g., English). What is said about the narrative and its structure must ultimately find its support in the words of the author and the way they are grammatically construed.

*Summary.* The goal of biblical interpretation (hermeneutics) is to find the author's intent in his verbal meaning. One must seek to understand the meaning of the words and sentences the author uses. We do that by understanding his words within the context of the grammar of biblical Hebrew, or a good translation, and the literary shape of the whole of the Pentateuch (verbal meaning). Our clues to the author's big idea are to be sought in those things about which the author most often writes and which seem most important to him. Ultimately, we discover the meaning of a book such as the Pentateuch by reading it and asking the right questions. Behind our quest for the (hu-

---

[7]See Wolfgang Richter, *Exegese als Literaturwissenschaft: Entwurf einer alttestamentlichen Literaturtheorie und Methodologie* (Göttingen: Vandenhoeck & Ruprecht, 1971), pp. 179-87.

[8]See John H. Sailhamer, "Genesis," in *The Expositors Bible Commentary*, ed. Tremper Longman III and David E. Garland, rev. ed. (Grand Rapids: Zondervan, 2008), 1:161-62.

man) author's intent is the conviction that the divine intention of Scripture *(mens dei)* is to be found in the human author's intent *(mens auctoris)*.

As noted above, the exegetical warrant for my understanding the message of the Bible, and the Pentateuch in particular, is to be found in a fourfold linkage of perspectives at four textually based levels: verbal, narrative technique, narrative world, thematic structure. An exegetically warranted interpretation of a biblical text such as the Pentateuch must be grounded in each of these levels of narrative.

***Biblical theology and composition.*** In seeking to find and describe the theology of the Pentateuch, I have focused on the final shape of the HB as the Tanak. This raises the question of whether a biblical theology that includes both the Tanak and the NT is possible. Can a theology of the whole OT as the Tanak play a role in a Christian understanding of biblical theology? Is there an exegetically warranted unity between the HB as Tanak and the NT?

*The "final shape" of the Old Testament.* My working definition of the "final shape" of the OT is that it was the compositional and canonical shape of the HB at the time it became part of an established community committed to its preservation. This occurred for the OT before the first century B.C. That is not an absolute date, since there were multiple and diverse communities at that time, and each community would have looked on their Hebrew Scriptures as "the Bible." Given the community nature of ancient texts such as the Tanak, one would expect to find multiple "final shapes" of the HB coming out of the pre-Christian era, and that is what we do find in the history of these texts. For the most part, the textual variants that exist among these communities are not merely textual, but also reflect genuine theological diversity at that early era.

The two categories of "composition" and "canon" help us form models of how an ancient author might have composed books and arranged them in intentional shapes such as in the OT (Tanak). The notion of the interrelationships between texts and communities is called "consolidation." It is an attempt to respond to recent observations about the nature of ancient written texts and the influence they have on and receive from the communities that preserve them. Religious communities such as Judaism and Christianity derive their essential identity from texts. Biblical texts receive their final shape from such communities. Communities endorse and impose restrictions on their foundational texts. In this book I have explored the idea that the consolidation of OT texts includes elements of composition and canonization. Communities not only produce canonical texts, they also create (compositionally) new texts.

The traces of text-communities and their beliefs often are reflected in the textual history of the OT. Ancient manuscripts, such as those from the Dead Sea area, and various versions, such as the LXX and the Targumim, give ample evidence that biblical interpretation in the pre-Christian era was anything but uniform. Pre-Christian communities varied distinctly in their understanding of the biblical texts, and such differences often made their way into the final (canonical) shape of the Tanak as variant texts. Beyond textual criticism's concern for reconstructing "original" manuscripts, the value of textual variants in ancient biblical texts lies in the fact that they give us a profile of the theology of the various communities that preserved the variants now extant. We know from textual variants preserved by such groups that in the first century there were still many unsettled questions. Such texts reflect different views about the "coming one" (Messiah) and the place of the Mosaic law. Much of the additional poetic material in the Pentateuch is linked to other sections of text by further cross-referencing and compositional seams growing out of Genesis 1–11. Those kinds of links provide further support for the notion that the composition of Genesis 1–11 is closely related to the composition of the Pentateuch as a whole. Many of the same kinds of explanatory details and additional commentary are found in the poems of Numbers 24. They provide an additional look into the meaning and message of the Pentateuch.

The compositional shaping of the poems in the Pentateuch serves to advance its central theological themes. Those themes are reinforced by brief explanatory comments throughout the text. These same themes are echoed throughout the rest of the OT Scriptures. The numerous interpretive comments in the poems further serve to align them with specific NT theolegomena, such as the importance of daily private reading of Scripture as the source of divine wisdom and understanding the will of God and the role of Scripture as a replacement of the divine presence at the temple (Acts 28:23). Thus, in the Pentateuch the themes of salvation and the eternal reign of God are cast along lines that stress the NT hope of an individual priesthood of believers—

for example, "This is *my* God" (Ex 15:2).[9] The innertextual allusions to the Genesis narratives in Exodus 15 point unmistakably to God's work of creation as depicted in the Genesis narratives (Gen 2). The creation account of the Genesis narratives is recast in terms of God's building a place for his sanctuary *(miqqĕdāš)* in Jerusalem.

*Creation and salvation.* In the Pentateuch, as elsewhere in the Bible, the twin themes of "creation" and "salvation" are inseparably linked. This is expressed compositionally at the macrolevel in the fact that the Pentateuch begins with an account of creation (Gen 1:1) and reaches its culmination in the salvation story of the exodus (Ex 14). I have also shown that the poem in Exodus 15 summarizes God's acts of creation and redemption by grounding its view of salvation in creation. I have further argued that creation and "this-worldliness" as such do not express the last word about salvation in the poem. Ultimately, the author elevates his view of God and salvation by shifting attention to the notion of God as the eternal king (Ex 15:18). The meaning of salvation expressed in Exodus 15 is that of the individual's relationship to the eternal God. The compositional macrostructure of the Pentateuch (Gen 1–Ex 15) is a witness to the centrality of creation in the biblical notion of salvation, but it is also left open to another theme that is also deeply embedded in the early narratives of Genesis: the blessing of eternal life. The Genesis narratives are clear that what was lost in the fall was not only access to the garden, but also, more importantly, access to the tree of life "in the midst of the garden" (Gen 2:9). The cherubim were placed to guard access to the "tree of life" (Gen 3:22-24), not merely access to the garden. It is thus not without purpose that the earliest biblical "salvation history" (Gen 1–Ex 15) concludes by returning to the hope of eternal life that lies in the idea of God as the eternal king (Ps 133:3).

---

[9]The same tendency can be seen in Hannah's psalm in 1 Samuel 2:10.

## Author Index

## Subject Index

# Scripture Index

## Genesis

**Job**



**Psalms**



**Proverbs**



**Ecclesiastes**



**Isaiah**



**Jeremiah**